Vegetarian Journal's Guide to

NATURAL FOODS RESTAURANTS

in the U.S. and Canada

Vegetarian Journal's Guide to

NATURAL FOODS RESTAURANTS

in the U.S. and Canada

Expanded 4th Edition

With Forewords by Moby and Lindsay Wagner

From The Vegetarian Resource Group
Edited by Keryl Cryer and Debra Wasserman

The
VRg VEGETARIAN
Resource Group

Baltimore, Maryland

Please note: The contents of *Vegetarian Journal's Guide to Natural Foods Restaurants in the U.S. and Canada* and our other publications, including web information, are not intended to provide personal medical advice. Medical advice should be obtained from a qualified health professional. We often depend on restaurant, product, and ingredient information from company statements. For this book, surveys are often completed by outside parties. It is impossible to be 100 percent sure about a statement, info can change, people have different views, and mistakes can be made. This is especially in the case of restaurants, which frequently open, close, and change. Please use your own best judgement about whether a meal selection or establishment is suitable for you. To be sure, do further research or confirmation on your own.

Vegetarian journal's guide to natural foods restaurants in the U.S. and Canada/
    the Vegetarian Resource Group; forewords by Moby and Lindsay Wagner.—
    4th ed.
    ISBN: 0-931411-27-0 (paperback)
    1. Vegetarian restaurants—United States—Guidebooks.   2. Natural foods
    restaurants—United States—Guidebooks.   3. Vegetarian restaurants—
    Canada—Guidebooks.   4. Natural foods restaurants—Canada—Guidebooks.
    I. Vegetarian Resource Group.   II. Vegetarian Journal.

Library of Congress Control Number: 2004115398
ISSN: 1553-426X

Printed in the United States of America

10   9   8   7   6   5   4   3   2   1

Table of Contents

Natural Foods Restaurants in the United States

Natural Foods Restaurants in Canada

Acknowledgments

As you can imagine, putting together a natural foods restaurant guide of this proportion is a tremendous task. This huge project would have been impossible without the help of many individuals. A very grateful "thank you" to these members of The Vegetarian Resource Group, readers of *Vegetarian Journal,* and others who contributed their efforts for the creation of this guide:

Zel and Reuben Allen ✦ Gail Appleson ✦ Nava Atlas ✦ Carmen Austin
Carol Barnett ✦ T. G. Barnhill ✦ Dennis Bayomi at VegDining.com
Phil Becker ✦ Nancy Berkoff, RD, EdD, CCE ✦ Ann Berwald ✦ Mike Billian
Ruth Blackburn ✦ Elizabeth Brandt ✦ Dan Brook ✦ Therese Bzdok
Ellen Campbell ✦ Andrea Caylor ✦ Trevor Chin ✦ Julie Covington ✦ Jessica Dadds
Juan Deguara ✦ Curtis and Paula Eakins of Health Seminars Unlimited
Janet Erickson and the Vegetarian Society of South Jersey ✦ Deer and Justice Fields
Kay Filler ✦ Erica Frank ✦ Bruce Friedrich at PETA ✦ Ed Goldstein ✦ Ellen Helms
Jacquie Hilton ✦ Suzanne Havala Hobbs, DrPH, RD ✦ Susan Huesken
Stephanie Huggins ✦ Jim Jeske and St. Louis Vegetarian Society ✦ Amy Jordens
Steve Kaufman and Vegetarian Advocates ✦ Matthew Koch, President of Road's End
Organics, Inc. ✦ Jay B. Lavine, M.D. ✦ Mark Machlis ✦ Reed Mangels, PhD, RD
Lynn Manheim at Letters for Animals ✦ Jayn and Tom Meinhardt ✦ Vesanto Melina
Roger Millen ✦ Jeff Morrison ✦ Kay Newhouse ✦ Lindsey Nielsen ✦ Jack Norris
Jim Oswald ✦ Myriam Parham ✦ Patty Park ✦ Bob Orabona and Jessica Patton
at Friends of Animals ✦ Michael and Denise Pfalzer ✦ Andrea Posner
Don Robertson ✦ Elizabeth Rockwell ✦ Juana Rogers and the Sacramento
Vegetarian Society ✦ Stewart Rose, Amanda Strombom, and the Vegetarians
of Washington ✦ Stephanie Schueler ✦ Kaz L. Sephton and the San Antonio
Vegetarian Society ✦ Bonnie Shwery ✦ Nan and Walter Simpson ✦ Anna Stacholy
Jay Sutliffe ✦ Oleta Thomas ✦ Seth Tibbott, President of Turtle Island Foods
The Toronto Vegetarian Association ✦ The Vegetarian Society of El Paso
The Vegetarian Society of Houston ✦ Amy Wasserman ✦ Marilyn Weaver
Zoe Weil ✦ Lige Weill and Vegetarian Awareness Network USA
Vernon Weir ✦ Randall White ✦ Michael Worsham
Ken Ziff at the Vegetarian Dining Club

The staff of The VRG would like to extend a very special thanks to the following individuals:

Kim Birnbaum • Jim and Maggie Dunn • Heather Gorn • David Herring
Evelyn Kimber and the Boston Vegetarian Society • Ernie Kopstein
Roger Lowe • Lisa Martin • Jane Michalek • Eben Packwood
Susan Petrie • Beth Preiss • Chloë Ringer • Rita Rovner • Brad Scott
Rudy Shur and Square One Publishers • Lin Silvan • Dave Wolven

We would also like to acknowledge the Avery Publishing Group for producing the first three editions of this volume.

Foreword

travelling as a vegan is a blessing and a curse. on one hand (the blessing part...), i've been able to eat at some of the most remarkable restaurants in the world, from cafe8 in tokyo to real food daily in l.a. to la truffe in paris (now closed and turned into a baskin-robbins...ah well, such is life) to teany in nyc (sorry, shameless plug for my own restaurant...). ok, so that's the blessing part.

the curse part has been finding these (and myriad other) amazing restaurants. over the years, i've tried to learn how to say 'i'm a vegan' in a lot of different languages, but not always with great success. in fact at one point in the early '90s, i went around germany telling people in hotels that i needed a vegetarian restaurant because i was celibate... i had misunderstood a translation guide and somehow confused 'celibate' for 'vegan.'

so as i was saying, for every amazing experience (finding millenium in san francisco, finding this great vegan buffet restaurant overlooking the harbor in stockholm, finding a tiny restaurant run by an old man and his wife in geneva, etc.), there's been the experience of trying to eat in, say, tulsa (nice place, but not exactly an abundance of vegan eateries). so a guide such as this (which covers the u.s and canada, i know) becomes invaluable to the travelling vegan/vegetarian. for although it has become easier over the years to be a travelling vegan/vegetarian, it's still not easy. so thanks, vrg, for helping to keep the travelling vegan/vegetarians of the world happy and well-fed.

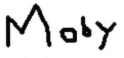

moby

Foreword

I am so excited to be writing a foreword for an entire book of restaurants in the United States that cater to vegetarians. I may seem easily pleased. However, I've been a performer struggling to maintain a vegetarian lifestyle for over twenty years. Here's what a good number of those years on the road looked like...

Limousine drives up to the Ritz-Carlton. Chauffeur opens the door. Doorman approaches. "Welcome, Ms. Wagner, glad to have you with us." The Bellman leads the way to the luxurious suite. "Where shall I put the bags?" I reply, "those three go in the bedroom. THAT BAG stays here." After lifting THAT BAG off the trolley, the bellman is clearly relieved it isn't going very far. And there I am, on location for a film and in one of the finest hotels in the country unpacking THAT BAG. Out comes my two-burner hot plate, two stainless steel pans, brown rice, adzuki beans, tamari sauce, Bragg's amino acid, whole-wheat tortillas, and of course, the ever-present cayenne pepper.

Life was rough in the '70s and '80s for vegetarians on the road. Eventually I learned to inquire (first thing) about the ethnic restaurants in town. (Most other countries around the world seem to understand nutrition without such a heavy carnivorous bent.) That made life much easier and resulted in setting off far fewer smoke alarms.

I now can take my *Guide to Natural Foods Restaurants* with me (in a much smaller bag) and know that my children and I will have a much easier time traveling and working in a healthy, sated way.

God bless the *Guide to Natural Foods Restaurants!*

Lindsay Wagner

Introduction

When we compiled the first edition of this guide in 1993, vegetarians were beginning to find more than cheese sandwiches when traveling. More than ten years later, times sure have changed, with almost every restaurant offering some type of vegetarian choice. The word "vegan" is common on many menus in some areas. Even fast food chains are dabbling in vegetarian options. However, this book is a tool for consumers who want to visit and support restaurants that seem to go more out of their way for vegetarians.

As a Co-Director of The Vegetarian Resource Group and the Managing Editor of *Vegetarian Journal,* I have been on the road quite a bit. Although I haven't eaten at every restaurant in this book, I'm surprised by how many I have visited. Each establishment has its own unique and enjoyable ambiance.

Often, I would enjoy dining with the owner and/or chef of the restaurant. During our sometimes lengthy discussions, I learned a great deal about what it takes to successfully run a natural foods restaurant these days. Few restaurants actually survive past the initial year or two. More often, restaurants that fail are underfinanced, situated in a poor location, or poorly managed. A good idea can be hurt by an unexpected dip in the economy. The owner/manager may have started a natural foods restaurant for the right reasons but simply underestimated the amount of energy and money it takes to compete in the industry. Other underfinanced natural foods restaurants are surviving simply through perseverance. The owner(s) make personal sacrifices to promote vegetarianism and keep the restaurant open to the public. In many ways, these individuals are vegetarian activists.

In compiling this restaurant guide, we obtained information through various channels. Member of The Vegetarian Resource Group continue to supply us with most of the data you'll find in this book. Many of our members are business travelers and vacationers who visit restaurants often. We've received information from airline pilots, CEOs of large companies, college students, retirees spending the summer traversing America, and others who simply enjoy dining out whenever possible. Interestingly, much enthusiasm towards the book has come from male vegetarians, who in the past were not as excited about buying vegetarian cookbooks and preparing meals at home.

Information for this book also comes via many local vegetarian and animal rights organizations. These groups often notify us of new vegetarian dining spots opening up in their community. Restaurants are surprised to receive our survey before they have even opened up their doors!

Today, there are frequently several vegetarian and/or vegan restaurants in cities. Therefore, we give a wider selection of purely vegetarian establishments in these locations. Outside of urban centers, we list dining spots that have a large vegetarian selection on their menu, even though they are not completely vegetarian restaurants. In most cases, these establishments offer at least ten creative vegetarian options. An exception might be made in very rural locations that have few restaurants.

The information in this guide is listed alphabetically by state or province, then city, then restaurant. At the beginning of each description, the italicized phrase indicates the type of restaurant (e.g. vegetarian, vegan, Chinese, Italian, etc.). This is followed by detailed information. For symbol explanations, see the key box on the bottom of various pages throughout the book.

For those especially good restaurants, you'll notice a Reviewer's Choice symbol (✪) following their name. Restaurants receiving this honor have received rave reviews from many individuals. This usually means that both their service and food are excellent on a consistent basis. Since vegetarians have different tastes, readers may have chosen restaurants with very different styles or cuisines.

Each restaurant and vacation spot in this book was sent a survey to complete and asked to return it along with a copy of their menu. For restaurants that did not respond, a follow-up phone call was made to obtain the necessary data. For each entry, we tried to gather as much information as possible; however, keep in mind that chefs and management change, and this can affect the food served. Also, as you probably know, restaurants often modify their hours of operation. If you have to travel a great distance to dine at a specific restaurant, you may want to call ahead to make sure the information has remained the same since last reported to us.

Finally, if you do find a place we've missed or that has closed, please let us know! We are only able to compile this guide with the help of individuals such as yourself, and we'd love your help in keeping the listings current. For your convenience, a form is included in the back of the book for updates. You can also easily send corrections and suggestions for new additions to us via the Internet. Go to <www.vrg.org> and use our online restaurant survey form. Also check this website for an updated list of restaurants.

According to Vegetarian Resource Group polls, between 2 and 3 percent of Americans are vegetarians. That is they never eat meat, fish, and fowl. Approximately 6 percent don't eat red meat. However, many times that amount of people are open to vegetarian meals if the food tastes good. The hard work of business owners and your patronage means these restaurants can have a positive impact on people's health, animals' lives, and the environment.

Thank you for supporting vegetarian establishments when you dine out. We hope this book makes your dining experience and travels more enjoyable.

Debra Wasserman

Co-Director, The Vegetarian Resource Group (www.vrg.org)
Publisher of *Vegetarian Journal*

Vegetarian Journal's Guide to

NATURAL FOODS RESTAURANTS

in the U.S. and Canada

Natural Foods Restaurants

Below are the symbols and primary abbreviations that will provide you with important information about each entry.

> ✪ Reviewer's Choice
> (This is an establishment that a vegetarian visiting an area should visit for at least one meal.)

> • Vegetarian Restaurant
> (No meat, fowl, or fish served.)

> • • Vegan Restaurant
> (No meat, fowl, fish, dairy products, eggs, or honey served.)

> $ Less than $6 for an average meal

> $$ $6-$12 for an average meal

> $$$ More than $12 for an average meal

> VISA Visa Card accepted

> MC MasterCard accepted

> DISC Discover Card accepted

> DC Diner's Club accepted

> Non-alcoholic Non-alcoholic drinks served

> Fresh juices Freshly squeezed in the restaurant, e.g., carrot juice

An abbreviated version of the above codes can be found on the bottom of various pages throughout the guide.

In addition, at the beginning of a number of the larger city entries, there appears a listing of towns, suburbs, and/or localities that are in close proximity to the respective city. The names within these listings can be used to locate additional restaurants in these neighboring areas.

For this book, surveys are often completed by outside parties. It is impossible to be 100 percent sure about a statement, info can change, people have different views, and mistakes can be made. Especially in the case of restaurants, they open, close, and change. Please use your own best judgement about whether a product or establishment is suitable for you. To be sure, do further research or confirmation on your own.

Alabama

BIRMINGHAM

(For restaurant listings in the surrounding areas, see Homewood and Hoover.)

Golden India Restaurant
Summit Square Shopping Center
279 W. Valley Ave., Birmingham, AL 35209   (205) 940-9030
Indian. Located three miles from the University of Alabama at Birmingham, this Indian restaurant offers about 20 vegetarian dishes. **Open daily for dinner. Open Monday through Saturday for lunch. Full service, vegan options, $-$$.**

• Golden Temple Natural Grocery & Café
1901 11th Ave., S., Birmingham, AL 35205   (205) 933-6333
Vegetarian. Sandwiches, salads, drinks, and daily specials are offered at this quick-service vegetarian café. Low-salt meals are also available. **Open Monday through Saturday. Closed Sunday. Limited service, vegan options, fresh juices, take-out, VISA/MC, $.**

The Pita Stop
1106 12th St., S., Birmingham, AL 35205   (205) 328-2749
Lebanese. Enjoy Middle Eastern dishes, such as hummus, baba ghanouj, tabbouleh, and falafel. **Open Monday through Thursday for lunch and dinner. Open Friday for lunch. Open Saturday for dinner after sundown. Closed Sunday. Limited service, take-out, $-$$.**

The Purple Onion
1717 10th Ave., S., Birmingham, AL 35205   (205) 933-2424
Middle Eastern. The Purple Onion serves traditional Middle Eastern cuisine. **Open Monday through Saturday for lunch and dinner. Closed Sunday. Limited service, vegan options, $.**

Standard Bistro
3 Mt. Laurel Ave., Birmingham, AL 35242   (205) 995-0512
Bistro. Standard Bistro offers a relatively large amount of vegetarian options for this area, including several unique salads, asparagus dishes, and a mushroom, leek, and goat cheese tart. Chef Michael can also make vegetarian or vegan versions of many of the menu's other offerings upon request, and about 90 percent of the ingredients they use are organic. Patio seating is available when weather permits. The bar area at this establishment is open daily. **Open Tuesday through Saturday for lunch and dinner. Closed Sunday and Monday. Full service, vegan options, beer/wine/alcohol, catering, VISA/MC/AMEX/DISC/DC, $$$.**

Surin of Thailand/Surin West
1918 11th Ave., S., Birmingham, AL 35205   (205) 324-1928
64 Church St., Birmingham, AL 35213   (205) 871-4531
Thai. This formal restaurant offers sushi, stir-fries, and many traditional Thai dishes. Nearly everything on their menu can be made vegetarian or vegan upon request. **Open daily for lunch and dinner. Full service, vegan options, beer/wine/alcohol, VISA/MC/AMEX, $$$.**

`HOMEWOOD`

The Purple Onion Deli & Grill

479 Green Springs Hwy., Homewood, AL 35209   **(205) 941-9979**

Middle Eastern. See description under Birmingham, AL.

`HOOVER`

Ali Baba Persian Restaurant

110 Centre At Riverchase, Hoover, AL 35216   **(205) 823-2222**

Persian. Located in the Birmingham suburb of Hoover, this restaurant has several vegetarian options. You can feast on starters like Hummus, Baba Ghanouj, Kashk o' Bademjan (fried and stewed eggplant with garlic, mint, onion, spices, and whey), or the Shirazi Salad (a Persian dish made with cucumbers, tomatoes, onions, mint, and parsley mixed with lemon juice and olive oil). Entrées include the Vegetarian Kabob and the "Create your own Vegetarian Plate" from choices like Falafel, Tabbouleh, and the appetizers and salads listed above. They also have an on-line store where customers can buy hard-to-find Middle Eastern spices. **Open Tuesday through Saturday for dinner. Open Sunday for lunch buffet and dinner. Closed Monday. Full service, vegan options, fresh juices, espresso/cappuccino, beer/wine, VISA/MC/AMEX/DISC, $$-$$$.** www.alibabarst.com

`HUNTSVILLE`

•• Eden's Delicacies

2413 Jordan Ln., NW, Huntsville, AL 35816   **(256) 721-9491**

Vegan/Caribbean. This restaurant serves flavorful Caribbean entrées, such as roti, and American favorites, such as veggie burgers, as well. They also offer vegan side dishes, including collard greens, cornbread, and pinto beans, and a host of desserts. Health seminars and a library are also available. **Open Sunday through Friday for lunch and dinner. Closed Saturday. Full service, $-$$.**

India Palace

420 Jordan Ln., NW, Huntsville, AL 35805   **(256) 536-3360**

Indian. If you choose the economic buffet or items from the regular vegetarian menu, you can enjoy such mouthwatering dishes as eggplant purée with peas, basmati rice, lentil soup, broccoli, potato and tomato stew, and chutneys. **Open daily for lunch and dinner. Full service, vegan options, take-out, catering, buffet, $-$$.**

Jamo's Juice and Java

413 Jordan Ln., Huntsville, AL 35805   **(256) 837-7880**

Bistro. Jamo's serves Middle Eastern and American fare with several vegetarian options. Try the Vegetarian B.L.T. and the soups, which are always vegetarian. **Open daily for three meals. Limited service, take-out, VISA/MC/DISC.**

Restaurant codes: ✪ Reviewers' Choice • Vegetarian Restaurant •• Vegan Restaurant
Restaurant prices: **$** less than $6 **$$** $6-$12 **$$$** more than $12
Credit Cards Accepted: VISA - VISA MC - MasterCard AMEX - American Express
DISC - Discover DC - Diner's Club

Rosie's Cantina
7540 Memorial Pkwy., SW, Ste. R, Huntsville, AL 35802   **(256) 382-3232**
6125 University Dr., NW, Huntsville, AL 35806   **(256) 922-1001**
Mexican. Rosie's offers both vegetarian and non-vegetarian fare in an open, authentic, and family-style Mexican restaurant. Try the vegetable burrito with mushrooms, zucchini, onions, bell peppers, and beans. Also note that the rice and beans used in vegetarian dishes are prepared without chicken broth, as opposed to the meat dishes. **Open daily for lunch and dinner. Full service, $-$$.**

Surin of Thailand
975 Airport Rd., SW, Huntsville, AL 35802   **(256) 213-9866**
Thai. See description under Birmingham, AL.

• Veggie Factory Plus
3620 Governors Dr., SE, Huntsville, AL 35805   **(256) 534-0109**
Vegetarian fast food/take-out. This is Huntsville's only vegetarian and vegan "drive-thru." Enjoy the famous "Parker Burger," "chicken" or "fish" sandwiches, and a host of vegetarian and vegan side dishes. **Open Monday through Friday for lunch and dinner. Closed Saturday and Sunday. Take-out, vegan options, $-$$.**

Alaska

ANCHORAGE

Aladdin's
4240 Old Seward Hwy., Anchorage, AK 99503   **(907) 561-2373**
Mediterranean. About 35 percent of the dishes served at Aladdin's each night are vegetarian, which is no surprise since every dish that is or can be made vegetarian is clearly marked. These includes appetizers like Dolma (stuffed grape vine leaves with rice and herbs) and Spanakopita (layers of spinach and feta cheese baked in filo dough); dips like Hummus and Tsatsiki (yogurt, cucumber, and garlic); and salads like Casbah-Style (fire-roasted bell peppers and eggplant tossed with tomatoes, onions, and olive oil) and Fattush (Lebanese-style salad with fried pita and a mint-lemon dressing). For entrées, consider unique dishes like the North African-inspired Couscous Maghrebin, the Vegetables and Fruit Curry, or the Vegetarian Mousaka (eggplant, mushrooms, tomatoes, zucchini, and tofu baked with bechamel sauce). **Open Tuesday through Saturday for dinner. Closed Sunday and Monday. Full service, vegan options, special drinks, beer/wine, catering, $$-$$$.** www.aladdinsak.com

Bear Tooth Theatrepub
1230 W. 27th, Anchorage, AK 99503   **(907) 276-4200**
American. Bear Tooth Theatrepub offers an array of vegan, vegetarian, and non-vegetarian pizzas; burritos; salads; appetizers; smoothies; and more in their full service restaurant, or they can delivery the tasty meals to a second-run movie theater nearby. **Open daily for lunch and dinner. Full service, vegan options, counter service, delivery, take-out, reservations not taken, non-smoking, non-alcoholic beverages, smoothies, beer/wine/alcohol, VISA/MC/ AMEX/DISC/DC, $$.** www.beartooththeatrepub.net

•• Enzyme Express

1330 E. Huffman Rd., Anchorage, AK 99515   **(907) 272-5433**

Vegan. This restaurant offers a vegan buffet, veggie burgers, soups, and a variety of raw foods dishes. **Open Monday through Friday for lunch and dinner. Open Saturday for brunch and lunch. Closed Sunday.** Limited service, fresh juices, smoothies, MC, $$.

The Marx Brothers Café

627 W. 3rd Ave., Anchorage, AK 99501   **(907) 278-2133**

Regional. Marx Brothers offers some vegetarian options, such as the Grilled Vegetables & Lentils, and is also willing to prepare special meals for vegetarians. Herbs, spices, lettuce, and edible flowers are grown on the premises in the summer. **Open daily for dinner in the summer. Open Monday through Saturday for dinner in the winter. Closed Sunday in winter.** Full service, wine/beer, catering, VISA/MC, $$$. www.marxcafe.com

Middleway Café

1200 West Northern Lights Blvd., Anchorage, AK 99503   **(907) 272-6433**

Natural foods. This mostly vegetarian establishment is home to a juice bar and offers wraps, tofu scrambles, organic granola, grain-and-soy burgers, burritos, and more. Daily vegan specials are available. **Open daily for three meals.** Limited service, vegan options, fresh juices, smoothies, espresso, $$.

FAIRBANKS

Gambardella's Pasta Bella

706 2nd Ave., Fairbanks, AK 99701   **(907) 456-3417**

Italian. The Gambardellas pride themselves on generations of fabulous Italian food. Vegetarian entrées are conveniently indicated on the menu. Examples include Pasta Marinara, Fettuccini Alfredo, Eggplant Parmesan, Pesto Pasta, and gourmet pizza. **Open Monday through Saturday for lunch and dinner. Open on Sundays in the summer.** Full service, espresso/cappuccino, wine/beer, take-out, VISA/MC, $-$$.

HOMER

Fresh Sourdough Express Bakery and Café

1316 Ocean Dr., Homer, AK 99603   **(907) 235-7571**

Natural foods deli. The Fresh Sourdough Express Bakery and Café offers diners exclusively organic foods in a quaint, cozy, informal atmosphere. The only full-line bakery and restaurant in Homer, The Express boasts everything from the owners' own line of cocoa to a "Pizzaz" of the day (pizza on sourdough), as well as several different cakes, cookies, and breads. **Open daily for three meals.** Full service, take-out, espresso/cappuccino, smoothies, VISA/MC, $$-$$$. www.freshsourdoughexpress.com

JUNEAU

Fiddlehead Restaurant & Bakery

429 W. Willoughby Ave., Juneau, AK 99801   **(907) 586-3150**

Natural foods. Fiddlehead offers full gourmet natural foods. The menu include salads, omelets, sandwiches, soups, bean burgers, and entrées. The restaurant also displays local artwork, and there is live piano music evenings with a weekend jazz band. The upstairs dining room offers a view of Mt. Juneau. **Open daily. Full service, vegan options, fresh juices, wine/beer/alcohol, take-out, non-smoking, VISA/MC/AMEX, $$.**

PETERSBURG

Helse Restaurant
17 Sing Lee Alley, Petersburg, AK 99833   **(907) 772-3444**

Natural foods. Helse's reputation is based on its soup and homemade bread specials, offered every day. Helse offers three vegetarian sandwiches (two of which are vegan), a tofu salad, and a garden salad. A natural foods store is located adjacent to the restaurant. **Open daily for breakfast through early dinner. Full service, vegan options, espresso/cappuccino, take-out, $$.**

Arizona

COTTONWOOD

•Greenhouse Café
1124 N. Main St., Cottonwood, AZ 86326   **(520) 639-4420**

Vegetarian. Greenhouse Café only uses rennetless cheese and does not serve eggs. Menu items include excellent breakfast choices, such as tofu scramble, biscuit and gravy, and pancakes. Other items include salads, grilled Reuben sandwiches (tempeh, swiss cheese, mustard, and sauerkraut), Boca burgers, chili, pizza, and Mexican entrées, such as enchiladas and burritos. **Open daily for three meals. Full service, vegan options, fresh juices, special drinks, smoothies, espresso/cappuccino, vegan options, $-$$.**

FLAGSTAFF

(For restaurant listings in the surrounding areas, see Sedona.)

Café Espress
16 N. San Francisco St., Flagstaff, AZ 86001   **(520) 774-0541**

Natural foods. A café, bakery, and gallery all in one, Café Espress' menu is actually a little newspaper with ads and interesting info. You can feed your body and your mind with a variety of vegetarian foods and facts about the area. Options include soups, sandwiches, chili, and hot entrées, plus a salad bar. Café Espress also prepares fresh baked breads, pastries, and desserts. **Open daily for three meals. Full service, vegan options, fresh juices, wine/beer, take-out, VISA, $.**

Macy's European Coffee House & Bakery
14 S. Beaver St., Flagstaff, AZ 86001   **(520) 774-2243**

Coffeehouse. This mostly vegetarian café offers fresh pastas and sauces made from scratch, as well as soups, salads, and sandwiches. **Open daily for three meals. Limited service, vegan options, non-alcoholic, espresso/cappuccino, no credit cards, $. www.macyscoffee.com**

Mountain Oasis

11 E. Aspen, Flagstaff, AZ 86001 **(520) 214-9270**

International. Flagstaff is a major stop on the way to the southern rim of the Grand Canyon. Mountain Oasis is located in its historic downtown and specializes in international cuisine. Natural foods are used to prepare items such as garden scrambler with tofu and seasoned veggies, grilled portobello mushroom sandwiches, organic tempeh burgers, falafel sandwiches, and Japanese-style nori rolls. A juice bar is also available. **Open daily for three meals. Full service, take out, reservations recommended for dinner, macrobiotic/vegan options, espresso/ capuccino, smoothies, soymilk, wine/beer/alcohol, VISA/MC/AMEX/DC, $$-$$$.**

PHOENIX

(For restaurant listings in the surrounding areas, see Tempe.)

India Palace

16842 N. 7th St., Phoenix, AZ 85022 **(602) 942-4224**

Indian. India Palace offers a variety of vegetarian options. **Open daily for lunch and dinner. Full service, vegan options, take-out, VISA/MC/AMEX/DISC/DC, $$.**

Indian Delhi Palace

5050 E. McDowell Rd., Phoenix, AZ 85008 **(602) 244-8181**

Indian. Indian Delhi Palace offers many vegetarian dishes, including Roasted Eggplant, Garbanzo Beans with Ginger, Fresh Okra with Onions, Cauliflower and Potatoes, Samosas, and fresh breads. **Open daily for lunch and dinner. Full service, wine/beer/alcohol, take- out, VISA/MC/AMEX/DISC/DC, $$.**

Persian Garden Café

1335 W. Thomas Rd., Phoenix, AZ 85013 **(602) 263-1915**

Persian. Though not vegetarian, this restaurant serves a wide range of vegetable-based soups, vegetable stir-fries, tofu dishes, eggplant dishes, hummus, and Middle Eastern specialties. You may want to try the Spinach Herb or Spud Burger for lunch and the Vegetable Stew Eggplant for dinner. Be sure to leave room for some homemade vegan desserts, like carrot cake, cheesecake, and Persian Saffron Rice Pudding. Near Veterans Convention Center and the State Fair Grounds. **Open Monday through Saturday for lunch and dinner. Closed Sunday. Full service, vegan/macrobiotic options, fresh juices, espresso/cappuccino, soymilk, beer/wine, reservations recommended, take-out, catering, VISA/MC/AMEX/DISC/DC, $$$.**

• Supreme Master Ching Hai Vegetarian House

3239 E. Indian School Rd., Phoenix, AZ 85018 **(602) 264-3480**

Vegetarian/Chinese. Enjoy a wide range of vegan Chinese dishes, including Hot and Spicy Beancurd (Matpo Tofu), Heaven Rice Rolls, Sizzling Rice Soup, and Broccoli with Chinese Mushrooms. Lunch specials are available. **Open Tuesday through Saturday for lunch and dinner. Closed Sunday and Monday. Full service, vegan options, take-out, VISA/MC, $-$$.**

Taste of India

1609 E. Bell Rd., B4, Phoenix, AZ 85022 **(602) 788-3190**

Indian. Taste of India offers a wide selection of vegetarian entrées. **Open daily for lunch and dinner. Full service, vegan options, take-out, VISA/MC/AMEX/DISC, $$.**

That's A Wrap

2022 N. 7th St., Phoenix, AZ 85004   **(602) 252-5051**

Sandwich and salad shop. This restaurant offers soups, salads, wraps, and rice bowls. One of the owners is a vegetarian, and the menu clearly indicates which items are vegetarian or vegan. Also, they will substitue tofu for meat in any of there dishes, making for a lot of variety. **Open Monday through Saturday for lunch and dinner. Closed Sunday. Counter service, vegan options, smoothies, take-out, $$.**

Yusef's

15236 N. Cave Creek Rd., Phoenix, AZ 85032   **(602) 867-2957**

Middle Eastern. This combination grocery, restaurant, and deli serves vegetarian dishes, including falafel, vegetarian grape leaves, and tabbouleh salad. **Open Monday through Saturday for lunch and dinner. Closed Sunday. Full service, vegan options, take-out, VISA/MC/AMEX/DC, $.**

SEDONA

Lotus Garden

Bashas' Shopping Center

164-H Coffee Pot Dr., Sedona, AZ 86336   **(520) 282-3118**

Chinese. Lotus Garden offers more than 15 vegetarian dishes, including Mushrooms and Chinese Greens, Eggplant with Garlic Sauce, Tofu in Brown Sauce, and Braised String Beans. **Open daily for lunch and dinner. Full service, vegan options, take-out, $$.**

Oaxaca Restaurante and Cantina

231 N. Hwy. 89A, Sedona, AZ 86336   **(602) 282-4179**

Mexican. Oaxaca offers regional and Southwestern entrées, featuring blue-corn and whole-wheat tortillas. Heart-healthy dishes and vegetarian meals are planned by a registered dietitian. All food is repared fresh daily without additives or animal fat. **Open daily. Full service, espresso/cappuccino, wine/beer/alcohol, take-out, VISA/MC/DISC, $$.**

Thai Spices

2986 W. Hwy. 89A, Sedona, AZ 86336   **(520) 282-0599**

Thai. Vegetarians can dine on Pad Thai (a rice noodle, vegetable, and tofu dish), Thai Fried Rice, vegetable curry, organic brown rice, and other dishes at Thai Spices. **Open Monday through Saturday for lunch and dinner. Open Sunday for dinner only. Full service, vegan options, take-out, VISA/MC, $$.**

TEMPE

Byblos Restaurant

3332 S. Mill Ave., Tempe, AZ 85282   **(520) 894-1945**

Middle Eastern. Dine on delicious Middle Eastern cuisine, including hummus, tabbouleh, falafel, stuffed grape leaves, and more. **Open Monday through Saturday for lunch and dinner. Open Sunday for dinner. Closed holidays. Full service, non-alcoholic wine/beer, wine/beer/alcohol, VISA/MC/AMEX/DC, $$.**

Delhi Palace
933 E. University Dr., Ste. 103, Tempe, AZ 85281   **(602) 921-2200**
Indian. Delhi Palace offers many vegetarian options. **Open daily for lunch and dinner. Full service, vegan options, take-out, VISA/MC/AMEX/DISC/DC, $$.**

Desert Greens Café
234 W. University Dr., Tempe, AZ 85282   **(480) 968-4831**
Natural foods deli. The Desert Greens Café is located within Gentle Strength, a natural foods co-op market. The deli strives to provide vegetarian, vegan, and macrobiotic choices in a healthy, pleasing atmosphere. Featured are award-winning muffins, soups, fresh sandwiches, daily specials, and desserts. **Open daily for lunch. Sunday brunch only. Limited service, vegan/macrobiotic options, take-out, VISA/MC, $.**

Pita Jungle
1250 E. Apache Blvd., Tempe, AZ 85281   **(520) 804-0234**
Natural foods. Enjoy a wide variety of Middle Eastern dishes, including pita sandwiches and salads. **Open daily for three meals. Full service, vegan options, take-out, $.**

Sahara Middle Eastern Restaurant
808 S. Mill Ave., Tempe, AZ 85281   **(480) 966-1971**
Middle Eastern. The family-run restaurant offers several vegetarian dishes, including hummus, baba ghanouj, tabbouleh, salads, stuffed grape leaves, falafel, and more. **Open Monday through Saturday for lunch and dinner. Open Sunday for dinner except in the summer. Full service, vegan options, catering, take-out, $-$$.**

Saigon Healthy Cuisine
820 S. Mill Ave., Tempe, AZ 85281   **(520) 967-4199**
Vietnamese. Vegetarian Spring Rolls, Papaya Vegetable Soup, Vegetable Pineapple Stew, and Spicy Lemongrass Vegetarian Delight are a few of the many vegetarian options found on this restaurant's menu. **Open Monday through Saturday for lunch and dinner. Closed Sunday. Limited service, vegan options, take-out, $.**

•• Veggie Fun
2240 N. Scottsdale Rd., #8, Tempe, AZ 85281   **(480) 941-9003**
Vegan/Chinese. This restaurant offers dishes made with mock meats and a stir-fry bar, where patrons can choose the ingredients and watch as their dish is prepared. Save room for their vegan soft serve ice cream for dessert. **Open Monday through Friday for lunch and dinner. Open Saturday and Sunday for dinner only. Limited service, take-out, VISA/MC, $$.**

TUCSON

• Casbah Teahouse
628 N. 4th Ave., Tucson, AZ 85705   **(520) 740-0393**
Vegetarian/Middle Eastern. The Casbah Teahouse is a vegetarian restaurant with a Middle Eastern flair. They serve many organic foods in a setting that includes Afghani rugs, pillows, and gypsy-style bellydancing. Their dishes include Shepherd's Pie, Tofu Quiche, Gypsy Stew, Reuben Burgers, organic bagels, organic potato salad, cashew gravy, and more. They even

offer soy margarine and tofu cream cheese. **Open daily for lunch and dinner. Full service, vegan options, outdoor smoking only, take-out, catering, fresh juices, espresso/capuccino, smoothies, soymilk, VISA/MC, $.** www.casbahteahouse.com

China-Thai Cuisine
6502 E. Tanque Verde, Tucson, AZ 85715   **(520) 885-6860**
Chinese/Thai. China-Thai Cuisine serves about eight vegetable dishes, as well as tofu veg-etable soup, in a totally non-smoking environment. **Open for lunch and dinner. Full service, take out, delivery, VISA/MC/AMEX/DISC/DC, $$.**

Frog and Firkin
874 E. University Blvd., Tucson, AZ 85719   **(520) 623-7507**
American. English pub atmosphere with a large outdoor patio, located close to the University of Arizona. Menu items include veggie and vegan pizzas. **Open daily for lunch through late dinner. Full service, wine/beer/alcohol, VISA/MC/AMEX/DISC/DC, $$.**

The Garland Restaurant
119 E. Speedway Blvd., Tucson, AZ 85705   **(520) 792-4221**
Chinese. The Garland, selected as the Best of Tucson for "Vegetarian Fine Dining," offers international cuisine in an informal setting. This long-established restaurant offers dishes such as "Tom Soya" and "Tofu Normandy" on the menu. **Open daily for three meals. Full service, macrobiotic/vegan options, fresh juices, smoothies, soymilk, wine/beer, catering, VISA/MC/DISC/DC, $$.**

• Govinda's
711 E. Blacklidge Dr., Tucson, AZ 85719   **(520) 792-0630**
Vegetarian. Govinda's offers a natural foods buffet featuring international dishes, fresh juices, and a sandwich bar. Most of the dishes are vegan, including items like Veggie Croquettes in Spinach Sauce, Mock Fish Fillet with Almond Tartar Sauce, and Vegetarian Lasagna. They serve only vegan food on Thursday night. **Open Wednesday through Saturday for lunch and dinner. Open Tuesday for dinner only. Closed Sunday and Monday. Cafeteria, vegan options, take-out, VISA/MC, $$.**

Guilin Restaurant
3250 E. Speedway, Tucson, AZ 85716   **(520) 320-7768**
Chinese. Menu includes over 80 tofu and vegetarian dishes. Located across from "The Loft" movie cinema. **Open daily for lunch and dinner. Full service, vegan options, take-out, non-smoking, fresh juices, soymilk, special drinks, wine/beer, non-alcoholic wine/beer, VISA/MC/AMEX, $$.**

La Indita
622 N. 4th Ave., Tucson, AZ 85705   **(520) 792-0523**

Mexican. "La Indita," an affectionate term for a little female Indian in Spanish, features the unique recipes of its own "little Indian woman," Maria Garcia, a Tarascan Indian from Michoacan, Mexico. The restaurant offers a mixture of traditional Mexican food, popular Indian fry breads, and Maria Garcia's own family recipes. No lard is used, and vegetarian items are indicated on the menu. Patio dining available. **Open daily for lunch and dinner. Full service, vegan options, fresh juices, wine/beer, take-out, $.**

Lotus Garden Restaurant
5975 E. Speedway, Tucson, AZ 85712   **(520) 298-4553**

Chinese. Specializes in Cantonese and Szechwan cuisine. Menu items are made to order and can be adjusted to special needs. Contemporary décor with new age music and patio. **Open daily for lunch and dinner. Full service, vegan options, informal atmosphere, suitable for business entertaining, non-smoking, take-out, catering, reservations recommended, wine/beer, non-alcoholic wine/beer, VISA/MC/AMEX/DISC/DC, $$.**

Magpies Gourmet Pizza
605 N. 4th Ave., Tucson, AZ 85705   **(520) 628-1661**
7315 N. Oracle, Tucson, AZ 85704   **(520) 297-2712**
5625 W. Cortaro Farms Rd., Tucson, AZ 85710   **(520) 744-0440**
4654 E. Speedway, Tucson, AZ 85712   **(520) 795-5977**
7157 E. Tanque Verde Rd., Tucson, AZ 85715   **(520) 546-6526**
105 S Houghton Rd., #149, Tucson, AZ 85748   **(520) 751-9949**

Pizza. This award-winning pizzaria offers a lacto "all vegetarian menu" but will be happy to use soy cheese upon request for no extra charge. **Open daily for lunch and dinner. Full service, delivery, take-out, beer and wine patio, "take & bake," VISA/MC/AMEX/DISC/DC, $-$$$.** www.magpiesgourmetpizza.com

Maya Quetzal
429 N. 4th Ave., Tucson, AZ 85705   **(520) 622-8207**

Guatemalan. Maya Quetzal's vegetarian options include tamales made with corn and rice, masa stuffed with spinach and red bell pepper sauce, and chiles releños stuffed with spinach and walnuts. **Open Monday through Saturday for lunch and dinner. Closed Sunday. Full service, vegan options, catering, take-out, VISA/MC, $-$$.**

New Delhi Palace
6751 E. Broadway Blvd., Tucson, AZ 85710   **(520) 296-8585**

Indian. This restaurant offers several Northern Indian-style vegetarian dishes. **Open daily for lunch and dinner. Full service, vegan options, fresh juices, wine/beer/alcohol, VISA/MC/AMEX/DC, $$$.**

New Life Café
4841 E. Speedway, Tucson, AZ 85712   **(520) 795-7862**
Natural foods. Try the traditional Southwestern flavors of guacamole tostadas and chili tostadas, or one of the tempeh, tofu, or garden burgers served at this largely vegetarian café. Open Monday through Saturday for lunch and dinner. Closed Sunday. Limited service, vegan options, fresh juices, smoothies, Visa/MC/DISC, $$.

Shish Kebab House of Tucson
5855 E. Broadway Blvd., Tucson, AZ 85711   **(520) 745-5308**
Middle Eastern. Authentic home-cooking from grandma's recipes. Open daily for lunch and dinner. Full service, non-smoking, informal atmosphere, reservations recommended, espresso/cappucino, wine/beer/alcohol, VISA/MC/AMEX/DISC, $$.

Tork's Café and Market
3502 E. Grant Rd., Tucson, AZ 85716   **(520) 325-3737**
Middle Eastern. Tork's Café offers many vegetarian options. Open Monday through Saturday for lunch and dinner. Closed Sunday. Counter service, $$.

Arkansas

EUREKA SPRINGS

Dairy Hollow House
515 Spring St., Eureka Springs, AR 72632   **(501) 253-7444**
Natural foods. Enjoy fine dining and contemporary Southern cuisine at this award-winning country inn and restaurant. The vegetarian owners make sure the soups are vegetarian, and there is always at least one vegetarian selection for a main course. Dairy Hollow House is willing to accommodate vegans with notice. Dinner is served at one seating at 7 p.m. Open nightly from April 1st to December 31st and on weekends during February and March. Full service, reservations required, formal, VISA/MC/AMEX/DISC/DC, $$$.

Mud Street Espresso Café
22G S. Main St., Eureka Springs, AR 72632   **(501) 253-6732**
Café. Located in the historic downtown area, this café offers an extensive vegetarian menu. Dishes include scones or sour cream pancakes for breakfast, Eggplant Tosca for lunch, and Korma Curry and Mushroom Tosca for dinner. Open Thursday through Tuesday for three meals. Closed Wednesday. Full service, take-out, informal atmosphere, special drinks, espresso/cappuccino, wine/beer/alcohol, $$.

The Oasis
53 Spring St., #C, Eureka Springs, AR 72632   **(501) 253-0886**
Mexican. Home of the original Ark-Mex cuisine. All natural and freshly prepared items include a green olive, tomato, and garlic burrito and vegetarian fajitas. Open daily for brunch and lunch. Full service, vegan options, take out, $.

Sparky's Roadhouse Café
147 E. Van Buren, Eureka Springs, AR 72632 **(501) 253-6001**
American. Along with traditional café fare, Sparky's Roadhouse Cafe serves up tabbouli, Gardenburgers, and enchiladas. In the winter, diners can sit beside a wood stove on the patio. Sparky's prides itself on its "kitschy" decor. **Open Monday through Saturday for lunch and dinner. Closed Sundays and from February 1st to March 17th. Full service, vegan options, non-alcoholic wine/beer, wine/beer/alcohol, VISA/MC/DISC, $$.**

FAYETTEVILLE

Racha Restaurant
2334 N. College Ave., Fayetteville, AR 72703 **(479) 251-7072**
Thai. Turn to the back page of Racha's menu, and you will find the Vegetarian Corner, featuring appetizers, soups, noodle dishes, curries, and entrées. Try the Tofu Coconut Soup with mushrooms, tofu, lemongrass, and ginger simmered in lime juice and coconut milk; Rana (large noodles topped with mixed vegetables and gravy); or the Garlic Pepper Tofu. Save room for the Fried Bananas or the Sweet Mango with Sticky Rice for dessert. **Open Tuesday through Sunday for lunch and dinner. Closed Monday. Full service, vegan options, take-out, VISA/MC/DISC, $$.**

The Village Epicureans
440 Mission, Fayetteville, AR 72701 **(501) 444-0010**
Natural foods. The Village Epicureans serves ethnic dishes, soups, sandwiches, and more in a friendly atmosphere. Organic produce is used when available. **Open Monday through Friday for lunch. Closed Saturday and Sunday. Limited service, vegan/macrobiotic options, fresh juices, catering, take-out, $$.**

LITTLE ROCK

Wild Oats
3000 S. Rodney Parham Rd., Little Rock, AR 72205 **(501) 221-2331**
Natural foods deli. Formerly Beans, Grains, & Things, this deli is located in a Wild Oats health foods store. **Open daily. Limited service, VISA/MC, $.**

California

ALBANY

• Mother Nature Vegetarian Cuisine
843 San Pablo Ave., Albany, CA 94706 **(510) 528-5388**
Vegetarian/Chinese. This restaurant serves many unique Chinese dishes, including several mock meat dishes. **Open Wednesday through Monday for lunch and dinner. Closed Tuesday. Full service, vegan options, fresh juices, non-alcoholic beer, wine/beer, $$.**

ALHAMBRA

• Vege House
1400 E. Valley Blvd., Alhambra, CA 91801   **(626) 293-8169**
Vegetarian/Chinese. Enjoy mock "meat" dishes and traditional Chinese vegetable dishes at Vege House. **Open daily for lunch and dinner. Full service, vegan options, take-out, $$.**

• Vegetarian Wok
529 E. Valley Blvd., #128, Alhambra, CA 91801   **(626) 288-6069**
Vegetarian/Chinese. This totally vegetarian Chinese restaurant offers creative dishes using gluten, yams, or mushrooms in place of meat, chicken, and fish. **Open daily for lunch and dinner. Full service, vegan options, take-out, VISA/MC, $$.**

ALTADENA

•• O' Happy Days
2283 N. Lake Ave., Altadena, CA 91001   **(626) 797-0383**
Vegan. This self-described "vegan homestyle restaurant," located inside a natural foods store, offers soups, salads, sandwiches, and entreés in an informal atmosphere. **Open Monday through Saturday for lunch through early dinner. Closed Sunday. Cafeteria, soymilk, $.**

ANAHEIM

• Rasthal Vegetarian Cuisine
2751 W. Lincoln Ave., Anaheim, CA 92801-6332   **(714) 527-3800**
Vegetarian/Indian. Far from your typical vegetarian South Indian restaurant, Rasthal's menu includes veggie stews, kaju karela (cashews, bitter gourds, and coconut oil), upma (chili-laced farina), tomato-stuffed uttapams, kachori (donut-hole sized fritters stuffed with brown lentils), and thali. This restaurant offers lunch and evening buffets. **Open Tuesday through Sunday. Closed Monday. Full service, vegan options, take-out, VISA/MC, $-$$.**

Thai & Thai Restaurant
150 E. Katella Ave., Anaheim, CA 92802   **(714) 635-3060**
Thai. Only a 20-minute walk from Disneyland and the Anaheim Convention Center, Thai & Thai offers 11 items on its "Vegetarian Lovers" menu, such as Spicy Mint Tofu, Stir-Fried Glass Noodles, or Tofu with Pepper & Garlic. They also serve a $4.95 Lunch Express on weekdays. Be sure to ask that they don't use fish sauce when ordering. **Open daily for lunch and dinner. Full service, vegan options, beer/wine, delivery, VISA/MC/AMEX, $-$$.**

• Yogiraj
3107 W. Lincoln Ave., Anaheim, CA 92801   **(714) 995-5900**
Vegetarian/Indian. With a relaxed atmosphere, Yogiraj specializes in North Indian, Gujarati, and South Indian foods, including sada mysora dhosa (rice crepes with chutney), masala paper dhosa (rice crepes with potato and onion), and pau bhaji (mashed vegetables marinated in a spicy garlic sauce). **Open Tuesday through Sunday for lunch and dinner. Closed Monday. Full service, VISA/MC, $.**

ARCATA

Day Break Café
768 18th St., Arcata, CA 95521   **(707) 826-7543**

Natural foods. Enjoy a wide range of natural foods served at this café. Local organic products are used when available. **Open Sunday through Thursday for breakfast and lunch. Open Friday and Saturday for three meals. Full service, vegan options, fresh juices, espresso/cappuccino, take-out, MC, $.**

Spoons Take-Out Kitchen, Arcata Co-op
811 I St., Arcata, CA 95521   **(707) 822-5947**

Natural foods deli. Spoons is a deli-style kitchen in a natural foods co-op supermarket. Ethnic foods, salads, and entrées are offered, most of which are meatless. Locally grown organic foods are used whenever possible. **Open daily. Deli-style, vegan options, fresh juices, wine/beer, take-out, $.** www.northcoastco-op.com

• Wildflower Café and Bakery
1604 G St., Arcata, CA 95521   **(707) 822-0360**

Vegetarian/macrobiotic. Wildflower features gourmet vegetarian and macrobiotic foods, using local organic fruits and vegetables when possible. Feast on the Nut Loaf Sandwich, West Indian Curry, Mushroom Stroganoff, or one of the many other vegetarian selections. The fresh-baked breads and sweets are excellent. **Open Monday through Saturday for three meals. Open Sunday for lunch. Full service, macrobiotic/vegan options, fresh juice, catering, no credit cards, $.**

ARTESIA

• Annapurna Cuisine
17631 Pioneer Blvd., Artesia, CA 90701   **(562) 403-2200**

Vegetarian/Indian. This restaurant offers a buffet featuring appetizers, lemon rice, curry dishes, dosas, and much more. **Open daily for three meals. Full service, vegan options, take-out, VISA/MC/AMEX/DISC, $$.**

• Udupi Palace
18635 Pioneer Blvd., Artesia, CA 90701   **(562) 860-1950**

Vegetarian/Indian. Udupi Palace's authentic South Indian dishes include iddly (steamed rice and lentil patties), rasam (spicy soup), a variety of dosai (crepes), uthappan (Indian pancakes), thali, and curries. **Open Tuesday through Sunday for lunch and dinner. Closed Monday. Full service, informal atmosphere, reservations recommended, VISA/MC/AMEX, $$.**

• Veggie's Delight, Co.
11736 166th St., Artesia, CA 90701   **(562) 860-4789**

Vegetarian/Chinese. This deli and bakery offers box lunches prepared daily with steamed brown or white rice, deli-style Chinese foods, Chinese cookies, and an eggless sponge cake. **Open Tuesday through Saturday for lunch and dinner. Closed Sunday and Monday. Take-out, vegan options, $.**

•Woodlands Indian Cuisine
11833 Artesia Blvd., Artesia, CA 90701 (562) 860-6500
Vegetarian/Indian. Specializing in dosai. Open Tuesday through Sunday for lunch and dinner. Closed Monday. Full service, vegan options, catering.

AUBURN

David's Thai Cuisine
13338 Lincoln Way, Auburn, CA 95603   **(530) 888-6444**
Thai. David's Thai Cuisine has specialized in southern Thai dishes for more than a decade at this location. Open Tuesday through Friday for lunch and dinner. Open Saturday for late lunch through dinner. Closed Sunday and Monday. Full service, vegan options, special drinks, beer/wine/alcohol, VISA/MC, $$.

•Latitudes
130 Maple St., #11, Auburn, CA 95603-5035   **(530) 885-9535**
Vegetarian/natural foods. Offering multicultural cuisine with an excellent vegetarian selection, Latitudes features a tropical décor with indoor and outdoor dining, an extensive microbrewery, and California wine selection. Family dining is welcome. Open Monday, Wednesday, Thursday, and Friday for lunch and dinner. Open Tuesday and Saturday for dinner only. Open Sunday for brunch. Full service, vegan options, fresh juices, catering, take-out, VISA/MC/AMEX, $$-$$$.

BERKELEY

•Ashkenaz Music and Dance Café
1317 San Pablo Ave., Berkeley, CA 94702   **(510) 525-5054**
Vegetarian. Ashkenaz's atmosphere is highlighted by live music and dancing six nights a week with sumptuous foods, such as vegetarian stew, tofu sandwiches, chips and salsa, fruit, and bagels. Open Tuesday through Sunday for late evening service only. Closed Monday. Limited service, fresh juices, non-alcoholic beer, wine/beer, $$.

Blue Nile
2525 Telegraph Ave., Berkeley, CA 94704   **(510) 540-6777**
Ethiopian. The Blue Nile serves authentic Ethiopian cuisine in a warm and inviting environment. Vegetarian dishes are clearly indicated and described. Open daily. Full service, vegan options, wine/beer, take-out, VISA/MC, $-$$.

Café Intermezzo
2442 Telegraph Ave., Berkeley, CA 94704   **(510) 849-4592**
Natural foods. This restaurant serves mostly vegetarian food, including soups, salads, and sandwiches. Open daily. Full service, fresh juices, wine/beer, take-out, $.

•• Cha-Ya Restaurant
1686 Shattuck Ave., Berkeley, CA 94709   **(510) 981-1213**
Vegan/Japanese. Located near the UC-Berkeley campus, Cha-Ya uses centuries-old cooking

traditions to prepare their authentic Japanese meals. **Open Tuesday to Sunday for dinner. Closed Monday. Full service, counter service, beer/wine, VISA/MC, $$.**

Elmwood Natural Foods
2944 College Ave., Berkeley, CA 94705   **(510) 841-3871**
Natural foods deli. This organic grocery offers soup, sandwiches, and take-out macrobiotic meals. Non-dairy, whole-grain desserts and baked goods made without refined sugar are also available. **Open daily. Counter service, macrobiotic, take-out, VISA/MC, $.**

• Govinda's
2334 Stuart St., Berkeley, CA 94705   **(510) 644-2777**
Vegetarian. Govinda's offers a vegetarian all-you-can-eat buffet. **Open Tuesday through Saturday. Closed Sunday and Monday. $.**

Lanesplitter Pub
2033 San Pablo Ave., Berkeley, CA 94702   **(510) 845-1652**
Pizza. Lanesplitter offers New York-style thin crust pizza and a large selection of micro-brewed beers on tap. **Open Sunday through Thursday for early dinner through late night. Open Friday and Saturday for lunch through late night. Closed Monday. Full service, vegan options, beer/wine, VISA/MC/DISC, $$.** www.lanesplitterpub.com

Long Life Vegi House
2129 University Ave., Berkeley, CA 94704   **(510) 845-6072**
Chinese. Though Vegi House does serve a few fish dishes, its menu has more than 100 vege-tarian entrées, including mock chicken, beef, or pork; tofu and vegetarian soups; and appe-tizers like Pot Stickers and Fresh Garlic Seaweed Salad. Even the pickiest of eaters should find something they like here! No MSG is used. **Open daily. Full service, vegan options, wine/beer, catering, take-out, VISA/MC/AMEX/DISC, $$.**

Maharani India Restaurant
1025 University Ave., Berkeley, CA 94710   **(510) 848-7777**
Indian. This Indian restaurant has an extensive vegetarian menu. **Open daily. Full service, vegan options, wine/beer, take-out, VISA/MC/AMEX/DISC, $$.**

• Michael's American Vegetarian Diner
2650 Telegraph Ave., Berkeley, CA 94704   **(510) 548-0600**
Vegetarian/American. Michael's serves vegetarian versions of traditional diner fare, such as mock "tuna" melts, chili dogs, and Reuben sandwiches, in a '50s-style diner, complete with jukeboxes at the booths. Ninety percent of the extensive menu can be prepared vegan. **Open daily for three meals. Full service, vegan options, take-out, soymilk, beer, non-alco-holic beer, organic wine, VISA/MC, $$.**

• Raw Energy Organic Juice Café
2050 Addison St., Berkeley, CA 94704   **(510) 665-9464**

Vegetarian juice bar. In addition to juices, smoothies, and nut milks, the menu here includes muesli, soups, salads, sandwiches, raw pizzas, and desserts. **Open Monday through Friday for three meals. Closed Saturday and Sunday.** Counter service, vegan options, fresh juices, smoothies, special drinks, take-out, no credit cards, $. www.rawenergy.net

• Smart Alec's Intelligent Fast Food
2355 Telegraph Ave., Berkeley, CA 94704   **(510) 704-4000**

Vegetarian. A fast food atmosphere encapsules Smart Alec's veggie burgers, gourmet salads, and low-fat French fries. **Open daily for three meals.** Limited service, vegan options, fresh juices, espresso/cappuccino, wine/beer, $$.

• Smokey Joe's Café
1620 Shattuck Ave., Berkeley, CA 94709   (no phone)

Vegetarian. Open since 1973, Smokey Joe's Café claims to be the first vegetarian restaurant in the Bay Area. This earthy establishment offers omelets, pancakes, French toast, tofu scramble, oatmeal, home fries, a BBQ veggie sandwich, and much more. Many of their dishes involve beans, eggs, and sprouts. **Open daily for breakfast and lunch.** Full service, vegan options, fresh juices, $$. www.smokeyjoesberkeley.com

• Vegi Food, Inc.
2083 Vine St., Berkeley, CA 94709   **(510) 548-5244**

Vegetarian/Chinese. Enjoy this all-vegetarian establishment. **Open daily. Open Monday for dinner only.** Full service, $$.

Vital Vittles
2810 San Pablo Ave., Berkeley, CA 94702   **(510) 644-2022**

Bakery. This certified organic and kosher bakery offers breads that vary from 12-Grain to Sesame Millet. **Open daily.** Take-out, $.

Whole Foods Market
3000 Telegraph Ave., Berkeley, CA 94705   **(510) 649-1333**

Natural foods deli. You will find both vegetarian and vegan options in this deli. **Open daily.** Cafeteria, fresh juice, take-out, VISA/MC, $-$$.

`BEVERLY HILLS`

• • Real Food Daily ✪
242 S. Beverly Dr., Beverly Hills, CA 90212   **(310) 858-0880**

Vegan. Real Food Daily's philosophy is that healthy food prepared with gourmet style and hands-on care improves not only the health of the individual but also that of the planet. You can dine on such items as lentil-walnut paté, millet croquettes, seitan fajitas, black bean burritos, tempeh Reubens, vegetable pot pies, salads, chocolate cake, and tofu cheesecake. **Open daily for lunch and dinner.** Full service, fresh juices, smoothies, soymilk, espresso/cappucino, beer/wine, take-out, VISA/MC/AMEX, $$. www.realfood.com

BOULDER CREEK

The Common Way Café
13070 Hwy. 9, Boulder Creek, CA 95006 **(408) 338-2105**
Natural foods. Located in True Nature Foods, this café offers a large selection of vegan food and organic baked goods. **Open daily for three meals. Limited service, vegan options, take-out, $-$$.**

CALISTOGA

Calistoga Inn Restaurant & Brewery
12150 Lincoln Ave., Calistoga, CA 94515 **(707) 942-4101**
California. This restaurant features vegetarian black bean chili, two veggie sandwiches, as well as vegetarian appetizers and entrées. **Open daily for three meals. Full service, catering, vegan options, beer/wine, $$-$$$.**

CAMARILLO

China Palace
341 Arneill Rd., Camarillo, CA 93010 **(805) 987-4234**
Chinese. Ask for China Palace's separate vegetarian menu, and you'll be a very happy diner. Enjoy both soy- and gluten-based dishes, as well as noodle and vegetable delights. **Open daily for lunch and dinner. Full service, vegan options, take-out, VISA/MC/AMEX, $$.**

CAMPBELL

Bread of Life
1690 S. Bascom Ave., Campbell, CA 95008 **(408) 371-5000**
Health foods store deli. Bread of Life offers a salad bar with more than 40 items, including sushi, quiche, and cakes. Also available are more than 30 salads, 20 desserts, and 20 sandwiches. **Open daily for breakfast and lunch. Limited service, fresh juices, take-out, VISA/MC/DISC, $.**

Royal Taj India Cuisine
1350 Camden Ave., Campbell, CA 95008 **(408) 559-6801**
Indian. Thirteen vegetarian specialties are available at this restaurant offering authentic Indian cuisine at five locations. Royal Taj also offers pakoras, samosas, dahl soup, salads, and many Indian breads. **Open daily for lunch and dinner. Full service, vegan options, wine/beer, take-out, VISA/MC/AMEX/DISC, $.**

•• Tasty Vegetarian Cuisine
2455 S. Winchester Blvd., Campbell, CA 95008 **(408) 374-9791**
Vegan/Chinese. Patrons here can enjoy a wide variety of vegan Chinese dishes, some of which use tofu or gluten. **Open daily for lunch and dinner. Full service, VISA/MC, $$.**

•Follow Your Heart Natural Foods & Café ✪
21825 Sherman Way, Canoga Park, CA 91303   **(818) 348-3240**
Vegetarian. This restaurant offers an excellent selection of natural vegetarian foods made without eggs, sugar, or harmful additives. Dishes include salads with a creative selection of dressings, sandwiches, entrées with vegetarian (rennet-free) cheese, tofu dishes, burritos, and other vegetarian favorites. Beverages include juices, teas, and shakes. They also offer a full breakfast menu and weekend brunch. **Open daily for three meals. Full service, vegan options, fresh juices, BYOB, take-out, VISA/MC, $$.** www.followyourheart.com

Book Café
1475 41st Ave., Capitola, CA 95010   **(408) 462-4415**
Natural foods. The Book Café features lasagna, soups, deli salads, and pastries. **Open Monday through Saturday. Closed Sunday. Counter service, $.**

•Dharma's Restaurant
4250 Capitola Rd., Capitola, CA 95010   **(408) 462-1742**
Vegetarian. A smiling cow wearing dark sunglasses graces the front of Dharma's menu. This is followed by statistics on the number of rainforest acres and cows saved by eating Dharma's vegetarian burgers. No bull! This serious mission with a sense of humor and excellent food is a combination worth exploring. Dharma's offers a wide range of international vegetarian dishes, including Mexican, Italian, Chinese, Japanese, and Thai, in addition to the old American standbys, great muffins, and desserts. The majority of the food is organic. **Open daily for three meals. Cafeteria, vegan options, limited service, fresh juices, espresso, wine/beer, take-out, $.** www.dharmaland.com

•New Beet Café
1210 41st Ave., Capitola, CA 95010   **(831) 479-7987**
Vegetarian. Located inside New Leaf Community Market, New Beet Café offers rice plates, wraps, and salads. Their "Morning Scramble" is made with vegetables, tofu, roasted potatoes, and toast. **Open daily for three meals. Limited service, vegan options, fresh juices, espresso/cappuccino, smoothies, soymilk, $.** www.newleaf.com

Café Stravaganza
241 Crossroads Blvd., Carmel, CA 93921   **(831) 625-3733**
Café. Café Stravaganza has many vegetarian options, such as Veggie Melt, Eggplant Sandwich, Dolmas, Homemade Gaspacho, Veggie Fusili, Pasta Puttanesca, and Pasta Primavera. **Open daily for lunch and dinner. Full service, vegan options, take-out, VISA/MC/AMEX.**

Grill On Ocean Avenue
Ocean Ave. and Lincoln Ln., Carmel, CA 93921   **(831) 624-2569**
California-style. For fine, fresh, and upscale dining, try the Grill on Carmel's quaint Ocean

Avenue in Carmel. The restaurant's giant windows are kept open so customers can enjoy the ocean air on pleasant afternoons, which are common for the area. The Grill is ideal for those in the mood to be pampered. **Open daily for lunch and dinner. Full service, reservations taken, fireplace, $$-$$$.**

La Dolce Vita
San Carlos St. and 7th Ave., Carmel, CA 93923   **(831) 624-3667**
Italian. Live the sweet life in this authentic Italian restaurant with outdoor seating and delicious cuisine. **Open daily for lunch and dinner. Full service, beer/wine/alcohol, $-$$$.**

The Power Juice and Food Company
173 Crossroads Blvd., Carmel, CA 93921   **(831) 626-6577**
Juice bar/café/bakery. The Power Juice and Food Company offers veggie-friendly fare in a casual atmosphere. **Open daily for three meals. Counter service, macrobiotic/vegan options, take-out, fresh juices, $.**

CARMICHAEL

Honey Bee Asian Restaurant
6301 Fair Oaks Blvd., Carmichael, CA 95608   **(916) 483-0341**
Chinese. This restaurant is a real gem hiding in a suburban strip mall. Ask for their huge listing of vegetarian (mostly vegan) options, many made from vegetable-based mock meats. **Open daily for lunch and dinner. Full service, vegan options, take-out, VISA/MC, $-$$.**

CERRITOS

• Madras Tiffin
11321 E. 183rd St., Cerritos, CA 90701   **(562) 924-0879**
Vegetarian/Indian. This South Indian vegetarian restaurant offers samosas, pakoras, poories, crepes, and stuffed patties. **Open Tuesday through Sunday. Closed Monday. Full service, vegan options, wine/beer, take-out, VISA/MC, $.**

•• Vegi Wokery
11329 183rd St., Cerritos, CA 90703   **(562) 809-3928**
Vegan/Chinese. The Vegi Wokery has more than 80 different menu items, including the chef's specialties, Vegetarian Carnival and Bean Curd Feast. **Open for lunch and dinner Monday through Saturday. Closed Sunday. Full service, take-out, fresh juices, $$.**

CHATSWORTH

• Woodlands
9840 Topanga Canyon Blvd., Chatsworth, CA 91311   **(818) 998-3031**
Vegetarian/Indian. Specializing in South Indian cuisine, this restaurant offers masala dosa, uthappam, and much more. **Open Tuesday through Sunday for lunch and dinner. Closed Monday. Full service, vegan options, $$.**

CHICO

• Café Sandino
817 Main St., Chico, CA 95928   **(530) 894-6515**

Vegetarian. Home of "Today's Tamales," Café Sandino is a vegetarian restaurant that strives to use organically grown ingredients and utilizes unrefined canola and olive oils. **Open Monday through Saturday for lunch and dinner. Closed Sunday. Full service, vegan options, fresh juices, wine/beer, take-out, $-$$.**

CHULA VISTA

•• Cilantro Live!
315 3rd Ave., Chula Vista, CA 91910   **(619) 827-7401**

Vegan/raw foods. This establishment is San Diego County's first organic, vegan, and 100 percent raw restaurant. The menu offers appetizers, soups, salads, wraps, entrées, and desserts, including the Walnut Mushroom Loaf, Roma Raw-violis, and Coconut-Carob Dream Parfait. They also feature books, nutritional supplies, and free health lectures every Wednesday night. **Open daily for lunch and dinner. Full service, fresh juices, smoothies, take-out, VISA/MC/AMEX/DISC/DC, $$. www.cilantrolive.com**

COLTON

Maharajah India Cuisine
1091 S. Mt. Vernon Ave., Ste. G, Colton, CA 92324   **(909) 824-5493**

Indian. Maharajah offers a wide selection of vegetarian entrées. Be sure to sample some the Indian breads as well. **Open Wednesday through Friday, Sunday, and Monday for lunch and dinner. Open Saturday for dinner only. Closed Tuesday. Full service, vegan options, non-alcoholic beer, beer, VISA/MC/DISC, $$.**

CONCORD

Swagat Indian Cuisine
1901 Salvio St., Concord, CA 94520   **(510) 685-2777**

Indian. Swagat offers traditional northern and southern Indian dishes during its lunch buffet and for dinner. Try a Dal Curry (lentils made with spinach and tomatoes), Aloo Saag (spinach and potato cooked with mild spices), and Navratan Koorma (nine vegetables in a mild cream sauce). Reservations recommended. Swagat also hosts tango, swing, and social dance lessons in the evenings. **Open daily for lunch and dinner. Full service, vegan options, beer/wine/ alcohol, take-out, catering, VISA/MC/AMEX/DISC/DC, $$.**

CORONA DEL MAR

Mayur
2931 E. Coast Hwy., Corona del Mar, CA 92625   **(714) 675-6622**

Indian. Mayur offers several vegetarian entrées, including vegetable jalfrezi, dahl, roasted eggplant, and creamed spinach with cheese. **Open daily for lunch and dinner. Full service, vegan options, take-out, VISA/MC/AMEX, $$.**

CORONADO

Viva Nova

1138 Orange Ave., Coronado, CA 92118 **(619) 435-2124**

Health foods store deli. Enjoy salads, daily soups, burritos, healthy sandwiches, vegetable juices, and smoothies at Viva Nova. At the time of publishing, this establishment was for sale, so call ahead for more details. **Open daily for breakfast through early dinner. Limited service, vegan options, fresh juices, smoothies, take-out, $.**

COSTA MESA

Mother's Market & Kitchen

225 E. 17th St., Costa Mesa, CA 92627 **(949) 631-4741**

Natural foods. Mother's menu is vegetarian, except for tuna. Centrally located within a natural foods store, the restaurant offers a wide assortment of delicious appetizers, salads, entrées, pastas, sandwiches, and ethnic and side dishes. A children's menu is also available. **Open daily for three meals. Full service, fresh juices, espresso/cappuccino, non-alcoholic wine/beer, take-out, $.**

• Native Foods ○

2937 Bristol St., Costa Mesa, CA 92626 **(714) 751-2151**

Vegetarian. Native Foods uses tempeh, seitan, and textured vegetable protein (TVP) to make many of the dishes found at this mostly vegan restaurant. Try the Jerk Burger made with spicy grilled seitan, a mock fish sandwich called the Moby Dick, Indonesian tempeh chips, or Japanese buckwheat noodle stir-fry called Yakisoba. **Open Monday through Saturday for lunch and dinner. Closed Sunday. Full service, vegan options, macrobiotic/vegan options, espresso/cappucino, catering, take-out, $$.** www.nativefoods.com

COVINA

• Covina Tasty

1063 N. Citrus Ave., Covina, CA 91722 **(626) 332-8816**

Vegetarian. Serving all vegetarian "fast food" since 1961, Covina Tasty offers burgers, hot dogs, sandwiches, burritos, tacos, and desserts. Careful, though, since some of the smoothies do contain egg whites. **Open daily for lunch through late night. Limited service, vegan options, juices, smoothies, take-out, $.**

CRESCENT CITY

Good Harvest Café

700 N. Crest Dr., Crescent City, CA 95531 **(707) 465-6028**

Natural foods deli. Good Harvest Café has a vegetarian-friendly bakery and vegetarian items for every meal, including veggie burgers, club sandwiches, and veggie links. **Open Monday through Saturday for breakfast and lunch. Open Sunday for brunch. Full service, take-out, fresh juices, espresso/cappuccino, special drinks, beer/wine, $$.**

CUPERTINO

Hobee's Restaurant
21267 Stevens Creek Blvd., Cupertino, CA 95014   **(408) 255-6010**
Restaurant chain. Hobee's features a variety of Mexican favorites, veggie patties, black bean chili, and a salad bar to accompany any meal. **Open daily. Full service, fresh juices, wine/beer, take-out, VISA/MC, $$.**

• Kokila's Kitchen
20956 Homestead Rd., Cupertino, CA 95014   **(408) 777-8198**
Vegetarian/Indian. Located near Hwy. 85 and 280, this restaurant was twice voted "Best Indian Vegetarian Restaurant" by "Veg News Magazine of San Francisco." Its predominately Gujarat and Thali menu is 80 percent vegan. Specialties include a great navratan kurma (with potatoes, raisins, carrots, homemade cheese, and cashews), undhiyu (vegetable stew), ginger-spiked potatoes, kadhi (a soupy, yogurt-based dish thickened with chickpea flour), traditional breads, and gulab jamun (deep-fried fritters soaked in sugar syrup). Call ahead to make sure specific dishes will be available that day. **Open Tuesday through Sunday for lunch and dinner. Closed Monday. Buffet, vegan options, reservations recommended, fresh juices, soymilk, take-out, VISA/MC, $-$$.** www.kokilaskitchen.com

DAVIS

Noodle Express
301 G St., Davis, CA 95616   **(530) 753-7755**
Chinese. Noodle Express carries an extensive vegetarian menu with items such as Szechuan Tofu, Kung-Pao diced vegetable, and Hong Kong-Style Vegetarian Chow Mein. **Open Tuesday through Sunday for lunch and dinner. Closed Monday. Full service, take-out, no MSG, $.**

DUNCANS MILLS

The Blue Heron
25300 Steelhead Blvd., Duncans Mills, CA 95430   **(707) 865-9135**
Ethnic foods. The Blue Heron features international dishes, salads, and pasta dishes. **Open daily in the summer. Call for winter hours. Full service, wine/beer/alcohol, take-out, VISA/MC, $$$.**

EAGLE ROCK

• Fatty's & Co.
1627 Colorado Blvd., Eagle Rock, CA 90041   **(323) 255-3367**
Vegetarian. Located in a former garage, Fatty's is a great place to enjoy a soy latte or full meal. Breakfast offerings include hot oatmeal, bagel melts, and a host of coffees, teas, and hot chocolate. For lunch or dinner, try the Far East Noodle Salad, hummus, pizza, great sandwiches, or one of the two daily soups, one of which is always vegan. On Friday and Saturday nights, they offer sushi, such as the Fatty's Roll with mango, tofu, Japanese radish, red bell pepper, and black sesame seeds on the outside. This restaurant does not actually

advertise itself as vegetarian, so it's a great way to introduce meateaters to the cuisine. **Open Wednesday through Monday for three meals. Open Tuesday for breakfast and lunch. Limited service, vegan options, espresso/cappuccino, $$.**

EL SEGUNDO

•Papillon Vegetarian Cuisine and Grill
408 Main St., El Segundo, CA 90245   **(310) 640-0408**
Vegetarian/Asian. Papillon serves a variety of Chinese and Filipino dishes, including Vegetarian Pork Adobo and Vegetarian Escabeche, which tastes like salmon in sweet and sour sauce. **Open daily for lunch and dinner. Full service, vegan options, fresh juices, smoothies, VISA/MC/AMEX, $$.**

ELK GROVE

The Oasis Express
9253 Gem Crest Way, Elk Grove, CA 95624   **(916) 444-6199**
International. Offering Mediterranean, North African, and Italian dishes, The Oasis' menu includes some great veggie options. The Thurshi-Zucchini dip sounds fabulous, as well as the Swiss Chard and Spinach Salad. **Open Monday through Thursday for lunch. Open Friday for lunch and dinner. Open Saturday for dinner. Closed Sunday. Limited service, catering, special drinks, $-$$.**

ENCINITAS

Kim's Restaurant
745 1st St., #103, Encinitas, CA 92024   **(760) 942-4816**
Vietnamese/Chinese. Although the menu is mostly meat-based, more than 40 items are listed in the vegetarian section, such as Napa cabbage with mock chicken soup and tofu chop suey. **Open Tuesday through Sunday for lunch and dinner. Closed Monday. Full service, take-out, wine/beer, $$.**

Roxy Restaurant and Ice Cream
517 S. Coast Hwy. 101, Encinitas, CA 92024   **(760) 436-5001**
Natural foods. International fare is featured. **Open daily. Full service, vegan options, take-out, fresh juices, wine/beer/alcohol, VISA/MC/AMEX/DISC, $$.**

•Swami's Café and Juice Bar
1163 S. Coast Hwy. 101, Encinitas, CA 92024   **(760) 944-0612**
Vegetarian. This vegetarian restaurant offers salads and a wide variety of entrées, including curried vegetables, black bean burritos, and mock meat dishes. **Open daily for three meals. Counter service, vegan options, fresh juices, smoothies, catering, take-out, $.**

Restaurant codes: ✪ Reviewers' Choice   • Vegetarian Restaurant   •• Vegan Restaurant
Restaurant prices: **$** less than $6   **$$** $6-$12   **$$$** more than $12
Credit Cards Accepted: VISA - VISA   MC - MasterCard   AMEX - American Express
DISC - Discover   DC - Diner's Club

• The Vegetarian

431 W. 13th Ave., Ste. M, Escondido, CA 92025   **(760) 740-9596**

Vegetarian. The Vegetarian is a self-serve establishment that offers a salad bar, soups, chili, veggie tamales, burgers, sandwiches, and more. They purchase fresh organic food from local organic farms. **Open Monday through Friday for breakfast and lunch. Open Saturday for lunch. Closed Sunday. Counter service, vegan options, fresh juices, take-out, $-$$.**

(For restaurant listings in the surrounding areas, see Arcata.)

Gabriel's

216 East St., Eureka, CA 95501   **(707) 445-0100**

Italian. Gabriel's, located in Old Town Eureka, serves spinach pies, vegetarian soups, salads, whole-wheat pizza, and various vegetarian entrées. **Open Monday through Saturday for lunch and dinner. Closed Sunday. Full service wine/beer, take-out, VISA/MC/AMEX/ DISC, $$.**

Tomo Japanese Restaurant

2120 4th St., Eureka, CA 95501   **(707) 444-3318**

Japanese. Tomo serves Japanese country-style whole food as well as traditional and non-fish sushi. Most entrées are available without meat. **Open Monday through Saturday for lunch and dinner. Closed Sunday. Full service wine/beer, macrobiotic/vegan options, VISA/MC/ DISC, $$.**

• Sunflower Natural Foods Drive-In

10344 Fair Oaks Blvd., Fair Oaks, CA 95628   **(916) 967-4331**

Vegetarian. Sunflower is a vegetarian fast food place that emphasizes raw foods. Offerings include burgers, burritos, chili, and sandwiches. Sunflower is adjacent to a park. **Open daily. Limited service, take-out, VISA/MC/DISC, $.**

•• Lydia's Lovin' Foods

31 Bolinas Rd., Fairfax, CA 94930   **(415) 258-9678**

Vegan/raw foods. Lydia's offers a menu of great raw, organic vegan dishes in a friendly, laid-back atmosphere. Also, many of their cereals, breads, and snacks are available to purchase on their website. **Open Wednesday through Monday for three meals. Closed Tuesday. Full service, macrobiotic options, fresh juices, smoothies, soymilk, take-out, catering, $$.** www. lydiasorganics.com

FORT BRAGG

(For restaurant listings in the surrounding areas, see Mendocino.)

Samratt
548 S. Main St., Fort Bragg, CA 95437   **(707) 964-0386**
Indian. Samratt has excellent service and fantastic vegetarian Indian offerings, including curry dishes, lentil dishes, and more. **Open daily for lunch and dinner. Full service, vegan options, wine/beer, VISA/MC/AMEX, $$.**

Viraporn's Thai Café
500 S. Main St., Fort Bragg, CA 95437   **(707) 964-7931**
Thai. This café, located in a converted streetcar, offers vegetarian curry dishes, Pad Thai, fried rice, Coconut Lemongrass Soup, and Thai salads. It can be quite crowded in the evenings. **Open Monday through Saturday for lunch and dinner. Closed Sunday. Full service, vegan options, non-alcoholic wine/beer, wine/beer, $$.**

FOUNTAIN VALLEY

• Au Lac Vegetarian Restaurant
16563 Brookhurst St., Fountain Valley, CA 92708   **(714) 418-0658**
Vegetarian/Asian. Specializing in Vietnamese and Chinese cuisine, Au Lac offers such delights as vegetarian "salmon" and clay pot tofu sensation. All dishes are prepared without eggs, wine, or MSG. **Open Tuesday through Sunday for lunch and dinner. Closed Monday. Full service, vegan options, reservations recommended, fresh juices, soymilk, non-alcoholic wine/beer, VISA/MC/AMEX/DISC, $$.** www.aulac.com

FREMONT

Hobee's
39222 Fremont Blvd., Fremont, CA 94538   **(415) 796-4779**
Restaurant chain. See description under Cupertino, CA.

FULLERTON

Chin Ting
1939 Sunnycrest Dr., Fullerton, CA 92635   **(714) 738-1978**
Chinese. Chin Ting offers several vegetarian dishes. **Open Sunday through Friday for dinner only. Open Saturday for lunch and dinner. Full service, vegan options, take-out, VISA/MC/AMEX/DISC/DC, $$.**

Rutabegorz
211 N. Pomoma Ave., Fullerton, CA 92632   **(714) 871-1632**
International. Specializing in homemade food, this bohemian-style coffeehouse has an extensive coffee menu, as well as veggie burritos, pastas, spinach lasagna, and stuffed mushrooms. **Open Monday through Saturday. Closed Sunday. Full service, vegan options, fresh juices, wine/beer/alcohol, $$.**

GARBERVILLE

Woodrose Café
911 Redwood Dr., Garberville, CA 95440   **(707) 923-3191**
Natural foods. This café's many vegetarian options contain cheese and eggs. Organic and local ingredients are used. **Open Monday through Friday for breakfast and lunch. Open Saturday and Sunday for breakfast only. Full service, vegan options, fresh juices, non-alcoholic beer, wine/beer, take-out, $.**

GARDEN GROVE

•Thuyên Viên
11080 Magnolia St., Garden Grove, CA 92841   **(714) 638-8189**
Vegetarian/Asian. The menu here features Asian-style vegetarian cuisine, including Thai, Vietnamese, and Chinese dishes. **Open daily for three meals. Full service, vegan options, no credit cards, $$.**

GLENDALE

•Glendale Adventist Medical Center
1509 Wilson Terr., Glendale, CA 91206   **(818) 409-8090**
Vegetarian. The vegetarian menu changes daily. **Open daily for three meals. Cafeteria, take-out, $.**

GOLETA

Good Earth
5955 Calle Real, Goleta, CA 93117   **(805) 683-6101**
Natural foods. This restaurant offers soups and salads, casseroles, stir-fries, and Mexican specialties. **Open daily for three meals. Full service, wine/beer, catering, take-out, VISA/MC/AMEX/DISC, $$.**

GRANADA HILLS

••Vegetable Delight
17823 Chatsworth St., Granada Hills, CA 91344   **(818) 360-3997**
Vegan/Chinese. This Chinese restaurant's entirely vegan menu offers exotic dishes, such as vegetarian squid with celery and mock hot braised veggie shrimp made from gluten or soy products. Vegetable dishes, including Crisp Fried Chinese Mushrooms and Szechuan Broccoli, are also available. **Open Monday through Friday for lunch and dinner. Open Saturday and Sunday for dinner only. Full service, vegan options, non-alcoholic wine/beer, beer, take-out, VISA/MC/AMEX, $$.**

Restaurant codes: ✪ Reviewers' Choice   • Vegetarian Restaurant   •• Vegan Restaurant
Restaurant prices: **$** less than $6   **$$** $6-$12   **$$$** more than $12
Credit Cards Accepted: VISA - VISA   MC - MasterCard   AMEX - American Express
DISC - Discover   DC - Diner's Club

GUERNEVILLE

•• Sparks Vegan Foods
16248 Main St., Guerneville, CA 95446   **(707) 869-8206**

Vegan. Concentrating on organic vegetarian fare, Sparks offers a unique menu, including Pancakes, French Toast, Biscuits and Gravy, Seasonal Salad with Maple-Mustard Dressing, a Tofu "Egg" Salad Sandwich, Tempeh Reubens, BBQ Seitan Kebabs, Lemon Rice Pudding with Blackberry Sauce, Coconut Chocolate Macaroons, and Organic Lemonade. They also serve soups, pizza or pasta specials of the day, and baked goods. Wheat-free options are noted on the menu. **Open Monday, Tuesday, Thursday, and Friday for lunch. Open Saturday and Sunday for brunch. Call for dinner hours. Closed Wednesday. Full service, fresh juices, special drinks, take-out, catering, $$.** www.sparksrestaurant.com

HACIENDA HEIGHTS

• Garden Fresh Restaurant
16034 Gale Ave., Hacienda Heights, CA 91745   **(626) 968-2279**

Vegetarian/Chinese. This informal restaurant offers a wide range of vegetarian dishes, including Kung Po Tofu, Spicy Tofu, Family Tofu (with broccoli, mushrooms, and cabbage), and Yuba with tomatoes, celery, mushrooms, or other vegetables. They offer lunch specials consisting of two to four items and a choice between white and brown rice, as well as special stir-fries for dinner. **Open daily for lunch and dinner. Closed first Sunday of every month. Full service, vegan options, fresh juices, soymilk, take-out, $.**

HARBOR CITY

Chan Thai Cuisine
1605 W. Pacific Coast Hwy., #106, Harbor City, CA 90710   **(310) 325-0844**

Thai. A beautiful dining room complements delicious Thai curry, stir-fried entrées, and various specials. **Open Monday through Saturday for lunch and dinner. Open Sunday for dinner only. Full service, vegan options, wine/beer, catering, take-out, VISA/MC, $-$$.**

HERMOSA BEACH

• The Spot Natural Food Restaurant
110 Second St., Hermosa Beach, CA 90254   **(310) 376-2355**

Vegetarian. This friendly "local" beach restaurant offers only vegetarian fare with many vegan items. Specialties include burritos, veggie burgers, and "Steamers" (steamed vegetable plates) with tasty sauces. **Open daily for lunch and dinner. Limited service, vegan options, take-out, VISA/MC, $$.**

HOLLYWOOD

• Paru's Indian Vegetarian Restaurant
5140 Sunset Blvd., Hollywood, CA 90027   **(323) 661-7600**

Vegetarian/Indian. At Paru's, most of the main dishes are non-dairy, and corn oil is used for cooking. A brunch special is offered on Saturday and Sunday. **Open daily for lunch and dinner. Full service, wine/beer, special drinks, take-out, VISA/MC, $$.**

HUNTINGTON BEACH

Alisan
16482 Bolsa Chica St., Huntington Beach, CA 92649   **(714) 840-0036**
Chinese. Diners have raved about the excellent food at this restaurant. Alisan specializes in "legume creations," as well as soy-based "meats." Organic ingredients are used whenever possible. **Open daily for lunch and dinner. Full service, vegan options, $$.** www.alisan naturalfood.com/index.html

•• Bodhi Tree Vegetarian Café
501 Main St., Huntington Beach, CA 92648   **(714) 969-9500**
Vegan/Vietnamese. Located near the Huntington Beach Pier, this restaurant offers authentic Vietnamese dishes made with organic ingredients. **Open daily for lunch and dinner. Full service, fresh juices, smoothies, soymilk, special drinks, VISA/MC/AMEX/DISC, $$.**

• Good Mood Food Deli Café
5930 Warner Ave., Huntington Beach, CA 92649   **(714) 377-2028**
Vegetarian. This café and catering business offers raw and living gourmet European-style foods. Specialties include Arugula Salad with Oranges, Olive Pâté and Golden Flaxseed Crackers, Tomato and Spinach Lasagne, Macadamia Cheese Balls with Pistachio Custard, Asparagus with Crème de Coco, Pecan Pie filled with Cherries, Black Forest Cake, and Marzipan Triangles. **Open Tuesday through Saturday for three meals. Closed Sunday and Monday. Full service, vegan/macrobiotic options, espresso/cappuccino, non-dairy milks, delivery, catering.** www.goodmoodfood.com

•• Happy Veggie Vegetarian Restaurant
7251 Warner Ave., Huntington Beach, CA 92847   **(714) 375-9505**
Vegan. Happy Veggie is a family-owned and operated establishment with a casual, family-friendly environment. It offers spring and summer rolls, salads, and soups made with noodles, vegetables, and/or fake meats. Entrées include Szechwan Soy Chicken Strips, Eggplant Tofu with Basil, Pineapple Soy Beef, Sizzling Soy Salmon, and 1000 Layer Tofu (braised tofu with potatoes, carrots, and eggplant served in a clay pot). Lunch specials are offered on weekdays. **Open Monday through Saturday for lunch and dinner. Closed Sunday. Full service, soymilk, VISA/MC, $-$$.** www.happyveggie.net

Mother's Market and Kitchen
19770 Beach Blvd., Huntington Beach, CA 92648   **(714) 963-6667**
Natural foods. See description under Costa Mesa, CA.

Tosh's Mediterranean Cuisine
16871 Beach Blvd., Huntington Beach, CA 92647   **(714) 842-3315**
Middle Eastern. Filled with Turkish art, Tosh's menu includes a vegetarian section. Options include fried eggplant; spinach-filled phyllo; leeks with carrots, onions, rice and feta, and garbanzo beans cooked with vegetables served on rice pilaf. Greek and Arabic dishes are also served. **Open Tuesday through Saturday for lunch and dinner. Open Sunday for dinner only. Closed Monday. Full service, reservations recommended on weekends, wine/beer, VISA/MC/ AMEX/DISC/DC, $$-$$$.**

IRVINE

Clay Oven
15435 Jeffrey Rd., Irvine, CA 92714   **(949) 552-2851**
Indian. Clay Oven takes a healthy approach to Indian cooking, offering nine vegetable
entrées. **Open daily for lunch and dinner. Full service vegan options, VISA/MC/AMEX/
DISC, $$.**

Mother's Market & Kitchen
2963 Michelson Dr., Irvine, CA 92715   **(949) 752-6667**
Natural foods. See description under Costa Mesa, CA.

Rutabegorz
4610 Barranca Pkwy., Irvine, CA 92714   **(714) 733-1444**
International. See description under Fullerton, CA.

• Veggie & Tea House
14988 Sand Canyon, Studio #1, Irvine, CA 92618   **(949) 559-0577**
Vegetarian/Chinese. This restaurant would probably be vegan if not for eggs in a few of their
dishes. Vegan items are clearly marked on the menu. Unique offerings include Opo Squash
Tempera, Teriyaki Potatoes, Soy Crepes, and Fried Rice served in a pineapple shell. They
mostly use organic produce, much of which is grown on their own farm. **Open daily for
lunch and dinner. Limited service, non-smoking, take-out, catering, VISA/MC/AMEX/
DISC, $$.** www.veggieandteahouse.com

•• The Wheel Of Life
14370 Culver Dr., #2G, Irvine, CA 92604   **(949) 551-8222**
Vegan/Thai. The Wheel of Life is a warm, inviting informal restaurant with Thai and Chinese
dishes. Entrées include stuffed tofu delights, pad Thai, curries, Thai salads, a variety of veggie "fish" dishes, and dishes made from soy meats created from their own recipes. No MSG
is used. **Open Wednesday through Monday for lunch and dinner. Closed Tuesday. Full
service, take-out, espresso, soymilk, special drinks, VISA/MC, $$.**
www.wheelofliferestaurant.com

LA JOLLA

• Ché Café
UCSD, 9500 Gilman Dr., Student Ctr. 0323-C, La Jolla, CA 92093   **(858) 534-2311**
Vegetarian. This is a not-for-profit vegetarian collective on the UCSD campus. Ché Café
serves mostly vegan foods and hosts live music shows on most weekends. **Open on
Wednesday. Call for others times. Limited service, vegan options, take-out, $.**

Daily's Fit and Fresh
8915 Towne Center Dr., La Jolla, CA 92122   **(858) 453-1112**
Natural foods. All items on the menu contain 10 grams of fat or less per serving, and many
are vegetarian. Thai Noodle Salad, Three-Bean and Corn Chili, fresh veggie pizza, grilled
eggplant and zucchini, and a garden vegetable burger are among the tasty but lean vegetarian

options you'll find here. **Open daily for lunch and dinner. Limited service, vegan options, smoothies, take-out, catering, VISA/MC, $.**

• Galoka Gallery Restaurant
5662 La Jolla Blvd., La Jolla, CA 92037   **(858) 551-8610**

Vegetarian/Indian. This restaurant, gallery, jazz venue, and full bar lounge offers a fine dining menu of traditional Indian dishes and foods epitomizing their signature Indo-fusion style. They offer mock meat dishes, as well as vegan entrées and desserts. In addition to the restaurant, this establishment hosts live music, from jazz to dance to hip-hop. **Open Thursday through Sunday for dinner. Full service, vegan options, wine/beer/alcohol, take-out, VISA/MC/AMEX, $$-$$$.** www.galoka.com

Royal Thai Cuisine
737 Pearl St., La Jolla, CA 92037   **(858) 551-8424**

Thai. Offers a variety of vegetarian Thai dishes made with soy or mushrooms, according to your preference. **Open daily for lunch and dinner. Limited service, catering, espresso, $$-$$$.**

LAGUNA BEACH

• Café Zinc
350 Ocean Ave., Laguna Beach, CA 92651   **(949) 494-6302**

Vegetarian. Café Zinc offers soups, salads, and mini- and full-sized pizzas. Indoor and outdoor seating is available. **Call for hours. Counter service, wine/beer, take-out, $.**

• Gauranga's
285 Legion St., Laguna Beach, CA 92651   **(949) 494-7029**

Vegetarian. If you're hungry, Gauranga's all-you-can-eat vegetarian buffet might be just what you need. The steam table includes two soups, brown and basmati rice, steamed veggies, pasta and sauce, mixed Indian-style veggies, and entrées that vary daily. All entrees are prepared vegan on Tuesday and Thursday. No eggs are used. **Open Monday through Saturday for lunch. Closed Sunday. Cafeteria, vegan options, take-out, VISA/MC, $.**

Natraj Cuisine of India
998 S. Coast Hwy., Laguna Beach, CA 92651   **(949) 497-9197**

Indian. Natraj offers 13 vegetable dishes, including Bainghan Aloo and Channa Masala. **Open daily. Full service, vegan options, $$-$$$.**

•• The Stand Natural Foods Restaurant
238 Thalia St., Laguna Beach, CA 92651   **(949) 494-8101**

Vegan. If you're looking for a restaurant with a commitment to quality and excellent vegan food, then The Stand is for you. In business for more than 27 years, The Stand offers a wide selection of international salads, sandwiches, side orders, burritos, tamales, entrées, and treats. All foods are vegan and made without refined sugar, salt, or artificial ingredients. **Open daily for three meals. Limited service, fresh juices, take-out, outdoor seating only, $.**

LAGUNA WOODS

Mother's Market & Kitchen
24165 Paseo de Valencia, Laguna Woods, CA 92653   **(949) 768-6667**
Natural foods. See description under Costa Mesa, CA.

LAKEPORT

•• Nature's Bounty Vegan Restaurant
495 N. Main St., Lakeport, CA 95453   **(707) 263-4575**
Vegan. Nature's Bounty serves healthy fast food and organic fruits, vegetables, grains, and
nuts are used whenever possible. **Open Monday through Friday for breakfast and lunch.**
Closed Saturday and Sunday. Limited service smoothies, fresh juices, take-out, VISA/MC/
AMEX/DISC, $.

LOMA LINDA

Kool Kactus Café
24957 Redlands Blvd., Loma Linda, CA 92354   **(909) 796-1545**
Mexican. Enjoy a wide variety of Mexican dishes from the vegetarian menu at Kool Kactus.
Open daily for lunch and dinner. Limited service, catering, take-out, VISA/MC/DISC, $.

• Loma Linda University Medical Center Café
Anderson and Barton Rds., Loma Linda, CA 92354   **(714) 824-4365**
Vegetarian. The cafeteria offers soups, salads, casseroles, and mock meat dishes. **Open daily.**
Cafeteria, vegan options, take-out, $.

LOMITA

•• House of Vege
2439 Pacific Coast Hwy., Lomita, CA 90717   **(310) 530-1180**
Vegan/Chinese. House of Vege has a regular menu and an all-you-can-eat menu. Everything
is prepared fresh, and there are many unique entrées. Suitable for business entertaining.
Open daily for lunch and dinner. Full service, vegan options, take-out, $$-$$$.

LONG BEACH

The Original Park Pantry
2104 E. Broadway, Long Beach, CA 90803   **(562) 434-0451**
California. The Original Park Pantry offers vegetarian light fare, including a steamed fresh
vegetable plate, vegetarian chili, and pasta of the day with marinara sauce. **Open daily for
three meals.** Full service, counter service, take-out, VISA/MC/AMEX/DISC, $-$$.

• Papa Jon's Natural Market & Café
5006 E. Second St., Long Beach, CA 90803   **(562) 439-1059**
Vegetarian café. Located inside a health foods market, Papa Jon's wants "every customer
happier when they leave than when they arrived." They just might succeed with large help-

ings of teriyaki tofu, tempeh burgers, potato corn chowder, potato burritos, vegetarian sushi rolls, and shepherd's pie. The all-vegan Spinach Lasagne is exceptional in both size and flavor. **Open daily for three meals. Limited service, vegan options, fresh juices, smoothies, take-out, VISA/MC, $-$$.** http://papajons.micronpcweb.com/

Star of Siam
2109 E. Broadway, Long Beach, CA 90803   **(562) 439-1564**
Thai. This traditional Thai restaurant has a vegetarian menu that includes veggie egg rolls, coconut milk soup, hot and sour soup, spicy eggplant, vegetable tempura, garlic or sweet and sour tofu, vegetable pad Thai, pineapple vegetable fried rice (with or without eggs), seasonal vegetables, and much more. They also offer vegetarian versions of their other entrées, including noodle dishes, rice dishes, and curries. **Open Wednesday through Monday for lunch and dinner. Closed Tuesday. Full service, vegan options, beer/wine, special drinks, VISA/ MC/AMEX/DISC/DC, $-$$$.** www.starofsiamonline.com

LOS ANGELES

(For restaurant listings in the surrounding areas, see Alhambra, Altadena, Anaheim, Artesia, Beverly Hills, Canoga Park, Cerritos, Chatsworth, Corona del Mar, Costa Mesa, Covina, Eagle Rock, El Segundo, Fountain Valley, Fullerton, Garden Grove, Glendale, Granada Hills, Hacienda Heights, Harbor City, Hermosa Beach, Hollywood, Huntington Beach, Irvine, Laguna Beach, Laguna Woods, Lomita, Long Beach, Mar Vista, Meiner Oaks, Monterey Park, Newport Beach, North Hollywood, Northridge, Norwalk, Orange, Pacific Palisades, Pasadena, Rancho Palos Verdes, Redondo Beach, Reseda, Riverside, Rosemead, Rowland Heights, San Dimas, San Gabriel, Santa Ana, Santa Monica, Sherman Oaks, South El Monte, South Pasadena, Studio City, Tarzana, Topanga Canyon, Tustin, Upland, Venice, Ventura, West Covina, West Hollywood, Westminster, Westwood, and Whittier.)

Angeli-Caffe-Pizzeria
7274 Melrose Ave., Los Angeles, CA 90046   **(323) 936-9086**
Italian. This is one of the best Italian restaurants in Los Angeles. About half the light, healthy, and tasty menu is vegetarian, and many dishes can be made vegan. **Open Monday through Friday for lunch and dinner. Open Saturday and Sunday for dinner only. Full service, take-out, catering, espresso/cappuccino, non-alcoholic beer, wine/beer, VISA/MC/AMEX, $$-$$$.**

• Beverly Hills Juice
8382 Beverly Blvd., Los Angeles, CA 90048   **(323) 655-8300**
Vegetarian/juice bar. They offer fresh juices and some foods prepared from local organic produce. Shakes and wheatgrass drinks are made to order. Tahini, sauerkraut, hummus, sushi, applesauce, dairy-free ice cream, and other treats are prepared on the premises. **Open Monday through Saturday for breakfast through early dinner. Closed Sunday. Take-out, fresh juices, VISA/MC, $.**

•• California Vegan
7300 W. Sunset Blvd., Los Angeles, CA 90046   **(323) 874-9079**
Vegan/Thai. This restaurant offers appetizers, soups, salads, entrées, noodle and rice dishes, curries, burgers, wraps, and desserts. Choices include raw spring rolls, BBQ Tofu, Spicy Vege Chicken Salad, Cowboy (seitan) Dinners, Soy Fish with Sweet & Sour Sauce, Cali-

fornia Fried Rice (with pineapple, raisins, and cashews), Lentil Burgers, and wheat-free pancakes. They also offer lunch specials, such as lentil loaf, vegetables, or curries with your choice of tofu, soy chicken, veggie pepper steak, seitan, or soy fish. All items are organic and free of white sugar and MSG. **Open daily for lunch through late dinner. Full service, fresh juices, soymilk, special drinks, take-out, delivery, VISA/MC, $$.**

Don's Fountain of Health
3606 W. Sixth St., Los Angeles, CA 90020   **(213) 387-6621**

Natural foods. Sample the veggie burgers, chili, freshly squeezed juices, and cakes and cookies made on the premises. **Open Monday through Friday for breakfast and lunch. Closed Saturday and Sunday. Full service, fresh juices, take-out, catering, $.**

Eat a Pita
465 N. Fairfax Ave., Los Angeles, CA 90036   **(213) 651-0188**

Mediterranean. Eat a Pita offers many vegetarian selections, including tabbouleh, hummus, baba ghanouj, and falafel. Seating is outdoors in a casual, friendly environment. **Open daily for lunch and dinner. Counter service, vegan options, take-out, $.**

Electric Lotus
4656 Franklin Ave., Los Angeles, CA 90026   **(888) 565-6887**

Indian. Electric Lotus offers a good selection of vegan entrées, such as tofu curry, vegetable pakora (deep-fried batter dipped vegetables), and malai kofta (vegetable balls in curry sauce), as well as many vegetarian appetizers and soups. Valet parking during dinner service. **Open daily for lunch through late evenings. Full service, vegan options, take-out, VISA/MC, $$.**

Fiddler's Bistro
6009 W. Third St., Los Angeles, CA 90036   **(323) 931-8167**

Bistro. Fiddler's Bistro offers several dishes for vegetarians. They have a vegetarian burrito, sautéed spinach, and a bistro caliente made with vegetables, beans, stuffed grape leaves, hummus, and tabbouleh. You might also try the Fresno Vegetarian Grape Leaves and baba ghanouj. **Open daily for three meals. Full service, take-out, reservations recommended for Sunday brunch, espresso/cappuccino, non-alcoholic beer, wine/beer/alcohol, VISA/MC/ AMEX, $$.**

Go Veggie
5462 S. Centinela Ave., Los Angeles, CA 90066   **(310) 577-0167**

Juice bar. Menu items include self-service vegetarian salad bar and soups, though the salad bar also has some fish and chicken dishes as well. They also offer sandwiches, like a tofu burger and their grilled veggies with basil and feta. **Open daily for lunch and early dinner. Limited service, fresh juices, smoothies, soymilk, take-out, catering, VISA/MC, $.**

• Govinda's
3764 Watseka Ave., Los Angeles, CA 90034   **(310) 836-1269**

Vegetarian. Located at a Hare Krishna temple, Govinda's offers a salad bar; freshly baked whole wheat bread; sandwiches; Mexican dishes; hot entrées such as tofu filet, nut loaf, and vegetable lasagna; Indian dishes; and pizza. This establishment prides itself on catering to vegans and serves many dairy-free items. It is located near Sony Studios in Culver City.

Open Monday through Saturday for lunch and dinner. Closed Sunday. Buffet, vegan options, fresh juices, special drinks, take-out, catering, VISA/MC/AMEX/DISC, $. www.hare krishnaLA.com

Inaka Natural Foods Restaurant

131 S. La Brea Ave., Los Angeles, CA 90036   **(213) 936-9353**

Macrobiotic. No eggs or dairy products are used, and foods are vegetarian except for some fish dishes. Brown rice and different beans are featured with vegetables. **Open Monday through Friday for lunch and dinner. Open Saturday for dinner only. Closed Sunday. Full service, vegan options, wine/beer, take-out, VISA/MC, $.**

India's Tandoori

5947 W. Pico Blvd., Los Angeles, CA 90035   **(213) 936-2050**

Indian. India's Tandoori has a vegetarian section on the menu, plus vegetarian appetizers like samosas and onion balls. Fresh clay-oven-baked breads are a specialty here. **Open daily. Full service, vegan options, fresh juices, wine/beer, take-out, VISA/MC, $.**

• Luna Tierra Sol Café

2501 W. 6th St., Los Angeles, CA 90057   **(213) 380-4754**

Vegetarian/Mexican. Luna Tierra Sol Café is a worker-owned business that provides a place for the people of East L.A. to meet and for artists and musicians to express themselves. They also happen to offer a great variety of Mexican foods designed for both vegetarians and vegans. Breakfast items include Chilaquiles (sliced corn tortillas sautéed with mushrooms and topped with red sauce and cheese) & Eggs; Big Bomb Breakfast Sandwich (egg, avocado, cheese, lettuce, tomato, and sprouts); Vegetarian Xorizo (sausage) & Eggs; and Tofu Scramble made with potatoes, spinach, mushrooms, green onions, and tomatoes. For lunch and dinner, there are the traditional choices like bean or veggie burritos, soft tacos, and guacamole. However, there are also unique items like Veggie, Tofu, and Avocado Quesadillas; Vegetarian Tamales; Burritos á la Mexicana with two eggs, tomatoes, mushrooms, and green onions; and the Chimmie Hendrix (a giant chimmichanga). Try their Chocolate Banana Thang Smoothie or one of their three varieties of potatoes: spicy Homeboy Fries, Homegirl Fries flavored with rosemary, and Rudegirl Fries, Homeboy Fries drowned in red sauce and covered in melted cheese. **Open daily for three meals. Limited service, vegan options, fresh juices, cappuccino/espresso, smoothies, $. www.lunatierrasol.com**

•• Mr. Wisdom Hari Krishna Restaurant

3526 W. Slauson Ave., Los Angeles, CA 90043   **(323) 295-1517**

Vegan deli in a natural foods store. This organic café in a health foods store features salads, soups, veggie burgers, a bean dish served over brown rice and steamed vegetables, and more. **Open Monday through Saturday for three meals. Closed Sunday. Limited service, fresh juices, take-out, $-$$.**

Newsroom Café

120 N. Robertson Blvd., Los Angeles, CA 90048   **(310) 652-4444**

Natural foods. Mingle with the stars, college kids, and families in this comfortable, healthy restaurant, which takes its name from its many TVs broadcasting CNN and silent radios printing out newsworthy information constantly. Try the fat-free, sugar-free, dairy-free hotcakes for breakfast, a freshly-made veggie burger or daily vegetarian soup for lunch, or vegan tamales for dinner. There is also a vegan frozen dessert. **Open daily for three meals.** Limited service, vegan options, fresh juices, espresso, non-alcoholic beer, take-out, VISA/ MC/AMEX/DISC, $-$$.

Osteria Romana Orsini
9575 W. Pico Blvd., Los Angeles, CA 90035   **(310) 277-6050**
Italian. Osteria features a large selection of meatless items. **Open Monday through Saturday for lunch and dinner. Closed Sunday.** Full service, wine/beer/alcohol, take-out, VISA/MC/ AMEX, $$-$$$.

Santé La Brea
345 N. La Brea Ave., Los Angeles, CA 90036   **(323) 968-0412**
Natural foods. Santé La Brea offers pizza with vegan cheese and many other entrées. Almost all items on the menu can be modified to be vegetarian or vegan. An outdoor patio is available for year-round dining. **Open daily for three meals.** Full service, take-out, catering, reservations recommended, vegan options, fresh juices, espresso/cappuccino, soymilk, beer/wine, VISA/MC/AMEX/DISC/DC, $$.

• Tokyo Teriyaki
2518 S. Figueroa St., Los Angeles, CA 90007   **(213) 747-6880**
Vegetarian/Asian. Tokyo Teriyaki serves vegetarian Chinese, Japanese, and Korean cuisine, including vegan teriyaki, veggie beef, and veggie orange chicken. **Open Monday through Friday for lunch and dinner. Closed Saturday and Sunday.** Full service, vegan options, VISA/MC/AMEX/DISC, $$.

•• Vegan Express
3217 Cahuenga Blvd., W., Los Angeles, CA 90068   **(323) 851-8837**
Vegan/Thai. This restaurant offers vegan Thai-American cuisine and uses organic ingredients whenever available. **Open daily for lunch and dinner.** Full service, smoothies, almond milk, catering, VISA/MC/AMEX/DISC, $$-$$$.

• White Memorial Medical Center
1720 Brooklyn Ave., Los Angeles, CA 90025   **(213) 268-5000 x1318**
Hospital cafeteria/vegetarian. This cafeteria is in a Seventh-day Adventist hospital. **Open daily.** Cafeteria, take-out, $$.

MAR VISTA

•• Venus of Venice
12034 Venice Blvd., Mar Vista, CA 90066   **(310) 391-7674**
Vegan. A casually elegant restaurant with soy sandwiches and organic pastas. The tables are decorated with music boxes and porcelain figurines. **Open Tuesday through Sunday for lunch and dinner. Closed Monday.** Full service, vegan options, catering, reservations recommended, fresh juices, smoothies, soymilk, special drinks, $$.

MEINER OAKS

The Farmer and The Cook
339 W. El Roblar Dr., Meiner Oaks, CA 93023   **(805) 640-9608**
Café. This organic market café offers fresh, organic produce, as well as soups, sandwiches, salads, smoothies, and more. **Open daily for three meals. Open Sunday for brunch through early dinner.** Limited service, vegan options, $. www.farmerandcook.com

MENDOCINO

Lu's Kitchen
45013 Ukiah Rd., Mendocino, CA 95460   **(707) 937-4939**
Mexican. Lu's Kitchen offers courtyard seating next to an old church that is now a health foods store. They use organic ingredients when available and never use lard in their beans. Try the sautéed portabello mushrooms, quesadillas, burritos, tacos, and more. We've been told that the vegan pesto is fantastic! **Open daily for lunch and dinner.** Limited service, vegan options, non-alcoholic beer, wine/beer, VISA/MC, $$.

Mendocino Café
10451 Lansing St., Mendocino, CA 95460   **(707) 937-2422**
California. Both indoor and outdoor seating is available at this café. Be sure to sample the Thai burrito. **Open daily for lunch and dinner.** Full service, vegan options, espresso/cappuccino, non-alcoholic beer, wine/beer, VISA/MC, $$.

• The Ravens at the Stanford Inn by the Sea
44850 Comptche Ukiah Rd., Mendocino, CA 95460   **(707) 937-5615**
Vegetarian/natural foods. Dishes at The Ravens are inspired by the restaurant's California-certified organic farm. The dining room offers a beautiful view of the ocean. For breakfast they serve such items as buckwheat waffles and eggs portobella, and the dinner menu includes Creole vegetables with blackened tofu. **Open Monday for breakfast and dinner. Open Tuesday and Wednesday for breakfast. Open Thursday and Friday for lunch and dinner. Open Saturday and Sunday for brunch and dinner.** Full service, reservations recommended, vegan/macrobiotic options, fresh juices, espresso/cappuccino, smoothies, soymilk, non-alcoholic wine/beer, wine/beer/alcohol, VISA/MC/AMEX/DISC/DC, $$$.

MENLO PARK

Flea Street Café
3607 Alameda de las Pulgas, Menlo Park, CA 94025   **(415) 854-1226**
Natural foods. The chef at this casually elegant restaurant will improvise to accommodate vegetarian requests. Organic produce is used. **Open daily for lunch and dinner. Open weekends for brunch.** Full service, vegan options, wine/beer, take-out, VISA/MC, $$$.

Fresh Choice
600 Santa Cruz Cove, Menlo Park, CA 94025   **(415) 323-4061**
American. The salad selection is extensive, and there is always one vegetarian soup and usually at least one vegetarian pasta. Fixed price covers everything, including bread and dessert. **Open daily.** Cafeteria, wine/beer, VISA/MC, $$.

Late for the Train
150 Middlefield Rd., Menlo Park, CA 94025   **(415) 321-6124**

Natural foods. Late for the Train is a very accommodating country-style restaurant that serves meals in the "wholest form possible," though most of the vegetarian dishes include dairy. Produce is organic when available. **Open daily. Full service, vegan options, espresso/cappuccino, wine/beer, take-out, VISA/MC, $$.**

MIDDLETOWN

Stonefront Restaurant
18424 Harbin Springs Rd., Middletown, CA 95461   **(707) 987-9012**

Natural foods. This restaurant is located in Harbin Hot Springs Resort. Daily dinner specials, salads, and soups are prepared with organically grown produce when available. **Open daily for breakfast and dinner. Cafeteria, vegan options, non-alcoholic beer, $-$$.**

MILPITAS

• Lu Lai Garden
210 Barber St., Milpitas, CA 95035   **(408) 526-9888**

Vegetarian. Enjoy delicious Hong Kong-style Chinese vegetarian cuisine, such as appetizers like Pot Stickers, Seaweed Bean Curd Rolls, and Veggie Egg Rolls. Also try one of 11 different types of soup offered, and a wide variety of entrées, including Chinese vegetables, bean curd, noodles, rice, and much more. **Open Wednesday through Monday for lunch and dinner. Closed Tuesday. Full service, vegan options, no credit cards, $$.**

• Milan Sweet Centre
296 S. Abel St., Milpitas, CA 95035   **(408) 946-2525**

Vegetarian/Indian. Feast on many traditional Indian items, as well as tofu kabobs and sweet and sour kabobs. **Open Monday for lunch. Open Tuesday through Sunday for lunch and dinner. Full service, take-out, VISA/MC/AMEX/DISC/DC, $.**

MONTEREY

Ama Rin Thai Cuisine
807 Cannery Row, Monterey, CA 93940   **(831) 373-8811**

Thai. Authentic Thai cuisine is presented with contemporary Thai ambiance. Sample a wide variety of Thai vegetarian dishes using organically grown local produce. Tofu can easily be substituted for meat in any dish. **Open daily for lunch and dinner. Full service, wine/beer, take-out, VISA/MC/AMEX/DISC, $$.**

Chef Lee's Mandarin House
2031 N. Fremont St., Monterey, CA 93940   **(408) 375-9551**

Chinese. Several vegetarian dishes, including Mushrooms with Chinese Greens, Spicy Bean Curd, and Mu Shu Vegetables, are offered at this restaurant. **Open daily for lunch and dinner. Full service, vegan options, catering, take-out, VISA/MC, $$.**

India's Clay Oven
150 Del Monte Ave., Monterey, CA 93940   **(408) 373-2529**
Indian. India's Clay Oven features more than a dozen vegetarian dishes. Open daily for lunch and dinner. Full service, vegan options, take-out, VISA/MC, $$.

• Vege2U
1126 Del Monte Ave., Monterey, CA 93940   **(831) 375-8343**
Vegetarian/natural foods. This informal "boutique deli" carries gourmet, organic foods, including raw, kosher, and bakery items. They also offer vegetarian pet products, non-alcoholic wine tastings, special cooking events, and a separate meditation room. Open Tuesday through Sunday for lunch and early dinner. Closed Monday. Deli-style, vegan options, smoothies, non alcoholic wine/beer, take-out, VISA/MC/AMEX/DISC, $$.

MONTEREY PARK

• Happy Family III
608 N. Atlantic Blvd., Monterey Park, CA 91754   **(626) 282-8986**
Vegetarian/Chinese. Happy Family offers a wide range of vegetarian Chinese dishes, including mock meat and fish entrées. No MSG is used, and an all-you-can-eat option is offered at dinner time. Open daily for lunch and dinner. Full service, vegan options, take-out, VISA/MC/AMEX/DISC/DC, $$-$$$.

MORENO VALLEY

Dragon House Restaurant
22456 Alessandro Blvd., Moreno Valley, CA 92507   **(714) 653-1442**
Chinese. Dragon House features a complete vegetarian menu. Don't be surprised when you see chicken, beef, and scallop dishes on the vegetarian menu since these options are made from soybean protein. Open daily for lunch and dinner. Full service, vegan options, wine/beer/alcohol, take-out, VISA/MC/AMEX, $$.

MOUNT SHASTA

Lily's
1013 S. Mt. Shasta Blvd., Mount Shasta, CA 96067   **(530) 926-3372**
California. Set in an old, refurbished house and displaying a view of Mt. Shasta, Lily's offers several vegetarian dishes, although very few vegan meals. Open daily for three meals. Full service, take-out, reservations recommended for Sunday brunch, alcohol, VISA/MC/AMEX/DISC, $$$.

MOUNTAIN VIEW

• Amarin Cuisine
156 Castro St., Mountain View, CA 94041   **(650) 938-8424**
Vegetarian/Thai. This restaurant offers vegetarian salads, soups, noodle dishes, and a host of curry dishes. Brown rice is available. Open daily for lunch and dinner. Full service, vegan options, VISA/MC, $$.

Amici's East Coast Pizzeria
790 Castro St., Mountain View, CA 94041 **(650) 961-6666**

Italian. It's difficult to find an Italian restaurant that caters to vegetarians, but Amici's is one delicious exception. You can choose from various pasta dishes, salads, and sandwich options, but do not miss the thin crust, brick-oven baked pizzas, available with non-dairy cheese substitutes and fresh veggies. Try the Cholesterol Council's National Bake-off choice, the new Asante Pizza, topped with soy mozzarella, spinach, broccoli, red onions, tomatoes, and fresh basil (no tomato sauce). **Open daily for lunch and dinner. Full service, take-out, delivery, VISA/MC/AMEX/DISC/DC, $-$$$.** www.amicis.com

Country Gourmet
2098 El Camino Real, Mountain View, CA 94040 **(650) 962-0239**

Natural foods. Country Gourmet serves veggie burritos, taco salad, and pasta dishes. **Open daily. Counter service, wine/beer, take-out, VISA/MC/DISC, $$.**

• Deedee's Indian Fast Food
2551 W. Middlefield Rd., Mountain View, CA 94043 **(650) 967-9333**

Vegetarian/Indian. This primarily vegan restaurant offers highly affordable food through its lunch buffet, counter service, and Sunday brunch. Choose from samosas, pakoras, rice dishes, vegetable entrées, traditional Indian breads, a veggie burger, desserts, and snacks. It also houses an Indian store. **Open daily for lunch. Counter service, vegan options, special drinks, take-out, delivery, VISA/MC/AMEX, $.** www.mydeedees.com/restaurant.htm

• Garden Fresh Vegetarian Restaurant
1245 W. El Camino Real, Mountain View, CA 94040 **(650) 961-7795**

Vegetarian/Chinese. This smoke-free establishment features a variety of vegan dishes, including spring rolls, scallion pancakes, steamed dumpling, vegetarian sushi, several soups, stir-fried brown rice with mixed vegetables, stuffed Chinese cabbage, tofu delight, and much more. **Open daily for lunch and dinner. Full service, vegan options, fresh juices, rice/soymilk, non-alcoholic beer, take-out, VISA/MC, $$.** http://waiter.com/garden/

Hobee's Restaurant
2312 Central Expy., Mountain View, CA 94043 **(650) 968-6050**

Restaurant chain. See description under Cupertino, CA. **Open daily. Full service, fresh juices, wine/beer, take-out, VISA/MC, $$.**

NEEDLES

Irene's Drive Inn
703 Broadway, Needles, CA 92363 **(619) 326-2342**

American. This is a typical fast-food hamburger place that offers window service. From a distance, there is no indication of the wonderful, large vegetarian tacos and burritos that are also available on the menu. This is certainly an oasis in the desert! You have the option of eating in your car or at the picnic tables outside. **Open daily. Limited service, fresh juices, take-out, $.**

NEWPORT BEACH

Royal Thai
4001 Pacific Coast Hwy., Newport Beach, CA 92663   **(714) 650-3322**
Thai. Royal Thai offers nine vegetarian entrées, plus appetizers, soups, and salads. **Open Monday through Friday for lunch. Open Saturday for dinner only. Open Sunday for brunch and dinner.** Full service, wine/beer/alcohol, VISA/MC/AMEX/DISC, $$.

Sage
2531 Eastbluff Dr., Newport Beach, CA 92660   **(949) 718-9650**
American. Sage offers a wide variety of options, from specialty pizzas to sweet potato fries. Among the vegetarian selections are Chinese saimin noodles with vegetables, grilled vegetable pizza, and Sage salad (roasted asparagus, leeks, scallions, maui onions, corn, summer squash, tomatoes, mixed greens, and red wine dijon vinaigrette). **Open daily for lunch and dinner.** Full service, vegan options, reservations required, $$.

NORTH HOLLYWOOD

Leonor's Mexican Food
11403 Victory Blvd., North Hollywood, CA 91606   **(818) 980-9011**
Mexican. Leonor's offers tostadas, tacos, enchiladas, quesadillas, and burritos made with soy cheese and soy "meats." It also serves pizza, sandwiches, and salads. This location is about 90 percent vegetarian, while their Studio City location is completely vegetarian. **Open daily for lunch and dinner.** Full service, vegan options, fresh juices, take-out, $-$$.

NORTHRIDGE

The Good Earth
19510 Nordhoff St., Northridge, CA 91324   **(626) 993-7306**
Natural foods. The Good Earth features Walnut Mushroom Au Gratin, Guatemalan Rice and Tofu, wok dishes, vegetarian burgers, burritos, tostadas, salads, vegetarian scramble, tofu scramble, eggplant sandwiches, and pasta primavera. **Open daily.** Full service, wine/beer, VISA/MC/AMEX, $$.

• Saam's A-1 Produce and Veggie Lovers' Deli
9043 Reseda Blvd., Northridge, CA 91324   **(818) 998-6900**
Vegetarian/Indian. Located inside a grocery, this buffet serves some of the tastiest Northern and Southern Indian food in the L.A. area. Their combination dinners are an outstanding value. **Open Monday through Friday for three meals. Open Saturday and Sunday for lunch and dinner.** Counter service, vegan options, $.

NORWALK

• Our Daily Bread Bakery
12201 Firestone Blvd., Norwalk, CA 90650   **(562) 863-6897**
Vegetarian/deli. The entrée menu rotates every 21 days, and there are 12 different soups, breads, cookies, macaroni and cheese, stuffed peppers, enchiladas, and quiche. **Open Monday**

through Thursday from late breakfast through early dinner. Open Friday for breakfast. Closed Saturday and Sunday. Counter service, vegan options, $.

• Golden Lotus
1301 Franklin St., Oakland, CA 94612   **(510) 893-0383**
Vegetarian/Vietnamese. Start your meal off with a Spring Roll, Vietnamese Veggie Pancakes, pot stickers, fried wontons, and more. Be sure to sample one of the numerous soups as well as a wide variety of creative entrées, many of which use wheat gluten and soy products. Open daily for lunch and dinner. Full service, vegan options, espresso/cappucino, non-alcoholic wine/beer, take-out, VISA/MC/DISC, $-$$.

Granny Feels Great
5020 Woodminster Ln., Oakland, CA 94602   **(510) 530-6723**
Natural foods. Granny's primarily offers sandwiches, but vegetarian options using cheese or dairy are also available. The menu also lists a salad plate, potato salad, and carrot-raisin salad. Open Monday through Saturday. Closed Sunday. Counter service, fresh juices, take-out, $.

Holyland Kosher Foods
677 Rand Ave., Oakland, CA 94610   **(510) 272-0535**
Kosher. Enjoy salads, hummus, tabbouleh, falafel, and stuffed grape leaves while sitting indoors or enjoying the sun outside. Open Sunday through Thursday for late lunch and dinner. Open Friday until noon. Closed Saturday. Full service, fresh juices, wine/beer, catering, take-out, $.

•• Layonna's Kitchen
358 11th St., Oakland, CA 94607   **(510) 628-0350**
Vegan/Chinese. Located in Oakland's Chinatown, the "East Bay Express" voted this Buddhist establishment the best vegetarian restaurant on the East Bay. Layonna's offers appetizers, soups, entrées, rice or noodle dishes, and an all-you-can-eat lunch buffet. Unique items include ginger 'fish' soup, twice-cooked 'pork,' Hainan 'drumsticks,' pan-fried 'codfish steak,' mustard green pickles and bean curd, and seaweed pinenut fried rice. No MSG, onion, or garlic is used. Also, the owners operate a Chinese vegetarian grocery with many exotic gourmet items at 443 8th St. Open Wednesday through Monday for lunch and dinner. Closed Tuesday. Full service, special drinks, take-out, VISA/MC, $-$$.

• MacRobiotic Grocery/Organic Café
1050 40th St., Oakland, CA 94608   **(510) 653-6510**
Vegetarian/macrobiotic. Gourmet macrobiotic food is prepared with organic ingredients by a team of internationally trained macrobiotic cooks. Every meal is unique. Desserts are made without refined sugars, honey, eggs, or dairy products. Open daily for three meals. Full service, macrobiotic/vegan options, catering, take-out, $$.

Nan Yang Rockridge
6048 College Ave., Oakland, CA 94618   **(510) 655-3298**
Burmese. The wide variety of vegetarian dishes includes Hot and Sour Soup, Fried Tropical

Squash, Stir-Fried Brussel Sprouts and Baby Corn, Stir-Fried Jicama, Burmese Cold Noodles, and more. Also, savor curry, black, coconut, or chili rice. **Open Tuesday through Sunday. Closed Monday. Full service, vegan options, wine/beer, take-out, VISA/MC, $$.**

• New World Vegetarian
464 8th St., Oakland, CA 94607   **(510) 444-2891**

Vegetarian/international. New World is a primarily vegan restaurant that offers veggie patties and dishes made from gluten, yam flour, and tofu, such as imitation BBQ pork and imitation eel. **Open daily for lunch and dinner. Full service, vegan options, reservations recommended, take-out, VISA/MC/AMEX/DISC, $$.** www.newworldvegetarian.com

• Vege House
369 12th St., Oakland, CA 94607   **(510) 465-4713**

Vegetarian/Vietnamese. Vege House makes all of their tofu and meat alternatives as well as soymilk fresh every day in the restaurant. Try the spicy tofu or Szechuan "Shrimp" with onions, carrots, and green beans, as well as many other delicious vegetarian and vegan options. **Open Monday through Saturday for lunch and dinner. Closed Sunday. Cafeteria, vegan options, fresh juices, smoothies, soymilk, non-smoking, take-out, VISA/MC/AMEX/ DISC/DC, $-$$.**

ORANGE

Tandoor Cuisine of India
1132 E. Katella Ave., Orange, CA 92667   **(714) 538-2234**

Indian. Minutes from Disneyland and the Anaheim Convention Center, Tandoor has a good selection of vegetarian Indian specialties including excellent appetizers, salad, rice dishes, and entrées. **Open daily. Full service, vegan options, take-out, $$.**

OROVILLE

Vega MacRobiotic Center
1511 Robinson St., Oroville, CA 95965   **(916) 533-7702**

Macrobiotic. Vega offers a variety of macrobiotic meals, ranging from simple to international gourmet. Meals are dependent upon which cooking course is in progress on the day you visit. **Open Monday through Friday. Closed Saturday and Sunday. Limited service, take-out, VISA/MC/AMEX, $$-$$$.**

OXNARD

A Good Thai and Peruvian Restaurant
722 N. Ventura Rd., Oxnard, CA 93030   **(805) 983-1514**

Thai/Peruvian. This restaurant has a vegetarian section that focuses more on Thai cuisine.

Restaurant codes: ✪ Reviewers' Choice   • Vegetarian Restaurant   • • Vegan Restaurant
Restaurant prices: **$** less than $6   **$$** $6-$12   **$$$** more than $12
Credit Cards Accepted: VISA - VISA   MC - MasterCard   AMEX - American Express
DISC - Discover   DC - Diner's Club

Items include a variety of soups, appetizers, and entrées. **Open daily for three meals. Full service, vegan options, non-alcoholic beer, beer/wine, $$-$$$.**

Chai's Thai Cuisine
2178 Saviers Rd., Oxnard, CA 93033 (805) 240-2462
Thai. Chai's Thai Cuisine has a separate vegetarian menu. **Open daily for lunch and dinner. Full service, take-out, VISA/MC, $$.**

PACIFIC GROVE

Tillie Gort's Café and Restaurant
111 Central Ave., Pacific Grove, CA 93950 (831) 373-0335
International. Tillie Gort's has California-style offerings, including hot and cold sandwiches, pasta, and two kinds of veggie burgers with your choice of toppings, and other vegetarian specialties. The café has an earthy, informal coffeehouse atmosphere that is suitable for business entertaining. **Open daily for lunch and dinner. Full service, take-out, non-smoking, vegan/macrobiotic options, soymilk, espresso/cappuccino, wine/beer, special drinks, VISA/MC/AMEX/DISC, $$.**

PACIFIC PALISADES

•• Seed Live Cuisine
17531 Posetano Rd., Pacific Palisades, CA 90272 (310) 454-0547
Vegan. Seed Live Cuisine offers raw, vegan, organic four-course meals for delivery and events. The menu changes weekly, but past dishes have included Pad Thai noodles made from fresh coconut, Thai curly beets served over pineapple lemongrass long grain wild rice, a spiced coconut sandwich with herb cheese and sliced avocado, peach pie with a date nut crust, and cinnamon rolls with walnuts, raisins, and glaze frosting. Those who prefer a restaurant dining experience can make reservations for their regular Sunday brunches at the Globe Restaurant. **Delivery only, reservations required for brunch, catering, $$$. www.seedcuisine.com**

PALM DESERT

• Native Foods ☉
73-890 El Paseo, Palm Desert, CA 92260 (760) 836-9396
Vegetarian. See description under Costa Mesa, CA.

• Veggie & Tea House
72281 Hwy. 111, Palm Desert, CA 92260 (760) 674-9579
Vegetarian/Chinese. See description under Irvine, CA.

PALM SPRINGS

• Café Totonaca
Nature's Rx Natural Health Food Market
555 S. Sunrise Way, Palm Springs, CA 92264 (760) 323-9487
Vegetarian/natural foods store deli. Located inside Nature's Rx Natural Health Food Market, Café Totonaca boasts a jungle décor and great service. Offerings include Whole Grain

Pancakes, Super Sprout Salad, Tofu Mock Egg Sandwiches, Tempeh Burgers, B.B.Q. Soy Chicken with Veggies, a Tofu Steak Platter, Soy Shrimp & Broccoli, and Veggies Azteca (steamed veggies with rice, beans, and salsa). Dairy-free shakes and smoothies are also available in flavors like Almond Pecan and Date. Near Living Desert Animal Park and the Palm Springs Aerial Tramway. **Open daily for three meals. Limited service, vegan options, fresh juices, special drinks, take-out, VISA/MC/AMEX/DISC, $$.**

• Native Foods ✪
1775 E. Palm Canyon Dr., Palm Springs, CA 92264   **(760) 416-0070**
Vegetarian. See description under Costa Mesa, CA. **Open Monday through Saturday for three meals. Closed Sundays and the month of August. Full service.**

PALO ALTO

•• Bay Leaf Café
520 Ramona St., Palo Alto, CA 94301   **(650) 321-7466**
Vegan. Bay Leaf Café, located in trendy downtown Palo Alto, offers vegan soups, sandwiches, salads, coffee, and 15 flavors of non-dairy ice cream. **Open daily. Limited service, vegan options, reservations not needed, cash only, take-out, $-$$.** www.thebayleaf.com

Country Sun Natural Foods Deli
440 California Ave., Palo Alto, CA 94306   **(415) 328-4120**
Health foods store deli. The Country Sun deli offers breakfast and lunch every day with a variety of vegetarian options. Organically grown grains, beans, fruits, and vegetables are used whenever possible. The menu features homemade vegetarian pizza, a wide variety of salads, hot entrées, vegetarian burgers, and sandwiches. **Open daily. Limited service, macrobiotic/vegan options, fresh juices, limited seating, take-out, $.**

Fresh Choice
379 Stanford Shopping Ctr., Palo Alto, CA 94304   **(415) 322-6995**
American. See description under Menlo Park, CA.

The Good Earth
1058 Elwell Ct., Palo Alto, CA 94303   **(415) 969-5051**
Natural foods. See description under Northridge, CA. **Open daily. Full service, wine/beer, VISA/MC/AMEX, $$.**

Hobee's
4224 El Camino Real, Palo Alto, CA 94306   **(650) 493-7823**
85 El Camino Real, Palo Alto, CA 94301   **(650) 327-4111**
Restaurant chain. See description under Cupertino, CA.

• Meekk's Dinner Tree
3750 Fabian Way, Palo Alto, CA 94024   **(650) 424-3900**
Kosher/vegetarian. Meekk's offers vegan, organic fare with inspiration from all over the world.

Try the salads, soups, entrées, appetizers and, definitely, the desserts! **Open Sunday through Thursday for three meals. Open Friday for lunch. Open Saturday for dinner. Full service, vegan options, catering, take-out, $$$.** www.meekkskitchen.com

Ming's

1700 Embarcadero Rd., Palo Alto, CA 94303   **(650) 856-7700**

Chinese. Offering an extensive vegetarian menu, Ming's is a fine dining experience for a reasonable price. Options include Sautéed Vegetarian "Scallops" with snow peas, and Vegetarian Cashew "Chicken" with soy gluten, roasted peanuts, bamboo shoots, carrots, celery, and bell pepper in chili and garlic sauce. **Open daily for lunch and dinner. Full service, take-out, delivery, $-$$.** www.mings.com

Molly Stone's

164 S. California Ave., Palo Alto, CA 94301   **(650) 365-8300**

Natural foods. Located across from the train station, Molly Stone's is a gourmet grocer with high quality produce, specialties, and natural foods. They have outdoor seating for those who wish to people-watch while they dine. **Open daily. Limited service, vegan options, $-$$$.**

Rojoz Gourmet Wraps

60 Town and Country Village, Palo Alto, CA 94301   **(650) 324-9727**

Mexican. Rojoz serves only the finest beans, vegetables, spices, and sauces prepared quickly, without compromising taste. The menu offers an array of vegetarian burritos, such as the Classic Veggie, stuffed with black beans, Aztec rice, sun-ripened tomato salsa, and homemade chunky guacamole; and the Taj Mahal, a vegan blend of curried red potatoes, julienne carrots, cabbage salsa, and jasmine rice. **Open Monday through Saturday for lunch and dinner. Closed Sunday. Limited service, vegan options, take-out, beer, $.**

• STO'A

3750 Fabian Way, Palo Alto, CA 94303   **(650) 424-3900**

Vegetarian. This upscale restaurant and wine bar offers innovative takes on classic Asian, Spanish, and Mediterranean cuisines. The menu varies seasonally, drawing on locally grown produce. Offerings include butternut squash bisque, maitake mushroom and chard wontons, housemade truffled spinach ravioli made with rennetless cheese, and black bean stew with a side of stuffed zucchini. Reservations recommended. **Open daily for lunch through late evening service. Full service, macrobiotic/vegan options, fresh juices, espresso/cappuccino, soymilk, beer/wine, non-alcoholic beer, special drinks, take-out, VISA/MC/AMEX, $$$.** www.stoarestaurant.com

Whole Foods Market & Deli

774 Emerson St., Palo Alto, CA 94301   **(415) 326-8676**

Natural foods deli. This gourmet natural foods deli offers 35 all-natural and organic salads. Specialty items include homemade vegetable knishes, pizzas, and vegetable sushi. There are also hot food selections, including vegan entrées, vegetable lasagna, and two daily soups. Breakfast is served and box lunches to-go are available. **Open daily. Deli-style, vegan options, fresh juices, wine/beer, catering, take-out, VISA/MC, $.**

World Wraps
201 University Ave., Palo Alto, CA 94301   **(415) 327-9777**
International. World Wraps offers a variety of sandwiches and smoothies. Try The Bombay
with curried vegetables and mango salsa, or the Mexican-style Sautéed Tofu wrap. **Open
daily.** Limited service, vegan options, fresh juices, smoothies, $.

Zao Noodle Bar
261 University Ave., Palo Alto, CA 94301   **(650) 328-1988**
California. Zao Noodles offers several vegetarian Spicy Black Bean with Vegetable Stir Fry,
Rice Noodles with Five Vegetables and Tofu, and Vegetable Pho. **Open daily for lunch and
dinner.** Full service, vegan options, VISA/MC, $$.

PALOMAR MOUNTAIN

• Mother's Kitchen
Junction S. 6th & S. 7th, Palomar Mountain, CA 92060   **(760) 742-4233**
Vegetarian juice bar. Any visitor to San Diego who drives up to see the famous Mt. Palomar
telescope will pass Mother's. It's the only eatery on the mountain. Within this rustic moun-
taintop cabin, you'll find soups, salads, sandwiches, and nutburgers. **Open Thursday through
Monday. Closed Tuesday and Wednesday.** Full service, fresh juices, smoothies, wine/beer,
take-out, $$.

PARADISE

• Feather River Hospital Cafeteria
5974 Pentz Rd., Paradise, CA 95969   **(916) 877-9361**
Vegetarian/cafeteria. Sample the Spinach Tortellini or Spaghetti, Mushroom Loaf, Zucchini
Quiche, Enchilada, or Garbanzo Casserole. Or visit the salad bar, pizza bar, and veggie
burger bar. **Open daily for lunch and dinner.** Cafeteria, take-out, $.

PASADENA

Clearwater Café
168 Colorado Blvd., Pasadena, CA 91105   **(818) 356-0959**
Natural foods. This smoke-free café offers many vegetarian dishes, such as Organic Brown
Rice Risotto with Lemon and Herbs, Chinese Long Beans with Black Bean-Ginger Sauce,
Mixed Grill of Vegetables with Creamy Polenta, Tempura Vegetables with Organic Ventura
Bananas and Ponzu Sauce, several salads, and more. Brunch served on weekends. **Open
daily for lunch and dinner.** Full service, vegan options, take-out, VISA/MC/AMEX, $$$.

The Good Earth
257 N. Rosemead Blvd., Pasadena, CA 91107   **(818) 351-5488**
Natural foods. See description under Northridge, CA. **Open daily.**

• Orean . . . The Health Express
817 N. Lake Ave., Pasadena, CA 91104   **(626) 794-0861**
Vegetarian. This vegetarian fast food restaurant offers meatless burgers, tacos, burritos,

tamales, chili dogs, shakes, "air fries," and more. Outdoor seating available. **Open daily for three meals. Take-out, smoothies, $-$$$.**

• Veggie & Tea House
600E Colorado Blvd., Pasadena, CA 91101   **(626) 396-3003**
Vegetarian/Chinese. See description under Irvine, CA.

PINOLE

The New Deli
624A San Pablo Ave., Pinole, CA 94564   **(510) 724-5335**
Natural foods/California-style. The New Deli offers many items made from scratch. Homemade salad dressings and vegetarian soups are prepared daily. **Open daily for breakfast and lunch. Limited service, smoothies, $-$$.**

PLEASANT HILL

Thai Village Restaurant
670-I Gregory Ln., Pleasant Hill, CA 94523   **(510) 256-0289**
Thai. This cozy restaurant will substitute bean curd in many of its authentic Thai dishes. Several different curries and vegetable sir-fries are served daily. **Open Monday through Saturday for lunch and dinner. Closed Sunday. Full service, non-alcoholic wine/beer, wine/beer, take-out, VISA/MC, $-$$.**

RANCHO PALOS VERDES

•• Vegan Terra Café
28901 S. Western Ave., #123, Rancho Palos Verdes, CA 90275   (310) 833-7977
Vegan. Vegan Terra Café boasts that it offers "vegan versions of all your favorite dishes," including soups, salads, sandwiches, wraps, California rolls, veggie burgers, veggie dogs, and unique Mexican dishes. There are also 'regional' specialties, like the Paris, Texas (French fries smothered in chili and salsa with a side of veggies); Salisbury Stack, which is covered in onions and mushrooms and comes with sides of mashed potatoes and veggies; Lasagna; Spaghetti & Wheat Balls; and the Mediterranean, falafel with hummus and tabbouleh. Even the sugar here is vegan. **Open Monday through Saturday for lunch and dinner. Closed Sunday. Limited service, vegan options, fresh juices, espresso/cappuccino, smoothies, take-out, VISA/MC/AMEX/DISC, $-$$.**

REDLANDS

Nature's Deli and Nutrition Center
202 E. State St., Redlands, CA 92373   **(909) 792-6556**
Natural foods deli. Nature's Deli and Nutrition Center offers tofu burgers, vegetable pita (tofu and spinach in a whole-wheat phyllo pastry), veggie avocado sandwiches, and a Mediterranean wrap. **Open Monday through Friday for lunch and dinner. Closed Saturday and Sunday. Counter service, vegan options, smoothies.**

REDONDO BEACH

•The Green Temple Vegetarian Restaurant
1700 S. Catalina Ave., #103, Redondo Beach, CA 90277   (310) 944-4525
Vegetarian. The Green Temple serves a variety of cuisines, including Mexican, Italian, and classic American. Their menu features daily soups, salads, quesadillas, rice and bean bowls, sides, sandwiches, burgers with choices like soy or white cheddar, and desserts, including Vanilla Rice Dream. Entrées include the Garden Burrito, Savory Steamers (brown rice, tofu, and veggies), a Shepherd Spud (a baked potato topped with vegetables, a veggie burger, and mushroom gravy), or the Mushroom Walnut Loaf. **Open Tuesday through Sunday for lunch and dinner. Closed Monday. Full service, vegan options, take-out, fresh juices, VISA/MC, $$.**

REDWOOD SHORES

Amici's East Coast Pizzeria
226 Redwood Shores Pkwy., Redwood Shores, CA 94065   (650) 654-3333
Italian. See description under Mountain View, CA

Hobee's Restaurant
1101 Shoreway Rd., Redwood Shores, CA 94002   (650) 596-0400
Restaurant chain. See description under Cupertino, CA.

RESEDA

•Garden Wok
6117 Reseda Blvd., Reseda, CA 91335   (818) 881-8886
Vegetarian/Chinese. The menu at this small, family-owned restaurant makes good use of mock meats, tofu, mushrooms, and other vegetables prepared wok-style. Offerings include Chicken Drum Sticks, Curry Veggie Beef, Veggie Meat Balls, Kung Pao Veggie Squid, and for dessert, Soy Delicious ice cream. **Open Monday through Saturday for lunch and dinner. Open Sunday for dinner only. Full service, vegan options, take-out, VISA/MC/AMEX/ DISC, $$.**

RIVERSIDE

Dragon House Restaurant
10466 Magnolia Ave., Riverside, CA 92505   (714) 354-2080
Chinese. See description under Moreno Valley, CA.

•Oasis Vegetarian Food
11550 Pierce St., Riverside, CA 92505   (909) 688-5423
Vegetarian. Oasis serves all vegetarian burgers and Latin American cuisine. It adjoins a vegetarian food market. Menu items include the Garden Supreme burger, pupusas (corn tortillas filled with vegetables), carnitas (soy "pork" burritos), tamales (stuffed corn husks), French fries, and many vegetarian sandwiches. **Open Sunday through Friday for lunch and dinner. Closed Sunday. Limited service, vegan options, smoothies, take-out, $.**

ROSEMEAD

Chameli
8752 Valley Blvd., Rosemead, CA 91770 **(626) 280-1947**
Indian. Listen to classical Indian sitar music while you enjoy ethnic food. Open daily for lunch and dinner. Full service, vegan options, wine/beer, catering, take-out, VISA/MC/ AMEX, $$.

• New Happy Family of Rosemead
8632 Valley Blvd., Rosemead, CA 91770 **(626) 288-5786**
Vegetarian/Chinese. This restaurant offers an all-you-can-eat menu with a large selection of tofu, yuba, and seitan dishes. A V.I.P. room for parties and meetings is also available. Open daily for lunch and dinner. Full service, vegan options, VISA/MC, $$.

ROWLAND HEIGHTS

• Happy Family Vegetarian Cuisine
18425 E. Colima Rd., 2F, Rowland Heights, CA 91748 **(626) 965-9923**
Vegetarian/Chinese. Happy Family Vegetarian Cuisine offers a light and airy atmosphere. Though the menu features many dishes containing mock meats, their specialty is the vege- tarian deep fried "chicken," which is made from mushrooms. Open daily for lunch and dinner. Full service, vegan options, takeout, VISA/MC/AMEX, $$.

SACRAMENTO

(For restaurant listings in the surrounding areas, see Auburn, Carmichael, Davis, Elk Grove, and Fair Oaks.)

Ernesto's Mexican Food
1901 16th St., Sacramento, CA 95814 **(916) 441-5850**
Mexican. Helpful servers will point out vegetarian options, such as Frida's Fajitas, the Navajo Bonanza Burrito, and Navajo Quesadillas. Also, the refried beans are vegan. Open daily. Full service, vegan options, beer/wine/alcohol, VISA/MC/AMEX/DISC/DC, $$$. www. ernestomexicanfood.com

Fox and Goose Public House
"The Building," 1001 R St., Sacramento, CA 95814 **(916) 443-8825**
Pub. This authentic British pub serves a plentiful array of vegan and vegetarian breakfast and lunch items, including pastries, vegetarian black bean chili and many homemade desserts. Open Monday through Saturday for three meals. Closed Sunday. Full service, vegan options, espresso/cappuccino, beer/wine, non-alcoholic beer/wine, special drinks, take-out, catering, VISA/MC/AMEX, $-$$. www.foxandgoose.com

Henry Nguyen Restaurant
1537 Howe Ave., Sacramento, CA 95825 **(916) 927-1014**
Vietnamese. This restaurant offers more than 25 delicious and affordable vegetarian entrées, and they state that they do not use MSG. Open daily for lunch and dinner. Full service, vegan options, VISA/MC/AMEX/DISC, $-$$.

Juliana's Kitchen

1401 G St., Sacramento, CA 95814-1503   **(916) 444-0966**

Middle Eastern. Juliana's Kitchen is a family-run business that specializes in a variety of vegetarian pita bread sandwiches from the Middle East. Salads, desserts, and organic juice selections are also on the menu. **Open daily for lunch and dinner. Limited service, vegan options, take-out, VISA/MC/AMEX/DISC, $.**

Ricci's Restaurant

705 J St., Sacramento, CA 95814   **(916) 442-6741**

Italian. The chefs at Ricci's are capable of creating any meal vegan or vegetarian. If you want something other than what is on the menu, just let the server know. **Open for lunch and dinner Monday through Friday. Open Saturday for dinner only. Closed Sunday. Full service, vegan options, special drinks, beer, wine, alcohol, VISA/MC/AMEX/DC, $$.**

Sacramento Natural Foods Co-op

1900 Alhambra Blvd., Sacramento, CA 95816   **(916) 455-2667**

Deli. Sacramento Co-op features a variety of soups, salads, sandwiches, and baked goods. **Open daily. Limited service, vegan options, VISA/MC/DISC, $. www.sacfoodcoop.com**

Taj Mahal

2355 Arden Way, Sacramento, CA 95825   **(916) 924-8378**

Indian. Taj Mahal features several vegetarian curry and tandoori dishes. **Open daily for lunch and dinner. Full service, wine/beer, VISA/MC/AMEX/DC, $$.**

SAN BERNARDINO

Lotus Garden

111 E. Hospitality Ln., San Bernardino, CA 92408   **(909) 381-6171**

Chinese. This Chinese restaurant offers many vegetarian options, including sizzling bean curd, diced vegetables with nuts, sautéed Chinese bok choy, mock meat and chicken dishes, and pan-fried noodles. **Open daily for lunch and dinner. Full service, vegan options, wine/beer/ alcohol, VISA/MC/DISC, $$.**

SAN CARLOS

Fon Yong

1065 Holly St., San Carlos, CA 94070   **(650) 637-9238**

Chinese. Fon Yong offers a large selection of vegetarian soups, appetizers, entrées, and rice and noodle dishes, some made with mock meats. **Open daily for lunch and dinner. Full service, vegan options, take-out, VISA/MC, $$.**

Restaurant codes: ✪ Reviewers' Choice   • Vegetarian Restaurant   •• Vegan Restaurant
Restaurant prices: **$** less than $6   **$$** $6-$12   **$$$** more than $12
Credit Cards Accepted: VISA - VISA   MC - MasterCard   AMEX - American Express
DISC - Discover   DC - Diner's Club

SAN DIEGO

(For restaurant listings in the surrounding areas, see Chula Vista, Coronado, Encinitas, and La Jolla.)

Café Athena

1846 Garnet Ave., San Diego, CA 92109 (858) 274-1140

Mediterranean. This Greek-style restaurant offers plenty of vegan options, and they're clearly marked with a "V" symbol. Try Skordalia (a spread made of potato and garlic blended with cilantro), Manitaria (smoked mushrooms blended with sweet peppers), lentil soup, marinated artichoke salad, or Iman Bayaldi (eggplant stuffed with raisins, walnuts, tomatoes, garlic, onion, and cilantro, topped with tomato sauce). **Open daily for lunch and dinner. Full service, vegan options, non-alcoholic beer, wine/beer, catering, take-out, VISA/MC/AMEX/DISC/DC, $-$$.**

Café India

3760-5 Sports Arena Blvd., San Diego, CA 92110 (619) 224-7500

Indian. Café India offers a vegetarian buffet daily. It is located in a shopping strip close to the arena. **Open Tuesday thorugh Sunday for lunch and dinner. Closed Monday. Full service, vegan options, catering, take-out, VISA/MC, $$.**

Casa de Pico

2754 Calhoun St., San Diego, CA 92110 (619) 296-3267

Mexican. Located in the heart of Bazaar Del Mondo Shopping Complex in old-town San Diego's historic state park, Casa de Pico offers many vegetarian options. A special menu for the health-conscious lists foods low in salt, fat, and cholesterol. Enjoy live mariachi music nightly on an open-air patio. **Open daily. Full service, wine/beer/alcohol, VISA/MC/AMEX/DISC, $-$$.**

• Charlie's Best Bread

1808 Garnet Ave., San Diego, CA 92109 (858) 272-3521

Vegetarian bakery. This bakery prepares some vegan breads and some vegetarian breads made with cheese or honey. Charlie's uses organic and stone-ground Montana wheat to make flour for the baked goods. They also sell their products at farmers' markets around the area. **Open daily. Take-out, vegan options, VISA/MC/AMEX/DISC, $.**

•• Eatopia

5001-A Newport Ave., San Diego, CA 92107 (619) 224-3237

Vegan. Serving a menu designed by a vegan food scientist, Eatopia offers fast and delicious plant-based, cholesterol-free, healthy, low-fat, and environmentally friendly foods. Try their pizzas, a soy seafood salad, the Cosmic Californian wrap (stuffed with spinach, tomato, avocado, scallions, olives, red peppers, and soy chicken or tofu), one of their raw food options, and more. Then, wash your meal down with one of their soymilk shakes or smoothies, or follow it up with some soft serve soy ice cream. **Open daily for three meals. Counter service, special drinks, no credit cards, $. www.eatopiaexpress.com**

• Gelato Vero Café
3753 India St., San Diego, CA 92103   **(619) 295-9269**

Vegetarian/coffeehouse. The menu is limited at this coffeehouse and gelato shop, but soups, salads, and fresh breads are available daily. **Open daily for breakfast through late night service.** Counter service, vegan options, fresh juices, take-out, AMEX, $.

• The Hare Krishna Temple Buffet & Boutique
1030 Grand Ave., San Diego, CA 92109   **(858) 483-2500**

Vegetarian. Each night is a different kind of cuisine, including Mexican, Indian, or Italian, at the Hare Krishna Temple Buffet. Though your first visit is free, the temple asks for a $5.00 donation each time you visit the Buffet thereafter. **Open Monday through Friday for dinner. Closed Saturday and Sunday.** Buffet, no credit cards, $.

• Jimbo's Vegetarian Restaurant
12853 El Camino Real, San Diego, CA 92130   **(858) 793-7755**

Vegetarian/natural foods. The menu offers items including enchiladas, Jamaican wraps, vegan cakes, and cookies. **Open daily.** Limited service, vegan options, take-out, fresh juices, espresso/cappuccino, smoothies, soymilk, special drinks, VISA/MC/DISC, $-$$.

Jyoti Bihanga
3351 Adams Ave., San Diego, CA 92116   **(619) 282-4116**

Natural foods. Jyoti Bihanga offers excellent vegetarian and macrobiotic foods in a serene atmosphere with a fountain, high arched ceiling, and 15-foot windows. Sample daily specials, homemade soups and desserts, and an all-you-can-eat Saturday breakfast buffet. **Open Monday through Saturday. Closed Sunday.** Full service, macrobiotic/vegan options, fresh juices, take-out, $-$$.

Lotsa Pasta
1762 Garnet Ave., San Diego, CA 92109   **(858) 581-6777**

Italian. This restaurant offers 12 different flavors of pasta cut to order and served with 18 different sauces, 15 of which are vegetarian, for more than 500 combinations. Wheat-free pasta is available. **Open daily.** Full service, vegan options, take-out, VISA/MC/AMEX/DISC, $$.

• Madras Café
9484 Black Mountain Rd., San Diego, CA 92126   **(858) 695-6229**

Vegetarian/Indian. This authentic South Indian vegetarian restaurant offers a menu of samosas, roti, masala dosa, idli, vada, curry dishes, and much more. **Open daily for lunch and dinner.** Full service, vegan options, fresh juices, smoothies, espresso/cappuccino, take-out, VISA/MC/AMEX/DISC/DC, $$. www.madras-café.com

• Ocean Beach Organic Food Market & Deli
4765 Voltaire St., San Diego, CA 92107   **(619) 224-1387**

Vegetarian deli. This deli in a health food store features vegan and raw foods. There is also a great selection of organic produce, cold salads, soups, entrées, sandwiches, baked goods, and desserts. **Open daily.** Take-out, vegan options, fresh juices, VISA/MC/DISC, $.

• Pokez Mex Vegetarian Restaurant

947 E St., San Diego, CA 92101 **(619) 702-7160**

Mexican. Great vegan options, live music, and spiritual and artistic awareness. **Open daily for three meals.** Full service, vegan options, take-out, catering, fresh juices, non-alcoholic beer/wine, beer/wine, soymilk, VISA/MC/AMEX/DISC, $$.

Ranchos

1830 Sunset Cliffs Blvd., San Diego, CA 92107 **(619) 226-7619**

Mexican. Great Mexican food in a very pleasant environment, with whole-wheat tortillas, no lard, and soy cheese as options. The vegan items are marked on the menu. **Open daily for three meals.** Full service, vegan options, smoothies, fresh juices, espresso/cappuccino, beer/wine, VISA/MC, $$.

Shmoozers

6366 El Cajon Blvd., San Diego, CA 92115 **(619) 583-1636**

Kosher. The menu is mostly vegetarian, with a few fish dishes. Offerings include pizza, Italian dishes, and Mexican dishes, all made with rennetless cheeses. Veggie burgers and side dishes available. **Open Sunday through Thursday for lunch and dinner. Closed Friday. Open Saturday after sundown.** Limited service, cafeteria, take-out, catering, VISA/MC/DISC, $.

• Stephanie's Bakery and Bohemia Strudel Factory

4879 Voltaire St., San Diego, CA 92107 **(619) 221-0285**

Vegetarian bakery. Here, you get two bakeries under one roof. Stephanie's is a 100 percent vegan bakery that creates breads, cakes, wedding and occasion cakes, cheesecakes, cookies, brownies, muffins, and more. Bohemia Strudel Factory specializes in both sweet and savory strudels, including cherry "cream cheese," black forest, pumpkin, and spinach herb. Some strudel flavors contain white sugar; others are 100 percent vegan. Selected items available by mail order. **Open Wednesday through Sunday for breakfast through late lunch. Closed Monday and Tuesday.** Limited service, vegan options, espresso/cappuccino, soymilk, take-out, catering, $$. www.stephaniesbakery.com

SAN DIMAS

• Veggie & Tea House

641 Arrow Hwy., San Dimas, CA 91773 **(909) 592-6323**

Vegetarian/Chinese. See description under Irvine, CA.

SAN FRANCISCO

(For restaurant listings in the surrounding areas, see Albany, Berkeley, Campbell, Concord, Cupertino, Fremont, Half Moon Bay, Menlo Park, Mountain View, Oakland, Palo Alto, Pleasant Hill, Redwood Shores, San Carlos, San Mateo, San Rafael, Soquel, and Sunnyvale.)

All You Knead

1466 Haight St., San Francisco, CA 94117 **(415) 552-4550**

American. All You Knead truly prepares all you need with homemade soups, salads, veggie sandwiches, veggie lasagna, tofu scramble, and veggie burritos. **Open daily.** $.

Amici's East Coast Pizzeria

2033 Union St., San Francisco, CA 94123   **(415) 885-4500**
Italian. See description under Mountain View, CA.

• Ananda-Fuara

1298 Market St., San Francisco, CA 94102-4801   **(415) 564-6766**
Vegetarian. This Sri-Chimnoy restaurant offers American and Indian-style foods, including
sandwiches, BBQ tofu burgers, pizza, curry dishes, salads, and a breakfast menu. Open
Monday, Tuesday, and Thursday through Saturday for three meals. Open Wednesday for
breakfast and lunch. Closed Sunday. Full service, macrobiotic/vegan options, fresh juices,
smoothies, take-out, $-$$. anandafuara.citysearch.com

• Bok Choy Garden

1820 Clement St., San Francisco, CA 94121   **(415) 387-8111**
Vegetarian/Chinese. Bok Choy Garden specializes in freshly prepared authentic regional
Chinese vegetarian cuisine without garlic, onion, or eggs. Open daily for lunch and dinner.
Full service, vegan options, fresh juices, soymilk, reservations recommended, take-out,
catering, VISA/MC, $$.

•• Café Gratitude

2400 Harrison St., San Francisco, CA 94110   **(415) 824-4652**
Vegan/raw foods. This earthy restaurant, which is 95 percent raw and mostly organic, offers
an array of appetizers, soups, salads, entrées, snacks, and desserts. An interesting note is that
every dish on the menu has a name that begins with "I Am." For example, the "I Am Bright-
Eyed" is seasonal fruit with young coconut, apple, and pecan porridge, the "I Am Friendly"
is an almond, celery, sea vegetable, and lemon paté, the "I Am Graceful" is quinoa with basil
pesto, the "I Am Passionate" is a raw pizza made with buckwheat crust and nut cheese, the
"I Am Giving" is butternut squash noodles, and the "I Am Surrendering" is walnut, date,
fig, and cacao fudge squares. Open Monday through Saturday for three meals. Open Sunday
for brunch. Full service, fresh juices, smoothies, organic beer/wine, special drinks, take-out,
VISA/MC/DISC, $$. www.withthecurrent.com/cafe.htm

Firefly

4288 24th St., San Francisco, CA 94114   **(415) 821-7652**
International. Firefly's veggie options include Roasted Tomato Soup with Semolina, Mixed
Greens with Roasted Shallot, Cheesy Risotto Cakes with Grilled Portabello Mushrooms,
Spicy Thai Coconut Curry Tofu, and vegetable stir-fry. Open daily for dinner. Full service,
wine/beer, reservations required, VISA/MC/AMEX, $$.

Fleur De Lys Restaurant

777 Sutter St., San Francisco, CA 94109   **(415) 673-7779**
French. Enjoy the feeling of dining in "an immense garden tent set in the French countryside,"
while feasting on dishes from the separate vegetarian menu. Such offerings include Ecuadorian
Quinoa, light Cauliflower Mousseline served with watercress sauce, and Ragout of Wild
Mushrooms in a potato shell. Open Monday through Saturday for dinner. Closed Sunday.
Full service, VISA/MC/AMEX/DISC/DC, $$$.

Gaylord India Restaurant

1 Embarcadero Ctr., San Francisco, CA 94111   **(415) 397-7775**
Ghirardelli Square, 900 N. Point St., San Francisco, CA 94109   **(415) 771-8822**
Indian. Gaylord offers world-renowned Indian cuisine with bread baked fresh in clay ovens. Vegetarian appetizers and meatless specialties are listed on the menu. **Open daily for lunch and dinner. Full service, vegan options, fresh juices, wine/beer, take-out, VISA/MC/ AMEX/DISC, $$.**

• Geranium

615 Cortland Ave. (Near Anderson), San Francisco, CA 94110   **(415) 647-0118**
Vegetarian. Located in Bernal Heights, this restaurant features a classy yet comfortable dining room and a tasty array of vegetarian comfort foods. The dinner menu offers a Bibb Lettuce Salad with candied pecans, blue cheese, and pears, Organic Orecchiette Pasta with dandelion greens and chickpeas, the All-American "Eat" Loaf, Polenta, a Japanese rice bowl, and Grilled Pizza topped with gorgonzola cheese, caramelized onions, and grapes. Weekend brunch options include pancakes, French toast, huevos rancheros and burritos made with scrambled eggs or tofu, veggie bacon, and veggie sausage links. **Open Tuesday through Friday for dinner. Open Saturday and Sunday for brunch and dinner. Closed Monday. Full service, vegan options, reservations suggested for parties of 6 or more, soymilk, beer/wine, take-out, VISA/MC, $$.** www.geraniumrestaurant.com

•• Golden Era Vegetarian Restaurant ✪

572 O'Farrell St., San Francisco, CA 94102   **(415) 673-3136**
Vegan/Asian. Located near Union Square Shopping Center, this restaurant offers a great menu of appetizers, soups, noodles, rice dishes, entrées, and desserts. Try the Vietnamese Crepes or the shredded soy "Chicken" Salad as a starter, the Tamarind or Sautéed Garlic "Beef," the Pineapple or Teriyaki "Salmon," or the Vegetarian Lamb Claypot. Then, top it off with the Vegan Mocha Chocolate Cake, the Caramel Flan, or a Salted Plum Lemonade. **Open daily for lunch. Full service, suitable for business entertainment, fresh juices, smoothies, soymilk, non-alcoholic beer, special drinks, take-out, VISA/MC, $$.** www.goldeneravegetarian.com

• Greens Gourmet Vegetarian Restaurant

Fort Mason, Bldg. A, San Francisco, CA 94123   **(415) 771-6222**
Vegetarian. Located in an old army warehouse, Greens offers beautiful views of the San Francisco Bay and the Coastal Mountain Range. Their menu includes salads, soups, appetizers, sandwiches, entrées, pizza, pasta, breakfast items, pastries, and desserts. Try some of their more unique dishes, such as the Sri Lankan Curry, Eggplant Gratin, and the Greens Asian Scramble. Reservations recommended. **Open Monday for dinner. Open Tuesday through Saturday for lunch and dinner. Open Sunday for brunch. Full service, vegan options, fresh juice, wine/beer, take-out, VISA/MC/DISC, $$$.** greensrest.citysearch.com

• Haveli Restaurant

35 6th St., San Francisco, CA 94103   **(415) 348-1381**
Vegetarian/Indian. If you like Indian food and are downtown, this is a good, cheap option. Their daily specials differ, but there are several dishes, such as all-you-can-eat thali, samosas, basmati rice, and pakoras, that are constants. Other items include Raswalle Aloo (spiced potatoes in tomato-based gravy) curry, Lal Chauri (kidney beans in tomato gravy), and

mung beans soup. Most of the food here is vegan, with corn oil used for frying, but a few of the breads and desserts are not. Suitable for business entertaining. **Open Monday through Thursday for lunch. Open Friday and Saturday for lunch and dinner. Closed Sunday. Full service, vegan options, take-out, catering, VISA/MC/AMEX/DISC, $-$$.**

•• Herbivore (The Earthly Grill)

983 Valencia St., San Francisco, CA 94110   **(415) 826-5657**
531 Divisadero St., San Francisco, CA 94117   **(415) 885-7133**

Vegan. Herbivore is an inexpensive, hip, vegan restaurant with a variety of ethnic dishes and a huge beverage selection with something for everyone. **Open daily for lunch and dinner. Full service, vegan options, fresh juices, espresso/cappuccino, non-alcoholic wine/beer, beer/wine/alcohol, smoothies, soymilk, special drinks, take-out, VISA/MC, $-$$.**

•• Hulu House

754 Kirkham St., San Francisco, CA 94122   **(415) 682-0826**

Vegan/Asian. This restaurant serves pan-Asian cuisine. **Open daily for lunch and dinner. Full service, take-out, catering, VISA/MC, $-$$.**

• Joubert's

4115 Judah St. at 46th Ave., San Francisco, CA 94122   **(415) 753-5448**

Vegetarian. Features authentic South African dishes like bredies (herbed baked beans) and potjiekos (mixed vegetables with varying sauces) and numerous entrées, chutneys, and desserts, some of which are vegan. **Open Wednesday through Sunday for dinner. Closed Monday and Tuesday. Full service, vegan options, formal atmosphere, reservations recommended, non-alcoholic beer/wine, beer/wine, VISA/MC/AMEX, $$$.**

•• Juicey Lucy's Organic Juice Bazaar

703 Columbus Ave., San Francisco, CA 94133   **(415) 786-1285**

Vegan/organic café/juice bar. Located in historic North Beach, Lucy's stands out as the only vegan restaurant among many Italian places and offers whole grain salads, bagels, bagel sandwiches, fresh fruit smoothies, and herbal teas in their earthy, informal establishment. Try the stir-fry with kale, tofu, onions, brown rice, and raisins. **Open daily for three meals. Full service, macrobiotic/vegan options, fresh juices, smoothies, soymilk, special drinks, take-out, catering, $-$$.** www.juiceylucy.com

•• Lombard Coffee Shop

1972 Lombard St., San Francisco, CA 94123   **(415) 923-1052**

Vegan/raw foods. This café offers a ethnically diverse menu of all raw options, except for the coffees, black and herbal teas, and soups. Appetizers include Zucchini Hummus, Sorta-Like Salmon Paté, Kimchi, and Daikon and Dried Apricots with crackers, and entrées include Asian Congee, Soba Noodles, Spinach Quiche, and a very filling Vegetable Marinated Lasagna. Make sure that you save some room for the desserts or snacks, though. The convincingly cheesy Lemon Cheesecake and the Black Forest Carob Brownies are highly recommended. Also, the works of rising young artists are often displayed at this café. **Open Tuesday and Wednesday for lunch. Open Friday through Sunday for lunch and dinner. Closed Monday and Thursday. Full service, fresh juices, special drinks, no credit cards, $-$$.**

• Lucky Creation Vegetarian Restaurant
854 Washington St., San Francisco, CA 94108 **(415) 989-0818**

Vegetarian/Chinese. Lucky Creation serves only vegetarian food because it is concerned about customers' health. The phrase "Health is Wealth" is even featured on the menu. Entrées include Sautéed Black Mushrooms with Chinese Greens and Meatless Diced Almond Chicken, plus 23 other healthy items. **Open Thursday through Tuesday. Closed Wednesday.** Full service, vegan options, wine/beer, take-out, $.

Maharani India Restaurant
1122 Post St., San Francisco, CA 94109 **(415) 775-1988**

Indian. See description under Berkeley, CA.

• Millennium Organic Cuisine ✪
580 Geary St., San Francisco, CA 94102 **(415) 345-3900**

Vegetarian. For upscale vegetarian dining, try Millenium, which features healthy meals prepared mainly with organic vegetables. The mostly vegan menu includes creations like Grilled Smoked Portobello Mushrooms, Thai Curry Torte, Turkish Tempeh, and Madras Tofu. **Open Tuesday through Friday for lunch and dinner. Open Saturday and Sunday for dinner only. Closed Monday.** Full service, macrobiotic options, espresso/cappuccino, non-alcoholic wine/beer, wine/beer/alcohol, catering, VISA/MC, $$-$$$. www.millennium restaurant.com

New Eritrea
907 Irving St., San Francisco, CA 94108 **(415) 681-1288**

Ethiopian. New Eritrea offers vegetarian entrées and appetizers served with injera (Ethiopian bread), as well as friendly service and a relaxed atmosphere. **Open daily for lunch and dinner.** Full service, vegan options, beer/wine, catering, VISA/MC/AMEX, $$.

• New Ganges Vegetarian Restaurant
775 Frederick St., San Francisco, CA 94117 **(415) 661-7290**

Vegetarian/Indian. New Ganges' offerings are light but exotic, with distinct flavors from Gujarat, India. You can go á la carte, or choose a special combination plate from the menu, which features dahl, curries, saffron rice, and other classic Indian appetizers. They have vegan desserts and, on Thursday through Saturday, live Indian music. **Open Tuesday through Saturday for dinner. Closed Sunday and Monday.** Full service, vegan options, wine/beer, take-out, VISA/MC/AMEX/DISC, $$.

Quetzal
1234 Polk St., San Francisco, CA 94109 **(415) 673-4181**

International. Quetzal carries an extensive variety of teas from all over the world. Vegetarian sandwiches and desserts also available. **Open daily for three meals.** Full service, vegan options, smoothies, special drinks, VISA/MC/AMEX, $$-$$$.

Rasoi
1037 Valencia St., San Francisco, CA 94110 **(415) 695-0599**

Indian. Rasoi offers traditional Indian entrées with a good vegetarian selection. **Open daily for dinner.** Full service, $$-$$$.

Ristorante Mereb
598 Guerrero St., San Francisco, CA 94110   **(415) 863-3031**
African. This restaurant serves vegetarian entrées and combos. Open daily for lunch and dinner. Full service, vegan options, fresh juices, espresso/cappuccino, $$-$$$.

• Shangri-La Chinese Vegetarian Restaurant
2026 Irving St., San Francisco, CA 94122   **(415) 731-2548**
Vegetarian/Chinese. Shangri-La offers dairy-free, kosher cuisine, including a large selection of soups, appetizers, mock meats, and some American dishes, in a peaceful Buddhist-inspired atmosphere. Try their Mongolian Beef for lunch or dinner and their delicious fried banana balls for dessert. Note that this restaurant is closed every first and third Wednesday of the month. Open daily for lunch and dinner. Full service, vegan options, reservations recommended, take-out, VISA/MC/AMEX, $.

Tai Chi
2031 Polk St., San Francisco, CA 94109   **(415) 441-6758**
Chinese. Tai Chi features Chinese pancakes, spring rolls, vegetable stir-fry, hot and sour cabbage, and dry braised green beans. Open daily. Full service, wine/beer, take-out, VISA/MC/AMEX, $.

Taiwan Restaurant
445 Clement St., San Francisco, CA 94118   **(415) 387-1789**
Chinese. Enjoy vegetarian dishes such as steamed dumplings, hot and sour fried rice, sweet and sour mock pork, and other mock meat dishes at this quaint Chinese restaurant. Open daily for lunch and dinner. Full service, wine/beer, take-out, VISA/MC/AMEX, $$.

Tortola
3640 Sacramento St., San Francisco, CA 94118   **(415) 929-8181**
Crocker Galleria, 50 Post St., San Francisco, CA 94108   **(415) 986-8678**
UCSF, 500 Parnassus Ave., San Francisco, CA 94122   **(415) 731-8670**
Stonestown Galleria, 3521 20th Ave., San Francisco, CA 94132   **(415) 929-8181**
Mexican. Tortola features vegetarian tacos, burritos, and tostadas daily. No lard is used in the beans. Open Tuesday through Sunday. Closed Monday. Full service, wine/beer, full bar, take-out, $$.

• Urban Forage
254 Fillmore St., San Francisco, CA 94117   **(415) 255-6701**
Vegetarian juice bar. Located in "The Haight" section, this earthy natural foods establishment and juice bar offers raw and vegan foods, with the exception of honey in a few desserts. Offerings include miso soup, salads, stuffed portobello mushrooms, wraps, sides, desserts, fruit drinks, and teas. Open Monday through Friday three meals. Open Saturday and Sunday for lunch and dinner. Counter service, vegan options, fresh juices, hemp milk, special drinks, non-smoking, take-out, catering, VISA/MC, $-$$. www.urbanforage.com

• Vege House
309 6th Ave., San Francisco, CA 94118   **(415) 668-0608**
Vegetarian/Vietnamese. See description under Oakland, CA. Take-out only $.

Vicolo Pizzeria
201 Ivy St., San Francisco, CA 94102 **(415) 863-2382**

Pizza. This pizzeria features cornmeal-crust pizza, wonderful salads, and vegetarian soups. Open daily for lunch and dinner. Limited service, non-alcoholic beer, wine/beer, take-out, VISA/MC/AMEX, $$.

Wu Kong Restaurant
101 Spear St., San Francisco, CA 94105 **(415) 957-9300**

Chinese. Among the options here are "Vegetable Goose" (tofu stuffed with mushrooms), other bean curd dishes, and vegetable dishes. Open daily for lunch and dinner. Full service, take-out, VISA/MC/AMEX, $$.

SAN GABRIEL

• Tea Shaker and Vegetarian Food
7258 Rosemead Blvd., San Gabriel, CA 91775 **(626) 287-5850**

Vegetarian. This restaurant offers vegan and macrobiotic options. Open Tuesday through Sunday for lunch and dinner. Closed Monday. Full service, reservations recommended, fresh juices, soymilk, special drinks, take-out, VISA/MC/AMEX/DISC, $.

• Veg Table
841 W. Las Tunas Dr., San Gabriel, CA 91776 **(626) 282-2282**

Vegetarian/Chinese. Located near Cal Tech, this restaurant serves vegetarian Chinese cuisine, including a variety of tofu dishes. Open Wednesday through Monday for lunch and dinner. Closed Tuesday. Full service, vegan options, no credit cards, $$.

•• Vegetarian Wok
1200 E. Valley Blvd., San Gabriel, CA 91801 **(626) 576-7930**

Vegan/Chinese. Vegetarian Wok offers more than 90 menu choices, from soup to mock meat dishes, served in a cafeteria atmosphere. Lunch specials are inexpensive. Open daily for lunch and dinner. Full service, VISA/AMEX, $$.

SAN JOSE

(For restaurant listings in the surrounding areas, see Boulder Creek, Milpitas, and Santa Clara.)

•• Di Da Vegetarian Fast Food
2597 Senter Rd., San Jose, CA 95111 **(408) 998-8826**

Vegan/Vietnamese. Located in a strip mall, Di Da offers a homey menu that includes Vietnamese-style soups, vegetable rolls, noodle dishes, and curry dishes. The jackfruit salad, sided with a chile-tamarind sauce, comes highly recommended. Open daily for three meals. Full service, no credit cards, take-out, $$.

• Di Lac Cuisine, A Vegetarian and Tofu Restaurant
1644 E. Capitol Expy., San Jose, CA 95121 **(408) 238-8686**

Vegetarian/Asian. Di Lac offers an extensive menu of Asian dishes made without eggs, meat, or MSG. The menu features such items as Vietnamese Veggie Crepes, Veggie Shark Fin Soup,

Thai Sweet & Sour Veggie Seafood Soup, Veggie Minced Crab & Shrimp Meat Vermicelli Soup, Veggie Kung Pao Chicken over Rice, Veggie Roasted Duck, Salted Pepper Veggie Squid, Eggplant with Veggie Beef, Sizzling Veggie Eel with Sweet Basil, and a Tofu Lovers' section. Also, save room for desserts like Non-Dairy Flan, Almond Tofu Jelly, or Pudding Tofu. **Open daily for three meals. Full service, vegan options, fresh juices, non-alcoholic beer, special drinks, VISA/MC, $-$$.** www.dilac.com

•Fresh n' Healthy Vegetarian Food To Go
388 E. Santa Clara St., San Jose, CA 95113   **(408) 286-6335**
Vegetarian/Vietnamese. The Vietnamese and international cuisine at this highly affordable restaurant includes fried rice, vegetable chow mein, and a host of mock meat dishes. Located one block north of Cal State-San Jose. **Open daily for three meals. Counter service, vegan options, take-out, no credit cards, $.**

Fresh Choice
1600 Saratoga Ave., San Jose, CA 95125   **(408) 866-1491**
American. See description under Menlo Park, CA.

•• Good Karma Vegan House
322 E. Santa Clara St., San Jose, CA 95112   **(408) 294-2694**
Vegan sandwich shop. Located in downtown San Jose, Good Karma offer soups, salads, mock lobster rolls, and stuffed tofu rolls, as well as a sandwich menu that changes daily. **Open daily for lunch and dinner. Full service, take-out, $.**

Hobee's Restaurant
680 River Oaks Pkwy., San Jose, CA 95134   **(408) 232-0190**
Restaurant chain. See description under Cupertino, CA.

•Vegetarian House
520 E. Santa Clara St., San Jose, CA 95112   **(408) 292-3798**
Vegetarian/Asian. This mostly vegan, gourmet restaurant offers a huge array of vegetarian offerings reflecting Chinese, Vietnamese, Thai, Middle Eastern, French, and other international cuisines. Choices include soups, spring rolls, vegetable tempura, hummus, vegetable quiche, shish kabobs, pizzas, pasta dishes, and mock chicken, beef, and fish entrées. In addition, this establishment is home to a beautiful art gallery featuring the work of Ching Hai. **Open daily for lunch and dinner. Full service, vegan options, fresh juices, wine/beer/alcohol, take-out, VISA/MC/AMEX/DISC, $$.** www.godsdirectcontact.com/vegetarian/

•White Lotus
80 N. Market St., San Jose, CA 95113   **(408) 977-0540**
Vegetarian/ethnic. The restaurant serves extremely flavorful fare, with the foods drawn from several cultures, especially Vietnamese. White Lotus utilizes many Eastern herbs and spices. The menu is mostly vegan, including the mock meats used for the beef, chicken, duck, pork, and fish dishes listed. **Open Tuesday through Sunday. Closed Monday. Full service, vegan options, take-out, VISA/MC/AMEX, $$.**

SAN LUIS OBISPO

Big Sky Café

1121 Broad St., San Luis Obispo, CA 93401   **(805) 545-5401**

California. This restaurant offers a variety of ethnic and original dishes. A wide range of spices and sauces are used to create unique cuisine. **Open daily for three meals. Full service, vegan options, espresso/cappuccino, soymilk, beer/wine, VISA/MC/AMEX, $$.**

Hobee's

1443 Calle Joaquin, San Luis Obispo, CA 93401   **(805) 549-9186**

Restaurant chain. See description under Cupertino, CA.

Jewel of India

2115 Broad St., San Luis Obispo, CA 93401   **(805) 543-3558**

Indian. Enjoy many vegetarian selections, including Samosas, Malai Kofta, Channa Masala, Gobbi Aloo, and Dahl Moong while sitting on the outdoor patio. **Open Monday through Saturday for lunch. Open daily for dinner. Full service, vegan options, take-out, VISA/MC, $$.**

Taj Palace

795 Foothill Blvd., Ste. A, San Luis Obispo, CA 93401   **(805) 543-0722**

Indian. Dine on several options, like Aloo Mutter, Dahl, Okra Masala, and Vegetable Korma at this vegetarian-friendly restaurant. **Open daily for lunch and dinner. Full service, vegan options, take-out, VISA/MC, $$.**

SAN MATEO

Amici's East Coast Pizzeria

69 Third Ave., San Mateo, CA 94401   **(650) 342-9392**

Italian. See description under Mountain View, CA.

The Good Earth

3190 Campus Dr., San Mateo, CA 94403   **(650) 349-0165**

Natural foods. See description under Northridge, CA. This location is near the San Francisco Airport.

SAN PABLO

• Vege House

1520 International Market Pl., San Pablo, CA 94806   **(510) 235-8343**

Vegetarian/Chinese. This restaurant features a huge selection of original vegetarian entrées, including deep fried crispy vege milk balls, twice-cooked vege "pork," and vege "chicken" and preserved radish noodle soup. **Open daily for lunch and dinner. Take-out, vegan options, fresh juices, $$.**

SAN RAFAEL

Amici's East Coast Pizzeria
1242 Fourth St., San Rafael, CA 94109   **(415) 455-9777**
Italian. See description under Mountain View, CA.

Bongkot Thai Express
857 4th St., San Rafael, CA 94901   **(415) 453-3350**
Thai. The Bongkot Thai Express features superior vegetarian dishes on the "Vegi Deluxe"
menu section, including curries, noodle dishes, and veggies with various Thai seasonings.
The setting includes hand painted mural walls reflecting the beauty of Thailand. **Open
daily for lunch and dinner. Full service, vegan options, buffet, take-out, delivery, VISA/
MC/AMEX/DISC, $-$$.**

• Paradise Vegetarian Restaurant
1444 4th St., San Rafael, CA 94901   **(415) 456-3572**
Vegetarian/Chinese/Vietnamese. This restaurant offers more than 100 vegan Chinese and
Vietnamese items (and an equal number of meat items). Don't miss the house salad or the
steamed "chicken" with ginger and green onions. **Open daily for lunch. Full service, vegan
options, take-out, VISA/MC, $$.**

SANTA ANA

Niki's Tandoori Express
3705 S. Bristol St., Santa Ana, CA 92704   **(714) 838-7615**
2031 E. 1st St., Santa Ana, CA 92705   **(714) 542-2969**
Indian. Niki's is a new concept in Indian cuisine with a fast food appeal. Some vegetarian
options are available. **Open daily. Cafeteria, wine/beer, take-out, $-$$.**

The Village Farmer
3851 S. Bear St., Santa Ana, CA 92704   **(714) 557-8433**
American. The Village Farmer offers some vegetarian options for a reasonable price. **Open
daily. Full service, wine/beer, take-out, VISA/MC/AMEX, $$.**

SANTA BARBARA

Galanga Thai Restaurant
507 State St., Santa Barbara, CA 93101   **(805) 899-3199**
Thai. Dine on more than 20 different vegetarian Thai dishes at this restaurant. Some dishes
contain oyster sauce, though. Ask your waitperson for help in avoiding such items. **Open
Thursday through Tuesday for lunch and dinner. Closed Wednesday. Full service, vegan
options, non-alcoholic beer, wine/beer, take-out, $-$$.**

The Natural Café and Juice Bar
508 State St., Santa Barbara, CA 93101   **(805) 962-9494**
Natural foods. The Natural Café is located in downtown Santa Barbara, five blocks away
from the Pacific Ocean. Dine on items such as vegetarian chili, guacamole with chips, spinach

salad, falafel pita, veggie stir-fry, tempeh tacos, and more. **Open daily for lunch and dinner. Full service, vegan options, fresh juices, take-out, $-$$.**

Sojourner Restaurant and Coffeehouse
134 E. Canon Perdido St., Santa Barbara, CA 93101   (805) 965-7922
Natural foods. Vegetarian options are scattered throughout the menu. Some international themes are favored, such as the Mediterranean Plate, Mexican fare, and curries. The Sojourner is now using vegetarian (rennetless) jack and cheddar cheese. Non-alcoholic specialty drinks, such as Mocha Frosted and Carob Supreme, are offered. **Open daily. Full service, vegan options, espresso/cappucino, wine/beer, take-out, $$.**

SANTA CLARA

Pasand India Cuisine
3701 El Camino Real, Santa Clara, CA 95051   (408) 241-5150
Indian. Authentic South Indian food is prepared with spices and herbs imported from India. Almost half of the menu lists various kinds of vegetarian dishes. Live classical Indian music is featured on Friday and Saturday evenings. **Open daily. Full service, vegan options, wine/beer, catering, take-out, VISA/MC/AMEX/DISC/DC, $$.**

SANTA CLARITA

India's Tandoori
23360 Valencia Blvd., Unit I, Santa Clarita, CA 91355   (805) 288-1200
Indian. See description under Los Angeles, CA.

SANTA CRUZ

• Asian Rose Café
1547 Pacific Ave., Santa Cruz, CA 95060   (408) 458-3023
Vegetarian. Customers can select from about 10 choices, and all items are served with rice. The café also has a salad bar. **Open Monday through Saturday. Closed Sunday. Limited service, vegan options, take-out, $$.**

The Bagelry
320-A Cedar St., Santa Cruz, CA 95060   (408) 429-8049
1636 Seabright Ave., Santa Cruz, CA 95060   (408) 425-8550
Bagel shop. This establishment bakes 20 kinds of bagels daily and can use them for a variety of both dairy and non-dairy sandwiches. There are also salads, vegan soups, vegan cookies, and a full selection of hot and cold beverages. Outdoor dining is available. **Open daily for three meals. Counter service, vegan options, fresh juices, take-out, $.**

Restaurant codes: ✪ Reviewers' Choice   • Vegetarian Restaurant   • • Vegan Restaurant
Restaurant prices: $ less than $6 $$ $6-$12 $$$ more than $12
Credit Cards Accepted: VISA - VISA   MC - MasterCard   AMEX - American Express
DISC - Discover   DC - Diner's Club

Hobee's Restaurant
The Galleria de Santa Cruz
740 Front St., Santa Cruz, CA 95060   (408) 458-1212
Restaurant chain. See description under Cupertino, CA.

Linda's Seabreeze Café
542 Seabright Ave., Santa Cruz, CA 95062   (408) 427-9713
American. Linda's is a charming place for breakfast and lunch on the way to the Santa Cruz
beach. Breakfast features pancakes, tofu scramble, and home fries. **Open daily for breakfast
and lunch.** Full service, vegan options, take-out, $.

• Malabar Café
1116 Soquel Ave., Santa Cruz, CA 95060   (408) 423-1717
Vegetarian/Indian. Malabar Café offers both Indian and Sri Lankan vegetarian dishes. **Open
Monday through Saturday. Closed Sunday.** Full service, $$.

New Leaf Deli
2351 Mission St., Santa Cruz, CA 95060   (408) 425-1306
Health foods store deli. While dining outdoors, you can enjoy approximately 20 sandwiches,
plus hot foods, cold deli salads, soups, and green salads. **Open daily.** Cafeteria, vegan options,
fresh juices, wine/beer, take-out, VISA/MC, $.

Royal Taj India Cuisine
270 Soquel Ave., Santa Cruz, CA 95062   (408) 427-2400
Indian. See description under Campbell, CA.

• Saturn Café
145 Laurel St., Santa Cruz, CA 95060   (831) 429-8505
Vegetarian/American. The café serves soups, salads, burgers, sandwiches, chili, and ratatouille
in an inviting atmosphere and has its own bakery. **Open daily until late night.** Counter
service, vegan options, espresso, wine/beer, take-out, $. www.saturncafe.com

• Staff of Life Natural Foods Market
1305 Water St., Santa Cruz, CA 95062   (408) 423-8041
Vegetarian/deli. This market includes a deli that offers burritos, falafels, sandwiches, and
soups. The featured entrée changes daily and is usually rice- or pasta-based. Various salads
and other items may be purchased separately. **Open daily.** Cafeteria, vegan options, fresh
juices, take-out, $.

Whole Earth
1156 High St., Santa Cruz, CA 95064   (831) 459-3066
Natural foods. Partake of muffins, scrambled tofu, soups, and salads. **Open daily.** Cafeteria,
vegan options, take-out, $.

SANTA MONICA

Anastasia's Asylum
1028 Wilshire Blvd., Santa Monica, CA 90401 **(310) 394-7113**
California. In addition to their menu, Anastasia's Asylum features specialty coffee drinks, unique décor, rotating art exhibits and a wide variety of nightly music performances. **Open daily. Limited service, vegan options, espresso/cappuccino, smoothies, soymilk, take-out, VISA/MC/AMEX, $$.**

Bistro of Santa Monica
2301 Santa Monica Blvd., Santa Monica, CA 90404 **(310) 453-5442**
Italian. The Bistro is a European-style restaurant featuring northern Italian cuisine. All items are prepared from scratch without salt, sugar, or preservatives. Vegetarian selections are offered in addition to items for guests with special dietary requirements. Fifteen types of pasta can be combined with numerous sauces listed under tomato, cream, olive oil, and specialty headings. **Open daily. Full service, vegan options, fresh juices, espresso/cappucino, wine/beer/alcohol, take-out, VISA/MC/AMEX/DISC, $$-$$$.**

• Chandni Vegetarian Cuisine of India
1909 Wilshire Blvd., Santa Monica, CA 90403 **(310) 828-7060**
Vegetarian/Indian. This vegetarian restaurant offers a wide range of Northern Indian appetizers, soups, breads, and entrées. **Open daily for lunch and dinner. Full service, vegan options, take-out, $-$$.**

•• Juliano's Raw
609 Broadway, Santa Monica, CA 90403 **(310) 587-1552**
Vegan. The menu here includes pizzas, sandwiches, vegan sushi, burritos, sangria, shakes, cookies, and pies. Sample dishes such as the Sea Witch soup with avocado and different sea weeds, the Rawvioli made with a pine-nut cheese, and the Strawberry Mousse Carob Tart. **Open daily for lunch and dinner. Full service, delivery, $$$.** www.rawrestaurant.com

Newsroom Café
530 Wilshire Blvd., Santa Monica, CA 90401 **(310) 319-9100**
Natural foods. See description under Los Angeles, CA.

•• Real Food Daily ✪
514 Santa Monica Blvd., Santa Monica, CA 90401 **(310) 451-7544**
Vegan. See description under Beverly Hills, CA.

Shambala Café
607 Colorado Ave., Santa Monica, CA 90401 **(213) 395-2160**
International. Sandwiches, pitas, and pizza offerings are augmented by an eclectic selection featuring Japanese, Mexican, Chinese, and Indian dishes. **Open daily. Cafeteria, take-out, $$.**

SANTA ROSA

East West Restaurant
2323 Sonoma Ave., Santa Rosa, CA 95405   **(707) 546-6142**
Natural foods. East West Restaurant serves international cuisine with a sumptuous Middle
Eastern flavor. It also offers non-dairy shakes and desserts. **Open daily for three meals. Full
service, vegan options, macrobiotic options, fresh juices, smoothies, take-out, VISA/MC/
DISC, $$.**

Fresh Choice
277 Santa Rosa Plaza, Santa Rosa, CA 95401   **(707) 525-0912**
American. See description under Menlo Park, CA.

Mistral Restaurant
1229 N. Dutton Ave., Santa Rosa, CA 95401   **(707) 578-4511**
Italian. Mistral Restaurant's menu includes antipasti, insalata, pasta, polenta, pizza, and spe-
cials. Lunch selections also include salads and sandwiches. Patio seating is available. **Open
Monday through Friday for lunch and dinner. Open Saturday and Sunday for dinner only.
Full service, wine, VISA/MC/AMEX/DISC, $$.**

SEBASTOPOL

• Slice of Life
6970 McKinley St., Sebastopol, CA 95472   **(707) 829-6627**
Vegetarian. Slice of Life serves organic whole-wheat crust pizza with creative toppings, veggie
burgers, sandwiches, ethnic cuisine, soups, salads, delicious desserts, plus much more. **Open
Tuesday through Sunday for lunch and dinner. Closed Monday. Full service, macrobiotic/
vegan options, fresh juices, non-alcoholic wine/beer, $-$$.**

Whole Foods Market
6910 McKinley St., Sebastopol, CA 95472   **(707) 829-9801**
Juice bar. This gourmet natural foods deli offers quick macrobiotic, vegetarian, and vegan
meals. **Open daily for three meals. Limited service, vegan options, take-out, fresh juices,
espresso/cappuccino, smoothies, soymilk, special drinks, VISA/MC/AMEX/DISC, $$.**

SEQUOIA NATIONAL PARK

Montecito-Sequoia Lodge Restaurant
King's Canyon National Park
8000 General Hwy., Sequoia National Park, CA 93633   **(800) 843-8677**
California. Country club buffet with vegetarian options, though the menu varies. Located
between King's Canyon and Sequoia National Parks. **Open daily for three meals. Buffet,
reservations recommended, fresh juices, espresso/cappuccino, beer/wine/alcohol, non-alco-
holic beer/wine, smoothies, soymilk, special drinks, VISA/MC/AMEX/DISC/DC, $$-$$$.**

SHERMAN OAKS

Grandma's Thai Kitchen
13230 Burbank Blvd., Sherman Oaks, CA 91401   **(818) 785-9036**
Thai. Grandma's Thai Kitchen offers 10 vegetarian entrées, including pad Thai noodles, mock chicken fried rice, spicy green beans, sweet and sour vegetables, and a tofu/rice medley. They also serve two vegetarian soups and five curry dishes using tofu or wheat gluten. Be sure to tell them not to use fish sauce. **Open daily for lunch and dinner. Full service, vegan options, take-out, wine/beer/alcohol, VISA/MC/AMEX/DISC/DC, $$.**

SOQUEL

The Bagelry
4763 Soquel Dr., Soquel, CA 95073   **(408) 462-9888**
Bagel shop. See description under Santa Cruz, CA.

Tortilla Flats
4616 Soquel Dr., Soquel, CA 95073   **(408) 476-1754**
Mexican. Rice, beans, or the "Flatland Mix" (made from a nut mixture) can be substituted for meat in the burritos and tostadas. **Open daily. Full service, wine/beer, take-out, VISA/ MC, $-$$.**

SOUTH EL MONTE

• Veggie Life Restaurant
9324 E. Garvey Ave., #8, South El Monte, CA 91733   **(626) 443-8687**
Vegetarian/Vietnamese. Veggie Life prepares authentic Vietnamese dishes, the majority of which are vegan. Various soy products are used in place of meat. **Open Tuesday through Sunday for lunch and dinner. Closed Monday. Full service, vegan options, non-alcoholic beer, soymilk, special drinks, VISA/MC/AMEX/DISC, $-$$.**

SOUTH LAKE TAHOE

Sprouts
Hwy. 50 & Alameda Ave., South Lake Tahoe, CA 96153   **(916) 541-6969**
Natural foods. This small café offers a wide variety of vegetarian dishes, including sandwiches, bagels, rice and beans, burritos, quesadillas, tempeh burgers, tostadas, soups, and salads. **Open daily for three meals. Limited service, fresh juices, espresso/capuccino, $.**

SOUTH PASADENA

Grassroots Natural Food Market and Kitchen
1119 Fair Oaks Ave., South Pasadena, CA 91030   **(818) 799-0156**
Natural foods. With an unusual variety of salads, dairy-free soups, tasty hot entrées, sandwiches, and a tempting selection of homemade muffins, Grassroots is a good choice. **Open Monday through Saturday. Closed Sunday. Cafeteria, vegan options, fresh juices, take-out, VISA/MC/AMEX, $.**

ST. HELENA

• St. Helena Health Center Dining Room
650 Sanitarium Rd., St. Helena, CA 94576   **(707) 963-6214**
Vegetarian. The food service is for participants at the health center, but non-participants can be accomodated with reservations. **Open daily for three meals. Cafeteria, reservations required.**

STUDIO CITY

The Good Earth
12345 Ventura Blvd., Studio City, CA 91604   **(818) 506-7400**
Natural foods. See description under Northridge, CA.

• Leonor's Mexican Food
12445 Moorpark St., Studio City, CA 91604   **(818) 762-0660**
Vegetarian/Mexican. See description under North Hollywood, CA. This location is 100 percent vegetarian. **Open Monday through Saturday for lunch and dinner. Closed Sunday.**

•• Playfood
11118 Ventura Blvd., Studio City, CA 91604   **(818) 784-4444**
Vegan/raw foods. Playfood is a fun, diner-style restauraunt that specializes in vegan cheese dishes and also vegan soft-serve ice cream. **Open Sunday through Friday for lunch through late night service. Call for Saturday hours. Full service, fresh juices, smoothies, soymilk, espresso/cappuccino, take-out, catering, VISA/MC/AMEX/DC, $$.** www.playfood.org

SUNNYVALE

• Bhavika's
1053 E. El Camino Real, Sunnyvale, CA 94087   **(408) 243-2118**
Vegetarian/Indian. Specializing in North Indian cuisine, this small, casual restaurant offers appetizers, entrées, and desserts. **Open Tuesday through Saturday for lunch and dinner. Open Sunday for three meals. Closed Monday. Counter service, take-out, no credit cards, $-$$.**

• Chaat House
839 E. El Camino Real, Sunnyvale, CA 94087   **(408) 733-9000**
Vegetarian/Indian. Chaat House offers soups, samosas, dahls, thalis, and an assortment of Indian breads. Indoor and outdoor seating available. **Open daily for lunch and dinner. Counter service, take-out, VISA/MC/AMEX, $.**

The Country Gourmet & Co.
1314 S. Mary Ave., Sunnyvale, CA 94087   **(408) 733-9446**
Natural foods. The Country Gourmet features baked goods, an extensive salad collection, and entrées that change daily. Everything is prepared from fresh ingredients with no preservatives or MSG. A couple of vegetarian entrées are featured nightly in addition to the regular menu selection, and there is a children's menu. **Open daily for three meals. Limited service, vegan options, fresh juices, wine/beer, take-out, VISA/MC, $$.**

•• Great Vegi Land
562 S. Murphy Ave., Sunnyvale, CA 94086   **(408) 735-8040**
Vegan/Chinese. Great Vegi Land specializes in mock meat dishes, such as smoked vegetarian fish and vegetarian meatballs. The dumplings and the vegetarian sushi come highly recommended. Open Monday through Saturday for lunch and dinner. Open Sundays for dinner only. Full service, take-out, fresh juices, VISA/MC/AMEX/DISC, $-$$.

Hobee's Restaurant
800 Ahwanee Ave., Sunnyvale, CA 94086   **(408) 524-3580**
Restaurant chain. See description under Cupertino, CA.

• Komala Vilas
1020 E. El Camino Real, Sunnyvale, CA 94087   **(408) 733-7400**
Vegetarian/Indian. Komala Vilas' menu includes idli, dosais, vadai, pongal, and much more. Open Wednesday through Monday for three meals. Closed Tuesday. Counter service, vegan options, take-out, VISA/MC. www.komalavilas.com

• Panchavati
460 Persian Dr., Sunnyvale, CA 95089   **(408) 734-9335**
Vegetarian/Indian. Choose from a large variety of traditional Indian dishes. Open daily for lunch and dinner. Full service, vegan options, take-out, VISA/MC, $-$$.

Royal Taj Indian Cuisine
889 E. El Camino Real, Sunnyvale, CA 94087   **(408) 720-8396**
Indian. See description under Campbell, CA.

• Saravana Bhavan Vegetarian Restaurant
1305 S. Mary Ave., Sunnyvale, CA 94087   **(408) 616-7755**
Vegetarian/Indian. Specializing in South Indian cuisine, Saravana Bhavan offers soups, Indian breads such as naan and roti, dosai, uttapham, curries, mushroom chops, channa cutlets, desserts, and a children's menu. Open daily for lunch and dinner. Full service, vegan options, fresh juices, catering, $$. www.saravanabhavan.com

• Udupi Palace
976 E. El Camino Real, Sunnyvale, CA 94087   **(408) 830-9600**
Vegetarian/Indian. This restaurant's menu includes dosas, masala dosa, iddly, sambar, and rice. Open daily for lunch and dinner. Full service, vegan options, VISA/MC, $-$$.

TARZANA

India's Tandoori
19006 Ventura Blvd., Tarzana, CA 91356   **(818) 342-9100**
Indian. See description under Los Angeles, CA.

TOPANGA CANYON

Inn of the Seventh Ray
128 Old Topanga Rd., Topanga Canyon, CA 90290   **(310) 455-1311**
California. Located near Topanga State Park and featuring creek-side dining, this restaurant offers gourmet American/French dishes in a romantic atmosphere. **Open daily for lunch and dinner. Open for breakfast Saturday.** Full service, vegan options, formal dinners, reservations recommended, macrobiotic options, espresso/cappuccino, non-alcoholic drinks, beer/wine, soymilk, special drinks, VISA/MC/AMEX/DISC/DC, $$$.

TUSTIN

Rutabegorz
158 W. Main St., Tustin, CA 92680   **(714) 731-9801**
International. See description under Fullerton, CA.

UPLAND

•Veggie Panda Wok
903-B W. Foothill Blvd., Upland, CA 91786   **(909) 982-3882**
Vegetarian/Chinese. This casual Chinese and Indonesian restaurant is mostly vegan and offers long lists of soups, vegetable and tofu dishes, veggie meats, veggie seafoods, and noodle and rice dishes. Options include Bean Curd with Barbeque Sauce, Almond Veggie Chicken, Spicy Onion Veggie Beef, and Cashew Veggie Shrimp. They also offer desserts like Soy Flan and Chocolate Truffle Pie. The few items that contain dairy products are clearly marked 'lacto.' **Open Sunday and Monday for dinner and Tuesday through Saturday for lunch and dinner.** Limited service, vegan options, fresh juices, smoothies, soymilk, special drinks, take-out, VISA/MC, $-$$. www.veggiepandawok.com

VENICE

The Dandelion Café
636 Venice Blvd., Venice, CA 90291   **(310) 821-4890**
California. Vegetarians can dine on Vegetarian Chili Tostadas, Vegetable Garden Melt (with cheese), Avocado Melt, quiche, and fresh fruit at this patio restaurant with a nice ocean breeze. **Open daily for breakfast and lunch.** Full service, vegan options, wine/beer/alcohol, VISA/MC/AMEX/DISC, $$.

Fig Tree Café
429 Ocean Front Walk, Venice, CA 90291   **(310) 392-4937**
Natural foods. Any dish can be made vegetarian to accommodate the customer, or choose from spinach nutburger, roasted eggplant and peppers, Santa Fe tostadas, and stir-fry pizzete (chapati pizza). **Open daily.** Full service, wine/beer, VISA/MC/AMEX/DISC, $$.

VENTURA

Tipps Thai Cuisine
512 E. Main St., Ventura, CA 93001   **(805) 643-3040**
Thai. Tipps has a full vegetarian menu featuring more than 20 entrées, plus appetizers, soups, and salads. Entrées include standard vegetable dishes, mock meats, curries, and noodle and rice dishes. No MSG is used in their food preparation. **Open Monday through Friday for lunch and dinner. Open Saturday for dinner. Closed Sunday. Full service, vegan options, wine/beer, take-out, VISA/MC/AMEX, $$.**

WEST COVINA

•One World Vegetarian Cuisine
178 S. Glendora Ave., West Covina, CA 91790   **(626) 917-2727**
Vegetarian. This restaurant offers an interesting menu of appetizers, soups, salads, sandwiches, rice and noodle dishes, and much more. Unique choices include grilled veggie beef teriyaki, barbequed veggie chicken drumsticks, eggplant with veggie ground meat, steamed veggie fish, a veggie smoked pepper ham sandwich, veggie turkey burgers, and a vegan banana-walnut cake. All dishes are egg-free and prepared with filtered water. **Open Monday through Saturday for lunch and dinner. Open Sunday from afternoon through dinner. Full service, vegan options, fresh juices, non-alcoholic beer/wine, cappuccino, take-out, VISA/MC, $$.** www.oneworldveggie.com

WEST HOLLYWOOD

Flowering Tree
8253 Santa Monica Blvd., West Hollywood, CA 90046   **(323) 654-4332**
Natural foods. The Flowering Tree has a large selection of vegetarian soups, burgers, appetizers, and specialties, as well as breakfast foods and desserts. **Open daily for three meals. Full service, vegan options, espresso/cappuccino, fresh juices, smoothies, special drinks, take-out, catering, $$.**

•• Real Food Daily ✪
414 N. La Cienega Blvd., West Hollywood, CA 90048   **(310) 289-9910**
Vegan. See description under Beverly Hills, CA.

•Sprout Café
8410 Sunset Blvd., West Hollywood, CA 90069   **(323) 848-2195**
Vegetarian. This comfortable, informal restaurant is right on the Sunset Strip. It offers an extensive menu, including Steak au Poive, a Hickory Smoked Burger, Tabbouleh, and the Tangy Tofu Rice Bowl. Almost everything on the menu can be made vegan. Add a Chocolate Shake for an extra special treat. **Open Monday through Friday. Closed Saturday and Sunday. Full service, vegan options, fresh juices, take-out, VISA/MC/AMEX/DISC, $-$$.**

WESTMINSTER

•Chez Rose Vegetarian Restaurant
7360 Westminster Blvd., Westminster, CA 92683-4253   (714) 890-9711
Vegetarian/French Vietnamese. The mostly vegan menu at this restaurant includes more than 100 different dishes made with vegetables, tofu, and mock meats. **Open daily for three meals. Full service, vegan options, no credit cards, $$.**

•Van-Hanh Restaurant
9455 Bolsa Ave., #D, Westminster, CA 92703   (714) 531-4661
Vegetarian/Vietnamese. Van-Hanh offers spring rolls, a wide array of rice dishes, house specials made with steamed or fried tofu, and hearty noodle soups. Unique fare includes Bitter Melon Soup and Vermicelli with Tofu Skin. The establishment also offers Family Tables, prix fixe meals for 4 to 10 people. **Open daily for three meals. Full service, fresh juices, special drinks (soybean milk, Vietnamese coffee drinks), take-out, $-$$.**

WESTWOOD

California Sunburger and Juice Bar
1001 Gayley Ave., Westwood, CA 90024   (310) 208-1020
Natural foods. Dine on vegan Sunburgers, falafel, soups, and salads with fresh juices and more. **Open daily for three meals. Limited service, vegan options, fresh juices, take-out, VISA/MC/AMEX, $-$$.**

Dr. J's Healthy and Tasty Fast Food Restaurant
1303 Westwood Blvd., Westwood, CA 90024   (310) 477-2721
Natural foods. Dr. J's offers foods with no sugar, dairy, wheat, or yeast, which is great for those with food allergies. Main dishes and soups are offered, as well as various snacks and specialty dishes. As of this writing, Dr. J's is up for sale, so call ahead. **Open daily for three meals. Cafeteria, vegan options, fresh juices, soymilk, smoothies, take-out, VISA/MC/ AMEX/DISC/DC, $-$$.** www.drjshealthnet.com

•Native Foods ۞
1110 1/2 Gayley Ave., Westwood, CA 90024   (310) 209-1055
Vegetarian. See description under Costa Mesa, CA. **Open daily for three meals.**

WHITTIER

•Veggie Bistro
6557 Comstock Ave., Whittier, CA 90601   (562) 907-7898
Vegetarian/Asian. This vegetarian eatery assures us that "all of our dishes including the ones with names such as 'beef, chicken, pork, fish and shrimp', etc. are healthy vegetarian entrées made from soy, wheat gluten, and other natural herbal ingredients." These include beef with pineapple, braised duck, steamed fish, and sweet and sour chicken. **Open Tuesday through Sunday for lunch and dinner. Closed Monday. Full service, vegan options, $$.**

WILLITS

• Harvest Bounty
212 S. Main St., #23, Willits, CA 95490   **(707) 459-9647**
Vegetarian. Organic produce is used in salads, and fresh-baked cornbread complements
homestyle meals. **Open daily for lunch. Full service, fresh juices, $.**

Tsunami
50 S. Main St., Willits, CA 95490   **(707) 459-4750**
Asian. Dinner and lunch menu headings include sushi, salads, side orders, grilled, Cajun,
colache, and tempura. All categories list vegetable and tofu selections, and vegetarian specials are also offered. Dishes are all carefully prepared from scratch with natural ingredients,
and most vegetables are locally and organically grown. Some dessert selections are prepared
without dairy, sugar, or eggs. Beverages include local microbrewery beers, coffee, and wine.
Dine on the patio amidst Japanese maple trees, plum trees, and flowers. **Open daily. Full
service, wine/beer, take-out, reservations recommended, $$.**

YREKA

Nature's Kitchen
412 S. Main St., Yreka, CA 96097   **(530) 842-1136**
Natural foods. Nature's Kitchen is located inside a health food store. Try the veggie chiliburger
with the apple and walnut salad. **Open Monday through Saturday for lunch. Closed Sunday.
Full service, vegan options, take-out, fresh juices, cappuccino, smoothies, soymilk, VISA/
MC/DISC, $$.**

Colorado

ASPEN

• Explore Booksellers & Bistro
221 E. Main St., Aspen, CO 81611   **(970) 925-5338**
Vegetarian. This sophisticated gourmet vegetarian restaurant and European-style bistro
is located under the same roof as a contemporary bookstore. Each day, a different ethnic
specialty is featured, in addition to the standard offerings of soups, a salad bar, tofu burgers,
and steamed veggies. **Open daily for lunch and dinner. Full service, vegan options, children's
menu, wine/beer, espresso, take-out, VISA/MC, $$.**

AURORA

Fong Lynn
1780 S. Buckley Rd., Aurora, CO 80017   **(303) 745-9111**
Chinese. Fong Lynn features tofu dishes. **Open daily for lunch. Full service, wine/beer/alcohol,
take-out, VISA/MC/AMEX, $.**

• Masalla

3140 S. Parker Rd., Aurora, CO 80014   **(303) 755-6272**

Vegetarian/Indian. This restaurant's menu includes samosas, steamed iddly cakes, dosas, a lentil and rice dish, curries, Indian breads, and much more. **Open daily for lunch and dinner. Full service, vegan options,** VISA/MC/AMEX/DISC, $$. www.masalla.com

Star of India

3102 S. Parker Rd., A-10, Aurora, CO 80014   **(303) 755-1921**

Indian. Star of India offers numerous vegetarian entrées and a large selection of breads. **Open daily for lunch and dinner. Full service, reservations recommended, vegan/macrobiotic options, special drinks, wine/beer/alcohol, take-out, catering,** VISA/MC/AMEX/DISC/DC, $$.

Wild Oats Markets

12131 E. Iliff Ave., Aurora, CO 80014   **(303) 695-8801**

Natural foods. This natural food market offers vegetarian and organic products, as well as an organic salad bar, juice bar, and dining area. **Open daily. Limited service, vegan options,** $-$$.

BOULDER

(For restaurant listings in the surrounding areas, see Lafayette.)

Alfalfa's Market

1651 Broadway St., Boulder, CO 80302   **(303) 442-0909**

Natural foods. Sandwiches, salads, and fresh baked goods are offered. **Open daily. Cafeteria, vegan options, take-out, catering,** VISA/MC, $.

• Café Prasad

Boulder Co-op Market, 1904 Pearl St., Boulder, CO 80302   **(303) 447-2667**

Vegetarian/natural foods. This organic, vegetarian café offers vegan baked goods and drinks all day, as well as soups, sandwiches, and other natural foods from their kitchen for lunch and dinner. On Friday evenings, they host live acoustic music. The co-op itself is very active, both in the community and politically, and hosts yoga classes, dance sessions, film nights, and a therapy room. **Open daily for three meals. Limited service, vegan options, fresh juices, smoothies, espresso, take-out,** VISA/MC/AMEX/DISC, $-$$. www.bouldercoop.com

Casa Alvarez

3161 Walnut St., Boulder, CO 80301   **(303) 546-0630**

Mexican. The menu has a vegetarian section featuring specialties such as spinach enchiladas, tofu fajitas, tofu tacos, and guacamole tostadas. **Open daily for lunch and dinner. Full service, beer/wine/alcohol, take-out, catering,** VISA/MC/AMEX, $$. http://casaalvarez.citysearch.com/1.html

Dot's Diner

1333 Broadway St., Boulder, CO 80302   **(303) 449-1323**

Natural foods. Dot's bases its reputation on its homestyle breakfasts, which are served through lunchtime every day. The lunch menu includes daily specials, Mexican dishes, grilled sandwiches, and a variety of vegetarian entrées. **Open daily for lunch and breakfast. Full service, fresh juice, espresso/cappucino, take-out,** no credit cards, $.

Ed's Juice Joint
1433 Pearl St. Mall, Boulder, CO 80302 (303) 541-0897
Juice bar/café/bakery. Located in downtown Boulder on the Pearl Street walking mall, Ed's Juice Joint offers an extensive juice menu and a variety of non-dairy milk choices. The menu also lists various vegetarian and vegan sandwiches, bagels, soy yogurt, granola, salads, and homemade soups with mostly organic ingredients. Patio seating is available. **Open daily for breakfast through early dinner. Counter service, vegan options, fresh juices, smoothies, soymilk, special drinks, non-smoking, take-out, VISA/MC, $.**

Golden Buff
1725 28th St., Boulder, CO 80301 (303) 442-2800
Natural foods. Enjoy many vegetarian items. **Open daily for three meals. Full service, fresh juice, wine/beer, take-out, VISA/MC, $-$$.**

Himalaya's Restaurant
2010 14th St., Boulder, CO 80302 (303) 442-3230
International. The cuisine here includes Indian, Nepali, and Tibetan food. Fresh breads are baked in the restaurant's tandoor oven. Lunch is buffet-style, with four vegetarian dishes. **Open daily. Full service, wine/beer, take-out, VISA/MC, $$.**

Illegal Pete's
1320 College Ave., Boulder, CO 80302 (303) 444-3055
1447 Pearl St., Boulder, CO 80302 (303) 440-3955
Mexican. Illegal Pete's offers decent vegetarian options at a cheap price. Try the vegetarian tacos, primavera veggie salad, veggie green chile, or "The Big Potato." **Open daily for lunch and dinner. College Ave. location open late on weekends. Full service, beer/alcohol, take-out, delivery, VISA/MC/AMEX/DISC, $.** www.illegalpetes.com

José Muldoon's
1600 38th St., Boulder, CO 80301 (303) 449-4543
Mexican. Santa Fe-style and authentic Mexican vegetarian fare includes appetizers, soups, salads, sandwiches, burgers, a tostada bar, and vegetarian specials. Patio dining is available. **Open daily for lunch and dinner. Open Sunday for brunch. Full service, vegan options, wine/beer/alcohol, take-out, VISA/MC/AMEX, $-$$.**

Ras Kassa's
2111 30th St., Boulder, CO 80301 (303) 447-2919
Ethiopian. Ras Kassa's offers vegetarian entrées and combination plates in a cozy authentic dining room or on its patio when weather permits. Options include Engudai (shiitake and button mushrooms with a splach of red wine), Metátesh (spicy sweet potato stew), Yemeser Wot (spicy organic red lentils), and Ki Ser Ena Denech (beets and potatoes). **Open daily for dinner. Full service, vegan options, reservations recommended, beer/wine/alcohol, VISA/MC/AMEX/DISC/DC, $$-$$$.** www.raskassas.com

Rudi's Restaurant
4720 Table Mesa Dr., Boulder, CO 80303 (303) 494-5858
Natural foods. Rudi's offers ethnic specialties and an extended gourmet vegetarian menu, as

well as a bakery, café, and espresso bar. **Open Tuesday through Sunday for lunch and dinner. Open Saturday and Sunday for brunch. Closed Monday. Full service, espresso, wine/beer, catering, VISA/MC/DISC, $$.**

Siamese Plate & Sumida's Sushi Bar
1575 Folsom St., Boulder, CO 80302   **(303) 447-9718**
Thai. Their vegetarian menu has a good selection of appetizers, soups, and entrées. Vegetarian versions of many of the regular menu items are available as well. **Open daily for lunch and dinner. Full service, wine/beer/alcohol, take-out, $$.**

Sunflower - Natural Fine Dining
1701 Pearl St., Boulder, CO 80302   **(303) 440-0220**
Natural foods. Serving an eclectic menu with a Far Eastern influence, Sunflower offers meals for vegans and vegetarians. The restaurant takes great pride in its selection of high quality organic ingredients. **Open daily for lunch and dinner. Open Sunday for brunch. Full service, reservations recommended, macrobiotic/vegan options, fresh juices, espresso/cappuccino, smoothies, soymilk, beer/wine/alcohol, special drinks, catering, VISA/MC/AMEX, $$$.**

Turley's
2350 Arapahoe Ave., Boulder, CO 80302   **(303) 442-2800**
American. Turley's is one of those "great American melting pot" restaurants that happens to have a decent amount of vegetarian options. Their menu features black bean quesadillas, black bean chili, sesame tofu and spinach salad, Thai tofu and vegetable, Grilled Quinoa Cakes, and vegetarian lasagna. Any of their cheese dishes can be made with soy cheese upon request, and they even have a kids' menu featuring a veggie burger. **Open daily for three meals. Full service, fresh juices, smoothies, take-out, VISA/MC, $-$$.**

Walnut Café
3073 Walnut St., Boulder, CO 80301   **(303) 447-2315**
Natural foods. Whether you're in the mood for a Boulder-sized muffin, huevos rancheros, or a veggie burger, the "Nut" has what you're looking for. The café cooks up a special soup, quiche, and omelette every day and has an espresso menu with 16 drinks. **Open daily for breakfast and lunch. Open Tuesday through Sunday for dinner. Full service, fresh juices, espresso, take-out, VISA/MC/DISC, $.**

Whole Foods Market
2301 30th St., Boulder, CO 80301   **(303) 545-6611**
Natural foods. This gourmet natural foods deli offers 35 all-natural and organic salads. Specialty items include homemade vegetable knishes, pizzas, and vegetable sushi. There are also hot food selections, including vegan entrées, vegetable lasagna, and two daily soups. Breakfast is served and box lunches to-go are available. **Open daily. Limited service, vegan options, fresh juices, wine/beer, catering, take-out, VISA/MC, $.**

Wild Oats Markets
2584 Baseline Ave., Boulder, CO 80303   **(303) 499-7636**
Natural foods. See description under Aurora, CO.

Young's Place Asian Cuisine
1083 14th St., Boulder, CO 80302 (303) 447-9837
Asian. Korean, Japanese, Chinese, and Mongolian cuisines are served at Young's Place. The Mongolian Barbecue has tofu and vegetable options, and there are some other vegetarian selections. **Open Monday through Saturday. Closed Sunday. Full service, take-out, $.**

BRECKENRIDGE

Amazing Grace Natural Foods
213 Lincoln Ave., Breckenridge, CO 80424 (970) 453-1445
Health foods store deli. Located in a historic building, Amazing Grace has a chalkboard menu that lists a soup du jour, veggie sandwiches, and garden salads. **Open daily for lunch and dinner. Counter service, fresh juices, smoothies, take-out, $.**

Red Orchid
206 N. Main St., Breckenridge, CO 80424 (970) 453-1881
Chinese. Red Orchid offers Szechuan, Hunan, and Mandarin cuisines. Some vegetarian dishes include braised bean curd, moo shu vegetables, and szechuan eggplant. **Open daily for lunch and dinner. Full service, vegan options, deck dining, wine/beer/alcohol, take-out, VISA/MC, $$.**

COLORADO SPRINGS

(For restaurant listings in the surrounding areas, see Manitou Springs.)

Dale Street Café
115 E. Dale St., Colorado Springs, CO 80903 (719) 578-9898
Natural foods. All-natural, freshly-prepared foods include appetizers, salads, pasta, and some Mediterranean dishes. **Open daily for lunch and dinner. Full service, non-alcoholic beer, wine/beer/alcohol, take-out, VISA/MC, $$.**

Gertrude's
2625 W. Colorado Ave., Colorado Springs, CO 80904 (719) 471-0887
Natural foods. Menu items include vegetarian Eggs Benedict, a variety of breakfast burritos, spinach salad, Belgian ravioli (stuffed with spinach, three cheeses, and covered with roasted red pepper basil sauce), ratatouille, tofu or tempeh marinated in soy sauce and orange juice, and a veggie cheesesteak sandwich. **Open daily for three meals. Closed Monday for dinner. Full service, vegan options, $$-$$$.**

Golden Dragon Restaurant
903 S. 8th St., Colorado Springs, CO 80906 (719) 632-3607
Chinese. Golden Dragon offers vegetarian appetizers, soup, and entrées. No MSG is used, and the restaurant is willing to accommodate special diets (may require advance notice). **Open daily for lunch and dinner. Full service, vegan options, wine/beer/alcohol, take-out, VISA/MC/AMEX/DISC, $$.**

José Muldoon's
222 N. Tejon St., Colorado Springs, CO 80903   **(719) 636-2311**
Mexican. See desciption under Boulder, CO.

The Olive Branch
23 S. Tejon St., Colorado Springs, CO 80903   **(719) 475-1199**
Natural foods. Vegetarian, "heart healthy," and other items are served. **Open daily for three meals. Full service, fresh juices, take-out, VISA/MC/AMEX/DISC, $.**

Wild Sage
The "Q"-McHugh Commons
1090 N. Cascade Ave., Colorado Springs, CO 80903   **(719) 389-7000**
Natural foods/juice bar. Located on the campus of Colorado College, Wild Sage offers salads, baked potatoes, sandwiches, soups, bean chili, vegan fries, and side items. Offerings include the Global Infusion (Israeli couscous and French lentil veggie salad), the Eggless Salad Sagewish, Lemon Tahini or Sesame Citrus dressings, and vegan Oatmeal or "Chocolate Hip" cookies. Dishes that are non-dairy, vegan, and/or organic are clearly marked with codes on the menu. **Open daily for lunch through late night. Limited service, vegan options, fresh juices, espresso/cappuccino, smoothies, soymilk, beer, take-out, catering, $-$$.** www.wild sagefoods.com

DENVER

Beau Jo's Pizza
2710 S. Colorado Blvd., Denver, CO 80222   **(303) 758-1519**
Pizza. A visit to Beau Jo's will undoubtedly be worth the trip, whether you eat or not. Seventeen years worth of napkin art is displayed at the restaurant. But if you do want to eat, the pizza options are just as interesting. You can choose from 16 vegetarian toppings, as well as a tofu pizza, which is vegan. There is also a soup and salad bar. **Open daily for lunch and dinner. Full service, vegan options, wine/beer/alcohol, take-out, VISA/MC/ AMEX/DISC, $$.**

Chinook Tavern
265 Detroit St., Denver, CO 80206   **(303) 394-0044**
International. Chinook Tavern offers unique vegetarian entrées, salads, and pastas, such as wild mushroom ravioli or polenta with sundried tomatoes. This health conscious establishment uses organic ingredients whenever possible and does not use MSG. **Open Monday through Saturday for lunch and dinner. Closed Sunday. Full service, VISA/MC/AMEX/ DISC/DC, $-$$$.**

City Spirit Café
1434 Blake St., Denver, CO 80202   **(303) 575-0022**
Natural foods. Everything served here is made from scratch with minimal use of fats. Organic items are available. Entrées include organic tamales, Cityburritos, and Urbanachos. Live music on weekends. **Open late daily. Full service, vegan options, wine/beer/alcohol, take-out, $.**

Delhi Darbar

1514 Blake St., Denver, CO 80202 **(303) 595-0680**

Indian. The daily buffet lunch offers primarily vegetarian foods, and the extensive vegetarian dinner menu is accompanied by fresh baked breads. **Open daily for lunch and dinner. Full service, vegan options, wine/beer/alcohol, take-out, VISA/MC/AMEX/DISC/DC, $$.**

Good Friends

3100 E. Colfax Ave., Denver, CO 80206 **(303) 399-1751**

Natural foods. They offer a wide selection of moderately priced foods. Over half of the menu is vegetarian, including dishes such as eggplant salad, stir-fry, Mexican entrées made without lard, and salads. **Open daily for lunch and dinner. Full service, wine/beer/alcohol, take-out, VISA/MC/AMEX/DISC, $-$$.**

Goosetown Tavern

3242 E. Colfax Ave., Denver, CO 80206 **(303) 399-9703**

International. Located across the street from the Bluebird Theater, Goosetown Tavern has sandwiches and numerous salads served in a homey atmosphere. **Open daily for lunch and dinner. Limited service, vegan options, non-alcoholic beer/wine, beer/wine/alcohol, VISA/MC/AMEX/DISC/DC, $$.**

• Govinda's Vegetarian Buffet

New Badarikasrama, 1400 Cherry St., Denver, CO 80220 **(303) 333-5462**

Vegetarian. This is an all-you-can-eat vegetarian buffet in the Govinda's tradition. It offers a salad bar, rice, breads, steamed vegetables, and international entrées. They do not use eggs, and only vegetarian (rennetless) cheese is served. Tuesdays and Thursdays are vegan days, when all items are non-dairy. **Open Monday through Saturday. Closed Sunday. Buffet, vegan options, take-out, VISA/MC, $.**

Handlebar and Grill

305 S. Downing St., Denver, CO 80209 **(303) 778-6761**

International. Enter into a cyclist's dream at Handlebar and Grill's bicycle-themed restaurant, which offers seven vegetarian entrées, salads, nachos, sandwiches, veggieburger, burritos, stir-fry, and more. **Open Monday through Friday for lunch and dinner. Open Saturday through Sunday for brunch. Full service, fresh juices, $-$$.** www.handlebarandgrill.com

The Hornet

76 Broadway, Denver, CO 80203 **(303) 777-7676**

Afghan. Across from the historic Mayan Theatre, The Hornet offers salads, vegetarian side dishes, vegetarian sandwiches, vegetarian burgers, along with creative drinks and live entertainment. **Open daily for lunch through late dinner. Limited service, beer/wine/alcohol, VISA/MC/AMEX/DC, $-$$.**

Illegal Pete's

1530 16th St., #101, Denver, CO 80202 **(303) 623-2169**

Mexican. See description under Boulder, CO.

• India's Harvest
3095 S. Peoria St., Unit D, Denver, CO 80014   **(303) 751-8571**
Vegetarian/Indian. This is the only vegetarian fast food restaurant in Denver, serving food that is best available on the beaches of Bombay, such as Pani Poori, Bhel, Pav Bhaji, and Dosas. **Open Wednesday through Sunday for lunch and dinner. Closed Monday and Tuesday.** Counter service, cappuccino, non-smoking, take-out, VISA/MC/DISC, $$.

Jerusalem Restaurant
1890 E. Evans Ave., Denver, CO 80210   **(303) 777-8828**
Middle Eastern. The Middle Eastern food offered at this restaurant includes many vegetarian appetizers and couple of "combo" dishes that make a satisfying meal. A special section of the menu lists the vegetable dishes. **Open daily. Open 24 hours on Friday and Saturday.** Full service, vegan options, take-out, VISA/MC/AMEX, $.

Mediterranean Health Café
2817 E. 3rd Ave., Denver, CO 80206   **(303) 399-2940**
Mediterranean. The primarily vegetarian menu offers falafel, hummus, veggie burger, vegetarian chili, and sandwiches. Fish is the only non-vegetarian food served. **Open daily.** Full service, vegan options, kosher, take-out, VISA/MC/AMEX, $.

Mercury Café
2199 California St., Denver, CO 80205   **(303) 294-9281**
American. The Mercury Café is one of Denver's eclectic hot spots. The menu boasts many vegetarian specialties, such as Susan Jane's Tofu Chop, Grilled Tempeh with black bean sauce, and Dinah's Tofu and Vegetables, as well as a 3000 sq. ft. ballroom available for events, dance classes, open mic nights, poetry slams, belly dancing, and a host of other events. If you're in Denver, the Mercury Café is not to be missed! **Open Tuesday through Sunday for dinner. Open Saturday and Sunday brunch. Closed Monday.** Full service, reservations recommended, no credit cards, $-$$. www.mercurycafe.com

• Rosewood Café
Porter Hospital, 2525 S. Downing St., Denver, CO 80210   **(303) 778-5881**
Vegetarian. The Rosewood Café offers an exciting, varied kosher menu that changes daily. Most food, including baked goods, is freshly prepared. The public is welcome! **Open daily.** Cafeteria, vegan options, fresh juices, take-out, no credit cards, $.

• Satsang Café
1665 Pearl St., Denver, CO 80203   **(303) 832-4118**
Vegetarian. This small vegetarian café offers veggie sandwiches, many with a Middle Eastern flavor. Also enjoy soups and desserts. **Open Monday through Friday for breakfast and lunch. Open Sunday for lunch. Closed Saturday.** Full service, vegan options, take-out, $-$$.

Seoul Food
701 E. 6th Ave., Denver, CO 80203   **(303) 837-1460**
Korean. Seoul Food serves authentic Korean cuisine with vegetarian and health-oriented selections. **Open daily for lunch and dinner.** Full service, wine/beer, take-out, VISA/MC, $.

T-WA Inn
555 S. Federal Blvd., Denver, CO 80219   **(303) 922-4584**
Vietnamese. The special vegetarian section on the menu features 14 entrées, including vegetables with rice noodles, tofu with lemon grass, curry, and eggplant dishes. **Open daily for lunch and dinner.** Full service, vegan options, wine/beer/alcohol, VISA/MC/AMEX, $$.

Tommy's Thai
3410 E. Colfax Ave., Denver, CO 80206   **(303) 377-4244**
Thai. This restaurant, located near the Bluebird Theater, offers Thai and limited Chinese cuisine made to order. **Open Monday through Saturday for lunch and dinner. Closed Sunday.** Full service, vegan options, take-out, catering, $.

Walnut Café
338 E. Colfax Ave., Denver, CO 80203   **(303) 832-5108**
Natural foods. Tofu is available as a meat, cheese, or egg substitute. **Open daily for breakfast and lunch.** Full service, take-out, $.

• Watercourse Foods
206 E. 13th Ave., Denver, CO 80203   **(303) 832-7313**
Vegetarian. This simple urban oasis offers vegan biscuits and gravy, and tempeh burgers. Macrobiotic dinners are served Monday nights. **Open daily for breakfast and lunch. Open Saturday and Sunday for brunch.** Limited service, vegan/macrobiotic options, espresso/cappuccino, soymilk, VISA/MC, $$. www.watercoursefoods.com

Whole Foods Market
2375 E. 1st Ave., Denver, CO 80206   **(720) 941-4100**
Natural foods. See description under Boulder, CO.

Wild Oats Markets
1111 S. Washington St., Denver, CO 80210   **(303) 733-6201**
Natural foods. See description under Aurora, CO.

Wolfe's Barbecue
333 E. Colfax Ave., Denver, CO 80203   **(303) 831-1500**
Barbecue. Traditional hole-in-the-wall (their words, not ours!) barbecue offering vegan BBQ entrées and side dishes. Wolfe's even has coleslaw without mayonnaise! **Open Monday through Friday for lunch and dinner. Closed Saturday and Sunday.** Limited service, vegan options, take-out, VISA/MC, $.

ENGLEWOOD

Twin Dragon Restaurant
3021 S. Broadway, Englewood, CO 80110   **(303) 781-8068**
Asian. Their extensive menu offers approximately 15 vegetable and tofu options. **Open daily for lunch and dinner.** Full service, vegan options, wine/beer/alcohol, take-out, VISA/MC/AMEX/DISC, $$.

Molly B's

200 Moraine Ave., Estes Park, CO 80517   **(970) 586-2766**

Natural foods. Vegetarian selections include pasta, stir-fry, lasagna, and daily specials. Baked goods are prepared on the premises. **Open daily for lunch and dinner. Full service, vegan options, fresh juices, wine/beer, take-out, VISA/MC/AMEX, $$.**

Cozzola's Pizza

241 Linden St., Fort Collins, CO 80524   **(970) 482-3557**

1112 Oakridge Dr., Fort Collins, CO 80525   **(970) 229-5771**

Pizza. Cozzola's offers gourmet pizza with whole-wheat, herb, or white crusts, plus a variety of sauces and toppings—even soy cheese! Some of the sauces do contain cheese, so vegans should inquire first. **Open Tuesday through Sunday. Closed Monday. Full service, vegan options, take-out, no credit cards, $.**

Fort Collins Food Co-op

250 E. Mountain Ave., Fort Collins, CO 80524   **(970) 484-7448**

Natural foods deli. This small take-out deli is in a natural foods market. **Open Monday through Saturday. Closed Sunday. Counter service, fresh juices, take-out, no credit cards, $.** www.ftcfoodcoop.com

Rainbow Ltd.

212 W. Laurel St., Fort Collins, CO 80521   **(970) 221-2664**

Natural foods. You will find several veggie items available on Rainbow's menu. **Open daily. Full service, wine/beer, take-out, VISA/MC, $.**

Rio Grande Mexican Restaurant

149 W. Mountain Ave., Fort Collins, CO 80524   **(970) 224-3049**

Mexican. Rio Grande serves authentic Mexican foods with sauces made fresh daily. All bean dishes are made with black beans and without lard. **Open daily. Full service, vegan options, wine/beer/alcohol, take-out, VISA/MC/DISC, $$.**

Good Pastures Restaurant & Lounge

733 Horizon Dr., Grand Junction, CO 81506   **(970) 243-1175**

International. Good Pastures offers a varied menu geared to please any appetite and takes pride in serving dishes free of chemicals, dyes, and preservatives. **Open daily for three meals. Full service, vegan options, fresh juices, wine/beer/alcohol, take-out, VISA/MC/AMEX/DISC, $$.**

• Sundrop Grocery

321 Rood Ave., Grand Junction, CO 81501   **(970) 243-1175**

Vegetarian/deli. Sundrop's fare is pre-made sandwiches, including tofuna, guacamole, veggie pita, bagel sandwiches, and more. **Open Monday through Saturday. Closed Sunday. Take-out, vegan options, $.**

GREENWOOD VILLAGE
Alfalfa's Market
5910 S. University Blvd., Greenwood Village, CO 80121   **(303) 798-9699**
Natural foods. See description under Boulder, CO.

GUNNISON
The Firebrand Deli
108 N. Main St., Gunnison, CO 81230   **(970) 641-6266**
Deli. This deli serves gourmet sandwiches, soups, and salads. They also offer waffles topped with syrup and bananas or with vanilla yogurt. **Open daily for breakfast and lunch. Limited service, vegan options, catering, take-out, espresso/cappuccino, wine/beer, $.**

IDAHO SPRINGS
Beau Jo's Pizza
1517 Miner St., Idaho Springs, CO 80452   **(303) 567-4376**
Pizza. See description under Denver, CO.

LAFAYETTE
Casa Alvarez
502 S. Public Rd., Lafayette, CO 80026   **(888) 634-6457**
Mexican. See description under Boulder, CO.

Efrain's Mexican Restaurant
101 E. Cleveland Ave., Lafayette, CO 80026   **(303) 666-7544**
Mexican. Mexican food is prepared fresh daily, and vegetarian items are clearly indicated on the menu. **Open daily for lunch and dinner. Full service, vegan options, take-out, VISA/MC, $.**

LAKEWOOD
Namaste
3355 S. Wadsworth Blvd., Lakewood, CO 80227   **(720) 963-4005**
Indian. With over a dozen vegetarian entrées, soups, and appetizers, Namaste offers authentic Indian cuisine, friendly service, and a warm atmosphere. **Open Monday through Saturday for lunch and dinner. Open Sunday for lunch only. Full service, special drinks, non-alcoholic beverages, beer/wine/alcohol, VISA/MC/AMEX, $-$$$.** www.namasterestaurant.com

---

Restaurant codes: ✪ Reviewers' Choice   • Vegetarian Restaurant   • • Vegan Restaurant
Restaurant prices: **$** less than $6   **$$** $6-$12   **$$$** more than $12
Credit Cards Accepted: VISA - VISA   MC - MasterCard   AMEX - American Express
DISC - Discover   DC - Diner's Club

LITTLETON

Alfalfa's
5910 S. University Blvd., Littleton, CO 80121   **(303) 798-9699**
Natural foods. A natural foods store with deli, bakery, pizza bar, and juice bar. Open daily for three meals. Cafeteria, fresh juices, cappuccino, take-out, catering, VISA/MC/DISC, $$.

LONGMONT

Ichi Ban Japanese Restaurant
1834 N. Main St., Longmont, CO 80501   **(303) 772-6882**
Japanese. Ichi Ban features authentic Japanese foods with vegetarian options, such as egg rolls, vegetable tempura, and noodle dishes. Open Tuesday through Sunday for lunch and dinner. Closed Monday. Full service, wine/beer, take-out, VISA/MC, $$.

LOUISVILLE

Karen's Kitchen
700 Main St., Louisville, CO 80027   **(303) 666-8020**
Natural foods. Features eggplant Parmesan, burritos, lasagna, and salads. Open daily. Open Sunday for brunch. Full service, vegan options, wine/beer, take-out, $$.

MANITOU SPRINGS

Adam's Mountain Café
110 Canon Ave., Manitou Springs, CO 80829   **(719) 685-1430**
Natural foods. This award-winning restaurant with a scenic view features southwestern entrées, including a breakfast burrito, the Small Planet burger, and Vegetarian Colorado. Open daily. Full service, vegan options, wine/beer, take-out, $$.

•• Organic Earth Café
1124 Manitou Ave., Manitou Springs, CO 80829   **(719) 685-0986**
Vegan. The completely vegan Organic Earth Café is near Soda Springs Park at the far end of downtown Manitou Springs, an artistic community near Colorado Springs. Its menu features sumptuous soups, salads, appetizers, hemp waffles, sandwiches, wraps, pitas, hand-made pizza, burgers, curries, desserts, raw drinks, and daily specials. Its scenic location lends itself to outdoor dining, if you aren't in the mood to enjoy its Victorian tea room décor. Open daily for breakfast through late night service. Full service, fresh juices, smoothies, espresso, special drinks, organic beer/wine. www.organicearthcafe.com

MORRISON

Red Rocks Grill
415 Bear Creek Ave., Morrison, CO 80465   **(303) 697-9290**
Mexican. The Red Rocks Grill is located in downtown Morrison, near the base of the rocky mountains and near the Red Rocks Amphitheater and Park. The restaurant offers a variety of vegetarian fare, including Veggie Fajitas, Chili Rellenos, Vegetarian Taco Salad, and the

restaurant's Special Green Chili. All items can be made vegan upon request. **Open daily for three meals. Full service, vegan options, wine/beer/alcohol, take-out, VISA/MC/DISC, $-$$.** www.officeonweb.com/suite103/redrocks.htm

TELLURIDE

Gregor's Bakery & Café
217 E. Colorado Ave., Telluride, CO 81435   **(970) 728-3334**
Natural foods. This restaurant serves a variety of creative vegetarian foods and features a bakery. **Open daily. Limited service, beer, take-out, $$.**

VAIL

Poppyseeds Café and Catering
2161 N. Frontage Rd., Vail, CO 81657   **(970) 476-5297**
Café. The Poppyseeds Café offers some vegetarian options, such as veggie Homemade Lasagna and veggie Smothered Burritos. **Open Monday through Saturday for lunch and early dinner. Closed Sunday. Catering.** http://vail.net/poppyseeds/

WESTMINSTER

La Casa Loma Café
710 W. 120th St., Westminster, CO 80234   **(303) 450-6906**
Mexican. La Casa Loma's menu features low-cholesterol foods that include many Mexican and American dishes. No lard is used in the beans or green chili. Vegetarian options are on the menu, and the restaurant is willing to accommodate special diets. **Open Monday through Saturday. Closed Sunday. Full service, vegan options, wine/beer/alcohol, take-out, VISA/MC, $.**

WHEAT RIDGE

Gemini Restaurant
Loehmann's Plaza
4300 Wadsworth Blvd., Wheat Ridge, CO 80033   **(303) 421-4990**
Natural foods. An extensive menu offers appetizers, salads, soups, sandwiches, quiche, pasta, and Mexican dishes, all of which can be prepared vegetarian. A children's menu is also available. **Open daily for three meals, weekend brunch. Full service, vegan options, fresh juices, wine/beer/alcohol, take-out, VISA/MC, $$.**

WINTER PARK

Carvers Bakery Café
93 Cooper Creek Way, Winter Park, CO 80482   **(970) 726-8202**
American. For breakfast, enjoy a veggie burrito, granola, and fresh fruit cup. Lunch features tempeh burgers, veggie burgers, grilled veggie sandwiches, vegetarian chili, vegetable linguini, salads, and more. **Open daily for breakfast and lunch. Full service, fresh juices, espresso/cappuccino, catering, take-out, VISA/MC/AMEX/DISC/DC, $$.**

Connecticut

BRIDGEPORT

(For restaurant listings in the surrounding areas, see Fairfield and Norwalk.)

• Bloodroot ✿
85 Ferris St., Bridgeport, CT 06605   **(203) 576-9168**
Vegetarian. Situated on an inlet in Long Island Sound, Bloodroot is "a feminist restaurant and bookstore with a seasonal vegetarian menu." This menu changes every three to four weeks to take advantage of foods in season. Outdoor dining on the herb terrace is available. **Open Tuesday and Thursday through Sunday. Closed Monday and Wednesday. Limited service on the weekdays, full service on weekends,** vegan options, wine/beer, no credit cards, $$. www.bloodroot.com

BROOKFIELD

Pancho's & Gringo's Mexican Restaurant
77 Federal Rd., Brookfield, CT 06804   **(203) 775-0096**
Mexican. A separate vegetarian menu includes chimichangas, black bean soup, vegetable fajitas, as well as several other vegetarian items. **Open daily for lunch and dinner. Full service,** espresso/cappuccino, smoothies, catering, take-out, VISA/MC/AMEX/DC, $-$$.

DANBURY

Sesame Seed
68 W. Wooster St., Danbury, CT 06810   **(203) 743-9850**
Natural foods. Middle Eastern dishes, broccoli strudel, spinach dumplings, and vegetable pie are featured at the Sesame Seed. **Open Monday through Saturday. Closed Sunday. Full service,** non-alcoholic beer, wine/beer, take-out, $-$$.

EAST HARTFORD

• Woodland
838 Silver Ln., East Hartford, CT 06118   **(860) 568-8800**
Vegetarian/Indian. Woodland's menu offers something for everyone who enjoys Indian cuisine. Try spicy dishes like the chili-pepper-powered sambhar soup, the green chili pakora, or the aloo gobi, or you may want to feast on one of 10 different kinds of dosai, all of which are seasoned with cumin, turmeric and black mustard seeds. However, this restaurant's specialty is its light, delicious breads, including batura and parathas. **Open daily for lunch and dinner. Full service,** vegan options.

FAIRFIELD

Fairfield Diner and Vegetarian Enclave
90 Kings Hwy. Cut Off, Fairfield, CT 06430   **(203) 335-4090**
American. Located near Exit 24 off I-95, this diner offers a wide range of vegetarian and vegan dishes, including Middle Eastern cuisine, tempeh Reuben sandwiches, grilled polenta,

grilled tofu, veggie burgers, grilled portobello mushroom sandwiches, and veggie chili. They also serve vegan chocolate cake. **Open daily for three meals. Full service, vegan options, VISA/MC/AMEX/DISC, $-$$.**

GLASTONBURY

Garden of Light Natural Foods Market

2858 Main St., Glastonbury, CT 06033   **(203) 657-9131**

Natural foods deli. Award-winning vegan chef Ken Bergeron supervises this store's deli. Organic ingredients are used whenever possible. Enjoy a full salad bar, fresh baked goods, and hot dishes sold mostly by the pound. **Open daily. Counter service, vegan/macrobiotic options, fresh juices, catering, take-out, VISA/MC, $$.**

GREENWICH

Chola

107-109 Greenwich Ave., Greenwich, CT 06830   **(203) 869-0700**

Indian. This restaurant is owned and operated by the same people who run Chola in New York City. However, the menus are slightly different. Sample the Aloo Dilruba, Nilgiri Korma, Chana Dal, or Tofu Kadai. **Open daily for lunch and dinner. Full service, catering, take-out, delivery, beer/wine/alcohol, carrot juice, soymilk, buffet, reservations taken, VISA/MC/AMEX/DISC/DC, $$-$$$.** www.fineindiandining.com/cholagr.htm

GUILFORD

Shoreline Diner and Vegetarian Enclave

345 Boston Post Rd., Guilford, CT 05437   **(203) 458-7380**

American. Located near Exit 59 off I-95, this restaurant is owned and operated by the people who run the Fairfield Diner in Fairfield, CT. They have the exact same menu and options available. **Open daily for three meals. Full service, vegan options, VISA/MC/AMEX/DISC, $-$$.**

HARTFORD

(For restaurant listings in the surrounding areas, see East Hartford, Glastonbury, Middletown, Rocky Hill, and West Hartford.)

Lion's Den

403 1/2 Woodland St., Hartford, CT 06112   **(860) 241-0512**

Caribbean. Though this restaurant serves fish, its mostly vegetarian menu features many dishes made from steamed vegetables and soy products. **Open Monday through Saturday for three meals. Closed Sunday. Counter service, vegan options, take-out, catering, no credit cards, $-$$.**

KILLINGWORTH

The Country Squire

243-247 Rte. 80, Killingworth, CT 06419   **(860) 663-3228**

International. Housed in an historic 18th century inn, the restaurant is located in a period carriage barn. Although not a vegetarian restaurant, they do cater to the needs of vegetarians, listing menu items that can be made both vegetarian and vegan. These include the Artichoke Hearts and Granny Smith Apples and the Smoky Eggplant Caviar. **Open Wednesday through Sunday for lunch and dinner. Closed Monday and Tuesday. Full service, catering, reservations required, vegan options, fresh juices, espresso/cappuccino, smoothies, soymilk, non-alcoholic wine/beer, wine/beer/alcohol, VISA/MC/AMEX/DISC/DC, $$.**

It's Only Natural Restaurant
386 Main St., Middletown, CT 06457   **(203) 346-9210**
Natural foods. This restaurant serves international gourmet vegetarian and macrobiotic meals, featuring fresh baked bread and desserts. It also features an outdoor patio in a small mall. **Open Monday through Saturday for lunch and dinner. Open the first Sunday of the month for brunch. Full service, vegan options, catering, take-out, VISA/MC, $$.**

Mamoun's Falafel Restaurant
324 Main St., Middletown, CT 06457   **(860) 346-4646**
Middle Eastern. Mamoun's has an informal atmosphere with Middle Eastern décor. Located just a few blocks from the Connecticut River, this restaurant makes everything fresh daily, including favorites such as Tabbouleh, Stuffed Grape Leaves, and Baba Ghanouj, as well as specialties such as Moujedrha, Ful Mudammas, and Kibbeh without meat. **Open daily for lunch and dinner. Full service, take-out, catering, fresh juices, $-$$. www.mamounsfalafel.com**

• Udupi Bhavan
749 Saybrook Rd., Middletown, CT 06457   **(860) 346-3355**
Vegetarian/Indian. This South Indian restaurant offers curries, crepes, rice dishes, and much more. They are very accommodating and will gladly make most of the dishes vegan upon request. **Open Tuesday through Sunday for lunch and dinner. Closed Monday. Full service, vegan options, catering, no credit cards, $.**

(For restaurant listings in the surrounding areas, see Fairfield, Guilford, Killingworth, Old Saybrook, and Southington.)

Avanti's
45 Grove St., New Haven, CT 06511   **(203) 777-3234**
Italian. Avanti's is an Italian restaurant and pizzeria with several vegan options. **Open Monday through Saturday. Closed Sunday. Full service, vegan options, espresso/cappuccino, wine/beer, take-out, VISA/MC, $$.**

Claire's Corner Copia
1000 Chapel St., New Haven, CT 06510   **(203) 562-3888**
Eclectic. Described as one of "America's Oldest Vegetarian Restaurants" (although the menu does contain some animal items). Visitors to New Haven should stop by and check out the BBQ Tofu, Soy Beef Fajitas, risotto, and soups that Claire's has to offer. The website also

has updates on special events and recipes. **Open daily for three meals. Cafeteria, vegan options, catering, take-out, counter, $$. www.clairescornercopia.com**

Edge of the Woods
379 Whalley Ave., New Haven, CT 06511   **(203) 787-1055**
Health foods store deli. Partake of vegetarian fare with some vegan choices and baked goods. **Open daily. Cafeteria, fresh juices, take-out, $.**

House of Chao
898 Whalley Ave., New Haven, CT 06515   **(203) 389-6624**
Chinese. House of Chao offers many vegan options and is accustomed to adjusting the menu for vegetarians. **Open daily for lunch and dinner. Full service, vegan options, take-out, $$.**

India Palace
65 Howe St., New Haven, CT 06511   **(203) 776-9010**
Indian. There's a vegetarian menu section to choose from, plus vegetable pakora, samosas, soup, breads, and desserts. **Open daily for lunch and dinner. Full service, vegan options, wine/beer, take-out, $$.**

Mamoun's Falafel Restaurant
85 Howe St., New Haven, CT 06511   **(203) 562-8444**
Middle Eastern. See description under Middletown, CT. **Open daily. Limited service, vegan options, take-out, $.**

Rainbow Garden
1022 Chapel St., New Haven, CT 06511   **(203) 777-2390**
Natural foods. Hot and cold vegetarian sandwiches along with ethnic entrées, daily specials, and soups are available at Rainbow Garden. Menu changes daily and there are many vegan entrées offered in a smoke- and alcohol-free environment. **Open daily. Vegan options, self-service, take-out, VISA/MC/AMEX, $.**

NORWALK

The Lime Restaurant
168 Main Ave., Rte. 7, Norwalk, CT 06851   **(203) 846-9240**
American/international. This restaurant has many eclectic dishes from around the world, including Tofu in Oriental Orange Sauce, Soy Carrot Loaf, and Black Bean Burritos. **Open daily for lunch and dinner. Full service, vegan options, reservations recommended, fresh juices, non alcoholic beer/wine, beer/wine/alcohol, MC/AMEX/DC, $$$. www.lime restaurant.com**

OLD SAYBROOK

Saigon City
1315 Boston Post Rd., Old Saybrook, CT 06475   **(860) 388-6888**
Vietnamese/Thai. When you want authentic Vietnamese or Thai cuisine, the only road to travel leads to Saigon City in Old Saybrook. The menu has a full page of vegetarian options,

including Thai Coconut Tofu with Veggies and Pad Thai. **Open Tuesday through Sunday for lunch and dinner. Closed Monday. Full service, non-smoking, take-out, VISA/MC/ AMEX, $$-$$$.**

ROCKY HILL

Rasoi Grill

1860 Silas Deane Hwy., Rocky Hill, CT 06067   **(860) 529-5252**
Indian. This Indian restaurant offers a variety of vegetarian favorites. **Open daily for lunch. Open Tuesday through Sunday for dinner. Open weekends for brunch. Full service, buffet, take-out, $$.**

SOUTHBURY

Señor Pancho's Mexican Restaurante

Union Square Mall, Southbury, CT 06488   **(203) 262-6988**
Mexican. A separate vegetarian menu includes chimichangas, black bean soup, vegetable fajitas, as well as several other vegetarian items. **Open daily for lunch and dinner. Full service, espresso/cappuccino, smoothies, catering, take-out, VISA/MC/AMEX/DC, $-$$.**

SOUTHINGTON

El Sombrero

Oak Hill Mall, Southington, CT 06489   **(203) 621-9474**
Mexican. A separate vegetarian menu includes chimichangas, black bean soup, vegetable fajitas as well as several other vegetarian items. **Open daily for lunch and dinner. Full service, espresso/cappuccino, smoothies, catering, take-out, VISA/MC/AMEX/DC, $-$$.**

WEST HARTFORD

Tapas

1150 New Britain Ave., West Hartford, CT 06040   **(203) 521-4609**
Mediterranean. Tapas offers platters, eclectic pizzas, side orders, salads, and daily specials for lunch and dinner. Patio dining is available in good weather. **Open daily. Full service, vegan options, wine/beer, take-out, VISA/MC/AMEX, $$.**

Restaurant codes: ✪ Reviewers' Choice   • Vegetarian Restaurant   •• Vegan Restaurant
Restaurant prices: **$** less than $6   **$$** $6-$12   **$$$** more than $12
Credit Cards Accepted: VISA - VISA   MC - MasterCard   AMEX - American Express
DISC - Discover   DC - Diner's Club

Delaware

DOVER

El Sombrero
655 N. DuPont Hwy., Dover, DE 19901 **(302) 678-9445**
International. El Sombrero features a vegetarian menu with vegetable fajitas, lasagna, samosas, and other items. **Open daily for lunch and dinner. Full service, vegan options, wine/beer/ alcohol, take-out, VISA/MC/AMEX/DISC, $$.**

HOCKESSIN

Capriotti's
120 Lantana Square Shopping Ct.
Rt.7 & Valley Rd., Hockessin, DE 19707 **(302) 234-2322**
Deli. Capriotti's is more than just a regular deli; it features vegetarian options such as vegetarian turkey and ham hoagies, veggie burgers and hot dogs, and veggie tuna for subs and sandwiches. **Open daily for lunch and dinner. Limited service, vegan options, take-out, $.**

NEW CASTLE

Capriotti's
708 W. Basin Rd., New Castle, DE 19720 **(302) 322-6797**
Deli. See description under Hockessin, CT.

NEWARK

(For restaurant listings in the surrounding areas, see Hockessin, New Castle, and Wilmington.)

Capriotti's
614 Newark Shopping Center, Newark, DE 19711 **(302) 454-0200**
Deli. See description under Hockessin, CT.

King's Chinese Restaurant
Meadowwood Shopping Ctr.
2671 Kirkwood Hwy., Newark, DE 19711 **(302) 731-8022**
Chinese. Chef and owner Bob Chang invites you to explore his new menu of homemade soups, tasty appetizers, and vegetarian entrées. King's extensive vegetarian menu features many Chinese dishes, including mock meat and exotic mushroom entrées. The restaurant is very flexible and willing to prepare whatever you request. King's is located in the Meadowwood Shopping Center, but it is difficult to see from the highway, as you must drive around the side of the shopping center to find it. **Open daily for lunch and dinner. Full service, vegan options, wine/beer/alcohol, take-out, VISA/MC/AMEX/DISC, $$.**

Newark Co-op
280 E. Main St., Newark, DE 19711 **(302) 368-5894**
Natural foods deli. This successful food co-op also offers a small deli where you can purchase

pre-made cold salads and sandwiches. **Open Monday through Saturday. Closed Sunday. Vegan options, take-out, $. www.newarknaturalfoods.com**

Sinclair's Café
177 E. Main St., Newark, DE 19711   **(302) 368-7755**
American. Sinclair's divides its lunch menu into selections for "Omnivores" and "Vegetarians." The vegetarian items include veggie burgers, Reubens, bean burritos, and a grilled cheddar and chutney sandwich. **Open daily for breakfast and lunch. Full service, espresso/cappuccino, VISA/MC/AMEX/DISC/DC, $.**

REHOBOTH BEACH

Chez La Mer
210 Second St., P.O. Box 788, Rehoboth Beach, DE 19971   **(302) 227-6494**
French. While at this beach resort town, enjoy a gourmet vegetarian meal on Chez La Mer's country French dining area, enclosed sun porch, or rooftop deck. Ask for the separate vegetarian menu, which includes dishes like Sautéed Medallions of Seitan finished with white wine, lemon, shiitake mushrooms, and capers. Try the Wild Mushroom Loaf made with porcini and button mushrooms, baked into a loaf, or feast on one of several other vegetarian entrées, soups, and appetizers. **Open daily for dinner. Full service, vegan options, espresso/ cappuccino, wine/beer/alcohol, $$$.**

• Planet X
35 Wilmington Ave, Rehoboth Beach, DE 19971   **(302) 226-1928**
Vegetarian. This vegetarian café is located near the popular summer destination of Rehoboth Beach. **Open daily for three meals. Full service, vegan options, fresh juices, take-out, catering, $.**

WILMINGTON

Capriotti's
510 N. Union St., Wilmington, DE 19805   **(302) 479-9818**
Deli. See description under Hockessin, CT.

Indian Paradise
1710-A Newport Gap Pike, Wilmington, DE 19808   **(302) 999-0855**
Indian. This restaurant is located near Prices Corner Shopping Complex. They offer a huge vegetarian selection, including cauliflower and potatoes, chickpeas and spinach, and broccoli sautéed with garlic and ginger. **Open daily for lunch and dinner. Full service, vegan options, catering, take-out, $$.**

Restaurant codes: ✪ Reviewers' Choice • Vegetarian Restaurant •• Vegan Restaurant
Restaurant prices: **$** less than $6 **$$** $6-$12 **$$$** more than $12
Credit Cards Accepted: VISA - VISA MC - MasterCard AMEX - American Express
DISC - Discover DC - Diner's Club

Washington DC

(For restaurant listings in the surrounding areas, see Bethesda, Capitol Heights, College Park, Gaithersburg, Greenbelt, Langley Park, Rockville, Silver Spring, Spencerville, Takoma Park, and Wheaton in Maryland, and Arlington, Falls Church, Herndon, Manassas, McLean, Reston, South Arlington, Springfield, and Vienna in Virgina.)

Aditi Indian Cuisine

3299 M St., NW, Washington, DC 20007-3632   **(202) 625-6825**

Indian. Sample vegetarian appetizers, soup, entrées, breads, and desserts. **Open Tuesday through Sunday for lunch and dinner. Open Monday for dinner only. Full service, vegan options, fresh juices, wine/beer/alcohol, take-out, VISA/MC/AMEX/DISC, $$.**

• Amma Vegetarian Kitchen

3291 M St., NW, Georgetown, Washington, DC 20007   **(202) 625-6625**

Vegetarian/Indian. Small restaurant with a number of South Indian specialties, such as dosa (a thin rice crepe served with sambar and coconut chutney), puri bhaji (fried breads filled with potato), and rasam (a spicy soup). **Open daily for lunch and dinner. Full service, vegan options, take-out, catering, special drinks, VISA/MC/AMEX/DISC/DC, $.**

Asia Nora Organic Cuisine

2213 M St., NW, Washington, DC 20037   **(202) 797-4860**

Natural foods. The Asia Nora serves multi-ethnic new American cuisine using all organic ingredients. Vegetarian appetizers, salads, and entrées are offered. Menu changes seasonally. **Open Monday through Friday for lunch for dinner. Open Saturday for dinner only. Closed Sunday. Full service, vegan options, fresh juices, wine/beer/alcohol, take-out, VISA/MC, $$-$$$.** www.noras.com

Asylum

2471 18th St. NW, Washington, DC 20009   **(202) 319-9353**

Biker bar. This establishment offers vegan pizza, veggie chili, sandwiches, and a vegan brunch that includes pancakes, French toast, and tofu scramble. **Open Monday through Friday for dinner only. Open Saturday and Sunday for brunch and dinner. Limited service, vegan options, beer/wine/alcohol, VISA/MC, $$.** www.asylumdc.com

Bombay Club

815 Connecticut Ave., NW, Washington, DC 20006-4008   **(202) 659-3727**

Indian. Regional Indian cuisine is served in club-like ambiance. Varied vegetarian dishes are featured from all of India. **Open daily for lunch and dinner. Full service, wine/beer/alcohol, take-out, VISA/MC/AMEX, $$.**

City Lights of China

1731 Connecticut Ave., NW, Washington, DC 20009   **(202) 265-6688**

Asian. Request the special vegetarian menu at City Lights, and you'll be pleased to find a wide assortment of delicious vegetarian appetizers, entrées, and soups that include mock meat dishes, as well as other vegetarian Chinese foods. **Open daily for lunch and dinner. Full service, vegan options, wine/beer/alcohol, take-out, VISA/MC/AMEX, $$.** www.city lightsofchina.com

•• Everlasting Life Health Complex Restaurant
2928 Georgia Ave. NW, Washington, DC 20001   **(202) 232-1700**
Vegan deli. Though part of the health complex, this vegan restaurant/health foods/juice
bar near Howard University is open to the public. The menu features both raw and cooked
foods, such as pizzas, fresh baked breads, cookies, cakes, and pies. They also offer an array
of sandwiches, including a Battered Tofu Sandwich, a Gluten Roast Sandwich, a Tofu Salad
Sandwich, and Veggie Burgers. Save room for the vegan soft serve ice cream. **Open daily
for lunch and dinner. Cafeteria, fresh juices, smoothies, special drinks, take-out, VISA/MC/
AMEX/DISC, $-$$. www.everlastinglife.net**

Fasika's Ethiopian Restaurant
2447 18th St., NW, Washington, DC 20009   **(202) 797-7673**
Ethiopian. Fasika's has a vegetarian menu section, featuring salads, vegetable, and grain dishes.
**Open daily for dinner. Full service, vegan options, wine/beer/alcohol, take-out, VISA/MC/
AMEX/DC, $$.**

Ghana Café
2465 18th St., NW, Washington, DC 20009   **(202) 387-3845**
African. Ghana Café offers many vegetarian dishes, including Banku (fermented corn balls),
FuFu (plantain and cassava), and Wakye (rice and beans). They also are home to some of
DC's best African and reggae bands. **Open daily for lunch and dinner. Full service, vegan
options, $-$$.**

Harmony Café
3287 1/2 M St., NW, Washington, DC 20007   **(202) 338-3886**
Chinese. At Harmony you can get any item on the menu made with a meat analogue. Try
the Orange Veggie Chicken or the Veggie Shrimp with Cashew Nut. **Open daily for lunch
and dinner. Full service, VISA/MC, $-$$.**

Himalayan Grill
1805 18th St., NW, Washington, DC 20009   **(202) 986-5124**
Nepalese. The Himalayan Grill is the only Tibetan/Nepalese restaurant in the Washington
Metro area. Enjoy the soupy Dal and many other ethnic goodies. **Open daily for lunch and
dinner. Full service, special drinks, beer/wine/alcohol, reservations recommended, VISA/
MC/DISC/DC, $-$$.**

Honest to Goodness Burritos
1500 K St. NW At 15th St., Washington, DC 20005   **(202) 276-1799**
Mexican. This popular sidewalk lunch cart is very vegetarian friendly. The lines can be long,
but that's because all of the food is made fresh there with your choice of beans, tortillas, and
hot sauce. The Georgia Peach Vidalia Onion comes highly recommended. **Open Monday
through Friday for lunch. Closed Saturday and Sunday. Take-out only, vegan options, $.**

India Gate
2408 18th St., NW, Washington, DC 20009-2004   **(202) 332-0141**
Indian. Enjoy various vegetarian appetizers, soups, entrées, homemade breads, and salads.

Open daily for lunch and dinner. Full service, vegan options, wine/beer/alcohol, take-out, VISA/MC/AMEX/DC, $$.

• Indian Delight

1100 Pennsylvania Ave., NW, Washington, DC 20004 (202) 371-2295
Union Station, 50 Massachussetts Ave., NE,
   Washington, DC 20001 (202) 842-1040
1101 Connecticut Ave., NW, Washington, DC 20036 (202) 463-7121

Vegetarian/Indian. Eleven vegetarian entrées, plus appetizers, soup, salad, and dessert are offered on the Indian Delight menu. Daily specials are also available. The Pennsylvania Avenue restaurant is located inside an old post office. Please note that the Connecticut Avenue location now offers meat dishes as well as vegetarian fare, but the meat and meatless meals are still kept separate. **Open daily for lunch and dinner. Cafeteria, vegan options, take-out, no credit cards, $.**

Indian Kitchen

3506 Connecticut Ave., NW, Washington, DC 20008 (202) 966-2541

Indian. South Indian and exotic dishes are featured. Appetizers, vegetable entrées, special dishes, and breads are included on the menu. Indoor and outdoor seating. **Open daily for lunch and dinner. Limited service, vegan options, $.**

• Java Green

1020 19th St., NW, Washington, DC 20036 (202) 775-8899

Vegetarian. Java Green's predominately vegan menu includes salads, soups, wraps, panini sandwiches, rice bowls, combination lunches, and vegan desserts. Unique dishes include the veggie Chicken Chili, the Boolgogi Rice Wrap made with veggie beef, and the Veg D.C. panini sandwich with soy ham, soy cheese, lettuce, tomato, and vegan mayo. **Open Monday through Friday for three meals. Open Saturday for brunch and early dinner. Closed Sunday. Limited service, vegan options, smoothies, soymilk/rice milk/multi-grain milk, special drinks, take-out, catering, VISA/MC/AMEX, $.** www.javagreen.net

Julia's Empanadas

2452 18th St., NW, Washington, DC 20020 (202) 328-6232

Mexican. The spinach, broccoli, and cheese or vegetarian-style empanadas are just a few of the creations offered at Julia's. The ingredients in the vegetarian empanadas are changed weekly. **Open daily for lunch and dinner. Limited service, vegan options, take-out, $.**

•• Juliette's Vegetarian and Vegan Meals

3155 Mt. Pleasant St., NW, Washington, DC 20010 (202) 518-2665

Vegan. At Juliette's, all food is vegan and made from scratch. Some of the favorites include Onion Quiche, Tofu Croquettes, and Apple Pie. **Open daily for lunch and dinner. Take-out, macrobiotic options, reservations are required, VISA/MC, $$-$$$.**

Lebanese Taverna

2641 Connecticut Ave. NW, Washington, DC 20008 (202) 265-8681

Lebanese. Various Middle Eastern appetizers and salads plus approximately four vegetarian entrées are available. **Open Monday through Saturday for lunch and dinner. Open Sunday for dinner only. Full service, outdoor café, $$-$$$.**

Luna Grill & Diner
1301 Connecticut Ave., NW, Washington, DC 20009   **(202) 835-2280**
American/international. Located near Dupont Circle, their menu has a decent selection of vegetarian items for a diner. These include salads, three-bean vegetarian chili, soups, veggie burgers, pasta, sandwiches, and desserts like fresh fruit. Chili and soups are served in bread bowls. **Open daily for three meals. Full service, vegan options, VISA/MC/AMEX, $$.**

Madras Restaurant
3506 Connecticut Ave., NW, Washington, DC 20008   **(202) 966-2541**
Indian. Madras is mostly a vegetarian restaurant with a few non-vegetarian dishes. **Open daily for lunch and dinner. Cafeteria, take-out, VISA/MC/AMEX/DISC/DC, $.**

Red Sea Ethiopian Restaurant
2463 18th St., NW, Washington, DC 20009   **(202) 483-5000**
Ethiopian. Red Sea uses a rich variety of native herbs and spices to flavor the authentic Ethiopian cuisine. Diners eat in the traditional manner, using fingers and pieces of Ethiopian bread called injera to wrap and eat food. The menu clearly explains the various dishes. Several vegetarian appetizers and entrées are offered. **Open daily for lunch and dinner. Full service, vegan options, wine/beer/alcohol, take-out, VISA/MC/AMEX, $$.**

Restaurant Nora
2132 Florida Ave., NW, Washington, DC 20008   **(202) 462-5143**
Natural foods. Restaurant Nora is an organic restaurant serving multi-ethnic new American cuisine. The menu changes daily, and every evening, an organic vegetarian plate is offered. There also is a selection of vegetarian appetizers and salads, and the restaurant is willing to accommodate special diets. **Open Monday through Saturday for dinner. Closed Sunday. Full service, reservations recommended, formal but no dress code, fresh juices, wine/beer/ alcohol, VISA/MC/AMEX, $$$.** www.noras.com

• Secrets of Nature Health Food Center
3923 S. Capitol St., SW, Washington, DC 20032   **(202) 562-0041**
Vegetarian/natural foods. Secrets of Nature offers a wide variety of veggie rolls, sandwiches, salads, soups, barbeque, desserts, and more. Be sure to sample their Saturday brunch menu, too. **Open Monday through Saturday for three meals. Closed Sunday. Counter service, fresh juices, macrobiotic/vegan options, catering, take-out, VISA/MC/AMEX/DISC, $.** www.secretsofnature.net

Skewers
1633 P St., NW, Washington, DC 20036-1403   **(202) 387-4005**
Middle Eastern. Skewers features vegetable kebabs, falafel, hummus. **Open daily. Full service, vegan options, wine/beer/alcohol, take-out, VISA/MC/AMEX, $$.**

• Snack 'A' Shack
2608 Georgia Ave., NW, Washington, DC 20036   **(202) 387-3469**

Vegetarian juice bar. Located across from Howard University School of Business, Snack 'A' Shack serves all natural smoothies, veggie sandwiches, and raw vegan dishes. **Open daily for three meals.** Limited service, vegan options, $.

•• Soul Vegetarian Café
2608 Georgia Ave., NW, Washington, DC 20001   **(202) 328-SOUL**

Vegan. The cover of the menu for Soul Vegetarian Café says it all: "All Vegan!!! All the Time!!!" Try the Garvey burger made from vegetable protein and spices, the Liberia Burger made from black-eyed peas and West African flavoring, a BBQ tofu sub, or one of the many other choices, including desserts like tofu cheesecake. **Open Monday through Saturday for lunch and dinner. Open Sunday for brunch.** Limited service, smoothies, soymilk, VISA/MC, $-$$. www.kingdomofyah.com/sv.htm

•• Sticky Fingers
1904 18th St., NW, Washington, DC 20009   **(202) 299-9700**

Vegan bakery. The people behind Sticky Fingers have "veganized" traditional dessert favorites, including chocolate and carrot cakes, cheesecakes, cupcakes, cookies, and cinnamon buns. **Open Tuesday through Saturday for lunch and dinner. Open Sunday for lunch through late afternoon. Closed Monday.** Counter service, take-out, VISA/MC/AMEX/DISC, $-$$$. www.stickyfingersbakery.com

Stoup's of Athens
1825 I St., NW, Washington, DC 20006-5403   **(202) 223-1169**

Greek. Authentic Greek cuisine is served along with vegetarian dishes, such as a vegetable platter, spinach pie, stuffed cabbage, and soups. **Open Monday through Saturday. Closed Sunday.** Vegan options, wine/beer, take-out, no credit cards, $.

Taj Mahal
1327 Connecticut Ave., NW, Washington, DC 20036   **(202) 659-1544**

Indian. As Washington's oldest Indian restaurant, Taj Mahal has been serving the nation's capital since 1965. A special section of the menu offers vegetarian cuisine from northern India. Vegetarian appetizers, soups, and desserts are also available. **Open daily for dinner. Open Monday through Friday for buffet lunch.** Full service, vegan options, wine/beer/ alcohol, take-out, VISA/MC/AMEX/DISC, $$.

Teaism
2009 R St., NW, Washington, DC 20009   **(202) 667-3827**
400 8th St., NW, Washington, DC 20004   **(202) 638-6010**
800 Connecticut Ave., NW, Washington, DC 20006   **(202) 835-2233**

Teahouse. This unique restaurant, located in the Dupont Circle area of D.C., offers many dishes with an eastern flavor, including veggie bento boxes, Chinese noodle and tofu salad, Indian vegetable curry, cilantro scrambled tofu, and Plum Ochazuke (Japanese rice and tea soup). You can also sample more than 20 different varieties of tea. **Open daily for three meals. Connecticut Ave. location open Monday through Friday for two meals and after-noon tea.** Deli-style, take-out, non-smoking, VISA/MC/AMEX, $-$$. www.teaism.com

Wellness Café

325 Pennsylvania Ave., SE, Washington, DC 20003-1147   **(202) 543-2266**

Natural foods. Macrobiotic and vegetarian sandwiches, soups, salads, and snacks are available for take-out at Wellness Café. Menu items include sushi, soba, hijiki, chiraci, various bean and grain soups, and veggie burgers. **Open Monday through Saturday. Closed Sunday.** Limited service, vegan options, take-out only, VISA/MC, $.

Yes! Natural Gourmet

3425 Connecticut Ave., NW, Washington, DC 20008   **(202) 363-1559**
1825 Columbia Rd., NW, Washington, DC 20009   **(202) 462-5150**

Natural foods. Soups, sandwiches, and fresh-squeezed juices are featured at Yes! **Open daily.** Take-out, fresh juices, VISA/MC/AMEX, $.

Zed's Ethiopian Cuisine

1201 28th St., NW, Washington, DC 20007-3513   **(202) 333-4710**

Ethiopian. As is customary with Ethiopian foods, no utensils are used at Zed's; patrons use traditional bread, injera, to pick up food during a meal. Various vegetarian options are available. **Open daily.** Full service, vegan options, wine/beer/alcohol, take-out, VISA/MC/AMEX, $.

Zorba's Café & Carry Out

1612 20th St., NW, Washington, DC 20009-1001   **(202) 387-8555**

Greek. Zorba's serves a variety of ethnic vegetarian dishes, such as fasolakia, falafel, spanakopita, and fasolia. **Open daily for lunch and dinner.** Counter service, vegan options, wine/beer, take-out, VISA/MC/AMEX, $. www.zorbascafe.com

Florida

ALTAMONTE SPRINGS

Bangkok Restaurant

260 Douglas Ave., Altamonte Springs, FL 32714   **(407) 788-2685**

Thai. Be sure to request their vegetarian menu, and you'll find six vegetarian Thai entrées. **Open daily for lunch and dinner.** Full service, take-out, $$.

Chamberlin's Natural Foods

Goodings Plaza
1086 Montgomery Rd., Altamonte Springs, FL 32714   **(407) 774-8866**

Natural foods. Salad bar, vegetarian deli, smoothies, homemade soup and veggie chili, frozen yogurt, hot and cold sandwiches, and hot vegetarian entrées are offered. **Open daily.** Counter service, vegan options, fresh juices, take-out, $.

Kohinoor

The Village Shoppes
249 W. Hwy. 436, #1093, Altamonte Springs, FL 32714   **(407) 788-6004**

Indian. This Indian restaurant offers a wide variety of vegetarian dishes, including a puréed vegetable soup with spices and lentil soup; vegetable samosas; various chutneys; Indian breads; and more than ten entrées. **Open Tuesday through Sunday for lunch and dinner. Closed Monday. Full service, vegan options, $$.**

•• Maracas Valley Vegetarian Restaurant
851 W. State Rd. 436, #1037, Altamonte Springs, FL 32714   (407) 786-1960

Vegan. You will find many dishes made with substitute meat products at this restaurant, including barbecue flavored items, Italian pasta dishes, and more. **Open Sunday through Friday for lunch and dinner. Closed Saturday. Full service, catering, take-out, VISA/MC/AMEX/DISC/DC, $$.**

BIG PINE KEY

Good Food Conspiracy
US 1 Mile Marker 30.2, Big Pine Key, FL 33043   (305) 872-3945

Natural foods. The next time you find yourself driving in the Florida Keys, be certain to stop at this natural foods market and juice bar. Dine on vegetarian soups, pita sandwiches, salads, smoothies, and more. **Open daily for three meals. Full service, take-out, VISA/MC/AMEX/DISC, $$.**

BOCA RATON

• Bombay Café
628 Glades Rd., Boca Raton, FL 33431   (561) 750-5299

Vegetarian. Bombay Café offers cheap, delicious Indian-style vegetarian dishes and some vegan options as well. **Open Monday through Saturday. Closed Sunday. Full service, vegan options, reservations not needed, take-out, VISA, $.**

Eilat Café
6853 SW 18th St., Boca Raton, FL 33433   (407) 368-6880

Mediterranean. Eilat Café offers a wide variety of Middle Eastern- and Italian-style dishes, including falafel, hummus, Turkish salad, pasta dishes, and gourmet pizza. This is a kosher establishment. **Open Sunday through Thursday for lunch and dinner. Open Friday for lunch. Open Saturday after sundown for dinner. Vegan options, take-out, $$. www.eilat cafe.com**

Pine Garden Restaurant
1668 N. Federal Hwy., Boca Raton, FL 33432   (561) 395-7534

Chinese. Pine Garden offers a different menu for their vegetarian customers with dishes made from seitan, tempeh, and tofu. These include Cantonese Steak, Veggie Ham with Assorted Vegetables in Szechuan or Black Bean Sauce, Aromatic Jade Soy Chicken or Gluten Beef, and Honey Walnut Soy Chicken. **Open daily for lunch and dinner. Full service, vegan options, beer/wine, non-smoking, VISA/MC/DISC, $$.**

Restaurant codes: ✪ Reviewers' Choice   • Vegetarian Restaurant   •• Vegan Restaurant
Restaurant prices: **$** less than $6   **$$** $6-$12   **$$$** more than $12
Credit Cards Accepted: VISA - VISA   MC - MasterCard   AMEX - American Express
DISC - Discover   DC - Diner's Club

BONITA SPRINGS

For Goodness Sake
9118 Bonita Beach Rd., Bonita Springs, FL 34135   **(239) 992-5838**
Natural foods deli. For Goodness Sake offers sandwiches, salads, and a soup du jour that is almost always vegan. Popular items include a sunshine burger, a barbeque tempeh burger, and eggless salad. **Open Monday through Saturday for lunch and dinner. Open Sunday for lunch.** Limited service, vegan options, fresh juices, smoothies, take-out, VISA/MC/AMEX/DISC, $$.

CASSELBERRY

Chamberlin's Natural Foods
Lake Howell Sq., 1271 Semoran Blvd., Casselberry, FL 32707   **(407) 678-3100**
Natural foods. See description under Altamonte Springs, FL.

CLEARWATER

Bunny Hop Café
Nature's Food Patch, 1225 Cleveland St., Clearwater, FL 33775 (727) 443-6703
Natural foods store. Located inside Nature's Food Patch, the Bunny Hop Café serves international vegetarian and macrobiotic foods in a coffeehouse atmosphere. High-fiber, low-fat cooking, fresh veggies and fruit, salad bar, veggie burgers, stir-fries, smoothies, desserts, and more are offered. **Open Monday through Saturday for three meals. Closed Sunday.** Full service, vegan options, fresh juices, take-out, VISA/MC, $-$$.

Lonni's Sandwiches, Etc.
601 Cleveland St., Clearwater, FL 33755   **(727) 441-8044**
Natural foods. This restaurant offers several vegetarian options, including Wild Rice Soup, sandwiches, salads, and more. **Open Monday through Friday for lunch. Closed Saturday and Sunday.** Counter service, take-out, catering, $$. www.lonnissandwiches.com

Thai Basil
4445 E. Bay Dr., Clearwater, FL 33764   **(727) 532-6108**
Thai. A favorite of area vegetarians, this restaurant offers appetizers and entrées made with mixed vegetables, tofu, rice noodles, and or rice. Sometimes, it also has interesting desserts, such as fried bananas drizzled with raspberry sauce. **Open Monday through Friday for lunch and dinner. Open Saturday for dinner only. Closed Sunday.** Full service, vegan options, beer/wine, VISA/MC/DISC, $-$$.

COCOA

Gardener's Cottage Natural Kitchen
902 Florida Ave., Cocoa, FL 32922   **(321) 631-2030**
Natural foods. Gardener's Cottage is a health mercantile as well as a natural kitchen offering antique nutrition books, garden gifts, and much more. **Open Monday through Friday for lunch and early dinner. Open Saturday for lunch only. Closed Sunday.** Full service, vegan options, fresh juices, espresso/cappuccino, smoothies, soymilk, VISA/MC, $.

COCONUT GROVE

The Last Carrot
3133 Grand Ave., Coconut Grove, FL 33133   **(305) 445-0805**
Natural foods. Sandwiches, spinach pies, salads, and various fresh juices and smoothies are served. Open daily for lunch and dinner. Counter service, vegan options, fresh juices, take-out, cash only, $.

DESTIN

Royal Orchid
11275 Emerald Coast Pkwy., Destin, FL 32541   **(850) 650-2555**
Thai. Located beside Seascape Golf Course, Royal Orchid offers an exotic menu, including a separate section with over nine vegetarian entrées. For a delicious experience, try Pad-Pak Tofu with a Cucumber Salad. **Open Monday through Thursday for lunch and dinner. Open Friday through Sunday for dinner only.** Full service, vegan options, take-out, $-$$.

DUNEDIN

Casa Tina Gourmet Mexican and Vegetarian Cuisine
369 Main St., Dunedin, FL 34698   **(727) 734-9226**
Mexican. Most of the dishes at this award-winning restaurant are available vegetarian or vegan style. No lard or animal stock is used in any sauces or beans. *Tampa Bay Magazine* has consistently voted this the best Mexican restaurant. **Open Tuesday through Sunday for lunch through late night service. Closed Monday.** Full service, vegan options, fresh juices, wine/beer, non-alcoholic wine/beer, take-out, catering, VISA/MC/AMEX/DISC/DC, $$-$$$. www.casatinas.com

Jerusalem Café
1140 Main St., Dunedin, FL 34698   **(727) 736-8438**
Middle Eastern/Kosher. Feast on falafel, baba ghanouj, hummus, veggie chopped liver, New York quality bagels, tabbouleh, Mediterranean salads, soups, sandwiches, and more. **Open Sunday through Thursday for three meals. Open Friday for breakfast and lunch. Closed Saturday.** Deli-style, vegan options, catering, VISA/MC/AMEX/DISC, $-$$.

Lonni's Sandwiches, Etc.
1153 Main St., Dunedin, FL 34698   **(727) 734-0121**
Natural foods. See description under Clearwater, FL. **Open Monday through Saturday for lunch only.**

FORT LAUDERDALE

(For restaurant listings in the surrounding areas, see Boca Raton, Hollywood, and Pembroke Pines.)

Healthy Bites Grill
21300 St. Andrews Blvd., Fort Lauderdale, FL 33433   **(561) 338-6294**
American. Healthy Bites redefines fast food by offering alternatives to the unhealthy norm.

Dine on their baked fries, grilled tofu club, fresh smoothies, and many more quick veggie meals inside the restaurant or in the comfort of your own home; it even has a drive-thru. Additional locations to open soon in West Boca Raton and North Fort Lauderdale. **Open daily for lunch and dinner. Limited service, vegan options, fresh juices, smoothies, $-$$.** www.hexs.com/root/index.html

Nature Boy Health Foods
220 E. Commercial Blvd., Fort Lauderdale, FL 33308   **(954) 776-4696**
Natural foods/macrobiotic. Nature Boy serves vegetable and fruit salads, sandwiches, soups, and side orders. **Open Monday through Saturday for lunch. Closed Sunday. Full service, vegan options, fresh juices, smoothies, take-out, delivery, VISA/MC, $.**

•• Sublime World Vegetarian Cuisine ✪
1431 N. Federal Hwy., Ft. Lauderdale, FL 33304   **(954) 615-1431**
Vegan café. For the ultimate in upscale vegan dining in a fresh, chic setting, Sublime is the place to go. The executive chef at this completely organic restaurant will individually prepare entrées such as Rigatoni Bolognese, Wild Mushroom Stroganoff, Raw Nut Loaf, Summer Corn Enchiladas, and Pad Thai. Or try a house specialty like Sublime Piccata, made with seitan, rutabaga mash, lemon caper beurre-blanc, haricot verts, and toasted almonds. Also available are sushi, pizzas, and a wide variety of organic salads. **Open daily for three meals. Full service, fresh juices, wine/beer/alcohol, take-out, VISA/MC/AMEX/DISC/DC, $$-$$$.** www.sublimeveg.com

Whole Foods Market
2000 N. Federal Hwy., Fort Lauderdale, FL 33305   **(954) 565-RICE**
Natural foods. Enjoy the soup and salad bar in this natural foods store. **Open daily. Limited service, vegan options, fresh juices, wine/beer, VISA/MC/AMEX/DISC, $-$$.**

FORT MYERS

(For restaurant listings in the surrounding areas, see Bonita Springs.)

Thai Gardens
7091-15 College Pkwy., Fort Myers, FL 33907   **(813) 275-0999**
Thai. Several vegetarian entrées including Vegetable Curry, Sautéed Vegetables with Bean Curd, Veggie Fried Rice, and more. **Open daily for lunch and dinner. Full service, vegan options, wine/beer, VISA/MC/AMEX/DISC/DC, $.**

GAINESVILLE

(For restaurant listings in the surrounding areas, see High Springs.)

• Book Lover's Café
505 NW 13th St., Gainesville, FL 32601   **(352) 384-0090**
Vegetarian. Book Lover's Café has an extensive selection of vegan desserts. Their entrées include Vegan Lasagna and Sage Lentil Loaf. **Open daily for lunch and dinner. Limited service, vegan options, fresh juices, $.**

Chop Stix Café
3500 SW 13th St., Gainesville, FL 32608   **(352) 367-0003**
Japanese. Chop Stix Café offers vegetarian sushi and other Pan Asian favorites, such as Thai Curry Fried Tofu. Open Monday through Saturday for lunch and dinner. Closed Sunday. Limited service, vegan options, catering, take-out, smoothies, $-$$.

•Radha's Vegetarian Café
125 NW 23rd St., Ste. 17, Gainesville, FL 32609   **(352) 378-2955**
Vegetarian/Indian. This mostly vegan Krishna establishment offers great meals in its restaurant, as well as frozen entrées, dry Indian groceries, gifts, and more. Open Monday through Saturday for lunch and early dinner. Closed Sunday. Full service, vegan options, take-out, VISA/MC/AMEX/DISC, $.

HIGH SPRINGS

The Great Outdoors Café
65 N. Main St., High Springs, FL 32643   **(904) 454-2900**
Natural foods. Located just off I-75 in north Florida, this café offers a diverse array of foods, like fresh salads, pastas, vegetarian entrées, and desserts. No smoking is allowed. Open daily. Full service, vegan options, wine/beer, take-out, VISA/MC, $$.

HOLLYWOOD

Jerusalem Pizza Of Hollywood
5650 Stirling Rd., #16, Hollywood, FL 33021   **(954) 964-6811**
Pizza. This family eatery has many vegetarian options. Open daily for three meals. Take-out, vegan options, non-smoking, VISA/MC/AMEX/DISC/DC, $-$$.

Sara's Kosher Restaurant
3944 N. 46th Ave., Hollywood, FL 33021   **(954) 986-1770**
Kosher/natural foods. This kosher dairy restaurant offers a wide selection of vegetarian dishes, including fake "meat" dishes, quiche, pizza, salads, sandwiches, Middle Eastern platters, and more. Open Sunday through Thursday for three meals. Open Friday for breakfast and lunch. Open Saturday for late dinner. Full service, vegan options, fresh juices, espresso/cappuccino, wine/beer, catering, take-out, VISA/MC/AMEX/DISC, $-$$.

INDIAN ROCKS BEACH

Thai-Pan Alley
2300 Gulf Blvd., Indian Rocks Beach, FL 33785   **(727) 593-3663**
Thai. Choose your level of spiciness, from no stars to five stars, for the Vegetable Deluxe, Vegetable Curry, Veggie Pad Thai, Veggie Fried Rice, or one of the several other dishes that can be prepared without meat. Open Monday through Saturday for lunch and dinner. Open Sunday for dinner only. Full service, take-out, VISA/MC, $.

JACKSONVILLE

(For restaurant listings in the surrounding areas, see Orange Park.)

Health Shoppe
12620-16 Beach Blvd., Jacksonville, FL 32257   **(904) 641-4410**
Natural foods. Veggie sandwiches, including a tofu Reuben, hummus, and veggie burger, are offered, as well as various salads. **Open Monday through Saturday for lunch. Closed Sunday.** Limited service, vegan options, take-out, $.

• Heartworks Gallery & Café
820 Lomax St., Jacksonville, FL 32204   **(904) 355-6210**
Vegetarian. Heartworks is often voted the best vegetarian restaurant in Jacksonville. Their affordable lunch menu includes the carrot dog, vegetable pizza, black bean burritos, vegetarian lasagna, the soup de jour, and daily specials. Dinner includes a rotating menu of gourmet entrées, while Sunday brunch includes fresh-fruit pancakes and spinach-omelet pies. They also offer vegan pastries. **Open Monday through Wednesday for lunch. Open Thursday and Friday for lunch and dinner. Open Saturday for lunch. Open Sunday for brunch. Full service, vegan options, soymilk, espresso/cappuccino, reservations required for large groups, no credit cards, $-$$$.

Pattaya Thai Restaurant
10916 Atlantic Blvd., Jacksonville, FL 32225   **(904) 646-9506**
Thai. Choose from more than 20 vegetarian Thai dishes, including Spring Rolls, Vegetable Tofu Soup, Curry Fried Rice, Mixed Vegetables with Tofu, Sweet and Sour Vegetables, and various curries. **Open Tuesday through Friday for lunch and dinner. Open Saturday and Sunday for dinner only. Closed Monday.** Full service, wine/beer/alcohol, VISA/MC/AMEX/DC, $$.

KEY WEST

(For restaurant listings in the surrounding areas, see Big Pine Key.)

• The Café
509 Southard St., Key West, FL 33040   **(305) 296-5515**
Vegetarian. One reader called this funky yet quaint establishment "a must for vegetarians and non-vegetarians alike." The menu, which is half vegan, includes grilled portobello salads, handmade spring rolls, vegan BBQ wings, great homemade veggie burgers, stir-fies, and much more. The service is excellent, and there is live music on Thursday nights. **Open Monday through Saturday for lunch and dinner. Closed Sunday.** Full service, vegan options, smoothies, soymilk, espresso/cappuccino, beer/wine, take-out, delivery, VISA/MC, $$.

•• Sugar Apple Juice Bar and Veggie Deli
917 Simonton St., Key West, FL 33040   **(305) 292-0043**
Vegan. Take-out a wide range of delicious vegetarian fare and fresh juices from this establishment, located in a natural foods store. Enjoy tempeh sandwiches, veggie burgers, baked tofu, barbecued tofu, tofu lasagna, plus much more at reasonable prices. **Open Monday through Saturday for lunch. Closed Sunday.** Take-out, fresh juices, $-$$.

Thai Cuisine
513 Greene St., Key West, FL 33040 **(305) 294-9424**
Thai. About a dozen vegetarian options are available on their menu, including Pad Thai, vegetarian spring rolls, fried tofu, soups, vegetable curry dishes, and noodle dishes. **Open daily for lunch and dinner. Full service, take-out, VISA/MC, $$.**

KISSIMMEE

Punjab Indian Restaurant
3404 W. Vine St., Kissimmee, FL 34741 **(407) 931-2449**
Indian. Choose from several vegetarian appetizers, soups, and a complete list of vegetarian curries at Punjab Indian Restaurant. The dishes are made to order. **Open Tuesday through Saturday for lunch and dinner. Open Sunday and Monday for dinner only. Full service, vegan options, take-out, reservations required, fresh juices, catering, VISA/MC/AMEX/ DISC, $$.**

LARGO

The Health Nut Café
The Health Nut Natural Foods & Supplements
11883 Indian Rocks Rd., Largo, FL 33774 **(727) 517-7442**
Natural foods deli. The Health Nut Café, located inside the Health Nut Natural Foods Store, offers organic salads, lunches, take-out dishes, and more. **Open Monday through Saturday for three meals. Open Sunday for brunch. Deli-style, vegan options, fresh juices, smoothies, take-out, VISA/MC/AMEX/DISC, $.**

Pioneer Natural Foods
12788 Indian Rocks Rd., Largo, FL 33774 **(727) 596-6600**
Natural foods. This deli and juice bar offers vegetarian sandwiches, salads, and hot dishes. The hummus sandwich comes highly recommended. **Open daily for three meals. Counter service, vegan options, fresh juices, smoothies, take-out, VISA/MC/AMEX, $.**

•• Sai Indian Restaurant
1300 E. Bay Dr., Largo, FL 33771 **(727) 559-7005**
Vegan/Indian. This affordable restaurant serves traditional southern Indian foods, including Indian pancakes, utthapam, curries, and breads. They also offer a buffet for approximately $6 per person. **Open Wednesday through Monday for lunch and dinner. Closed Tuesday. Full service, take-out, VISA/MC/DISC, $.**

Tum Nuk Thai
11002 Seminole Blvd., Largo, FL 33778 **(727) 397-7759**
Thai. This restaurant has a good selection of vegetarian, macrobiotic, and vegan entrées. Offerings include Sautéed Mixed Vegetables, Sautéed Bean Curd with Mixed Vegetables, Panang Curry, and Siam Tofu with Thai Chili Sauce. The Amazing Eggplant is highly recommended. **Open Monday through Friday for lunch and dinner. Open Saturday and Sunday for dinner only. Full service, vegan options, take-out, VISA/MC/DISC/DC, $$.**

Ali Baba

1155 W. St. Rd. 434, Longwood, FL 32750 **(407) 331-8680**

Middle Eastern. Ali Baba has been consistently voted the best Middle Eastern restaurant in Central Florida. They have a separate vegetarian menu which includes Falafel, Hummus, and Dolmehs. **Open daily for lunch and dinner. Full service, vegan options, fresh juices, beer/wine, VISA/MC, $-$$.**

(For restaurant listings in the surrounding areas, see Cocoa.)

Community Harvest Café

1405 Highland Ave., Melbourne, FL 32935 **(321) 254-4966**

Natural foods. At Community, dine on eggless multi-grain pancakes, organic granola, tempeh or tofu salad, hummus sandwiches, veggie burgers, and more. Daily vegetarian lunch specials are made with organic beans, grains, and when available, organic produce. Hot and cold sandwiches include nut and grain burgers, tofu surprise, and a BLT made with soy bacon and eggless mayo. Live acoustic music on Friday nights. **Open Monday through Friday for three meals. Open Saturday for breakfast and lunch. Closed Sunday. Full service, vegan options, smoothies, fresh juices, macrobiotic options, take-out, VISA/MC, $.**

(For restaurant listings in the surrounding areas, see Coconut Grove, Hollywood, Miami Beach, North Miami, and North Miami Beach.)

• Govinda's

3220 Virginia St., Miami, FL 33133 **(305) 445-8689**

Vegetarian. This Hare Krishna-style restaurant serves mainly Indian cuisine but also Italian food and desserts. It is said to be an excellent value for the price. **Open daily for lunch and dinner. Full service, vegan options, buffet, VISA/MC/AMEX/DISC, $.**

Granny Feelgood's

25 W. Flagler St., Miami, FL 33130 **(305) 377-9600**

Natural foods. Granny Feelgood's makes a special effort to offer the freshest, healthiest foods available. Organic produce is offered and the menu selections (sandwiches, soups, salads, desserts, and international entrées) emphasize low-fat, low-cholesterol, and low-sodium foods. **Open Monday through Friday. Closed Saturday and Sunday. Full service, vegan options, fresh juices, take-out, $.**

• The Honey Tree

5138 Biscayne Blvd., Miami, FL 33137 **(305) 759-1696**

Vegetarian. This vegetarian natural foods restaurant offers organic food whenever possible. **Open daily for lunch and dinner. Limited service, vegan options, take-out, non-smoking, fresh juices, smoothies, soymilk, catering, VISA/MC/AMEX/DISC, $$.**

MIAMI BEACH

13th Street Café
227 13th St., Miami Beach, FL 33139　　　　　　　　**(305) 672-8169**

Natural foods. Enjoy the "Carmen Miranda" motif at this café that serves fresh juices and smoothies, as well as vegetarian sandwiches and specialties. **Open daily for three meals. Full service, fresh juices, smoothies, take-out, $.**

Pacific Time
915 Lincoln Rd., Miami Beach, FL 33139　　　　　　　**(305) 534-5979**

Asian. If you find yourself in the South Miami Beach area and you're looking for an upscale restaurant that serves vegetarian options, you may want to try Pacific Time. Offerings include organic greens with tomatoes and herbs served with fennel bread; steamed asparagus with endive and yamabuki miso vinaigrette; sautéed Japanese eggplant and haricots with Thai red curry sauce; noodles with porcini shiitake mushrooms, artichokes, tomatoes, and blanched garlic in a miso/truffle broth; and sautéed steamed vegetables with rice. **Open daily for dinner. Full service, vegan options, reservations recommended, fresh juices, espresso/cappuccino, non-alcoholic wine/beer, wine/beer/alcohol, VISA/MC/AMEX, $$$.**

•• Sunshine and Aj's Food Without Fire
747 4th St., Miami Beach, FL 33139　　　　　　　　**(305) 674-9960**

Vegan/raw foods. The raw menu here includes salads, chilled soups, sandwiches, pizza, lasagna, nori rolls, frozen desserts, and fresh fruit pies. **Open Monday through Saturday for lunch and dinner. Open Sunday for brunch. Full service, fresh juices, smoothies, take-out, catering, VISA/MC/AMEX, $$.**

NAPLES

For Goodness Sake
2464 Vanderbilt Beach Rd. Ext., Naples, FL 34109　　　　**(239) 597-0120**

Natural foods deli. See description under Bonita Springs, FL.

Nature's Garden Organic Café & Market
2089 9th St. N., Naples, FL 34102　　　　　　　　**(239) 643-7600**

Natural foods café. This café offers delicious and creative sandwiches, such as the "yamoli" and the "humdinger" (a wrap of chickpeas, spinach, and tomato), and 24 different salads, including a tabbouleh, wild rice, and arugula salad and a wheatberry salad. Hot lunch entrées include brown rice adzuki bean burgers and quinoa stuffed peppers. **Open daily for three meals. Call for seasonal hours. Limited service, vegan options, fresh juices, smoothies, take-out, VISA/MC/DISC, $$.**

Sun Splash Café
850 Neapolitan Way, Naples, FL 33940　　　　　　　**(239) 434-7221**

Natural foods. At least two different entrées are offered at this café that uses all organically grown produce, tofu mayonnaise, and no refined sugars or artificial sweeteners in their menu of chilled salads. Try the Thai Tempeh Salad, Curried Red Lentil Salad, or "Eggless" Tofu

Salad. They also offer a 30-item salad bar. **Open daily for lunch and dinner. Cafeteria, vegan options, smoothies, catering, VISA/MC/DISC, $$.**

NORTH MIAMI

Sara's Kosher Restaurant
2214 NE 123rd St., North Miami, FL 33181   **(305) 891-7272**
Kosher/natural foods. See description under Hollywood, FL.

NORTH MIAMI BEACH

Artichokes Natural Cuisine
3055 NE 163rd St., North Miami Beach, FL 33160   **(305) 945-7576**
International. Vegetarian, macrobiotic, and Pritikin dishes are served at this popular neighborhood restaurant. The menu includes appetizers, salads, entrées, and desserts. **Open nightly for dinner. Full service, vegan options, fresh juices, wine/beer, take-out, VISA/MC/ AMEX/DC, $$.**

Kebab Indian Restaurant
514 NE 167th St., North Miami Beach, FL 33162   **(305) 940-6309**
Indian. Kebab is recommended by the Vegetarian Gourmet Society in Florida as serving "the best Indian vegetarian foods that we have ever tasted." Dishes are made fresh, and special diets are accommodated. **Open daily. Full service, vegan options, wine/beer, take-out, VISA/MC/AMEX, $$.**

ORANGE PARK

Granary Deli
1738 Kingsley Ave., Orange Park, FL 32073   **(904) 269-7350**
Natural foods. The Granary Deli is located in the Granary Whole Foods store. This primarily vegetarian deli offers soups, sandwiches, salads, and much more. Organic ingredients are used when available. **Open Monday through Saturday for lunch and early dinner. Closed Sunday. Limited service, vegan/macrobiotic options, fresh juices, catering, take-out, $.**

ORLANDO

(For restaurant listings in the surrounding areas, see Altamonte Springs, Casselberry, Kissimmee, Longwood, and Oviedo.)

4, 5, 6
657 N. Primrose Dr., Orlando, FL 32803   **(407) 898-1899**
Chinese. Vegetarian egg rolls, soups, and 20 non-dairy vegetarian dishes with brown rice are available. MSG is not used in food preparation. **Open daily for lunch and dinner. Full service, vegan options, take-out, wine/alcohol, VISA/MC, $.**

Bee Line Diner
Peabody Hotel, 9801 International Dr., Orlando, FL 32819   **(407) 352-4000**
International. This diner features a vegetarian section on the menu that includes chili, lasagna,

falafel, and veggie burgers. **Open 24 hours a day. Full service, take-out, non-alcoholic wine/ beer, wine/beer/alcohol, VISA/MC/AMEX/DISC/DC, $$.**

Chamberlin's Market and Café
7600 Dr. Phillips Blvd., Orlando, FL 32819   **(407) 352-2130**
Natural foods. See description under Altamonte Springs, FL.

•Florida Hospital Cafeteria
601 E. Rollins St., Orlando, FL 32803   **(407) 897-1793**
Vegetarian/cafeteria. A deli, a taco bar, and a soup and salad bar are featured; low-fat and low-salt entrées are available at this cafeteria. **Open 24 hours daily. Cafeteria, take-out, $.**

•Garden Café
810 W. Colonial Dr., Orlando, FL 32804   **(407) 999-9799**
Vegetarian/Chinese. Located near Disney World, the Garden Café offers an all-vegetarian menu. Their philosophy is "Forgo the meat without giving up the taste." You can choose from vegan Chinese standards, such as Hot and Sour Soup, or be adventurous and try Braised Vegetarian Shark's Fin with Wild Bamboo Pith Soup. Their entrées are made with soy and wheat gluten mock meats, including Rainbow Shrimp, Sweet and Sour Chicken, and Satay Beef. **Open daily for lunch and dinner. Full service, $-$$.**

Green Earth Health Foods
2336 W. Oakridge Rd., Orlando, FL 32809   **(407) 859-8045**
Natural foods. The café offers fresh soups, chili, sandwiches, salads, and smoothies. It is "dedicated to serving wholesome foods with no chemicals or preservatives" and uses organic products whenever possible. All food is prepared on the premises and is low-salt and low-fat. Green Earth is located in Oakridge Plaza. **Open Monday through Friday. Closed Saturday and Sunday. Limited service, vegan options, fresh juices, VISA/MC, $.**

Passage to India
5532 International Dr., Orlando, FL 32819   **(407) 351-3456**
Indian. Choose from several vegetarian appetizers, soups, and 12 vegetarian entrées. **Open daily for lunch and dinner. Full service, take-out, non alcoholic wine/beer, wine/beer, VISA/MC/AMEX/DISC, $.**

Punjab Indian Restaurant
7451 International Dr., Orlando, FL 32819   **(407) 352-7887**
Indian. See description under Kissimmee, FL.

•Taste Of India
9251 S. Orange Blossom Trail, Orlando, FL 32837   **(407) 855-4622**
Vegetarian/Indian. Taste of India has dishes available for Jain, Buddhist, and Swaminarayan faiths. Along with their Indian menu, they also offer dishes from East Africa, Mexico, and Italy. **Open Tuesday through Sunday for lunch and dinner. Closed Mondays. Limited service, vegan options, macrobiotic options, fresh juices, smoothies, beer/wine/alcohol, non-smoking, VISA/MC/AMEX/DISC/DC, $.**

ORMOND BEACH

English Rose Tea Room

49 W. Granada Blvd., Ormond Beach, FL 32174   **(386) 672-7673**

International. This traditional tea room has a vegetarian selection on its menu, which includes a Vegan Lasagna and Vegan Tofu Manicotti. **Open Monday through Saturday for lunch. Closed Sunday. Full service, vegan options, catering, $-$$.** www.englishrosetearoom.com

OVIEDO

Chamberlin's Market and Café

1170 Oviedo Marketplace Blvd., Oviedo, FL 32765   **(407) 359-7028**

Natural foods. See description under Altamonte Springs, FL.

PALM BEACH

(For restaurant listings in the surrounding areas, see Boca Raton and West Palm Beach.)

•Sunrise Natural Foods

233 Royal Poinciana Way, Palm Beach, FL 33480   **(305) 655-3557**

Macrobiotic. Sunrise's selections include soup, egg rolls, spinach pies, and artichoke pasta for take-out. **Open Monday through Saturday for lunch and dinner. Closed Sunday. Take-out, non-alcoholic beer/wine, VISA/MC/AMEX, $.**

PALM HARBOR

•Consciousness Blossoms

3390 Tampa Rd., Palm Harbor, FL 34684   **(727) 789-1931**

Vegetarian. This is the only entirely vegetarian cafeteria in the Tampa Bay area. Committed to serving healthy and delicious vegetarian meals, the menu offers Neatloaf, barbeque tempeh or tofu sandwiches, veggie Reubens, tofu scramble, oatmeal, and more. This restaurant closes for two weeks in mid-April and two weeks at the end of August annually. **Open Tuesday through Sunday for breakfast and lunch. Closed Monday. Cafeteria, macrobiotic/vegan options, smoothies, take-out, catering, no credit cards, $$.**

PEMBROKE PINES

•Indian South Cuisine

7855 Pines Blvd., Pembroke Pines, FL 33024   **(954) 322-8353**

Vegetarian/Indian. This authentic South Indian restaurant offers vegetable dishes, Indian pancakes, rice specialties, and more. **Open daily for lunch and dinner. Full service, vegan options, fresh juices, smoothies, take-out, VISA/MC/AMEX/DISC, $$.**

Restaurant codes: ✪ Reviewers' Choice   • Vegetarian Restaurant   •• Vegan Restaurant
Restaurant prices: **$** less than $6   **$$** $6-$12   **$$$** more than $12
Credit Cards Accepted: VISA - VISA   MC - MasterCard   AMEX - American Express
DISC - Discover   DC - Diner's Club

PENSACOLA

(For restaurant listings in the surrounding areas, see Destin.)

Ever'man Natural Foods
315 W. Garden St., Pensacola, FL 32501   **(850) 438-0402**
Natural foods deli. Open since 1973, this cooperative offers vegetarian options in its deli. Open Monday through Saturday. Closed Sunday. Take-out, vegan options, $.

Hip Pocket Deli
4130 Barrancas Ave., Pensacola, FL 32507   **(904) 455-9321**
Deli. Try any of their vegetarian subs, sandwiches, or pitas, as well as their vegetarian calzone made with broccoli, cauliflower, and various cheeses. **Open Monday through Saturday for breakfast and lunch. Closed Sunday. Take-out, catering, $.**

SARASOTA

Bangkok Restaurant
4791 Swift Rd., Sarasota, FL 34231   **(941) 922-0703**
Thai. Great care is taken in the selection of over 30 native herbs and spices in order to present the rich cultural atmosphere of Thailand. Vegetarian entrées include Red or Green Curry Vegetables, Pad Puck (stir-fried vegetables with fresh napa and savory cabbage), and Garlic Tofu. Dessert items include Honey Bananas and Thai Custard. **Open Monday through Friday for lunch and dinner. Open Saturday and Sunday for dinner only. Full service, vegan options, reservations recommended, non-smoking, VISA/MC, $$.**

Fandango
Siesta Key, 1266 Old Stickney Point Rd., Sarasota, FL 34242   **(941) 346-1711**
International. Fandango has it all, from Middle Eastern to Caribbean to Indian. Try the Thai Rice with Tofu, the Black Bean Hummus, or the award-winning vegetarian chili. **Open daily for lunch and dinner. Limited service, vegan options, wine/beer/alcohol, non-alcoholic beer, VISA/MC, $-$$$.**

Lonni's Sandwiches, Etc.
1535 Main St., Sarasota, FL 34236   **(941) 363-9222**
Natural foods. See description under Clearwater, FL.

ST. AUGUSTINE

The Manatee Café
525 State Rd. 16, #106, St. Augustine, FL 32084   **(904) 826-0210**
Natural foods. "Manatee" says it all with part of the restaurant's profits being donated to efforts to save the manatees. This café uses organic ingredients when available. Try their tofu Reuben sandwich, Middle Eastern dishes, veggie burgers, stir-fry, soups, salads, and more. **Open Tuesday through Sunday for breakfast and lunch. Open Thursday through Saturday for dinner. Closed Monday. Full service, vegan options, take-out, fresh juices, espresso/cappuccino, VISA/MC/DISC, $$.** www.manateecafe.com

A New Dawn
110 Anastasia Blvd., St. Augustine, FL 32084   **(904) 824-1337**
Juice bar. This juice bar has a mostly vegetarian menu. Enjoy an eggless egg salad sandwich with fresh carrot juice made to order. **Open daily for lunch. Limited service, take-out, fresh juices, $.**

ST. PETERSBURG

Ajanta Indian Cuisine
5005 34th St. N., St. Petersburg, FL 33714   **(727) 525-6581**
Indian. Feast on a wide array of traditional Indian options at Ajanta. The Tampa Bay Vegetarians voted this establishment its Restaurant of the Year for 2002. **Open daily for lunch and dinner. Full service, vegan options, beer, VISA/MC/AMEX/DISC, $$-$$$.**

Ben Thanh Restaurant
2880 34th St. N., St. Petersburg, FL 33713   **(727) 522-6623**
Vietnamese. More than 15 vegetarian options can be found at this restaurant, including a Vietnamese Crepe stuffed with bean sprouts and bean curd; Asparagus Soup with Rice; Curry Bean Curd; Rice Vermicelli with Tofu; and Spring Rolls. **Open Monday, Tuesday, Thursday, and Friday for lunch and dinner. Open Saturday and Sunday for three meals. Closed Wednesday. Full service, VISA/MC/AMEX, $.**

Evos Healthy Burgers
2631 4th St. N., St. Petersburg, FL 33704   **(727) 571-3867**
American. This restaurant is the future of fast food (fast food with a conscience). The menu includes salads with organic field greens, wraps, soy burgers, veggie burgers, baked "airfries," and smoothies. **Open daily for lunch and dinner. Limited service, vegan options, smoothies, beer, non-smoking, VISA/MC/AMEX/DISC/DC, $. www.evos.com**

Lonni's Sandwiches, Etc.
133 1st St. N., St. Petersburg, FL 33701   **(727) 894-1944**
Natural foods. See description under Clearwater, FL.

Nature's Finest Foods
6651 Central Ave., St. Petersburg, FL 33707   **(727) 347-5682**
Natural foods. This supermarket-type establishment offers a large salad bar with organic produce, soups, bean stew, vegetable pizzas, sanwiches, and vegan lasagna. **Open daily. Limited service, macrobiotic/vegan options, fresh juices, smoothies, VISA/MC, $.**

Rollin' Oats Natural Foods Café
2842 9th St. N., St. Petersburg, FL 33705   **(727) 895-4910**
Natural foods café. This café specializes in vegetarian and vegan dishes, including vegan desserts. Their menu offers a wide range of salads, sandwiches, burgers, and entrées, such as Seitan Fajitas, Szechuan Smoked Tofu, Black Bean Burritos, pasta dishes, and much more. Their Sunday brunch also has an array of vegetarian and vegan options. **Open Monday through Saturday for three meals. Limited Sunday hours. Limited service, macrobiotic/vegan**

options, fresh juices, smoothies, soymilk, espresso, take-out, catering, VISA/MC/AMEX/DISC, $.

Saffron's

1700 Park St. N., St. Petersburg, FL 33710 **(727) 345-6400**

Caribbean. Located on the water, this café features live music daily and other entertainment. Vegetarian dishes include Jamaican Stewed Peas (vegetarian chili served over rice) and "garden steaks" (Take Away the Meat and Add the Heat!). Try the Creole or Jerked Vegetables for a real taste of the Caribbean. **Open daily for lunch and dinner. Sunday brunch. Full service, catering, VISA/MC/AMEX/DISC, $$.**

Thai-Am Restaurant

6040 4th St. N., St. Petersburg, FL 33703 **(727) 522-7813**

Thai. At Thai-Am, choose from a huge number of vegetarian dishes, including Spring Rolls, Tofu Coconut Milk Soup, Cashew Nut Salad, curry dishes, and much more. You can't go wrong, but be sure to avoid those dishes containing oyster sauce. **Open Monday through Saturday for lunch and dinner. Closed Sunday. Full service, vegan options, take-out, $-$$.**

STUART

Heavenly Harvest

Monterey Shopping Plaza
455 W. Monterey Rd., Stuart, FL 34994 **(561) 781-2220**

Natural foods. Prepared with organic ingredients, this restaurant offers vegetarian and vegan fare that is prepared seperately from the rest of the menu. Try the Oven "Fried" Rice topped with herb roasted tofu and scallions. **Open daily for lunch and dinner. Full service, vegan options, fresh juices, soymilk, smoothies, beer/wine, non-smoking, VISA/MC, $$-$$$.**

Nature's Way Café

25 SW Osceola St., Stuart, FL 34994 **(772) 220-7306**

Juice bar. Nature's Way offers fresh fruits, salads, and roll-up sandwiches in a historic downtown area. **Open Monday through Friday for breakfast through early dinner. Open Saturday for lunch through early dinner. Closed Sunday. Limited service, fresh juices, smoothies, $.**

TALLAHASSEE

• Higher Taste Vegetarian Café, Buffet, & Bakery

411 St. Francis St., Tallahassee, FL 32301 **(850) 894-4296**

Vegetarian. This Krishna establishment offers soups, organic salads, entrées, desserts, and more. Try their chickpea stew, barbequed haloumi, quiche, stromboli, calzones, or spanakopita. And save room for some of their heavenly baked goods, such as focaccia, banana bread, cinnamon rolls, or cakes. Organic produce is used when available. Outdoor dining is available. **Open Monday, Tuesday, and Thursday for lunch. Open Wednesday and Friday for lunch and dinner. Closed Saturday and Sunday. Buffet, vegan options, fresh juices, private parties, take-out, VISA/MC, $-$$. www.highertaste.us**

New Leaf Market and Café
1235 Apalachee Pkwy., Tallahassee, FL 32301   **(850) 942-2557**
Natural foods deli. Located in the Parkway Shopping Center, the deli counter at this natural foods market offers a wide variety of salads and sandwiches, including a rice salad, Szechuan noodles, fruit salad, and hummus sandwiches. **Open Monday through Saturday. Closed Sunday. Take-out, fresh juices, smoothies, catering, $.**

• Organic Living
123 E. 5th Ave., Tallahassee, FL 32311   **(850) 222-7171**
Vegetarian/natural foods. This completely certified organic restaurant offers a blend of American sandwiches with Korean fare. **Open Monday through Friday for lunch and dinner. Full service, vegan options, macrobiotic options, $-$$.**

TAMPA

(For restaurant listings in the surrounding areas, see Clearwater, Dunedin, Indian Rocks Beach, Largo, Palm Harbor, and St. Petersburg.)

Abby's Health & Nutrition
14374 N. Dale Mabry Hwy., Tampa, FL 33618   **(813) 265-4951**
Natural foods deli. This deli in a health foods store has both vegetarian and vegan options, including potato pancakes, many tofu items, and vegan cheesecake. **Open daily for lunch and dinner. Limited service, vegan/macrobiotic options, fresh juices, smoothies, soymilk, espresso, take-out, catering, VISA/MC/AMEX/DISC/DC, $-$$.**

Angithi
2047 E. Fowler Ave., Tampa, FL 33612   **(813) 979-4889**
Indian. From Alu Matar to Lahari Alu, Anghiti covers the bases for vegetarian meals. **Open Tuesday through Sunday for lunch and dinner. Closed on Monday. Full service, vegan options, fresh juices, VISA/MC/AMEX/DISC, $-$$.**

Evos Healthy Burgers
609 S. Howard St., Tampa, FL 33606   **(813) 258-3867**
157 Westmore Plaza, Tampa, FL 33609   **(813) 282-4982**
American. See description under St. Petersburg, FL.

Jasmine Thai
13248 N. Dale Mabry Hwy., Tampa, FL 33618   **(813) 968-1501**
1947 W. Lumsden Rd., Tampa, FL 33511   **(813) 662-3635**
Thai. Enjoy both vegetarian and macrobiotic options at this Thai restaurant. **Open daily for lunch and dinner. Full service, vegan/macrobiotic options, wine/beer/alcohol, non-alcoholic wine/beer, catering, VISA/MC/AMEX/DISC, $$.**

The Laughing Cat
1811 15th St. N., Tampa, FL 33605   **(813) 241-2998**
Italian. The Laughing Cat's menu includes freshly-made gnocchi, fettuccini, pappardelle. Pasta primavera, and portobello mushroom dishes. Though some of their pastas contain eggs,

the spaghetti, linguini, penne, and farfelle (bowtie) pastas are vegan. The fresh-baked breads is one of this restaurant's signatures. **Open Monday for lunch only. Open Tuesday through Friday for lunch and dinner. Open Saturday for dinner only. Closed Sunday. Full service, vegan options, espresso/capuccino, wine/beer, catering, VISA/MC/AMEX/DISC, $$$.**

Lonni's Sandwiches, Etc.
513 E. Jackson St., Tampa, FL 33602   **(813) 223-2333**
Natural foods. See description under Clearwater, FL.

The Natural Kitchen (The N.K. Café)
4100 W. Kennedy Blvd., Tampa, FL 33609   **(813) 874-2233**
Natural foods. Originally a vegetarian restaurant, The N.K. Café now offers chicken and fish. However, there is still a decent selection of vegetarian fare, including non-dairy vegetable lasagna, couscous with chunky vegetables, and many other vegetarian and vegan options. No chemicals, preservatives, or processed food are used. **Open Monday through Saturday for lunch and dinner. Closed Sunday. Full service, vegan options, fresh juices, smoothies, wine/beer, non-alcoholic wine/beer, take-out, catering, VISA/MC/AMEX/DISC, $$.**

Nature's Harvest Market and Deli
1021 N. MacDill Ave., Tampa, FL 33607   **(813) 873-7428**
Natural foods deli. This deli has a daily rotation of vegan entrées, an array of vegetarian entrées, and vegetarian side dishes, soups, and sandwiches. **Open daily for three meals. Limited service, vegan/macrobiotic options, fresh juices, smoothies, soymilk, espresso, take-out, catering, VISA/MC/AMEX/DISC, $-$$.**

Ovo Café
1907 E. 7th Ave., Tampa, FL 33605   **(813) 248-9849**
Bistro. Located in a historic building, this restaurant offers an artist's ambiance. They offer several vegetarian entrées, including Classic Perogies, and are more than willing to accommodate vegetarian and vegan diners. **Open Monday for lunch and dinner. Open Tuesday through Saturday for lunch through late evening service. Open Sunday for brunch. Full service, vegan options, reservations recommended, take-out, VISA/MC/AMEX/DISC/DC, $$-$$$.** www.ovocafe.com

Trang Viet Cuisine
1524 E. Fowler Ave., Tampa, FL 33612   **(813) 979-1464**
Vietnamese. The menu here has many unique vegetarian and vegan dishes, including vegan fish, vegan chicken, veggie drumsticks, and some delightful stir-fries. The owners grow many of their own herbs and some of the fruit used at the restaurant. **Open Monday through Saturday for lunch and dinner. Closed Sunday. Full service, vegan options, wine/beer/alcohol, non-alcoholic wine/beer, take-out, catering, VISA/MC/DISC/DC, $-$$.**

Viva La Frida Café y Galleria
5901 N. Florida Ave., Tampa, FL 33604   **(813) 231-9199**
Mexican. Named and designed to honor artist Frida Kahlo, this restaurant offers authentic Sonoran cuisine but is famous for its more creative items. Dishes include Frida Fried Green Tomatoes, Artichoke and Brie Enchiladas, Nopalito & Mango Quesadillas, and Salad

Burritos. Monday, Wednesday, and Thursday nights are "Starving Artist" (discount) nights. The restaurant also hosts live poetry readings, music, films, and art exhibits. **Open Wednesay through Monday for dinner. Closed Tuesday. Full service, vegan options, wine/beer, non-alcoholic wine/beer, special drinks, take-out, catering, VISA/MC/AMEX/DISC, $-$$$.** www.seminoleheights.com/storefronts/vlf/VivaHome.asp

WEST PALM BEACH

Thai Bay Restaurant
1900 Okeechobee Blvd., West Palm Beach, FL 33409   (561) 640-0131
Thai. Thai Bay offers traditional Thai food, such as panang curry, red curry, and pad Thai. They list tofu as a substitution for meat on the menu, but remember to tell them to leave off the fish sauce. **Open Monday through Saturday for lunch and dinner. Closed Sunday. Full service, take-out, VISA/MC/AMEX/DISC/DC, $$.**

Wild Oats Market
7735 S. Dixie Hwy., West Palm Beach , FL 33405   (561) 585-8800
Natural foods deli. Wild Oats Markets offer salads, sandwiches, and other ready-made vegetarian and vegan options. **Open daily. Limited service, $-$$.** www.wildoats.com

WINTER PARK

Chamberlin's Natural Foods
Winter Park Mall, 430 N. Orlando Ave., Winter Park, FL 32789   (407) 647-6661
Natural foods. See description under Altamonte Springs, FL.

Power House
111 E. Lyman Ave., Winter Park, FL 32789   (407) 645-3616
Natural foods. Enjoy sandwiches, salads, soup, vegetarian chili, and a wide variety of shakes and smoothies from Power House. **Open daily. Limited service, vegan options, $.**

Georgia

ATHENS

Bluebird Café

493 E. Clayton St., Athens, GA 30601-2708   **(706) 549-3663**

Natural foods. Vegetarian dishes with a Mexican flair are included on the Bluebird Café menu. Entrées such as burritos, quesadillas, and enchiladas as well as salads, quiches, sandwiches, and desserts are offered. **Open daily for breakfast and lunch. Full service, vegan options, take-out, no credit cards, $.**

•The Grit

199 Prince Ave., Athens, GA 30601   **(706) 543-6592**

Vegetarian. According to one visitor, The Grit is "part of the funky Athens scene." This establishment serves global dishes like Indian Samosas, Mexican Mondo Burritos, Lentil Burgers, and the Middle-E Platter with Mediterranean favorites hummus and falafel, as well as several other eclectic dishes. Be sure to try their vegan gravy! Enjoy eating in their artistic dining room, complete with tin ceiling and mosaic tile floor. **Open daily for lunch and dinner. Full service, vegan options, espresso/cappuccino, $$.**

ATLANTA

(For restaurant listings in the surrounding areas, see Chamblee, Decatur, Duluth, Marietta, Norcross, and Stone Mountain.)

Arden's Garden

985 Monroe Dr. NE, Atlanta, GA 30308   **(404) 817-6624**

1117 Euclid Ave., NE, Atlanta, GA 30307   **(404) 827-0424**

3757 Roswell Rd., Atlanta, GA 30342   **(404) 844-4477**

Juice bar. Wheatgrass, carrot-spinach, and frozen or soft smoothies are among a wide variety of fresh-made vegetable and fruit juice options. **Open daily. Counter service, non-smoking, take-out, catering, VISA/MC, $.** www.ardensgarden.com

Broadway Café

2168 Briarcliff Rd., Atlanta, GA 30329   **(404) 329-0888**

Kosher. Broadway Café is a Kosher restaurant featuring Broadway music and memorabilia. They serve various vegetarian and vegan ethnic cuisines, including Chinese, Italian, and Middle Eastern. Smoking allowed. **Open Sunday through Thursday for lunch and dinner. Open Friday for lunch. Closed Saturday. Full service, vegan options, fresh juices, espresso/ cappuccino, take-out, catering, VISA/MC/AMEX/DISC, $-$$.**

Burrito Art

1451 Oxford Rd. NE, Atlanta, GA 30307   **(404) 627-4433**

1950 Howell Mill Rd. NW, Atlanta, GA 30318   **(404) 425-0030**

Mexican. This Tex-Mex establishment features fresh, made-to-order vegetarian and vegan burritos, as well as salads and side dishes. They only use 100 percent vegetable oil. The Oxford Rd. location is near Emory Univeristy. **Oxford Rd. location: Open Monday through**

Saturday for dinner only. Howell Mill Rd. location: Open daily for lunch and dinner. Full service, vegan options, beer/wine, VISA/MC/AMEX/DISC, $-$$.

•Café Sunflower ✪

5975 Roswell Rd., #353, Atlanta, GA 30328   **(404) 256-1675**
2140 Peachtree Rd. NW, Atlanta, GA 30309   **(404) 352-8859**

Vegetarian. Elegant décor and beautifully presented dishes like Stuffed Mushrooms, Wild Mushroom Fettuccine, or Vegan Carrot Cake make dining a pleasure at this mostly vegan café. **Open Monday though Saturday for lunch and dinner. Closed Sunday. Full service, vegan options, Take-out, fresh juices, VISA/MC/AMEX/DISC, $-$$.**

•Cameli's Vegan/Vegetarian Restaurant

1263 Glenwood Ave. SE, Atlanta, GA 30060   **(404) 622-9926**

Vegetarian. This mostly vegan restaurant offers huge portions for small prices. They offer several soups, an excellent salad bar with vegan dressings, and a host of entrées. The grilled portabella mushrooms over mashed potatoes comes highly recommended. **Open daily for lunch and dinner. Full service, vegan options, beer/wine, VISA/MC, $.**

•Green Sprout Vegetarian Cuisine

1529 Piedmont Ave., Atlanta, GA 30324   **(404) 874-7373**

Vegetarian/Chinese. Green Sprout is yet another addition to great (and cheap!) vegetarian cuisine in Atlanta. Almost all of their dishes are vegan, and those with eggs can usually be made without them. Try their Seaweed Tofu Roll, Spicy Eggplant with Garlic Sauce, "Chicken" Curry, or divine Portabello Mushroom with Sweet Sesame Sauce. This restaurant is located in Clear Creek Mall across from Ansley Mall. **Open daily for lunch and dinner, Full service, vegan options, fresh juices, take-out, VISA/MC/AMEX, $-$$.**

•Govinda's

1287 S. Ponce de Leon Ave., NE, Atlanta, GA 30306   **(404) 377-8680**

Vegetarian. Govinda's offers an all-you-can-eat vegetarian buffet with all meals. **Open Monday through Saturday. Closed Sunday. Buffet, vegan options, take-out, $.**

•Little China

5750 Roswell Rd. NE, Atlanta, GA 30342   **(404) 252-8878**

Vegetarian/Chinese. Located at the Days Inn hotel off I-285, Sam's offers an extensive menu of vegetarian items. All dishes are prepared using gluten or soy protein as a substitute, and with delicacies such as Roast Duck, Braised Lamb Meat, and Prawn in Chile Sauce, Sam's is a dining experience not to be missed. **Open daily for lunch and dinner. Full service, vegan options, take-out, catering, VISA/MC/AMEX, $$.** www.samsvegetarianparadise.com

•Lush

913 Bernina Ave., Atlanta, GA 30307   **(404) 223-9292**

Vegetarian. Located in Inman Park, Lush is a modern, upscale restaurant with greenery as part of its décor. The menu features Jicama Citrus Salad with blueberry cumin vinaigrette, Potato, Corn, and Caramelized Vidalia Onion "Latke," Mock Lobster Ravioli, Oatmeal-Raisin Spring Rolls, and Banana Pound Cake. Their brunch often includes Whole Wheat Maple Praline Pancakes, Chipotle Scrambled Tofu Tostadas, and Sweet Potato Hash Browns.

The only thing that keeps this restaurant from being vegan is some animal products in its soy cheese. Also, join others for garlic foccacia bread, sliced fruit, and spicy fried chickpeas at their "after-work socials" on Wednesday and Fridays evenings. **Open Tuesday and Wednesday for dinner. Open Thursday and Friday for lunch and dinner. Open Saturday for dinner. Open Sunday for brunch. Closed Monday. Full service, vegan options, fresh juices, wine, special drinks, VISA/MC, $$-$$$.** www.lushcafe.com

Nuts 'N Berries
4274 Peachtree Rd. NE, Atlanta, GA 30319   (404) 237-6829
Natural foods. This whole-foods restaurant offers home-baked goods, sandwiches, salads, side dishes, chili, and soup. They also have a health foods store. **Open Monday through Saturday for lunch. Closed Sunday. Limited service, vegan options, non-smoking, fresh juices, take-out, VISA/MC, $.**

R Thomas Deluxe Grill
1812 Peachtree St. NW, Atlanta, GA 30309   (404) 881-0246
Natural foods. This café offers vegetarian tacos and burgers, as well as pasta dishes. **Open 24 hours. Full service, vegan/macrobiotic options, fresh juices, espresso/cappucino, VISA/MC/ AMEX/DISC/DC, $-$$.**

Ria's Bluebird Café
421 Memorial Dr. SE, Atlanta, GA 30312   (404) 521-3737
Café. Many of the menu items here have both meat and vegetarian options. Breakfast, which is served all day, may include pancakes, the Bionic Breakfast (with potatoes, veggies, and a spicy tofu sauce), country fried tempeh, biscuits and gravy, vegan sweet potao cakes, veggie grits, and a side of soysage. For lunch, have the soup of the day, a salad with or without grilled tempeh, a barbeque tofu sanwich, a tempeh Reuben, a Harvest sanwich with oven-roasted vegetables, or a spinach, grilled corn, and potato quesadilla. Outdoor seating available. **Open daily for breakfast and lunch. Full service, vegan options, fresh juices, espresso, VISA/MC, $-$$.**

Sevananda Co-op Natural Foods Market
467 Moreland Ave. NE, Atlanta, GA 30307   (404) 681-2831
Natural foods deli. Sevananda is the Southeast's largest consumer-owned cooperative. Its deli has a salad bar and a hot bar with creative, mostly vegan ethnic foods on weekdays and hosts a vegetarian brunch bar on Saturdays and Sundays. They also offer organic coffees and teas, and their bakery is the only 100 percent vegan one in Atlanta. **Open Monday through Friday for lunch and early dinner. Open Saturday and Sunday for brunch. Counter service, vegan options, non-smoking, take-out, VISA/MC/AMEX, $.** www.sevananda.com

Shipfeifer
1814 Peachtree St., Atlanta, GA 30309   (404) 875-1106
Mediterranean. Wraps, salads, platters, side dishes, Mediterranean pizza, and desserts are included on the Shipfeifer menu. All food is prepared fresh to order. Outdoor patio dining is also available. **Open Monday through Friday for lunch. Closed Saturday and Sunday. Full service, vegan options, non-smoking, wine/beer, take-out, VISA/MC/AMEX, $-$$.**

•• Soul Vegetarian
879 Ralph David Abernathy Blvd. SW, Atlanta, GA 30310   **(404) 752-5194**
652 N. Highland Ave., Atlanta, GA 30306   **(404) 875-0145**
Vegan. Soul has its own unique gluten creation called "kalebone" that is made into burgers, "furters," steaks, and salads. Soul's many other original dishes—soups, lentil burgers, Veggie Patties, Tofu Filet, Veggie Gyros, salads, and desserts—are sure to keep your taste buds happy. Children's dinner is also available. **Open daily for lunch and dinner. Highland Ave. location closed on Monday. Full service, fresh juices, take-out, catering, VISA/MC/AMEX, $. www. everlastinglife.net**

Teaspace
1133-B Euclid Ave. NE, Atlanta, GA 30307   **(404) 577-9793**
Eclectic. This mostly vegetarian restaurant serves a variety of dishes in a hip, speakeasy atmosphere. Try the Massaman Curry or the Wakame Salad. **Open daily for late lunch and dinner. Full service, vegan options, take-out, beer/wine/alcohol, VISA/MC/AMEX/DISC/DC, $-$$.**

• Veggieland
211 Pharr Rd. NE, Atlanta, GA 30305   **(404) 231-3111**
Vegetarian. This restaurant is nearly all vegan, except for the soy cheese. Its menu features delicious low-salt, low-calorie, sugar-free foods, including starters, salads, veggie burgers, and sandwiches. Filtered water is even used for the ice cubes! **Open Monday through Saturday for lunch and dinner. Closed Sunday. Full service, vegan options, non-smoking, fresh juices, take-out, VISA/MC/AMEX, $-$$.**

CHAMBLEE

•• Harmony Vegetarian Chinese Restaurant
4897 Buford Hwy., Ste. 109, Chamblee, GA 30341   **(770) 457-7288**
Vegan/Chinese. Enjoy vegetarian Chinese cuisine including taro dumplings, cold sesame noodles, spinach and bean curd soup, noodle platters, hot pot specials, and more. They also serve mock meats such as "chicken" and "fish." **Open Wednesday through Monday for lunch and dinner. Closed Tuesday. Full service, vegan options, non-smoking, fresh juices, take-out, VISA/MC/AMEX/DC, $$.**

COLUMBUS

•• Country Life Vegetarian Restaurant
1217 Eberhart Ave., Columbus, GA 31906   **(404) 323-9194**
Vegan. The fare here is "healthy foods that taste good," with a menu that changes daily. A buffet lunch and a soup and salad bar are available. They have a health food store as well, which is also open on Sundays. **Open Monday through Friday for lunch. Closed Saturday and Sunday. Limited service, non-smoking, take-out, VISA/MC/DISC, $.**

DECATUR

• Indian Delights
1707 Church St., Decatur, GA 30030   **(404) 296-2965**
Vegetarian/Indian. Enjoy a wide variety of vegetarian Indian dishes, including specialities from

the nation's south. **Open Tuesday through Sunday for lunch and dinner. Closed Monday. Limited service, vegan options, take-out, catering, $.**

• Madras Saravana Bhavan
2179 Lawrenceville Hwy., Decatur, GA 30033 **(404) 636-4400**

Vegetarian/Indian. Only 4 miles from Stone Mountain, this restaurant specializes in south Indian foods like masala dosas (crepes made with rice and lentils), but they also offer uthappams (Indian-style pancakes), special curries, rice dishes, and whole wheat breads. The menu is mostly vegan, except for some curry dishes and desserts made with dairy products. The restaurant can host meetings and is suitable for business entertaining. Reservations are required on weekends and recommended for larger groups. **Open daily for lunch and dinner. Full service, vegan options, fresh juices, beer/wine, special drinks, VISA/MC/AMEX/DISC/DC, $$.** www.madrassaravanabhavan.com

• Rainbow Natural Foods & Restaurant
2118 N. Decatur Rd., Decatur, GA 30033 **(404) 636-5553**

Natural foods. Sandwiches and soups are featured along with daily specials. Lunch is full service, but the self-serve salad and hot bars are open until 8 p.m. **Open Monday through Saturday for lunch. Closed Sunday. Limited service, vegan options, non-smoking, fresh juices, take-out, VISA/MC, $.**

Thai-1-On Café
1359 Clairmont Rd., Decatur, GA 30033 **(404) 728-0504**

Thai. This Thai restaurant is cozy with live plants and soft music. They can substitute tofu for meat in the dishes; don't forget to ask them to omit the fish sauce. **Open Tuesday through Sunday for lunch and dinner. Closed Monday. Full service, non-smoking, wine/beer, non-alcoholic beer, $$.**

• Udipi Café
1850 Lawrenceville Hwy., Decatur, GA 30033 **(404) 325-1933**

Vegetarian/Indian. The authentic South Indian cuisine here includes dosai, creamy baigan bartha, and dip poori. Also, try their daily lunch buffet. **Open daily for lunch and dinner. Full service, non-smoking, VISA/MC, $-$$.**

DULUTH

• Madurai Kitchen
3455 Peachtree Industrial Blvd., Ste. 840, Duluth, GA 30096 **(770) 622-3051**

Vegetarian/Indian. Madurai Kitchen serves North and South Indian home-cooking in a casual atmosphere. They also offer daily lunch specials and children's meals. This is the only full service vegetarian Indian restaurant in Gwinnett County. **Open daily for lunch and dinner. Full service, vegan options, take-out, VISA/MC/AMEX/DC, $$.**

Roly Poly-Rolled Sandwiches
3675 Satellite Blvd., Ste. 1000, Duluth, GA 30096 **(770) 623-3355**

American. All sandwiches rolled in a 12-inch flour tortilla; over a dozen are vegetarian. **Open Monday through Saturday. Closed Sunday. Limited service, non-smoking, $.**

MACON

• Eden'z Vegetarian Cuisine
617 Poplar St., Macon, GA 31201   **(478) 745-3336**

Vegetarian. The menu, which is vegan except for some honey, includes Fried Plantains, Roti, BBQ Steaks, Sesame Chicken, and vegan ice cream. Eden'Z is located downtown between 1st and 2nd St., half a block from City Hall. **Open Sunday for brunch. Open Monday through Thursday for lunch and early dinner. Open Friday for lunch. Closed Saturday. Full service, vegan options, soymilk, smoothies, take-out, delivery, catering, VISA/MC, $-$$.**

MARIETTA

• Vatica
1475 Terrel Mill Rd. SE, Ste. 105, Marietta, GA 30067   **(770) 955-3740**

Vegetarian/Indian. Vatica offers fresh daily Indian food at a very reasonable price. The Gujurati Thali, an all-you-can-eat lunch or dinner specialty, consists of one variety of Dahl (kathor, lentil) or Kadhi (curd preparation), two to three varieties of vegetables, salad, puri or roti, and chutney or pickles. Appetizers are also available. Vatica is an affordable way to enjoy a good, home-cooked meal. **Open daily for lunch and dinner. Full service, vegan options, take-out, catering, VISA/MC/AMEX, $$.** www.indiagourmet.com

NORCROSS

•• Fung's Vegetarian Chinese Restaurant
4975 Jimmy Carter Blvd., Norcross, GA 30393   **(770) 925-8322**

Vegan/Chinese. Located at Green's Corner Shopping Center, this restaurant's chef has more than 20 years experience preparing Chinese cuisine. The menu offers many mock "meats," as well as appetizers, soups, traditional entrées, rice, and noodle dishes. **Open Tuesday through Sunday for lunch and dinner. Closed Monday. Full service, soymilk, take-out, VISA/MC/AMEX, $-$$.**

SAVANNAH

Brighter Day Deli
1102 Bull St., Savannah, GA 31401   **(912) 236-4703**

Natural foods deli. This deli is located in Brighter Day Natural Foods store and offers fresh juices and vegetarian or macrobiotic options with international flavor. Enjoy a view of historic Forsyth Park while dining in a restored 1911 building with hardwood floors and a pleasant atmosphere. **Open Monday through Saturday for lunch. Closed Sunday. Limited service, vegan/macrobiotic options, fresh juices, take-out, VISA/MC/AMEX/DISC, $-$$.**

STONE MOUNTAIN

The Basket Bakery, Inc.
6655 Memorial Dr., Stone Mountain, GA 30083   **(770) 498-0329**

Café. You'll find a veggie burger, as well as a few other vegetarian options, at this European-style café. **Open Tuesday through Saturday for three meals. Open Sunday for brunch and dinner. Closed Monday. Full service, VISA/MC/AMEX, $$.**

Hawaii

AIEA

• Down To Earth Deli
98-131 Kaonohi St., Aiea, HI 96701   **(808) 488-1375**
Vegetarian/natural foods store deli. This deli offers a wide variety of made-to-order treats, including a Mock Chicken Salad Wrap, a Vegetarian Reuben, and a Fresh Mex Burrito. In addition, the deli also has a salad and hot food bar featuring organic ingredients whenever possible. **Open daily for three meals. Deli-style, vegan options, fresh juices, smoothies, soymilk, organic coffee, take-out, VISA/MC, $$.** www.downtoearth.org

HALEIWA

• Paradise Found Café
Celestial Natural Foods
66-443 Kamehameha Hwy., Haleiwa, HI 96712   **(808) 637-4540**
Vegetarian. Minutes from the beaches on the North Shore of Oahu, Paradise Found offers organic and locally grown produce whenever possible. The menu is mostly vegan and includes soy mayo and soy cheese. Try their soups, the BBQ tempeh calzone, tofu walnut sandwich, or the ginger teriyaki tempeh burger. **Open daily for lunch and early dinner. Full service, vegan/macrobiotic options, fresh juices, smoothies, soymilk, special drinks, take-out, $-$$.**

HANALEI

(For restaurant listings in the surrounding areas, see Kilauea.)

Post Cards Café
5-5075 Kuhio Hwy. # A, Hanalei, HI 96714   **(808) 826-1191**
Natural foods. Enjoy a wide variety of vegetarian dishes in a charming "old Hawaii" setting. Featured dishes include Marinated Grilled Italian Veggies, Thai Spring Rolls, Polenta Triangles, Nori Rolls, Taro Burgers (made from grated taro, tempeh, and whole grains), enchiladas, quesadillas, soups, salads, and much more. **Open daily for dinner only. Full service, vegan options, fresh juices, espresso, VISA/MC/AMEX, $$-$$$.**

HILO

Abundant Life Natural Foods & Café
292 Kamehameha Ave., Hilo, HI 96720   **(808) 935-7411**
Natural foods. This establishment offers a full deli with a hot table that is 97 percent vegetarian, except for one dish that contains fish and tuna sanwiches. Most of the ingredients

---

Restaurant codes: ✪ Reviewers' Choice   • Vegetarian Restaurant   •• Vegan Restaurant
Restaurant prices: **$** less than $6 **$$** $6-$12 **$$$** more than $12
Credit Cards Accepted: VISA - VISA   MC - MasterCard   AMEX - American Express
DISC - Discover   DC - Diner's Club

are organic, and they offer lots of vegan options, raw dishes, and desserts. **Open Monday through Saturday for three meals. Open Sunday for brunch through early dinner. Counter service, vegan options, fresh juices, take-out, VISA/MC/AMEX, $-$$.** www.abundantlife naturalfoods.com

Island Naturals Market & Deli
303 Makaala St., Hilo, HI 96720   **(808) 935-5533**
Natural foods deli. The Island Naturals Market & Deli offers local Hawaiian-style and inter-national dishes. They have sandwiches and hot and cold buffet-style foods. Specials change daily. **Open daily for three meals. Limited service, vegan/macrobiotic options, fresh juices, smoothies, wine/beer/alcohol, take-out, VISA/MC/AMEX/DISC, $.**

HONOLULU

(For restaurant listings in the surrounding areas, see Aiea.)

Chiang Mai Thai Restaurant
2239 S. King St., Honolulu, HI 96826   **(808) 941-1151**
Thai. Here you will find exotic northern Thai cuisine with a full vegetarian menu, and we mean full! The front of the menu says, "Vegetarians Welcome," and their excellent meatless selection reflects this. You'll find an impressive array of appetizers, salads, soups, noodle and rice dishes, and other tofu and vegetable entrées. **Open daily for lunch and dinner. Full service, vegan options, wine/beer, take out, VISA/MC/AMEX, $.**

• Down To Earth Deli
2525 S. King St., Honolulu, HI 96826   **(808) 947-7678**
Vegetarian/natural foods store deli. See description under Aiea, HI.

• Govinda's
51 Coalho Way, Honolulu, HI 96817   **(808) 595-3947**
Vegetarian. This highly affordable buffet, located on a lovely three-acre estate in the hills of Nuuano, was formerly called Gauranga's Vegetarian Dining Club. Govinda's features a full salad bar, homemade whole-grain bread, fresh baked cookies, Mung Dahl soup, brown and jasmine rice, and more. A different ethnic theme is featured for each night of service. **Open Monday through Saturday for lunch and dinner. Closed Sunday. Buffet, vegan options, fresh juices, take-out, VISA/MC, $.** www.iskcon.net/hawaii

Heidi's Bistro and Deli
1001 Bishop St., Honolulu, HI 96813   **(808) 536-5344**
900 Fort St. Mall, Honolulu, HI 96813   **(808) 536-4123**
California. Heidi's offers an extensive selection of vegetarian options, including pizza, salads, and sandwiches, such as zucchini melts, grilled eggplants, veggie panini grill, wraps, and veggie burgers. They also sell vegetarian party platters, such as a breakfast panini tray, bagel trays, a gourmet wraps tray, and a fresh fruit tray. **Open Monday through Friday for three meals. Full service, vegan options, reservations recommended, smoothies, espresso/cappuc-cino, wine/beer, non-alcoholic wine/beer, special drinks, take-out, delivery, catering, VISA/ MC/AMEX/DISC, $-$$.** www.heidiscatering.com

I Love Country Café

451 Piikoi St., Honolulu, HI 96814   (808) 596-8108
4211 Waialae Ave., Honolulu, HI 96816   (808) 735-6965

Hawaiian. This café features a number of vegetarian and vegan entrées, water-cooked chow mein, stir-fries, tofu burgers, Thai vegetable curry, and chili. **Open daily for lunch and dinner.** Limited service, vegan options, smoothies, catering, VISA/MC/AMEX/DISC, $$.

India Bazaar Madras

2320 S. King St., Honolulu, HI 96826   (808) 949-4840

Indian. Indian Bazaar features a menu of South Madras-style Indian cuisine that is nearly all vegetarian. The food is good yet inexpensive. **Open daily for lunch and dinner.** Cafeteria, BYOB, take-out, $.

Keo's In Waikiki

Ward Centre, 1200 Ala Moana Blvd., Honolulu, HI 96814   (808) 523-0014
1726 S. King St., Honolulu, HI 96826   (808) 941-6184

Thai. Gourmet Thai cuisine is served in a casually elegant, tropical garden setting. Vegetarian appetizers, salads, entrées, and curry dishes are available on the menu. Also, any item can be made vegetarian because all food is cooked to order. **Open nightly for dinner. Open Monday through Saturday for lunch.** Full service, vegan options, wine/beer/alcohol, take-out, VISA/MC/AMEX/DISC/DC, $$.

•• Legend Vegetarian

100 N. Beretania St. #109, Honolulu, HI 96817   (808) 532-8218

Vegan/Chinese. Formerly Buddhist Vegetarian Restaurant, the extensive menu at this restaurant includes vegetarian Dim Sum and other great Chinese dishes. It is located in the Chinese Cultural Plaza. **Open Thursday through Tuesday for lunch and dinner. Closed Wednesday.** Full service, take-out, catering, VISA/MC, $$.

Mekong Restaurant

1295 S. Beretania St., Honolulu, HI 96814   (808) 591-8841

Thai. The oldest Thai restaurant in Hawaii, Mekong includes vegetarian dishes on the menu. **Open daily for dinner. Open Monday through Friday for lunch.** Full service, non-smoking, BYOB, take-out, VISA/MC/AMEX/DISC/DC, $-$$.

New Ja Ja Restaurant

1210 Dillingham Blvd., #14, Honolulu, HI 96817   (808) 845-8886

Chinese. New Ja Ja specializes in Northern Chinese cuisine, including many spicy dishes. **Open daily for three meals.** Full service, reservations recommended, soymilk, take-out, VISA/MC, $$.

Payao Thai Cuisine

500 Ala Moana Blvd. # 1 E, Honolulu, HI 96813   (808) 521-3511

Thai. Located on restaurant row, Payao Thai has two pages on the menu of sumptuous vegetarian dishes to choose from, including Crispy Thai Vegetarian Noodle, Sa-The Tofu, and

Royal Tofu Soup. **Open Monday through Saturday for lunch and dinner. Open Sunday for dinner only. Full service, non-alcoholic and alcoholic wine/beer, VISA/MC/AMEX/DISC/ DC, $$.**

Pineland Chinese Restaurant
1236 Keeaumoku St., Honolulu, HI 96814   **(808) 955-2918**
Chinese. Pineland features a special vegetarian menu with dishes such as Hot and Sour Noodles in Soup, Fried Bean Curd with Szechuan Orange Flavor, and Eggplant with Spicy Hunan Garlic Sauce. **Open Monday through Saturday for dinner. Closed Sunday. Full service, vegan options, BYOB, take-out, $.**

Ruffage Natural Foods
2443 Kuhio Ave., Honolulu, HI 96815   **(808) 922-2042**
Natural foods. Ruffage offers a full sushi menu as well as other natural foods treats. Try the Vege Chili or an Avocado Burger. **Open Monday through Saturday for lunch and dinner. Closed Sunday. Full service, vegan options, fresh juices, smoothies, soymilk, take-out, VISA/MC, $-$$.**

Yen King Chinese Restaurant
Kahala Mall, 4211 Wailae Ave., Honolulu, HI 96816   **(808) 732-5505**
Chinese. Szechuan, Mandarin, and Shanghai cuisines are featured at Yen King. The back page of the Yen King menu lists 30 vegetarian dishes, including soups, assorted vegetable and noodle entrées, mock meats, and gluten dishes. MSG is not used in food preparation, but you may have to request that they not use chicken stock. **Open daily. Full service, vegan options, wine/beer/alcohol, take-out, VISA/MC/AMEX, $$.**

KAHULUI

•Down To Earth Deli
305 Dairy Rd., Kahului, HI 96732   **(808) 877-2661**
Vegetarian/natural foods store deli. See description under Aiea, HI.

KAILUA

•Down To Earth Deli
201 Hamakua Dr., Kailua, HI 96734   **(808) 262-3838**
Vegetarian/natural foods store deli. See description under Aiea, HI.

•Pali Gardens Restaurant
Castle Medical Center, 640 Ulukahiki St., Kailua, HI 96734   **(808) 263-5500**
Vegetarian. The Castle Medical Center, as part of the Seventh-day Adventist Hospital System, specializes in preparing low-fat vegetarian dishes. Winner of "Best Vegetarian Restaurant" award in Kailua in 1998, the Pali Gardens Restaurant offers a wide range of local and international foods. Meals are served in a cafeteria setting with a view of Windward Oahu's Koolau Mountains. **Open Monday through Friday for three meals. Open Saturday for lunch and dinner. Open Sunday for lunch only. Cafeteria, vegan options, fresh juices, smoothies, soymilk, non-smoking, cooking classes, $.**

Willow Tree Restaurant
25 Kaneohe Bay Dr., Kailua, HI 96734 **(808) 254-1139**
Korean. Willow Tree Restaurant serves a wide variety of Korean dishes and is willing to accommodate vegetarians by substituting tofu for meat in some of their dishes. Request no chicken or fish sauce, though. **Open daily for lunch and dinner. Full service, take-out,** VISA/MC, $$.

KAPAA

•• The Blossoming Lotus ✪
4504 Kukui St., Kapaa, HI 96746 **(808) 822-7678**
Vegan. The Blossoming Lotus offers transformational music and art, a great variety of international herbal teas, and a menu of "Vegan World Fusion Cuisine." Offerings includes Rainbow Spring Rolls, Green Papaya Salad, Cosmic Corn Bread, Incan Quinoa Salad, Indian Dahl Fusion, Tempeh Reubens, Wholly Hummus Wrap with tofu or breadfruit, Stuffed Bread Du Jour, and the Thousand Petal Lotus, which lets you select up to four items to create your own pupu platter. Some raw foods items are also available. **Open daily for lunch and dinner. Full service, fresh juices, soymilk, take-out, catering, VISA/MC/AMEX/DISC/ DC, $$.** www.blossominglotus.com

KIHEI

• Arya Bhavan
2508 W. Devon Ave., Kihei, HI 96753 **(773) 274-5800**
Vegetarian/Indian. This vegetarian restaurant specializes in Northern- and Southern-style Indian cuisine. Dishes include Tadka Dal (lentils cooked with ginger, garlic and spices), Tandoori Gobi (cauliflower marinated and cooked in a tandoori oven), Potato Batani Korma (fried dumplings of lentils in a gravy of poppy seeds, chilies, and garlic), and many rice specialities. Good buffet. **Open daily for lunch and dinner. Full service, vegan options, fresh juices, VISA/MC/AMEX/DISC, $$.**

Hawaiian Moons Natural Foods
2411 S. Kihei Rd., Kihei, HI 96753 **(808) 875-4356**
Natural foods. Located across from Kama'ole Beach, this deli has a salad bar and market. **Open daily for three meals. Cafeteria, fresh juices, espresso/cappuccino, smoothies, soymilk, alcoholic and non-alcoholic wine/beer, take-out, catering, VISA/MC/AMEX/DC, $$.**

Joy's Place
1993 S. Kihei Rd., Kihei, HI 96753 **(808) 879-9258**
Natural foods. Located in the Island Surf Building next to the Pacific Ocean. Dishes are prepared with organic and locally grown ingredients. Menu items include vegan vegetable soup, avocado salad roll, black bean salad wrap, and pesto wrap. **Open Monday for breakfast and lunch. Open Tuesday through Saturday for three meals. Closed Sunday. Limited service,** VISA/MC, $.

KILAUEA

Mango Mama's
4460 Hookui Rd., Kilauea, HI 96754   **(808) 828-1020**
Juice bar. Mango Mama's claim to have "the best smoothies on the Hawaiian Islands," as well as fresh carrot and pineapple juices. For breakfast they offer bagels with non-dairy "butter," and for lunch try the Teriyaki Tofu sandwich or the Veggie Burger with avocado. **Open daily for breakfast and lunch. Take-out, vegan options, $.**

LAHAINA

• Down To Earth Deli
193 Lahainaluna Rd., Lahaina, HI 96761   **(808) 667-2855**
Vegetarian/natural foods store deli. See description under Aiea, HI.

MAKAWAO

• Down To Earth Deli
1169 Makawao Ave., Makawao, HI 96768   **(808) 572-1488**
Vegetarian/natural foods store deli. See description under Aiea, HI.

MAUI

(For restaurant listings in the surrounding areas, see Kahului and Kihei.)

Cheeseburger In Paradise
811 Front St., Lahaina, Maui, HI 96761   **(808) 661-4855**
American. From the sound of its name, you would never expect Cheeseburger in Paradise to offer vegetarian food. However, it does list a tofu burger, a gardenburger, a Lahaina grilled cheese, and the Sort of Tuna Melt in its vegetarian section. This restaurant is located on the beach and offers live music during the evening. **Open daily for lunch and dinner. Full service, smoothies, wine/beer/alcohol, VISA/MC/AMEX, $$.**

Royal Thai Cuisine
1280 S. Kihei Rd., Kihei, Maui, HI 96753   **(808) 874-0813**
Thai. Although not a vegetarian restaurant, Royal Thai Cuisine offers more than 25 vegetarian entrées. A great selection for reasonable prices. **Open Monday through Friday for lunch and dinner. Closed Saturday and Sunday. Full service, take-out, VISA/MC/AMEX, $-$$.**

Thai Chef Restaurant
Lahaina Shopping Center
880 Front St., Lahaina, Maui, HI 83702 (808) 667-2814
Thai. Thirteen authentic Thai vegetarian entrées, including tofu, curry, and vegetable dishes, are offered in a relaxed, cozy atmosphere. The chef is willing to accommodate special diets and can prepare any of the regular dishes without meat. **Open daily. Full service, vegan options, take-out, fresh juices, non-alcoholic beer, take-out, VISA/MC/DC, $$.**

PAIA

• Fresh Mint
115 Baldwin Ave., Paia, HI 96779   **(808) 579-9144**

Vegetarian/Vietnamese. Fresh Mint offers a cool, comfortable place to sit and take in good vegetarian food. The menu includes the signature "Fresh Mint" salad with soy shrimp or soy crab and veggies tossed with pineapple sauce, bamboo soup with tofu and veggie ham, golden mock chicken curry, veggie beef with lemon grass, and the Vietnamese Burrito with Grilled (mock) Fish. **Open daily for lunch and dinner, Full service, vegan options, VISA/ MC, $-$$.**

Idaho

BOISE

Addie's
501 W. Main St., Boise, ID 83702   **(208) 388-1198**

American. This casual restaurant offers vegetarian options like salads, veggie burgers, and veggie sausage. They serve breakfast at all times. **Open daily for breakfast and lunch. Full service, take-out, VISA/MC/AMEX, $.**

• Kulture Klatsch
409 S. 8th St., Boise, ID 83702   **(208) 345-0452**

Vegetarian. The menu at Kulture Klatsch has it all. It marks with a "V" which meals are vegan and includes a "Not Milk" vegan section. Try the Ginger Tofu wrap or the Lotus Tofu Scramble with brown rice and bean sprouts. **Open daily for three meals. Full service, vegan options, fresh juices, soymilk, $-$$.**

Illinois

ARLINGTON HEIGHTS

• Chowpatti Vegetarian Restaurant
1035 S. Arlington Heights Rd., Arlington Heights, IL 60005   (847) 640-6162

Vegetarian. This family-owned vegetarian restaurant serves international fare—American, Italian, French, Mexican, and Middle Eastern dishes. Everything is homemade and prepared fresh. **Open Tuesday through Saturday for lunch and dinner. Open Sunday for dinner only. Closed Monday. Full service, take-out, catering, fresh juices, totally non-smoking, reservations recommended for large groups, VISA/MC/AMEX/DISC, $-$$.**

BATAVIA

Al's Café and Creamery
5 Webster St., Batavia, IL 60510   **(630) 406-8855**

Café. Al's Café and Creamery provides a charming ambience in which to sample many imaginative soups and sandwiches for vegetarians and non-vegetarians alike. The creamery features special malts and shakes, and a fountain menu that lets you create your own sundaes.

CHAMPAIGN

Basmati
302 S. 1st St., Champaign, IL 61820   **(217) 315-8877**
Indian. More than a dozen vegetarian options appear on Basmati's menu, including various vegetable curry dishes. **Open Monday through Saturday for lunch and dinner. Open Sunday for dinner only. Full service, take-out, $$.**

Fiesta Café
216 S. First St., Champaign, IL 61820   **(217) 352-5902**
Mexican. You will find many vegetarian options here. **Open daily for lunch and dinner. Full service, wine/beer/alcohol, take-out, VISA/MC/AMEX/DISC, $.**

CHICAGO

(For restaurant listings in the surrounding areas, see Evanston, Oak Park, Skokie, and Westmont.)

Addis Abeba
3521 N. Clark St., Chicago, IL 60657   **(312) 929-9383**
Ethiopian. Try the Kinche (European-style wheat pilaf seasoned with kibbeh), Gomen (spinach cooked in onions and cardamom), or one of the several other vegetarian entrées. **Open daily for dinner. Full service, vegan options, non-alcoholic beer, wine/beer/alcohol, VISA/MC/AMEX/DISC, $-$$.**

• Alice and Friends Vegetarian Café
5812 N. Broadway, Chicago, IL 60660   **(773) 275-8797**
Vegetarian. Alice and Friends serves light Asian fare that is mostly vegan; the only non-vegan items being those that have honey. All items made with honey are marked on the menu and can be changed upon request. Sample Korean and Japanese fare such as Bi Bim Bop, Don Ka Su, or Lemon Tofu. **Open Monday through Friday for three meals. Open Saturday for lunch and dinner. Closed Sunday. Full service, vegan options, take-out, fresh juices, smoothies, wine/beer, VISA/MC/AMEX, $$.**

•• Amitabul
6207 N. Milwaukee Ave., Chicago, IL 60646   **(773) 774-0276**
Vegan/Korean. When the Amitabul on Southport came under new ownership, the chefs from the old location moved to Milwaukee Ave. and opened this restaurant. Enjoy unique vegan Korean cuisine at this terrific restaurant. Portions are huge, and the food is creatively presented. Try Maki Rolls, Vegan Tofu Young, vegan egg rolls, grilled dumplings, soups, vegan pancakes made from various batters, noodle-based dishes, plus much more. **Open daily for lunch and dinner. Full service, macrobiotic/vegan options, fresh juices, wine, VISA/MC/AMEX, $-$$.**

Bukhara
2 E. Ontario St., Chicago, IL 60611   **(312) 943-0188**

Indian. Bukhara offers candlelight dinners and prepares its food in clay ovens. Vegetarian options include peppers stuffed with vegetables, nuts, and dried fruit; dahl; potatoes with a rich stuffing of raisins, cashews, green chiles, and spices; and various delicious Indian breads. Open daily for lunch and dinner. Full service, vegan options, wine/beer/alcohol, take-out, VISA/MC/AMEX, $$.

Café Selmarie
4729 N. Lincoln Ave., Chicago, IL 60625   **(773) 989-5595**

Café. Vegetarian options include vegetarian chili and soups. Open Tuesday through Sunday for three meals. Closed Monday. Full service, espresso/cappuccino, take-out, VISA/MC/AMEX, $$.

• The Chicago Diner ✪
3411 N. Halsted St., Chicago, IL 60657   **(773) 935-6696**

Vegetarian. The Chicago Diner, the hub for the animal rights movement in the Midwest, serves an eclectic assortment of international vegetarian fare without preservatives, processes, or artificial foods. The owners have traveled extensively and are dedicated to promoting healthy eating for the sake of humans, the planet, and animals. A breakfast menu and a kids' menu are also available, as is patio dining during the summer. Fresh organic produce is purchased whenever possible. Open daily. Full service, vegan options, fresh juices, non-alcoholic beer, organic wine/beer, take-out, VISA/MC/AMEX/DISC, $$. www.veggiediner.com

Club Lucky
1824 W. Wabanesia Ave., Chicago, IL 60622   **(773) 227-2300**

Italian. Start your meal with the Club Lucky Veggie Antipasti, then choose from such favorites as spicy homemade penne arrabiata and eggplant parmigiana. Open daily for lunch and dinner. Full service, take-out, espresso/cappuccino, non-alcoholic and alcoholic beer/wine/alcohol, VISA/MC/AMEX/DISC/DC, $$$.

• Earwax
1564 W. Milwaukee Ave., Chicago, IL 60622   **(773) 772-4019**

Vegetarian. Enjoy a funky but friendly atmosphere with an Eastern European circus motif. Breakfast items include granola and yogurt, oatmeal, and bagels. For lunch and dinner, sample various salads, hummus on pita bread, tempeh burgers, veggie burgers, veggie burritos, spinich pies, and falafel sandwiches. Daily specials are also offered. Open Monday through Thursday for lunch and dinner. Open Friday through Sunday for brunch and dinner. Full service, vegan options, espresso/cappuccino, non-alcoholic wine/beer, wine/beer/alcohol, VISA/MC, $-$$.

• Eat Your Hearts Out
1835 W. North Ave., Chicago, IL 60622   **(773) 235-6361**

Vegetarian. The food is just as fascinating as the atmosphere at this restaurant, decorated with chandeliers, red velvet, wrought iron chains, and a Liberace-style candelabra at a table that seats six to twelve. Tempting creations include Black Bean Hummus, Vegetarian Gumbo, and Thai Wild Rice Noodles with stir-fried vegetables and peanut sauce. Open Monday

through Friday for lunch and dinner. Open weekdays for brunch. Full service, espresso/
cappuccino, smoothies, VISA/MC/AMEX, $$$.

Feast
1616 N. Damen Ave., Chicago, IL 60622   **(773) 772-7100**
International. Feast considers itself a "neighborhood restaurant with a global beat." For dinner
try the mixed baby greens with grilled asparagus or the penne pasta with pine nuts and sun-
dried tomatoes. **Open daily for dinner. Open Saturday and Sunday for brunch. Full service,
vegan options, espresso/cappucino, smoothies, beer/wine/alcohol, VISA/MC, $$$.**

Foodlife
835 N. Michigan Ave., Chicago, IL 60611   **(312) 335-3663**
Natural foods. This unique restaurant is set up with 13 different kitchen areas, almost like
a food court, with names like "Mother Earth Grains" (which is mostly vegetarian), Asian,
"Mighty Nice," and "Miracle Juice Bar." Dishes found at these areas range from soy burgers
to portabello mushrooms to Tuscan veggies and much more. A very unique dining experience. **Open daily for three meals. Limited service, vegan options, fresh juices, espresso/
cappuccino, VISA/MC/AMEX, $$.**

Gaylord India Restaurant
678 N. Clark St., Chicago, IL 60610   **(312) 664-1700**
Indian. Indian food is freshly prepared using no canned or processed ingredients. **Open daily
for lunch and dinner. Full service, vegan options, wine/beer/alcohol, take-out, VISA/MC/
AMEX, $$.**

Gourmand Coffeehouse
728 S. Dearborn St., Chicago, IL 60605   **(312) 427-2610**
Coffeehouse. The menu at Gourmand has a decent amount of vegetarian options, such as
Mexican Red Beans and Rice, Spinach Lasagna, and Vegetable Burrito. **Open Monday
through Saturday for lunch and dinner. Closed Sunday. Limited service, vegan options,
soymilk, espresso/cappucino, smoothies, beer/wine/alcohol, Amex, $-$$.**

Green Zebra
1460 W. Chicago Ave., Chicago, IL 60622   **(312) 243-7100**
Natural foods. This hip yet intimate restaurant is almost entirely vegetarian, with a concen-
tration on raw foods and organics. The seasonal menu often includes Jerusalem artichoke
soup; curry-spiced eggplant potstickers with pickled cucumbers; an avocado panna cotta
made with tomato gelée, créme fraiche, and sweet corn chips; shiitake mushrooms rolled
in cabbage and potatoes; and Hawaiian heart of palm with kaffir lime and Thai basil chili.
Reservations recommended. **Open daily for dinner. Full service, vegan options, wine,
VISA/MC/AMEX, $$$.**

Heartland Café
7000 N. Glenwood, Chicago, IL 60626   **(773) 465-8005**
Natural foods. Open since 1976, this restaurant serves "good wholesome foods for the mind
and body" in a comfortable environment. Feast on appetizers, soups, salads, sandwiches,
burritos, quesadillas, pizza, and vegetarian specialties. There is late-night music and dancing

on winter weekends and outdoor dining during warm months. The café is accompanied by a general store that features holistic and political magazines, and merchandise. **Open daily for three meals. Full service, vegan options, fresh juices, smoothies, soymilk, cappuccino/espresso, wine/beer/alcohol, take-out, VISA/MC/AMEX, $$.** www.heartlandcafe.com

John's Place
1202 W. Webster Ave., Chicago, IL 60614   **(773) 525-6670**

American. Try the vegetarian chili, soba noodles, veggie burrito, or one of the other vegetarian options. **Open Tuesday through Sunday for lunch and dinner. Open Saturday and Sunday for brunch. Full service, fresh juices, espresso/cappuccino, VISA/MC/AMEX, $$.**

•• Karyn's Fresh Corner
1901 N. Halsted Ave., Chicago, IL 60614   **(312) 255-1590**

Vegan. This "living foods" restaurant has no oven but serves creative vegan dishes like Broccoli Soup, Sunny Sea Salad made with seaweed and pine nuts, Karyn's Cashew Supreme (formerly mock tuna), Raw Apple Pie, and scones made with a tofu base. **Open daily for three meals. Full service, smoothies, $-$$.**

Kopi, A Traveler's Café
5317 N. Clark St., Chicago, IL 60640   **(773) 989-5674**

Café. Decorated with clocks that show the time in different zones around the world and an area with pillow seating and low tables where customers must remove their shoes, the owners of this establishment aim to show customers many different world cultures in one café. While taking in all the sights, don't forget to try one of the international dishes on the mostly vegetarian menu. Also, the home of an international shop selling travel books, clothing, jewelry, and arts and crafts from around the world. **Open daily for three meals. Full service, vegan options, fresh juices, espresso/cappuccino, VISA/MC, $-$$.**

Mama Desta's Red Sea
3216 N. Clark St., Chicago, IL 60657   **(312) 935-7561**

Ethiopian. The restaurant is decidedly decorated to create an African ambiance, with crafts and paintings from Africa, plus bamboo-and-reed-covered walls. **Open daily for lunch and dinner. Full service, vegan options, wine/beer/alcohol, take-out, VISA/MC/AMEX, $$.**

• The Mother Earth Café & Organic Juice Bar
3111 N. Ashland Ave., Chicago, IL 60657   **(773) EAR-THLY**

Vegetarian. Part of Healing Earth Resources bookstore/giftstore, this vegetarian café features specialties like tempeh salad, a macro plate, veggie burgers, and a variety of juices and smoothies. **Open daily for lunch and dinner. Limited service, vegan options, fresh juices, smoothies, take-out, VISA/MC/AMEX, $-$$.**

• Mysore Woodlands
2548 W. Devon Ave., Chicago, IL 60659   **(773) 338-8160**

Vegetarian/Indian. Mysore Woodlands specializes in Southern Indian cuisine. Options include a variety of appetizers, soups, uthappam (Indian style pancakes), dosai (rice crepes filled with vegetables and legumes), curries, rice, bread, and more. **Open daily for lunch and dinner. Full service, vegan options, VISA/MC, $-$$.**

A Natural Harvest
7122 S. Jeffery Blvd., Chicago, IL 60649   **(773) 363-3939**
Natural foods. Soups, salads, sandwiches, and other entrées are prepared on-site daily. The
restaurant specializes in vegetable proteins; vegetarian burgers, steaklets, and hot dogs are
sold by the pound. **Open Monday through Saturday. Closed Sunday. Limited service, fresh
juices, take-out, VISA/MC/AMEX/DISC, $.**

Old Jerusalem
1411 N. Wells St., Chicago, IL 60610   **(312) 944-0459**
Middle Eastern. For over 20 years, Old Jerusalem has been serving Middle Eastern favorites
from falafel to hummus to baklava. There is a vegetarian section on the menu with appetizers
and entrées available. **Open daily lunch and dinner. Full service, take-out, fresh juices,
VISA/MC/AMEX/DC, $$.**

The Original Mitchell's Restaurant
101 W. North Ave., Chicago, IL 60610   **(312) 642-5246**
Natural foods. Mitchell's prides itself in its delicious breakfasts, known nationwide for such
foods as vegetarian sausage, non-dairy whole-wheat pancakes, giant homemade muffins,
and omelettes. Mitchell's has daily vegetarian lunch and dinner specials as well, including
Oatmeal Walnut Burgers and great chili. **Open daily for three meals. Full service, vegan
options, fresh juices, wine/beer, take-out, VISA/MC, $.**

• Pattie's Heart-Healthy
Inside Saks Fifth Ave.
700 N. Michigan Ave., 8th Fl. Food Court, Chicago, IL 60661   **(312) 751-7777**
Vegetarian. The menu at Pattie's includes breakfast items, sandwiches, soups, pizza, calzones,
specials, and sweets. It also lists grams of fat and calories for each item. **Open daily. Counter
service, vegan options, fresh juices, espresso/cappuccino, take-out, no credit cards, $.**

Pegasus Restaurant and Tavern
130 S. Halsted St., Chicago, IL 60661   **(312) 226-4666**
Greek. A local patron recommends Pegasus' excellent all-vegetable entrées and mentions that
the restaurant has more vegan selections than any other restaurant in "Greek town." **Open
daily for lunch and dinner. Full service, vegan options, $$.**

Pita-Ria
441 N. La Salle Dr., Chicago, IL 60610   **(312) 645-1310**
Middle Eastern. Pita Ria offers vegetarian combination plates with choices of falafel, hummus,
stuffed grape leaves, spinach pie, baba ghanouj, tabbouleh salad, and more. **Open Monday
through Friday for three meals. Open Saturday for lunch. Closed Sunday. Limited service,
reservations not needed, take-out, non-smoking, VISA/MC/AMEX/DISC, $$.**

Reza's Restaurant
432 W. Ontario St., Chicago, IL 60610   **(312) 664-4500**
Persian. There are more than 20 clearly listed vegetarian appetizers at Reza's, including
Vegetable Casserole, Roasted Zucchini in Tomato Sauce, and Eggplant Steak. Vegetarian
platters are also served, as well as six different veggie combination lunches. Reza's also offers

an elegant '20s style décor, outdoor seating when weather permits, and a seated bar. **Open daily for lunch and dinner. Full service, vegan options, catering, take-out, delivery, VISA/ MC/AMEX/DISC/DC, $$.**

Russian Tea Room
77 E. Adams St., Chicago, IL 60604   **(312) 360-0000**

Russian. This elegant, upscale Russian restaurant offers unmatched hospitality and a good selection of vegetarian and vegan options. Several traditional vegetarian appetizers and entrées are clearly marked on the menu, including dishes like potato pancakes, grilled portobello mushrooms, Baked Eggplant stuffed with sautéed vegetables, Mung Bean and Vegetable Stew, stuffed green bell peppers, and many others. **Open Monday through Friday for three meals. Open Saturday and Sunday for lunch and dinner. Full service, vegan options, espresso/cappuccino, wine/beer/alcohol, reservations recommended, VISA/MC/AMEX/DISC/DC, $$$.**

• Soul Vegetarian
205 E. 75th St., Chicago, IL 60619   **(773) 224-0104**

Vegetarian. Various ethnic dishes are featured at Soul Vegetarian, including African, Middle Eastern, and American fare. Examples include Vegetarian Ribs, Tofu Fish, Sunflower-Seed Burger, and Split Pea and Chickenless Noodle Soup. Except for the occasional use of honey, the dishes are vegan. **Open daily, reservations accepted. Full service, vegan options, fresh juices, take-out, VISA, $$.**

Star Of Siam
11 E. Illinois St., Chicago, IL 60611   **(312) 670-0100**

Thai. All dishes can be prepared without meat or with tofu or veggie substitutes. **Open daily for lunch and dinner. Full service, vegan options, wine/beer/alcohol, take-out, VISA/MC/ AMEX/DISC.**

• Udupi Palace
2543 W. Devon Ave., Chicago, IL 60659   **(773) 338-2152**

Vegetarian. This vegetarian restaurant features traditional southern Indian cuisine. They recommend the Masala Dosa as the "most popular item," but they also feature vegetarian appetizers, breads, soups curries, rice specialties, and entrées. **Open daily for lunch and dinner. Full service, vegan options, fresh juices, catering, take-out, VISA/MC/AMEX/DISC/DC, $$.**

•• Vegetarian Express Gourmet
3031 W. 111th St., Chicago, IL 60655   **(773) 238-2599**

Vegan. The chef at Vegetarian Express trained at Soul Vegetarian before opening his own location. Unlike Soul Vegetarian, Vegetarian Express Gourmet uses no honey in any of its dishes. Located in Chicago's South Side, this restaurant serves a wide variety of vegan soul food, such as the Jerk Tofu, Seitan Steak Sandwich, and a variety of raw salads and juices. **Open Tuesday through Sunday for lunch and dinner. Weekends are buffet service only. Limited service, take-out, catering, $$.**

• Victory's Banner
2100 W. Roscoe St., Chicago, IL 60618   **(773) 665-0227**

Vegetarian/American. This mostly ovo-lacto vegetarian restaurant offers some variations on standard American breakfast and lunch fare. **Open daily for breakfast and lunch. Full service, vegan options, take-out, $-$$.**

ELGIN

Al's Café & Creamery
43 Fountain Sq., Elgin, IL 60120   **(847) 742-1180**

Café. See description under Batavia, IL. This location is housed in a historic building. **Open Monday through Saturday for lunch and dinner. Closed Sunday. Full service, wine/beer, take-out, VISA/MC/AMEX, $$.**

Jalapeños
7 Clock Tower Plaza, Elgin, IL 60120   **(847) 468-9445**

Mexican. The authentic, fresh-cooked Mexican cuisine is mostly vegetarian with a limited vegan selection. **Open daily for lunch and dinner. Full service, vegan options, wine/beer/ alcohol, take-out, $$.**

EVANSTON

•Blind Faith Café ✪
525 Dempster St., Evanston, IL 60201   **(847) 328-6875**

Vegetarian. The Chicago area is fortunate to benefit from this fantastic restaurant. Service is excellent, and the food is always delicious. Vegans can enjoy several seitan dishes, including a terrific barbecue sandwich, noodle-based dishes with tofu, plus much more. Be sure to sample their vegan chocolate cake. **Open daily for three meals. Full service, macrobiotic/ vegan options, fresh juices, wine/beer, catering, take-out, VISA/MC/AMEX, $$.**

Dave's Italian Kitchen
1635 Chicago Ave., Evanston, IL 60201   **(847) 864-6000**

Italian. Dave's serves homemade pasta and bread, salad, sandwiches, pizza, calzones, and Italian specialties. **Open daily. Full service, vegan options, wine/beer, take-out, no credit cards, $-$$.**

MOLINE

Le Mekong Restaurant
1606 Fifth Ave., Moline, IL 61265   **(309) 797-3709**

Asian. Traditional curry dishes, tofu, and mock meats are featured in the vegetarian menu section. **Open daily. Full service, vegan options, wine/beer/alcohol, take-out, VISA/MC/ AMEX, $$.**

NORMAL

•Coffee World Coffeehouse
114 E. Beaufort St., Normal, IL 61761   **(309) 452-6774**

Vegetarian. Everyone in the community enjoys this coffeehouse, known as "a meeting place off the Illinois State University campus." Enjoy one of the many coffee blends and a creative vegetarian meal of charbroiled tofu, falafel pita, or one of the many other vegetarian dishes on the menu. **Open daily for three meals. Limited service, vegan options, espresso/cappuccino, VISA/MC, $.**

OAK PARK

Khyberpass
1031 Lake St., Oak Park, IL 60301 (708) 445-9032
Indian. Enjoy classical Indian music as you dine on a wide variety of dishes, including spicy vegetable dishes, garbanzo beans and potatoes, vegetable rice dishes, and more. **Open daily for lunch and dinner. Full service, vegan options, take-out, wine/beer, VISA/MC/AMEX, $$.**

PEORIA

(For restaurant listings in the surrounding areas, see Peoria Heights.)

• One World Coffee and Cargo
1245 W. Main St., Peoria, IL 61606 (309) 672-1522
Vegetarian/coffeehouse. This restaurant's eclectic menu has vegetarian dishes marked with the symbol of the one Earth and vegan dishes with two. Enjoy music from a live band, poetry, or theater—depending on when you're there—and be sure to check out the international gift shop. **Open daily for three meals. Full service, vegan options, espresso/cappuccino, take-out, VISA/MC/DISC/DC.** www.oneworld-cafe.com

PEORIA HEIGHTS

Cyd's Sendsationals
4607 N. Prospect Rd., Peoria Heights, IL 61614 (309) 685-1100
Take-out only. A quick stop and you can enjoy gourmet vegetarian meals including veggie sandwiches and veggie lasagna. **Open Monday through Saturday for lunch and dinner. Closed Sunday. Take-out.**

PRINCETON

Jaya Juice Bar
509 S. Main St., Princeton, IL 61356 (815) 875-1751
Juice bar. Experience the goodness of fruit in wild combinations, the tastiness of vegetables blended as one, as well as a few delicious vegetarian sandwiches and wraps. **Open Monday through Saturday for lunch. Closed Sunday. Limited service, vegan options, $.**

ROCKFORD

Mary's Market
4431 E. State St., Rockford, IL 61108 (815) 397-7291
American. Enjoy several vegetarian dishes at this café, including raisin/walnut French toast for breakfast and salads, roasted vegetable focaccia, veggie burgers, grilled vegetables, pasta dishes, roasted portobello mushrooms, and more. **Open daily for three meals. Full service, vegan options, VISA/MC/AMEX/DISC, $-$$.**

SKOKIE

Slice of Life Bistro
4120 W. Dempster St., Skokie, IL 60076   **(847) 674-2021**
Kosher/natural foods. Slice of Life is an Italian/dairy kosher restaurant that serves fish and vegetarian foods. An eclectic menu lists a wide variety of appetizers, salads, soups, pasta, sandwiches, and vegetarian entrées. A children's section is on the menu. Monday is Mexican night and features several vegetarian entrées. **Open daily for lunch and dinner. Full service, fresh juices, espresso/cappuccino, wine/beer/alcohol, take-out, $$.**

SPRINGFIELD

Holy Land Diner
518 E. Adams St., Springfield, IL 62701   **(217) 544-5786**
Middle Eastern. Enjoy Greek and Lebanese food as you listen to Lebanese music. Try spinach pies, stuffed grape leaves, Middle Eastern salads, hummus, baba ghanouj, falafel, vegetarian shish kebabs, and more. **Open Monday through Saturday for lunch and dinner. Closed Sunday. Full service, vegan options, catering, take-out, fresh juices, non-alcoholic wine/ beer, VISA/MC, $$.**

URBANA

•• Red Herring Vegetarian Restaurant
1209 W. Oregon St., Urbana, IL 61801   **(217) 367-2340**
Vegan. The only vegetarian restaurant in Urbana is a non-profit educational food service. All foods are made from scratch, and organic ingredients are used when possible. The menu features international dishes and homemade baked goods. **Open Monday through Thursday for lunch. Open Friday for lunch and dinner. Closed Saturday and Sunday. Cafeteria, take-out, VISA/MC/AMEX, $.**

Strawberry Fields
306 W. Springfield, Urbana, IL 61801   **(217) 328-1655**
Natural foods store. This natural foods store has a café, deli, bakery, and an in-house nutritionist. You can easily make a meal out of their vegetarian chili, soup, salad, sandwich, calzone, pizza, quiche, and other choices. **Open Monday through Saturday for three meals. Open Sunday for lunch through early dinner. Limited service, vegan options, smoothies, soymilk, espresso/cappuccino, special drinks, take-out, catering, VISA/MC, $$.** www.strawberry-fields.com

WEST DUNDEE

China Palace
840 W. Main St., West Dundee, IL 60118   **(847) 428-8888**
Chinese. The management here is willing to accommodate vegetarians and will substitute tofu for meat in any dish. **Open daily. Full service, vegan options, wine/beer/alcohol, take-out, VISA/MC/AMEX, $.**

WESTMONT

•Mysore Woodlands

6020 S. Cass Ave., Westmont, IL 60559   **(630) 769-9663**
Vegetarian/Indian. See description under Chicago, IL.

•Shree Vegetarian Restaurant

655 N. Cass Ave., Westmont, IL 60559   **(630) 655-1021**
Vegetarian/Indian. A varied and extensive menu of well-prepared Indian foods is served in a friendly atmosphere. Incense and Indian music enhance the dining experience. Open Thursday through Sunday. Reservations required Friday through Sunday. Full service, fresh juices, BYOB, take-out, AMEX, $.

Indiana

BLOOMINGTON

Encore Café

316 W. 6th St., Bloomington, IN 47404   **(812) 333-7312**
American/eclectic. Owned by a natural foods co-op in town, the Encore Café's menu changes daily and includes many vegetarian options in an Art Deco environment. It is located near Indiana University. Open daily for lunch through late dinner. Cafeteria, vegan options, espresso/cappuccino, wine/beer, take-out, VISA/MC/AMEX, $$.

Laughing Planet

322 E. Kirkwood, Bloomington, IN 47408   **(812) 323-2233**
Mexican. Located near Indiana University, Laughing Planet specializes in whole foods and internationally-themed burritos, such as Jamaican, Southwestern, Thai, and Tibetan. Options include baked tofu and soy cheese. Open daily for lunch and dinner. Limited service, vegan options, fresh juices, espresso/cappuccino, smoothies, soymilk, $.

CHESTERTON

Taste Of Thailand

425 Sand Creek Dr. N., Chesterton, IN 46304   **(219) 921-0092**
Thai. This restaurant's vegetarian options include Tofu Soup, Seaweed Soup with Tofu, salads, six types of curry, and noodle dishes. Or try something from "The Vegetarian Touch" section, such as Tofu Pad Thai, Vegetable or Tofu Fried Rice, Royale Tofu in yellow bean sauce, or the Vegetable Lovers (14 vegetables stir-fried and served over jasmine rice). Open Tuesday through Friday for lunch and dinner. Open Saturday for dinner. Open Sunday for lunch and dinner. Closed Monday. Full service, vegan options, smoothies, take-out, VISA/MC/AMEX/DISC/DC, $-$$.

(For restaurant listings in the surrounding areas, see Chesterton and Valparaiso.)

Twin Happiness Restaurant
1188 N. Main St., Crown Point, IN 46307   **(219) 663-4433**
Chinese. Twin Happiness offers a large variety of vegetable and tofu dishes. Corn oil is used for cooking, and the staff is willing to accommodate requests for low-salt or low-fat foods. **Open daily. Full service, wine/beer/alcohol, take-out, VISA/MC/AMEX/DISC/DC, $$.**

India Palace
4213 Lafayette Rd., Indianapolis, IN 46254   **(317) 298-0773**
Indian. Many vegetarian options, including appetizers, side dishes, and many breads, are joined by such entrées as Paneer and Brijani. **Open daily for lunch and dinner. Full service, wine/beer, take-out, VISA/MC/AMEX/DISC/DC, $$.**

Three Sisters Café
6360 Guilford Ave., Indianapolis, IN 46220   **(317) 257-5556**
Café. Three Sisters offers some great veggie treats. Try the house favorite, The Three Sisters Loaf, which is made with black beans and wild rice. **Open Tuesday through Sunday for lunch and dinner. Closed Monday. Limited service, vegan options, $-$$.**

• Udupi Café
4225 Lafayette Rd., Indianapolis, IN 46254   **(317) 299-2127**
Vegetarian/Indian. Udupi Café offers southern Indian vegetarian cuisine. **Open Tuesday through Thursday for lunch and dinner. Open Friday for lunch only. Open Saturday and Sunday for lunch and dinner. Closed Monday. Full service, reservations recommended, wine/beer/alcohol, take-out, catering, VISA/MC/AMEX/DISC/DC, $$.**

Billy Jack's Café & Grill
2904 Calumet Ave., Valparaiso, IN 46383   **(219) 477-3797**
Eclectic. Vegetarian options here include Grilled Portobello Mushroom appetizers, Parsley-Garlic Tortellini, Gourmet Vegetarian Pizza, Pesto Pizza, Black Pepper Linguine, Mushroom Ravioli, Vegetarian Stew, a Veggie Wrap, a Grilled Portobello Sandwich, and Fresh Fruit Sorbet. Ask the waitstaff if a particular dish can be made vegan. **Open daily for lunch and dinner. Full service, take-out, catering, VISA/MC/AMEX/DISC, $$.**

Restaurant codes: ✪ Reviewers' Choice   • Vegetarian Restaurant   • • Vegan Restaurant
Restaurant prices: **$** less than $6   **$$** $6-$12   **$$$** more than $12
Credit Cards Accepted: VISA - VISA   MC - MasterCard   AMEX - American Express
DISC - Discover   DC - Diner's Club

Iowa

AMES

Café Lovish
2512 Lincoln Way, Ames, IA 50010 **(515) 292-9900**
Natural foods. Café Lovish offers a wide selection of vegetarian dishes, many of which feature Mexican fare or other ethnic foods. The restaurant is located near Iowa State University. Open daily for lunch and dinner. Full service, $$.

The Pizza Kitchens
120 Hayward Ave., Ames, IA 50014 **(515) 292-1710**
Pizza. Among the gourmet pizza and Italian pasta dishes serverd here are two vegetarian pizzas and two pastas. Pizza Kitchens is located near Iowa State University. Open daily for lunch and dinner. Full service, espresso/cappuccino, take-out, $$.

DAVENPORT

The Greatest Grains On Earth
1600 Harrison St., Davenport, IA 52803 **(319) 323-7521**
Natural foods. Food, which can be ordered by the piece or by the pound, includes items such as pizza, enchiladas, burritos, spinach potato pies, sandwiches, soups, side dishes, and desserts. Open daily. Deli-style, vegan options, fresh juice, take-out, $.

DES MOINES

(For restaurant listings in the surrounding areas, see Urbandale.)

Á Đông Restaurant
1511 High St., Des Moines, IA 50309 **(515) 284-5632**
Vietnamese. This restaurant features a separate vegetarian menu that includes appetizers, egg and spring rolls, soups, noodles, and rice dishes. Interesting offerings include the Bo Kho Chay (tofu and vegetable stew over noodles), Com Tau Hu Xao Hanh (Mongolian tofu over rice), Com Tau Hu Don Chay (stuffed tofu with a sweet and sour topping), and the Banh Xeo Chay (tofu and vegetables in Vietnamese pancakes). Open Tuesday through Sunday for lunch and dinner. Closed Monday. Full service, vegan options, take-out, VISA/MC, $-$$$.

Campbell's Nutrition Center
4040 University Ave., Des Moines, IA 50311 **(515) 277-6351**
Health foods store deli. Campbell's features a variety of vegetarian sandwiches. Open Monday through Saturday. Closed Sunday. Deli-style, take-out, $.

Sheffield's
10201 University Ave., Des Moines, IA 50325 **(515) 224-6774**
Natural foods. Dine on a choice of vegetarian soups, sandwiches, and quesadillas. Open Monday through Saturday. Closed Sunday. Full service, vegan options, fresh juice, wine/beer, take-out, VISA/MC/AMEX, $.

A Taste Of Thailand
215 E. Walnut St., Des Moines, IA 50309   **(515) 282-0044**

Thai. The authentic Thai cuisine includes an extensive vegetarian menu section. Vegetable soups, spring rolls, Thai salad, and various vegetarian entrées make up the selection at this restaurant. **Open Monday through Saturday. Closed Sunday. Full service, vegan options, fresh juices, wine/beer, take-out, VISA/MC, $.**

FAIRFIELD

India Café
50 W. Burlington Ave., Fairfield, IA 52556   **(641) 472-1792**

Indian. The menu at India Café includes 16 vegetarian entrées, including their special Vegetarian Thali. **Open daily for lunch and dinner. Full service, vegan options, fresh juices, special drinks, reservations required, VISA/MC/DISC, $$.**

IOWA CITY

(For restaurant listings in the surrounding areas, see North Liberty.)

• Masala Indian Vegetarian Cuisine
9 S. Dubuque St., Iowa City, IA 52240   **(319) 338-6199**

Vegetarian/Indian. Vegetarian and vegan entrées with vegetables, lentils, and more are served at Masala. Also enjoy homemade tandoori Indian-style breads. **Open Monday through Friday for lunch and dinner. Open Saturday for brunch. Closed Sunday. Full service, vegan options, espresso/cappuccino, non-alcoholic wine/beer, wine/beer, take-out, catering, VISA/MC/DISC, $$.**

• The Red Avocado
521 E. Washington St. #3, Iowa City, IA 52240   **(319) 351-6088**

Vegetarian/natural foods. Located near the University of Iowa, The Red Avocado offers a wide variety of dishes. Approximately 99 percent of the ingredients used are certified organic. Good choices include the TLT, Emerald Stew and Rice, Vegetable & Tempeh Stir-Fry with Rice, and the Torpedo Burrito. The Red Avocado also displays artwork by local artists and offers music on various weeknights. **Open Tuesday through Sunday for lunch and dinner. Closed Monday. Full service, macrobiotic/vegan options, take-out, fresh juices/smoothies, soymilk, $$.** www.theredavocado.com

NORTH LIBERTY

Great Midwestern Ice Cream Co.
3411 Forest Dr. NE, North Liberty, IA 52317   **(319) 337-7243**

Ice cream/sandwich shop. Some vegetarian soups, sandwiches, and pastries are offered at this ice cream shop. No smoking. **Open daily. Cafeteria, take-out, $.**

Restaurant codes: ✪ Reviewers' Choice   • Vegetarian Restaurant   • • Vegan Restaurant
Restaurant prices: **$** less than $6   **$$** $6-$12   **$$$** more than $12
Credit Cards Accepted: VISA - VISA   MC - MasterCard   AMEX - American Express
DISC - Discover   DC - Diner's Club

URBANDALE

New Delhi Palace

3225 NW 86th St., Urbandale, IA 50322 **(515) 278-2929**

Indian. New Delhi Palace features a special vegetarian menu section with eight entrées plus appetizers and soup. Fresh Indian breads are baked in clay ovens. **Open daily for lunch and dinner. Full service, vegan options, fresh juice, wine/beer, take-out, VISA/MC, $$.**

Kansas

KANSAS CITY

(For restaurant listings in the surrounding areas, see Mission, Overland Park, Prairie Village, Shawnee, and Shawnee Mission in Kansas, and Kansas City in Missouri.)

LAWRENCE

Community Mercantile Co-op

901 Mississippi St., Lawrence, KS 66044 **(785) 843-8544**

Deli. Vegetarian options include veggie burgers, a salad bar, organic fruits and vegetables, breads, and more. **Open Monday though Saturday. Closed Sunday. Full service, fresh juices, espresso/cappuccino, take-out, $-$$.**

Paradise Café

728 Massachusetts Ave., Lawrence, KS 66044 **(913) 842-5199**

Natural foods. "Good Real Food" is made from scratch and includes homemade breads and desserts, and entrées based on various ethnic dishes from Italy, India, and Mexico. Breakfast menu includes vegan options **Open daily for three meals. Full service, take-out, VISA/MC/ DISC, $$.**

Z-Teca

743 Massachusetts St., Lawrence, KS 66044 **(785) 865-0700**

Mexican. Z-Teca is a fast food chain that serves vegetarian-friendly options. Entrées are prepared fresh daily without lard or animal fats. Menu items include grilled vegetable tacos, salads, and vegetable or bean burritos. **Open daily. Limited service, take-out, $.**

MISSION

Z-Teca

6852 Johnson Dr., Mission, KS 66202 **(913) 831-1000**

Mexican. See description under Lawrence, KS.

OVERLAND PARK

Bombay Café

9036 Metcalf Ave., Overland Park, KS 66212 **(913) 341-0415**

Indian. Authentic Indian cuisine in a three-star restaurant. Menu items include Baingan

Bartha (eggplant baked on an open flame) and Vegetable Korma (combination of vegetables cooked with nuts, raisins, and fresh spices). **Open daily for lunch and dinner. Full service, VISA/MC/AMEX/DISC, $$.**

India Palace
9918 W. 87th St., Overland Park, KS 66212   **(913) 381-1680**
Indian. Feast on appetizers such as Aloo Takki (fried potato patties); main dishes such as Vegetarian Thali, Chana Masala (chick peas with tomatoes, onions, and spices), and Bhindi Masala (okra with onions, garlic, ginger, and spices); and a wide range of fresh-baked Indian breads. **Open daily for lunch and dinner. Full service, VISA/MC/AMEX/DISC, $$.**

Z-Teca
9220 Metcalf Ave., Overland Park, KS 66212   **(913) 648-2500**
Mexican. See description under Lawrence, KS.

PRAIRIE VILLAGE

Martha's Café
4515 W. 90th St., Prairie Village, KS 66207   **(913) 385-0354**
Ethiopian. Yellow split peas in a curry sauce, Red Lentil Purée with Berbere Sauce, and a few other vegetarian specialties are available. All of these dishes are prepared vegan. **Open Tuesday through Sunday for lunch and dinner. Closed Monday. Full service, vegan options, espresso/ cappuccino, catering, take-out, VISA/MC/AMEX, $.**

Sister's Café
5313 W. 94th Terr., Prairie Village, KS 66207   **(913) 381-9615**
Natural foods. Adjacent to a health foods store, this homey café features heart-healthy foods and daily specials. **Open Monday through Saturday. Closed Sunday. Limited service, fresh juices, take-out, VISA/MC/AMEX, $.**

SHAWNEE

Taste Of India
6010 Niemon Rd., Shawnee, KS 66203   **(913) 631-7876**
Indian. Taste of India is a one-of-a-kind restaurant in the Kansas City area. They offer a daily lunch buffet. **Open daily for lunch and dinner. Limited service, take-out, catering, reservations recommended, VISA/MC/AMEX/DISC, $$.**

SHAWNEE MISSION

Shawnee Mission Medical Center
9100 W. 74th St., Shawnee Mission, KS 66201   **(913) 676-2496**
Hospital cafeteria. Many vegetarian entrées and side dishes are available every day at this cafeteria. **Open daily. Cafeteria, take-out, $.**

WICHITA

Dinky Deli
2929 E. Central Ave., Wichita, KS 67214   **(316) 683-6078**
Natural foods. Try the "Tempeh-tation" or the totally non-dairy Tex-Mex Lasagna at this
deli located inside a natural foods store. **Open Monday through Friday for lunch. Closed
Saturday and Sunday. Full service, vegan options, fresh juices, take-out, VISA/MC, $.**

Kentucky

LEXINGTON

Alfalfa
557 S. Limestone, Lexington, KY 40508   **(606) 253-0014**
International. A casual atmosphere surrounds a menu that varies daily but stresses international and regional fare. Vegetarian entrées, salads, home-baked bread, and desserts are
always offered. **Open daily. Full service, vegan options, wine/beer, take-out, $-$$.**

Good Foods Market & Café
455-D Southland Dr., Lexington, KY 40503   **(859) 278-1813**
140 E. Main St., Inside The Library, Lexington, KY 40507   **(859) 422-6802**
Natural foods café. Good Foods Market Café offers a full-service coffee bar featuring organic
equal exchange coffee as well as espressos, chai, and Ghiradelli hot chocolate; full-service
smoothie and juice bars with made-to-order fresh juices, including carrot and wheat grass,
and fruit smoothies; and a self-serve salad bar with fresh, make-your-own green salads and
a variety of homemade cold salads. The self-service hot bar features vegan and vegetarian
soups, entrées, casseroles, and vegetables. Made-to-order sandwiches and fresh sushi (seafood
or vegetarian) are made daily. Also available are combinations boxes and miso soup. **Café is
open daily for lunch and dinner and Sunday for brunch. Cafeteria, vegan options, catering,
VISA/MC/AMEX/DISC, $$.** www.goodfoodscoop.com

LOUISVILLE

Grape Leaf
2217 Frankfort Ave., Louisville, KY 40206   **(502) 897-1774**
Middle Eastern. When dining at Grape Leaf, try dining on the patio surrounded by growing
grapes. Check out the Vegan Dolmas or Vegetarian Mousakah. **Open Tuesday through
Saturday for lunch and dinner. Closed Sunday and Monday. Full service, vegan options,
fresh juices, smoothies, VISA/MC/AMEX/DISC/DC, $$.**

• Rainbow Blossom Natural Foods & Deli
3608 Springhurst Blvd., Louisville, KY 40241   **(502) 339-5090**
3738 Lexington Rd., Louisville, KY 40207   **(502) 896-0189**
Vegetarian/deli. Rainbow Blossom is dedicated to providing an alternative to those who seek
healthy and convenient gourmet foods to go. Offering many vegan items, this vegetarian deli

is take-out only. The foods are made with high-quality products using organic ingredients when possible. Open Monday through Saturday for three meals. Open Sunday for lunch and dinner. Take-out, vegan options, fresh juices, VISA/MC, $.

Ramsi's Café

1293 Bardstown Rd., Louisville, KY 40204   **(502) 451-0700**

International. Ramsi's offers many vegetarian options, including roasted vegetable sandwiches, Capellini Marinara, and Vegetarian Lasagna, just to name a few. Open daily for lunch and dinner. Full service, vegan options, catering, beer/wine, VISA/MC/AMEX, $$.

Third Avenue Café

1164 S. Third St., Louisville, KY 40206   **(502) 585-CAFÉ**

American. This cute, cozy restaurant in Old Louisville serves meat, but its substantial vegan menu includes some of the best options in the area. Feast upon items such as the gigantic black bean burger, grilled portabella and veggie sandwich, hummus veggie delight, veggie club, veggie reuben with vegan thousand island dressing, BBQ tofu sandwich, and spinach salad with tofu. Afterward, you have your choice of wonderful vegan cheesecake, chocolate cappuccino cake, chocolate raspberry cake, cookies, and sometimes even homemade soy ice cream. Open Monday through Saturday for lunch and dinner. Closed Sunday. Full service, vegan options, soymilk, beer/wine, espresso/cappuccino, take-out, VISA/MC, $$.

Louisiana

NEW ORLEANS

The Apple Seed Shoppe, Inc.

336 Camp St., New Orleans, LA 70130   **(504) 529-3442**

Natural foods. The Apple Seed is located in downtown New Orleans, three blocks from the French Quarter. The restaurant offers a healthy lunchtime fare of salads, soups, and sandwiches and an atmosphere that's suitable for business entertaining. No reservations are required. Open Monday through Friday for lunch. Closed Saturday and Sunday. Limited service, vegan options, fresh juices, smoothies, BYOB, take-out, delivery, $$.

Back To The Garden

833 Howard Ave., New Orleans, LA 70113   **(504) 522-8792**

Natural foods. Dine on a veggie stir-fry over brown rice, bean chili, hearty salads, vegetarian tacos, and fruit smoothies at Back to the Garden, which is located near Lee Circle. Open Monday through Saturday for breakfast and lunch. Closed Sunday. Counter service, vegan options, fresh juices, smoothies, take-out, $.

Café Angeli

1141 Decatur St., New Orleans, LA 70116   **(504) 566-0077**

International. Café Angeli's menu includes omelettes; waffles; bagels; breakfast pizzas; hummus; baba ghanouj; spicy tomato spreads; green and pasta salads; portobello, roasted eggplant, and artichoke and spinach sandwiches; veggie pita rolls; and specialty pizzas. Open Monday through Thursday for lunch through late night. Open 24 hours on weekends. Full service, vegan options, espresso/cappuccino, special drinks, VISA/MC, $-$$. www.fourgreat restaurants.com/angeli

The Gumbo Shop
630 St. Peter St., New Orleans, LA 70115 **(800) 554-8626**

Creole/Cajun. In the vegetarian-unfriendly French Quarter, this restaurant was an oasis in the desert. It has several veggie entrées of Creole-Cajun origin, including gumbo z' herbs, vegetarian po-boys, and even a vegetarian special of the day. It was the only opportunity we found, as vegetarians, to try versions of these regional favorites. Attire is typically informal. **Open daily for lunch and dinner.** Full service, macrobiotic/vegan options, fresh juices, espresso/cappuccino, beer/wine, take-out, VISA/MC/AMEX/DISC/DC, $$. www.gumboshop.com

Juan's Flying Burrito
2018 Magazine St., New Orleans, LA 70130 **(504) 569-0000**

4724 S. Carrollton Ave., New Orleans, LA 70119 **(504) 486-9950**

Mexican. A Creole-Mex Taqueria, Juan's offers an "Eat Your Veggies" menu, including veggie quesadillas, tacos, and fajitas. You might also consider the Veggie Punk (pinto bean burrito with potatoes, jalapenos, cheese, salsa, rice, and lettuce), the Supergreen (a burrito with spinach, onions, peppers, broccoli, mushrooms, and sliced avocado in a spinach tortilla), Spinach Garlic Mushroom Enchiladas, and much more. **Open daily for lunch through late dinner.** Full service, vegan options, take-out, beer/wine/alcohol, VISA/MC/AMEX/DISC, $-$$.

Lebanon's Café
1506 S. Carrollton Ave., New Orleans, LA 70130 **(504) 862-6200**

Middle Eastern. The menu at Lebanon's Café includes hummus, bab ghanouj, vegetarian grape leaves, and several other Middle Eastern favorites, along with vegetarian entrées like the Falafel Plate, Vegetarian Plate, Vegetarian Cabbage Rolls, and more. **Open daily for lunch and dinner.** Full service, vegan options, take-out, catering, $-$$.

Nirvana Indian Cuisine
4308 Magazine St., New Orleans, LA 70116 **(504) 894-9797**

Indian. Nirvana offers a daily lunch buffet with plenty of vegetarian options. **Open daily for lunch and dinner.** Full service, vegan options, smoothies, espresso/cappuccino, beer/wine/alcohol, VISA/MC/AMEX/DISC, $-$$.

SHREVEPORT

Earthereal Restaurant & Bakery
3309 Line Ave., Shreveport, LA 71104 **(318) 865-8947**

Natural foods/macrobiotic. Salads, many unique sandwiches, tacos with soymeat or avocado, and daily specials are offered on the Earthereal menu. **Open Monday through Friday for lunch. Closed Saturday and Sunday.** Limited service, macrobiotic/vegan options, fresh juices, take-out, VISA/MC, $.

Healthy Planet

678 Egan St. (At Louisiana Ave.), Shreveport, LA 71101   (318) 425-0706

Natural foods/juice bar. This earthy natural foods store and juice bar is located in the old historic district of Shreveport. In addition to vegetable drinks, smoothies, and non-dairy shakes, they feature organic salads and a soup of the day. Try one of their sandwiches or burgers, such as their guacamole burger or the Mediterranean (whole wheat flatbread with marinated artichokes, black olives, and other veggies). Or have a Mexican dish, such as the Too Hip Burrito (with hummus, refried beans, salsa, and veggies) or the Navajo Nachos (organic blue chips, beans, peppers, purple onions, and non-dairy cheese). Outdoor dining available. Also, check out their organic gardening supplies and non-toxic household cleaning products. **Open Monday through Thursday for breakfast through early dinner. Open Friday for breakfast and lunch. Closed Saturday and Sunday.** Limited service, vegan options, fresh juices, smoothies, soymilk, take-out, cash only, $.

Maine

BAR HARBOR

(For restaurant listings in the surrounding areas, see Ellsworth.)

Café Bluefish

122 Cottage St., Bar Harbor, ME 04609   (207) 288-3696

International. Formerly Quiet Earth, Café Bluefish serves gourmet international cuisine in a charming European-style atmosphere. Vegetarian and non-dairy entrées are available. **Open daily for dinner in summer.** Full service, wine/beer/take-out, VISA/MC, $$.

•• Eden Vegetarian Café

78 West St., Bar Harbor, ME 04609   (207) 288-4422

Vegan café. Eden is an entirely vegan and organic café that features produce from local farms. They offer an eclectic mix of elegant dishes, including shepherd's pie, crimson lentil dahl with stewed lady fingers, chapati on roasted banana leaves, and eggplant Napolean with roasted kale and oven-dried tomatoes. **Open Monday through Saturday for dinner. Closed Sunday.** Full service, beer/wine, VISA/MC, $$$. www.barharborvegetarian.com

BELFAST

90 Main St.

90 Main St., Belfast, ME 04915   (207) 338-1106

Natural foods/macrobiotic. Quality natural foods using organic produce are served when in season. Daily specials and desserts, as well as black bean enchiladas, pasta dishes, salads, and vegetarian soups are featured. Outdoor dining is available in the summer. **Open daily for lunch and dinner.** Full service, vegan options, fresh juices, take-out, VISA/MC, $$.

Belfast Co-op Deli

123 High St., Belfast, ME 04915   (207) 338-2532

Natural foods. Belfast Co-op serves three vegetarian entrées daily, as well as salads and breads.

Open daily for breakfast and lunch. Limited service, fresh juices, take-out, $. www.belfast coop.com

Darby's

105 High St., Belfast, ME 04915   **(207) 338-2339**

Natural foods. Darby's has operated continuously since 1845 with the original walls, ceiling, and antique bar. Macrobiotic specials are offered daily. **Open daily. Full service, wine/beer/ alcohol, take-out, VISA/MC, $$.**

BETHEL

• Café Dicocoa

Main St., Bethel, ME 04217   **(207) 824-5282**

Vegetarian. Café DiCocoa is a self-proclaimed "funky and hip natural foods eatery." Located in an 1880s Victorian farmhouse, this café has a full bakery and holds cooking and baking classes. They are kid-friendly and do vegetarian catering. **Open year-round with seasonal hours. Full service, vegan options, fresh juices, smoothies, espresso/cappucino, soymilk, catering, VISA/MC/DISC/DC, $-$$.** www.cafedicocoa.com

BIDDEFORD

New Morning Natural Food Market and Café

230 Main St., Biddeford, ME 04005   **(207) 282-1434**

Natural foods. The café offers an ever-changing selection of creative entrées. A wide variety of sandwiches is available on sourdough bread from a local bakery. There are also homemade soups and chili. **Open Monday through Friday. Closed Saturday and Sunday. Limited service, vegan options, fresh juices, take-out, $.**

ELLSWORTH

The Riverside Café

151 Main St., Ellsworth, ME 04605   **(207) 667-7220**

American. Enjoy breakfast or lunch in a totally non-smoking environment at the Riverside Café. The restaurant offers a separate vegetarian menu, including The Illusive Tofu Scramble, The TLT, and 151 Main, a vegan French toast dish. **Open daily for breakfast and lunch. Full service, vegan options, counter service, fresh juices, espresso/cappuccino, soymilk, smoothies, take-out, $-$$.**

FREEPORT

The Corsican Restaurant

9 Mechanic St., Freeport, ME 04032   **(207) 865-9421**

Natural foods. Homemade vegetarian soups, unique whole-wheat pizza, calzones, and fresh baked breads are offered daily. Delicious pies and cakes are also available for dessert. No smoking is allowed. **Open daily for lunch and dinner. Full service, wine/beer, take-out, $$.**

PORTLAND

(For restaurant listings in the surrounding areas, see Biddeford and Freeport.)

Bagel Works, Inc.
15 Temple St., Portland, ME 04101   **(207) 879-2425**
Bagel deli. More than 16 varieties of bagels are offered with various topping options, including cream cheeses, Tofutti spreads, salads, and other vegetarian combinations. Only natural
ingredients without preservatives are used. Bagel Works is environmentally conscious and
socially active in its community. **Open daily. Counter service, vegan options, fresh juices,**
take-out, $.

Pepperclub
78 Middle St., Portland, ME 04101   **(207) 772-0531**
Regional. The Pepperclub menu is approximately 50 percent vegetarian and 50 percent fish.
There is always at least one vegan entrée offered daily. **Open daily for dinner. Full service,**
wine/beer, take-out, VISA/MC, $$.

Silly's
40 Washington Ave., Portland, ME 04102   **(207) 772-0360**
Natural foods. A small restaurant with a colorful atmosphere, Silly's has delicious food, with
a variety that includes hummus, falafel, sesame noodles, pizza, Jamaican beans and rice, and
sandwiches. The patio is open during the summer for dining. **Open daily for lunch and**
dinner. Full service, vegan options, $.

Victory Deli and Bake Shop
1 Monument Way, Portland, ME 04102   **(207) 772-7299**
Deli. This New York-style deli, café, and bakery emphasizes preparation of food items from
scratch. Veggie salads, sandwiches, falafel, and veggie burgers are offered. A whole-grain
bakery and organic vegetables are offered in the summer. **Open Monday through Friday for**
three meals. Open Saturday and Sunday for breakfast and lunch. Full service, fresh juices,
wine/beer, take-out, $.

Walter's Café
15 Exchange St., Portland, ME 04101   **(207) 871-9258**
American. Walter's Café offers regional cuisine that is prepared fresh daily in the exhibition-
style kitchen. Walter's offers friendly, courteous service in a casual but professional atmos-
phere. **Open daily for lunch and dinner. Full service, wine/beer, take-out,**
VISA/MC/AMEX, $$.

The Whole Grocer
127 Marginal Way, Portland, ME 04101   **(207) 774-7711**
Natural foods deli. Whole Grocer has two featured soups daily, plus freshly baked muffins,
sandwiches, and salads. Sometimes desserts are offered here. **Open daily. Counter service,**
vegan options, wine/beer, take-out, $.

SOUTH HARPSWELL

J. Hathaways

Rte. 123, South Harpswell, ME 04079   **(207) 833-5305**

American. Recommended by a local patron, this restaurant has a terrific vegetarian lasagna and a meatless chili topped with cornbread. The bean soup is also delicious. **Open Tuesday through Sunday for dinner. Closed Monday. Full service, vegan options, $$.**

VASSALBORO

• Elaine's Starlight Oasis

452 Taber Hill Rd., Vassalboro, ME 04989-3050   **(207) 288-3287**

Vegetarian. Elaine's is noted as being Mount Desert Island's only vegetarian restaurant. Try the Spiced Island Tofu, the "Beef" (seitan) Burgundy, or Eggplant Casserole, or Tempeh Parmesan, and wash it down with one of their many Maine microbrewed beers. **Open daily for dinner. Full service, vegan options, soymilk, beer/wine/alcohol, $$. www.starlightoasis.com**

WOOLWICH

Little Lad's Basket Bakery & Café

US Rt. 1, Woolwich, ME 04578   **(207) 442-0759**

Vegetarian/natural foods. This café features homemade soups, sandwiches, and dinners. The baked goods are vegan, except for a few that contain honey. **Open Monday through Friday for lunch in the summer. Call for winter hours. Limited service, vegan options, $.**

Maryland

ANNAPOLIS

India's Restaurant

257 West St., Annapolis, MD 21401   **(410) 263-7900**

Indian. Located in Annapolis' historic district and known for its relaxed, elegant fine dining, India's offers a menu of vegetarian specialties. Entrées include Malai Kofta (mixed vegetable balls cooked in onion and tomato sauce) and Bayngan Bhurta (whole eggplants cooked on skewers, chopped, then mixed with tomatoes, onions, and spices). Reservations recommended. **Open daily for lunch and dinner. Full service, beer/wine/alcohol, take-out, catering, VISA/MC/AMEX, $$$.**

Mexican Café

975 Bay Ridge Rd., Annapolis, MD 21403   **(410) 626-1520**

Mexican. The Mexican Café offers several vegetarian options, and their beans do not contain lard. **Open daily for lunch and dinner. Full service, vegan options, wine/beer, take-out, VISA/MC, $-$$.**

Potato Valley Café
47 State Cir., #100, Annapolis, MD 21401   **(410) 267-0902**
Café. This café offers gourmet stuffed potatoes, as well as sandwiches and salads. Their "South of the Valley" potato includes beans, papaya, corn, lime, cilantro, peppers, and garlic butter. Open Monday through Saturday for lunch and dinner. Closed Sunday. Limited service, vegan options, espresso/cappuccino, soy milk, $$.

Sun & Earth Foods
1933 West St., Annapolis, MD 21401   **(410) 266-6862**
Natural foods. This natural foods store features vegetarian sandwiches and organic produce. Open Monday through Saturday for breakfast through early dinner. Open Sunday for brunch. Take-out, vegan options, $.

BALTIMORE

(For restaurant listings in the surrounding areas, see Columbia, Ellicott City, Owings Mills, Pikesville, Randallstown, Timonium, and Towson.)

Akbar
823 N. Charles St., Baltimore, MD 21201   **(410) 539-0944**
Indian. Akbar features authentic Indian cuisine with a wide variety of vegetarian dishes. This restaurant has consistently given great service. Open daily for lunch and dinner. Full service, vegan options, wine/beer/alcohol, catering, take-out, VISA/MC/AMEX/DISC, $$-$$$.

Al Pacino Café
900 Cathedral St., Baltimore, MD 21201   **(410) 962-8859**
6080 Falls Rd., Baltimore, MD 21209   **(410) 377-3132**
Middle Eastern/pizza. With a New York City-type atmosphere, this bustling café has great-tasting Middle Eastern food, steaming-hot pita bread, and unique pizza combinations, such as pizza served with curry. All pizza is available without cheese or with soy cheese. Falls Road location is take-out only. Open daily for lunch and dinner. Full service, vegan options, take-out, VISA/MC, $$.

Ambassador Dining Room
3811 Canterbury Rd., Baltimore, MD 21210   **(410) 366-1484**
Indian. Located near the Johns Hopkins University Homewood campus, this Indian restaurant offers a formal environment with outdoor patio seating overlooking a garden (weather permitting). Enjoy a wide variety of vegetarian Indian dishes. The food tends to be spicy, so you may want to request that it be prepared mildly. Open daily for lunch and dinner. Full service, vegan options, wine/beer, catering, take-out, MC/AMEX, $$$.

Amer's Café
7624 Belair Rd., Baltimore, MD 21210   **(410) 668-5100**
Mediterranean. This fine Mediterranean café offers more than nine vegetarian varieties of gourmet pizza, salads, pastas, pitas, soups, and more. Also, check out the belly dancing every Friday night. Open daily for lunch and dinner. Full service, delivery, take-out, wheelchair access, VISA/MC/AMEX/DISC, $-$$$.

Brick Oven Pizza
800 S. Broadway, Baltimore, MD 21231 **(410) 563-1600**
Pizza. This pizza joint offers soy cheese upon request, as well as whole wheat crusts. Open daily for lunch and late dinner, Full service, take-out, $$.

Bombay Garden Indian Restaurant
5511 York Rd., Baltimore, MD 21212 **(410) 323-8440**
Indian. Bombay Garden features formal dining with Indian instrumental music in the background. The restaurant offers a nice vegetarian variety on the menu. Open Monday through Saturday for lunch and dinner. Open Sunday for dinner only. Full service, vegan options, wine/beer/alcohol, take-out, VISA/MC/AMEX/DISC, $$.

Café Bombay
114 E. Lombard St., Baltimore, MD 21202 **(410) 539-2233**
Indian. This cozy Indian restaurant offers Indian breads and many vegetarian entrées, including Vegetable Kofta, Okra and Onions, Eggplant Stir-Fry, and a Grilled Vegetable Kebab. Dishes are prepared with vegetable or olive oil. Open daily for lunch and dinner. Full service, vegan options, wine/beer/alcohol, catering, take-out, VISA/MC/AMEX/DISC/DC, $$.

Dalesio's Restaurant
829 Eastern Ave., Baltimore, MD 21202 **(410) 539-1965**
Italian. This restaurant is located in Little Italy and offers two vegan dishes and many vegetarian options. Open daily for dinner. Full service, $$$.

The Desert Café
1605 Sulgrave Ave., Baltimore, MD 21209 **(410) 367-5808**
Middle Eastern. An oasis in a sea of pit beef, the Desert Café offers light Middle Eastern fare in the Mt. Washington area of Baltimore. Patrons should be delighted with the offerings of zaater bread, mujaddarah, and falafel. Open Tuesday through Saturday for lunch and dinner. Open late on Friday and Saturday. Closed Sunday and Monday. Full service, vegan options, soymilk, catering, VISA/MC/AMEX, $$.

Ding How
631-637 S. Broadway, Baltimore, MD 21231 **(410) 327-8888**
Chinese. This Fell's Point Chinese restaurant offers many vegetarian items, including appetizers, soups, tofu, and vegetable entrées. Open daily for lunch and dinner. Full service, vegan options, wine/beer/alcohol, take-out, VISA/MC/AMEX/DISC/DC, $-$$.

Donna's Coffee Bar
2 W. Madison St., Baltimore, MD 21201 **(410) 385-0180**
University Of Maryland Hospital
    22 S. Greene St., Baltimore, MD 21201 **(410) 328-1962**
The Gallery, 200 E. Pratt St., Baltimore, MD 21202 **(410) 752-9040**
3101 St. Paul St., Baltimore, MD 21218 **(410) 889-3410**
Coffeehouse. One of Baltimore's staples, this restaurant serves a wide variety of options,

including a roasted vegetable sandwich, portobello mushroom sandwich, and penne with marinara. All dishes can be made without cheese upon request. **Open daily for lunch and dinner. Full service, espresso/cappuccino, take-out, catering, VISA/MC/AMEX/DC, $$.**

Egyptian Pizza
542 E. Belvedere Ave., Baltimore, MD 21212   **(410) 323-7060**
811 S. Broadway, Baltimore, MD 21231   **(410) 327-0005**
Middle Eastern/pizza. This pizzeria offers great-tasting Middle Eastern food, steaming-hot pita bread, and unique pizza combinations, such as pizza served with curry. All pizza is available without cheese or with soy cheese. **Open daily for lunch and dinner. Full service, vegan options, take-out, VISA/MC, $$.** www.egyptianpizza.com

The Helmand
806 N. Charles St., Baltimore, MD 21201   **(410) 752-0311**
Afghan. This restaurant has many vegetarian dishes on its menu, including Shornakhod (a potato, chickpea, and scallions salad with cilantro vinaigrette dressing), Dolma Murch (stuffed bell peppers), Aushak (leek ravioli), and Feereny (egg-free Afghan pudding). It is located 8 blocks north of the Inner Harbor and within two blocks of the Walters Art Gallery, the Peabody Conservatory, and the Washington Monument. **Open Tuesday through Sunday for dinner. Closed Monday. Full service, vegan options, take-out, catering, VISA/MC/AMEX/DISC, $-$$.** www.helmand.com

Indian Delight Restaurant
622 Frederick Rd., Baltimore, MD 21228   **(410) 744-4422**
Indian. Vegetable Samosa, Vegetable Korma, and curries are served, as well as many other vegetarian options. **Open daily for lunch and dinner. Full service, vegan options, fresh juices, catering, take-out, VISA/MC/AMEX/DISC/DC, $$.**

• Liquid Earth
1626 Aliceanna St., Baltimore, MD 21231   **(410) 276-7859**
Vegetarian. This quaint coffee and juice bar has a vegetarian menu with daily specials, including hearty soups, salads, and whole-grain breads. Sandwiches include a portobello mushroom, a veggie Reuben, a veggie BLT, and "The Picnic" with apples, pears, walnuts, caramelized onions, and your choice of dairy or vegan cheese on a baguette. Also, save room for their vegan chocolate cake. **Open daily for three meals. Limited service, vegan options, fresh juices, espresso/cappuccino, take-out, $-$$.**

Mughal Garden Restaurant
920 N. Charles St., Baltimore, MD 21201   **(410) 547-0001**
Indian. Sample vegetarian curries, dahls, and others vegetable creations, along with fresh baked tandoori breads. **Open daily for lunch and dinner. Full service, vegan options, take-out, wine/beer/alcohol, VISA/MC, $$.**

OK Natural Food Store
11 W. Preston St., Baltimore, MD 21203   **(410) 837-3911**
Natural foods. Located in the theater district near Penn Station, MICA, and the University of Baltimore, this natural foods store offers supplements, groceries, herbs, organic produce,

and boxed sandwiches for lunch. **Open Monday through Friday for three meals. Open Saturday for lunch and dinner. Open Sunday for lunch and early dinner. Take-out,** VISA/MC.

One World Café
100 W. University Pkwy., Baltimore, MD 21210   **(410) 235-5777**
Natural foods. Located on the ground floor of a high rise across the street from Johns Hopkins University Homewood campus, One World Café offers a wide variety of coffees, as well as vegetarian food, including chili, salads, soups, fresh breads and baked goods, and even vegan pancakes on weekends. A few fish dishes on the menu keep this restaurant from being completely vegetarian. **Open daily for three meals. Open late on Friday and Saturday. Full service, vegan options, fresh juices, smoothies, espresso/cappuccino, soymilk, beer/wine/alcohol, take-out, VISA/MC/AMEX, $-$$.**

Tashes Ankh
8045 Liberty Rd., Baltimore, MD 21244   **(410) 922-9196**
Caribbean. Located west of Baltimore's city limits, this restaurant offers several vegetarian dishes, including curry yuba, brown stew yuba, and stewed peas with rice and vegetables. **Open Monday through Saturday for three meals. Closed Sunday. Take-out, $-$$.**

Thai Restaurant
3316 Greenmount Ave., Baltimore, MD 21218   **(410) 889-6002**
Thai. Although the service and atmosphere are formal, dress is casual. There's a nice selection, and the restaurant will substitute tofu for meat in any of its dishes. The curry dishes are particularly good. **Open daily. Full service, wine/beer/alcohol, catering, take-out, VISA/MC, $.**

Tov Pizza
6313 Reisterstown Rd., Baltimore, MD 21215   **(410) 358-5238**
Kosher dairy. Tov's offers a unique blend of Middle Eastern and Italian cuisine. **Open Sunday through Thursday for lunch and dinner. Open Friday for lunch. Open Saturday for dinner.** Limited service, vegan options, take-out, delivery, catering, VISA/MC, $-$$.

•• The Yabba Pot
2433 St. Paul St., Baltimore, MD 21218   **(410) 662-TOFU**
Vegan/International. The Yabba Pot offers great international cuisine on a rotating menu in an atmosphere evoking a Caribbean café. Feast on curried vegetables, Asian BBQ tofu, Caribbean red beans with fennel rice, broccoli in coconut sauce, plantains, individual lemon zest bundt cakes, and much more. **Open Monday through Saturday for lunch and dinner. Closed Sunday. Limited service, fresh juices, take-out, catering, VISA/MC, $-$$.** www. empresscatering.com

---

Restaurant codes: ✪ Reviewers' Choice   • Vegetarian Restaurant   •• Vegan Restaurant
Restaurant prices: **$** less than $6   **$$** $6-$12   **$$$** more than $12
Credit Cards Accepted: VISA - VISA   MC - MasterCard   AMEX - American Express
DISC - Discover   DC - Diner's Club

BEL AIR

David's Natural Market II
3 Red Pump Rd., Bel Air, MD 21014   **(410) 803-0784**
Natural foods. This natural foods store offers vegetarian sandwiches and soups. Open Monday
through Saturday for lunch and dinner. Open Sunday for lunch and early dinner. Take-out,
vegan options, fresh juices, VISA/MC/AMEX/DISC/DC, $. www.davidsnaturalmarket.com

Hunan Chef Restaurant
5 Bel Air S. Pkwy., Bel Air, MD 21014   **(410) 838-2313**
Chinese. Hunan Chef offers several vegetarian dishes. Open Monday through Saturday for
dinner. Open Sunday for lunch and dinner. Full service, vegan options, take-out, VISA/
MC/AMEX, $$.

BELTSVILLE

El Mexicano
10413 Baltimore Ave., Beltsville, MD 20703   **(301) 572-4000**
Mexican. El Mexicano offers a separate vegetarian menu with a tamale platter, tacos, burritos,
enchiladas, quesadillas, and more. Also, lard is not used in their beans. Open for three meals
Monday through Friday. Open for lunch and dinner Saturday and Sunday. Full service,
vegan options, take-out, $.

BETHESDA

Bacchus Bethesda
7945 Norfolk Ave., Bethesda, MD 20814   **(301) 657-1722**
Lebanese. This Lebanese restaurant offers several vegetarian items, including stuffed grape
leaves, hummus, baba ghanouj, stuffed eggplant, eggplant salad, potato salad, cauliflower
and tahini dip, and falafel. Open daily. Full service, vegan options, wine/beer/alcohol,
catering, take-out, VISA/MC/AMEX, $$-$$$.

Thyme Square
4735 Bethesda Ave., Bethesda, MD 20814   **(301) 657-9077**
Natural foods. Thyme Square offers a wide range of natural foods dishes, including many that
are vegetarian. Try Vegetable Pot Stickers, Oven-Roasted Roma Tomatoes with Polenta, a
Mediterranean Platter, grilled vegetables, various soups and salads, pasta dishes, and wood-
burning oven-baked pizza. Open daily for lunch and dinner. Full service, vegan options,
fresh juices, take-out, espresso/cappuccino, VISA/MC, $$.

CAPITOL HEIGHTS

•• Soul Vegetarian Gourmet Restaurant
Everlasting Life Health Complex
9185 Central Ave., Capitol Heights, MD 20743   **(301) 324-6900**
Vegan. Located inside a wellness center, Soul Vegetarian is a completely vegan gourmet
restaurant with a bakery and a banquet hall. Their menu includes soups, salads, sandwiches,
pastas, and desserts. You can choose from appetizers like Spinach Dip or Hummus, and

follow those up with some Spinach Lasagna, Vegetarian Kabobs, or Grab Cakes (similar to crab cakes). **Open Tuesday through Sunday for lunch and dinner. Closed Monday. Full service, vegan options, fresh juices, special drinks, take-out, VISA/MC/AMEX/DISC, $$-$$$.** www.everlastinglife.net

CLARKSVILLE

• Great Sage
5809 Clarksville Sq. Dr., Clarksville, MD 21029   (443) 535-9400
Vegetarian. Located next to Roots Market, this restaurant serves soups, salads, sandwiches, and international entrées, most of which are created with organic foods. **Open daily for lunch and dinner. Full service, vegan options, fresh juices, smoothies, soymilk, espresso/ cappuccino, beer/wine, reservations for parties of 8 or more, take-out, VISA/MC/AMEX/ DISC/DC, $$-$$$.** www.great-sage.com

COLLEGE PARK

• Berwyn Café
5010 Berwyn Rd., College Park, MD 20740   (301) 345-9898
Vegetarian. Located near the University of Maryland in College Park, the Berwyn Café has been serving organic vegetarian food since 1973. The Berwyn Café offers favorites, such as the Tofu Steak, Tofu Gyro, and VLT, as well as a vegan breakfast on Saturdays and Sunday for brunch. In addition, the café features monthly music shows and a reading room. A definite must for anyone visiting the College Park area. **Open Tuesday through Friday for lunch and dinner. Open Saturday for three meals. Open Sunday for brunch. Closed Monday. Full service, vegan options, take-out, catering, fresh juices, $-$$.** www.berwyncafe.com

• • Sprouts
The Diner @ Ellicott
University Of Maryland, College Park, MD 20742   (301) 314-8010
Cafeteria. This food station inside The Diner @ Ellicott offers daily vegan selections for lunch and dinner. **Call for hours. Cafeteria, take-out, $.** www.dining.umd.edu/locations/ diner/

COLUMBIA

Akbar
9400 Snowden River Pkwy., Columbia, MD 21045   (410) 381-3600
Indian. See description under Baltimore, MD.

David's Natural Market
5430 Lynx La., Columbia, MD 21044   (410) 730-2304
Natural foods. See description under Bel Air, MD.

Hunan Manor
7091 Deepage Dr., Columbia, MD 21045   (410) 381-1134
Chinese. Hunan Manor offers many vegetarian dishes using mock "meat" and tofu. Be sure

to request details about their vegetarian specialties. **Open daily for lunch and dinner. Full service, vegan options, beer/wine/alcohol, take-out, VISA/MC, $$-$$$.**

• The Mango Grove ✪
6365 B Dobbin Rd., Columbia, MD 21045   **(410) 884-3426**

Vegetarian/Indian. Located in a shopping center near Friendly's restaurant, The Mango Grove offers unique South Indian vegetarian dishes. Be sure to try their Mango-Filled Dosai and vegetable curry dishes when you visit. **Open daily for lunch and dinner. Full service, vegan options, catering, take-out, VISA/MC/AMEX/DISC, $-$$.**

CUMBERLAND

Gehauf's
1268 National Hwy., Cumberland, MD 21502   **(301) 729-3300**

American. In a lovely airy setting, you'll find Spinach Salad, mixed salad with fresh vegetables, fresh fruit plates when in season, and a few vegetarian dishes, like vegetarian chili. **Open daily. Full service, wine/beer/alcohol, take-out, VISA/MC/AMEX, $$.**

ELLICOTT CITY

• Sarah and Desmond's Bakery Café
8198 Main St., Ellicott City, MD 21042   **(410) 465-9700**

Vegetarian bakery/coffeehouse. In the heart of historic Ellicott City, Sarah and Desmond's offers fresh baked goods, gourmet coffee and teas, along with vegetarian sandwiches and salads. Stop in for a treat after browsing the nearby antique shops and galleries. They also offer a kid-friendly room. **Open Tuesday through Sunday for breakfast and lunch. Closed Monday. Counter service, vegan options, espresso/cappuccino, smoothies, soymilk, take-out, catering, VISA/MC/AMEX/DC, $-$$.**

FREDERICK

Bombay Grill
137 N. Market St., Frederick, MD 21701   **(301) 668-0077**

Indian. Dine on Indian breads and vegetarian entrées, including vegetable kofta, potato dishes, and a grilled vegetable kabob. Dishes are prepared with vegetable or olive oil. **Open daily for lunch and dinner. Full service, vegan options, take-out, catering, wine/beer/alcohol, VISA/MC/DISC/DC, $$.**

• Common Market
5813 Buckeystown Pike, Frederick, MD 21701   **(301) 663-3416**

Vegetarian/natural foods store deli. Enjoy sandwiches made with organically grown foods and a juice bar. **Open daily for lunch. Limited service, fresh juices, take-out, $.**

Restaurant codes: ✪ Reviewers' Choice   • Vegetarian Restaurant   • • Vegan Restaurant
Restaurant prices: **$** less than $6   **$$** $6-$12   **$$$** more than $12
Credit Cards Accepted: VISA - VISA   MC - MasterCard   AMEX - American Express
DISC - Discover   DC - Diner's Club

Health Express & Gourment Vegetarian
1540 W. Patrick St., Frederick, MD 21701 **(301) 662-2293**
Health foods store deli. Sandwiches and homemade soups are the order of the day at Health Express. **Open daily for lunch. Limited service, fresh juices, take-out, $.**

Hunan Gourmet
915 W. Seventh St., Frederick, MD 21701 **(301) 695-0446**
Chinese. Hunan Gourmet offers a Vegetarian Menu with appetizers, soups, and vegetable dishes, and entrées made from mock chicken (gluten), beef (gluten puff), and pork (tofu jerky). They offer vegetarian versions of traditional Chinese cuisine like Kung Pao Chicken and Szechuan Beef, as well as unique items like Beef Mimosa (orange-flavored gluten puff and red pepper in a spicy brown sauce) and Sweet and Sour Spareribs (green pepper, carrots, pineapple, and dough staning in for the meat). Near Hood College and Frederick Memorial Hospital. **Open daily for lunch and dinner. Full service, vegan options, take-out, delivery, VISA/MC/AMEX, $$.**

Lotus Chinese Cuisine
107 Baughmans Ln., Frederick, MD 21702 **(301) 694-3388**
Chinese. Lotus offers authentic Chinese cuisine in a relaxed atmosphere. The menu has a vegetarian section, and the restaurant's staff will gladly accommodate vegetarians and vegans. **Open daily. Full service, vegan options, wine/beer, take-out, VISA/MC/DISC, $$.**

The Orchard
45 N. Market St., Frederick, MD 21701 **(301) 663-4912**
Natural foods. This completely non-smoking natural foods restaurant is located in the heart of downtown Frederick. **Open Tuesday through Saturday for lunch and dinner. Closed Sunday and Monday. Full service, vegan options, wine/beer, take-out, VISA/MC/AMEX, $$.**

Taurasos
6 East St., Frederick, MD 21701 **(301) 663-6600**
American. This popular restaurant has an elegant formal dining room and a casual pub. A special vegetarian menu is available upon inquiry. **Open daily for lunch and dinner.** $-$$$.

FROSTBURG

Gandalf's Restaurant
20 E. Main St., Frostburg, MD 21532 **(301) 689-2010**
International. Gandalf's lets you choose from grilled tofu squares, kitfo (vegetarian "meat-balls"), and falafel for appetizers, and seven specialty salads, many of which are vegan. There are vegetarian African, Mediterranean, and Thai dishes for entrées, as well as several vegan and vegetarian sandwiches, such as a soy Reuben. The restaurant uses organic ingredients whenever possible. **Open Monday through Saturday for dinner. Closed Sunday. Full service, vegan options, wine/beer, $-$$.**

Giuseppe's

11 Bowery St., Frostburg, MD 21532   **(301) 689-2220**

Italian. Located in a small town near a ski area, this unique Italian restaurant offers many lacto-ovo choices and a tasty plain sauce for vegans. Giuseppe's will accommodate special needs. **Open daily for dinner. Full service, vegan options, wine/beer/alcohol, take-out, VISA/MC/AMEX/DISC, $$.**

GAITHERSBURG

El Mexicano

12150 Darnestown Rd., Gaithersburg, MD 20878   **(301) 330-5620**

Mexican. See description under Beltsville, MD.

• Madras Palace

74 Bureau Dr., Gaithersburg, MD 20878   **(301) 977-1600**

Vegetarian/Indian. This restaurant specializes in both north and south Indian cuisine, including a variety of curries, dosa, and rice specialties. A buffet is served for lunch. **Open daily for lunch and dinner. Full service, fresh juices, take-out, catering, reservations recommended, VISA/MC, $$.**

Thai Sa-Mai Restaurant

8369 Snouffer School Rd., Gaithersburg, MD 20879-1502   **(301) 963-1800**

Thai. The menu features original spicy Thai foods and 30 vegetarian dishes made without MSG. *The Washingtonian* magazine named Thai Sa-Mai's curry the best. **Open Monday through Saturday for lunch and dinner. Closed Sunday. Full service, vegan options, wine/beer, take-out, VISA/MC, $$.**

GERMANTOWN

El Mexicano

12922 Middlebrook Rd., Germantown, MD 20874   **(301) 972-0500**

Mexican. See description under Beltsville, MD.

GREENBELT

China Pearl

7701 Greenbelt Rd., Greenbelt, MD 20770   **(301) 441-8880**

Chinese. The menu features vegetarian spring rolls, tempura, and 21 vegetarian Chinese selections. **Open daily for lunch and dinner. Full service, vegan options, alcohol, take-out, VISA/MC/AMEX/DISC.**

• Madras Palace

8839 Greenbelt Rd., Greenbelt, MD 20770   **(301) 552-3353**

Vegetarian/Indian. Specializes in south Indian cuisine, including idly, medhu vada, dosas, utthapam, soups, curries, thails, and breads. Two of the desserts and some drinks are dairy-based, but most of the menu is vegan. **Open Tuesday through Sunday for lunch and dinner. Closed Monday. Counter service, vegan options, special drinks, VISA/MC, $-$$.**

LANGLEY PARK

• Woodlands

8046 New Hampshire Ave., Langley Park, MD 20783 **(301) 434-4202**

Vegetarian/Indian. The Woodlands serves an ample selection of cuisine from southern India, such as curries, breads, appetizers, and regional delicacies. One of their specialties is "Woodlands Special Spring Dosai," made with vegetables and hot chutney-wrapped in a rice crepe. **Open Monday through Saturday for lunch and dinner. Closed Sunday. Full service, vegan options, special drinks, catering, VISA/MC/AMEX, $$.**

MONKTON

• Monkton Village Market

1900 Monkton Rd., Monkton, MD 21111 **(410) 472-9821**

Vegetarian. Located on the NCR Trail in Monkton near the Gunpowder River, Monkton Village Market is a great spot to visit to grab some soup, sandwiches, wraps, breakfast items (including vegan pancakes and tofu scramble), or dessert. **Open daily for three meals. Counter service, vegan options, take-out, catering, VISA/MC/DISC, $-$$.**

MONROVIA

Amigo's

11791 Fingerboard Rd., Monrovia, MD 21770 **(301) 865-0898**

Mexican. Amigo's offers six vegetarian entrées, including a Three Bean Salad, Veggie Fajitas, Spinach Enchiladas, and more. **Open daily for lunch and dinner. Full service, take-out, $-$$.**

OLNEY

Olney Ale House

2000 Olney-Sandy Spring Rd., Olney, MD 20832-1602 **(301) 774-6708**

Natural foods. This cozy restaurant with a fireplace during winter months offers several vegetarian dishes, such as chili, tofu and Sunburgers, salads, and homemade breads. It's very crowded on weekends, so expect a long wait. **Open Tuesday through Sunday. Closed Monday. Full service, vegan options, wine/beer, take-out, VISA/MC/DISC, $$.**

OWINGS MILLS

Egyptian Pizza

9161 Reisterstown Rd., Owings Mills, MD 21117 **(410) 902-9020**

Middle Eastern/pizza. See description under Baltimore, MD.

PASADENA

The Bangkok Oriental

8043-F Ritchie Hwy., Pasadena, MD 21122 **(410) 766-0973**

Thai. This restaurant offers a variety of Thai specialties, including Sautéed Spicy Vegetables; Mixed Vegetables with Tofu, Snow Peas, Baby Corn, and Black Mushrooms with Rice; and

Thai Curry Vegetables. **Open Monday through Saturday for lunch and dinner. Closed Sunday. Full service, take-out, VISA/MC/DISC, $$.**

Al Pacino Café
1809 Reisterstown Rd., Pikesville, MD 21208   **(410) 653-6868**
Middle Eastern/pizza. See description under Baltimore, MD.

Mr. Chan's Szechuan ✪
1000 Reisterstown Rd., Pikesville, MD 21208   **(410) 484-1100**
Chinese. One of the better Chinese dining experiences in the Baltimore area, Mr. Chan's has a wide variety of dishes from which to choose from. Some favorites include vegetable sushi, mushroom wonton soup, Yuba Teriyaki, Seitan with Walnuts, and Warm Protein Salad (with veggie ham and pine nuts). **Open daily for lunch and dinner. Full service, vegan options, take-out, catering, VISA/MC/AMEX, $$.**

Akbar Palace
3541 Brenbrook Dr., Randallstown, MD 21133   **(410) 655-1600**
Indian. See description under Baltimore, MD.

Szechuan Best
8625 Liberty Rd., Randallstown, MD 21133   **(410) 521-0020**
Chinese. This Chinese restaurant has an extensive vegetarian menu. **Open daily for lunch and dinner. Full service, vegan options, take-out, $$.**

Bombay Bistro
98 W. Montgomery Ave., Rockville, MD 20850   **(301) 762-8798**
Indian. Bombay Bistro serves vegetarian dishes from North and South India, including vegetable samosas, vegetable biryani, and oothapam (a savory pancake of lentils and rice with onions and tomato). **Open daily for lunch and dinner. Full service, vegan options, espresso/ cappuccino, take-out, VISA/MC, $$.**

•Café Masala
705 Baltimore Rd., Rockville, MD 20850   **(301) 294-2937**
Vegetarian/Indian. This restaurant offers a wide range of Indian-style vegetarian cuisine, such as grilled kabobs. **Open daily for lunch. Buffet, $$.**

Restaurant codes: ✪ Reviewers' Choice   • Vegetarian Restaurant   • • Vegan Restaurant
Restaurant prices: **$** less than $6   **$$** $6-$12   **$$$** more than $12
Credit Cards Accepted: VISA - VISA   MC - MasterCard   AMEX - American Express
DISC - Discover   DC - Diner's Club

•• The Vegetable Garden ✪
11618 Rockville Pk., Rockville, MD 20852 (301) 468-9301

Vegan/Chinese. If you are in the D.C. area and you like Chinese food, this restaurant is a must. It has dozens of vegan and vegetarian dishes, especially seitan and wheat gluten items, and interesting soups, such as Sizzling Rice. A non-fat menu is available. **Open daily for lunch and dinner. Full service, vegan options, fresh juices, wine/beer/alcohol, take-out, VISA/MC/ AMEX, $$.** www.thevegetablegarden.com

•Yuan Fu Vegetarian
798 Rockville Pike, Rockville, MD 20852 (301) 762-5937

Vegetarian/Chinese. Yuan Fu's owner, Chef Tai, has 20 years of experience with vegetarian cuisine. They make all of their mock meats, using wheat gluten, tofu, and tofu skin. The inexpensive lunch menu includes moo shi vegetables and "shrimp" chow mein. **Open daily for lunch and dinner. Full service, vegan options, $$.**

SILVER SPRING

Silver Palace
11311 Lockwood Dr., Silver Spring, MD 20904 (301) 681-9585

Chinese. The Palace offers many vegetarian entrées and has a large banquet room for groups. **Open daily. Full service, wine/beer/alcohol, VISA/MC/AMEX, $$.**

Thai Derm Restaurant
939 Bonifant St., Silver Spring, MD 20910 (301) 589-5341

Thai. The noodle specialities and all other dishes are made without MSG upon request. **Open Monday through Saturday. Closed Sunday. Full service, wine/beer, VISA/MC, $$.**

SPENCERVILLE

Edgewood Inn
16101 Oak Hill Rd., Spencerville, MD 20905 (301) 421-9247

American. Located in a historic house, Edgewood Inn offers a vegetarian buffet, including Nut Loaf, Eggplant Parmesan, Lasagna, Spinach Pie, Rice Casserole, Potato Salad, home-made breads, and Pineapple Cream Cake. **Call for hours. Buffet, catering, $$.**

TAKOMA PARK

Royal Bengal
6846 New Hampshire Ave., Takoma Park, MD 20912-4817 (301) 270-6054

Indian. Diners have a choice of 14 vegetarian dishes served with basmati rice. **Open daily for dinner. Open for lunch Monday through Friday. Full service, vegan options, beer.**

•Takoma Park Silver Spring Food Co-Op
201 Ethan Allen Ave., Takoma Park, MD 20912 (301) 891-COOP

Vegetarian/deli. This co-op has the area's largest olive selection, "direct from the grower." The deli only does take-out, with a selection of vegan, low-fat, low sodium, wheat-free, dairy-free, and other vegetarian foods. **Open daily. Take-out, macrobiotic/vegan options, VISA/MC, $.**

TIMONIUM

The Natural Café

2149 York Rd., Timonium, MD 21093   **(410) 560-3133**

Natural foods/juice bar. This self-server café has a chef on duty and offers homemade soup or chili daily. **Open Monday through Friday for lunch. Closed Saturday and Sunday.** Cafeteria, vegan options, fresh juices, take-out, VISA/MC/AMEX, $.

TOWSON

Purim Oak

321 York Rd., Towson, MD 21204   **(410) 583-7770**

Asian. This restaurant specializes in Korean, Japanese, and Chinese Cuisine. Some specialties include Vegetable Fried Rice, Soft Tofu Stew with vegetables, and Vermicelli with assorted vegetables and mushrooms. A buffet is also offered. **Open Monday through Friday for lunch. Open Saturday and Sunday for dinner.** Limited service, take-out, VISA/MC/AMEX/DISC, $$-$$$.

WHEATON

China Chef

11323 Georgia Ave., Wheaton, MD 20902-4619   **(301) 949-8170**

Chinese. This Chinese restaurant offers several vegetarian entrées. **Open daily for lunch and dinner.** Full service, wine/beer/alcohol, catering, take-out, VISA/MC/AMEX, $$.

Dusit Thai Cuisine

2404 University Blvd., Wheaton, MD 20902-4510   **(301) 949-4140**

Thai. Dusit features vegetable and tofu dishes, noodle entrées, and vegetarian soups. **Open daily for lunch and dinner.** Full service, wine/beer/alcohol, take-out, VISA/MC/AMEX, $.

Nut House Pizza

11419 Georgia Ave., Wheaton, MD 20902   **(301) 942-5900**

Kosher/pizza. Experience Nut House's pizza made with soy or kosher cheese, falafel, vegetarian burgers, and vegetarian pitas. **Open Sunday through Thursday for lunch and dinner. Open Friday until one hour before sundown. Open Saturday one hour after sundown to late night.** Limited service, take-out, catering, VISA/MC/AMEX, $.

Sabang Indonesian Restaurant

2504 Ennalls Ave., Wheaton, MD 20902   **(301) 942-7859**

Indonesian. Sabang features vegetarian reistafel that includes soup, dessert, and approximately 10 different vegetarian dishes. It's fun to go with a few friends. **Open daily for lunch and dinner.** Full service, vegan options, wine/beer/alcohol, take-out, VISA/MC/AMEX, $$-$$$.

Restaurant codes: ✪ Reviewers' Choice • Vegetarian Restaurant •• Vegan Restaurant
Restaurant prices: **$** less than $6 **$$** $6-$12 **$$$** more than $12
Credit Cards Accepted: VISA - VISA   MC - MasterCard   AMEX - American Express
DISC - Discover   DC - Diner's Club

Saigonese

11232 Grandview Ave., Wheaton, MD 20902   **(301) 946-8002**

Vietnamese. A large vegetarian menu features appetizers, soups, and several tofu and gluten dishes daily. Lunch specials are available on weekdays. **Open Monday through Friday for lunch and dinner. Open Saturday and Sunday for dinner only. Full service, $$.**

Massachusetts

ALLSTON

•• Grasshopper ✪

1 N. Beacon St., Union Sq., Allston, MA 02134   **(617) 254-8883**

Vegan/Asian. Grasshopper's menu offers a wide variety of mock meat entrees and imaginative vegetable dishes, attractively served. Appetizers, Vietnamese pizza, and monthly specials are especially recommended. **Open daily for lunch and dinner. Full service, $-$$.**

TJ's House of Pizza

487 Cambridge St., Union Sq., Allston, MA 02134   **(617) 787-9884**

Pizza. This modest pizza house offers a full vegan menu beyond their soy cheese pizzas. Vegan Buffalo fingers, BBQ chicken, sausage, meatballs, and more can be served as a dinner or adorn pizzas, pasta, subs, and calzones. **Open daily for lunch through late night. Full service, vegan options, take-out, delivery, $-$$.**

AMESBURY

• Hippie Chick Bakery

11 Elm St., Amesbury, MA 01913   **(978) 388-6644**

Vegetarian bakery. This European-style bakery uses organic ingredients whenever possible. They offer many vegan items, including seasonal gift packages and vegan wedding cakes. Items are available by mail-order. **Open Tuesday through Saturday for breakfast through early dinner. Closed Sunday and Monday. Take-out, vegan options, non-smoking, VISA/ MC, $-$$.** www.hippiechickbakery.com

AMHERST

(For restaurant listings in the surrounding areas, see Greenfield, Hadley, and Northampton.)

Amherst Chinese Foods

62 Main St., Amherst, MA 01002   **(413) 253-2813**

Chinese. Amherst Chinese grows their own organic vegetables on their own farm. **Open daily for lunch and dinner. Full service, non-smoking, wine/beer/alcohol, VISA/MC/AMEX/ DISC, $$.**

Bueno y Saño

46 Main St., Amherst, MA 01002   **(413) 253-4000**

Mexican. The name translates as "Good and Healthy," and this small restaurant lives up to its name. The menu mainly features burritos including fillings like seitan, grilled zucchini, and fresh spinach, as well as the standard beans and rice. Burritos can be ordered without cheese or sour cream. **Open daily for lunch and dinner. Counter service, vegan options, take-out, delivery, VISA/MC/AMEX, $. www.buenoysano.com**

Fresh Side

61 Main St., Amherst, MA 01002   **(413) 256-0296**

Variety. Fresh Side's menu features great tea rolls, rice and noodle dishes, salads, soups, and other dishes. **Open Monday through Saturday for lunch and dinner. Closed Sunday. Limited service, vegan options, take-out, $.**

Nick's Place

63 Main St., Amherst, MA 01002   **(413) 256-4643**

Eclectic. Nick's, which was formally Amber Waves, offers a great variety of New York deli-style and Southwestern vegetarian and vegan brunch items. Their menu includes a tofu scramble breakfast burrito with salsa and black beans, great vegan pancakes and French toast, and vegan omelettes made with soy sausage and your choice of veggies. **Open daily for breakfast and lunch. Full service, vegan options, fresh juices, smoothies, soymilk, espresso/ cappuccino, take-out, VISA/MC, $$. www.blacksheepdeli.com/niksmenu.htm**

ARLINGTON

Olive Branch

117 Broadway, Arlington, MA 02474   **(781) 646-4244**

Middle Eastern. Try the excellent maza plate, which is a trio of hummus, tabouli, and baba ghanouj served with pita bread. Also try the authentic, melt-in-your-mouth vegan dolmathes (stuffed grape leaves), mujadara (a simple yet tasty lentil and rice dish), and eggplant moussaka (a vegan take on the original). **Open Monday through Saturday for lunch and dinner. Closed Sunday. Full service, vegan options, take-out, fresh juices, VISA/MC, $$.**

BEVERLY

•• Organic Garden Restaurant and Juice Bar

294 Cabot St., Beverly, MA 01915   **(978) 922-0004**

Vegan. Organic Garden offers many living foods, including salads, soups, wraps, entrées, and desserts. Try the Ole Guacomole Burrito with wild rice, BBQ sauce, and creamy vegan "cheese," or the Mongolian with shiitake mushrooms and sun-dried tomatoes. **Open daily for lunch and dinner. Full service, fresh juices, smoothies, wine, VISA/MC/AMEX/DISC/ DC, $-$$. www.organicgardencafe.com**

BILLERICA

• Masalaa Boston Fine Indian Vegetarian Cuisine

786 Boston Rd., Billerica, MA 01821   **(978) 667-3443**

Vegetarian/Indian. Masalaa Boston's menu features a great variety of soups, salads, dosas, uthappams (lentil and rice batter pancakes), idly (rice cakes), thali, curry dishes, rice dishes, breads, desserts, and drinks. Unique offerings include Bisibella Bath (Indian rice cooked in lentil soup) and Sukku Kapi (traditional South Indian ginger coffee). **Open Tuesday through**

Sunday for lunch and dinner. Closed Monday. Full service, vegan options, reservations accepted, fresh juices, beer/wine, special drinks, take-out, catering, VISA/MC/AMEX/DISC, $-$$. www.masalaaboston.com

BOSTON

(For restaurant listings in the surrounding areas, see Allston, Arlington, Beverly, Billerica, Braintree, Brookline, Burlington, Cambridge, Concord, Dorchester, Framingham, Jamaica Plain, Lexington, Marblehead, Somerville, and Waltham.)

Addis Red Sea Ethiopian Restaurant
544 Tremont St., Boston, MA 02116   **(617) 426-8727**

Ethiopian. Sample authentic Ethiopian cuisine from the vegetarian appetizer and entrée selections on the menu. Open daily. Full service, vegan options, wine/beer, take-out, VISA/MC/AMEX, $-$$.

• Buddha's Delight ✪
5 Beach St., Boston, MA 02111   **(617) 451-2395**

Vegetarian/Asian. Located in Chinatown, Buddha's Delight has an extensive and exclusively vegan food menu that consists of inventive mock meat and seafood entrées made from tofu and gluten, as well as vegetable entrées, soups, and appetizers. Note that some beverages do contain dairy. Open daily for lunch and dinner. Full service, take-out, $$.

Burrito Max
642 Beacon St. (Kenmore Square), Boston, MA 02215   **(617) 266-8088**

Mexican. Burrito Max has its vegetarian options covered. Known for its Vegetarian Chili Big Burrito, you can try the Barbecued Tofu Burrito as well, or have any number of items made with your choice of whole-wheat or spinach tortillas. Open daily for lunch and dinner. Limited service, vegan options, $.

India Quality
484 Commonwealth Ave., Boston, MA 02215   **(617) 267-4499**

Indian. Half of the menu is vegetarian. Special breads baked freshly in clay ovens accompany their extensive vegetarian menu. Open daily for lunch and dinner. Full service, vegan options, take-out, VISA/MC/AMEX/DISC, $$.

Kashmir
279 Newbury St., Boston, MA 02116   **(617) 536-1695**

Indian. Vegetable Samosas, Aloo Palak, and several other vegetarian options are available at this Indian restaurant. Open daily for lunch and dinner. Full service, vegan options, take-out, VISA/MC/AMEX/DC, $$.

Milk Street Café
50 Milk St., Boston, MA 02109   **(617) 542-3663**

Kosher. Milk Street Café features many kosher-style vegetarian and vegan meals, including soups, salads, burritos, a Mediterranean platter, and hot entrées. The menu includes some fish dishes, but meat and poultry are not served. Open Monday through Friday for lunch and dinner. Closed Saturday and Sunday, Cafeteria, take-out, $.

Phoenicia
240 Cambridge St., Boston, MA 02114   **(617) 523-4606**

Middle Eastern. Vegetarian dishes on Phoenicia's menu include Pumpkin Kibby made with puréed pumpkin, cracked wheat, walnuts, and pine nuts; Broccoli-Noodle Casserole; Fasolia made with kidney beans, onions, and tomato sauce; and traditional Middle Eastern dishes, like falafel and hummus. **Open daily for lunch and dinner. Full service, vegan options, catering, take-out, VISA/MC/AMEX/DISC/DC, $-$$.**

Souper Salad
103 State St., Boston, MA 02107	**(617) 227-9151**
3 Center Plaza, Boston, MA 02108	**(617) 367-6067**
102 Water St., Boston, MA 02109	**(617) 367-2582**
101 Federal St., Boston, MA 02110	**(617) 357-9393**
126 High St., Boston, MA 02110	**(617) 542-3157**
209 Berkeley St., Boston, MA 02116	**(617) 350-5380**
364 Brookline Ave., Boston, MA 02215	**(617) 232-5599**

Restaurant chain. Souper Salad features a salad bar, soups, sandwiches, and entrées, all of which are fresh and homemade. It also has a decent selection of vegetarian options, including some Mexican dishes. **Open daily. Full service, vegan options, fresh juices, wine/beer, take-out, VISA/MC/AMEX, $.** www.soupersaladboston.com

Trident Café
338 Newbury St., Boston, MA 02115   **(617) 267-8688**

Café. This hip but comfy café and bookstore features a daily vegetarian special and many creative vegetarian dishes on the menu, such as cashew chili and Tibetan momos (dumplings). **Open daily for breakfast through late night. Full service, vegan options, take-out, VISA/MC/AMEX/DISC, $-$$.**

BRAINTREE

Souper Salad
South Shore Plaza Shopping Mall
250 Granite Ave., Braintree, MA 02184   **(781) 843-3870**

Restaurant chain. See description under Boston, MA.

BROOKLINE

•• Buddha's Delight Too!
404 Harvard St., Brookline, MA 02146   **(617) 739-8830**

Vegan/Asian. The sister restaurant of the Beach St. location, this popular establishment offers more than 150 Cambodian, Thai, Vietnamese, and Japanese dishes in varying price ranges. **Open daily for lunch and dinner. Full service, take-out, wine/beer, VISA/MC/AMEX, $-$$.**

BURLINGTON

Souper Salad
Burlington Mall, 100 Middlesex Tpke., Burlington, MA 01803   (781) 270-4133
Restaurant chain. See description under Boston, MA.

CAMBRIDGE

Bombay Club
56 JFK St., Cambridge, MA 02138   (617) 661-8100
Indian. Their vegetarian menu section features various curry dishes, dahl, and vegetable entrées. Open daily. Full service, vegan options, wine/beer, take-out, VISA/MC/AMEX, $$.

Christopher's Restaurant & Bar
1920 Massachusetts Ave., Cambridge, MA 02140   (617) 876-9180
Natural foods. Christopher's has combined mainstream American and Mexican fare with a variety of vegetarian dishes and a dedication to wholesome and healthful food. (The owner is a long-time vegetarian!) The restaurant uses ingredients that are free of preservatives and artificial colors. All sauces, dressings, salsa, and guacamole are homemade. Even the brewed decaf is prepared "Swiss water processed," and there are no dioxins in the coffee filters. Open daily for lunch and dinner. Full service, vegan options, wine/beer/alcohol, take-out, VISA/MC/DISC, $-$$.

Gandhi Restaurant
704 Massachussets Ave., Cambridge, MA 02139   (617) 491-1104
Indian. Ghandi's traditional Indian cuisine includes 11 vegetarian entrées, plus soups, appetizers, and south Indian dishes. Open daily for lunch and dinner. Full service, vegan options, wine/beer, take-out, VISA/MC, $$.

• Greater Boston Buddhist Cultural Center
950 Massachusetts Ave., Cambridge, MA 02180   (617) 547-6670
Vegetarian. This Vegetarian Restaurant and Tea House offers specialty appetizers and tea daily. The Cultural Center also offers vegetarian cooking classes. Open Tuesday through Sunday for lunch and early dinner. Closed Monday. Full service. www.gbbcc.org

Grendel's Restaurant
Harvard Square, 89 Winthrop St., Cambridge, MA 02138   (617) 491-1160
American/international. Located in an old fraternity house, Grendel's serves eclectic vegetarian meals, like spinach lasagne, burritos, Quesadillas, and a veggie burger. Open daily for lunch and dinner. Full service, espresso/cappuccino, smoothies, VISA/MC/AMEX/DISC/DC, $-$$.

The Helmand
143 1st St., Cambridge, MA 02141   (617) 492-4646
Afghan. Check under the vegetarian section of the menu for appetizers and entrées, including Kaddo Borawni (pan-fried then baked seasoned baby pumpkin), Sabzi Challo (spinach sautéed with Afghan seasoning), or one of the many other traditional vegetarian Afghan

meals. **Open Monday through Friday for lunch and dinner. Open Saturday and Sunday for dinner only. Full service, reservations recommended, VISA/MC/AMEX, $$.**

• Veggie Planet
47 Palmer St., Cambridge, MA 02138   **(617) 661-1513**
Vegetarian. This innovative, meat-free pizzeria offers dishes like Yummy Yam Pizza (curried roast sweet potatoes and spinach topped with cheddar and onion chutney), Red Peanut Curry Pizza (creamy coconut rice topped with tofu, broccoli, and red peanut curry sauce), and the Vegan Oddlot (topped with tomato sauce, spinach, basil, tofu ricotta, Calamata olives and fried garlic). Toppings can be served on organic pizza crust or rice. This restaurant also offers fresh soups and salads and a popular Sunday brunch. **Open daily for lunch and dinner. Limited service, vegan options, take-out, fresh juices, special drinks, no credit cards, $-$$.** www.veggieplanet.net

Whole Foods Market
115 Prospect St., Cambridge, MA 02140   **(617) 492-0070**
Fresh Pond Mall, 200 Alewife Brook Pkwy.
  Cambridge, MA 02138   **(617) 491-0040**
340 River St., Cambridge, MA 02139   **(617) 876-6990**
Natural foods deli. A wide variety of vegetarian and vegan foods are offered in the deli and on the salad bar. **Open daily. Counter service, vegan options, take-out, VISA/MC, $$.**

CENTERVILLE

Sprouts Café at Cape Cod Natural Foods
Bell Tower Mall, 1600 Rte. 28, Centerville, MA 02632   **(508) 771-8394**
Natural foods café. Lunches feature many vegetarian sandwiches, plus soups and salads. **Open daily for lunch. Limited service, vegan options, take-out, VISA/MC, $.**

CONCORD

The Natural Gourmet
98 Commonwealth Ave., Concord, MA 01742   **(978) 371-7573**
Natural foods deli. This deli serves many vegetarian and vegan items. Choose from soups; exotic salads, such as Quinoa with Pine Nuts and Apricots; and entrées. **Open daily. Take-out, vegan options, fresh juices, $.**

DORCHESTER

•• Café Mosheh
499 Washington St., Dorchester, MA 02124   **(617) 288-8813**
Vegan/soul food. This vegan soul restaurant offers breakfast items, such as veggie ham, veggie sausage, grits, and scrambled tofu. For lunch or dinner, choose from lentil soup, salads, BBQ tofu, teriyaki tofu, Soy Steak with Mushroom Gravy, Chickpea & Potato Curry, veggie lasagna, collard greens, Mac & Soy Cheesy Sauce, and more. And save some room for sweet potato pie or chocolate mousse pie for dessert. **Open Monday through Friday for three meals. Open**

Saturday for lunch and dinner. Closed Sunday. Limited service, fresh juices, take-out, no credit cards, $. www.cafemosheh.com

EAST SANDWICH

The Beehive Tavern
406 Rte. 6A, East Sandwich, MA 02537   **(508) 833-1184**
American. The Beehive features salads, dinner entrées, some Middle Eastern foods, and pasta. Open daily, seasonal hours. Full service, non-alcoholic beer, wine/beer/alcohol, VISA/MC, $$.

FITCHBURG

Bombay Tandoor Grill Restaurant
200 Lunenburg St., Fitchburg, MA 01420   **(978) 348-1699**
Indian. This establishment features exotic flavors of authentic Indian cuisine with delicacies from north and south India. Vegetarian menu items include vegetable pakoras and samosas, a mixed vegetable platter, palak paneer (chopped spinach with homemade cheese), Navratan Korma (nine mixed vegetables cooked in gravy with yogurt), and of course, a wide variety of Indian breads. The menu also includes a vegetarian luncheon special and an all-you-can-eat lunch buffet. Open daily for lunch and dinner. Full service, take-out, catering, reservations recommended, $$.

FOXBORO

Bangkok Café
369 Central St., Foxboro, MA 02035   **(508) 543-8424**
Thai. This café offers a wide selection of vegetarian Thai dishes, including appetizers, soups, salads, and entrées, several of which contain tofu. Open Monday through Saturday for lunch and dinner. Open Sunday for dinner only. Full service, vegan options, take-out, VISA/MC/AMEX, $$.

FRAMINGHAM

• Udupi Bhavan
417 Waverly St., Framingham, MA 01702   **(508) 820-0230**
Vegetarian/Indian. This is one of the most popular and one of the oldest Indian restaurants in New England. Feast on authentic South Indian vegetarian dishes, including Dosai, Vada, and Thali, and North Indian curries. Open Tuesday through Sunday for lunch and dinner. Closed Monday. Full service, vegan options, take-out, VISA/MC/AMEX/DISC/DC, $$.

GREAT BARRINGTON

Dos Amigos Mexican Restaurant
250 Stockbridge Rd., Great Barrington, MA 01230   **(413) 528-0084**
Mexican. Dos Amigos, located in the Berkshires, can easily accomodate vegetarian and vegan diets. The Mexican fare features vegetarian beans and the vegetarian sampler, both of which can be made vegan. Open daily for lunch and dinner. Full service, vegan options, take-out, $$.

GREENFIELD

Green Fields Market Co-op

144 Main St., Greenfield, MA 01301   **(413) 773-9567**

Natural foods. This deli inside Green Fields Co-op offers sandwiches made to order and fresh salads. **Open daily for lunch and dinner. Limited service, vegan options, soymilk, take-out, catering, VISA/MC/DISC, $.**

HADLEY

Whole Foods Market Café

Rt 9, Hadley, MA 01035   **(413) 586-9932**

Natural foods deli. See description under Cambridge, MA.

HYANNIS

Pavilion Indian Cuisine

511 Main St., Hyannis, MA 02601   **(508) 790-0985**

Indian. This restaurant offers several vegetarian entrées, including a mixed vegetable dish and a lentil dish. **Open daily for lunch and dinner. Full service, wine/beer, catering, take-out, VISA/MC/AMEX, $$.**

JAMAICA PLAIN

Bukhara

701 Centre St., Jamaica Plain, MA 02130   **(617) 522-2195**

Indian. Bukhara offers a vegetarian menu that includes 13 dishes. **Open daily for lunch and dinner. Open Saturday and Sunday for brunch. Full service, vegan options, $$-$$$.**

Center Street Café

669 Centre St., Jamaica Plain, MA 02130   **(617) 524-9217**

American/ethnic. This small, funky neighborhood restaurant serves an eclectic collection of Mexican, Thai, Indian, and American cuisine. **Open Monday through Friday for lunch and dinner. Open Saturday for dinner only. Closed Sunday. Full service, vegan options, take-out, $$.**

The Purple Cactus

674 Centre St., Jamaica Plain, MA 02130   **(617) 522-7422**

Mexican. The Purple Cactus offers Tofu Teriyaki Wraps and many other tasty vegetarian plates, including their own creation, Tofu Hummus. **Open daily for lunch and dinner. Counter service, vegan options, $.**

LEE

Cactus Café

54 Main St., Lee, MA 01238   **(413) 243-4300**

Mexican. Enjoy authentic Mexican dishes at Cactus Café, including guacamole and chips, burritos, enchiladas, quesadillas, and salads. **Open daily for lunch and dinner. Full service, fresh juices, espresso/cappuccino, non-alcoholic wine/beer, wine/beer, catering, take-out, MC/AMEX/DISC/DC, $$.**

LEXINGTON

Lemon Grass Thai Cuisine

1710 Massachusetts Ave., Lexington, MA 02173   **(781) 862-3530**

Thai. When dining at Lemon Grass, try the Tofu Pad Thai or the Vegetable Curry. They do not use fish sauce in the vegetarian entrées. **Open daily for lunch or dinner. Full service, vegan options, $-$$.**

MARBLEHEAD

•• Basil Chef Cuisine

Body and Soul, Village Shopping Center

13 R Bessom St., Marblehead, MA 01945   **(781) 864-9250**

Vegan. Basil Chef offers organic living foods, such as wraps, soups, and á la carte items. Ask about their special ginger house dressing and cinnamon buckwheat granola. **Open Monday through Saturday for breakfast through early dinner. Open Sunday for lunch through early dinner. Deli-style, vegan options, fresh juices, take-out.**

NANTUCKET

(For restaurant listings in the surrounding areas, see East Sandwich, Hyannis, Provincetown, Sandwich, and Woods Hole.)

Something Natural

50 Cliff Rd., Nantucket, MA 02554   **(508) 228-0504**

Bakery. Something Natural offers 20 varieties fresh-baked breads daily. Large sandwiches are made to order, and garden seating is available. **Open daily in summer. Counter service, take-out, $.**

NEWTON CENTER

Sabra Restaurant

45 Union St., Newton Center, MA 02159   **(617) 527-5641**

Middle Eastern. Sabra's offers falafel, hummus, baba ghanouj, and meatless grape leaves, as well as six vegetarian salads. **Open daily for lunch and dinner. Full service, wine/beer/alcohol, take-out, VISA/MC/AMEX, $-$$.**

NORTHAMPTON

•Bela Vegetarian Restaurant

68 Masonic St., Northampton, MA 01060   **(413) 586-8011**

Vegetarian/natural foods. Their chalkboard menu of affordable international and eclectic vegetarian cuisine changes every one to two days. Many listed are dairy-free entrées. Desserts include honey- and sugar-sweetened, dairy and dairy-free. Outdoor seating available when weather permits. They also allow local women to display their artwork in the restaurant. **Open Tuesday through Saturday. Closed Sunday and Monday. Full service, vegan options, non-smoking, take-out, $.**

• The Haymarket Café and Restaurant
185 Main St., Northampton, MA 01060   **(413) 586-9969**

Vegetarian. At Haymarket, all food is vegetarian, several items are vegan, and many menu items can be altered to be vegan. The restaurant downstairs serves soups, sandwiches, salads, and Middle Eastern dishes. Upstairs, you'll find a café featuring a juice bar, bakery, and coffee. **Restaurant open daily for lunch and dinner. Café open daily for three meals. Counter service, vegan options, fresh juices, espresso/cappuccino, take-out, $.**

Panda Garden
34 Pleasant St., Northampton, MA 01060   **(413) 584-3858**

Chinese. This restaurant has separate vegetarian and vegan menus from which diners can order classic vegetarian items, such as Buddhist Delight, or other dishes, such as Vegetarian Orange Flavored Beef and Vegetarian General Tso's Chicken. The All-Natural Vegetarian Foods menu items also contain no MSG, no cholesterol, no eggs, and no preservatives. **Open daily for lunch and dinner. Full service, vegan options, delivery, $-$$.**

Paul & Elizabeth's
150 Main St., Northampton, MA 01060   **(413) 584-4832**

Natural foods/macrobiotic. Paul & Elizabeth's, which is located downtown, offers food that is excellent, generously portioned, and reasonably priced. Some of their entrées contain dairy, but these are clearly labeled. The menu includes many vegan options. **Open daily for lunch and dinner. Full service, vegan options, non-alcoholic wine/beer, take-out, VISA/MC, $$.**

ORLEANS

Lo Cicero's Restaurant
Orleans Market Place, 134 Rte. 6A, Orleans, MA 02653   **(508) 255-7100**

Italian. This family restaurant serves macrobiotic, vegetarian, and vegan options. **Open daily for dinner. Full service, macrobiotic/vegan options, non-alcoholic wine/beer, wine/beer/ alcohol, catering, take-out, VISA/MC/AMEX/DC, $$.**

PITTSFIELD

House of India
261 North St, Pittsfield, MA 01201   **(413) 443-3262**

Indian. Many traditional vegetarian Indian dishes are available in the House of India. **Open daily for lunch and dinner. Full service, take-out, $$.**

POCASSET

Stir Crazy
626 MacArthur Blvd., Pocasset, MA 02559   **(508) 564-6464**

Asian. Stir Crazy's menu features Southeast Asian foods, specifically authentic Cambodian cuisine. The restaurant caters to vegetarians and is willing to accomodate special diets. Foods are prepared with 100 percent pure olive oil, using no artificial colors or MSG. **Open Tuesday through Sunday. Closed Monday. Full service, vegan options, take-out, VISA/MC, $$.**

PROVINCETOWN

• Café Crudite
366 Commercial St., #6, Provincetown, MA 02657   **(508) 487-6237**

Vegetarian café. Located in the Pilgrim House Complex with both street and water views, Café Crudite offers soups, salads, and delicious entrées, such as Indonesian Tofu and Vegetables, Pacific Rim Tempeh Sauté, Spicy Seitan and Vegetables, bean burritos, a macrobioitc plate, and much more. Be sure to try some of their vegan desserts, too. **Open daily for lunch and dinner during the summer. Limited hours in the spring and fall. Limited service, vegan/ macrobiotic options, fresh juices, espresso/cappuccino, non-alcoholic wine/beer, $$.** www.cafecrudite.com

The Martin House
157 Commercial St., Provincetown, MA 02657   **(508) 487-1327**

American. Located in the second oldest house in Provincetown (circa 1750), The Martin House offers a view of Provincetown Harbor and at least three vegetarian entrées, such as Spring Vegetable Paella or Wild Mushroom Ravioli with Fennel. **Open daily for dinner. Full service, vegan options, espresso/cappuccino, catering, VISA/MC/AMEX/DISC/DC, $$$.**

Napi's Restaurant
7 Freeman St., Provincetown, MA 02657   **(508) 487-1145**

International. Carousel horses, stained glass, and artwork decorate this restaurant, where you can enjoy Coconut Curry Stir-Fry, Syrian Falafel Melt, or one of the other international vegetarian options. **Open daily for dinner. Open for lunch October through April. Full service, vegan options, espresso/cappuccino, VISA/MC/AMEX/DISC/DC, $$$.**

• Tofu A Go-Go!
336 Commercial St., Provincetown, MA 02657   **(508) 487-6237**

International vegetarian. This restaurant, in Provincetown on Cape Cod, offers great menus for breakfast, lunch, and dinner. Choose from items like Tofu Florentine, vegan Biscuits and Gravy, or the Macro Breakfy (with brown rice, sesame seeds, scallions, and miso soup) for breakfast. Lunch offerings include Jamaica Jerk Seitan, salads, stir fries, burgers, burritos, and much more. The dinner menu builds upon the lunch one, adding entrées like Spicy Sesame Noodles, Indonesian Sauté, and Vegan Alfredo. **Call for seasonal hours. Full service, macrobiotic/vegan options, cooking classes, no credit cards, $-$$.** www.tofuagogo.com

SANDWICH

Marshland Restaurant
109 Rte. 6A, Sandwich, MA 02563   **(508) 888-9824**

American. Marshland features salads, sandwiches, dinner entrées, some Middle Eastern foods, and pasta. **Open Monday for breakfast and dinner. Open Tuesday through Sunday for three meals. Full service, non-alcoholic beer, wine/beer/alcohol, VISA/MC, $$.**

SHELBURNE FALLS

Copper Angel Café

2 State St., Shelburne Falls, MA 01370   **(413) 625-2727**

Natural foods. The atmosphere at Copper Angel Café is "heavenly," with over 100 angels in the dining room and a divine view of the famous bridge of Flowers and Deerfield River. In addition to the atmosphere, enjoy vegetarian dishes like the Angel Burger made from a blend of grains, nuts, and seeds; Grilled Tofu Sandwich; or Lentil Cutlets with Vegetarian Gravy. **Call for hours. Full service, vegan options, espresso/cappuccino, non-alcoholic wine/beer, take-out, VISA/MC, $-$$.**

• McCusker's Market and Bruncheon Deli

3 State St., Shelburne Falls, MA 01370   **(413) 625-9411**

Vegetarian/natural foods. McCusker's offers a large selection of vegetarian sandwiches, as well as many vegan options. Enjoy outdoor seating with a view of a "Bridge of Flowers," or take advantage of the picnic area out back. **Open daily for breakfast and lunch. Limited service, vegan options, VISA/MC/DISC, $.**

SOMERVILLE

India Palace

23 Union Sq., Somerville, MA 02143   **(617) 666-9770**

Indian. Dine on breads, vegetable samosas, and numerous vegetarian and vegan Indian entrées at India Palace. **Open Monday through Saturday for lunch and dinner. Open Sunday for dinner only. Full service, vegan options, take-out, $$.**

Johnny D's Uptown Restaurant

17 Holland St., Somerville, MA 02144   **(617) 776-2004**

American. You'll find several vegetarian options on this menu, including a few veggie sandwiches and vegetable and bean burritos. There is also a seperate brunch menu with items you can only get on the weekend, such as Grilled Marinated Tofu and Goat Cheese. **Open Monday through Friday for lunch through late night. Open Saturday and Sunday for breakfast through late night. Full service, vegan options, VISA/MC/AMEX/DISC, $-$$.**

SOUTH ATTLEBORO

Arbour-Fuller Hospital

231 Washington St., South Attleboro, MA 02703   **(508) 761-8500**

Cafeteria. This is a not-for-profit hospital owned and operated by the Seventh-day Adventist Church. **Open daily for lunch and dinner. Cafeteria, vegan options, take-out, no credit cards, $.**

Restaurant codes: ✪ Reviewers' Choice   • Vegetarian Restaurant   • • Vegan Restaurant
Restaurant prices: **$** less than $6   **$$** $6-$12   **$$$** more than $12
Credit Cards Accepted: VISA - VISA   MC - MasterCard   AMEX - American Express
DISC - Discover   DC - Diner's Club

WALTHAM

Bombay Mahal Restaurant
458 Moody St., Waltham, MA 02453   **(781) 893-9988**
Indian. Bombay Mahal serves both north and south Indian cuisine, as well as a nice selection of vegetarian entrées. **Open daily for lunch and dinner. Full service, vegan options, take-out, catering, fresh juices, special drinks, beer/wine, VISA/MC/AMEX/DISC/DC, $-$$.**

•• Carambola
663 Main St., Waltham, MA 02451   **(781) 899-2244**
Vegan/Cambodian. Try the Carambola Salad with starfruit and basil, or the Kuy Tieu Chah with bean sprouts, rice noodles, and freshly roasted peanuts. **Open Monday through Friday for lunch and dinner. Open Saturday and Sunday for dinner only. Full service, vegan options, VISA/MC/AMEX/DISC/DC, $-$$.**

• Masao's Kitchen
582 Moody St., Waltham, MA 02453   **(781) 647-7977**
Vegetarian. The choice of foods and cooking methods are based on macrobiotic teachings, using organic vegetables. No refined sugar, preservatives, irradiated or genetically-modified foods, or tropical oils are used. **Open Monday through Saturday for lunch and dinner. Closed Sunday. Full service, vegan options, fresh juices, take-out, catering, VISA/MC, $$.** www.masaoskitchen.com

WEST STOCKBRIDGE

Truc Orient Express ✪
3 Harris St., West Stockbridge, MA 01266   **(413) 232-4204**
Vietnamese. Truc Orient Express offers a seperate vegetarian menu that includes Marinated Tofu over Fine Rice Noodles, Tofu with Lemon Grass, Sweet and Sour Mushrooms, Vegetarian Fried Rice, soups, salads, and more. **Open daily for lunch and dinner. Closed Tuesday in winter. Full service, wine/beer/alcohol, catering, take-out, VISA/MC/AMEX/DISC, $$-$$$.**

WESTMINSTER

The 1761 Old Mill Restaurant
Rte. 2A, E., Westminster, MA 01473   **(978) 874-5941**
Family dining. The Old Mill Restaurant offers delicious vegetarian meals in a country setting. Relax beside the brook and enjoy the old saw mill. **Open Tuesday through Saturday for lunch and dinner. Open Sunday for brunch, dinner, and late night service. Closed Monday. Full service, wine/beer/alcohol, VISA/MC/AMEX/DISC, $$-$$$.**

WOODS HOLE

Fishmonger's Café
56 Water St., Woods Hole, MA 02543   **(508) 540-5376**
Natural foods. Fishmonger's offers a full range of vegetarian dishes, as well as home-baked

goods. Open Wednesday through Monday for three meals. Open Tuesday for lunch and dinner only. Full service, wine/beer, VISA/MC, $$-$$$.

WORCESTER

The Gentle Lentil

800 Main St., Worcester, MA 01610   **(508) 753-8663**

Natural foods. A restaurant for people who believe in wholesome, vegetarian-inspired food that's exciting, ethnically diverse, and satisfyingly delicious. **Open Wednesday through Saturday for lunch and dinner. Open Tuesday for lunch only. Open Sunday for brunch only. Closed Monday. Full service, vegan options, catering, fresh juices, smoothies, VISA/ MC/AMEX/DISC, $-$$.**

• Lily Pad

755 Grafton St., Worcester, MA 01604   **(508) 890-8899**

Vegetarian/Chinese. They offer an extensive menu of vegetarian appetizers and entrées, including many made with mock meats. Menu items include sour bamboo soup, tempura udon, and "chicken" with lemon grass and chili. Spicy dishes can be altered to suit diners' tastes. **Open daily for lunch and dinner. Full service, take-out, catering, smoothies, soymilk, $$.**

Living Earth

232 Chandler St., Worcester, MA 01609   **(508) 753-1896**

Natural foods. Although not strictly vegetarian, there is a large selection of fine natural vegetarian and vegan dishes, and they offer several dairy-free desserts. **Open daily for lunch and dinner. Full service, take-out, catering, fresh juices, smoothies, espresso/cappuccino, non-alcoholic beer, VISA/MC/AMEX/DISC, $-$$.**

•• Quan Yin Vegetarian

56 Hamilton St., Worcester, MA 01604   **(508) 831-1322**

Vegan. Chinese, Indian, Thai and Vietnamese foods are served in a comfortable atmosphere. Feast on fresh salads, soups, rice, and noodle dishes as well as several tofu options. Additional entrées include meat analogs, such as vegetable "chicken, pork, or shrimp." **Open Monday through Saturday for lunch and dinner. Closed Sunday. Full service, take-out, soymilk, $-$$.**

Michigan

ANN ARBOR

(For restaurant listings in the surrounding areas, see Canton, Dearborn Heights, Farmington Hills, and Livonia.)

The Blue Nile
221 E. Washington St., Ann Arbor, MI 48104   **(734) 998-4746**
Ethiopian. Their authentic Ethiopian cuisine includes many vegetarian options. The all-you-can-eat Vegetarian Meal includes cabbage, collard greens, and red, green, and yellow lentils. Open daily. Full service, vegan options, wine/beer/alcohol, non-smoking, VISA/MC/AMEX/DISC, $$-$$$.

• Chia Shiang Restaurant
2016 Packard St., Ann Arbor, MI 48104   **(734) 741-0778**
Vegetarian/Chinese. Chia Shiang serves delicious Vegetarian Pot Stickers, Spring Rolls, and vegetarian entrées. Only a few dishes contain eggs. **Open daily for lunch and dinner.** Full service, vegan options, take-out, VISA/MC/AMEX, $$.

Del Rio
122 W. Washington St., Ann Arbor, MI 48104   **(734) 761-2530**
International. This hip restaurant serves up mainly vegetarian Mexican, American, and Italian cuisine, including salads, nachos, wheat crust pizzas, tempeh burgers, and quesadillas. **Open Sunday through Friday for dinner through late night service. Open Saturday for lunch through late night service.** Full service, vegan options, no credit cards, $-$$.

• Earthen Jar
311 S. 5th Ave., Ann Arbor, MI 48104   **(734) 327-9464**
Vegetarian. This restaurant is located near the Ann Arbor District Library. Meals are served buffet-style and you pay by the pound. A wide range of dishes are offered. **Open Monday through Saturday for lunch and dinner. Closed Sunday.** Limited service, vegan options, take-out, $$.

Inn Season Café ✿
211 E. Washington St., Ann Arbor, MI 48104   **(734) 302-7701**
Café. Even some non-vegetarians call this the best restaurant in Michigan. Though fish can be ordered specially, the menu itself is vegetarian, offering items like Scrambled Tofu, Black Bean Avocado Quesadillas, Three Mushroom Walnut Pizza, Seitan Sandwiches sautéed with onions and tamari, Cashew Ginger Stir-Fry, organic salads, and much more. Sugar-free desserts are also served. Note that the soy cheese here is not vegan. With dimly lit chandeliers, hardwood floors, and lace curtains, this restaurant is a great place for a special occasion. **Open Tuesday through Saturday for lunch and dinner. Open Sunday for brunch. Closed Monday.** Full service, macrobiotic/vegan options, fresh juices, espresso/cappuccino, beer/wine/alcohol, non-alcoholic beer, non-smoking, take-out, VISA/MC/AMEX/DISC/DC, $$.
www.innseasoncafe.com

People's Food Co-op and Café Verde
216 N. 4th Ave., Ann Arbor, MI 48104   **(734) 994-9174**
Café. Café Verde at People's Food Co-op features a Food Bar with super-fresh organic salad ingredients, hot soups, sides, beans and rice, vegetarian sandwiches, and entrées. Some hot items are only available for lunch and dinner, but you can enjoy bagels with dairyless cream cheese, hummus, or sunflower sprouts or their vegan and dairyless cookies, cakes, and pastries at any time. **Open daily for three meals. Counter service, vegan options, espresso/cappuccino, soymilk, non-smoking, take-out, VISA/MC/AMEX/DISC/DC, $.** www.peoplesfood.coop/storecafe.html

• Seva
314 E. Liberty St., Ann Arbor, MI 48104   **(734) 662-1111**
Vegetarian/Mexican. We've been told Seva offers some of the best Mexican food in Michigan, and it's all vegetarian! Menu headings include small courses, salads, soups, Mexican specialties, Oriental specialties, sandwiches, omelettes, beverages and blended drinks. Vegan options are clearly indicated on the menu. As an appetizer, try the Yam Fries or the Cold Sesame Noodles. For an entrée, enjoy the Melanzana Rustico (grilled eggplant over noodles with olive oil). **Open Monday through Friday. Open Saturday and Sunday for brunch. Full service, vegan options, wine/beer/alcohol, catering, take-out, VISA/MC/DISC, $$.**

Shalimar
307 S. Main St., Ann Arbor, MI 48104   **(734) 663-1500**
Indian. Vegetarian options are available at this restaurant, which features Indian and Mexican foods. **Open daily for lunch and dinner. Full service, vegan options, non-alcoholic beer, wine/beer/alcohol, take-out, VISA/MC, $.**

Whole Foods Market & Deli
2398 E. Stadium Blvd., Ann Arbor, MI 48104   **(734) 971-3366**
2789 Plymouth Rd., Ann Arbor, MI 48105   **(734) 769-0900**
Natural foods deli. This gourmet natural foods deli offers organic salads, vegan entrées, daily soups, a salad bar, and a bakery. **Open daily for three meals. Deli-style, vegan options, fresh juices, take-out, VISA/MC, $-$$.**

BERRIEN SPRINGS

• Andrews University
Campus Center, U.S. Hwy. 31 N., Berrien Springs, MI 49104   **(616) 471-3161**
Vegetarian/cafeteria. Cyclical menu changes feature soups, main dishes, hot food selections, plus an extensive salad bar and desserts. Soy- and gluten-based meat analogs are utilized in many dishes. **Open daily during school year. Call for summer hours. Cafeteria, $.**

CANTON

Good Food Company Deli
Canton Corners Shopping Center
42615 Ford Rd., Canton, MI 48187   **(248) 362-0886**
Juice bar/deli. Good Food Company's deli serves vegetarian, vegan, and organic entrées and

has a bakery that features vegan cookies. The atmosphere is earthy and informal. **Open Monday through Saturday for three meals. Open Sunday for lunch and early dinner.** Cafeteria, vegan/macrobiotic options, fresh juices, soymilk, smoothies, non-smoking, take-out, VISA/MC, $.

La Shish

1699 N. Canton Center Rd., Canton, MI 48187   **(734) 983-9000**
Lebanese. La Shish offers a stunning décor and many vegetarian dishes, all of which are noted on the menu. Choose from dishes like Rice Almond Salad, Spinach Fatoosh, Baba Ghanouj, Hummus with Sautéed Pine Nuts, the Falafel Plate, Mjadra (lentils and cracked wheat cooked with onions and olive oil), or the Lentil, Potato, or Tomato Kibbee. **Open daily for lunch and dinner.** Full service, vegan options, fresh juices, smoothies, special drinks, take-out, delivery, catering, VISA, $-$$. www.lashish.com

DEARBORN

La Shish

13250 Rotunda Dr., Dearborn, MI 48120   **(313) 441-2900**
22039 Michigan Ave., Dearborn, MI 48124   **(313) 562-7200**
12918 Michigan Ave., Dearborn, MI 48126   **(313) 584-4477**
Lebanese. See description under Canton, MI.

DEARBORN HEIGHTS

La Pita

22435 Michigan Ave., Dearborn Heights, MI 48124   **(313) 565-7482**
Middle Eastern. This restaurant, known for its good food and service, serves hummus, tabbouleh, baba ghanouj, falafel, and other favorites. Parking is arranged for customers. **Open daily for lunch and dinner.** Full service, vegan options, take-out, VISA/MC/AMEX/DISC/ DC, $$-$$$.

DETROIT

(For restaurant listings in the surrounding areas, see Dearborn, Farmington Hills, Ferndale, Grosse Pointe, Harper Woods, Livonia, Roseville, Royal Oak, Southfield, Troy, Warren, and West Bloomfield.)

The Blue Nile

508 Monroe St., Detroit, MI 48322   **(313) 964-6699**
Ethiopian. See description under Ann Arbor, MI. **Open Friday through Tuesday for dinner. Closed Wednesday and Thursday.**

Don Pedro's

24366 Grand River Ave., Detroit, MI 48219   **(313) 537-1450**
Mexican. Vegetarian dining is easy at Don Pedro's, as there is no lard in the beans and no chicken broth in the rice. There is a nice atmosphere. **Open daily for dinner. Open Saturday and Sunday for lunch.** Full service, vegan options, wine/beer/alcohol, take-out, VISA/MC/AMEX/DISC, $$.

Traffic Jam and Snug
511 W. Canfield St., Detroit, MI 48201   **(313) 831-9470**
Natural foods. The menu changes weekly at this natural foods eatery, but there are always vegetarian entrées and usually vegan options as well. Seasonal and local foods are emphasized. Homemade breads and brews are also offered. The service here is friendly. **Open Monday through Saturday. Closed Sunday. Full service, vegan options, fresh juices, wine/beer, take-out, VISA/MC/DISC, $$.**

EAST GRAND RAPIDS

Osta's Lebanese Cuisine
2228 Wealthy SE, East Grand Rapids, MI 49506   **(616) 456-8999**
Lebanese. Osta's offers a variety of vegetarian selections. Choose from appetizers like cucumber lebneh (Lebanese yogurt, diced cucumber, garlic, and mint) to lubyee (green beans sautéed with tomatoes, onions, and garlic in tomato sauce). Entrées include moudardara (lentils and rice sautéed in olive oil and onion) and hummus sandwiches made from pita bread. **Open Tuesday through Friday for lunch and dinner. Open Saturday for dinner only. Closed Monday and Sunday. Full service, vegan options, take-out, VISA/MC/DISC, $$.**

EAST LANSING

Beggar's Banquet
218 Abbott Rd., East Lansing, MI 48823   **(517) 351-4540**
American. Located near the north side of the Michigan State University campus, this restaurant offers a decent selection of vegetarian options in an environment decorated with paintings and sculptures by local artists. You can choose from the "Vegomatic" Sandwich, Three-Bean Vegetarian Chili, Vegetarian Manicotti, a Wild Mushroom Napolean, the Spinach and Dried Cherry Salad with walnuts and bleu cheese, and more. Note that the Black Bean Burger does contain eggs. **Open daily for lunch and dinner. Full service, vegan options, VISA/MC/AMEX/DISC. www.beggarsbanquet.com**

Sultan's Place
Hannah Plaza, 4790 S. Hagadorn Rd., East Lansing, MI 48823   (517) 333-4444
Middle Eastern/Mediterranean. This restaurant offers about 20 vegetarian options, including stuffed grave leaves, hummus, baba ganouj, and falafel. **Open Sunday though Friday for lunch and dinner. Open Saturday from late afternoon through dinner. Full service, vegan options, fresh juices, VISA/MC/AMEX, $-$$.**

FARMINGTON HILLS

Anita's Kitchen
31005 Orchard Lake Rd., Farmington Hills, MI 48018   **(248) 855-4150**
Lebanese. The menu features falafel and hummus, as well as black bean soup and vegetarian

---

Restaurant codes: ✪ Reviewers' Choice   • Vegetarian Restaurant   •• Vegan Restaurant
Restaurant prices: **$** less than $6   **$$** $6-$12   **$$$** more than $12
Credit Cards Accepted: VISA - VISA   MC - MasterCard   AMEX - American Express
DISC - Discover   DC - Diner's Club

chili. Open daily for lunch and dinner. Full service, vegan options, take-out, VISA/MC/ AMEX/DISC, $-$$$.

La Shish
37610 W. 12 Mile Rd. (At Halsted Rd.)
Farmington Hills, MI 48331   **(248) 553-0700**
Lebanese. See description under Canton, MI.

Shalimar
29200 Orchard Lake Rd., Farmington Hills, MI 48334   **(248) 626-2982**
Indian. See description under Ann Arbor, MI.

• Udipi Vegetarian
29210 Orchard Lake Rd., Farmington Hills, MI 48334-2965   **(248) 626-6021**
Vegetarian/Indian. This restaurant serves South Indian vegetarian dishes, including iddly, lentil soup, masala dosais, uthappams, curry dishes, rice dishes, Indian breads, desserts, and more. They also offer a daily lunch buffet. **Open daily for lunch and dinner. Full service, vegan options, special drinks, catering, VISA/MC, $-$$. www.udipirestaurant.com**

FERNDALE

Om Café
23136 N. Woodward Ave., Ferndale, MI 48220   **(248) 548-1941**
Macrobiotic. The Om Café offers terrific macrobiotic food, including a good range of vegetarian and vegan dishes. **Open Monday through Saturday for lunch and dinner. Closed Sunday. Full service, vegan options, non-smoking, $.**

GRAND RAPIDS

(For restaurant listings in the surrounding areas, see East Grand Rapids.)

Bombay Cuisine
1420 Lake Dr., SE, Grand Rapids, MI 49506   **(616) 456-7055**
Indian. This casual yet romantic Indian and Pakistani restaurant is among the best in the area. It offers a wide range of vegetarian fare, including Kafta Dilkush (vegetarian dumplings), Saag (spinach stuffed bread), Kormas, Kabobs, and Onion Bajia. **Open Sunday and Monday for lunch and dinner. Closed Tuesday. Open Wednesday through Friday for lunch and dinner. Open Saturday for dinner only. Full service, vegan options, beer/wine/alcohol, non-alcoholic beer, take-out, VISA/MC/AMEX/DISC, $$-$$$.**

• Gaia Coffee House
209 Diamond St., Grand Rapids, MI 49506   **(616) 454-6233**
Vegetarian. This restaurant is actually vegetarian, though most of the regulars are not. Gaia offers delightfully fresh food, including the veggie hash, which is a mound of colorful vegetables smothered in melted cheese and blended with a hint of garlic (can be made vegan). Many of the menu items are made fresh in house, including focaccia and corn breads, as well as the infamous Gaia cookies (which are vegan) and chock-full of everything that makes cookies so good. House recipe soups and nightly dinner specials ranging from polenta to

pasta, keep even the most carnivorous coming back for more. Featured dishes include the mean green burrito, sundried tomato-artichoke dip, and the suicide juice to drink. **Open daily for three meals. Open Sunday for brunch. Full service, vegan options, fresh juices, soymilk, smoothies, espresso/cappucino, take-out, macrobiotic options, VISA/MC, $$.**

• Little Africa
956 E. Fulton, Grand Rapids, MI 49503   **(616) 222-1169**
Vegetarian/Ethopian. This excellent restaurant serves delicious, mostly vegan dishes, including spiced peas, gomen (greens), potatoes, cabbage, lentiles, split peas, flax seed dishes, and beets with injera, Ethopian bread that is used instead of utensils. Juices, coffees, and teas are also available. **Open daily for lunch and dinner. Full service, vegan options, take-out, no credit cards, $.**

GROSSE POINTE

Atom's Juice Café
345 Fisher Rd., Ste. B, Grosse Pointe, MI 48230   **(313) 885-0095**
Juice bar. Atom's Juice Café serves fruit juices, smoothies, tea and coffee, soups, salads, and healthy snacks. It is also the first certified Green Restaurant in Michigan, meaning that they recycle, use eco-friendly carry-out containers and cleaning supplies, and are otherwise environmentally aware. **Open Monday through Saturday for lunch and early dinner. Open Sunday for brunch. Take-out, vegan options, fruit juices, smoothies, special drinks.** www. atomsjuicecafe.cafeprogressive.com

HARBERT

Café Gulistan
13581 Red Arrow Hwy., Harbert, MI 49115   **(269) 469-6779**
Middle Eastern. Located near Lake Michigan and a popular antiquing area, Café Gulistan offers many vegetarian and vegan options amidst its Middle Eastern and Mediteranean fare. Their menu includes sautéed vegetable dishes, baba ganouj, tabbouli, falalel, and much more. Reservations recommended. **Call for seasonal hours. Full service, vegan options, fresh juices, espresso/cappuccino, beer/wine/alcohol, take-out, catering, VISA/MC/AMEX/DISC, $$-$$$.**

HARPER WOODS

Steve's Back Room
19872 Kelly Rd., Harper Woods, MI 48225   **(313) 527-7240**
Middle Eastern. This Middle Eastern Restaurant offers an array of vegetarian meals. Try the Bulgur and Beans, Grapeleaves, or Meatless Kousa. **Open Monday through Saturday for lunch and dinner. Closed Sunday. Limited service, vegan options, VISA/MC/AMEX/ DISC/DC, $-$$.**

KALAMAZOO

Just Good Food Deli
Rose St. Market, 303 N. Rose St., Kalamazoo, MI 49007   **(616) 383-1033**
Natural foods deli. This natural foods store's deli offers friendly service and such vegetarian

options as soups, salads, freshly-made sandwiches, and veggie pesto pastas. **Open Monday through Friday for breakfast through early dinner. Open Saturday for lunch. Closed Sunday. Counter service, macrobiotic/vegan options, non-smoking, take-out, VISA/MC/AMEX, $.**

Mi Ranchito

3112 S. 9th St., Kalamazoo, MI 49009   **(269) 375-5861**
3806 S. Westnedge Ave., Kalamazoo, MI 49008   **(269) 343-7262**

Mexican. Mi Ranchito offers a seperate vegetarian menu that includes enchiladas, quesadillas, fajitas, burritos, tamales, chili rellenos, and many other traditional Mexican dishes at good prices. They use corn oil for all frying, and no preservatives, artificial ingredients, lard, animal fats, or chicken broth is used in the preparation of any of the dishes. **Open daily for lunch and dinner. Full service, vegan options, catering, take-out, VISA/MC/DISC, $-$$.**

LANSING

(For restaurant listings in the surrounding areas, see East Lansing.)

Apple Jade

300 N. Clippert St., Lansing, MI 48912   **(517) 332-1111**

Chinese. This Chinese restaurant offers Vegetarian Pot Stickers, as well as many other vegetarian entrées. **Open daily for lunch and dinner. Full service, take-out, VISA/MC, $$.**

LIVONIA

La Shish

37367 6 Mile Rd., Livonia, MI 48152   **(734) 464-8200**

Lebanese. See description under Canton, MI.

MARQUETTE

Sweet Water Café

517 N. 3rd St., Marquette, MI 49855   **(906) 226-7009**

Café. This establishment offers quite a few vegan options for one that isn't vegetarian. For breakfast, choose from items like the Café Scramble (herbed tofu, broccoli, tomatoes, and onions served with potatoes and toast) or the Hot Winter Grain Cereal (oatmeal, wheatberries, brown rice, and millet topped with dried apricots, raisins, and toasted almonds). Lunch and dinner selections include Tabbouleh, the Hammondsport (greens topped with cauliflower, orange, and raisins), Tofu Stir-Fry, and the Trio Plate of Beans and Rice, Salsa, & Vegetables. They offer at least one vegetarian soup each day and have a children's menu. They are convenient to Northern Michigan University and close to the coast of Lake Superior. **Open Monday and Tuesday for breakfast and lunch. Open Wednesday through Sunday for three meals. Full service, vegan options, fresh juices, espresso/cappuccino, soymilk, beer/wine/ alcohol, VISA/MC/DISC.** www.sweetwatercafe.org

---

Restaurant codes: ✪ Reviewers' Choice   • Vegetarian Restaurant   • • Vegan Restaurant
Restaurant prices: **$** less than $6   **$$** $6-$12   **$$$** more than $12
Credit Cards Accepted: VISA - VISA   MC - MasterCard   AMEX - American Express
DISC - Discover   DC - Diner's Club

OTSEGO

Mi Ranchito Tres

108 E. Allegan St., Otsego, MI 49078   (269) 692-6008
Mexican. See description under Kalamazoo, MI.

ROSEVILLE

La Shish

Gratiot @ Masonic, 32088 Gratiot Ave., Roseville, MI 48066   (586) 415-0500
Lebanese. See description under Canton, MI.

ROYAL OAK

• Inn Season Café

500 E. Fourth St., Royal Oak, MI 48067   (248) 547-7916
Café. See description under Ann Arbor, MI. This location is 7 miles northwest of Detroit.
Open Tuesday through Saturday for dinner. Closed Sunday and Monday.

SOUTHFIELD

Jerusalem Pizza

62025 Greenfield Rd., Southfield, MI 48076   (248) 552-0088
Kosher. Jerusalem Pizza is a certified kosher pizza restaurant. Their vegetarian options
include the Veggie Meatball Sandwich, Falafel Calzone, and Potato Jerusalem Pie. **Open
daily for lunch and dinner. Limited service, vegan options, catering, take out, $.**

TROY

Good Food Company Deli

74 W. Maple Rd., Troy, MI 48084   (248) 362-0886
Juice bar/deli. See description under Canton, MI. This location is in one of the largest
health food stores in the Detroit area.

La Shish

3720 Rochester Rd., Troy, MI 48083   (248) 457-1111
Lebanese. See description under Canton, MI.

Whole Foods Market & Deli

2880 W. Maple Rd., Troy, MI 48084   (248) 649-9600
Natural foods deli. See description under Ann Arbor, MI.

UNION CITY

• Creative Health Institute

918 Union City Rd., Union City, MI 49094   (517) 278-5837
Vegetarian/living foods. Sample a living foods buffet that includes assorted sprouts, organic

indoor greens, seed cheeses, raw vegetable dishes, soups, and salads. **Call for hours. Buffet, vegan options, $.**

WARREN

La Shish
32401 Van Dyke Ave. (Near 14 Mile Rd.), Warren, MI 48093   (586) 977-2177
Lebanese. See description under Canton, MI.

WEST BLOOMFIELD

La Shish
6303 Orchard Lake Rd., West Bloomfield, MI 48322   (248) 538-0800
Lebanese. See description under Canton, MI.

Whole Foods Market & Deli
7350 Orchard Lake Rd., West Bloomfield, MI 48322   (248) 538-4600
Natural foods deli. See description under Ann Arbor, MI.

Minnesota

ANOKA

Lakewind's Anoka Food Co-op Grocery & Café
1917 2nd Ave. S., Anoka, MN 55303   (763) 427-4340
Natural foods café. Anoka serves various international vegetarian foods, including veggie burgers, spanakopita, quiche, wild rice stir-fry, soups, salads, sandwiches, pies, cookies, cakes, and more. **Open Monday through Friday for lunch. Closed Saturday and Sunday. Cafeteria, vegan options, fresh juices, take-out, $.**

BLAINE

Organica Cafeteria
Aveda Corporation, 4000 Pheasant Ridge Dr., Blaine, MN 55449   (763) 783-4069
Organic natural foods. Located at Aveda Corporation Headquarters, this employee cafeteria is open to the public and offers many vegetarian entrées, soups, salads, and sandwiches. **Open Monday through Friday for breakfast and lunch. Closed Saturday and Sunday. Cafeteria, vegan options, fresh juices, take-out, catering, $.**

BLOOMINGTON

Tandoor Restaurant
8062 Morgan Cir. S., Bloomington, MN 55431   (952) 885-9060
Indian. Their menu features many vegetarian offerings, including appetizers, Channa Aloo (chickpeas and potato), Yellow Dahl (lentils), Bhindy (Okra) Masala, Malai Kofta (veggie

rolls with cashews and raisins), Bangan Barta (puréed eggplant with onions, tomatoes, and peas), Mushroom Palak (with spinach in curry), and a vegetarian combination platter. **Open Monday through Saturday for lunch and dinner. Closed Sunday. Full service, vegan options, wine/beer, non-alcoholic beer, take-out, catering, $$-$$$.** www.tandoormn.com

COLUMBIA HEIGHTS

•Udupi Café
4920 Central Ave. NE, Columbia Heights, MN 55421   (763) 574-1113
Vegetarian/Indian. This fully vegetarian Indian restaurant offers a variety of authentic dishes, many of which are vegan. House specials and desserts, as well as South Indian Thali, Vegetable Biriyani, and Dhal Curry, are featured. **Open daily for lunch and dinner. Full service, vegan options, catering, $$.**

DULUTH

The New Scenic Café
5461 N. Shore Dr., Duluth, MN 55804   (218) 525-6274
Eclectic. A passion for interesting and beautiful foods combined with an interest in the cuisines of the world set the stage for the fare at the New Scenic Café. This culinary global fusion includes a variety of vegetarian and vegan options. Reservations are recommended. **Opens daily for three meals. Full service, vegan options, fresh juices, beer/wine, non-alcoholic beer/wine, special drinks, VISA/MC/DISC, $$-$$$.** www.ScenicCafe.com

Taste of Saigon
DeWitt-Seitz Marketplace, 94 Lake Ave. S., Duluth, MN 55802   (218) 727-1598
Vietnamese. The Taste of Saigon offers a selection of vegetarian dishes, including tofu and mock meat items. **Open Monday through Saturday. Closed Sunday. Full service, vegan options, take-out, $-$$.**

EDINA

The Good Earth
3460 W. 70th St., Edina, MN 55450   (612) 925-1001
Natural foods. The Good Earth is a casual, welcoming restaurant with a spiritual feel. Tea, cinnamon, and citrus fill the air in a totally non-smoking environment. Fresh baked goods are offered daily. **Open daily for three meals. Limited service, vegan options, fresh juices, smoothies, soy and rice milk, beer/wine, MC/AMEX/DISC/DC, $$.** www.goodearth.com

HASTINGS

Professor Java's Coffeehouse and Deli
202 E. Second St., Hastings, MN 55033   (651) 438-9962
Coffeehouse. This deli offers several vegetarian sandwich options, such as the Department of Agriculture Vegetarian and the Black Bean Salsa Burger. They also feature a veggie chili. **Open Monday through Saturday for breakfast through early dinner. Open Sunday for lunch. Counter service, vegan options, smoothies, $.**

MANKATO

The Coffee Hag

329 N. Riverfront Dr., Mankato, MN 56001 **(507) 387-5533**

Coffeehouse. Customers say that Coffee Hag presents fast healthy, deli-style food at a fair price. Each day features a new menu of vegetarian and vegan items, including soups, salads, sandwiches, and calzones. Located in the historic old downtown, the café offers a unique cultural and dining experience. Regional artists, musicians, and poets find The Coffee Hag a welcome oasis to present their art amid acres of cornfields. **Open daily for three meals. Limited service, vegan options, take-out, espresso/cappuccino, soymilk, catering, $.**

MAPLEWOOD

Taste Of India

1745 Cope Ave., Maplewood, MN 55109 **(651) 773-5477**

Indian. This restaurant offers several vegetarian offerings, including a dinner for two. Dishes can be made mildly spiced to extra hot at a diner's request. **Open daily for lunch and dinner. Full service, vegan options, reservations recommended, wine/beer, VISA/MC/AMEX/DISC/DC, $$.**

MINNEAPOLIS

(For restaurant listings in the surrounding areas, see Anoka, Blaine, Bloomington, Columbia Heights, Edina, Hastings, Maplewood, Minnetonka, Roseville, Spring Lake Park, St. Louis Park, and St. Paul.)

Asase Yaa Juice Bar & Global Gifts

2922 Bryant Ave. S., Minneapolis, MN 55408 **(612) 821-6484**

Juice bar. Asase Yaa, or Mother Earth in Ghanaian mythology, is interested in providing for the needs of all living beings. She takes a special interest in caring and providing for your nutritional needs. The restaurant uses organically-grown crops and offers fresh-squeezed fruit and raw vegetable juices, crisp salads, wraps, homemade soups, and other traditional Ghanaian healing dishes for your dining pleasure. **Open daily for three meals. Full service, vegan options, fresh juices, smoothies, espresso/cappuccino, $-$$.**

Binh Mink Restaurant

514 E. 60th St., Minneapolis, MN 55419 **(612) 869-1148**

Vietnamese/Chinese. Vegetable egg rolls, vegetable lo mein, bean curd selections, mock duck dishes, and mushroom chow mein are examples of menu items friendly to vegetarians. **Open Monday through Saturday for lunch and dinner. Open Sunday for dinner only. Full service, take-out, delivery, $.**

Café Brenda

300 1st Ave. N., Minneapolis, MN 55401 **(612) 342-9230**

Natural foods. Located in a restored warehouse in a historic district of downtown Minneapolis, Café Brenda prepares a good selection of vegetarian appetizers, sandwiches, and entrées. There are daily specials, plus a full á la carte menu and a children's menu. No smoking is allowed.

Open Monday through Saturday. Closed Sunday. Full service, vegan options, fresh juices, espresso, wine/beer/alcohol, non-alcoholic beer, take-out, VISA/MC/AMEX/DC, $$.

•• Ecopolitan
2409 Lyndale Ave. S., Minneapolis, MN 55405   **(612) 874-7336**

Vegan. Ecopolitan's menu consists entirely of raw, organic vegan foods and offers a nice variety of soups, salads, entrées, pizzas, and desserts. The clean, smoke-free environment is enhanced by the use of non-toxic paints and building materials. Dress is typically informal but suitable for business entertaining. Reservations are recommended. The restaurant also has an ecological shop that sells natural, non-toxic home and body products. Ecopolitan emphasizes education and social support and offers weekly events that emphasize health and sustainability on Mondays. **Open daily for three meals. Full service, vegan options, fresh juices, smoothies, non-alcoholic cocktails, take-out (please bring your own containers), VISA/MC, $$-$$$.** www.ecopolitan.net

Falafel King
701 W. Lake St., Minneapolis, MN 55408   **(612) 824-7887**

Middle Eastern. Try the tabbouleh salad with the Falafel King Combo (hummus, eggplant, king salad, potatoes, and falafel) at this highly-recommended establishment. **Open daily for lunch and dinner. Limited service, vegan options, fresh juices, $.**

French Meadow Bakery & Café
2610 Lyndale Ave. S., Minneapolis, MN 55408   **(612) 870-7855**

Café. French Meadow is a highly-recommended, casual café with a bakery that is renowned for its great-tasting, healthy breads. It offers a nice variety of vegetarian meals, from the Tempeh Fajita Wrap to the award-winning Vegan Black Bean Chili. Try the Vegan Fruit Crisp for dessert. The restaurant also features a large sidewalk café, which lends itself to an eclectic atmosphere and crowd. **Open daily for three meals. Limited service, vegan/macrobiotic options, fresh juices, smoothies, soymilk, espresso/cappuccino, beer/wine/alcohol, non-alcoholic beer/wine, catering, VISA/MC/AMEX, $$.** www.FrenchMeadow.com

Galactic Pizza
2917 Lyndale Ave. S., Minneapolis, MN 55408   **(612) 824-9100**

Pizza. Located in uptown Minneapolis, this colorful establishment touts itself as "pizza with a conscience." They use hemp for eveything from their menus to their pesto, and 90 percent of the pizzas are available as vegetarian or vegan, which substitutes gourmet mozzarella alternative for cheese and mock duck for chicken. Interesting offerings include the Alamo, with BBQ sauce, cheddar, and red peppers; the CSA, which uses fresh seasonal crops from the Natural Harvest Community Supported Agriculture; and the truly unique Paul Bunyan with morel mushrooms and wild rice. Pasta, salads, desserts, and soft drinks are also available. **Open daily for lunch through late night, Full service, vegan options, take-out, delivery, VISA/MC/AMEX/DISC, $$.** www.galacticpizza.com

It's Greek To Me
626 W. Lake St., Minneapolis, MN 55408   **(612) 825-9922**

Greek. To start things off, try the Fakes Me Spanaki soup with lentils and spinach. There are six vegetarian entrées, but you may want to try out the Vegetarian Mousaka and wash it down with a Greek Coffee. Open Tuesday through Sunday for lunch and dinner. Closed Mondays. Full service, vegan options, VISA/MC/AMEX/DC, $-$$.

The Lotus of Campus
313 Oak St., SE, Minneapolis, MN 55414   **(612) 331-1781**
Vietnamese. The Lotus has a vegetarian section on its menu. Open daily for lunch and dinner. Full service, beer, take-out, no credit cards, $.

Lotus-To-Go
Grant Mall, 113 Grant St., Minneapolis, MN 55403   **(612) 870-1218**
Vietnamese. Vegetarian options include tofu, vegetable, and mock meat dishes. No eggs are used in their dishes. Open daily. Take-out, vegan options, no credit cards, $.

Moghal's
1123 W. Lake St., Minneapolis, MN 55408   **(612) 823-2866**
Indian. The vegetarian menu at Moghal's is extensive and creative. Try the Mushroom Spinach Curry or the Mushroom Bhazee. Open daily for lunch and dinner. Full service, vegan options, catering, VISA/MC/AMEX/DISC/DC, $-$$.

Organica Deli
400 Central Ave. SE, Minneapolis, MN 55414   **(612) 378-7413**
Organic natural foods. This deli, located in an educational center, serves organic bean burritos, sandwiches, and special entrées each day. Open Tuesday through Friday. Closed Saturday through Monday. Cafeteria, vegan options, fresh juices, take-out, $.

Ping's Szechuan
1401 Nicollet Ave. S., Minneapolis, MN 55403   **(612) 874-9404**
Chinese. Located near the Convention Center, Ping's serves vegetarian entrées, including some made with mock duck. The restaurant is willing to make substitutions for any dish. Open daily for lunch and dinner. Full service, vegan options, wine/beer/alcohol, take-out, VISA/MC/AMEX/DISC/DC, $$.

Pizza Luce
3200 Lyndale Ave. S., Minneapolis, MN 55408   **(612) 827-5978**
119 N. Fourth St., Minneapolis, MN 55401   **(612) 333-7359**
Pizza. Pizza Luce features many vegan and vegetarian options, including vegan pizzas, sandwiches, appetizers, salads, pasta, and a vegan desert. The atmosphere is totally non-smoking, and the dress is typically casual. Lyndale location open daily for lunch and dinner. N. Fourth St. location open Monday through Saturday for lunch through late night service. Full service, vegan options, fresh juices, beer/wine, take-out, VISA/MC/AMEX/DISC, $$. www.pizzaluce.com

Seward Community Café
2129 E. Franklin Ave., Minneapolis, MN 55404   **(612) 332-1011**
Natural foods. The Seward Café is located on the corner across from the Seward Co-op and offers sandwiches, soups, salads, and desserts in a cafetaria/café atmosphere. Patio dining is available. Open daily for three meals. Cafeteria, vegan options, take-out, $.

St. Martin's Table
2001 Riverside Ave., Minneapolis, MN 55454   **(612) 339-3920**
Natural foods. St. Martin's Table is a nonprofit restaurant/bookstore with various political titles and resources on peace. Lunches are served by volunteers so that all tips go to hunger-related causes. The chalkboard menu has two soups daily, three sandwiches, and special salads. Fresh baked goods made from scratch are also featured. Bring your own container for take-out. **Open Monday through Saturday. Closed Sunday. Full service, take-out, $.**

Tao Natural Foods & Books
2200 Hennepin Ave. S., Minneapolis, MN 55405   **(612) 377-4630**
Juice bar/deli. The Tao has a small juice bar and deli in front of its natural foods store. Daily sandwich and soup specials are offered, along with a great selection of books, herbs, vitamins, and health and beauty products. Tao is located next to an eco-store. **Open daily. Limited service, fresh juices, take-out, $.**

Triple Rock Social Club
629 Cedar Ave., S., Minneapolis, MN 55454   **(612) 333-7399**
American. This corner bar has two owners, one who eats meat and one who is vegan. So the menu has an equal number of meat and vegan dishes. Among the veggie items are Vegan French Toast, Vegan Meatloaf, and a Tofu Down Home BBQ Sandwich, but they can make most items vegan unless otherwise noted. The restaurant is non-smoking, with a typically casual atmosphere. **Open daily for lunch and dinner. Full service, vegan options, fresh juices, soymilk, espresso/cappuccino, beer/wine/alcohol, non-alcoholic beverages, take-out, VISA/MC/AMEX/DISC, $$.**

Wedge Community Co-op Deli
2105 Lyndale Ave. S., Minneapolis, MN 55405   **(612) 871-3993**
Natural foods deli. The Wedge Co-op has a deli counter in the back with a wonderful selection of salads, sandwiches, and some soups. **Open daily for three meals. Take-out, vegan options, VISA/MC, $. www.wedge.coop**

MINNETONKA

The Marsh Restaurant
15000 Minnetonka Blvd., Minnetonka, MN 55345   **(612) 935-2202**
Health club restaurant. The highly-recommended Marsh Restaurant serves some vegetarian foods. All muffins and breads are baked from scratch on-site, using a minimum of processed foods. **Open daily. Cafeteria, fresh juice, wine/beer, take-out, VISA/MC, $$.**

ROSEVILLE

Good Earth

1901 W. Hwy. 36, Roseville, MN 55113   **(651) 636-0956**

Natural foods. See description under Edina, MN.

SPRING LAKE PARK

Lotus Garden

8478 Central Ave. NE, Spring Lake Park, MN 55432   **(612) 780-9524**

Vietnamese. They offer a large selection of vegetarian entrées, including several dishes with mock meats or tofu, vegetarian eggrolls, and spring rolls. No MSG is used. The staff is willing to accommodate special dietary needs. **Open Monday through Saturday for lunch and dinner. Open Sunday for dinner only.** Full service, fresh juices, non-smoking, wine/beer, non-alcoholic wine/beer, take-out, VISA/MC, $$.

ST. LOUIS PARK

Taste Of India

5617 Wayzata Blvd., St. Louis Park, MN 55416   **(952) 541-4865**

Indian. See description under Maplewood, MN.

ST. PAUL

Babani's Kurdish Restaurant

544 St. Peter St., St. Paul, MN 55102   **(651) 602-9964**

Kurdish. This Kurdish restaurant offers dishes such as Vegetarian Bakla, Garbanzo Shilla, Biryani, and Dolma. For a real kick, try the Kurdish Tea. **Open Monday through Friday for lunch and dinner. Open Saturday and Sunday for dinner only.** Full service, vegan options, VISA/MC/AMEX/DISC, $-$$.

Everest On Grand

1278 Grand Ave., St. Paul, MN 55105   **(651) 696-1666**

Nepalese. The menu at this restaurant is 75 percent vegetarian. Choose from the veggie soup, momo (dumplings), many curry dishes, combination plates, rice dishes, and desserts. **Open daily for lunch and dinner.** Buffet, vegan options, fresh juices, beer/wine, non-alcoholic beer, special drinks, $. www.hotmomo.com

Khyber Pass Café

1571 Grand Ave., St. Paul, MN 55105   **(651) 690-0505**

Afghan. Vegetarian options include Shorwa, a vegetarian vegetable soup; Aush made with whole green peas and kidney, garbanzo, and mung beans; Shola, Mung Beans, and Rice topped with Chutney; as well as a few other á la carte items. **Open Tuesday through Saturday for lunch and dinner. Closed Sunday and Monday.** Full service, $$.

Lotus Victoria Crossing

867 Grand Ave., St. Paul, MN 55105   **(651) 228-9156**

Vietnamese. The Lotus Victoria offers 25 vegetarian entrées. Try the Vietnamese Mock-Duck

Noodle Salad or the Vietnamese Eggroll Salad. **Open daily for lunch and dinner. Full service, vegan options, take-out, $-$$.**

Mississippi Market Delicatessen

1810 Randolph Ave., St. Paul, MN 55105   **(651) 690-0507**
622 Selby Ave., St. Paul, MN 55104   **(651) 310-9499**
Natural foods deli. You will find several veggie options here. The Randolph Ave. location is a grab-and-go deli only. **Open daily for lunch and dinner. Buffet, vegan options, smoothies, take-out, VISA/MC, $. www.msmarket.org**

ST. PETER

St. Peter Food Co-op and Deli

119 W. Broadway Ave., , St. Peter, MN 56082   **(507) 931-4880**
Natural foods deli. The shop offers self-serve soups and entrées, plus a cooler stocked with pre-made sandwiches and salads. Fresh baked goods are also available. **Open daily. Cafeteria, vegan options, take-out, $.**

Mississippi

JACKSON

Bravo

4500 I-55 N., Jackson, MS 39211   **(601) 982-8111**
Italian. Bravo's vegetarian menu includes Grilled Portobello Mushrooms with White Bean Hummus, Polenta Smothered with Herb-Infused Mushrooms, or Rigatoni with Roma Tomatoes. **Open daily for lunch and dinner. Full service, vegan options, $$-$$$.**

• High Noon Café

Rainbow Whole Foods Co-op
4147 Northview Dr., Jackson, MS 39206   **(601) 366-1602**
Vegetarian. Open since 1982, the High Noon Café serves only vegan food every day except Saturday, which is a "vegetarian day." Typical offerings include organic whole-wheat pizzas with soy cheese, burritos, veggie burgers, mock chicken salad sandwiches, hummus plates, nori rolls, organic breads, and much more. **Open Monday through Saturday for lunch. Closed Sunday. Buffet, vegan options, vegan/macrobiotic options, fresh juices, smoothies, take-out, VISA/MC/AMEX/DISC, $-$$. www.rainbowcoop.org/menu.htm**

OXFORD

• Harvest Café & Bakery

1112 Van Buren Ave., Oxford, MS 38655   **(601) 236-3757**

Vegetarian café. Harvest Café & Bakery has a completely vegetarian menu featuring black bean chili, soups, salads, hummus sandwiches, tempeh Reubens, pasta dishes, and more for lunch or dinner, and whole-wheat pancakes and waffles for Sunday brunch. This establishment also supports sustainable agriculture, recycling, and local artists. **Open Sunday and Monday for breakfast and lunch. Open Tuesday through Friday for three meals. Closed Saturday. Full service, non-alcoholic wine/beer, wine/beer/alcohol, vegan options, take-out, $-$$.**

Missouri

CHESTERFIELD

Crazy Bowls and Wraps

1627 Clarkson Rd., Chesterfield, MO 63017   **(314) 519-7277**

American. This Missouri chain offers a fair number of vegetarian options. Try the Veggie Barbecue Wrap or the Tofu Veggie Bowl. As for drinks, go for the Raspberry Smoothie. **Open daily for lunch and dinner. Limited service, vegan options, smoothies, $.**

CLAYTON

Crazy Bowls and Wraps

39 N. Central Ave., Clayton, MO 63105   **(314) 727-9727**

American. See description under Chesterfield, MO.

India's Rasoi

7923 Forsyth Blvd., Clayton, MO 63105   **(314) 727-1414**

Indian. The menu at India's Rasoi includes 11 vegetarian dishes. Try the Bharta (eggplant with tomatoes and onions) or the Aloo Gobi (cauliflower and potatoes sautéed in herbs and spices). **Open daily for lunch and dinner. Full service, vegan options, catering, $-$$.**

COLUMBIA

International Café

209 Hitt St., Columbia, MO 65201   **(573) 449-4560**

International/Greek. One local patron recommends the appetizer combo as the best-bet dish at this establishment, which specializes in international and Greek cuisine. Patio dining is available. **Open Monday through Saturday for lunch and dinner. Limited service, $.**

• Main Squeeze

28 S. 9th St., Columbia, MO 65201   **(573) 817-5616**

Vegetarian/natural foods. The Main Squeeze uses organic foods and locally grown products as much as possible. Inside the restaurant you'll find a plaster wall of handprints from local vegetarians and natural foods supporters. They have daily specials, such as stuffed peppers and noodle salads, as well as a juice bar. **Open Monday through Saturday for three meals. Closed Sunday. Limited service, take-out, catering, macrobiotic options, fresh juices, smoothies, soymilk, special drinks, VISA/MC, $$.**

KANSAS CITY

(For restaurant listings in the surrounding areas, see Kansas City, Mission, Overland Park, Prairie Village, Shawnee, and Shawnee Mission in Kansas.)

Blue Bird Bistro

1700 Summit St., Kansas City, MO 64108   **(816) 221-7559**
Natural foods. Blue Bird offers organic foods available from local farmers. For dinner try the Curried Vegetable triangle. If you are there for lunch or brunch, check out the Basil Bruchetta or the Biscuits with Savory Mushroom Gravy. **Open Monday through Friday for lunch. Open Friday and Saturday for dinner. Open Saturday and Sunday for brunch. Full service, vegan options, catering, take-out, espresso/cappucino, smoothies, beer/wine, VISA/MC/ DISC/DC, $-$$.**

Eden Alley Café

707 W. 47th St., Kansas City, MO 64112   **(816) 561-5415**
Café. Eden Alley was voted "Healthiest Menu" in *Kansas City Magazine* in 2001 and 2002. Though they do serve a few fish specials, they are careful that there is no cross contamination between meals. The daily menu features dishes like Tomato Bisque, Apple Cranberry Salad, Falafel Platters, a vegan Spinach and Mushroom Loaf, and a veggie burger. Past specials have included Mexican dishes like vegan Soft Tacos and Black Bean Tostadas made with TVP, African Stew, Potato Cannelloni, Pesto Mushrooms, and Zucchini Cake topped with a smokey tomato aioli. **Open Monday through Saturday for lunch and dinner. Closed Sunday. Full service, vegan options, fresh juices, soymilk, espresso/cappuccino, take-out, catering, $$.** www.edenalley.com

Great India

1706 W. 39th St., Kansas City, MO 64111   **(816) 753-3331**
Indian. Several vegetarian entrées and numerous breads are offered. Northern Indian cooking spiced to each customer's request. Special meals may be requested. **Open Tuesday through Sunday for lunch and dinner. Closed Monday. Full service, delivery, catering, informal atmosphere, suitable for business entertaining, vegan options, wine/beer/alcohol, VISA/ MC/AMEX/DISC/DC, $$.**

Papagallo

3535 Broadway St., Kansas City, MO 64111   **(816) 756-3227**
Middle Eastern. Papagallo was voted "Best Falafel" by *The Kansas City Star.* **Open Tuesday through Sunday for lunch and dinner. Closed Monday. Full service, smoothies, soymilk, beer/wine/alcohol, VISA/MC/AMEX/DISC/DC, $$$.**

Z-Teca

2450 Grand Ave., Ste. 143, Kansas City, MO 64108   **(816) 474-7779**
Mexican. Z-Teca is a fast food chain that serves vegetarian friendly options. Entrées are

prepared fresh daily without lard or animal fats. Menu items include grilled vegetable tacos, salads, and vegetable or bean burritos. **Open daily. Limited service, take-out, $.**

SPRINGFIELD

Market Place Café
307 S. National Ave., Springfield, MO 65806 **(417) 865-9897**
Italian. The menu at Market Place Café offers appetizers, salads, soups, and desserts. Vegetarian pizza options include the Mediterranean (with artichoke hearts and black olive pesto), the James tomatoes, zucchini, and carmelized onions), and the Californian (fresh spinach leaves and garlic). Or choose a pasta dish, such as the Santa Fe Ravioli (cheddar cheese, black olives, and green onions in a cream sauce). **Open daily for lunch and dinner. Full service, vegan options, beer/wine/alcohol, take-out, VISA/MC/AMEX/DISC, $$.**

• Wellspring Café
300 W. McDaniel St., Springfield, MO 65804 **(417) 865-1818**
Vegetarian. This all-vegetarian café serves veggie burgers, salads, falafel, sandwiches, quiche, and baked potatoes. They also offer a range of vegan fare, including desserts, as well as organic coffee. **Open Monday through Friday for lunch. Closed Saturday and Sunday. Full service, vegan options, take-out, fresh juices, catering, VISA/MC/AMEX.**

ST. LOUIS

(For restaurant listings in the surrounding areas, see Clayton, Chesterfield, and University City.)

Caldwell's At The Plaza
94 Plaza Fronterac, St. Louis, MO 63131 **(314) 997-8885**
American. At Caldwell's, dine on fresh pizza made in a wood-burning stove, a Mediterranean sampler dish, Sautéed Vegetable Pilaf, salads, veggie sandwiches, plus more. Vegan dishes are clearly marked on the menu. **Open daily for lunch and dinner. Full service, vegan options, catering, take-out, espresso/cappuccino, non-alcoholic beer, wine/beer/alcohol, MC/AMEX/ DC, $$.**

Crazy Bowls and Wraps
3852 Lindell Blvd., St. Louis, MO 63108 **(314) 533-9727**
American. See description under Chesterfield, MO.

Curry In A Hurry
612 Olive St., St Louis, MO 63101 **(314) 241-7900**
Indian. See description under India's Rasoi in Clayton, MO. **Open daily for lunch.**

• Eternity Vegetarian Deli & Juice Bar
11 S. Euclid Ave., St. Louis, MO 63108 **(314) 454-1851**
Vegetarian deli. This deli has a great selection of vegetarian, vegan, and raw deli sandwiches; battered vegetable combo baskets; veggie pizza; soups; and vegan desserts. The salads and the veggie gyros come particularly highly recommended. Outdoor seating available. **Open Monday through Saturday for lunch and dinner. Closed Sunday. Counter service, vegan options, fresh juices, smoothies, take-out, catering, VISA/MC/AMEX/DISC, $.**

• Govinda's
3926 Lindell Blvd., St. Louis, MO 63108   **(314) 535-8085**

Vegetarian. Located on the grounds of a Krishna temple, Govinda's features a wide variety of vegetarian foods. **Open daily for lunch and dinner. Buffet, vegan options, fresh juices, take-out, $.** www.govindas.org

Hacienda Mexican Restaurant
9748 Manchester Rd., St. Louis, MO 63119   **(314) 962-7100**

Mexican. Dine indoors and outdoors in a fun atmosphere with terrific food. Items are prepared from scratch, including chips made on premise. Be sure to request their separate vegetarian menu, and you'll find quesadillas, chili, black bean soup, salads, veggie pizza made on a tortilla, fajitas, tacos, and more. **Open daily for lunch and dinner. Full service, vegan options, take-out, non-alcoholic wine/beer, wine/beer/alcohol, VISA/MC/AMEX/DISC/DC, $$.**

House Of India
8501 Delmar Blvd., St. Louis, MO 63124   **(314) 567-6850**

Indian. Enjoy a wide selection of vegetarian Indian dishes in a warm environment. **Open daily for lunch and dinner. Full service, wine/beer/alcohol, VISA/MC/AMEX/DISC/DC, $$.**

India's Rasoi
4569 Laclede Ave., St. Louis, MO 63108   **(314) 361-6911**

Indian. See description under Clayton, MO.

• The Peacock Café and Market
2137 Barrett Station Rd., St. Louis, MO 63131   **(314) 965-3822**

Vegetarian/Indian. A favorite of local vegetarians, this establishment is half Indian and South Asian café and half market. The café serves great food that is both fresh and inexpensive, including dosas, breads, and kheer (sweet rice pudding dessert) that is not to be missed. Also, the market offers food, music, and natural healing products. **Open Tuesday through Sunday for lunch and dinner. Closed Monday. Counter service, vegan options, BYOB, take-out, VISA/MC/AMEX/DISC, $.** www.thepeacockcafe.com

Pho Grand Vietnamese Restaurant
3195 S. Grand Blvd., St. Louis, MO 63118   **(314) 664-7435**

Vietnamese. This is considered one of the best Vietnamese restaurants in the area, and it's one of the most affordable as well. They have many vegetarian items, with large portions that will give you a lot of bang for your buck. Vegetarian selections include tofu with ginger and onions, with hot chiles or lemongrass, or with special tomato sauce; snowpeas with garlic and sesame oil; Chinese broccoli with garlic sauce; and bun (vermicelli noodle) dishes. **Open Wednesday through Monday for lunch and dinner. Closed Tuesday. Full service, vegan options, reservations recommended, wine/beer, special drinks, VISA/MC/AMEX/DISC, $-$$.** www.phogrand.com

Saleem's Restaurant
6501 Delmar Blvd., St. Louis, MO 63130   **(314) 721-7947**

Lebanese. Vegetarian appetizers, platters, and eggplant dishes are offered at Saleem's. **Open**

Monday through Saturday. Closed Sunday. Full service, wine/beer/alcohol, take-out, VISA/MC/DISC, $$.

Tangerine
1405 Washington Ave., St. Louis, MO 63103   **(314) 621-PEEL**
Café. Check out this appealing lounge for a taste of music and vegetarian fare, such as stuffed mushrooms, pizza, and pasta. It is not solely vegetarian, since there is fish available on the menu. You must be 21 or older to enter. No cover charge Tuesday through Thursday. **Open Tuesday through Saturday for dinner. Closed Saturday and Sunday. Full service, beer/wine/alcohol, special drinks, $-$$.** www.saucecafe.com/tangerine

UNIVERSITY CITY

Brandt's Market & Cafe
6525 Delmar Blvd., University City, MO 63130   **(314) 727-3663**
Natural foods. Eggplant Parmigiana, veggie burger, black bean chili, spring rolls, pizza, and other options are available for vegetarians. There is live music provided nightly. **Open daily. Full service, vegan options, fresh juice, wine/beer/alcohol, VISA/MC/AMEX/DISC, $$.**

Crazy Bowls and Wraps
7353 Forsyth, University City, MO 63130   **(314) 725-5030**
American. See description under Chesterfield, MO.

Fitz's Restaurant
6605 Delmar Blvd., University City, MO 63106   **(314) 726-9555**
International. This root beer microbrewery and restaurant offers a wide variety of vegetarian dishes, including grilled veggie sandwiches; veggie burritos; vegan black beans and rice; couscous burgers; pasta and red sauce with artichokes, mushrooms, and spinach; and more. **Open daily for lunch and dinner. Full service, vegan options, espresso/cappuccino, VISA/MC/DISC, $$.**

Red Sea
6511 Delmar Blvd., University City, MO 63112   **(314) 863-0099**
Ethiopian. Red Sea offers several vegetarian Ethiopian dishes. **Open Wednesday through Saturday for lunch and dinner. Open Sunday through Tuesday for dinner only. Full service, non-alcoholic wine/beer, wine/beer/alcohol, catering, take-out, VISA/MC/AMEX/DISC, $$.**

Montana

BOZEMAN

Community Food Co-op
908 W. Main St., Bozeman, MT 59715   **(406) 587-4039**
Natural foods. Indoor and outdoor seating is available at this deli, which offers an incredible view of the Bridger Mountains in a park-like setting. Vegetarian options are seasonally and locally based. Smoking is not allowed. **Open daily for lunch and dinner. Counter service,**

macrobiotic/vegan options, fresh juices, organic coffee and tea, take-out, VISA/MC/AMEX, $. www.bozocoop.com

CORWIN SPRINGS

The Four Winds @ Cinnabar
752 Hwy. 89 S., Corwin Springs, MT 59030   **(406) 848-7893**
Natural foods deli. Located near Yellowstone and Grand Teton, The Four Winds offers soups and sandwiches from their all-day deli and a whole foods lunch buffet. Also available is organic produce and groceries, camping needs, and gifts. **Open daily for lunch and dinner.** Deli-style, espresso, fresh juices. www.the4winds.com

HAMILTON

Spice Of Life
163 S. Second St., Hamilton, MT 59840   **(406) 363-4433**
International. Spice of Life offers a variety of sandwiches, entrées, pasta, soups, salads, appetizers, and desserts. Some meatless options include the Veggie Burger, Linguine, or the Sesame Noodle Salad, to name a few. **Open Monday for lunch. Open Tuesday through Friday for lunch and dinner. Open Saturday for dinner. Closed Sunday. Full service,** VISA/MC/AMEX, $-$$$. www.bitterroot.net/spice/left.ihtml

HELENA

Real Food Store Deli
501 Fuller Ave., Helena, MT 59601   **(406) 443-5150**
Natural foods deli. This natural foods deli offers sandwiches, soups, salads, and a hot food bar. Options at the hot food bar have included fajitas, enchiladas, sweet and sour tofu, and pad Thai. **Open daily for lunch and dinner. Limited service, vegan options,** VISA/MC, $-$$. www.realfoodstore.com

MISSOULA

China Garden
2100 Stephens Ave., Missoula, MT 59801   **(406) 721-1795**
Chinese. This restaurant uses no MSG in food preparation. Vegetarian options include vegetable sautées, soups, vegetable and noodle dishes, Vegetarian Foo Young, and Vegetable Fried Rice. **Open Tuesday through Sunday for lunch and dinner. Closed Monday. Full service,** take-out, VISA/MC/AMEX, $$.

• Mr. Goodburger's
1555 Liberty Ln., Missoula, MT 59808   **(406) 549-5552**
Vegetarian fast food/take-out. This fast food joint offers veggie burgers based on the cuisines of several American cities. Enjoy the Memphis with BBQ sauce, the Kansas City with grilled mushrooms and garlic chips, and of course, the Honolulu with ginger, nori, pineapple, and mango chutney. The menu also includes baked tater tots and vegetarian bean chili. **Open Monday through Saturday for lunch. Closed Sunday. Limited service, vegan options,** smoothies, take-out, $. www.mrgoodburgers.com

The Mustard Seed

419 W. Front St., Missoula, MT 59802 **(406) 728-7825**

Contemporary Oriental. The Mustard Seed offers a separate vegetarian menu that includes sushi, spring rolls, wok dishes, and tofu and vegetable dishes with various sauces. Smoking is not allowed. **Open daily for lunch and dinner. Full service, non-alcoholic wine/beer, wine/beer/alcohol, take-out, VISA/MC/AMEX/DISC, $.**

WHITEFISH

Truby's Wood Fired Pizza

115 Central Ave., Whitefish, MT 59937 **(406) 862-4979**

Pizza. Located near Glacier and Whitefish Lake, Truby's offers brick oven-fired pizza, pasta, and more. **Open Monday through Saturday for lunch and dinner. Open Sunday for dinner only. Full service, wine/beer, VISA/MC/AMEX/DISC/DC, $-$$.** www.whitefishmt.com/dining/truby/index.html

Nebraska

LINCOLN

Crane River Brewpub and Café

200 N. 11th St., Lincoln, NE 68508 **(402) 476-7766**

American. Vegetarian entrées and appetizers are marked on menu. Also, several handcrafted ales are on tap. **Open daily for lunch through late evening service. Full service, vegan options, informal atmosphere, suitable for business entertaining, wine/beer/alcohol, VISA/MC/AMEX/DISC/DC, $-$$.**

Maggie's Vegetarian Wraps

311 N. 8th St., Lincoln, NE 68502 **(402) 477-3959**

Bakery. You'll find wraps, a bakery full of muffins and cookies, and pleasant service at Maggie's. **Open daily for three meals. Counter service, vegan options, VISA/MC/DISC.**

Open Harvest Natural Foods Grocery

1618 South St., Lincoln, NE 68502 **(402) 475-9069**

Deli. This co-op and deli offers many vegan and vegetarian selections, natural and bulk foods, organic produce, vitamins, and herbs. Soy, gluten, and frozen food options are also available. **Open daily for three meals. Deli-style, vegan options, espresso.**

The Oven
201 N. 8th, Ste. 117, Lincoln, NE 68508   **(402) 475-6118**
Indian. The Oven provides fine dining and Indian food with a very good selection for vege-
tarians. **Open daily. Full service, vegan options, wine/beer/alcohol, VISA/MC/AMEX, $$.**

Taj Mahal Cuisine Of India
5500 Old Cheney Rd., Ste. 4, Lincoln, NE 68516   **(402) 420-1133**
Indian. Several traditional Indian vegetarian entrées are served. **Open Tuesday through
Saturday for lunch and dinner. Open Sunday for dinner only. Closed Monday. Full service,
vegan options, take-out, catering, casual, non-smoking, wine/beer/alcohol, reservations rec-
ommended, VISA/MC/AMEX/DISC, $$.**

OMAHA

Indian Oven
1010 Howard St., Omaha, NE 68102   **(402) 342-4856**
Indian. The hallmark of Indian Oven's cuisine is the "Tandoori Cuisine" cooked in its clay
oven. Included on the menu are stuffed and plain tandoor breads, Pakoras, Papadums, and
Samosas, as well as various other vegetarian options. **Open daily. Full service, fresh juices,
wine/beer/alcohol, take-out, VISA/MC/AMEX, $$.**

McFoster's Natural Kind Café
302 S. 38th St., Omaha, NE 68131   **(402) 345-7477**
Natural foods. Enjoy falafel, almond milk-based soups, and more at McFoster's. Acoustic
music and patio service are provided. **Open Monday through Saturday for lunch and dinner.
Closed Sunday. Full service, vegan options, fresh juices, take-out, VISA/MC, $-$$.**

Nevada

LAS VEGAS

Gandhi India's Cuisine
4080 Paradise Rd., #9, Las Vegas, NV 89109   **(702) 734-0094**
Indian. Rated one of the best restaurants in Las Vegas, this establishment has an extensive
menu, including an all-you-can-eat buffet. Offerings include appetizers (such as vegetable
samosas and onion bhaji), vegetarian entrées (such as matter paneer and mushroom bhajee),
a wide range of breads, and regional specialties. **Open daily for lunch and dinner. Full service,
reservations recommended, non-alcoholic beer, wine/beer, VISA/MC/AMEX/DC, $$.**

•• Go Raw Café
2381 E. Windmill Ln., Las Vegas, NV 89123   **(702) 450-9007**
2910 Lake E. Dr., Las Vegas, NV 89107   **(702) 254-5382**
Vegan/raw foods. The menu includes mock salmon sushi, cream of carrot and avocado
soup, enchiladas, burritos, a spinach ricotta-like dish, neat loaf, and pizza. On any given
day, dessert offerings may include mango parfait, apple pie, fudge, and carob-banana pie.

Open Monday through Saturday for lunch and dinner. Closed Sunday. Take-out, fresh juices, smoothies, catering, delivery, VISA/MC/AMEX/DISC, $$. www.gorawcafe.com

Komol Restaurant

953 E. Sahara Ave., Las Vegas, NV 89104 (702) 731-6542

Thai. This Thai restaurant offers an extensive vegetarian menu, including seitan and tofu dishes. Open daily for lunch and dinner. Full service, take-out, $.

La Scala Restaurant

1020 E. Desert Inn Rd., Las Vegas, NV 89109 (702) 699-9980

Italian. This all-organic Italian restaurant offers pesto-grilled tofu with roasted peppers, tofu stuffed shells, and gnocchi (potato dumplings) with tomato sauce. Open daily for dinner. Full service, VISA/MC/AMEX/DISC, $$-$$$.

• Long Life Vegetarian Restaurant

4130 S. Sandhill Rd., #A4, Las Vegas, NV 89121 (702) 436-4488

Vegetarian/Chinese. Their extensive vegetarian lunch and dinner menu includes pork, beef and chicken alternatives. They also offer a large selection of meatless appetizers, such as spring rolls, vegetable potstickers, and veggie wonton soup. Everything is MSG-free. Open daily for lunch and dinner. Full service, vegan options, take-out, VISA/MC, $$.

Mediterranean Café & Market

4147 S. Maryland Pkwy., Las Vegas, NV 89119 (702) 731-6030

Mediterranean. This restaurant offers courtyard dining. Traditional dishes include falafel, hummus, tabbouleh, and salads. They also offer spinach pie, pasta, several vegetarian sandwiches, and a vegetarian platter. Open daily for lunch and dinner. Full service, vegan options, take-out, catering, reservations recommended, beer/wine/alcohol, VISA/MC/AMEX/DISC, $$.

• Rainbow's End Natural Foods & Café

1120 E. Sahara Ave., Las Vegas, NV 89104 (702) 737-7282

Natural foods. Rainbow's End offers veggie burgers, sandwiches, soups, and entrées. Open Monday through Saturday for breakfast and lunch. Closed Sunday. Counter service, $.

Shalimar Fine Indian Cuisine

3900 Paradise Rd., Las Vegas, NV 89109 (702) 796-0302

Indian. Shalimar offers more than 20 vegetarian Indian dishes prepared in a tandoor oven. Open daily for dinner. Open Saturday and Sunday for lunch. Full service, non-alcoholic beer, wine/beer/alcohol, VISA/MC/AMEX/DISC/DC, $$.

Wild Oats Café

7500 W. Lake Mead Blvd., Las Vegas, NV 89128 (702) 942-1500

Natural foods deli. The deli in this natural foods market offers soups, salads, sandwiches, and more. Open daily for three meals. Cafeteria, vegan options, take-out, fresh juices, smoothies, soymilk, VISA/MC/AMEX/DISC, $-$$. www.wildoats.com

RENO

Anthony's Dandelion Deli and Catering
1170 S. Wells Ave., Reno, NV 89502   **(775) 322-6100**
Natural foods. Anthony's offers vegan soup and chili, wheat-free and dairy-free dishes, baked goods, and more at reasonable prices. Open Monday through Saturday for breakfast and lunch. Closed Sunday. Limited service, vegan options, fresh juices, espresso/cappuccino, catering, take-out, $$.

Café de Thai
7499 Longley Ln., Reno, NV 89511   **(775) 829-8424**
Thai. They offer a selection of vegetarian entrées and are willing to make any other dish on the menu vegetarian. Open Wednesday through Saturday for lunch and dinner. Closed Sunday through Tuesday. Full service, take-out, reservations recommended, non-smoking, suitable for business entertaining, fresh juices, beer/wine, non-alcoholic beer/wine, VISA/MC, $$.

Deux Gros Nez
249 California Ave., Reno, NV 89503   **(702) 786-9400**
Natural foods. A wide variety of vegetarian cuisine is offered daily. Located on the second floor of the building, this establishment features a tremendous collection of cycling jerseys hanging on its walls. Open daily for three meals. Counter service, vegan options, fresh juices, espresso/cappuccino, take-out, $-$$.

Pneumatic Diner
501 W. 1st St., Reno, NV 89503   **(775) 786-8888 x 106**
Natural foods. This diner is located upstairs in the wonderful Truckee River Lodging House at the corner of 1st and Ralston Sts. It offers Middle Eastern and Mexican-style dishes in an eclectic environment. Open daily for three meals. Full service, vegan options, fresh juices, espresso/cappuccino, wine/beer, take-out, VISA/MC/DISC, $$.

New Hampshire

CONCORD

Bagel Works, Inc.
42 N. Main St., Concord, NH 03301   **(603) 226-1827**
Bagel deli. More than 16 varieties of bagels are offered with various topping options, including cream cheeses, Tofutti spreads, salads, and other vegetarian combinations. Only natural ingredients without preservatives are used. Bagel Works is environmentally conscious and

---

socially active in its community. **Open daily. Counter service, vegan options, fresh juices, take-out, $.**

DURHAM

The Bagelry
One Mill Rd. Plaza, Durham, NH 03824 **(603) 868-1424**
American. Seventeen varieties of bagels are available at The Bagelry, as well as salads, bagel sandwiches, and other vegetarian options. **Open daily. Counter service, vegan options, take-out, $.**

KEENE

Bagel Works, Inc.
120 Main St., Keene, NH 03431 **(603) 357-7751**
Bagel deli. See description under Concord, NH.

•• Country Life Vegetarian Restaurant
15 Roxbury St., Keene, NH 03431 **(603) 357-3975**
Vegan. Country Life is a self-serve vegan establishment with many different options. **Open Sunday through Friday for lunch. Closed Saturday. Limited service, take-out, $$.**

MANCHESTER

(For restaurant listings in the surrounding areas, see Concord.)

Bagel Works, Inc.
581 Second St., Manchester, NH 03102 **(603) 647-6560**
Bagel deli. See description under Concord, NH.

MEREDITH

For Every Season
67 Main St., Meredith, NH 03253 **(603) 279-8875**
Natural foods deli. This restaurant, located in the beautiful Lakes Region of New Hamsphire, offers homemade soups and salads in a casual, kid-friendly environment. Breakfast is served all day. Garden deck seating is available. **Open daily for breakfast and lunch during summer. Open Tuesday through Saturday during winter. Limited service, vegan options, take-out, BYOB, $.**

NORTH CONWAY

Café Chimes
20 Cranmore Rd., North Conway, NH 03860 **(603) 356-5500**
Natural foods. "Homemade" and "natural" are the passwords at Café Chimes, which features soups, salads, quiche, pizza, grain dishes, and specials. The café's wheat mill grinds wheat berries daily to create unique whole-wheat bread. **Call for hours. Full service, $.**

PORTSMOUTH

(For restaurant listings in the surrounding areas, see Durham.)

Bagel Works, Inc.
9-11 Congress St., Portsmouth, NH 03801   **(603) 431-4434**
Bagel deli. See description under Keene, NH.

•• The Juicery
51 Hanover St., Portsmouth, NH 03801   **(603) 431-0693**
Vegan deli/juice bar. This vegan juice bar offers all-natural smoothies, soups, chili, and vegan
wraps. Currently, it's take-out only, but the owners hope to add seating in the near future.
Open daily for breakfast through early dinner. Dinner hours are later during summer months.
Take-out, fresh juices, smoothies, VISA/MC/AMEX/DISC, $-$$.

New Jersey

ALLENDALE

Harvest Café
53 W. Allendale Ave., Allendale, NJ 07401   **(201) 818-4190**
Natural foods. This informal café serves dishes based on vegetables, legumes, herbs, and grains.
Enjoy stir-fries with tofu or tempeh, sandwiches, and other options. **Open Monday for lunch.**
Open Tuesday through Saturday for three meals. Open Sunday for breakfast and lunch.
Limited service, vegan options, espresso/cappuccino, catering, take-out, VISA/MC, $$.

BELMAR

• Veggie Works
817 Belmar Plaza, Belmar, NJ 07719   **(908) 280-1141**
Vegetarian. This mostly vegan restaurant features an international menu with choices like
egg rolls, stuffed grape leaves, tacos, and falafels, but if you're in the mood for some good
ol' American food, try the vegetarian meatloaf with mashed potatoes and vegan gravy. There
are also blackboard specials every night including vegan desserts. **Open Tuesday through**
Friday for lunch and dinner. Open Saturday and Sunday for dinner only. Closed Monday.
Full service, vegan options, fresh juices, smoothies, take-out, VISA/MC/AMEX/DISC, $$.

BRICK

Sentosa Restaurant
2063 E. Rte. 88, Brick, NJ 08724   **(732) 892-9595**
Chinese. This restaurant offers numerous vegetarian offerings, including Malaysian entrées
served with brown rice and dishes made with soy protein "meats" or tofu. **Open Tuesday**
through Sunday for lunch and dinner. Closed Monday. Full service, vegan options, take-out,
delivery, non-smoking, VISA/MC/DISC, $-$$.

CAPE MA

(For restaura   Stone Harbor and Wildwood.)

Fruit O

309 Be   **(609) 898-2211**
Café. Fi   is along with their regular fare. **Seasonal**
hours.   ces, $-$$.

CH

Al

Pin   ke, Cherry Hill, NJ 08003   **(609) 427-0888**
Mo   , couscous, and other Middle Eastern favorites are available
on Al Khimah's menu. **Open daily for lunch and dinner. Full service, take-out, VISA/MC,**
$-$$$.

• Evergreen Health Cuisine

2087 E. Marlton Pk., Cherry Hill, NJ 08003   **(856) 751-8599**
Vegetarian. This restaurant is run by three generations of vegetarians. Enjoy a wide variety
of different ethnic cuisine, including Italian, Chinese, Mexican, and Middle Eastern dishes.
Most dishes are vegan. **Open Tuesday through Sunday for lunch and dinner. Closed**
Monday. Full service, vegan options, take-out, VISA/MC/AMEX, $$.

•• Singapore Vegetarian Restaurant

219 Berlin Rd., Cherry Hill, NJ 08034   **(609) 795-0188**
Vegan/Chinese. This vegan restaurant is connected to the renowned Singapore Vegetarian
Restaurant in downtown Philadelphia. The food and service come highly recommended.
Open daily for lunch and dinner. Full service, vegan options, VISA/MC/AMEX, $$.

CHESTER

The Health Shoppe

Chester Spring Shopping Center, Rte. 206, Chester, NJ 07930   **(908) 879-7555**
Deli. Enjoy a nice variety of sandwiches, some hot entrées, and a salad bar at the Health
Shoppe. **Open daily for three meals. Limited service, vegan options, fresh juices, VISA/**
MC/DISC, $.

CLEMENTON

Tandoor Palace Restaurant

Plaza 30, 328 White Horse Pike, Clementon, NJ 08021   **(609) 435-1234**
Indian. Dine on vegetable samosas, freshly baked Indian breads, and a choice of more than
10 vegetarian entrées. **Open daily for lunch and dinner. Full service, take-out, VISA/MC/**
AMEX, $$.

DELRAN

Szechuan King

3025 Rt. 130 S., Delran, NJ 08075   **(609) 764-0096**

Chinese. At Szechuan King, you can select from several items in the vegetarian section of the menu. **Open daily for lunch and dinner. Full service, vegan options, take-out, VISA/ MC/AMEX/DISC/DC, $-$$.**

DENVILLE

Café Metro

60 Diamond Spring Rd., Denville, NJ 07834   **(973) 625-1055**

Café. Café Metro offers a diverse menu with vegetarian and vegan options, including stir-fries, grilled and steamed vegetables, soups, and salads in a completely smoke-free environment. Reservations are recommended. **Open Monday through Friday for lunch and dinner. Open Saturday and Sunday for dinner only. Full service, vegan options, catering, take-out, fresh juices, espresso/cappuccino, smoothies, BYOB, outdoor seating, VISA/MC/AMEX/DC, $$.** www.TheCafeMetro.com

EAST BRUNSWICK

Bombay Gardens

1020 Rt. 18, East Brunswick, NJ 08816   **(908) 613-9500**

Indian. Bombay Gardens offers a variety of vegetarian Indian dishes, including many South Indian dishes. **Open daily for lunch and dinner. Full service, vegan options, Take-out, $$.**

EAST RUTHERFORD

Park and Orchard Restaurant

240 Hackensack St., East Rutherford, NJ 07073   **(201) 939-9292**

Eclectic. Park and Orchard was voted "Best Restaurant in Northern New Jersey" by readers of "New Jersey Magazine." There's an award-winning wine list and an excellent eclectic menu. **Open Monday through Friday for lunch and dinner. Open Saturday for dinner only. Open for Sunday late lunch and dinner. Full service, fresh juices, wine/beer/alcohol, take-out, VISA/MC/AMEX/DISC, $$$.**

EGG HARBOR TOWNSHIP

The Pearl Garden

6041 Black Horse Pike, Egg Harbor Township, NJ 08234   **(609) 646-7072**

Chinese. The Pearl Garden has a separate vegetarian section on their menu offering several soups, vegetarian egg rolls and dumplings, and about 20 entrées. **Open daily for lunch and**

Restaurant codes: ❂ Reviewers' Choice   • Vegetarian Restaurant   • • Vegan Restaurant
Restaurant prices: **$** less than $6   **$$** $6-$12   **$$$** more than $12
Credit Cards Accepted: VISA - VISA   MC - MasterCard   AMEX - American Express
DISC - Discover   DC - Diner's Club

dinner. Full service, vegan options, wine/beer/alcohol, take-out, VISA/MC/AMEX/DISC/ DC, $$.

ELIZABETH

Jerusalem Restaurant
150 Elmora Ave., Elizabeth, NJ 07202 **(908) 289-0291**
Kosher/natural foods. Enjoy kosher Middle Eastern vegetarian food, as well as pizza, salads, and more. **Open Sunday through Thursday for lunch and dinner. Open Friday for lunch only. Closed Saturday.** Limited service, vegan options, catering, take-out, $.

HAINESPORT

Hainesport Health Haven
Rt. 38 and Lumberton Rd., Hainesport, NJ 08036 **(609) 267-7744**
Lunch bar. Enjoy the pleasant atmosphere in this fully stocked natural foods store. The lunch bar is very willing to accommodate special diets, and there are many vegetarian options. **Open Monday through Friday for lunch through early dinner. Open Saturday for brunch. Closed Sunday.** Limited service, take-out, VISA/MC, $.

HAMILTON

•Vasanta Bhavan
3800 Quakerbridge Rd., Hamilton, NJ 08619 **(609) 586-7899**
Vegetarian/Indian. The slogan for this Indian establishment is "the best dosas and rotis under one roof." The menu includes soups, uthappam, kababs, curries, puttus, masala dishes, pizzas, combination plates, and desserts. "Healthy Alternative" and children's menus are available. Their website is especially helpful, offering links to descriptions and suggested accompaniments for every dish. **Open daily for lunch and dinner.** Full service, vegan options, special drinks, take-out, catering, $-$$. www.vasantabhavan.us/dynamicdata/

HILLSBOROUGH

Culinary Creations
434 Rte. 206 S., Hillsborough, NJ 08876 **(908) 281-3894**
Café. Enjoy a friendly and casual atmosphere while dining on homemade lentil burgers, black bean burgers, fresh grilled vegetable sandwiches, and daily meatless specials and soups prepared by graduates of the Culinary Institute of America. **Open Monday through Friday for three meals. Open Saturday and Sunday for breakfast and lunch.** Limited service, vegan options, catering, take-out, special drinks, espresso/cappuccino, VISA/MC/AMEX/DISC, $.

HOBOKEN

Hoboken Farm Boy
127 Washington St., Hoboken, NJ 07030 **(201) 656-0581**
Primarily vegetarian deli. Farm Boy offers deli-style service with an extensive vegetarian menu, including sandwiches, burgers, baked tofu, soups, black bean chili, plus more.

Seating is very limited. **Open daily for lunch and dinner. Deli-style, fresh juices, take-out, catering, VISA/MC/AMEX, $.**

ISELIN

• Udupi Authentic Indian Vegetarian Cuisine
1380 Oak Tree Rd., Iselin, NJ 08830   **(908) 283-0343**
Vegetarian/Indian. Udupi offers several vegetarian Indian specialties. **Open daily for lunch and dinner. Full service, take-out, VISA/MC/DISC, $-$$.**

LAKE HIAWATHA

• Vegetarian Garden
48 N. Beverwyck Rd., Lake Hiawatha, NJ 07034   **(973) 402-8883**
Vegetarian/Chinese. Healthy kosher and all-natural vegetarian and vegan Chinese dishes are served daily. **Open daily for lunch and dinner. Full service, vegan options, catering, take-out, fresh juices, soymilk, VISA/MC/AMEX/DISC/DC, $-$$.**

LAWRENCEVILLE

Palace of Asia
400 Mercer Mall, Lawrenceville, NJ 08648   **(609) 987-0606**
Indian. Many vegetarian specialties, including samosas, pakoras, masalas, and vegetable biryani, are featured at Palace of Asia. **Open daily for lunch and dinner. Full service, vegan options, fresh juices, wine/beer/alcohol, take-out, VISA/MC/AMEX/DISC/DC, $$.**

LITTLE SILVER

• Healthfair
625 Branch Ave., Little Silver, NJ 07739   **(732) 747-3140**
Vegetarian. Located in a natural foods store, Healthfair offers an organic salad bar, macrobiotic lunches, vegetarian sandwiches, hot foods, organic breads, fresh juices, vegan desserts, and more. **Open Monday through Friday for three meals. Open Saturday for breakfast and lunch. Open Sunday for brunch only. Limited service, vegan options, take-out, $$.**

LIVINGSTON

Jerusalem Restaurant
99-101 W. Mt. Pleasant Ave., Livingston, NJ 07016   **(793) 533-1424**
Kosher/natural foods. See description under Elizabeth, NJ.

MANTOLOKING

Café La Playa
34 Hwy. 35, Mantoloking, NJ 08738   **(732) 892-7170**
Natural foods café. A popular, casual spot located across from the beach cooks up gourmet veggie burgers, overflowing salads, and burritos using all fresh ingredients. It is also equipped

with pool tables, a bar, and video game room. **Open daily for lunch and dinner. Full service, vegan options, catering, take-out, cappuccino, beer/wine/alcohol, reservations recommended, VISA/MC/AMEX, $$.**

MARLTON

Mexican Food Factory
601 W. Rte. 70, Marlton, NJ 08053 **(856) 983-9222**
Mexican. Mexican food in a casual atmosphere. **Open daily for lunch and dinner. Full service, beer/wine/alcohol, VISA/MC/AMEX, $$$.**

Zagara's
501 Route 73 S., Marlton, NJ 08053 **(609) 983-5700**
Natural foods. Zagara's hot bar selections differ daily but have included Mushroom Barley Soup with Vegetable Stock, Vegetarian Navy Bean Soup, Rice Tempeh with Pineapple Salsa, and Seitan and Broccoli. **Open daily for three meals. Buffet, vegan options, take-out, fresh juices, smoothies, catering, VISA/MC/AMEX, $$.**

METUCHEN

Radhana's Thai Kitchen
10 Pearl St., Metuchen, NJ 08840 **(908) 548-9747**
Thai. A separate vegetarian menu includes appetizers, soups, and entrées for lunch and dinner. Try the Thai Tempura, Tofu Coconut Milk Soup, Gluten Curry, or one of several other vegetarian dishes. **Open Tuesday through Sunday for lunch and dinner. Closed Monday. Full service, vegan options, take-out, VISA/MC, $-$$.**

MONTCLAIR

• Udupi Village
511 Bloomfield Ave., Montclair, NJ 07042 **(973) 233-1905**
Vegetarian/Indian. This restaurant serves North and South Indian cuisines, including soups, dosais, curries, and Indian breads. **Open daily for lunch and dinner. Full service, fresh juices, take-out, VISA/MC/AMEX/DISC, $$-$$$.** www.udupivillage.com

MORRISTOWN

• Chand Palace
79 Washington St. (Rt. 24W), Morristown, NJ 07960 **(201) 539-7433**
Vegetarian/Indian. Chand Palace offers a wide variety of vegetarian Indian food, including baked breads, vegetable curries, rice specialties, and more. The restaurant does not use eggs in its dishes. **Open Wednesday through Monday for lunch and dinner. Closed Tuesday. Full service, vegan options, take-out, $$.** www.chandpalace.com

The Dietworks
41 Morris St., Morristown, NJ 07960 **(201) 538-0328**
Ethnic foods. Look for menu items marked with a "V" for vegetarian. Try the Ratatouille Casserole, Black Bean Moussaka, Mushroom Lasagna Polonaise, or vegetable calzones.

There are also vegetarian specials that change daily. **Open Monday through Saturday for lunch and dinner. Closed Sunday. Full service, vegan options, espresso/cappuccino, delivery, catering, take-out, VISA/MC/AMEX, $-$$.**

The Health Shoppe
66 Morris St., Morristown, NJ 07960   **(201) 538-9131**
Deli. See description under Chester, NJ.

NEW BRUNSWICK

(For restaurant listings in the surrounding areas, see East Brunswick, Hamilton, Hillsborough, Metuchen, and Piscataway.)

The Round Grill
1 Penn Plaza (Rte. 7), New Brunswick, NJ 08901   **(732) 828-3337**
Mongolian. Located in Ferren Mall, this restaurant allows you to select fresh, raw vegetables from the food bar, coat them with a variety of sauces, and hand them to a chef who will stir-fry them on a large, flat grill. The set menu also has some vegetarian entrées. **Open Monday through Saturday for lunch and dinner. Open Sunday for dinner only. Full service, take-out, reservations recommended, suitable for business entertainment, non-smoking, special drinks, VISA/MC/AMEX/DISC, $$.**

•• Zafra Vegetarian Restaurant
46 Paterson St., New Brunswick, NJ 08901   **(732) 214-1005**
Vegan/American/Caribbean. Right off the New Jersey Turnpike, this casual restaurant offers up vegan versions of traditional American fare with a Caribbean twist. All of the food is vegan, with the exception of dairy cheese added to items by request only. Patrons can choose from Cheesesteaks, Chicken Parmesan, Creole Seitan, or the popular Plantain Tofu Croquettes (breaded and served with a sweet sauce). Also, vegan desserts are made on the premises. **Open Monday through Friday for lunch and dinner. Open Saturday for dinner. Closed Sunday. Full service, soymilk, special drinks, BYOB, catering, private parties, VISA/MC/AMEX, $-$$.**

OAKHURST

Changmao Sakura
214 Roosevelt Ave., Oakhurst, NJ 07755   **(908) 517-8889**
Kosher/Asian. This kosher restaurant offers both Chinese and Japanese cuisine, including several vegetarian dishes. Enjoy Broccoli with Garlic Sauce, Tofu in Brown Sauce, String Beans with Garlic Sauce, and Vegetarian Lo Mein. **Open Sunday through Thursday for dinner. Open Saturday one and a half hours after sunset. Closed Friday. Full service, vegan options, take-out, $$-$$$.**

OCEAN CITY

Bridges Restaurant
3050 Shore Rd., Ocean City, NJ 08226   **(609) 398-5858**
American. Dine along the waterfront of the Great Egg Harbor Bay at Bridges, a mainstream

for lunch and dinner. Closed Sunday. Full service, vegan options, fresh juices, BYOB, catering, take-out, $$.

RUNNEMEDE

Li's Peking Chinese Restaurant
Runnemede Plaza
835 E. Clements Bridge Rd., Runnemede, NJ 08078   **(609) 939-4440**
Chinese. Li's has an excellent vegetarian menu with appetizers, many soups, and entrées featuring vegetable, tofu, and mock meat. Foods are low in salt and prepared without MSG. Open daily. Full service, vegan options, BYOB, take-out, VISA/MC/AMEX, $$.

SCOTCH PLAINS

• Udupi Authentic Indian Vegetarian Cuisine
2540 Rte. 22E, Scotch Plains, NJ 07076   **(908) 233-5511**
Vegetarian/Indian. See description under Iselin, NJ.

STONE HARBOR

Green Cuisine
302 96th St., Stone Harbor, NJ 08247   **(609) 368-1616**
Natural foods. This restaurant has been serving delicious healthy food for more than 10 years. Menu selections include gourmet sandwiches, exotic salads, and beautiful fresh fruit selections. Vegetarian items, such as hummus pita, tabbouleh salad, and veggie burgers, are very popular. No credit cards. Open daily for three meals. Full service, fresh juice, BYOB, take-out, $$.

TEANECK

Chopstix
172 W. Englewood Ave., Teaneck, NJ 07666   **(201) 833-0200**
Chinese. This kosher Chinese restaurant offers take-out only. Vegetarian dishes include 10 different soups, vegetable egg rolls, scallion pancakes, dumplings, noodle and rice dishes, and many tofu dishes. Open Sunday through Thursday for lunch and dinner. Closed Friday and Saturday. Take-out, catering, fresh juices, VISA/MC/AMEX/DISC/DC, $$.

• Veggie Heaven
473 Cedar Ln., Teaneck, NJ 07666   **(201) 836-0887**
Vegetarian/Chinese. See description under Parsippany, NJ.

TOMS RIVER

•• East Coast Vegan
313-A W. Water St., Toms River, NJ 08753-6530   **(732) 473-9555**
Vegan. This restaurant serves a good variety of vegan wraps and sandwiches, such as a Tempeh Reuben, a Philly Cheese Fake, and the No Harm-No Foul, an un-chicken salad sandwich. Entrées are made with tofu, tempeh, or seitan, served with the vegetable of the day and a

choice of pasta or brown rice, and often covered with white country gravy and soy sausage, Yankee (mushroom) gravy, a Cajun-Creole sauce, or Floribbean curry. The staff uses nearly all organic products to make their delicious creations. **Open Monday through Saturday for lunch and dinner. Closed Sunday. Full service, soymilk, take-out, VISA/MC/AMEX/DISC, $-$$.**

Natural Foods Vegetarian Café

675 Batchelor St., Toms River, NJ 08753   **(732) 240-0024**

Natural foods. Located inside a natural foods store, this mostly vegetarian café features many unique dishes like a Vegan German Platter, Veggie Loaf Platter, and Tempeh and Chickpea Curry. **Open Monday through Friday for lunch. Closed Saturday and Sunday. Limited service, vegan options, take-out, VISA/MC/AMEX/DISC, $.**

WILDWOOD

Shakespeare's Café Of Earthly Delights

101 W. Rio Grande Ave., Wildwood, NJ 08260   **(609) 522-8147**

Natural foods. Shakespeare's promises that all of their "food is made daily on the premises from the freshest of all natural ingredients." They offer several vegetarian and vegan sandwiches, as well as salads and side orders. Options include veggie burgers, "eggless egg" salad, falafel, and hummus. **Open daily for three meals during the summer and for limited hours during the winter. Full service, vegan options, take-out, smoothies, special drinks, $.**

New Mexico

ALBUQUERQUE

• Annapurna

513 San Mateo NE, Albuquerque, NM 87108   **(505) 254-2424**

Vegetarian/Indian. This Ayurvedic cuisine and chai house offers many traditional Indian dishes and also has a boutique with Indian clothing. **Open Monday through Wednesday for breakfast through early dinner. Open Thursday through Saturday for three meals. Closed Sunday. Full service, vegan options, non-smoking, VISA/MC, $-$$.**

Bangkok Café

5901 Central Ave. NE, Albuquerque, NM 87108   **(505) 255-5036**

Thai. An entire vegetarian menu section that includes appetizers, soups, curry dishes, wok-fried dishes, rice and noodles, and desserts is available at Bangkok Café. All of the foods may be prepared from mild to spicy. **Open daily. Full service, vegan options, wine/beer, take-out, $$.**

Barry's Oasis Restaurant & Lounge

6337 Avenida La Costa NE, Albuquerque, NM 87109   **(505) 884-2324**

Mediterranean. Oasis features a collection of foods from France, Italy, Greece, and Spain. Vegetarian entrées include hummus, falafel, tabbouleh, moussaka, and pasta dishes. Desserts are homemade. There's live entertainment Wednesday through Saturday evenings. Reservations are recommended. **Open Monday through Saturday for lunch and dinner. Open Sunday for dinner only. Full service, vegan options, wine/beer/alcohol, take-out, VISA/ MC/AMEX/DISC, $$-$$$.**

Bodhi Tree Restaurant

127 Harvard Dr. SE, Albuquerque, NM 87106   (505) 260-0919

Indian. About one-third of the items on Bodhi Tree's menu are vegetarian, and only vegetable oil is used. There's patio dining with lots of shade. **Open daily. Full service, fresh juices, take-out, $$.**

El Patio Restaurant

142 Harvard Dr. SE, Albuquerque, NM 87106   (505) 268-4245

Mexican. Located near the University of New Mexico, this restaurant has vegetarian green and red chili and usually offers a daily veggie special. Try a vegetarian burrito with fresh avocados, tomatoes, and vegetarian beans. **Open daily. Full service, vegan options, wine/ beer, take-out, VISA/MC, $.**

India Kitchen Restaurant

6910 Montgomery Blvd. NE, Albuquerque, NM 87109   (505) 884-2333

Indian. Soups, appetizers, and 11 vegetarian entrées are on the India Kitchen menu. Everything is prepared fresh to order daily. **Open daily for dinner only. Full service, vegan options, wine/beer, VISA/MC/AMEX/DISC, $.**

India Palace

4410 Wyoming Blvd. NE, Albuquerque, NM 87111   (505) 271-5009

Indian. Highly recommended by both "Fodor's" and "The New York Times," India Palace offers deliciously prepared vegetable dishes made with only the finest spices and sauces. They also have a lunch buffet. **Open daily for lunch and dinner. Full service, catering, beer/wine, $-$$$.**

La Montanita Co-op Supermarket

3500 Central Ave. SE, Albuquerque, NM 87106   (505) 265-4631

Health foods store deli. La Montanita's deli features a wide variety of hot soups, healthy salads, entrées, and sandwiches. **Open daily. Deli-style, vegan options, fresh juices, take-out, $.** www.lamontanita.com

Punjab Restaurant

4801 Central Ave. NE, Albuquerque, NM 87108   (505) 255-9895

Indian. A wide selection of vegetarian appetizers and entrées are offered at Punjab. **Open Monday through Saturday for lunch and dinner. Open Sunday for dinner only. Full service, vegan options, take-out, catering, VISA/MC/AMEX/DISC, $-$$.**

Richard's Mexican Restaurant

3301 Menaul Blvd. NE, Albuquerque, NM 87107   (505) 881-1039

Mexican. Hearty breakfasts are available, as are options on a separate vegetarian lunch menu, including vegetarian tacos, chili, burritos and brown rice. **Open Monday through Saturday for breakfast and lunch. Closed Sunday. Full service, $-$$.**

Siam Café

5500 San Mateo Blvd. NE #101, Albuquerque, NM 87109   (505) 883-7334

Thai. Siam Café offers a separate vegetarian menu with specialty appetizers, soups, salads, and curry dishes. Try tofu and vegetables sautéed with vegetables in green curry or hot and sour mushroom soup with lemon grass, onion, galanga, tomato, and lime leaves. **Open Monday through Saturday for lunch and dinner. Closed Sunday. Full service, $$.**

•Twenty Carrots Natural Foods Café

2110 Central Ave. SE, Albuquerque, NM 87106   (505) 242-1320

Vegetarian. This café is located alongside a natural foods market. Enjoy delicious soups and salads, as well as a wide variety of veggie burgers, vegetarian sushi, tamales, and much more. **Open Monday through Saturday for three meals. Open Sunday for breakfast and lunch. Limited service, vegan/macrobiotic options, fresh juices, take-out, VISA/MC, $$.**

Wild Oats Community Market

11015 Menaul Blvd. NE, Albuquerque, NM 87112   (505) 275-6660
2103 Carlisle Blvd. NE, Albuquerque, NM 87110   (505) 260-1366
6300 San Mateo Blvd. NE, Albuquerque, NM 97109   (505) 823-1933

Natural foods deli. Enjoy daily hot vegetarian entrées, such as Tofu Fried Rice, Veggie Tamales, Tofu Foo Young, Roasted Rosemary Tempeh, Tofu Stroganoff, and more. Cold salads include mustard tempeh, veggie burgers, barbecue tempeh, and more. Also enjoy their juice bar, salad and soup bar, and pizza bar. **Open daily for three meals. Limited service, vegan options, fresh juices, espresso/cappuccino, take-out, catering, VISA/MC/AMEX/DISC, $-$$.**

LAS CRUCES

••The Herbal Hand Vegetarian Eatery

1801 Avenida de Mesilla, Las Cruces, NM 88005   (505) 523-2652

Vegan. The Herbal Hand offers soups, salads, sandwiches, and entrées. Examples include green chile soup, black bean and jicama salad, BBQ tofu sandwiches, and meatless meatloaf. This restaurant uses organic ingredients whenever possible. **Open Monday through Saturday for lunch and dinner. Closed Sunday. Full service, fresh juices, smoothies, soymilk, take-out, VISA/MC, $$.**

SANTA FE

Baja Tacos

2621 Cerrillos Rd., Santa Fe, NM 87501   (505) 471-8762

Mexican. Enjoy fast, healthy, and fresh Mexican food with no preservatives or additives. There's a vegetarian menu available. **Open daily for three meals. Counter service, vegan options, BYOB, take-out, $.**

Blue Corn Café

133 Water St., Santa Fe, NM 97501   (505) 984-1800

Mexican. Blue Corn's vegetarian options include tamales, fajitas, and veggie-fajita burritos.

Open daily for lunch and dinner. Full service, vegan options, wine/beer/alcohol, VISA/MC/AMEX/DISC/DC, $$.

Café Pasqual's

121 Don Gaspar, Santa Fe, NM 87501 (505) 983-9340

Natural foods. A Santa Fe classic, Café Pasqual's is known for its breakfasts and delicious Southwestern fare. They pay particular attention to quality and authenticity. The menu is based on simple ingredients, such as red and green chiles, pinto beans, garlic, onions, blue and yellow cornmeal, and white cheese. There is a decent selection for vegetarians, and specials are offered. Open daily for three meals. Full service, fresh juices, wine/beer, take-out, VISA/MC, $$-$$$.

Cloud Cliff Bakery & Restaurant

1805 Second St., Santa Fe, NM 87501 (505) 983-6254

Natural foods. Cloud Cliff integrates contemporary arts with fresh foods. The management works closely with local farmers and uses organically grown grains in European breads and alternative pastries. Open daily. Full service, fresh juice, wine/beer, take-out, VISA/MC, $$.

Hunan Chinese Restaurant

2440 Cerrillos Rd., Santa Fe, NM 87505 (505) 471-6688

Chinese. If you need a break from Southwestern cuisine, you can find a wide variety of vegetarian Hunan- and Peking-style Chinese foods at this restaurant. Appetizers, soups, and 16 vegetarian entrées are offered to delight your taste buds. Open daily for lunch and dinner. Full service, vegan options, wine/beer, take-out, VISA/MC, $$.

India House

2501 Cerrillos Rd., Santa Fe, NM 87501 (505) 471-2651

Indian. Try some of India House's vegetable samosas, pakoras, or any of its other vegetable dishes. Open daily for lunch and dinner. Full service, vegan options, VISA/MC/AMEX/DISC, $$.

Longevity Café

112 W. San Francisco St., Santa Fe, NM 87501 (505) 986-0403

Café. Located in the historic district of Santa Fe, Longevity Café is a Zen-style teahouse and café. In addition to teas, herbal elixirs, and tonics, they offer Asian-inspired meals and desserts. Open daily. Vegan options, $-$$. www.LongevityCafe.com

Szechwan Restaurant

1605 Juan Tabo Blvd. NE, Santa Fe, NM 87112 (505) 299-9133

Chinese. Ten vegetable and tofu entrées, such as Broccoli with Hot Garlic Sauce and Sizzling Bean Curd, are included on the menu. Appetizers, soup, and daily vegetarian specials are also offered. Open daily for lunch and dinner. Full service, vegan options, wine/beer, take-out, VISA/MC, $$.

• Tamale Molly

323 Aztec St., Santa Fe, NM 87501 (877) 509-1800

Vegetarian/ethnic. Feast on handmade vegetarian tamales made from only the finest, freshest ingredients. All profits are donated to various organizations aimed at helping the hungry, the homeless, and others in need. **Open Tuesday through Saturday for lunch. Closed Sunday and Monday. Vegan options, shipping, $-$$.** www.tamalemolly.com

Tecolote Café

1203 Cerrillos Rd., Santa Fe, NM 87501   **(505) 988-1362**

Mexican. Known for its breakfasts, Tecolote features fresh baked goods and original atole-pinon hot cakes made with blue cornmeal and roasted pine nuts. The café offers various Mexican classics with a New Mexican twist on its lunch menu. Beans and chili sauces are made with pure soy oil and no lard. The work of local artists is displayed on the walls. **Open Tuesday through Sunday for breakfast and lunch. Closed Monday. Full service, fresh juices, wine/beer, take-out, VISA/MC/AMEX/DC, $.**

Whistling Moon Café

402 N. Guadalupe St., Santa Fe, NM 87501   **(505) 983-3093**

Mediterranean. Feast on Middle Eastern cuisine, including hummus and tabbouleh, as well as pizza, salads, and more. **Open Monday through Friday for lunch and dinner. Open Saturday and Sunday for brunch only. Full service, espresso/cappuccino, non-alcoholic wine/beer, wine/beer, catering, take-out, $-$$.**

Wild Oats Market

1090 S. St. Francis Dr., Santa Fe, NM 87501   **(505) 983-5333**
1708 Llano St., Santa Fe, NM 87505   **(505) 473-4943**

Natural foods deli. This deli has vegetarian options and a large selection of breads and pastries. **Open daily. Deli-style, fresh juices, take-out, VISA/MC, $.**

TAOS

Amigos Café

326 Paseo Del Pueblo Sur, Taos, NM 87571   **(505) 758-8493**

Natural foods/juice bar. This establishment offers large portions of food made with organic ingredients in an informal environment. **Open daily for lunch. Limited service, vegan options, fresh juices, $.**

Apple Tree Restaurant

123 Bent St., Taos, NM 87571   **(505) 758-1900**

Natural foods. Salads, soups, appetizers, and specials all include options for vegetarians. The red and green chili and the beans are vegetarian. Foods are prepared using the freshest ingredients available and reflecting a variety of ethnic persuasions. **Open Mondy through Saturday for lunch and dinner. Open Sunday for brunch only. Full service, vegan options, espresso/cappuccino, wine/beer, take-out, VISA/MC/AMEX, $-$$$.**

The Café Tazza

122 Kit Carson Rd., Taos, NM 87571   **(505) 758-8706**

Café. Cafe Tazza is an espresso bar with locally made ethnic vegetarian tamales, vegetarian chili, plus daily soup specials and Italian espresso. They also offer great magazines, exhibits in a photo gallery, and courtyard seating in summer. No credit cards. **Open daily. Limited service, espresso, take-out, $.**

• Sheva Café
812B Del Pueblo Norte, Taos, NM 87571   **(505) 737-9290**

Vegetarian/Middle Eastern. Enjoy a wide variety of authentic Middle Eastern vegetarian dishes and other delicacies at the Sheva Café. **Open Monday through Thursday for lunch and dinner. Open Friday for lunch only. Open Saturday night for performances. Open Sunday for brunch only. Catering, take-out, $-$$.**

Taos Pizza Outback
712 Paseo del Peublo Norte, Taos, NM 87571   **(505) 758-3112**

Pizza. This restaurant serves gourmet pizza with toppings, such as dried tomatoes, spinach, artichoke, and pineapple. Pasta and salads are also on the menu. **Open daily for lunch and dinner. Full service, wine/beer, take-out, VISA/MC, $$.**

New York

(For restaurant listings in the surrounding areas, see Clifton Park.)

BFS Catering Café Restaurant
1736 Western Ave., Albany, NY 12203   **(518) 452-6342**

Mediterranean. Enjoy stuffed grape leaves, soup, salads, falafel, hummus, tabbouleh, and sandwiches at this café. **Open Monday through Saturday for three meals. Open Sunday for breakfast and lunch. Full service, vegan options, espresso/cappuccino, take-out, catering, $.**

Bomber's Burrito Bar
258 Lark St., Albany, NY 12210   **(518) 463-9636**

Mexican. Bomber's offers huge vegetarian burritos, all of which can be made vegan, and a different vegan burrito special each month. All can be rolled in your choice of chili, spinach, tomato, or whole wheat tortillas. Other interesting items include a peanut butter and jelly taco, barbequed Tofu Fries (with or without cheese), and Vegan Chili Fries. **Open daily for three meals. Full service, vegan options, beer/wine/alcohol, take-out, VISA/MC/AMEX, $.** www.bombersburritobar.com

El Loco Mexican Café
465 Madison Ave., Albany, NY 12210   **(518) 436-1855**

Mexican. El Loco offers no-lard refried beans, veggie brown Mexican rice, veggie chili and soups, blue cornbread, and a host of items can be prepared vegetarian. The restaurant has a funky atmosphere, outdoor patio dining, and interesting t-shirts. **Open Tuesday through Saturday for lunch and dinner. Open Sunday for late lunch and dinner. Closed Monday. Full service, wine/beer/alcohol, catering, take-out, VISA/MC/AMEX, $$.**

LuLu's Café

288 Lark St., Albany, NY 12210   **(518) 436-5660**

Bistro. Located near a stretch of cool shops between Madison and Central Avenues, LuLu's has a bar downstairs, a bistro upstairs, and a very nice art gallery on the third floor. The menu consists of some very unusual original dishes on a menu that is always at least half vegetarian. They serve some of the best coffee in Albany, and the desserts are excellent. **Open daily for dinner through late night. Full service, vegan options, wine/beer, take-out, VISA/MC/ AMEX/DISC, $$.**

Mamoun's

206 Washington Ave., Albany, NY 12210   **(518) 434-3901**

Mediterranean. Mamoun's serves creative vegetarian dishes, including cooked spinach with a tahini sauce served over rice, lentils and bulgur served with a salad, couscous with steamed vegetables, falafel, hummus, baba ghanouj, stuffed grape leaves, a spicy eggplant dish, and vegetarian sandwiches. **Open daily for lunch and dinner. Full service, vegan options, take-out, fresh juices, $-$$.**

• Shades of Green

187 Lark St., Albany, NY 12210   **(518) 434-1830**

Vegetarian. Voted the "Best Vegetarian Restaurant" in "Metroland" from 1995 through 2002, Shades of Greens offers a wide variety of soups, salads, and sandwiches, as well as special hot entrées, vegetarian chili, Mexican dishes, vegetarian burgers, organic rice bowls, and much more. **Open Monday through Saturday for lunch and dinner. Closed Sunday. Full service, vegan options, fresh juices, soymilk, smoothies, take-out, $.**

ALBERTSON

Vincent's Restaurant & Pizzeria

1004 Willis Ave., Albertson, NY 11507   **(516) 621-7530**

Italian. Vincent's offers several vegetarian dishes, including a Cheeseless Potato Pizza. **Open daily for lunch and dinner. Full service, vegan options, catering, take-out, wine/beer, VISA/ MC/AMEX/DISC, $$.**

AMHERST

Mighty Taco

6888 Transit Rd., Amherst, NY 14221   **(716) 632-1072**
9360 Transit Rd., Amherst, NY 14051   **(716) 568-1143**
5495 Sheridan Dr., Amherst, NY 14221   **(716) 565-1954**
3190 Niagara Falls Blvd., Amherst, NY 14228   **(716) 695-1899**

Mexican. This regional fast food chain is a great solution for those looking for a quick meal. The beans that Mighty Taco uses are vegetarian. All tacos and burritos can be made without cheese upon request. **Open daily for lunch and dinner. Limited service, take-out, $.** www.mightytaco.com

Taste Of India
3093 Sheridan Dr., Amherst, NY 14226 **(716) 886-4000**
Indian. This restaurant offers the most authentic dishes, each prepared with a variety of spices to create a distinct and individual flavor. Their fresh ingredients are skillfully cooked to preserve a low-fat, high nutritional value and prepared for your taste from mild to medium to hot. All entrées are served with Basmati rice. **Open daily for lunch and dinner. Full service, catering.**

Teta's Middle Eastern Cuisine
9370 Transit Rd., Amherst, NY 14051 **(716) 636-5944**
Middle Eastern. This Middle Eastern restaurant specializes in Lebanese cuisine, such as hummus, falafel, baba ghanouj, tabbouleh, spinach pies, stuffed grape leaves, fava beans, and desserts. **Open Monday through Saturday for lunch and dinner. Open Sunday for dinner only. Full service, vegan options, beer/wine, take-out, VISA/MC/AMEX/DISC, $.**

Thai Bistro
1009 Niagara Falls Blvd., Amherst, NY 14226 **(716) 832-2361**
Thai. This large, upscale restaurant has an extensive vegetarian menu, including Thai salads, spring rolls, pad Thai, curry dishes, and mock meat entrées. The menu features a full listing of all ingredients, and all food is made-to-order. **Open Monday through Friday for lunch and dinner. Open Saturday and Sunday for dinner only. Full service, VISA/MC/AMEX, $$-$$$.**

AMITYVILLE

• Santosha Vegetarian Restaurant
40 Merrick Rd., Amityville, NY 11701 **(516) 598-1787**
Vegetarian. Long Island's oldest vegetarian restaurant features international vegetarian cuisine, such as Tofu Scallop Platter, Seventh Dynasty, and quesadillas. **Open Tuesday through Sunday for dinner. Closed Monday. Full service, vegan options, dairy and non-dairy cappuccino, take-out, catering, VISA/MC/AMEX, $$$.**

BINGHAMTON

(For restaurant listings in the surrounding areas, see Johnson City.)

•• King David's Royal Foodcourt
101 1/2 Trafford Rd., Binghamton, NY 13901 **(607) 723-0837**
Vegan. Doors open only once a month, but it's worth the wait. You'll enjoy a vegan feast, which could include any number of dishes on the rotating menu, including Thai Tempeh Kebabs, Shepherd's Pie, and Vegan Chocolate Almond Cheesecake. Personal catering is available on a regular basis. **Call for hours. Full service, vegan options, reservations required, fresh juices, catering, $-$$.**

Restaurant codes: ✪ Reviewers' Choice • Vegetarian Restaurant •• Vegan Restaurant
Restaurant prices: **$** less than $6 **$$** $6-$12 **$$$** more than $12
Credit Cards Accepted: VISA - VISA MC - MasterCard AMEX - American Express
DISC - Discover DC - Diner's Club

Whole in the Wall
43 S. Washington St., Binghamton, NY 13903   **(607) 722-5138**
Natural foods. Whole in the Wall serves tofu, tempeh, and Middle Eastern dishes; fresh-baked breads and bagels; and soups made from scratch. Examples include miso, spicy vegetarian chili, stir-fried vegetables with tofu, tempeh, or both, tempura, and pita pockets. All non-vegetarian items are cooked separately, and the restaurant can accommodate special diets. For dessert, try a slice of pie, made with fresh fruit and a whole-wheat crust. Live music is featured on Saturday night. **Open Tuesday through Saturday for lunch and dinner. Closed on Sunday and Monday. Full service, reservations recommended on weekends and for large parties, macrobiotic/vegan options, fresh juices, $$. www.wholeinthewall.com**

BREWSTER

Jaipore Royal India Cuisine
280 Rt. 22, Brewster, NY 10509   **(914) 277-3549**
Indian. Jaipore is located in an historic Victorian manor and offers more than 15 vegetarian entrées, including rice dishes, freshly baked breads, vegetable curry dishes, and more. **Open daily for lunch and dinner. Full service, vegan options, catering, wine/beer/alcohol, take-out, VISA/MC/AMEX, $$.**

BRIGHTON

Golden Dynasty Chinese Restaurant
Loehmann's Plaza, 1900 S. Clinton Ave., Brighton, NY 14618   (585) 442-6340
Chinese. This restaurant has a separate vegetarian menu, including Sautéed Green Beans, lightly fried Spinach Tofu, and about a dozen soy protein dishes. **Open daily for lunch and dinner. Full service, vegan options, take-out, catering, VISA/MC/AMEX, $$.**

BROOKLYN

Back To Nature
535 Kings Hwy., Brooklyn, NY 11223   **(718) 339-0273**
Kosher/natural foods. Most of the menu items at Back to Nature are vegetarian, but there are a few fish dishes. Try the Vegetable Kibbeh, Tofu Vegetable Salad, hummus sandwich, veggie burger deluxe, vegetable stir-fry with tempeh, or one of the many other creative meals. **Open Sunday through Friday for lunch and dinner. Open Saturday after sundown until midnight. Full service, vegan options, Fresh juices, espresso/cappuccino, take-out, VISA/ MC/AMEX, $$.**

•Bliss
191 Bedford Ave. (Between N. 6th and N. 7th Sts.)
Brooklyn, NY 11211   **(718) 599-2547**
Vegetarian. Bliss is a casual little dining spot located in Williamsburg, an artistic community in Brooklyn. The atmosphere is casual, and you can fill up on such vegetarian favorites as portobello mushroom sandwiches, a marinated tofu club sandwich, curry supreme, or the bliss bowl. If you live in or are visiting the area, Bliss has free deliveries with a $10 minimum order. **Open daily for three meals. Open Saturday and Sunday for brunch. Full service, vegan options, fresh juices, espresso/cappuccino, soymilk, no credit cards, take-out, delivery, $$.**

• D'ital Shak

989 Nostrand Ave., Brooklyn, NY 11225   (718) 756-6557
305 Halsey St., Brooklyn, NY 11216   (718) 573-3752

Vegetarian. D'ital Shak is another Brooklyn haven for vegetarians. Try the natural vegetarian patties. **Open 24 hours a day. Full service, vegan options, fresh juices, take-out, delivery, catering, $$.**

•• Foodswings

295 Grand St., Brooklyn, NY 11211   (718) 388-1919

Vegan. This socially-conscious vegan fast food joint in Williamsburg serves soups, salads, heroes, burgers, hot dogs, and desserts. Unique offerings include the No Chicken Caeser Salad, Fried "Shrimp," and Mock Beef Quesadillas. **Open daily for lunch through late night. Counter service, catering, VISA/MC, $$.** www.foodswings.net

• The Greens Vegetarian Restaurant

128 Montaque St., Brooklyn, NY 11201   (718) 246-1288

Vegetarian/Chinese. Located near the Borough Hall subway stop, this certified kosher Chinese restaurant offers several soups, tofu and seitan dishes, and much more. Try the Vegetarian Boat appetizer sampler, the raw Large Greens Salad with soy protein and pineapple, and the Peking Style Vegetarian Cutlet, which is a tofu loaf with pancakes, brown rice, and vegetables. **Open daily for lunch and dinner. Full service, vegan options, reservations accepted, fresh, juices, take-out, VISA/MC, $-$$.**

•• IMHOTEP's Health and Living

734 Nostrand Ave. (Between Park and Prospect)
Brooklyn, NY 11216   (718) 493-2395

Vegan/West Indian. This organic restaurant offers delicious veggie ribs and more. **Open Monday through Saturday for three meals. Closed Sunday. Cafeteria, take-out, VISA/MC/ AMEX, $$.**

Kar Too Restaurant

5908 Ave. N, Brooklyn, NY 11234   (718) 531-8811

Chinese. At Kar Too, savor sautéed string beans with pickled cabbage, Tangy and Spicy Tofu, and spinach sautéed with Fu-U sauce. Brown rice is available upon request. **Open daily for lunch and dinner. Buffet, wine/beer, take-out, VISA/MC/AMEX, $$.**

King Falafel

7408 3rd Ave., Brooklyn, NY 11209   (718) 745-4188

Middle Eastern. Half of the menu at King Falafel is dedicated to vegetarian sandwiches and platters, including hummus, fried cauliflower, stuffed grape leaves, and falafel. **Open daily for lunch and dinner. Full service, vegan options, fresh juices, espresso/cappuccino, catering, take-out, $-$$.**

Moustache Pizza

405 Atlantic Ave., Brooklyn, NY 11217   (718) 852-5555

Middle Eastern. Behind this small neighborhood restaurant is a quaint garden setting with tables and umbrellas. Bread is baked when ordered. The pizza here is made using vegan pita bread instead of traditional pizza dough. **Open daily. Limited service, vegan options, special drinks, $.**

Mr. Falafel Restaurant
226 Seventh Ave., Brooklyn, NY 11215   **(718) 768-4961**
Middle Eastern. This restaurant serves primarily Mediterranean food of an Egyptian style at an affordable price. Try the Koshery, Falafel, Greek Salads, Hummus, Baba Ghanouj, and vegetable lasagna. **Open daily for lunch and dinner. Full service, fresh juices, cappuccino, special drinks, take-out, AMEX, $.**

Steve and Sons Bakery and Caterers, Inc.
9305 Church Ave., Brooklyn, NY 11212   **(718) 498-6800**
Ethnic/American. This restaurant offers vegetarian patties and turnovers, vegetarian stew, vegetarian barbecue West Indian ribs, vegetable steaks, and gluten in wine sauce, among many other selections. **Open Sunday through Thursday for three meals. Open Friday for breakfast and lunch. Open Saturday for dinner. Full service, fresh juices, beer, $$.**

•• Strictly Vegetarian
2268 Church Ave. (Between Bedford and Flatbush)
Brooklyn, NY 11226   **(718) 284-2543**
Vegan/Caribbean. The menu here changes daily, but items often include tofu stew and chickpea stew. **Open Monday through Saturday for lunch and dinner. Call for Sunday hours. Counter service, vegan options, take-out, no credit cards, $$.**

• Vegetarian Palate
258 Flatbush Ave. (Between Prospect Pl. and St. Mark's)
Brooklyn, NY 11217   **(718) 623-8808**
Vegetarian/Chinese. Known simply as VP by regular customers, Vegetarian Palate offers veggie Chinese cuisine, including spring rolls, mock meat dishes, and noodle dishes. And you may want to save room for some soy ice cream for dessert. **Open daily from lunch through late night. Full service, vegan options, take-out, VISA/MC/AMEX, $$.**

•• Veggie Castle
2242 Church Ave. (Between Flatbush and Bedford)
Brooklyn, NY 11226   **(718) 703-1275**
Vegan/Caribbean. Located in a former White Castle restaurant, Veggie Castle offers a variety of vegan "fast food items." Try the veggie burgers and the vegan mac and cheese, along with a variety of juices. **Open daily for three meals. Limited service, vegan options, fresh juices, take-out, $.**

Weiss's Restaurant
1146 Coney Island Ave., Brooklyn, NY 11230   **(718) 421-0184**
Kosher. Weiss's Restaurant serves kosher dairy cuisine with added vegetarian dishes, such as Tofu Primavera, Vegetables & Linguine, and Vegetarian Chopped Liver. You might want to order an egg cream to go with your meal. **Open Sunday through Thursday for lunch and**

dinner. In winter, open Saturday 90 minutes after sundown. Full service, wine/beer/alcohol, take-out, catering, $$.

BUFFALO

(For restaurant listings in the surrounding areas, see Amherst, Depew, Hamburg, Lockport, Niagara Falls, Orchard Park, Tonawanda, and Williamsville.)

Amy's Place
3234 Main St., Buffalo, NY 14214 (716) 832-6666
Natural foods/American/Middle Eastern. About one-half of the menu is vegetarian. **Open daily for three meals. Full service, take-out, $.**

Feel Rite Deli
3912 Maple Rd., Buffalo, NY 14226 (716) 834-3385
5425 Transit Rd., Buffalo, NY 14221 (716) 636-1000
Natural foods deli. This deli, located within a natural foods store, is one of the few safe havens for vegetarians in Buffalo, NY. Try the TLT, Feel Lite Bagel, Hummus Stuff-It, or the Tofu Cheddar (soy cheddar available upon request). **Open Monday through Saturday for three meals. Open Sunday for lunch and early dinner. Counter service, vegan options, take-out, fresh juices, smoothies, VISA/MC, $.**

Mighty Taco
345 Amherst St., Buffalo, NY 14207 (716) 447-9228
2367 Delaware Ave., Buffalo, NY 14216 (716) 871-8670
1762 Sheridan Dr., Buffalo, NY 14223 (716) 332-0324
2245 Walden Ave., Buffalo, NY 14225 (716) 681-3633
Mexican. See description under Amherst, NY.

Pano's Restaurant
1081 Elmwood Ave., Buffalo, NY 14222 (716) 886-9081
Greek. Pano's is one of Buffalo's institutions. The restaurant moved up the street from its previous location and is now able to accommodate many more customers. Pano's serves breakfast at any hour and has a vegetarian menu that features stuffed grape leaves, falafel, a white bean salad, and spinach and rice. **Open 24 hours daily. Full service, beer/wine/alcohol, outdoor seating, take-out, VISA/MC/AMEX/DISC, $-$$.**

Saigon Café
1098 Elmwood Ave., Buffalo, NY 14222 (716) 883-1252
Vietnamese/Thai. This restaurant, located in Buffalo's trendy Elmwood district, features some of the best cuisine that southeast Asia has to offer. The menu features a "vegetarian corner," with such specialties as Vegetable Rainbow, Tamarind Tofu, Eggplant Curry, and vegetarian

---

Restaurant codes: ✪ Reviewers' Choice • Vegetarian Restaurant • • Vegan Restaurant
Restaurant prices: **$** less than $6 **$$** $6-$12 **$$$** more than $12
Credit Cards Accepted: VISA - VISA MC - MasterCard AMEX - American Express
DISC - Discover DC - Diner's Club

green curry. **Open daily for lunch and dinner. Full service, take-out, VISA/MC, $-$$.** www.thesaigoncafe.com

CAMBRIDGE

Park 56

56 N. Park St., Cambridge, NY 12816   **(518) 677-8096**

American. This mostly non-vegetarian restaurant in fact caters to vegetarians with dishes like Walnut Rice Loaf, Tempeh Reuben, Tempeh Parmesan, and veggie burgers. **Open daily for lunch and dinner. Open Sunday for brunch. Full service, wine/beer, non-alcoholic beer, take-out, catering, VISA/MC/AMEX/DISC, $-$$.**

CEDARHURST

Natural Gourmet

546 Central Ave., Cedarhurst, NY 11516   **(516) 569-7609**

Natural foods. Natural Gourmet is a kosher restaurant offering many vegetarian dishes, including homemade soups, salads, lasagna, sandwiches and burgers, vegan desserts, and more. **Open Sunday through Thursday for lunch and dinner. Open Friday for breakfast and lunch. Closed Saturday. Limited service, macrobiotic/vegan options, fresh juices, take-out, catering, VISA/MC/AMEX, $$.**

CLIFTON PARK

Antipasto's

1028 Rt. 146 (At 146A), Clifton Park, NY 12065   **(518) 383-1209**

Italian. This restaurant has been called "a vegetarian's delight," and with good reason. Most dishes have wheat-free pasta options and/or can be altered to suit vegan guests. The menu includes appetizers, an "always vegetarian friendly" soup of the day, salads, and vegetarian versions of classic pasta dishes. In addition to traditional toppings, you can choose items like chick peas, pine nuts, and veggie bacon, pepperoni, sausage, or meatballs for a gourmet pizza. Or try an entrée from the "Very Vegetarian" menu, such as The Paul McCartney (Tofu Parmigian), Burrito Grande, or The Ultimate Veggie Sausage Burger. **Open daily for dinner. Full service, vegan options, wine/beer, non-alcoholic beer, take-out, catering, no credit cards, $$-$$$.** www.antipastos.com

CORNING

Medley's Café

88 W. Market St., Corning, NY 14830   **(607) 936-1685**

Natural foods. This eclectic, primarily vegetarian café serves many different ethnic dishes. Music is provided Thursday, Friday, and Saturday evenings. **Open Monday through Saturday for lunch and dinner. Closed Sunday. Full service, vegan options, wine/beer, non-alcoholic wine/beer, VISA/MC/AMEX/DISC/DC, $-$$.**

Restaurant codes: ✪ Reviewers' Choice   • Vegetarian Restaurant   • • Vegan Restaurant
Restaurant prices: **$** less than $6   **$$** $6-$12   **$$$** more than $12
Credit Cards Accepted: VISA - VISA   MC - MasterCard   AMEX - American Express
DISC - Discover   DC - Diner's Club

DELHI

Quarter Moon Café
53 Main St., Delhi, NY 13753 (607) 746-6562

Café. Most options on Quarter Moon's menu are vegetarian. A variety of soups, sandwiches, platters, and daily specials are offered. **Open Monday through Saturday for lunch. Open Sunday for brunch. Full service, vegan options, take-out, $.**

DEPEW

Mighty Taco
1435 French Rd., Depew, NY 14043 (716) 656-0721

Mexican. See description under Amherst, NY.

FAYETTEVILLE

Wegman's Market Café
6789 E. Genesse St., Fayetteville, NY 13066 (315) 446-2950

American. The café inside Wegman's Market is quite spectacular. Feast on pasta, Chinese dishes, pizza, and more. **Open daily for lunch and dinner. Counter service, vegan options, fresh juices, take-out, catering, VISA/MC/AMEX/DISC, $-$$.**

FREEVILLE

Kiraku Rose Restaurant & Organic General Store
17D Railroad Rd., Freeville, NY 13068 (607) 844-8813

Macrobiotic. Located just northeast of Ithaca, this warm, friendly restaurant offers beautiful organic, macrobiotic cuisine that is primarily vegan, though they do occasionally serve fish. The menu, which the chef artfully prepares, changes daily. They serve lunch, as well as evening special gourmet meals that you may only attend with reservations. These special dinners are five-course affairs, so plan on staying at least two hours. **Open Tuesday through Saturday for lunch and for dinner with a reservation. Closed Sunday and Monday. Full service, macrobiotic/vegan options, soymilk, special drinks, $$-$$$.** www.kirakullc.com

GARDEN CITY

Akbar
2 South St., Garden City, NY 11530 (516) 248-5700

Indian. Akbar has a good vegetarian selection with at least four vegan entrées; three others have some dairy. Spicy food is available upon request. **Open daily for lunch and dinner. Full service, vegan options, $$.**

GARDINER

Bistro Mountain Store
3124 Rt. 44/55, Gardiner, NY 12525 (845) 255-2999

Natural foods deli. Located within a grocery store at the foot of the Shawangunk Cliffs, this full service deli features homemade salads, omelets, bagels, soymilk, soy ice cream, and grilled tofu. The store also has mountain bike rentals for $35 per day. This establishment is run by the same people who manage the Main Street Bistro in New Paltz, NY. **Open daily for three meals. Deli-style, take-out, VISA/MC/DISC, $-$$.**

GLEN COVE

Rising Tide Natural Market

42 Forest Ave., Glen Cove, NY 11542   **(516) 676-7895**

Natural foods. This take-out only market makes a huge variety of vegan salads and sandwiches, including Lemon Seitan, Tofu Teriyaki, barbecue tempeh, and vegetarian chili. **Open daily for three meals. Take-out, vegan options, fresh juices, catering, VISA/MC, $.**

GREAT NECK

Earth's Harvest

5 Great Neck Rd., Great Neck, NY 11021   **(516) 829-8605**

Health foods store deli. Several veggie options are offered. **Open daily. Limited service, macrobiotic options, VISA/MC, $.**

Garden of Plenty

4 Wellwyn Rd., Great Neck, NY 11021   **(516) 482-8868**

Ethnic foods. Garden of Plenty offers unique vegetarian dishes like Sautéed Chinese Spinach, Snow White Chow Fun Rolls, Fish Fantasy (made from bean curd), and Enoki Mushrooms. **Open daily for lunch and dinner. Full service, $$.**

HAMBURG

Mighty Taco

5999 S. Park Ave., Hamburg, NY 14075   **(716) 649-8177**

Mexican. See description under Amherst, NY.

HUNTINGTON

Tortilla Grill

335 New York Ave., Huntington, NY 11743   **(516) 423-4141**

Mexican. This Mexican restaurant clearly indicates on the menu the dishes suitable for vegetarians. The beans do not contain lard. **Open Tuesday through Sunday for lunch and dinner. Closed Monday. Counter service, $.**

ITHACA

(For restaurant listings in the surrounding areas, see Freeville and Trumansburg.)

ABC Café

308 Stewart Ave., Ithaca, NY 14850   **(607) 277-4770**

Natural foods. The Apple Blossom Café, or ABC, serves up vegetarian favorites like the ABC Burger, Tempeh Reuben, and Broccoli Cashew Stir-Fry. They also feature Sunday brunch, seasonal menus, free music Tuesday night, and monthly art shows. **Open Tuesday through**

Sunday. Closed Monday. Counter service, macrobiotic/vegan options, espresso, smoothies, wine/beer, take-out, $-$$.

Aladdin's Natural Eatery

100 Dryden Rd., Ithaca, NY 14850   (607) 273-5000

Natural foods. Aladdin's offers great soups, sandwiches, pasta dishes, salads, and more. **Open daily for three meals.** Full service, vegan options, fresh juices, wine/beer, take-out, $-$$.

Collegetown Bagels

329 Pine Tree Rd., East Hill Plaza, Ithaca, NY 14850   (607) 273-1036
Triphammer Mall, N. Triphammer Rd., Ithaca, NY 14850   (607) 257-2255
400 N. Meadow St., Ithaca, NY 14850   (607) 273-4975

Bakery. The bagel sandwiches are made with everything from portobello mushrooms to seitan to avocado. They also offer bagels with Tofutti cream "cheese." **Open daily for three meals.** Limited service, vegan options, VISA/MC, $. www.collegetownbagels.com

• Harvest Deli

171 E. State St., Center Ithaca, The Commons, Ithaca, NY 14850   (607) 272-1961

Vegetarian. Located in a food court in the Commons, Harvest Deli offers a healthy alternative for people who are on-the-go specializing in dairy- and egg-free breakfast and lunch. Try the Tofu Scramble (with seitan "bacon"), Tofu Rancheros, and and rosemary-seasoned homefries. The grilled sub of the week ranges from the Spicy Seitan Cuban Sub to the Artichoke & Roasted Red Pepper sandwich to the Cajun-style seitan/BBQ and breaded tofu cutlet. Other offerings include wraps, soups (miso and daily special), salads, and bakery items like vegan muffins. **Open daily for breakfast and lunch.** Limited service, fresh juices, smoothies, take-out, catering, $. www.harvestdeli.com

Ithaca Bakery

400 N. Meadow St., Ithaca, NY 14850   (607) 273-7110

Bakery. This bakery is located on Rt. 13 in the historic west end of Ithaca. Besides breads and pastries, they have a selection of vegetarian sandwiches, including the Cayuga Croissant (with avocado, tomato, mushrooms, sprouts, and parsley-garlic dressing), Sapsucker Woods (portobello with sprouts, roasted red peppers, and aioli dressing on multi-grain), and Varna Vegan (lemon teriyaki seitan on oatmeal wheat bread with fresh spinach, tomato, and balsamic vinaigrette). **Open daily for three meals.** Limited service, vegan options, espresso/cappuccino, take-out, catering, VISA/MC, $. www.ithacabakery.com

Juna's Café

146 E. State St., Ithaca, NY 14850   (607) 256-4292

Eclectic. Juna's Café is the sister restaurant of the Harvest Deli. There are many options available, including a pita platter featuring the hummus of the day, an Asian wrap with tempeh and brown rice, a veggie turnover, and a Mediterranean wrap. **Open daily.** Limited service, vegan options, live music, espresso/cappuccino, soymilk, take-out, $. www.junascafe.com

Moosewood Restaurant ✪

DeWitt Building, 215 N. Cayuga St., Ithaca, NY 14850   (607) 273-9610

Natural foods. Moosewood is a cooperatively owned and managed restaurant with a menu that changes daily, rotating through the hundreds of dishes featured in the restaurant's cook-books.The menu offers gourmet and natural foods cuisine with ethnic specialties on Sunday nights and features homemade desserts, Bully Hill 100% New York State Grape Juice, and Yuengling beer, ale, and porter. There is a friendly ambiance, and seasonal outdoor terrace dining is available. **Open daily. Open on Sunday for dinner only. Full service, wine/beer, take-out, catering, VISA/MC, $$.**

Thai Cuisine
501 S. Meadow St. (Rte. 13), Ithaca, NY 14850   **(607) 273-2031**
Thai. Thai Cuisine's vegetarian menu includes such items as curry dishes, sweet and sour dishes, tofu dishes, noodle dishes, soups, salads, and more. **Open Monday through Thursday for dinner. Open Friday through Sunday for lunch and dinner. Full service, wine/beer/alcohol, take-out, $$.**

JOHNSON CITY

HealthBeat Natural Foods and Deli
214 Main St., Johnson City, NY 13790   **(607) 797-1001**
Natural foods. This deli is located in the back of a natural foods store. Both hot entrées and cold dishes are available. **Open Monday through Friday for three meals. Open Saturday for breakfast and lunch. Closed Sunday. Counter service, vegan options, take-out, VISA/MC, $.**

LITTLE NECK

• Zen Pavilion
251-15 Northern Blvd., Little Neck, NY 11362   **(718) 281-1500**
Vegetarian. This restaurant serves exotic, gourmet-style vegetable cuisine in both formal and informal atmospheres. **Open daily for lunch and dinner. Full service, vegan options, fresh juices, espresso/cappuccino, non-alcoholic beer/wine, reservations recommended, non-smoking, VISA/MC/AMEX/DC, $$.**

LOCKPORT

Mighty Taco
5691 S. Transit Rd., Lockport, NY 14094   **(716) 434-8211**
Mexican. See description under Amherst, NY.

LOCUST VALLEY

Charlie's Restaurant
324 Forest Ave., Locust Valley, NY 11560   **(516) 676-6229**
American. Charlie's offers pasta dishes, personalized pizzas, and calzones made with a whole-wheat crust, vegetarian sandwiches, and tofu dishes. **Open daily for dinner through late night. Full service, wine/beer/alcohol, take-out, VISA/MC/AMEX/DISC, $$.**

LONG ISLAND

(For restaurant listings on Long Island, see Albertson, Amityville, Cedarhurst, Garden City, Glen Cove, Great Neck, Huntington, Little Neck, Locust Valley, Merrick, Montauk, Oceanside,

Plainview, Riverhead, Sag Harbor, Sayville, Syosset, West Hempstead, and Westbury. For restaurant listings in the surrounding areas, see New York City.)

MAHOPAC

• Mrs. Green's Natural Market
Lake Plaza, Rt. 6, Mahopac, NY 10541   **(914) 626-0533**
Vegetarian/natural foods. A wide range of organic vegetarian, vegan, and fat-free dishes, as well as a bakery, are available at Mrs. Green's. **Open daily. Limited service, vegan options, fresh juices, take-out, VISA/MC/AMEX/DISC, $.**

MAMARONECK

•• Organica Garden
136 Mamaroneck Ave., Mamaroneck, NY 10543   **(914) 777-3450**
Vegan. Organica Garden's menu includes Eggplant Napoleon, Swiss Chard Roll (pinto beans, rice, and vegetables over a mushroom ragout), Spiced Jerk Tempeh, and several wraps. They also offer desserts and indoor and outdoor patio dining. **Open Wednesday through Monday for lunch and dinner. Open for brunch on Sunday. Closed Tuesday. Full service, vegan options, fresh juices, smoothies, soymilk, take-out, catering, VISA/MC/AMEX, $-$$.**

MANHATTAN

(For restaurant listings in the surrounding areas, see New York City.)

• 18 Arhans
227 Centre St., New York, NY 10015   **(212) 941-8986**
Vegetarian. Located in the rear of a Buddhist temple, this small restaurant boasts an extensive menu for a good price. Seating is extremely limited, so take-out might be a better option. **Open daily for lunch and dinner. Counter service, soymilk, take-out, catering, $-$$.**

535
535 Laguardia Pl., New York, NY 10012   **(212) 254-1417**
Natural foods. 535 is a take-out restaurant that offers many vegetarian options, including veggie burgers, hummus, falafel, and salads. **Open daily for lunch and dinner. Take-out, $.**

•• Angelica Kitchen ✿
300 E. 12th St., New York, NY 10003   **(212) 228-2909**
Vegan. This restaurant uses 95 percent organic ingredients. Daily specials are offered along with excellent homemade cornbread and tahini dressing. Angelica's has been rated highly by many New Yorkers. **Open daily for lunch and dinner. Full service, macrobiotic/vegan options, fresh juices, smoothies, take-out, $$.**

Apple Restaurant
17 Waverly Pl., New York, NY 10003   **(212) 473-8888**
Vietnamese. This restaurant uses separate cooking equipment when preparing vegetarian foods. There are many interesting natural food choices, including Yam Tempura, Watercress Salad, Tempeh Burger, Stir-Fried Cabbage with Soba Noodles, BBQ Seitan, and more. It also fea-

tures Karaoke sing-a-long. **Open daily for lunch and dinner. Full service, wine/beer/alcohol, catering, take-out, VISA/MC/AMEX, $$.**

• Ayurveda Café
706 Amsterdam Ave., New York, NY 10025   **(212) 932-2400**

Vegetarian/Indian. Located at 94th St., this restaurant offers Indian vegetarian cuisine. **Open daily for lunch and late dinner. Full service, take-out, catering, delivery, suitable for business entertaining, reservations recommended, VISA/MC/AMEX/DC, $$.**

B & H Dairy Restaurant
127 Second Ave., New York, NY 10003   **(212) 505-8065**

Kosher. This kosher restaurant offers daily soup and sandwich specials, omelets, sandwiches, salads, soups, baked goods, and desserts. Hot entrées include vegetarian stuffed cabbage and vegetarian chili. This establishment does serve fish. **Open daily. Limited service, vegan options, fresh juices, no credit cards, take-out, $.**

Benny's Burritos
93 Ave. A, New York, NY 10014   **(212) 254-3286**

113 Greenwich Ave., New York, NY 10014   **(212) 727-0584**

Mexican. Benny's serves Cal-Mex-style cuisine in a kitschy '50s atmosphere. The food contains no preservatives, lard, or MSG. Options for the burritos or other entrées include non-dairy tofu sour cream, whole wheat tortillas, and brown rice. **Open daily for lunch and dinner. Full service, vegan options, wine/beer/alcohol, take-out, catering, $$.**

Bonobo's
18 E. 23rd St. (at Madison Ave.), New York, NY 10010   **(212) 505-1200**

Natural foods. Opened in October 2003, this restaurant includes an almost all organic menu that includes daily specials and create-your-own wraps. The majority of the offerings are raw dishes, most of which are vegan but also a few that are made with honey. The dining area features a natural setting with wood floors, brick walls, and a skylight. Located across the street from Madison Square Park. **Open for lunch and dinner. Call for hours. Counter service, smoothies, take-out, vegan options, VISA/MC/AMEX, $$.**

Café Boulud
20 E. 76th St., New York, NY 10021   **(212) 772-2600**

French. This elegant restaurant offers gourmet vegetarian options, including herb-stuffed artichokes, five-potato and market vegetable cocotte, and crisp chickpea fries. **Open Tuesday through Saturday for lunch. Open daily for dinner. Full service, reservations recommended, beer/wine/alcohol, VISA/MC/AMEX, $$$.** www.danielnyc.com

---

Restaurant codes: ✪ Reviewers' Choice • Vegetarian Restaurant • • Vegan Restaurant
Restaurant prices: **$** less than $6 **$$** $6-$12 **$$$** more than $12
Credit Cards Accepted: VISA - VISA MC - MasterCard AMEX - American Express
DISC - Discover DC - Diner's Club

• Café Viva Herbal Pizzeria

179 Second Ave. (between 11th and 12th Sts.)
New York, NY 10003   (212) 420-8801
64 E. 34th St. (between Park and Madison Aves.)
New York, NY 10016   (212) 779-4350
2578 Broadway (between 97th and 98th Sts.)
New York, NY 10025   (212) 663-8482

Vegetarian pizzeria. This establishment has a great selection of pizzas, including some made with wheat-free crusts. Choose from items such as seitan pepperoni, soy sausage, organic vegetables, homemade mozzarella, and tofu. Casein-free soy cheese is available for vegans. The menu also includes salads, sandwiches, pastas with seitan meat sauce, calzones, ravioli, and more. The restaurant only uses unbleached flour, sea salt, filtered water, and natural sweeteners. Kosher options available. **Open daily for lunch through late night service. Full service, vegan options, fresh juices, take-out, delivery, VISA/MC/AMEX/DC, $.**

• Candle Café ✪

1307 3rd Ave. (near 75th St.), New York, NY 10021   (212) 472-0970

Vegetarian café. "Vegetarianism is taken to a whole new level" at this mostly vegan restaurant that serves unique dishes like a Grilled Rosemary Tempeh Sandwich and a Grilled Tempeh Portabello Burger, as well as a rotating selection of entrées, such as Seitan Toastadas, Lentil Croquettes, and Hijiki Caviar. Desserts include dairy- and egg-free muffins and cookies. **Open daily for lunch and dinner. Full service, vegan options, fresh juices, smoothies, wine/ beer, espresso/cappuccino, take-out, delivery, catering, VISA/MC, $$.** www.candlecafe.com

• Candle 79 ✪

124 E. 79th St. (between Lexington and Third Aves.)
New York, NY 10021   (212) 537-7179

Vegetarian. This fine dining establishment, owned by the same people as Candle Café, serves a menu of Autumn Vegetable Salad, raw Tomato Tartare, Fennel-Crusted Tempeh, Zucchini Enchiladas, Asian Pear-Marinated Grape Tart, and much more. **Open daily for lunch and dinner. Full service, vegan options, fresh juices, smoothies, wine/beer, espresso/cappuccino, take-out, delivery, catering, VISA/MC, $$-$$$.** www.candlecafe.com/candle79.html

•• Caravan of Dreams

405 E. 6th St. (between First Ave. and Ave. A)
New York, NY 10009   (212) 254-1613

Vegan. The menu here offers include Black Bean Chili, Corn Polenta with Sweet Potato and Leek Sauce, and Grilled Marinated Tofu. Many dishes are wheat-free, and the water is osmosis-filtered. The staff at Caravan is committed to using only organically grown ingredients whenever available and to designing balanced dishes for healthful eating. The restaurant also features live music nightly, an art gallery, lectures, and various classes. **Open daily until late night. Full service, vegan options, fresh juices, espresso/cappuccino, VISA/MC/AMEX, $-$$.**

Chola

232 E. 58th St. (near Second Ave.), New York, NY 10022   (212) 688-4619

Indian. The restaurant offers many vegetarian options, a lunch buffet, and vegetarian lunch boxes to-go. Sample the Chola Peshawari, Sabji Sag Malai, Vegetable Biryani, or if you're feeling adventurous, the Vegetable Vindaloo. Chola is a sister restaurant of Jaipore Royal Indian Cuisine in Brewster, NY, and Bombay Bar & Grill in Westport, CT. **Open daily for lunch and dinner. Full service, beer/wine/alcohol, take-out, delivery, catering, gift certificates available, VISA/MC/AMEX/DISC/DC, $$-$$$.** www.fineindiandining.com/cholany.htm

• Counter Vegetarian Restaurant & Wine Bar

105 First Ave. (between 6th and 7th St.), New York, NY 10003   (212) 982-5870

Vegetarian/American. This mostly organic restaurant opened in New York's East Village in March of 2003. Menu items include a fried mushroom appetizer, a grilled seitan burger with smoked onions, a Southern Po' Boy sandwich with barbeque sauce, tofu-based Cape Cod cakes, and spinach mushroom crepes. Sunday brunch includes items like wheat-free banana pancakes. Wines that contain honey are clearly marked on the wine list. **Open Tuesday through Sunday for lunch through late night. Closed Monday. Full service, vegan options, wine/beer, VISA/MC/AMEX, $$$.**

• Dimple

11 W. 30th St., New York, NY 10003   (212) 643-9464

Vegetarian/Indian. Varied menu with breakfast items and options from all regions of India, including an extensive section of sweets and snacks sold by the pound. The menu features exotic menu items, such as Bhel Purl (puffed crisps served with potatoes, beans, sauce, and mint water), Usal Pav (white beans topped with onions, corriander, sauces, and Indian noodles), Undhiu (mixed vegetables with nuts and coconut), as well as traditional items like vegetable samosas, uthappams, and dosas. **Open Monday through Friday for three meals. Open Saturday and Sunday for lunch and dinner. Full service, suitable for business entertainment, special drinks, take-out, delivery, catering, $-$$.**

•• Franchia Tea House and Restaurant

12 Park Ave. (between 34th and 35th Sts.), New York, NY 10016   (212) 213-1001

Vegan/Korean. Franchia, an offshoot of the nearby upscale vegan Korean restaurant Hangawi, was designed with waxed floors, low tea tables, and intricately carved wooden sliding doors to evoke a mountain-temple-style traditional tearoom. It features a vegetarian kitchen specializing in soups; vegetarian sushi; green-tea-flavored pancakes, noodles, salads, and bread; soy and grain "meat" dumplings; sautéed rice cakes; pumpkin noodles; and desserts, including soy ice cream and soy cheesecake. In addition, you may buy their teas and other items in the gift shop and through their website. **Open daily for lunch and dinner. Full service, suitable for business entertaining, take-out, delivery, VISA/MC/AMEX, $-$$$.** www. franchia.com

• Friday Night Dinner Club

The Natural Gourmet Cookery School, 48 W. 21st St., 2nd Fl.
New York, NY 10010   (212) 645-5170

Vegetarian/natural foods. Enjoy a five-course vegetarian meal served by a chef instructor and students of the Chef's Training Program. The food is whole, fresh, natural, and seasonal, as well as high-fiber, low-fat and cholesterol-free. No refined sugar is used. Communal seating and a new fixed menu each week. In addition, baked desserts, frozen yogurt, and non-dairy frozen desserts are available at reasonable prices, and there's a large selection of herbal teas.

Open Friday only. Closed major holidays. Full service, reservations required, BYOB, catering, take-out, VISA/MC/AMEX, $$$. www.naturalgourmetschool.com

Galaxy Global Eatery
15 Irving Pl., New York, NY 10003 **(212) 777-3631**

International. Located near Gramercy Park, this restaurant's menu uses symbols to show if an item is vegetarian or vegan, or if it contains hemp. Dishes include MediterAsian Raw Nut'n Fruit Salad, Sea Squares (lemon tahini grilled tofu, seaweed caviar, and bamboo rice), Seitan Enchiladas, Hempnut Edamame Cakes, Luna Lasagna Rolls, Hempnut Veggie Burgers, and more. **Open daily for three meals, including late dinner. Full service, vegan options, smoothies, soymilk, beer/wine/alcohol, take-out, catering, VISA/MC, $-$$.** www.galaxyglobaleatery.com

• Gobo
401 Ave. Of The Americas (between Waverly Pl. and 8th St.)
New York, NY 10014 **(212) 255-3242**

Vegetarian/Asian. The sons of Zen Palate's owners are behind this sophisticated Greenwich Village eatery. The open kitchen turns out artful international dishes, such as crispy spinach and soy cheese wontons, green tea noodle miso soup with seitan, white beans and cremini mushroom casserole, wild rice and tempeh wrapped in collard greens with pomegranate sauce, avocado tartare with wasabi-lime sauce, and butternut squash risotto with toasted almonds. **Open daily for lunch through late night service. Full service, vegan options, fresh juices, smoothies, beer/wine, VISA/MC/AMEX/DC, $$-$$$.** www.goborestaurant.com

•• Govinda's Vegetarian Buffet
Near 3 E. 52nd St. (at 5th Ave.), New York, NY 10019 **(212) 679-9573**

Vegan/Indian. This food cart offers all of the scrambled tofu, potato and cauliflower curry, sweet potatoes, yams, semolina, and polenta that you can eat for a only $5 a visit. **Open Monday through Friday for breakfast and lunch. Closed Saturday and Sunday. Limited service, take-out, no credit cards, $.**

The Great American Health Bar
35 W. 57th St. (between 5th and 6th Aves.)
New York, NY 10019 **(212) 355-5177**

Natural foods. Known for its fresh-squeezed juices and homemade soups, the Health Bar offers a wide variety of vegetarian entrées, such as Eggplant Parmesan, Pizza of the Day, and Pasta of the Day, and sandwiches, such as The Garden Patch, hummus, falafel, and avocado. **Open daily. Full service, vegan options, fresh juices, catering, take-out, $.**

Hana Restaurant
675 9th Ave., New York, NY 10036 **(212) 582-9742**

Korean. Hana offers a separate vegetarian menu that includes Korean and Japanese specialties. The menu features Jap Cahe (vegetables with rice noodles), Hana Noodle (stir-fried noodles), Woo Dong (soup with noodles and vegetables), and four types of vegetarian sushi. **Open Monday through Saturday for lunch and dinner. Closed Sunday. Full service, vegan options, fresh juices, wine/beer, VISA/MC/AMEX, $$.**

•• Hangawi ☉

12 E. 32nd St., New York, NY 10016   **(212) 213-0077**

Vegan/Korean. This upscale vegan restaurant serves traditional Korean dishes in a serene setting, with ancient decor and traditional folk music. Shoes must be removed at the door. There is a fixed price menu that comes with starters, appetizers, entrée, and dessert. An á la carte menu is also available with several other options, including salads, soups, rice and noodle dishes, stews, and much more. A fun fact about this restaurant is that birthday honorees are dressed in traditional Korean attire for their meals and photographed by the staff. **Open daily for lunch and dinner. Full service, VISA/MC/AMEX/DC, $$$.** www.hangawi restaurant.com

The Health Nuts

1208 2nd Ave. (between 63rd and 64th Sts.)
New York, NY 10021   **(212) 593-0116**
835 2nd Ave. (between 44th and 45th Sts.)
New York, NY 10017   **(212) 490-2979**
2141 Broadway (between 75th and 76th Sts.)
New York, NY 10023   **(212) 724-1972**
2611 Broadway (between 98th and 99th Sts.)
New York, NY 10025   **(212) 678-0054**

Natural foods. A natural deli and juice bar are situated inside a large health food store. Freshly-prepared gourmet vegetarian salads, pasta, grains, hot foods, pizza, soups, pastries, cakes, and snacks are available. Sometimes, a vegan cheesecake is even offered. **Open daily. Counter service, vegan options, fresh juices, take-out, VISA/MC/AMEX, $.**

• Healthy Chelsea

248 W. 23rd St., New York, NY 10011   **(212) 691-0286**

Vegetarian. Located between 7th and 8th Ave., their menu items include tofu and collard greens, and special "immunity" drinks. **Open Monday through Friday for three meals. Open Sunday for lunch and dinner. Closed Saturday. Limited service, cafeteria, vegan/macrobiotic options, fresh juices, smoothies, special drinks, $.**

Herban Kitchen

290 Hudson St., New York, NY 10013   **(212) 627-2257**

Organic natural foods. This restaurant, with a country atmosphere, offers Vegetarian Grain Burgers, Smoked Tofu Clubs, Vegetarian German Sauerbraten and Red Cabbage, Tempeh Scaloppini served over Linguini, and Quinoa Bean Loaf served with Braised Greens. The menu changes daily depending on the season, and the ingredients used in the creations come from local family farms whenever possible. Home delivery of weekly meals is also available. **Open Monday through Friday for lunch and dinner. Open Saturday for dinner only. Closed Sunday. Full service, vegan options, fresh juices, smoothies, take-out, catering, VISA/MC/AMEX/DISC, $$.**

• House of Vegetarian

68 Mott St., New York, NY 10013   **(212) 226-6572**

Vegetarian/Chinese. House of Vegetarian offers a menu free of meat, chicken, seafood, and

MSG. The restaurant serves more than 200 dishes with many different meat imitations. There are assorted mock chicken dishes using pineapple, lemon, mango in season, and yams; mock iron steak; imitation fish; vegetarian egg rolls; and more. **Open daily. Full service, macrobiotic/vegan options, take-out, $-$$.**

Josie's Restaurant and Juice Bar
300 Amsterdam Ave. (near 74th St.), New York, NY 10023   (212) 769-1212
Natural foods. Located near 74th Street, Josie's offers several dairy-free vegetarian dishes using organic products when available. You could start your meal with their Grilled Vegetable Salad with Mesclun Greens or their Roasted Butternut Squash/Sweet Potato Soup with toasted pumpkin seeds. Veggie entrées include Vegetable Meatloaf with brown rice, red beans, wheat gluten, and rosemary with mashed potatoes; Marinated Portobello Mushroom Fajitas with Tomato Avocado Salsa on a whole wheat tortilla; and baked sweet potato with tamari brown rice, steamed broccoli, roasted beets, and a tahini sauce. Josie's uses recycled materials for dining, including napkins and paper towels. **Open daily for lunch and dinner. Full service, vegan options, fresh juices, wine/beer/alcohol, non-alcoholic wine/beer, take-out, catering, VISA/MC/AMEX/DC, $$-$$$.**

• Kate's Joint
58 Ave. B, New York, NY 10009   (212) 777-7235
Vegetarian. Kate's menu includes Southern Fried Unchicken Cutlets, tofu buffalo wings, whole-grain hot oven pizza, veggie chili, mock popcorn shrimp with "secret sauce," grilled barbeque mock chicken, and mock shepherd's pie seasoned with herbs and covered with mashed potatoes. The atmosphere here is typically casual, and the décor is East Village funky. **Open daily for three meals with late evening service. Full service, vegan options, fresh juices, soymilk, cappuccino/espresso, wine/beer, non-alcoholic wine/beer, take-out, delivery, VISA/MC/AMEX/DISC, $$.**

Life Café
343 E. 10th St., New York, NY 10009   (212) 477-8791
Natural foods. Made famous during some pivotal scenes in "Rent," Life Café has plenty of local color and great food. It's tiny and fills up fast, but the food is worth the crowd. Many offerings are vegetarian or vegan. **Open daily for three meals. Open Saturday and Sunday for brunch. Full service, vegan options, fresh juices, wine/beer/alcohol, take-out, VISA/MC/DC, $$.**

Life Thyme Natural Market
416 6th Ave., New York, NY 10011   (212) 420-9099
Natural foods. Located between 8th and 9th Streets, this natural market features one of NYC's largest selections of organic produce, natural personal care items, all-natural deli (including a 100% organic salad bar and hot bar), and an all-vegan kosher bakery. Sweet selections include cookies, cakes made-to-order, raw fruit cheesecakes, and more! **Open daily for lunch and dinner. Market open during breakfast hours. Limited service, vegan options, fresh juices, smoothies, soymilk, special drinks, take-out, catering, VISA/MC/AMEX, $$.**

• Liquiteria
170 2nd Ave. (At 11th St.), New York, NY 10012   (212) 358-0300
Vegetarian/juice bar. Besides a huge selection of fresh juices, like organic carrot or cantaloupe,

the menu offers a vegetarian sandwich menu with items like Chickenless Chicken, Hummus, and Nori Rolls. **Open daily for three meals. Full service, vegan options, fresh juices, smoothies, take-out, $.**

• Madras Café
79 2nd Ave. (between 4th and 5th Sts.)
New York, NY 10003   **(212) 254-8002**
Vegetarian/Indian. Another great south Indian vegetarian restaurant in the heart of Manhattan. Try the Rava Idli, Madras Curried Soy Chunks, or the Mysore Rava Masala Dosa. **Open daily for lunch and dinner. Full service, vegan options, VISA/MC/AMEX/DISC, $$.**

• Madras Mahal
104 Lexington Ave., New York, NY 10016   **(212) 684-4010**
Vegetarian/Indian. Madras Mahal features kosher South Indian vegetarian cooking near Manhattan's Little India section. Try South Indian dosai, spicy curries from Western India, fluffy breads, and much more. Some dishes are made with dairy products, but eggs are not used. **Open daily for lunch and dinner. Full service, vegan options, non-alcoholic beer, special drinks, take-out, catering, VISA/MC/AMEX/DC, $$.**

Mana Restaurant
646 Amsterdam Ave. (between 91st and 92nd Sts.)
New York, NY 10024   **(212) 787-1110**
Japanese. Mana, which is vegetarian except for fish, offers Japanese natural and macrobiotic cooking without sugar, chemicals, preservatives, or dairy products. Filtered water and organic ingredients are used. **Open Monday through Saturday for lunch and dinner. Closed Sunday. Full service, macrobiotic/vegan options, BYOB, take-out, no credit cards, $$.**

Meskerem Ethiopian Restaurant
468 W. 47th St., New York, NY 10036   **(212) 664-0520**
Ethiopian. Located near Times Square and the theater district, the dishes are served on injera (Ethiopian bread). Menu items include miser alecha (split lentils dipped with ginger) and shiro wat (highly seasoned chickpeas in berbere sauce). **Open for lunch and late dinner. Full service, reservations recommended, espresso/cappuccino, wine/beer, take-out, VISA/MC/DISC, $$.**

• New Saravana Bhavan Dosa Hut
102 Lexington Ave. (between 27th and 28th Sts.)
New York, NY 10016   **(212) 725-7466**
Vegetarian/Indian. This restaurant, which is certified kosher, offers South Indian dosas, North Indian pakoras, traditional breads, and much more. **Open daily for lunch and dinner. Full service, VISA/MC/AMEX/DISC/DC, $$.**

• The Organic Grill
123 1st Ave. (between 7th St. and St. Mark's Pl.)
New York, NY 10003   **(212) 477-7177**
Vegetarian. The Organic Grill boasts that "99.9% of our foods are prepared using clean, sustainably raised materials." For a tasty treat, try the BBQ Seitan Sandwich, Eggplant

Caponata with Herb Crostini, or the Vegan Wheat-Free Waffles. All cheese dishes can be made with vegan cheese. Orders and reservations can be placed from The Organic Grill's website. **Open daily for lunch and dinner. Full service, vegan options, fresh juices, smoothies, espresso/cappuccino, delivery, take-out, catering, VISA/MC/AMEX, $$-$$$.** www.theorganicgrill.com

Our Kitchen

520 E. 14th St. (between Aves. A and B), New York, NY 10009   (212) 677-8018
Chinese. This restaurant has a plethora of vegetarian options, including Basil Ginger Eggplant, Vegetarian's Sesame Chicken, a Tofu Casserole, vegetable spinach dumplings, and veggie wontons. **Open Monday through Saturday for lunch and dinner. Open Sunday and holidays for dinner. Full service, beer, delivery, take-out, VISA/MC/AMEX, $$.**

Ozu Restaurant

566 Amsterdam Ave., New York, NY 10024   (212) 787-8316
Macrobiotic. The menu here, which is primarily Japanese, includes soups, breads, salads, and entrées featuring tofu, grains, noodles, tempura, and vegetables. Also, there are daily entrées and dessert specials. Fish is served here as well. **Open daily. Full service, macrobiotic/vegan options, beer/organic wine, take-out, VISA/MC, $$.**

• Pommes Frites

123 2nd Ave. (between 7th St. and St. Mark's Pl.)
New York, NY 10003   (212) 674-1234
Regional. Pommes Frites offers Belgian fried potatoes with 30 sauce options, some of which are vegan. **Open daily for lunch and dinner. Take-out, vegan options, $.**

• Pongal

110 Lexington Ave. (between 27th and 28th Sts.)
New York, NY 10016   (212) 696-9458
Vegetarian/Indian. Pongal specializes in southern Indian cuisine, so you will find items like dosai and crepes, made with fermented batters that are stuffed with potatoes and other vegetables. This restaurant is certified kosher. **Open daily for lunch and dinner. Full service, vegan options, take-out, VISA/MC/AMEX/DISC/DC, $$.**

•• Pure Food and Wine

54 Irving Pl. (near 17th St.), New York, NY 10003   (212) 477-1010
Vegan/raw foods. This upscale restaurant serves up raw cucumber summer rolls with green papaya and watermelon; soft corn tortillas with chili-spiced beans, avocado, tomato-lime salsa, and vegan sour cream; gnocchi made from red beets; green-curry noodles made from coconut; and spelt crust and pignoli cheese pizzas in a garden setting that seats 80. As an environmentally friendly establishment, it prides itself on its organic wines and even offers utensils made from corn and wheat for take-out orders. **Open daily for lunch and dinner, Full service, fresh juices, smoothies, organic wine, take-out, VISA/MC/AMEX, $$$.**

Quantum Leap

88 W. 3rd St., New York, NY 10012   (212) 677-8050
Natural foods. Many tasty vegan and vegetarian dishes are served in this relaxed and homey

atmosphere. Ask about the house dressing and natural pies. Fish is prepared in a separate area. **Open daily for lunch and dinner. Full service, vegan options, $$.**

• Quintessense Restaurant

263 E. 10th St. (between 1st Ave. and Ave. A)
New York, NY 10009   **(646) 654-1823**
353 E. 78th St. (between 1st and 2nd Aves.), New York, NY 10021 (212) 734-0888
566 Amsterdam Ave. (between 87th and 88th)
New York, NY 10024   **(212) 501-9700**
Vegetarian. This internationally-flavored restaurant uses only organic ingredients to prepare their dishes. All meals are based on living foods philosophies. Options include dips, salads, soup, pasta, nori rolls, and desserts. The only thing that keeps Quintessense from being completely vegan is the use of honey in some dishes. **Open Tuesday through Sunday for dinner only. Closed Monday. Full service, vegan options, fresh juices, catering, VISA/MC/ AMEX, $-$$.**

• Red Bamboo Vegetarian Soul Café

140 W. 4th St. (between MacDougal St. and 6th Ave.)
New York, NY 10012   **(212) 260-1212**
Vegetarian/soul food. Located near Washington Square Park and many NYU buildings, Red Bamboo is a soul food restaurant with the same owner as its neighbor Vegetarian's Paradise 2. Its menu includes unique vegetarian and vegan entrées, including Caribbean Jerk Spiced Seitan, Creole Soul Chicken, Maryland Fried Scallops, Salmon Teriyaki, Citrus Beef with Asparagus, Butterfly Soy Chops, and Quesadillas. They also offer appetizers, soups, salads, sandwiches, pasta dishes, specialty rices, and sides like Sweet Potato Fries, Collard Greens with Veggie Ham, and Mango Salsa. **Open daily for lunch through late night service. Full service, vegan options, take-out, delivery, VISA/MC/AMEX/DISC, $-$$.** www.redbamboo-nyc.com

• Sacred Chow

522 Hudson St., New York, NY 10014   **(212) 337-0863**
Vegetarian deli. Although pricey, this prepared foods deli is definitely worth checking out. Almost completely vegan, except for the occasional use of honey, gourmet dishes include Fennal Soysage with Roasted Garlic Tomatoes; Dill Pickle Tempeh with Juniper Berries and Tarragon and Grilled Vegetables; Seitan Robai; and Wheat Berries with Tamarind Glaze. Fresh-made juices and milks include orange blossom almond milk and organic orange juice available daily. **Open daily for lunch and dinner. Limited service, vegan options, fresh juices, take-out, VISA/MC/AMEX, $$.**

• The Sanctuary

25 1st Ave. (between 1st and 2nd Sts.), New York, NY 10003   (212) 780-9786
Vegetarian. Offering "a unique experience in enlightened dining," the Sanctuary has an extensive menu with an international flavor. Visitors can sample such exotic dishes as Japanese Harmless Ham, Krishna's Delite, Marinated "Un-Turkey" dinner, and Barbecued Veggie "Ribs." The restaurant features live acoustic music on Friday and Saturday nights. **Open Tuesday through Sunday for lunch and dinner. Open for brunch on weekends. Closed Mondays. Full service, macrobiotic/vegan options, reservations recommended for large**

groups, fresh juices, smoothies, espresso/cappuccino, non-alcoholic beer/wine, take-out, VISA/MC/AMEX, $-$$.

Souen Restaurant

28 E. 13th St. (near Univeristy Pl.), New York, NY 10003   **(212) 627-7150**

Macrobiotic/natural foods. Sample Souen's various seitan, tofu, and tempeh entrées. Appetizers, soups, salads, tempura, and noodle dishes with the option of udon or soba noodles are also offered. Note that fish is served here. There are indoor and outdoor gardens. **Open daily. Full service, macrobiotic/vegan options, fresh juices, organic wine/beer, take-out, VISA/ MC/AMEX, $$-$$$.**

•• Strictly Roots

2058 Adam Clayton Powell Blvd., New York, NY 10027   **(212) 864-8699**

Vegan. Strictly Roots is an all-natural restaurant that "serves nothing that crawls, walks, swims, or flies." Located near the famous Apollo Theater in Harlem, this restaurant features many fine organic juices, soups, sandwiches and pastries. Try the Sweet Potato Pudding Gluten Sandwich, or Tofu in Plum Sauce. Strictly Roots is not to be missed! **Open daily for lunch and dinner. Limited service, vegan options, fresh juices, take-out, VISA/MC/AMEX/DISC, $-$$.**

• Teany

90 Rivington St. (between Ludlow and Orchard Sts.)
New York, NY 10002   **(212) 475-9190**

Vegetarian. Musician Moby's popular vegetarian restaurant, with its modern lime-green, white, and yellow modern décor, offers a variety of vegetarian cuisine, including cold nectarine and cantaloupe soup, faux turkey clubs, Middle Eastern dishes, desserts, and interesting teas. **Open daily for breakfast through late night. Limited service, vegan options, $-$$.** www.teany.com

Temple In The Village Restaurant

74 W. 3rd St. (between Laguardia Pl. and Thompson St.)
New York, NY 10012   **(212) 475-5670**

Natural foods/macrobiotic. This small, buffet-style health food restaurant caters to macrobiotics and vegetarians with vegetables, noodles, seven grain rice, and teas. All foods are prepared on the premises. Seating is limited. Note that one fish dish is served. **Open Monday through Saturday for lunch and dinner. Closed Sundays. Cafeteria, BYOB, catering, take-out, $.**

• Thali Vegetarian Cuisine

28 Greenwich Ave., New York, NY 10011   **(212) 367-7411**

Vegetarian/Indian. This small restaurant has a menu that changes daily. All food is prepared fresh that day. Limited seating is available. **Open daily for lunch and dinner. Full service, vegan options, take-out, catering, cash only, $$-$$$.**

•• Tiengarden

170 Allen St. (between Stanton and Rivington Sts.)
New York, NY 10002   **(212) 388-1364**

Vegan/Chinese. Located near E. Houston St., many of the dishes here feature tofu or seitan with a Chinese/Asian accent. **Open Sunday through Friday for lunch and dinner. Closed Saturday. Full service, soymilk, take-out, $$.**

•Udipi Palace

103 Lexington Ave. (between 27 and 28 Sts.)
]New York, NY 10016   **(212) 889-3477**
Vegetarian/Indian. This restaurant serves South Indian cuisine, including soups, dosai, curries, and Indian breads. **Open daily for lunch and dinner. Full service, vegan options, take-out, VISA/MC/AMEX/DISC/DC, $$.**

••Uptown Juice Bar

54 W. 125th St. (between 5th and Lenox Aves.)
New York, NY 10027   **(212) 987-2660**
116 Chambers St. (between Church St. and W. Broadway)
New York, NY 10007   **(212) 964-4316**
Vegan. Don't let the name fool you. This place is much than organic fruit and vegetable juices. The menu features blueberry pancakes; tofu omelets; mock breakfast meats; hot soups and stews; mock chicken, beef, turkey, or fish salads, wraps, and sandwiches; shepard's pie; curry duck; Cajun of barbeque tofu; lasagna; veggie steak; side dishes; and much more. They also offer a full line of vegan pastries and baked goods, including breads, carrot cake, soy cheesecake, pies, muffins, doughnuts, and more. **Harlem location open daily for three meals. TriBeCa location open Monday through Friday for three meals. Open Saturday for breakfast through early dinner. Closed Sunday. Counter service, fresh juices, smoothies, soymilk, special drinks, take-out, catering, $$.** www.uptownjuicebar.com

•Vatan Indian Restaurant

409 3rd Ave. (near 29th St.), New York, NY 10016   **(212) 689-5666**
Vegetarian/Indian. Decorated to evoke a Gujarati village, diners at Vatan remove their shoes to sit on fluffy cushions surrounding a central courtyard. They offer an all-you-can-eat dinner featuring dishes, such as samosas, batatavada (fried potato balls in chickpea flour batter), bhaji (chickpeas and spinach), and khichdi (lentils, rice, and vegetables). You may also order from a four-course prix fixe menu that includes appetizers, soups, rice, entrées, and desserts. No children under 10 allowed. **Open Tuesday through Sunday for dinner only. Closed Monday. Full service, vegan options, reservations recommended, VISA/MC/AMEX, $$$.** www.vatanny.com

••Vegetarian Dim Sum House

24 Pell St., New York, NY 10013   **(212) 577-7176**
Vegan/Chinese. This restaurant in Manhattan's Chinatown features Dim Sum all day. Try Rice Flour Rolls, Spring Rolls, various dumplings, sweet cakes, fresh juices, and more. **Open daily for lunch and dinner. Full service, fresh juices, take-out, $-$$.**

•Vegetarian Paradise 2

144 W. 4th St., New York, NY 10012   **(212) 260-7141**
Vegetarian/Chinese. An extensive, mostly vegan menu features exquisite Chinese vegetarian cuisine. The menu includes hot and cold appetizers, salads, desserts, and many entrée categories, such as bean curd, greens, mock meat, mushroom, wheat gluten, noodle, and rice.

In addition, they feature hot clay pots and house specials, such as Crispy Fish Divine (made from soy protein), Stuffed Lotus Leaf, and Spinach Dumpling. It's not be missed!! You'll find it near the W. 4th St. subway stop on the A/B/C/D/E/F trains. **Open daily for lunch and dinner. Full service, vegan options, fresh juices, catering, take-out, VISA/MC/AMEX/ DISC, $$.**

• Vegetarian Paradise 3
33-35 Mott St., New York, NY 10013 **(212) 406-6988**
Vegetarian/Chinese. See description under Vegetarian Paradise 2 in New York, NY.

Village Natural Food Corp.
46 Greenwich Ave., New York, NY 10011 **(212) 727-0968**
Natural foods. This spacious Greenwich Village restaurant offers whole grains only and has daily specials. They have many vegetarian dishes, but they also serve fish. **Open daily for lunch and dinner. Full service, take-out, $$.**

• Whole Earth Bakery & Kitchen
130 St. Marks Pl., New York, NY 10009 (212) 677-7597
Vegetarian bakery. The menu, which is mostly vegan, includes muffins, cookies, brownies, and much more. Some avocado, tofu, and tempeh sandwiches are also offered. **Open daily. Take-out, vegan options, $.**

Yaffa Café
97 St. Marks Pl. (between 1st Ave. and Ave. A)
New York, NY 10009 **(212) 674-9302**
Natural foods. In the bohemian atmosphere of the East Village, vegetarian dishes include crepes, stir-fry, tofu, baba ghanouj, hummus, pasta, and a divine fruit salad. There's garden seating during the summer, as well as a sidewalk café. **Open 24 hours daily. Full service, vegan options, fresh juices, wine/beer, take-out, VISA/MC/AMEX, $$.**

• Zen Palate ✪
663 9th Ave., (at 46th St.), New York, NY 10036 **(212) 582-1669**
34 Union Sq. E., New York, NY 10003 **(212) 614-9345**
2170 Broadway (between 76th and 77th St.)
New York, NY 10024 **(212) 501-7768**
Vegetarian. In a minimalist atmosphere, the staff at Zen Palate offers beautifully presented dishes, such as Spinach Wonton Soup, Taro Spring Rolls, Vegetarian Squid, Zen Ravioli, Basiled Vegetarian Ham, Kale & Seaweed Salad, and tofu-based desserts, at its three locations. **Open daily for lunch and dinner. Full service, vegan options, fresh juices, soymilk, espresso/cappuccino, suitable for business entertaining, take-out, VISA/MC/AMEX, $$-$$$.** www.zenpalate.com

•• Zenith ✪
311 W. 48th St. (between 8th and 9th Aves.)
New York, NY 10036 **(212) 262-8080**
Vegan/Asian. Zenith is convenient to Times Square and a great possibility to accompany an evening of Broadway theater. Its menu lists unique vegan dishes, including Marinated

Seaweed, Thai Soup, Mesculin Organic Salad with a Miso-Mustard Dressing; Vegetarian Duck, Fireworks Squid, assorted vegetables with a mushroom steak wrapped and baked in a soybean crepe; Soybean Gluten prepared with carrots and potatoes in a mild curry sauce; steamed eggplant topped with black bean sauce; sautéed artichokes with basil; noodle and rice dishes; and much more. **Open daily for lunch and dinner. Full service, fresh juices, espresso/cappuccino, take-out, VISA/MC/AMEX/DISC/DC, $$-$$$.**

MERRICK

Tortilla Grill
53 Merrick Ave., Merrick, NY 11566   **(516) 668-9030**
Mexican. See description under Huntington, NY.

MILLERTON

Manna Dew Health Foods & Café
54 Main St., Millerton, NY 12546   **(518) 789-3500**
Natural foods deli. Manna Dew offers daily specials, which include curry tofu, steamed brown rice, and vegetables with peanut sauce. **Open Monday through Saturday for lunch and dinner. Closed Sunday. Counter service, macrobiotic/vegan options, fresh juices, soymilk, take-out, catering, VISA/MC, $-$$.**

MONTAUK

Naturally Good Foods & Café
38 S. Etna Ave., Montauk, NY 11954   **(631) 668-9030**
Natural foods café. Breakfast, lunch, and dinner are available at this café, where you'll also find a deli case, take-out, fresh baked goods daily, and fruit smoothies, along with a natural foods store. **Open daily for three meals. Limited service, vegan options, macrobiotic/vegan options, fresh juices, smoothies, take-out, AMEX, $.**

MT. KISCO

• Mrs. Green's Natural Market
686 Lexington Ave., Mt. Kisco, NY 10549   **(914) 242-9292**
Vegetarian/natural foods. See description under Mahopac, NY.

NEW PALTZ

• The Bakery
13 A N. Front St., New Paltz, NY 12561   **(913) 255-8840**
Vegetarian bakery. This bakery not only offers the usual muffins, scones, and crumb buns, but also interesting pastry items, such as Apricot Linzer Tart and Espresso Fudge Tort. Menu items include sandwiches, vegetarian burgers, vegetarian deli slices, fat-free chili, soups, and salads. There is also an outdoor café with a children's play area and gardens. **Open daily for three meals. Limited service, fresh juices, soymilk, espresso/cappuccino, VISA/MC/AMEX/DISC/DC, $.**

Main Street Bistro

59 Main St., New Paltz, NY 12561 (845) 255-7766

Natural foods. Located near Minnewaska State Park, this natural foods restaurant offers a variety of veggie burgers, a BLT with Fakin Bacon, some excellent veggie burritos, and a wide variety of tofu dishes. **Open Thursday through Monday for three meals. Open Tuesday and Wednesday for breakfast through early dinner.** Full service, vegan options, espresso/cappuccino, smoothies, soy milk, beer/wine, non-smoking, VISA/MC/AMEX/DISC, $-$$. www.mainstreetbistro.com

NEW YORK CITY

New York City actually consists of the five boroughs of Manhattan, Queens, Bronx, Brooklyn, and Staten Island. Most tourists tend to go to Manhattan, which is generally referred to as New York City. There are many, many restaurants in Manhattan. If you visit New York, it is easiest to explore the large variety of restaurants in Manhattan rather than to go off to other areas. You actually can have a fun walk across the Brooklyn Bridge to Brooklyn, and with a tour guide map find Brooklyn Heights, where there are numerous natural foods restaurants. You can also travel to other boroughs—except Staten Island—relatively easily by subway. If you choose to visit other places using mass transit, we would recommend that you start with Brooklyn and Queens. (Though part of New York City politically and via mass transit, these boroughs are geographically on Long Island.)

If you have a car, you can visit restaurants on Long Island. This can end up being a one- to three-hour drive, depending on traffic and how far out on Long Island you are going. If you are willing to make the trip, see entries under the towns: Albertson, Amityville, Cedarhurst, Garden City, Glen Cove, Great Neck, Huntington, Little Neck, Locust Valley, Merrick, Montauk, Oceanside, Plainview, Riverhead, Sag Harbor, Sayville, Syosset, West Hempstead, and Westbury.

Some New Jersey cities are also within the vicinity of Manhattan. See entries under Chester, Denville, East Rutherford, Elizabeth, Hoboken, Montclair, Morristown, Parsippany, Scotch Plains, and Teaneck. Hoboken is accessible by "PATH" trains from Manhattan. Buses also go from Manhattan to New Jersey cities.

For detailed listings of restaurants in New York City or the surrounding areas, refer to the individual boroughs or the areas listed above.

NIAGARA FALLS

(For restaurant listings in the surrounding areas, see Amherst, Buffalo, Lockport, Tonawanda, and Williamsville.)

Mighty Taco

2951 Military Rd., Niagara Falls, NY 14304 (716) 297-7198

Mexican. See description under Amherst, NY.

OCEANSIDE

Jandi's Organic Kitchen and Juice Bar

24 Atlantic Ave., Oceanside, NY 11572 (516) 536-5535

Organic café/juice bar. Try one of Jandi's many delicious organic vegetarian soups, salads, pizza, pasta, desserts, and more. Dishes prepared with soy cheese are vegan. **Open daily. Limited service, vegan options, $-$$.**

OLIVEREA

Full Moon Café
12 Valley View Rd., Oliverea, NY 12410   **(845) 254-5117**
Café. This café offers a cozy, rustic environment for breakfast and lunch on the weekends, and it serves guests at the unique Full Moon Resort Bed & Breakfast, as well as those attending special events. Breakfast at this inn's café can include vegetarian options like fresh baked goods, crepes or French toast, homemade granola, cereals, yogurt, and assorted fresh fruit. The dinner buffet begins with seasonal soups, such as roasted pumpkin or cannelloni bean, and is followed by yellow peppers stuffed with polenta, spinach and artichoke topped with pecorino, or cabbage leaves rolled with basmati brown rice and garlic tofu in red sauce. **Open Saturday and Sunday for breakfast. Open Saturday for dinner. Full service, $$-$$$.** www.fullmooncentral.com/cafe.html

Mountain Gate Indian Restaurant
212 McKinley Hollow Rd., Oliverea, NY 12410   **(845) 254-6000**
Indian. Mountain Gate offers a vegetarian buffet and features outdoor dining and hiking trails. **Open Wednesday through Monday for lunch and dinner. Closed Tuesday. Full service, fresh juices, smoothies, wine/beer/alcohol, espresso/cappuccino, reservations recommended, take-out, VISA/MC, $$.** www.mountaingatelodge.com

ONEONTA

The Autumn Café
244 Main St., Oneonta, NY 13820   **(607) 432-6845**
Natural foods. This American bistro offers daily specials and uses whole foods. All items are prepared on the premises. **Open Tuesday through Saturday for lunch and dinner. Open Sunday for brunch. Closed Monday. Full service, wine/beer, catering, take-out, VISA/MC/ AMEX, $-$$.**

ORCHARD PARK

Mighty Taco
3342 Southwestern Blvd., Orchard Park, NY 14127   **(716) 675-7260**
Mexican. See description under Amherst, NY.

PINE BUSH

•• Pure City
100 Main St., Pine Bush, NY 12566   **(845) 744-8888**
Vegan/Chinese. Pure City is a family-owned Chinese restaurant which offers a wide variety of delicious, MSG-free appetizers, soups, and 21 entrées. The menu includes the Pure City appetizer platter, Green Jade made with veggie ham, Ginger Veggie Nuggets, Bai-yeTofu (bean curd with a savory mild mushroom sauce), and excellent BBQ veggie ribs. Also, the décor is beautiful, the owners are great, the restaurant is clean, and all of the food is made fresh to order. **Open Tuesday through Saturday for lunch and dinner. Closed Sunday and Monday. Full service, suitable for business entertaining, take-out, VISA/MC, $$.**

PITTSFORD

Aladdin's Natural Eatery

8 Schoen Pl., Pittsford, NY 14534 (585) 264-9000

Natural foods. See description under Ithaca, NY.

PLAINVIEW

Hunan Cottage

135 Central Park Rd., Plainview, NY 11803 (516) 349-0390

Chinese. Their separate vegetarian menu offers 12 dishes using mock "meats" and more. Open daily for lunch and dinner. Full service, vegan options, take-out, VISA/MC, $$.

PLATTSBURGH

Lindsey's Casual Food & Spirits

446 Rte. 3, Plattsburgh, NY 12901 (518) 581-7750

American. Lindsey's offers a unique selection of dishes, such as eggplant stir-fry, grilled butternut squash, pan-fried tortellini, and a garden burger. The vegetables used by Lindsey's are seasonal. Open daily for lunch and dinner. Full service, beer/wine/alcohol, take-out, VISA/MC/AMEX/DISC, $$.

QUEENS

• Anand Bhavan

3566 73rd St. (near Roosevelt Ave.), Jackson Heights, NY 11372 (718) 507-1600

Vegetarian/Indian. This restaurant mostly serves South Indian cuisine, such as dosai and uthappam, but you can order some North Indian dishes here as well. Open daily for lunch and dinner. Full service, take-out, VISA/MC/AMEX/DISC/DC, $$$.

• Annam Brahma Restaurant

84-43 164 St., Jamaica Hills, NY 11432 (718) 523-2600

Vegetarian/Indian. This completely vegetarian restaurant offers dishes such as Vegetable Kebab, Vegetarian Casserole, and samosas. Open Thursday through Tuesday for lunch and dinner. Open Wednesday for lunch. Full service, vegan options, fresh juices, catering, take-out, $-$$.

• Bombay Sizzlers

248-03 Union Tpke., Bellerose, NY 11426 (718) 343-8499

Vegetarian/Indian. This restaurant serves a wide range of Indian dishes, including pakoras, dosa, uthappam, biryani, sizzling entrées, idli, dahl, breads, and specialty rices. However, the menu also includes other ethnic cuisines, such as Mexican (nachos, enchiladas), Italian (eggplant parmesan, lasagna), and Chinese (spring rolls, haka noodles), a children's menu,

---

desserts, and a variety of Indian drinks. **Open daily for lunch and dinner. Full service, vegan options, special drinks, take-out, delivery, VISA/MC/AMEX, $$.** www.bombaysizzlers.com

• Buddha Bodai Kosher Vegetarian Restaurant
42-96 Main St. (At Cherry Ave.), Flushing, NY 11355   (718) 939-1188
Vegetarian/Asian. Buddha Bodai is a unique dining experience in Flushing near the Botanical Gardens. All food preparation is monitored by rabbis and prepared in accordance with Jewish law. Patrons may wish to try the Braised Bean Curd Roll with Shiitake Mushroom, Sliced Dry Pressed Bean Curd with Black Pepper Sauce, or the Crispy Shredded Shiitake Mushroom & Broccoli with Brown Sauce. Only one meal on the menu is made with eggs. **Open daily for lunch and dinner. Full service, vegan options, fresh juices, smoothies, take-out, delivery, VISA/MC, $-$$$.**

• Dimple
35-68 73rd St., Jackson Heights, NY 11372   (718) 458-8144
Vegetarian/Indian. See description under Manhattan, NY.

• Dosa Hudd
4563 Bowne St., Flushing, NY 11355   (718) 961-5897
Vegetarian/Indian. This affordable establishment offers masala dosas, traditional breads, and other South Indian cuisine. **Open daily for lunch and dinner. Counter service, take-out, $.**

• Happy Buddha Vegetarian Restaurant
13537 37th Ave., Flushing, NY 11354   (718) 358-0079
Vegetarian/Chinese. Among the offerings here are soups, spring rolls, dumplings, a tofu casserole, noodle dishes, mock "meat" dishes, and much more. **Open daily for lunch and dinner. Full service, vegan options, soymilk, take-out, VISA/MC/AMEX, $-$$.**

India Corner
178-19 Union Tpke., Flushing, NY 11366   (718) 523-9682
Indian. This restaurant specializes in northern Indian cuisine. **Open Wednesday through Monday for lunch and dinner. Closed Tuesday. Full service, take-out, catering, VISA/MC/ AMEX/DISC, $$.**

Linda's Organic Kitchen and Market
81-22 Lefferts Blvd., Kew Gardens, NY 11415   (718) 847-2233
Natural foods deli. This small deli, located inside a natural foods store, sells mostly vegetarian food by the pound, including soups, vegetable korma, and other ethnic dishes. **Open Monday through Saturday for three meals. Open Sunday for brunch. Counter service, vegan options, take-out, VISA/MC/AMEX/DISC, $-$$.** www.lindasorganic.com

• The Oneness Fountain Heart Restaurant
157-19 72nd Ave., Flushing, NY 11367   (718) 591-3663
Vegetarian. Eclectic menu with unusual items, such as Duck Surprise (vegetarian duck with butter-braised broccoli, served with royal rice and pineapple sauce) and Portobello Mellow (grilled portobello mushrooms, red peppers, fresh spinach, and mozzarella in a spinach wrap). The menu also includes a soup-of-the-day, appetizers, salads, and desserts. **Open**

Thursday through Tuesday for lunch and dinner. Closed Wednesday. Full service, fresh juices, espresso/cappuccino, $$.

Quantum Leap
65-64 Fresh Meadows Ln., Fresh Meadows, NY 11365   **(718) 461-1307**
Natural foods. See description under Manhattan, NY.

Queens Health Emporium
159-01 Horace Harding Expy., Flushing, NY 11365   **(718) 358-6500**
Natural foods. This natural foods store offers a variety of hot and cold items, many using organic vegetables. The menu is veggie except for tuna salad. Entrées are available for take-out, and upstairs seating is also offered. **Open Monday through Saturday for three meals. Open Sunday for brunch.** Limited service, fresh juices, take-out, VISA/MC, $-$$.

• Smile of the Beyond
86-14 Parsons Blvd., Jamaica, NY 11432   **(718) 739-7453**
Vegetarian. Smile of the Beyond started as an ice cream parlor but now sells more traditional American breakfast items, plus Brown Rice Veggie Salad, mock meats, rice, and salads. **Open Monday through Saturday for breakfast and lunch. Closed Sunday.** Counter service, fresh juices, take-out, $.

RIVERHEAD

Green Earth Grocery Natural Foods Market
50 E. Main St., Riverhead, NY 11901   **(516) 369-2233**
Natural foods deli. This deli has several veggie options. **Open daily for lunch and dinner.** Limited service, vegan options, fresh juices, smoothies, take-out, VISA/MC/AMEX/DISC, $-$$.

ROCHESTER

(For restaurant listings in the surrounding areas, see Brighton, Pittsford, and Victor.)

• Atomic Eggplant
75 Marshall St., Rochester, NY 14607   **(585) 325-6750**
Vegetarian/natural foods. The eclectic menu features scrambled tofu; hummus; baba ghanouj; black bean chili with cornbread; veggie, spinach, or black bean burgers; barbequed tofu or tempeh; stir-fries; and much more. Virtually every item on the menu is vegan or can be made that way, including almost all of the desserts. **Open Monday through Saturday for lunch and dinner. Closed Sunday.** Full service, vegan options, fresh juices, smoothies, espresso/cappuccino, take-out, VISA/MC/AMEX/DISC, $-$$. www.theatomiceggplant.com

Dashen Ethiopian Restaurant and Bar
503 South Ave., Rochester, NY 14620   **(585) 232-2690**
Ethiopian. This spacious South Wedge restaurant offers such vegetarian items as gomen wat (collard greens and bracing garlic), kik alicha (yellow split pea stew), and yatakilt wat (a stew-soft trio of potatoes, cabbage, and carrots). **Open daily for lunch and dinner.** Full service, vegan options, non-smoking, wine/beer/alcohol, VISA/MC/AMEX/DISC, $$.

• India House Vegetarian Café
1009 S. Clinton Ave., Rochester, NY 14620   **(585) 271-0242**

Vegetarian/Indian. This restaurant offers Southern Indian cuisine, including many items not found in a typical Indian restaurant. Appetizers include dahivada (lentil and onion fritter) and soups like rasam (spicy lentil and tomato soup). A variety of dosai (crispy crepes), as well as curries (spinach made with paneer or tofu, for example), rices, breads, and desserts make this a unique place to eat. **Open daily for lunch and dinner. Full service, vegan options, suitable for business dining, non-smoking, reservations recommended, special drinks, wine/beer, VISA/MC/AMEX/DISC/DC, $$.**

The King and I
1475 E. Henrietta Rd., Rochester, NY 14623   **(716) 427-8090**

Thai. An extensive vegetarian and vegan menu includes an excellent Phat Thai and vegan ice creams made with coconut milk. The atmosphere is enchanting and the service is friendly. **Open daily for lunch and dinner. Full service, vegan options, non-smoking, special drinks, take-out, VISA/MC, $$.**

Mamasan's Restaurant
309 University Ave., Rochester, NY 14607   **(585) 262-4580**

Vietnamese. Mamasan's menu includes vermicelli and noodle salads, vegetable salads, curries, and more. **Open Monday through Saturday for lunch and dinner. Closed Sunday. Full service, take-out, $$.**

Savory Thyme Catering
220 Mt. Hope Ave., Rochester, NY 14620   **(585) 423-0750**

Catering. This company will cater an event, lunch, or meeting with vegetarian and vegan appetizers, spring rolls, salads, pasta dishes, brunch items, and desserts. Their entrée menu includes Spanakopita, Quiches, West African Peanut Stew, Tempeh and Shiitake Mushrooms, Tofu- or Cheese-filled Ravioli, and Moroccan Eggplant. Vegan items are noted, as are those that can be made vegan upon request. **Open for lunch for take-out. Call about catering events. Limited service, vegan options, no credit cards for take-out. www.savory-thyme.com**

• Skippy's Veg Out
742 South Ave., Rochester, NY 14620   **(585) 271-7590**

Vegetarian café. This location used to be home to the Slice of Life Café. Now, one of its cooks has taken it over and is creating many of the same favorites, such as Buffalo tempeh and biscuits & gravy. Other offerings include meatball subs and a Thanksgiving plate (fake turkey with stuffing and gravy). **Open Tuesday through Saturday for lunch and dinner. Closed Sunday and Monday. Full service, vegan options, take-out, catering, $.**

ROSENDALE

The Rosendale Café
435 Main St., Rosendale, NY 12472   **(914) 658-9048**

Natural foods café. This cafe offers a wide variety of events, including music, storytelling, and more. Their menu features soups, salads, vegetarian chili, sandwiches, pasta dishes, and other entrées which change daily. **Open Tuesday through Sunday for lunch and dinner. Closed Monday. Full service, vegan options, espresso/cappuccino, wine/beer, take-out, $$.**

SAG HARBOR

Provisions of Sag Harbor, Ltd.
Bay & Divisions St., Sag Harbor, NY 11963   **(516) 725-3636**
Natural foods deli. In this homey atmosphere, you'll find a salad bar with organic lettuce, and dishes such as Scrambled Tofu, an Organic Vegetable Pot Pie, and a Tempeh Reuben. **Open daily for three meals. Full service, vegan options, organic carrot juice, fresh juices,** VISA/MC/AMEX, $-$$.

SARATOGA SPRINGS

• Four Seasons Natural Foods Store & Café
33 Philadelphia St., Saratoga Springs, NY 12866   **(518) 584-4670**
Vegetarian. A wide variety of vegetarian and vegan dishes are offered daily, including hot and cold entrées, soups, salads, and fresh breads. **Open daily for lunch and dinner.** Cafeteria, vegan options, fresh juices, take-out, catering, VISA/MC/DISC, $$.

SAYVILLE

Cornucopia Natural Foods
39 Main St., Sayville, NY 11782   **(516) 589-9579**
Natural foods. This small café and deli located in a natural foods store offers fresh juices, soups, veggie burgers, sandwiches, salads, and more. **Open daily for lunch and early dinner.** Limited service, fresh juices, VISA/MC/AMEX/DISC, $.

SCARSDALE

• Mrs. Green's Natural Market
365 Central Park Ave., Scarsdale, NY 10583   **(914) 472-9675**
780 White Plains Rd., Scarsdale, NY 10583   **(914) 472-0111**
670 Post Rd., Scarsdale, NY 10583   **(914) 472-7900**
Vegetarian/natural foods. See description under Mahopac, NY.

STATEN ISLAND

Dairy Palace
2210 Victory Blvd., Staten Island, NY 10314   **(718) 761-5200**
Kosher dairy. This pizza and dairy restaurant features a Chinese menu, mock meat dishes, and an ice cream bar. Note, they do serve fish. **Open Sunday through Thursday for lunch and dinner. Open Friday until sunset. Open Saturday after sundown. Cafeteria, vegan options,** $$.

SYOSSET

Long Island Health Connection
520 Jericho Tpke., Syosset, NY 11791   **(516) 496-2528**
Natural foods deli. This deli offers veggie sandwiches, burgers, and main dishes. Organic

ingredients are used. **Open daily for lunch and dinner. Limited service, vegan options, fresh juices, take-out, VISA/MC/AMEX, $.**

SYRACUSE

(For restaurant listings in the surrounding areas, see Fayetteville.)

Aladdin's Natural Eatery
163 Marshall St., Syracuse, NY 13210   **(315) 471-4000**
Natural foods. See description under Ithaca, NY.

Alto Cinco
526 Westcott St., Syracuse, NY 13210   **(315) 422-6399**
Mexican. Alto Cinco uses no lard and no MSG in any of their foods. The rice and beans are vegetarian, and they have two vegan burritos on the menu. All sauces are made fresh daily. Alto Cinco also has a shorter dine-in menu, with a special vegetable platter featuring fall harvest vegetables and wild rice. **Open daily for lunch and dinner. Open Sunday for brunch. Full service, vegan options, wine, take-out, delivery, catering, $-$$.**

King David Restaurant
129 Marshall St., Syracuse, NY 13210   **(315) 471-5000**
Middle Eastern. This Middle Eastern style restaurant is in the heart of the Syracuse University area. **Open Monday through Saturday for lunch and dinner. Closed Sunday. Full service, wine/beer, VISA/MC/AMEX, $$.**

•• Nature's Kitchen
527 Charles Ave., Syracuse, NY 13209   **(315) 484-2143**
Vegan. Some of the delicious items on the menu at Nature's Kitchen include hickory baked tofu, broccoli and tofu with garlic sauce, Jamaican Jerk "chicken," barbeque-style "ribs," carrot cake, and cheesecake. **Open Sunday through Thursday for lunch and dinner. Open Friday until 90 minutes before sundown. Closed Saturday. Limited service, special drinks, $$.**

TONAWANDA

Mighty Taco
48 Main St., Tonawanda, NY 14150   **(716) 692-9155**
2309 Sheridan Park Edge Plz., Tonawanda, NY 14150   **(716) 833-3060**
Mexican. See description under Amherst, NY.

TRUMANSBURG

The Rongovian Embassy to The USA
1 W. Main St., Trumansburg, NY 14886   **(607) 387-3334**
Mexican. This is a casual restaurant with eclectic atmosphere and live music. Their menu includes veggie fajitas, pizza, burritos, and taco salad. A children's menu is available. **Open Tuesday through Sunday for dinner. Closed Monday. Full service, vegan options, suitable for business entertaining, wine/beer, non-alcoholic beer, special drinks, take-out, VISA/ MC/DISC, $$.**

UTICA

The Phoenician Restaurant

623 French Rd., Utica, NY 13413   **(315) 733-2709**

Middle Eastern. Vegetarian platters include falafel, fattoush, tabbouleh, and other Middle Eastern items. **Open Monday through Saturday. Closed Sunday. Full service, wine/beer, take-out, VISA/MC, $.**

VICTOR

China Court

6385 Victor-Manchester Rd. (Rt. 96), Victor, NY 14564   **(585) 924-1930**

Chinese. The vegan options here include mock meats. The lemon "chicken" comes particularly highly recommended. **Open Tuesday through Sunday for lunch and dinner. Closed Monday. Full service, vegan options, take-out, VISA/MC/AMEX/DISC, $-$$.**

WATKINS GLEN

Cascata Winery At The Professor's Inn

3651 Rt. 14, Watkins Glen, NY 14891   **(607) 535-8000**

American. They have several vegetarian and vegan options, including sandwiches, pasta, and even "Raspberry Soy Tofu with rice and vegetables." The menu notes for vegans to let the "server know, so that we may better meet your needs." **Open weekends only in winter. Open daily for three meals in summer. Full service, vegan options, smoothies, soymilk, espresso/cappuccino, beer/wine/alcohol, take-out, catering, $-$$.** www.cascatawinery.com

Glen Mountain Market

200 N. Franklin St., Watkins Glen, NY 14891   **(607) 535-6900**

Bakery. This bakery makes European-style breads and pastries fresh daily. Menu items include tofu burger, healthy hoagie, hummus, cheese sandwich, and PB&J. **Open Monday through Saturday for three meals. Open Sunday for breakfast and lunch. Limited service, vegan options, non-smoking, espresso/cappuccino, soymilk, special drinks, take-out, catering, $$.**

WEST HEMPSTEAD

Taj Mahal Restaurant

221 Hempstead Tpke., West Hempstead, NY 11552   **(516) 565-4607**

Ethnic foods. There are many veggie dishes served here. **Open Monday through Saturday for lunch and dinner. Open Sunday for dinner only. Full service, wine/beer/alcohol, VISA/MC/AMEX, $$.**

WESTBURY

• Zen Palate ✿

477 Old Country Rd., Westbury, NY 11590   **(516) 333-8686**

Vegetarian. See description under Manhattan, NY.

WHITE PLAINS

•Manna Foods, Inc.
171 Mamaroneck Ave., White Plains, NY 11552   **(914) 946-2233**
Vegetarian. Hot vegetarian Meatball Loaf, vegetarian Chicken Parmesan, and vegetarian stews made from organic ingredients are a few of the items available at Manna Foods. **Open Monday through Friday for lunch. Closed Saturday and Sunday. Full service, $-$$.**

WILLIAMSVILLE

Pizza Plant
8020 Transit Rd., Williamsville, NY 14221   **(716) 632-0800**
Pizza. Vegetarian items on the menu are indicated by a carrot. Choices include Bread Bowl Stew, chili, nachos, and a wide variety of pizzas. Whole-wheat, sesame, spinach, or garlic doughs are available. **Open daily. Full service, wine/beer, take-out, VISA/MC/AMEX/ DISC, $$.**

WOODSTOCK

Bluestone Country Foods
54-C Tinker St., Woodstock, NY 12498   **(914) 679-5656**
Natural foods deli. This deli features many vegetarian and vegan dishes, including several wheat-free items. Satisfy your appetite with one of their fresh juices, as well as a wide variety of soups, sandwiches, salads, and entrées. A few tables are available inside. **Open daily for lunch and dinner. Limited service, vegan options, fresh juices, catering, take-out, $-$$.**

•• In The Raw
65 Tinker St., Woodstock, NY 12498   **(845) 679-9494**
Vegan/raw foods. The menu includes the Woodstock in the Raw Wrap with mock tuna, Mexican Pizza atop a flourless almond flax crust, the sprouted Sun Burger, an organic Kale Avocado Salad, French Lentil Tabbouleh, Lime Tarts, Fruit Parfaits, Carob Cake with almond butter frosting, and shakes made with soymilk, rice milk, or their special Coconut-Almond Milk. **Open Friday through Tuesday for lunch through early dinner. Closed Wednesday and Thursday. Deli-style, fresh juices, smoothies, soymilk, take-out, $$.** www.woodstockintheraw.com

YORKTOWN HEIGHTS

•Mrs. Green's Natural Market
12 Triangle Shopping Center, Yorktown Heights, NY 10598   **(914) 962-4482**
Vegetarian/natural foods. See description under Mahopac, NY.

Restaurant codes: ❂ Reviewers' Choice • Vegetarian Restaurant •• Vegan Restaurant
Restaurant prices: **$** less than $6 **$$** $6-$12 **$$$** more than $12
Credit Cards Accepted: VISA - VISA MC - MasterCard AMEX - American Express
DISC - Discover DC - Diner's Club

North Carolina

ASHEVILLE

(For restaurant listings in the surrounding areas, see Black Mountain and Hendersonville.)

Café Max & Rosie's

52 N. Lexington Ave., Asheville, NC 28801   (828) 254-5342

Natural foods. Dine on a number of vegetarian and vegan dishes at Café Max & Rosie's, including Tempeh Parmigiana Sub, Fresh Fruit Fantasy, Mideast Bean Pita, Vegan Veggie Pita, fried rice, a veggie burger, plus much more. **Open Monday through Saturday for lunch and early dinner. Full service, vegan options, fresh juices, smoothies, take-out, $.** www.maxandrosies.com

Café Terra

65 Westgate Pkwy., Asheville, NC 28806   (828) 253-7656

Natural foods deli. Many vegetarian options are available at this natural foods deli. **Open daily. Counter service, vegan options, take-out, $.**

Flying Frog Café

76 Haywood St., Asheville, NC 28801   (828) 254-9411

International. This café offers everything from Cajun to Italian cuisine. **Open daily for dinner. Full service, beer/wine/alcohol, VISA/MC/AMEX/DISC/DC, $$$.**

• Laughing Seed Café

40 Wall St., Asheville, NC 28801   (704) 252-3445

Vegetarian. Enjoy a wide variety of international vegetarian dishes, including a Carribean Quesadilla, Mid-Eastern Pita Sandwich, Greek Salad, Kung Pao Tofu, tempeh fajitas, and more. Indoor and outdoor seating available. **Open Monday through Saturday for three meals. Open Sunday for brunch. Full service, fresh juices, macrobiotic/vegan options, take-out, VISA/MC/DISC, $$.**

• Rosetta's Kitchen

116 N Lexington Ave., Asheville, NC 28801   (828) 232-0738

Vegetarian. Rosetta's Kitchen has a wholesome atmosphere that is the perfect setting for its homestyle cooking. More than just a restaurant, Rosetta's has become a local gathering spot, with friendly staff, local art, downtown bicycle deliveries, and dedicated, environmentally conscious policies. **Open Tuesday through Sunday for lunch through late night service. Closed Monday. Full service, vegan options, beer/wine/alcohol, take-out, delivery, VISA/ AMEX, $.**

BLACK MOUNTAIN

• The Green Light Café

205 W. State St., Black Mountain, NC 28711   (828) 669-2444

Vegetarian. The menu includes soups, wraps, a Thai vegetable crepe, a Tempeh Reuben, daily specials, and desserts baked fresh daily. **Open Monday through Friday for lunch and dinner.**

Open Saturday and Sunday for brunch. Full service, vegan options, fresh juices, beer, no credit cards, $$.

BREVARD

• Bearfoot Café and Catering Company
430 Caldwell St., Brevard, NC 28712   **(704) 883-2220**

Vegetarian. Bearfoot Café is situated in the mountains and caters to campers and other visitors. Various ethnic cuisines are served, and outdoor dining is offered. **Open daily for three meals. Limited service, macrobiotic/vegan options, catering, fresh juices, $.**

BURNSVILLE

•• Planet Zen Café and Market
RR 3 Box 305, Burnsville, NC 28714   **(609) 391-2000**

Vegan. Planet Zen boasts a wide variety of vegetarian and organic meals, including Veggie Wraps, Zen Dogs, Un-Chicken salad sandwiches, soups, and smoothies of the day. **Open daily for three meals. Full service, vegan options, take-out, VISA, $-$$.**

CARY

• Udipi Café
590 E. Chatham St., Cary, NC 27511   **(919) 465-0898**

Vegetarian/Indian. Udipi Café serves appetizers, soups, dosai, curries, breads, and much more on its large lunch buffet and for dinner. Unique dishes include Shredded Coconut Utthappam and Chana Batura. They also offer on-line ordering and delivery. **Open Tuesday through Sunday for lunch and dinner. Closed Monday. Full service, special drinks, take-out, catering, delivery, VISA/MC, $-$$.** www.udipionline.com

• Woodlands
1305 NW Maynard Rd., Cary, NC 27513   **(919) 467-6020**

Vegetarian/Indian. Concentrating on Southern Indian cuisine, Woodlands offers samosas, dosas, puri, chana masala, uthappam, and more. None of the dishes contain eggs. **Open daily for lunch and dinner. Full service, vegan options, take-out, VISA/MC/AMEX, $.**

CHAPEL HILL

Margaret's Cantina
1129 Weaver Dairy Rd., Chapel Hill, NC 27514   **(919) 942-4745**

Southwestern. Margaret's veggie options include Very Vegetarian Nachos, hummus, vegetarian black bean chili, and a tempeh pita sandwich. **Open Monday through Saturday for lunch and dinner. Closed Sunday. Full service, vegan options, espresso/cappuccino, take-out, VISA/MC/AMEX/DC, $-$$.**

• Sage Vegetarian Café
1129 Weaver Dairy Rd., Chapel Hill, NC 27514   **(919) 968-9266**

Vegetarian/Middle Eastern. Sage Vegetarian Café offers a varied menu of soups, salads, sandwiches and wraps, entrées, and side dishes. Entrées include delicious black beans and rice, Persian Eggplant Paradise (made with split peas, saffron basmati rice, and fragrant spices), vegetable kabobs, and Persian pomegranate stew. Daily specials also available. Though there are many vegan options, eggs and cheese are used frequently. However, the friendly staff will happily answer questions about the ingredients. Outdoor seating is available. **Open daily for lunch and dinner. Full service, vegan options, take-out, $$.**

Saladelia Café
105 N. Columbia St., Chapel Hill, NC 27514 (919) 932-1020
Middle Eastern. The vegetarian and vegan options at Saladelia include the Vegetarian Gyro, Hummus Pocket, Mediterranean Eggplant Melt, stuffed grape leaves, and falafel. **Open daily for lunch and dinner. Limited service, vegan options, espresso/cappuccino, take-out, VISA/ MC/AMEX/DISC/DC, $.**

CHARLOTTE

Berrybrook Farm Natural Foods
1257 East Blvd., Charlotte, NC 28203 (704) 334-6528
Natural foods. Homemade soups, salads, and sandwiches are made fresh daily at this natural food grocery and deli. The menu at Berrybrook changes daily and is primarily vegetarian. **Open Monday through Saturday. Closed Sunday. Take-out, vegan options, fresh juices, VISA/MC/DISC, $.**

Café Verde At Talley's Green Grocery
1408-C East Blvd., Charlotte, NC 28203 (704) 334-9200
Natural foods. Café Verde offers ethnic, low-fat vegetarian, vegan, and non-vegetarian dishes, daily soups, a wonderful salad bar, sandwiches, and desserts made without refined sugars. Also, enjoy the best selection of beers in Charlotte. **Open daily. Cafeteria, vegan options, fresh juices, wine/beer/alcohol, take-out, VISA/MC, $.**

House of Chinese Gourmet
5608 Independence Blvd., Charlotte, NC 28212 (704) 563-8989
Chinese. Here's a deliciously inviting menu with more than 20 vegetarian entrées, plus soups and appetizers. Many tofu dishes are available, and MSG is omitted upon request. **Open daily. Full service, vegan options, wine/beer/alcohol, take-out, VISA/MC/AMEX, $$.**

India Palace
4515 E. Independence Blvd., Charlotte, NC 28212 (704) 568-7176
Indian. Authentic Indian cuisine is offered, and great care is taken in the preparation and use of spices. Nine vegetable entrées are featured on this menu. **Open daily for dinner. Full service, vegan options, take-out, VISA/MC/AMEX, $$.**

• The Peaceful Dragon Tea House and Cultural Center
12610 Steele Creek Rd., Charlotte, NC 28273   **(704) 544-1012**

Vegetarian/Asian. In addition to lectures, classes, and a spa, the Peaceful Dragon offers a wonderful vegetarian menu. Lunch options include Potato Samosa Wontons, Thai "Fish" Steaks, a Thai "Chicken" (seitan) Wrap, and Spicy "Shrimp" Stir-Fry. For dinner, choose from any of those dishes or from entrées like the "Chicken" Skewer Bowl, the Imperial Phoenix (sautéed shiitake and snow peas in brown sauce), or Ma Pao Tofu (tofu stir-fried with ginger and chili-garlic sauce served over brown rice and cool kale). The weekend brunch menu includes buckwheat pancakes, baked tofu and grits, eggs benedict made with veggie ham, and orange-scented French toast. **Open Monday through Saturday for lunch and dinner. Open Sunday for brunch. Full service, vegan options, beer/wine, special drinks, take-out, catering, $-$$. www.thepeacefuldragon.com**

Thai Cuisine Restaurant
3108 E. Independence Blvd., Charlotte, NC 28025   **(704) 532-7511**

Thai. Tofu can be substituted for the meat in any dish to create delicious vegetarian options. There also are some vegetarian appetizers, salads, and soups. No MSG or salt is used in the preparation of food. **Open daily. Full service, vegan options, wine/beer/alcohol, take-out, VISA/MC/AMEX, $$.**

Thai Taste
324 East Blvd., Charlotte, NC 28203   **(704) 332-0001**

Thai. You can choose to have many dishes on Thai Taste's menu, such as curries, stir-fries, and noodle dishes, made vegetarian, with or without eggs. Try the Pud Met Ma Muang (cashew nut) or the Khing Sod (fresh ginger) stir-fry, the Thai Salad with vegetables and fried tofu, or one of several vegetarian appetizers. **Open Monday through Friday for lunch and dinner. Open Saturday and Sunday for dinner only. Full service, vegan options, take-out, delivery, VISA/MC, $$.**

• Woodlands
7128 Albemarle Rd., Charlotte, NC 28227   **(704) 569-9193**

Vegetarian/Indian. One member called this "the best Indian restaurant in Charlotte," and it's not just because it's the only one that's all-vegetarian. The menu offers a wide range of appetizers, dosais, uthappam (Indian-style pancakes), pullavs (rice specialties), curries, breads, and desserts. Or order a dinner special that lets you choose from a combination of these selections. **Open Tuesday through Sunday for lunch and dinner. Closed Monday. Full service, vegan options, fresh juices, special drinks, catering, VISA/MC/AMEX/DISC, $-$$.**

DURHAM

Anotherthyme
109 N. Gregson St., Durham, NC 27701   **(919) 682-5225**

Seasonal. Enjoy gourmet seasonal cuisine at Anotherthyme with pasta, vegetarian, and non-vegetarian dishes. No red meat is served. **Open daily. Full service, fresh juices, wine/beer/alcohol, take-out, VISA/MC/AMEX, $$-$$$.**

Saladelia Café
4201 University Dr., Durham, NC 27707   **(919) 489-5776**
Middle Eastern. See description under Chapel Hill, NC.

GREENSBORO

(For restaurant listings in the surrounding areas, see Winston-Salem.)

•The Grapevine Cafe & Juice Bar
Guilford Village, 435 Dolley Madison Rd., Greensboro, NC 27410 (910) 856-0070
Vegetarian. Dine on fresh bread, soups, chili, stuffed pita pockets, salads, burgers, sandwiches, and delicious entrées at this cafe. They feature a monthly theme dinner highlighting one regional cuisine with international flavor. **Open Monday through Saturday for lunch and dinner. Closed Sunday. Full service, vegan options, fresh juices, non-alcoholic wine/beer, wine/beer, take-out, VISA/MC/AMEX/DC, $-$$.** www.gvinecafe.com

Sunset Café
4608 W. Market St., Greensboro, NC 27407   **(919) 855-0349**
Natural foods. At least four of the 16 entrées are vegetarian, and some are vegan. Examples include Russian Cheese Dumplings, Vegetarian Cheese Nut Loaf, Rice and Cheese Croquettes, Grilled Vegetable Kebabs, Vegetarian Lasagna, Spinach Manicotti, and more. Their blackboard menu changes daily. **Open daily. Full service, vegan options, wine/beer/alcohol, take-out, VISA/MC, $$.**

HENDERSONVILLE

•Blue Mountain Café
715 Old Spartanburg Hwy., Hendersonville, NC 28792   **(828) 693-0505**
Natural foods café. Located in the Hendersonville Co-op, this café serves sandwiches like the Café Veggie Burger, Tempeh Reuben, Veggie Roll-Up, and Herb Baked Tofu Sandwich. It also offers entrées, such as the Hummus Plate, Happy Buddha Plate, and seasonal platters. The Blue Mountain Café Organic Juice Bar offers a number of organic fruit and vegetable juices, allowing you to create your own blend, as well as tasty smoothies and tonics. Plus, their Grab n' Go case is stocked daily with sandwiches, salads, desserts, soups, and more. **Open Monday through Saturday for breakfast and lunch. Closed Sunday. Deli-style, vegan options, fresh juices, $-$$.** www.hendersonvillecoop.com/cafe.html

MORRISVILLE

Neomonde Bakery & Deli
10235 Chapel Hill Rd., Morrisville, NC 27560   **(919) 469-8009**
Middle Eastern. Neomonde serves Middle Eastern and American cuisine, including stuffed grape leaves, tabbouleh, spinach pie, chickpea salad, hummus, and baba ghanouj. **Open daily for lunch and dinner. Full service, vegan options, take-out, VISA, $.**

•Tower Restaurant
144 Morrisville Sq. Way, Morrisville, NC 27560   **(919) 465-2326**
Vegetarian/Indian. The menu includes samosas, pakoras, puri, vadai, dosais, utthappams,

masala dosas, curries, rice dishes, desserts for kids, and more. Lunch is a buffet, while dinner is served á la carte. This restaurant is located near the Morrisville Fire Station. **Open daily for lunch and dinner. Full service, special drinks, VISA/MC/AMEX/DISC/DC, $-$$.** www.towerindianrestaurant.com

RALEIGH

(For restaurant listings in the surrounding areas, see Cary, Chapel Hill, Durham, and Morrisville.)

Irregardless Café
901 W. Morgan St., Raleigh, NC 27603   **(919) 833-8898**
Natural foods. Irregardless Café presents a new menu each night featuring vegetarian, vegan, and non-vegetarian entrées. Fresh baked breads, cookies, and desserts are also available in this totally non-smoking environment. **Open Monday through Saturday. Open Sunday for brunch only. Full service, vegan options, espresso/cappuccino, wine/beer/alcohol, take-out, VISA/MC/AMEX, $-$$.**

Neomonde Bakery & Deli
3817 Beryl Rd., Raleigh, NC 27607   **(919) 828-1628**
Middle Eastern. See description under Morrisville, NC.

SYLVA

Lulu's Café
612 W. Main St., Sylva, NC 28779   **(828) 586-8989**
Café. Lulu's caries a variety of ethnic foods. The menu includes portobella and spinach pesto pitas, marinated tofu with peanut sauce (vegan), and a black turtle beans and saffron rice. A children's menu is available. **Open Monday through Saturday for lunch and dinner. Closed Sunday. Full service, vegan options, informal atmosphere, take-out, non-alcoholic beer, beer/wine, VISA/MC, $$.**

WINSTON-SALEM

Nawab Indian Cuisine
129 S. Stratford Rd., Winston-Salem, NC 27104   **(336) 725-3949**
Indian. Nawab features a large selection of vegetarian and vegan appetizers and entrées. Sample vegetable patia (vegetables cooked with sweet and sour mangos and a touch of ginger), palak paneer (spinach with or without Indian cheese), mushroom broccoli krahi (sautéed with vegetables, garlic, and herbs), Bombay potatoes, eggplant bharta (baked, then mashed and sautéed with garlic, onions, and tomatoes), and much more. Children's portions are often available for half the price of a regular entrée. **Open daily for lunch and dinner. Full service, vegan options, reservations recommended, beer/wine/alcohol, non-alcoholic beer, special drinks, take-out, VISA/MC/AMEX/DISC/DC, $$.** www.nawabonline.com

Restaurant codes: ✪ Reviewers' Choice • Vegetarian Restaurant •• Vegan Restaurant
Restaurant prices: **$** less than $6 **$$** $6-$12 **$$$** more than $12
Credit Cards Accepted: VISA - VISA MC - MasterCard AMEX - American Express
DISC - Discover DC - Diner's Club

North Dakota

FARGO

Café Aladdin
530 6th Ave. N., Fargo, ND 58102   **(701) 298-0880**
Middle Eastern. The menu includes vegetarian sandwiches and platters, such as falafel and lentil rice. **Open Monday through Saturday for lunch and dinner. Closed Sunday. Limited service, take-out, catering, $-$$.**

Full Circle Café
69 N. 4th St., Fargo, ND 58102   **(701) 271-0051**
American. This "non-profit restaurant" offers itself as an educational center as well as a transitional work site for people with disabilities. Their breakfast menu is served all day. **Open Monday through Saturday for breakfast and lunch. Closed Sunday. Full service, vegan options, take-out, fresh juices, soymilk, special drinks, $.**

Ohio

AKRON

(For restaurant listings in the surrounding areas, see Canton, Hudson, and North Canton.)

Aladdin's Eatery
782 W. Market St., Akron, OH 44303   **(330) 535-0110**
Middle Eastern. This local restaurant chain offers great Mediterranean and Middle Eastern dishes, including many vegetarian and vegan options. These include lentil soup, vegetarian chili, hummus, tabbouleh, salads, stuffed grape leaves, falafel, and six vegetarian rolled pita options. **Open daily for lunch and dinner. Full service, vegan options, fresh juices, smoothies, espresso/cappuccino, beer, take-out, VISA/MC/AMEX, $-$$.** www.aladdinseatery.com

Mustard Seed Market Café
West Market Plaza, 3885 W. Market St., Akron, OH 44333   **(216) 666-7333**
Natural foods/macrobiotic. Mustard Seed Market is one of the largest natural food stores in the midwest. The restaurant, located within the store, offers great natural food dishes. There is a strong emphasis on vegetarian dishes, including macrobiotic and vegan meals, but some seafood and poultry are also served. Mustard Seed Market uses organic foods and has the best produce department in town. **Open Sunday for brunch. Open Monday through Saturday for lunch and dinner. Full service, vegan options, fresh juices, smoothies, soymilk, espresso/cappuccino, wine/beer, take-out, catering, VISA/MC/DISC, $$.** www.mustardseedmarket.com

ATHENS

Casa Nueva and Cantina
4 W. State St., Athens, OH 45701   **(740) 592-2016**
Mexican. This worker-owned restaurant obtains its produce and food ingredients from local

farmers and has a rotating seasonal menu. Breakfast options include the Vegan Scrambler, soysage (made on the premises), and tofu bacon. They also have burritos, enchiladas, tacos, and other traditional favorites that can be made vegetarian by substituting marinated tofu. In addition, they offer salads and eight kinds of salsas. **Open daily for three meals. Full service, take-out, catering, vegan options, fresh juices, organic coffee, VISA/MC, $-$$.**

World's Best Bagels
31 N. Court St., Athens, OH 45701   **(740) 594-5506**
Bagel deli. World's Best Bagels offers 16 varieties of bagels, various cream cheeses, and even 11 types of creamy tofu spreads. Sandwiches, soups, and desserts help to make World's Best a bagel lover's paradise. **Open daily for breakfast through late evening service. Limited service, vegan options, carry-out, catering, delivery, $. www.worldsbestbagels.com**

BEREA

Nam Wah
392 W. Bagley Rd., Berea, OH 44017   **(216) 243-8181**
Vietnamese/Chinese. Nam Wah features a vegetarian menu with egg rolls, fried rice, lo mein, curry, and several other dishes. **Open daily for lunch and dinner. Full service, take-out, VISA/MC/AMEX/DC, $.**

• Tabor's Thyme Café
34 Park St., Berea, OH 44017   **(440) 243-1011**
Vegetarian. Tabor's Thyme Café serves a diverse selection of multicultural dishes. Menus change daily, but past items have included Walnut-Lentil Burgers, Tamales, Lentil Stew Magyar, Nut Steak with Mushroom Gravy, Wheatberry Salad, and Hoppin' John. Most of the items are low-fat and made with organic ingredients whenever possible. Also, they note on the menu which dishes are vegan and which can be made vegan. **Open Tuesday through Saturday for lunch and dinner. Closed Sunday and Monday. Full service, vegan options, organic coffee, $-$$.**

BOARDMAN

•• Flaming Ice Cube
7105 Lockwood Blvd., Boardman, OH 44512   **(330) 726-4766**
Vegan café. The Flaming Ice Cube is a vegan café, coffee shop, juice bar, and gift shop. They carry items such as vegan cookies, vegan jerkies, bath items, candles, books and CDs, yoga and meditation accessories, and more. **Open Monday through Saturday for lunch and dinner. Open Sunday for lunch and early dinner. Limited service, fresh juices, take-out, VISA/MC/DISC. www.flamingice.com**

BOWLING GREEN

•• Squeaker's Café & Health Food
175 N. Main St., Bowling Green, OH 43402   **(419) 354-7000**
Vegan. Named for the owner's pet guinea pig, Squeaker's is home to a restaurant and a health foods store where 90 percent of the products are organic. The menu at the café includes

soups, wraps, pizza, and daily specials, often made with produce from café's garden. Try their avocado bagel or curried tofu salad sandwich, perhaps with some cookies to finish off your meal. The owner donates a percentage of proceeds to environmental organizations. **Open daily for lunch and dinner. Full service, fresh juices, take-out, VISA/MC, $.**

CANTON

Gregory's Family Restaurant
2835 Whipple Ave., NW, Canton, OH 44708   **(330) 477-1296**

American. Named the "best in Canton," Gregory's offers a vegetarian menu, including some vegan dishes, in addition to their traditional restaurant fare. Their "home cooking" meatless selections include specialty appetizers, side dishes, entrées with vegan gravy, salads, sweets, and breakfast foods. **Open Monday through Friday for three meals. Open Saturday and Sunday for brunch. Full service, vegan options, cappuccino, VISA/MC, $$.**

Mulligan's
4118 Belden Village St., NW, Canton, OH 44718   **(330) 493-8239**

Pub. Located near the National Pro Football Hall of Fame, this turn-of-the-century Irish pub offers a separate vegetarian menu. This includes appetizers, salads, meatless chili, soups, veggie hot dogs, garden burgers, veggie deli sandwiches, burritos, pasta dishes, and rice and black beans. Try the Philadelphia "Steak" Sandwich, the Veggie "Chicken" Oriental Stir-Fry, the veggie "Chicken" Cacciatori, or the Junk Yard Dog with everything. **Open daily for lunch through late evening service. Full service, vegan options, smoothies, soymilk, espresso/cappuccino, beer/wine/alcohol, non-alcoholic beer/wine, special drinks, take-out, VISA/MC/AMEX, $-$$.**

CINCINNATI

Amol India Restaurant
354 Ludlow Ave., Cincinnati, OH 45220   **(513) 961-3665**

Indian. This Indian restaurant serves traditional dishes, many of which are vegetarian. Try the Bangan Bhartha, Aloo Chana Masala, Gajjar Mattar, or any of the other delicious selections. **Open daily for lunch and dinner. Full service, vegan options, beer/wine/alcohol, $-$$$.**

Andy's International Deli
906 Nassau St., Cincinnati, OH 45206   **(513) 218-9791**

American/international. Described as the "Best of Cincinnati," Andy's offers a wide variety of vegetarian salads, appetizers, and side dishes. Some selections include hummus, falafel, ratatouille, tabbouleh, dolmas, and spinach pie. **Open daily for three meals. Limited service, vegan options, catering, take-out, smoothies, beer/wine/alcohol, VISA/MC, $.**

Arnold's Bar & Grill
210 E. 8th St., Cincinnati, OH 45202   **(513) 421-6234**

American tavern. Arnold's is a unique turn-of-the-century tavern with good food, fresh ingredients, and a strong selection of vegetarian specials and soups. **Open Monday through Friday for lunch and dinner. Closed Saturday and Sunday. Full service, fresh juice, wine/beer/alcohol, take-out, $$.**

Cheng-I Cuisine
203 W. McMillan St., Cincinnati, OH 45219   **(513) 723-1999**
Chinese. Cheng-I is a traditional Chinese restaurant with an extensive vegetarian menu. The Vegetarian Spring Rolls were voted best vegetarian appetizer by "Cincinnati Magazine." **Open Monday through Saturday for lunch and dinner. Open Sunday for dinner. Full service,** vegetarian options, wine/beer/alcohol, catering, take-out, VISA/MC/AMEX/DISC/DC, $$.

Floyd's of Cincinnati, Inc.
129 Calhoun St., Cincinnati, OH 45219   **(513) 221-2434**
Middle Eastern. Various vegetarian Middle Eastern dishes, including tabbouleh, baba ghanouj, hummus, falafel sandwich, and salads are offered at Floyd's. **Open Monday through Saturday for lunch and dinner. Closed Sunday. Full service,** vegan options, take-out, $.

Indigo Casual Gourmet Café
2637 Erie Ave, Cincinnati, OH 45208   **(513) 321-9952**
American. Indigo offers a wide variety of vegetarian meals. On their menu, you can simply look for the "V" symbol, indicating a meatless dish. Located near Hyde Park Square, Indigo is earthy and informal, yet suitable for business entertaining. **Open daily for lunch and dinner. Full service,** beer/wine/alcohol, non-alcoholic beer/wine, VISA/MC/AMEX/DISC/DC, $$$.

Johnny Chan 2
11296 Montgomery Rd., Cincinnati, OH 45249   **(513) 489-2388**
Asian. An extensive selection of meatless dishes are available at Johnny Chan 2. Some include Bean Curd Vegetable Hot Pot, Yu Hsiang Eggplant, Spicy Szechuan String Beans, among many others. **Open daily for lunch and dinner. Buffet,** vegan options, senior discounts.

Lemon Grass Thai Cuisine
2666 Madison Rd., Cincinnati, OH 45208   **(513) 321-2882**
Thai. At Lemon Grass, you'll find a wide variey of dishes, including an entirely vegetarian section on the menu. Plus, nearly all other dishes can be prepared meatless, and if done so, the adaptation and modified price are listed directly on the menu! Reservations are recommended but not required at this informal restaurant. **Open Monday through Friday for lunch and dinner. Open Saturday and Sunday for dinner. Full service,** vegan options, VISA/MC/AMEX/DISC, $-$$.

• Manna Vegetarian Deli
633 Main St., Cincinnati, OH 45202   **(513) 241-8343**
Vegetarian deli. Located near the Aranoff Center, Manna offers such delicious dishes as Seven Bean Barley soup, Barcelona Sweet Pea Soup, a barbeque wrap, Adam's Barbeque Rib, a vegan Southwestern Chili Wrap, Vegetarian Lasagna, and Curry Tofu Chicken Salad. They also do special catering for pre-schools, holidays, business luncheons, and other events. **Open Monday through Friday for lunch. Closed Saturday and Sunday. Limited service,** vegan options, fresh juices, smoothies, catering, VISA/MC/AMEX/DISC, $. www.eat-better.com/deli

Mayura Restaurant
3201 Jefferson Ave., Cincinnati, OH 45220   **(513) 221-7125**
Indian. This Indian restaurant with its attached bar offers many vegetarian dishes. **Open**

Tuesday through Saturday for lunch and dinner. Closed Sunday and Monday. Full service, wine/beer/alcohol, catering, take-out, VISA/MC/AMEX/DISC, $$.

Mullane's Parkside Café
723 Race St., Cincinnati, OH 45202 **(513) 381-1331**
Natural foods. Located next door to the Cincinnati Shakespeare Festival, this restaurant can give vegetarians and their meat-eating friends great pre-performance meal offerings. The menu includes hummus and vegetables, the Veggieburger Through the Garden, a tofu bagel sandwich, and red beans and rice. Tofu or tempeh may be substituted in all entrées, such as spinach or vegetable sautés. **Open Monday through Friday for lunch and dinner. Open Saturday for dinner only. Closed Sunday. Limited service, vegan options, VISA/MC, $$.**

Myra's Dionysus
121 Calhoun St., Cincinnati, OH 45219 **(513) 961-1578**
International. Myra's has an extensive international menu, including Middle Eastern, Chinese, Greek, Brazilian, Mexican, Turkish, Indian, and Italian dishes.The menu features an incredible variety of excellent soups and many vegan selections. Outdoor seating is available. **Open Monday through Saturday for lunch and dinner. Open Sunday for dinner. Full service, vegan options, wine/beer, catering, take-out, $.**

Pacific Moon Café
8300 Market Pl., Cincinnati, OH 45242 **(513) 891-0091**
Chinese. This restaurant's menu features the history of the Chin family (who run Pacific Moon Café), facts about historic Hong Kong, and best of all, a vegetarian section with dishes like Vegetarian Hot and Sour Ribs, Szechuan Green Beans, and Ma Po Tofu. Outdoor dining near an herb garden is available. **Open daily for lunch and dinner. Full service, vegan options, non-alcoholic wine/beer, wine/beer, catering, take-out, VISA/MC/AMEX/DISC/DC, $$.** www.pacificmooncafe.com

Red Apple Deli & Café
6911 Miami Ave., Cincinnati, OH 45243 **(513) 271-6766**
Natural foods. The Red Apple Deli & Cafe offers Barbecue Tofu, Stir-Fry Vegetables with Rice, vegetarian chili, veggie burgers, veggie lasagna, various salads, and much more. **Open daily for lunch and dinner. Counter service, vegan options, fresh juices, take-out, VISA/MC/AMEX/DISC, $.**

Susan's Natural World
8315 Beechmont Ave., Cincinnati, OH 45255 **(513) 474-4990**
Natural foods. Susan's is a natural foods store with a juice bar. Two vegetarian soups are available daily, and there are numerous meatless sandwiches to choose from. Organic products are used when possible. **Open Monday through Saturday for lunch and dinner. Open Sunday for lunch. Limited service, vegan options, fresh juices, coffee, $.**

Tandoor India
8702 Market Place Ln., Cincinnati, OH 45242 **(513) 793-7484**
Indian. At Tandoor India, you'll find various vegetarian selections, including the vegetable samosas, mushroom mattar, and daal. This totally non-smoking, informal establishment

is located near King's Island, a local attraction. **Open Monday through Saturday for lunch and dinner. Closed Sunday. Full service, vegan options, take-out, special drinks, VISA/MC/ AMEX/DC, $$.** www.tandoor.com

• Udipi Café
7633 Reading Rd., Cincinnati, OH 45237   **(513) 821-2021**
Vegetarian/Indian. Udipi Café features highly affordable South Indian-style cuisine, including vegetable uthappam (Indian pancakes), dosas, and curries. The iddly (lentil and rice flour dumplings) and chana batura (bread and garbanzo beans) come highly recommended. Eggs are not used, but some of the recipes do employ yogurt. This restaurant offers a daily buffet. **Open Wednesday through Monday for lunch and dinner. Closed Tuesday. Full service, vegan options, VISA/MC, $$.**

What's For Dinner?
3009 O'Bryon St., Cincinnati, OH 45208   **(513) 321-4404**
Eclectic. Located near historic O'Bryonville on Madison Rd., What's for Dinner serves an award-winning veggie burger and meatless sloppy joes. While dining in the earthy atmos- phere, you'll find a daily variety of vegetarian casseroles, salads, and soups. **Open Monday through Saturday for lunch and dinner. Closed Sunday. Limited service, vegan options, take-out, catering, special drinks, VISA/MC/AMEX, $$.**

CLEVELAND

(For restaurant listings in the surrounding areas, see Berea, Cleveland Heights, Hudson, Independence, Lakewood, Middleburg Heights, North Olmsted, Solon, South Euclid, Westlake, and Willoughby.)

Ali Baba Restaurant
12021 Lorain Rd., Cleveland, OH 44111   **(216) 251-2040**
Middle Eastern. Ali Baba's menu features delicious Middle Eastern specialties created from recipes by the owner's grandmother. Their falafel, hummus, and baba ghanouj are outstand- ing. Brown rice, whole-wheat pitas, and all other foods are prepared without MSG, artificial flavorings, or preservatives. The hosts are friendly, cheerful, and accommodating. **Open Tuesday through Friday for lunch and dinner. Open Saturday for dinner only. Closed Sunday and Monday. Full service, catering, take-out, $$.**

Co-op Café
2130 Adelbert Rd., Cleveland, OH 44106   **(216) 368-3095**
Natural foods. Located inside a fitness center called One to One, this non-profit café is open to non-club members as well as club members. Dishes, made at Food Co-op a couple blocks away, include Middle Eastern fare, Tofu-Stuffed Ravioli, and the Power Burger. **Open Monday through Saturday for three meals. Closed Sunday. Limited service, vegan options, fresh juices, smoothies, take-out, $.**

Empress Taytu
6125 St. Clair Ave., Cleveland, OH 44103   **(216) 391-9400**
Ethiopian. Sample traditional vegetarian Ethiopian flavors with a serving of Lentils in Berbere Sauce or Mixed Legumes with Ginger Root, Rue Seed and Bishops Weed. Or just allow

yourself to be are immersed in authentic Ethiopian music, art, and culture. **Open Monday through Friday for lunch. Open Tuesday through Sunday for dinner. Full service, $$.**

• Limbo
12706 Larchmere Blvd., Cleveland, OH 44120 **(216) 707-3333**

Vegetarian. Limbo offers a great vegetarian menu of soups, salads, pizzas, sandwiches, entrées, and breakfast items. Try the Hummus and Pita with Black Olives and Cherry Tomatoes, a Mock Pepperoni and Mushroom pizza, a Four-Layer Spinach Lasagna, or a Falafel Burger with Lime Avocado Spread on a Knotted Sesame Bun. All dairy cheeses are rennet-free, and all eggs used are from free-range chickens that are hormone- and antibiotic-free. Smoking is limited to the patio and front porch areas. **Open Tuesday for breakfast and lunch. Open Wednesday through Saturday for three meals. Open Sunday for breakfast and lunch. Closed Monday. Limited service, vegan options, fresh juices, smoothies, soymilk, espresso/cappuccino, special drinks, take-out, catering, $.**

Shticks Kosher Dairy Restaurant
11291 Euclid Ave., Cleveland, OH 44106 **(216) 231-0922**

Kosher. This friendly kosher restaurant is located on the Case Western Reserve University campus. The menu is vegetarian apart from a few fish dishes. Try their homemade soups, unique wraps, falafel, and daily specials. **Open Monday through Thursday for lunch and dinner. Open Friday for lunch only. Closed Saturday and Sunday. Limited service, catering, $.**

CLEVELAND HEIGHTS

Aladdin's Eatery
12447 Cedar Rd., Cleveland Heights, OH 44106 **(216) 932-4333**

Middle Eastern. See description under Akron, OH.

Tommy's
1820 Coventry Rd., Cleveland Heights, OH 44118 **(216) 321-7757**

Greek. Cleveland Heights natives have told us Tommy's is the place to go. Service is always friendly, and the atmosphere is very enjoyable. Menu items include tofu scamble and meatless sausage links for breakfast; salads; pizzas; seitan, tempeh, and tofu sandwiches; veggie burgers and dogs; falafel; hummus; spinach or potato pies; and dairy-free ice cream. **Open daily for three meals. Full service, vegan options, fresh juices, smoothies, soymilk, take-out, VISA/MC, $-$$.** www.tommyscoventry.com

Yaakov's Kosher Restaurant
13969 Cedar Rd., Cleveland Heights, OH 44118 **(216) 932-8848**

Kosher. Excellent pizza, falafel, hummus, baba ghanouj, and eggplant Parmesan are featured at Yaakov's. **Open Sunday through Thursday for lunch and dinner. Open Friday for lunch. Open Saturday after sunset. Cafeteria, vegan options, take-out, $.**

Restaurant codes: ✿ Reviewers' Choice • Vegetarian Restaurant •• Vegan Restaurant
Restaurant prices: **$** less than $6 **$$** $6-$12 **$$$** more than $12
Credit Cards Accepted: VISA - VISA MC - MasterCard AMEX - American Express
DISC - Discover DC - Diner's Club

COLUMBUS

(For restaurant listings in the surrounding areas, see Gahanna and Reynoldsburg.)

Aladdin's Eatery
2931 N. High St., Columbus, OH 43202   **(614) 262-2414**
Middle Eastern. See description under Akron, OH.

• Annapurna Indian Vegetarian Restaurant
5657 Emporium Sq., Columbus, OH 43231   **(614) 523-3640**
Vegetarian/Indian. The menu includes samosas, curry dishes, and rice made with cashews, golden raisins, and green peas. You can choose from a buffet or order á la carte. The service here is friendly, and interesting tapestries liven up an otherwise bland décor. **Open Tuesday through Sunday for lunch and dinner. Closed Monday. Full service, vegan options, take-out, catering, VISA/MC, $$.**

• Benevolence
41 W. Swan St., Columbus, OH 43215   **(614) 221-9330**
Vegetarian. This is a highly environmentally-conscious business with an emphasis on fresh, natural ingredients. Lunch is served at large, meet-your-neighbor tables. Bread is baked fresh each morning, and soup and salad choices vary daily. **Open Monday through Saturday for lunch. Open Saturday for breakfast. Closed Sunday. Limited service, vegan options, take-out, non-smoking, VISA/MC, $$.**

•• Dragonfly Restaurant
247 King Ave., Columbus, OH 43201   **(614) 298-9986**
Vegan. This upscale, contemporary establishment use organic ingredients whenever possible to make their unique dishes. Offerings include Oyster Mushroom Caesar Salad, Mediterranean Pizza with marinated figs and grilled eggplant, Seitan and Tempeh Chorizo-Style, and the White Devil (chocolate mousse and coconut layer cake). **Open Tuesday through Saturday for lunch and dinner. Closed Monday. Full service, fresh juices, wine/beer, special drinks, non-smoking, take-out, catering, VISA/MC/AMEX/DISC, $$-$$$.** www.dragonflyneov.com

Estrada's Restaurant
240 King Ave., Columbus, OH 43201   **(614) 294-0808**
Mexican. Estrada's offers the best Mexican food in town—inexpensive, fresh, and good. There are many vegetarian and a few vegan options offered. Lard is not used in the preparation of the food. **Open Monday through Saturday for lunch and dinner. Closed Sunday. Full service, vegan options, catering, take-out, DISC, $.**

Nong's Hunan Express
1634 Northwest Blvd., Columbus, OH 43212   **(614) 486-6630**
Thai. Nong's offers a huge variety of vegetarian dishes, including soups and egg rolls. The atmosphere is casual and relaxed. **Open Monday through Friday for lunch and dinner. Open Saturday and Sunday for dinner only. Full service, vegetarian options, take-out, $$.**

Rigsby's Cuisine Volatile
698 N. High St., Columbus, OH 43215   **(614) 461-7888**
American. The atmosphere at Rigsby's is formal. The menu offers several vegetarian and a few vegan selections. **Open Monday through Saturday for lunch and dinner. Closed Sunday. Full service, vegan options, VISA, $$.**

Taj Mahal Indian & Pakistani Cuisine
2247 N. High St., Columbus, OH 43201   **(614) 294-0208**
Indian. Taj Mahal serves authentic Indian and Pakistani cuisine. Try any number of dishes from the Vegetarian Specialties section of the menu, including Matar Paneer, Chana Masala, Alu Gobi, and many more. Taste a vegetable samosa or a homemade dessert. **Open Tuesday through Sunday for lunch and dinner. Closed Monday. Buffet for lunch, full service for dinner, vegan options, $-$$$.**

• Udipi Café
2001 E. Dublin Granville Rd., Columbus, OH 43229-3510   **(614) 885-7446**
Vegetarian/Indian. This highly-recommended restaurant offers a wide range of primarily vegan Indian dishes, including soups, curries, and dosas, at inexpensive prices. The service is prompt, and the weekday lunch buffet is extremely popular. **Open Wednesday through Monday for lunch and dinner. Closed Tuesday. Full service, vegan options, VISA/MC, $-$$.**

• Whole World Restaurant and Bakery
3269 N. High St., Columbus, OH 43202   **(614) 268-5751**
Vegetarian/American. Whole World offers Tofu Sloppy Joes, veggie burgers, whole-wheat vegan pizzas, great vegetarian soups, and baked goods made without sugar. A wide variety of entrées is offered. **Open Tuesday through Sunday for lunch and dinner. Closed Monday. Full service, vegan options, BYOB, take-out, catering, $-$$.**

• Woodlands Vegetarian Restaurant
Olentangy Sq. Plaza, 816 Bethel Rd., Columbus, OH 43214   **(614) 459-4101**
Vegetarian/Indian. Located near Ohio State University, Woodlands offers a menu of South Indian food, including soups, pakoras, dosas, idlys, curried vegetables. The lentil crepes are especially good. **Open Tuesday through Sunday for lunch and dinner. Closed Monday. Full service, vegan options, take-out, catering, VISA/MC, $$.**

World's Best Bagels
714 N. High St., Columbus, OH 43215   **(614) 294-0567**
Bagel deli. See description under Athens, OH.

DAYTON

(For restaurant listings in the surrounding areas, see Fairborn, Kettering, Miamisburg, Springfield, and Yellow Springs.)

Euro Bistro
5524 Airway Rd., Dayton, OH 45431   **(513) 256-3444**
Natural foods. This smoke-free bistro offers freshly baked breads, specialty sandwiches, homemade salads, soups, quiche, and incredible cookies and cheesecakes. Outdoor seating

available in season. **Open Monday through Saturday. Closed Sunday. Limited service, catering, take-out, $.**

Little Saigon
1718 Woodman Dr., Dayton, OH 45420   **(937) 258-8010**
Vietnamese. An extensive list of vegetarian selections is offered at Little Saigon. Some meatless dishes include sweet and sour vegetable soup, mixed vegetables with black bean sauce, sate vegetable fried rice, or marinated mushrooms in a clay pot. **Open Monday through Saturday for lunch and dinner. Closed Sunday. Full service, vegan options, beer/wine, $-$$.**

FAIRBORN

Euro Bistro
1328 Kauffman Ave., Fairborn, OH 45324   **(513) 878-1989**
Natural foods. See description under Dayton, OH.

FINDLAY

•• Squeaker's Vegetarian Café
601 N. Main St., Findlay, OH 45840   **(419) 424-3990**
Vegan. See description under Bowling Green, OH.

GAHANNA

Aladdin's Eatery
1307 Stoneridge Dr., Gahanna, OH 43230   **(614) 472-2500**
Middle Eastern. See description under Akron, OH.

GRANDVIEW

Aladdin's Eatery
1423-B Grandview Ave., Grandview, OH 43212   **(614) 488-5565**
Middle Eastern. See description under Akron, OH.

HOLLAND

The Grape Leaf Diner
909 S. McCord Rd., #6, Holland, OH 43528   **(419) 868-9099**
Middle Eastern. Vegetarian options, which are marked with a grape leaf, include Vegetarian Stuffed Cabbage, Vegetarian Kebabs, Greek Spinach Pie, Mushroom Sauté, falafel, and several other items. **Open daily for lunch and dinner. Full service, vegan options, fresh juices, catering, take-out, VISA/MC/DISC, $-$$.**

HUDSON

Pad Thai
5657 Darrow Rd., Hudson, OH 44236-4013   **(330) 650-9998**
Thai. Pad Thai's menu includes appetizers, soups, noodle and fried rice dishes, and desserts.

It also features more than 40 vegetarian entrées, such as Basil Vegetarian Stir-Fry, Avocado Tofu, Garlic Eggplant, and Tofu or Vegetables made with yellow, green, or red curries. **Open daily for lunch and dinner. Full service, vegan options, reservations accepted, beer/wine/ alcohol, catering, VISA/MC/AMEX/DISC, $$.** www.pad-thairestaurant.com

INDEPENDENCE

Aladdin's Eatery
6901 Rockside Rd., Independence, OH 44131   **(216) 642-7550**
Middle Eastern. See description under Akron, OH.

KETTERING

• Kettering Hospital Cafeteria
3535 Southern Blvd., Kettering, OH 45429   **(513) 296-7262**
Hospital cafeteria/vegetarian. A changing menu offers both vegetarian and vegan options, vegetarian sandwiches and burgers, an extensive salad bar, fresh baked breads, and desserts. **Open daily for three meals. Cafeteria, vegan options, $.**

LAKEWOOD

Aladdin's Eatery
14536 Detroit Rd., Lakewood, OH 44107   **(216) 521-4005**
Middle Eastern. See description under Akron, OH.

MIAMISBURG

• Sycamore Hospital Cafeteria
2150 Leiter Rd., Miamisburg, OH 45342   **(513) 866-0551**
Vegetarian. This establishment offers a changing menu that includes both vegetarian and vegan options, vegetarian sandwiches, a salad bar, fresh baked breads, and desserts. **Open daily for three meals. Cafeteria, vegan options, $.**

MIDDLEBURG HEIGHTS

Aladdin's Eatery
18334 E. Bagley Rd., Middleburg Heights, OH 44130   **(440) 243-0800**
Middle Eastern. See description under Akron, OH.

NORTH CANTON

Bombay Sitar
4633 Belden Village St. NW, North Canton, OH 44718   **(330) 493-0671**
Indian. Bombay Sitar offers many vegetarian appetizers and entrées, including Vegetable Jal Frazi, Mushroom Matar (peas), Alo Chhole (potatoes and chickpeas), Alo Palak (potatoes and spinach), Bayngan Bharta (eggplant), and Bhindi Masala (orka). **Open daily for lunch and dinner. Full service, vegan options, catering, VISA/MC/AMEX/DISC, $$.** http://rrenner.home.igc.org/bombaysitar

NORTH OLMSTED
Kashmir Palace
26703 Brookpark Rd., North Olmsted, OH 44070   **(216) 779-5774**
Indian. Vegetarian selections include Chole, Matar Paneer, and curry dishes. **Open daily for dinner. Full service, smoothies, take-out, VISA/MC/AMEX/DISC, $$.**

REYNOLDSBURG
Sun Tong Luck Restaurant
6517 E. Livingston Ave., Reynoldsburg, OH 43068   **(614) 863-2828**
Chinese. Vegetarian dishes at Sun Tong include moo shu vegetable, vegetable lo mein, and Szechuan tofu. The friendly staff here is completely willing to accommodate special orders. **Open Tuesday through Saturday for lunch and dinner. Closed Sunday and Monday. Full service, vegan options, special drinks, VISA/MC/DISC, $-$$.**

SOLON
Mustard Seed Market Café
6025 Kruse Dr., Solon, OH 44139   **(440) 519-FOOD**
Natural foods/macrobiotic. See description under Akron, OH. This is the newer of the two locations.

SOUTH EUCLID
Peking Gourmet and Chinese Restaurant
13955 Cedar Rd., South Euclid, OH 44118   **(216) 397-9939**
Chinese. Peking's separate vegetarian menu includes 70 vegetarian and vegan items, some of which include mock meats. They even serve vegan cheesecake. **Open Monday through Saturday for lunch and dinner. Open Sunday for dinner. Full service, vegan options, wine/beer/alcohol, non-alcoholic wine/beer, take-out, VISA/MC/AMEX/DISC/DC, $.**

SPRINGFIELD
•• Strange Brew Coffee House
227 Cecil St., Springfield, OH 45503   **(937) 322-4233**
Vegan. This earthy restaurant serves non-dairy breakfasts such as Wheat-Meat Sausage with Biscuits and Gravy and Banana Walnut French Toast. Lunch and dinner items include Mr. Chic-A-Pea Potent No-Pocket Platter, mock tuna and mock egg salads, Miso Soup over Rice and Bok Choy, and a Blue Plate special. Also, they offer 50 different kinds of tea. **Open daily for three meals. Full service, take-out, fresh juices, macrobiotic options, espresso/cappuccino, smoothies, soymilk, $.** www.strangebrew4u.com

(For restaurant listings in the surrounding areas, see Bowling Green and Holland.)

Jalmer's Health Foods

1488 Sylvania Ave., Toledo, OH 43612 **(419) 478-7918**

Health foods store deli. Look for several veggie selections. **Open Monday through Saturday. Closed Sunday.** Limited service, fresh juices, take-out, VISA/MC, $.

Manos Greek Restaurant

1701 Adams St., Toledo, OH 43624 **(419) 244-4479**

Greek. At Manos, choose from several appetizers and main dishes, including Baked Garlic, Marinated Artichoke Hearts, Spinach Pie, Baked Butter Beans, and Vegetarian Gyro. **Open Monday through Friday for lunch and dinner. Open Saturday for dinner. Closed Sunday.** Full service, espresso/cappuccino, catering, VISA/MC/DISC/DC, $$.

Tandoor

2247 S. Reynolds Rd., Toledo, OH 43614 **(419) 385-7467**

Indian. Tandoor is located one mile away from exit 4 of the Ohio Turnpike. You will find a wide selection of vegetarian curry dishes and Indian breads. **Open for lunch and dinner.** Full service, vegan options, wine/beer/alcohol, take-out, VISA/MC, $$.

•• The Web of Life Natural Foods Market

25923 Detroit Rd., Westlake, OH 44145 **(440) 899-2882**

Vegan deli in a natural foods store. The Web of Life is an all-vegan, mostly organic restaurant, deli, and juice bar. Some of their many offerings include soups, Save the Fish Sticks, the Lasagna Dinner with salad, Open-Faced Tofurky, a Mediterranean Plate, vegan or oat burgers, tofu sandwiches, Meatless Meatball Subs, Falafel Roll-Ups, Veggie Dogs, Peanut Butter or Almond Butter n' Jelly sandwiches, pizzas made with vegan organic pizza dough, and Oats-creme Cones for dessert. **Open Monday through Saturday for three meals. Open Sunday for lunch and early dinner.** Limited service, fresh juices, smoothies, soymilk, special drinks, take-out, catering, VISA/MC/AMEX/DISC, $. www.weboflifewestlake.com

• Just Natural Health Foods

38669 Mentor Ave., Willoughby, OH 44094 **(440) 954-8638**

Vegetarian/natural foods. They offer delicious vegetarian and vegan breakfasts, lunches, and dinners for eat-in or carry-out, as well as a wide variety of groceries. **Open Monday through Friday for three meals. Open Saturday for brunch. Closed Sunday.** Counter service, vegan options, soymilk, smoothies, take-out, fresh juices, VISA/MC/DISC, $. www.justnatural healthfoods.com

Ha Ha Pizza

108 Xenia Ave., Yellow Springs, OH 45387   **(937) 767-2131**

Pizza. Ha Ha features homemade white or whole-wheat dough, sauce, and fresh vegetables. Several meat alternatives are offered. Soy cheese is available for the pizzas. **Open daily for lunch and dinner. Full service, vegan options, take-out, $.**

• Organic Grocery

230 Keiths Alley, Yellow Springs, OH 45387   **(937) 767-7215**

Vegetarian/natural foods. This vegetarian deli offers veggie chili, sandwiches, wraps, thick fruit drinks, hummus, and much more. Patio area with tables outside. This establishment is located near some local attractions, such as Antioch College, a skate park, and the eclectic and artsy village of Yellow Springs. **Open Monday through Saturday for three meals. Open Sunday for lunch. Take-out, vegan options, catering available, VISA/MC/AMEX/DISC, $.** www.folksites.com/organicgrocery

Sunrise Café

259 Xenia Ave., Yellow Springs, OH 45387   **(937) 767-1065**

Natural foods. This charming restored 1940s diner continues to expand its vegetarian offerings. They use fresh ingredients, and everything is made from scratch. **Open daily. Full service, vegan options, non-smoking, take-out, catering, VISA/MC, $.** www.sunrisecafe.com

Winds Café and Bakery

215 Xenia Ave., Yellow Springs, OH 45387   **(937) 767-1144**

Natural foods. Specialties include fresh baked breads and pastries, Scrambled Tofu, and a constantly changing menu that always includes several vegetarian selections. **Open Monday through Saturday for lunch and dinner. Open Sunday for brunch. Full service, vegan options, fresh juice, wine/beer/alcohol, take-out, VISA/MC/AMEX/DISC, $$-$$$.**

(For restaurant listings in the surrounding areas, see Boardman.)

Aladdin's Eatery

7325 South Ave., Youngstown, OH 44512   **(330) 629-6450**

Middle Eastern. See description under Akron, OH.

Oklahoma

The Earth Natural Foods & Deli

309 S. Flood St., Norman, OK 73069   **(405) 364-3551**

Natural foods deli. This deli offers sandwiches, salads, and drinks to-go. Seating is not available. **Open daily. Deli-style, vegetarian options, fresh juice, catering, take-out, VISA/MC/AMEX, $.**

OKLAHOMA CITY

(For restaurant listings in the surrounding areas, see Norman.)

Gopuram Taste of India

4559 NW 23rd St., Oklahoma City, OK 73127   **(405) 948-7373**

Indian. This restaurant serves both northern and southern Indian cuisine. They offer many selections for vegans daily and feature a vegetarian buffet every Wednesday night. Live sitar music is featured in the evenings. **Open daily for lunch and dinner. Full service, vegan options, non-alcoholic beer, wine/beer/alcohol, take-out, catering, VISA/MC/AMEX/ DISC/DC, $-$$.**

Grateful Bean Café

1039 N. Walker Ave., Oklahoma City, OK 73102   **(405) 236-3503**

Natural foods. Several vegetarian options for breakfast, lunch, and dinner are available, including Tofu Scramble, Nancy's Bean Burger, and Rob's Powerhouse Veggie. **Open Monday through Friday for lunch. Closed Saturday and Sunday. Full service, vegan options, smoothies, cappuccino, take-out, catering, VISA/MC/AMEX/DISC, $$.**

SULPHUR

•• Lifestyle Center Of America Restaurant

Rte. 1, Goddard Youth Camp Rd., Sulphur, OK 73086   **(800) 213-8955**

Vegan. Located amidst 1,700 acres of native forest and the picturesque lake of the Arbuckles, the world-class Lifestyle Center of America and restaurant is dedicated to ensuring a healthy life through the power of diet, exercise, and stress management. There are center tours every day at 2 p.m. **Open Sunday through Friday for three meals. Closed Saturday. Cafeteria, vegan options, reservations required, non-smoking, special drinks, VISA/MC, $$.** www.lifestylecenter.org

TULSA

Bangkok Restaurant

3313 E. 32nd Pl., Tulsa, OK 74135   **(918) 743-9669**

Thai. Try the Pad Thai Pak, made with oriental vegetables, ground peanuts, and egg, or the Ghang Ped Pak, made with red curry paste, oriental vegetables, and coconut milk. Any entrée on the menu can be prepared without meat. **Open Monday through Saturday for lunch and dinner. Closed Sunday. Full service, vegan options, VISA/MC/AMEX/DC, $$.**

Big Al's Subs and Health Foods

3303 E. 15th St., Tulsa, OK 74112   **(918) 744-5080**

Deli. Open since 1975 and smoke-free for more than 10 years, Big Al's has a separate vegetarian menu featuring a veggie loaf, several different types of salads, subs, and burritos. **Open Monday through Friday for lunch and dinner. Open Saturday for lunch. Closed Sunday. Buffet, vegan options, take-out, fresh juices, smoothies, $.**

Casa Laredo

1114 E. 41st St., Tulsa, OK 74105   **(918) 743-3744**
6526 E. 51st St., Tulsa, OK 74145   **(918) 610-0086**

Mexican. Casa Laredo has several vegetarian options available. Live music is provided six days a week. **Open daily for lunch and dinner. Full service, VISA/MC/AMEX/DISC, $-$$.**

Cedar's Import Restaurant and Deli

2606 S. Sheridan Rd., Tulsa, OK 74105   **(918) 835-5519**

Deli. Try the Lentil & Celery Soup, Falafel, Veggie Cabbage Roll Dinner, or Sampler Veggie Dinner. **Open daily for lunch and dinner. Limited service, vegan options, catering, $.**

Thai Chef Restaurant

9720 E. 31st St., Ste. G, Tulsa, OK 74146   **(918) 663-6576**

Thai. Explore the exotic flavors of Thailand at this restaurant, which boasts a varied menu with many vegetarian and vegan options prepared to fit your tastes. **Open Tuesday through Sunday for lunch and dinner. Closed Monday. Full service, vegan options, take-out, reservations recommended for large parties, non-smoking, soymilk, special drinks, beer, VISA/MC/AMEX/DISC/DC, $$.**

Oregon

ALOHA

Green Bean Café and Market

14125 SW Walker Rd., Aloha, OR 97006   **(503) 644-4442**

Health foods store deli. Part of a health foods store, the Green Bean Café is a casual spot with lots of candles, a vaulted ceiling, and sage-green walls with a hand-painted border of fruits and vegetables. Offerings include organic coffee drinks, speltbread, almond cheese, personal pizzas, and meat substitutes, such as vegetarian hot dogs and burgers, faux chicken-breast sandwiches, and a Tu-No salad. Also, the space is host to acoustic music on weekday evenings. **Open daily for three meals. Cafeteria, vegan options, smoothies, soymilk, VISA/MC/DISC, $.**

ASHLAND

Ashland Food Cooperative

237 N. First St., Ashland, OR 97520   **(541) 482-2237**

Deli. Located in the Historic Railroad District, Ashland's only natural foods co-op is dedicated to providing the highest quality organic produce and whole foods possible. Their deli offers hot soups, hot entrées, a sandwich bar, dips and spreads, grab-and-go foods, and fresh bakery items. **Open daily. Limited service, vegan options, fresh juices, take-out, VISA/MC/DISC, $-$$.** www.ashlandfood.coop

Geppetto's

345 E. Main St., Ashland, OR 97520   **(541) 482-1138**

Italian. Enjoy a wide selection of vegetarian meals at Geppetto's, including a Parmesan breaded tofu patty with spaghetti and pesto sauce, twice baked potatoes with your choice of toppings, marinated cucumber sandwiches, and great eggplant burgers. **Open daily for three meals. Full service, vegan options, fresh juices, wine/beer/alcohol, take-out, VISA/MC, $-$$$.** www.geppettosrestaurant.com

Greenleaf

49 N. Main St., Ashland, OR 97520   **(541) 482-2808**

Italian. Located in the refurbished, old downtown area, the Greenleaf has both a patio and view of the river. Suitable for business entertaining, the menu includes tofu burgers, Greek vegan and veggie chef salads, baked potatoes, pasta, and a vegetarian soup of the day. There is also a wide range of box lunches, fresh baked desserts, breakfast options including Tofu Scramble, and á la carte options. **Open daily for three meals. Full service, vegan options, non-smoking, espresso, beer/wine, catering, $-$$.** www.greenleafrestaurant.com

House of Thai Cuisine

1667 Siskiyou Blvd., Ashland, OR 97520   **(541) 488-2583**

Thai. This family-owned and operated restaurant offers a separate vegetarian menu. It was voted "Best Oriental restaurant in Ashland" in 1992. **Open Monday through Friday for lunch and dinner. Open Saturday and Sunday for dinner. Full service, wine/beer, take-out, catering, VISA/MC, $$.**

Jade Dragon

2270 Hwy. 66, Ashland, OR 97520   **(541) 482-8220**

Chinese/Thai. Jade Dragon offers an extensive, separate vegetarian menu with such delicious options as Black Bean Sauce Vegetables with Baked Tofu, Sautéed Broccoli in Garlic Sauce, and Cashews with Vegetables and Baked Tofu. **Open Monday through Saturday for lunch and dinner. Closed Sunday. Full service, $-$$.**

The Natural Café

358 E. Main St., Ashland, OR 97520   **(541) 488-5493**

Juice bar/café/bakery. The Natural Café and Juice Bar offers all-natural and mostly organic foods, as well as a large selection of vegetarian entrées, salads, sandwiches, and pasta. Try the tempeh tacos, which feature grilled soy tempeh and onions in a zesty red sauce on corn tortillas. You have your choices of toppings including cheddar and jack cheeses, shredded lettuce, and sprouts. **Open daily for lunch and dinner. Full service, vegan options, fresh juices, espresso, beer/wine, smoothies, $-$$.**

• Pilaf

18 Calle Guanajuato, Ashland, OR 97520   **(541) 488-7898**

Vegetarian. Located near Ashland Creek, Pilaf's international menu includes pakoras (potato fritters), Portobello Poorboys, Artichoke Panini Sandwiches, Fusion Burritos on a tomato tortilla, Papas ala Brava (chunky fried potatoes swirled with sour cream and hot pepper sauce), and Greek, Turkish, Middle Eastern, Vegan, or other sampler plates. For dessert, try the mango mousse, the vegan chocolate silk pie, or the baklava. Vegan menu items are noted. This restaurant also offers take-out platters for picnics. **Open Tuesday through Saturday for lunch and dinner. Open Sunday for brunch. Closed Monday. Full service, vegan options, soymilk, espresso/cappuccino, beer/wine, non-alcoholic beer/wine, take-out, catering, VISA/MC, $-$$.** www.globalpantry.com/pilaf/

Señor Sam's Mexican Grill

1634 Ashland St., Ashland, OR 97520   **(541) 488-1262**

Mexican. Señor Sam's grills delicious Mexican fare with a separate menu available for vegetarians. Try the spicy Veggie Tamale or the Veggie Fajita Burrito stuffed with rice, beans, green, red, and gold bell peppers, onions, and tomatoes. **Open daily for lunch and dinner. Full service, fresh juices, beer/wine/alcohol, $.**

ASTORIA

Cannery Café

1 6th St., Astoria, OR 97103   **(503) 325-8642**

American. Dine with a view of the Colombia River in this warm, clean, and creative café specializing in healthy homemade food. **Open daily for lunch and dinner. Full service,** reservations recommended, espresso/cappuccino, soymilk, beer/wine/alcohol, non-alcoholic beer/wine, catering, VISA/MC/DISC/DC, $$-$$$.

The Columbia Café

1114 Marine Dr., Astoria, OR 97103   **(503) 325-2233**

Natural foods. Here you'll find lots of delicious vegetarian and vegan food, including rice and veggie dishes, bean burritos, homemade pasta, and other international options. Salsas are made from all types of fruits and vegetables. Crepes are a specialty. **Open Sunday through Tuesday for breakfast and lunch. Open Wednesday through Saturday for three meals. Full** service, vegan options, fresh juices, wine/beer, non-alcoholic beer, $$.

BEAVERTON

Swagat Indian Cuisine

4325 SW 109th Ave., Beaverton, OR 97005   **(503) 626-3000**

Indian. Swagat offers traditional northern and southern Indian dishes during its lunch buffet and for dinner. Try a Dal Curry (lentils made with spinach and tomatoes), Aloo Saag (spinach and potatoes cooked with mild spices), and Navratan Koorma (nine vegetables in a mild cream sauce). Reservations recommended. Swagat also hosts tango, swing, and social dance lessons in the evenings. **Open daily for lunch and dinner. Full service, vegan options,** beer/wine/alcohol, take-out, catering, VISA/MC/AMEX/DISC/DC, $$.

Thai Orchid Restaurant

18070 NW Evergreen Pkwy., Ste. C, Beaverton, OR 97006   **(503) 439-6683**
16165 SW Regatta Ln., Beaverton, OR 97006   **(503) 617-4602**

Thai. Thai Orchid offers more than 40 vegetarian dishes, cooked in a traditional Thai manner with no MSG or hydrogenated oil added. Options include Pra Ram stir-fry (with broccoli and topped with peanut sauce), Pad Kai Yad Sai (a Thai Omelette made with ground tofu, onions, tomatoes, and bean sauce, wrapped in scrambled eggs), Evil Jungle Noodles (medium rice noodles on a bed of steamed cabbage with bean sprouts and curry sauce), soups, salads, curries, and more. **Open daily for lunch and dinner. Full service, VISA/MC/AMEX/DISC,** $$. www.thaiorchid.citysearch.com

BEND

Baja Norte
801 NW Wall St., Bend, OR 97701 (541) 385-0611

Mexican. Baja Norte offers a few vegetarian options, including artichoke quesadillas, veggie tacos, veggie burritos, veggie tostadas, and veggie fajitas. **Open daily for three meals. Limited service, take-out, $.** www.centormall.com/baja_norte

Colors - A Full Spectrum Eatery
1110 NW Newport Ave., Bend, OR 97701 (541) 330-8181

International. Colors is proud to be the only Central Oregon eatery to provide a third of its menu Vegan, a third Vegetarian, and a third Omnivore. This colorful and unique restaurant serves a wide variety of healthy and creative dishes inspired by cultures around the world. **Open Sunday and Monday for breakfast and lunch. Open Tuesday through Saturday for three meals. Full service, vegan options, beer/wine, $-$$.**

BRIDAL VEIL

Multnomah Falls Lodge Restaurant
50000 Historic Columbia River Hwy., Bridal Veil, OR 97010 (503) 695-2376

American. This is a standard American restaurant, but the menu does include items such as omelets, pancakes, whole oat grains oatmeal, dinner salads made with spinach or kale, a Garden burger, vegetarian rigatoni, and sweet potato fries. **Open daily for three meals. Full service, non-alcoholic beer, wine/beer/alcohol, VISA/MC/AMEX, $$.** www.multnomah fallslodge.com

CORVALLIS

The Beanery
500 SW 2nd St., Corvallis, OR 97330 (541) 753-7442
2541 NW Monroe St., Corvallis, OR 97330 (541) 757-0828

Coffeehouse. The Beanery features vegetarian lasagna, burritos, soups, salads, and desserts. **Open daily. Counter service, espresso/cappuccino, take-out, VISA/MC/DISC, $-$$.**

• Cha-Da Thai Restaurant
1945 NW 9th St., Corvallis, OR 97330 (541) 757-8223

Vegetarian/Thai. An extensive menu of vegetarian Thai entrées, appetizers and desserts is available at Cha-Da. Try the Southern Comfort Tofu, which is tofu, onions, sweet peppers, and peanuts sautéed in roasted chili sauce with a touch of red wine or even curry over jasmine rice. **Open daily for lunch and dinner. Full service, special drinks, no MSG, VISA/MC/DISC, $$.**

China Blue
2307 NW 9th St., Corvallis, OR 97330 (541) 757-8088

Chinese. China Blue has a large vegetarian selection, including Sweet and Sour Tofu and other tofu dishes. **Open Sunday through Friday for lunch and dinner. Open Saturday for dinner only. Full service, vegan options, take-out, $-$$.**

China Delight
325 NW 2nd St., Corvallis, OR 97330   **(541) 753-3753**
Chinese. Delight in China's vegetarian specialties like Spicy Sesame Tempeh or Tofu in Mandarin Sauce. **Open daily for lunch and dinner. Full service, take-out, non-smoking, no MSG, $$.**

Intaba's Kitchen
1115 SE Third St., Corvallis, OR 97333   **(541) 754-6958**
International. Enter into a world of gourmet organic cuisine at Intaba's Kitchen. Most of the menu is vegan, though they do serve some fish. The restaurant's hand-sculpted earthen oven is the birthplace of delicious whole-grain breads and build-your-own pizzas. Soups, salads, wraps, and vegan desserts are made from organic and locally grown ingredients. Unique items include Angelica's (wheat-free) Cornbread with Miso-Tahini Spread, Beer-Braised Seitan Stew, and the wood-fired Continental Wrap with basil-almond pesto, white bean spread, spinach, artichoke hearts, capers, and lemon drizzle. **Open Tuesday through Saturday for lunch and dinner. Open Sunday for brunch. Closed Monday. Full service, vegan options, fresh juices, soymilk, beer/wine, non-smoking, take-out, reservations needed for parties over six, VISA/MC, $$.** www.intabas.com

• Nearly Normal's Gonzo Cuisine
109 NW 15th St., Corvallis, OR 97330   **(541) 753-0791**
Vegetarian. This local restaurant has an extensive and diverse vegetarian menu. Great salads with seasoned tofu and homemade dressings as well as homemade desserts are featured. There are farm-fresh specials in the summertime. All visitors should have a Nearly Normal's experience while in the area! **Open Monday through Saturday for three meals. Closed Sunday. Limited service, vegan options, fresh juices, wine/beer/alcohol, take-out, catering, $-$$.**

EUGENE

(For restaurant listings in the surrounding areas, see Springfield.)

The Beanery
152 W. 5th St., Eugene, OR 97401   **(541) 342-3378**
2456 Hilyard St., Eugene, OR 97405   **(541) 344-0221**
Coffeehouse. See description under Corvallis, OR.

Café Yumm
5th St. Public Market, 296 E. 5th Ave., #108, Eugene, OR 97401 (541) 484-7302
Natural foods. International specialties include Tofu Punjabi — mango chutney, grilled curried tofu, and vegetables in a tortilla. **Open daily for lunch and dinner. Limited service, vegan options, $.**

Casablanca
5th St. Public Market, 296 E. 5th Ave., Eugene, OR 97401   **(541) 342-3885**
Middle Eastern. Enjoy a good selection of Middle Eastern vegetarian foods at Casablanca. **Open daily for lunch and dinner. Cafeteria, vegan options, take-out, $.**

The Glenwood Restaurants
1340 Alder St., Eugene, OR 97401 **(541) 343-8303**
2588 Willamette St., Eugene, OR 97405 **(541) 687-8201**
American. Enjoy a great variety of vegetarian options, including frittatas, waffles, vegetarian sausage, quiche, tofu or black bean burritos, veggie and/or tofu wraps, Garden burgers, pasta dishes, tempeh stir-fry, cabbage rolls, and much more. **Alder Street location open 24 hours daily. Willamette location open daily for three meals.** Limited service, vegan options, fresh juices, espresso/cappuccino, almond milk, wine/beer, reservations recommended, take-out, VISA/MC/AMEX/DISC, $. www.theglenwood.net

• Holy Cow Café
EMU Bldg. - Student Union, University Of Oregon-Eugene
1222 E. 13th Ave., Eugene, OR 97403 **(541) 346-2562**
Vegetarian café. Fun, festive, and feisty, Holy Cow Café offers an ever-changing range of daily specials, as well as a Mix-and-Match Menu that lets patrons choose from several kinds of tofus, veggies, noodles, beans, rice, potatoes, and sides. Cow Classics include items like Falafels; Chipotle BBQ Tofu Mash and Veggies; and Indian Soulfood (lentil dahl, vegetable curry, brown basmati rice, and apple ginger chutney). They offer Grab & Go items, two soups that change daily, and a salad bar, and they are also proud to announce they have just added pizza to their menu. **Open weekdays, but hours vary according to school schedule.** Limited service, vegan options, outdoor seating, non-smoking, soymilk, take-out, catering, $. www.emu.uoregon.edu/holy_cow_cafe.shtml

Keystone Café
395 W. 5th Ave., Eugene, OR 97401 **(541) 342-2075**
American. The Keystone Café serves breakfast at all times. Their specialty is their plate-sized pancake menu, which includes oatmeal/sesame, whole-wheat, corn/rice, and buckwheat barley varieties. **Open Monday through Friday for breakfast and lunch. Open Saturday and Sunday for breakfast only.** Full service, vegan options, fresh juice, take-out, catering, $.

• The LocoMotive Restaurant
291 E. 5th St., Eugene, OR 97401 **(541) 465-4754**
Vegetarian. LocoMotive Restaurant offers delicious dishes, including South Indian Lentil and Sherried Black Bean Soup, Sautéed Portobello Mushrooms, and Moroccan Couscous Stew over Steamed Semolina, made with organic produce when available. The menu changes weekly. **Open Wednesday through Saturday for dinner. Closed Sunday through Tuesday.** Full service, vegan options, reservations recommended, espresso/cappuccino, wine/beer, $$-$$$. www.thelocomotive.com

• Lotus Garden Vegetarian Restaurant
810 Charnelton St., Eugene, OR 97401 **(541) 344-1928**
Vegetarian/Chinese. Step into Lotus Garden for delicious vegetarian Chinese fare, such as Wheat Gluten with Pickled Napa, Bean Curd Sausage with Ginger, or Pineapple Veggie "Pork" for a reasonable price. **Open Wednesday through Monday for lunch and dinner. Closed Tuesday.** Full service, vegan options, no MSG, VISA/MC/DISC, $$.

Mekala's Thai Restaurant
1769 Franklin Blvd., Eugene, OR 97401   **(541) 342-4872**
Thai. Experience outstanding Thai vegetarian dishes containing no MSG. Only canola oil is used. Located in the 5th Street Public Market, the restaurant has a very nice atmosphere for daily dining. **Open Monday through Saturday for lunch and dinner. Open Sunday for dinner only. Full service, vegan options, fresh juices, wine/beer, take-out, catering, VISA/MC, $-$$.**

• Morning Glory Café
450 Willamette St., Eugene, OR 97401   **(541) 687-0709**
Vegetarian. This café serves breakfast all day. There is a vegan bakery on the premises, organics are used whenever possible, and even the ketchup is homemade. Breakfast menu includes vegan French toast, vegan biscuits and gravy, and vegan omelets. Lunch offers Zephyr's Marinated Tempeh, Baked Tofu Luna, or Jamaican Jerk Tempeh. On the side you can choose from Tantric Mushroom Gravy, Herbed Tofu Sour Creme, and Tofu Creme Fraiche. **Open Tuesday to Sunday for breakfast and lunch. Closed Monday. Limited service, vegan options, take-out, macrobiotic options, fresh juices, smoothies, soymilk, special drinks, $.**

• Planet Goloka
679 Lincoln St., Eugene, OR 97401   **(541) 465-4555**
Vegetarian/Indian. Planet Goloka's menu includes sandwiches, stir-fries, Garden and Boca burgers, and a selection of kava drinks. This establishment carries gifts and books and hosts kava ceremonies, live music, and chanting. **Open Monday through Friday for lunch and dinner. Open Saturday for brunch. Closed Sunday. Limited service, vegan options, fresh juices, smoothies, soymilk, special drinks, VISA/MC/AMEX/DISC, $.**

Poppi's Anatolia
992 Willamette St., Eugene, OR 97401   **(541) 343-9661**
Natural Foods/Mediterranean. This restaurant offers a wide variety of Mediterranean vegetarian dishes, including an Eggplant and Chickpea Stew, several curries, soups, and salads. **Open Monday through Saturday for lunch and dinner. Open Sunday for dinner only. Full service, wine/beer, non-alcoholic beer, take-out, VISA/MC, $$.**

Ring of Fire Restaurant and Lava Lounge
1099 Chambers St., Eugene, OR 97402   **(541) 344-6475**
Thai. Enter into the exotic with a variety of Thai noodles, curries, stir-fry, soups, and entrées topped with your choice of tofu or tempeh. For dessert, visit the lounge with its tempting cocktails and mixed drinks. **Open daily for lunch and dinner. Full service, vegan options, catering, take-out, fresh juices, beer/wine/alcohol, VISA/MC, $$-$$$.** www.ringoffire restaurant.com

• Sam Bond's Garage
407 Blair Blvd., Eugene, OR 97402   **(541) 431-6603**
Vegetarian/natural foods. Located in the historic district, Sam Bond's features live music and quality microbrews in its beer garden. Its organic menu changes daily but usually includes organic pizzas topped with choices like crimini mushrooms, spinach, sundried tomatoes, tofu, and more; vegan soups; salads; and appetizers. Children welcome until 8:30 p.m.

Open daily for dinner through late evening. Limited service, vegan options, fresh juices, beer/wine, VISA/MC, $. www.sambonds.com

Sweet Life Patisserie
855 Monroe St., Eugene, OR 97402   **(541) 683-5676**
Bakery. This establishment offers beautiful cakes and desserts made with the finest quality ingredients, including organic flours, all-natural German chocolate, pure extract flavorings, fresh flowers, and no artificial ingredients. Spelt and rice flour can be used in place of wheat flour. **Open daily. Limited service, vegan wedding cakes available, $-$$.**

GRANTS PASS

Sunshine Natural Food Café
128 SW H St., Grants Pass, OR 97526   **(541) 474-5044**
Natural foods. Enjoy Sunshine's organic salad bar and a buffet Tuesday through Friday. Open Monday through Saturday for breakfast through early dinner. Closed Sunday. Full service, vegan options, fresh juices, wine/beer, take-out, $.

GRESHAM

Thai Orchid Restaurant
120 N. Main Ave., Gresham, OR 97030   **(503) 491-0737**
Thai. See description under Beaverton, OR.

HILLSBORO

Thai Orchid Restaurant
4550 NE Cornell Rd., Hillsboro, OR 97229   **(503) 681-2611**
Thai. See description under Beaverton, OR.

HOOD RIVER

China Gorge Restaurant
2680 Old Columbia River Dr., Hood River, OR 97031   **(541) 386-5331**
Chinese. Enjoy authentic Szechuan and Hunan cuisines at China Gorge. Their Bean Curd Homestyle and Vegetarian Moo Shu are delicious, and you can dine while gazing over the Columbia River. **Open Tuesday through Sunday for lunch and dinner. Closed Monday. Full service, vegan options, take-out, VISA/MC/AMEX/DISC, $$.**

Mother's Market
106 Hwy. 35, Hood River, OR 97031   **(541) 387-2202**
Deli. Centrally located within a natural foods store, the restaurant offers a wide assortment of appetizers, organic salads, entrées, pastas, sandwiches, burgers, and ethnic and side dishes. **Open daily for three meals. Full service, fresh juices, smoothies, espresso/cappuccino, non-alcoholic wine/beer, take-out, $.**

Sun Garden Café
1816 NE Hwy. 101, Lincoln City, OR 97367   **(541) 557-1800**
Juice bar/café/bakery. Sun Garden Café offers vegetarian deli-style sandwiches and other options in a casual atmosphere. **Open Sunday through Thursday for breakfast and lunch. Open Friday and Saturday for three meals.** Full service, espresso, smoothies, fresh juice, beer/wine, VISA/MC/DISC, $$.

Mother Nature's Natural Foods and Café
298 Laneda Ave., Manzanita, OR 97130   **(503) 368-5316**
Natural foods café. Mother Nature's Natural Foods and Café features an all-organic café with homemade soups, daily specials, sushi, sandwiches, and salads. **Open Monday through Saturday for lunch and dinner. Closed Sunday.** Limited service, take-out, catering, reservations not taken, non-smoking, macrobiotic/vegan options available, fresh juices, smoothies, soymilk, beer/wine/alcohol, VISA/MC, $-$$. www.neahkahnie.net

Wild Wood Café
319 N. Baker St., McMinnville, OR 97128   **(503) 435-1454**
Café. This is a family-owned restaurant specializing in breakfast with a number of lunch options as well. Lunch includes a wide range of veggie burgers, a veggie melt, and salads. They make their own breads, granola, soups, and salsa. **Open Wednesday through Monday for breakfast and lunch. Closed Tuesday.** Full service, VISA/MC/AMEX, $.

Oceana Natural Foods Co-op
159 SE 2nd St., Newport, OR 97365   **(541) 265-8285**
Natural foods deli. You'll find homemade soups made without dairy or meat, some vegan sandwiches made daily, and an all-organic salad bar at this self-service co-op. **Open daily for three meals.** Take-out, vegan options, fresh juices, VISA/MC, $. www.oceanafoods.org

(For restaurant listings in the surrounding areas, see Aloha, Beaverton, Bridal Veil, Gresham, Hillsboro, and West Linn.)

Cup and Saucer Café
3566 SE Hawthorne Blvd., Portland, OR 97214   **(503) 236-6001**
Diner. Cup and Saucer is a true diner that serves breakfast all day, as well as hefty sandwiches, soups and salads for lunch and dinner. For a healthy escape from burgers and pies, try the wheat-free coffeecake. **Open daily for three meals.** Full service, vegan options, fresh juices, beer/wine, VISA/MC, $-$$.

• Divine Café

SW 9th Ave. Between Washington and Alder
Portland, OR 97233 **(503) 314-9606**

Vegetarian. A unique alternative to the parking lot "hot dog stand," a cart called the Divine Café serves vegetarian and vegan meals, such as smoked tofu sandwiches, soba salad in peanut sauce and "Heavenly Granola." Don't forget to check out one or all of the vegan desserts available as well. **Open Monday through Thursday for lunch and early dinner. Open Friday and Saturday for lunch and dinner. Closed Sunday. Take-out, vegan options, $.**

• Dogs Dig Deli

212 NW Davis St., Portland, OR 97209 **(503) 223-3362**

Vegetarian deli. Dig into Dogs Dig's delicious vegetarian and vegan twists on traditional sandwiches, salads, and desserts. Instead of an egg salad sandwich, try the organic tofu alternative with eggless mayo, or maybe even the 70% water sandwich with fresh veggies of your choice on whole grain, spelt, or pocket bread. **Open Monday through Friday for breakfast through early dinner. Closed Saturday and Sunday. Take-out, vegan options, smoothies, fresh juices, $.**

• Garden Café

Portland Adventist Medical Center
10123 SE Market St., Portland, OR 97216 **(503) 251-6125**

Vegetarian/natural foods. This is a full-service cafeteria offering vegetarian entrées, salad bar, fresh fruit bar, and a fast-food grill featuring 15 vegetarian sandwiches. Vegetarian meals have been served here for more than 100 years. Enjoy a wide variety of foods in a comfortable dining area with indoor and outdoor seating, just six blocks off Interstate 205. **Open daily for lunch and early dinner. Cafeteria, vegan options, take-out, catering, $.**

India Grill

2924 E. Burnside St., Portland, OR 97214 **(503) 236-1790**

Indian. With an eclectic array of Indian delicacies, India Grill also dedicates part of its menu to vegetarian specials, such as Saagalu (spinach cooked with potatoes) and Bengan Ki Sabji (stir-fried eggplant-potato-green herb combination). **Open daily for lunch and dinner. Full service, take-out, catering, VISA/MC/AMEX/DISC, $$.**

Iron Horse Restaurant

6034 SE Milwaukee Ave., Portland, OR 97202 **(503) 232-1826**

Mexican. Situated near Antique Row in the Sellwood District, Iron Horse provides fresh, festive, and authentic Mexican and Southwestern meals. Feast on dishes like mini tacos filled with beans or vegetables, seven-vegetable tacos, mushroom tamales, and traditional favorites. A vegan menu is available upon request. **Open Tuesday through Sunday for lunch and dinner. Closed Monday. Full service, vegan options, beer/wine/alcohol, take-out, VISA/MC/AMEX/DISC, $$.** www.portlandironhorse.com

---

Restaurant codes: ✪ Reviewers' Choice • Vegetarian Restaurant •• Vegan Restaurant
Restaurant prices: **$** less than $6 **$$** $6-$12 **$$$** more than $12
Credit Cards Accepted: VISA - VISA MC - MasterCard AMEX - American Express
DISC - Discover DC - Diner's Club

• Kalga Kafe

4147 SE Division St., Portland, OR 97209   **(503) 236-4770**

Vegetarian. Lit by candlelight, Kalga Kafe is the perfect spot for the late-night snackers, or maybe even those who just want a healthy dinner with a funky, eclectic atmosphere. This restaurant offers an impressive vegetarian and vegan menu from Japanese sushi rolls to Mexican dishes. Try the Asian stir-fry, a delicious mixture of bok choy, mushrooms, broccoli, tofu with ginger tamari, and black beans. Live DJs are featured on Monday and Wednesday nights. **Open Monday and Wednesday through Friday for lunch through late night. Open Saturday and Sunday for dinner through late night. Closed Tuesday. Full service, vegan options, $-$$.** www.kalgakafe.com

Kim Hong

4239 NE Fremont St., Portland, OR 97213-1149   **(503) 282-0456**

Vietnamese. Feast from an extensive Vietnamese menu, the majority of which is vegan. **Open Monday through Friday for lunch and dinner. Open Saturday and Sunday for dinner. Full service, vegan options, soymilk, VISA/MC/AMEX/DISC, $$.**

Nicholas Restaurant

318 SE Grand Ave., Portland, OR 97214-1117   **(503) 235-5123**

Middle Eastern. Nicholas serves Middle Eastern fare with a vast array of vegetarian options. Try the flavorful veggie kebab over rice or the thin-crust pizza topped with oregano, thyme, sumac, olive oil and sesame seeds. **Open daily for lunch and dinner. Full service, $-$$.**

Oasis Café

3701 SE Hawthorne Blvd., Portland, OR 97214   **(503) 231-0901**

Café. Although it offers an array of sandwiches, soups, salads, focaccia, and desserts, Oasis is known for its pizza. Wild Ride is a popular vegetarian option with artichoke hearts, tomatoes, onions and mushrooms, but it is also possible to design your own pizza with whichever toppings you desire. **Open daily for lunch and dinner. Limited service, delivery, take-out, VISA/MC/DISC, $-$$.**

Old Wives Tales

1300 E. Burnside St., Portland, OR 97214   **(503) 238-0470**

Ethnic foods. Enjoy Black Bean Stew, an Egyptian Loaf, Mexican dishes, a soup and salad bar, soy products, rice noodles, and much more. **Open daily for three meals. Full service, fresh juices, non-alcoholic wine/beer, wine/beer, take-out, VISA/MC/AMEX, $$.**

Paradox Palace Café

3439 SE Belmont St., Portland, OR 97214   **(503) 232-7508**

American. This mostly vegetarian/vegan, diner-style café is located in the heart of trendy Belmont district. All of the breads, sauces and desserts served here are dairy- and egg-free and many of the ingredients used are local and organic. Breakfast is served anytime and can include dishes such as the Breakfast Burrito, Corn Cakes, Scrambled Curry Tofu with Mixed Veggies or Biscuits & Almond Gravy. Lunch and dinner items range from Tacos non Carne or Tofurky Sandwich to Green Curry with Tofu or Fettucini Alfredo. While they do serve hamburgers, the patties are cooked on a skillet separate from other items. **Open daily for three meals, Full service, vegan options, no credit cards, $-$$.**

Plainfield Mayur ✪
852 SW 21st St., Portland, OR 97205   **(503) 223-2995**
Indian. Probably one of the most elegant Indian restaurants you'll find, Plainfield Mayur is located in one of Portland's landmark homes with table settings of fine European crystal, china, and full silver service. The menu includes a vegetarian section with delicious, original entrées, appetizers, and soup. Reservations recommended. Private dining rooms are available for business meetings or private gatherings. **Open daily for dinner. Full service, vegan options, wine/beer/alcohol, take-out, VISA/MC/AMEX/DISC, $$$. www.plainfields.com**

• The Purple Parlor
3560 N. Mississippi Ave., Portland, OR 97227   **(503) 281-3560**
Vegetarian. The Purple Parlor provides Portland with a refreshing approach to business and customer service. It offers a vast vegetarian and vegan menu, wholesome and healthy ingredients, and friendly service. Try the Coconut Green Curry, Pesto Polenta, or the many alternative breakfast options. **Open Tuesday through Sunday for breakfast and lunch. Closed Monday. Full service, vegan options, take-out, fresh juices, soymilk, cappuccino/espresso, VISA/MC, $. www.thepurpleparlor.com**

Saigon Kitchen
3829 SE Division St., Portland, OR 97202   **(503) 236-2312**
Thai. Although pricey, Saigon Kitchen prepares delicious and flavorful Thai dishes. **Open Monday through Saturday for lunch and dinner. Closed Sunday. Full service, beer/wine/ alcohol, VISA/MC/AMEX/DISC, $$-$$$.**

Swagat
2074 NW Lovejoy, Portland, OR 97209   **(503) 227-4300**
Indian. See description under Beaverton, OR.

Thai Orchid Restaurant
2231 W. Burnside St., Portland, OR 97219   **(503) 226-4542**
10075 SW Barbur Blvd., Portland, OR 97219   **(503) 452-2544**
Thai. See description under Beaverton , OR.

Thanh Thao Restaurant
4005 SE Hawthorne Blvd., Portland, OR 97214   **(503) 238-6232**
Vietnamese/Thai. Thanh Thao offers a wide selection of tofu, vegetable, eggplant, and mock meat entrées. Appetizers, soup, and noodle dishes are also available. **Open Wednesday through Monday for lunch and dinner. Closed Tuesday. Full service, vegan options, take-out, $-$$.**

• • Veganopolis
412 SW Fourth Ave., Portland, OR 97204   **(503) 226-3400**
Vegan. This restaurant was a few months from opening at press time, so you may want to contact them before visiting. They plan to serve gourmet tofu scrambles, an Original Seitan Caesar Sandwich, vegan Reubens, cashew chili, and vegan crepes with caramelized apples. Vegan baked goods will be made on-site daily. Their space will be home to great music and free wireless Internet access. **Open Monday through Saturday for lunch through early dinner. Closed Sunday. Cafeteria, espresso, take-out, VISA/MC, $$. www.veganopolis.net**

• Vege Thai
3272 SE Hawthorne Blvd., Portland, OR 97214 **(503) 234-2171**
Vegetarian/Thai. This restaurant offers traditional Thai cuisine made from mock meats, vegetables, and noodles. **Open daily for lunch and dinner. Full service, vegan options, VISA/MC, $$.** www.vegethai.com

• Vegetarian House
22 NW 4th Ave., Portland, OR 97209 **(503) 274-0160**
Vegetarian/Chinese. Located in historic Old Town/China Town, this vegetarian restaurant's menu includes unique items such as Corn & Tofu Coup, Chinese-Style Sesame Flat Bread, Veggie Chicken with Cashew Nuts, and Veggie Shredded Beef with Bell Pepper. Also featured are Veggie Kung Pao Shrimp, Veggie Crab Meat with Baby Bok Choy, Veggie Pork Fried Rice, Veggie Ham Pan-Fried Noodles, and, for dessert, Almond-Flavored Soft Tofu. The staff uses organic produce whenever available. Try the lunch buffet on weekdays for only $5.95. **Open daily for lunch and dinner. Full service, vegan options, VISA/MC/AMEX/DISC/DC, $$.** www.vegetarianhouse.com

Vita Café
3024 NE Alberta St., Portland, OR 97211 **(503) 335-8233**
American. This mostly vegetarian/vegan café in the Alberta Arts section of town serves a wide range of eclectic dishes, including breakfast items, which are served all day. Try their Vegan Chicken Fried Steak, Tofurkey Sandwich, and Vegan French Toast. Vita Café shares the same owners as Paradox Café, and their menu items are nearly identical. Their breads and desserts are also dairy and egg-free, and they have a nice selection of vegan cakes and pies available by the slice. **Open Tuesday and Wednesday for dinner only. Open Thursday to Monday for three meals. Full service, vegan options, fresh juices, take-out, $-$$.**

SALEM

India Palace Restaurant
377 Court St., NE, Salem, OR 97301 **(503) 371-4808**
Indian. Dine on several different vegetarian curries, as well as rice dishes and Indian bread from India Palace. **Open daily for lunch and dinner. Full service, vegan options, take-out, VISA/MC, $-$$.**

Kwan's Cuisine
835 Commercial St., SE, Salem, OR 97302 **(503) 362-7711**
Chinese. Choose from a full page of vegetable options, including Tofu Tomato with Sautéed Vegetables, Fresh Mushrooms and Snow Peas, and Diced Vegetables with Tofu and Roasted Almonds. Vegetable broth instead of chicken broth is available upon request. Mock chicken, beef, and BBQ pork is available for vegetarian dishes. **Open daily for lunch and dinner. Full service, vegan options, fresh juices, non-alcoholic wine/beer, special drinks, catering, take-out, VISA/MC/AMEX/DISC/DC, $-$$.**

The Off Center Café
1741 Center St., NE, Salem, OR 97301 **(503) 363-9245**
Natural foods. Enjoy Curried Tofu with Rice, Cuban Black Beans and Rice, plus much more

at this '50s style café. **Open Tuesday and Wednesday for breakfast and lunch. Open Thursday and Friday for three meals. Open Saturday for breakfast and dinner. Open Sunday for breakfast. Closed Monday. Full service, vegan options, $-$$.**

Thai Orchid Restaurant
Liberty Plaza, 285 Liberty St. NE, Salem, OR 97301   **(503) 391-2930**
Thai. See description under Beaverton, OR.

SEASIDE

Gregorio's Chicago Pan Pizza Co.
111 Broadway St., #2, Seaside, OR 97138   **(503) 738-5217**
Italian. Located only half a block from the Pacific Ocean, Gregorio's serves veggie pizzas, including the C.P. Vegetarian; Surf City with artichoke and sundried tomato; and the Meatless Taco Pizza. Unique toppings range from sauerkraut to pine nuts. Whole wheat dough is also available. **Open daily for lunch and dinner. Limited service, non-alcoholic beer, wine/beer, $$.**

SPRINGFIELD

Kuraya's Thai Cuisine
1410 Mohawk Blvd., Springfield, OR 97477   **(541) 746-2951**
Thai. Kuraya's offers many wonderful vegetarian selections. **Open daily for lunch and dinner. Full service, vegan options, wine/beer, take-out, catering, VISA/MC, $.**

WEST LINN

Thai Orchid Restaurant
18740 Willamette Dr., West Linn, OR 97068   **(503) 699-4195**
Thai. See description under Beaverton, OR.

Pennsylvania

ARDMORE

All Natural Eatery
30 E. Lancaster Ave., Ardmore, PA 19003   **(610) 896-7717**
Deli. All Natural Eatery uses only organic produce in their sandwiches and other dishes, which are offered for an affordable price. **Open Monday through Saturday for lunch and dinner. Closed Sunday. Take-out, vegan options, fresh juices, smoothies, VISA/MC, $.**

BALA CYNWYD

The Carrot Bunch
51 E. City Line Ave., Bala Cynwyd, PA 19004   **(215) 664-5231**
Natural foods. Enjoy several vegetarian options. **Open Monday through Saturday for lunch and dinner. Closed Sunday. Full service, fresh juices, take-out, VISA/MC, $.**

Shangri-La Inn
138 Montgomery Ave., Bala Cynwyd, PA 19004   **(610) 668-3228**
Chinese/Japanese. Shangri-La's large menu features a vegetarian selection with such delicacies as Szechuan Bean Curd, Mock Chicken with Cashew Nuts, and Curry Vegetables and Bean Curd. There are also a number of sushi rolls and soups. **Open daily for lunch and dinner. Full service, vegan options, $$-$$$.**

BETHLEHEM

•The Green Café
22 W. 4th St., Bethlehem, PA 18015   **(610) 694-0192**
Vegetarian/natural foods. The Green Café is a cooperatively-run restaurant that features a wide variety of international dishes, including Brazilian-Style Black Beans and Rice, West African Peanut Soup, Spicy Fried Tofu over Kale, vegetable biryani, falafel, and more. They offer an all-you-can-eat brunch on Sunday and musical events on Monday nights. **Open Tuesday through Saturday for lunch and dinner. Open Sunday for brunch. Closed Monday. Full service, macrobiotic/vegan options, fresh juices, $-$$.**

Jonathan's Liquids For Life
38 W. Broad St., Bethlehem, PA 18018   **(610) 882-0600**
Juice bar. This is the only juice bar in the Allentown/Bethlehem/Easton area. They serve a veggie sandwich and a peanut butter/fruit sandwich, as well as juices, smoothies, and health shakes. **Open Monday through Saturday for breakfast through early dinner. Closed Sunday. Limited service, soymilk, smoothies, $.**

CLARKS SUMMIT

Everything Natural
426 S. State St., Clarks Summit, PA 18411   **(570) 586-9684**
Natural foods store. The restaurant in this friendly, comfortable natural foods store has a

café atmosphere. Offerings include soups, sandwiches, teas and coffees, and desserts. Near Steamtown National Park, lakes, skiing, and other northwestern Pennsylvania attractions. **Open daily for three meals. Counter service, vegan options, non-smoking, take-out, VISA/MC/DISC, $.**

COCHRANVILLE

Taco Shells
3161 Limestone Rd., Rte. 10, Cochranville, PA 19330   (610) 593-5134

Mexican. Restaurants are limited in this area of southeastern PA, so finding Taco Shells, with its excellent homemade Mexican food in a small-town restaurant atmosphere, is a real treat. The rice and homemade salsa are delicious, and you can always get a filling vegetarian burrito or enchilada. **Open Tuesday through Friday for lunch and dinner. Closed Saturday through Monday. Full service, limited vegan options, BYOB, take-out, $.**

DELAWARE WATER GAP

The Gallery at the Watergap
760 Broad St. (Rt. 611), Delaware Water Gap, PA 18327   (570) 424-5565

Natural foods. The Gallery offers many vegetarian options, including Lentil Walnut Loaf, Udon Noodles with Beet Sauce, Chickpea Burgers, guacamole, hummus, gazpacho, pasta dishes, salads, and more. **Open Wednesday through Sunday for lunch and dinner. Closed Monday and Tuesday. Full service, macrobiotic/vegan options, fresh juices, take-out, $-$$.**

FORT WASHINGTON

Palace of Asia
285 Commerce Dr., Fort Washington, PA 19034   (215) 646-2133

Indian. Many vegetarian specialties, including vegetable biryani, samosas, pakoras, masalas, and other traditional vegetarian Indian dishes are featured at Palace of Asia. **Open daily for lunch and dinner. Full service, vegan options, fresh juices, wine/beer/alcohol, take-out, VISA/MC/AMEX/DISC/DC, $$.**

GETTYSBURG

• Jasper's Juice Works
51 Chambersburg St., Gettysburg, PA 17325   (717) 334-5553

Vegetarian/juice bar. Jasper's offers cold and hot foods, wraps, baked goods, and soup offerings that change daily. Of course, they also feature a variety of smoothies, teas, coffees, juices, and soy drinks. **Call for hours. Counter service, vegan options, $-$$. www.jaspersjuice works.com**

Restaurant codes: ✪ Reviewers' Choice   • Vegetarian Restaurant   • • Vegan Restaurant
Restaurant prices: **$** less than $6   **$$** $6-$12   **$$$** more than $12
Credit Cards Accepted: VISA - VISA   MC - MasterCard   AMEX - American Express
DISC - Discover   DC - Diner's Club

HARRISBURG

Passage to India

525 S. Front St., Harrisburg, PA 17104   **(717) 233-1202**

Indian. Choose from a large selection of vegetarian options, like Chana Masala (chickpeas cooked with onions, tomatoes, and spices) and Aloo Methi (potatoes cooked with mustard seed, fenugreek, and other spices) at this restaurant, which overlooks the Susquehanna River. **Open daily for three meals. Full service, vegan options, catering, take-out, VISA/MC, $$.**

HONESDALE

Nature's Grace Health Foods and Deli

947 Main St., Honesdale, PA 18431   **(570) 253-3469**

Health foods store deli. Nature's Grace serves homemade soups, enchiladas, salads, baked goods, hoagies, and other entrées available daily. **Open Monday through Saturday for lunch. Closed Sunday. Counter service, fresh juices, take-out, $.**

INDIANA

The Café At Back To Nature

2450 Warren Rd., Indiana, PA 15701   **(724) 349-1772**

Natural foods. Get back to nature in this friendly, clean café with breakfast available anytime, vegetarian and/or vegan salads made with organic ingredients, and sandwiches. Don't miss the fresh-ground organic coffee with free refills, herbal teas, and fresh fruit smoothies. **Open Monday through Friday for three meals. Open Saturday for breakfast and lunch. Closed Sunday. Limited service, vegan options, take-out, fresh juices, smoothies, soymilk, espresso/cappuccino, special drinks, VISA/MC, $.**

LANCASTER

A Loaf of Bread

16 McGovern Ave., Lancaster, PA 17602   **(717) 393-2445**

Bakery. Fresh breads made daily with only the finest organically-grown grains in a variety of types, such as fruit nut, multigrain, sun-dried tomato, and olive. Though primarily take-out, they do have a few small tables. **Open Tuesday through Friday for breakfast, lunch and early dinner. Open Saturday for breakfast and lunch. Closed Sunday and Monday. Take-out, non-smoking, fresh juices, $.**

Rhubarb's Market

1342 Columbia Ave., Lancaster, PA 17603   **(717) 392-0333**
1521 Lititz Pike, Lancaster, PA 17601   **(717) 390-3001**

Natural foods. Sample some of vegetarian sandwiches and snacks that Rhubarb's Natural Foods Market offers while you explore the store's other healthy selections. **Open Monday through Friday for three meals. Open Saturday for breakfast, lunch, and early dinner. Closed Sunday. Take-out, macrobiotic/vegan options, VISA/MC/AMEX/DISC, $.**

Taj Mahal
2080 Bennet Ave., Hechinger Plaza, Lancaster, PA 17601   **(717) 295-1434**
Indian. Vegetarian entrées are listed separately on Taj Mahal's extensive menu. Open daily for lunch and dinner. Full service, vegan options, take-out, VISA/MC, $$.

MALVERN

•• Su Tao Café
81 Lancaster Ave., Malvern, PA 19355   **(610) 651-8886**
Vegan/Chinese. Su Tao is one of the best restaurants in the area. They have a wonderful buffet and a beautiful salad bar with edamame, tofu skins, raw vegetables, homemade dressings, and fried bananas. Both casual and fine dining are available. Open daily for lunch and dinner. Full service, fresh juices, smoothies, macrobiotic options, reservations recommended, take-out, catering, non-smoking, VISA/MC/AMEX/DISC, $$. www.sutaocafe.com

MARSHALLS CREEK

Naturally Rite Restaurant and Natural Foods Market
Route 209, Marshalls Creek, PA 18335   **(570) 223-1133**
Natural foods. It's a pleasure to find this restaurant among the Pocono vacation spots. Among the wide variety of menu selections are Garden Burgers, Millet Croquettes, and Fettucini Pomadora. Desserts can be served with non-dairy ice cream. Informal and very casual, an outdoor patio is available in good weather. A health food store and clinic are connected to the restaurant. Open Wednesday through Monday for lunch and dinner. Open Tuesday for lunch only. Full service, fresh juices, catering, take-out, VISA/MC/AMEX/DC, $$.

MOOSIC

Amber
3505 Birney Ave., Moosic, PA 18507   **(570) 457-2700**
Indian. Amber offers many Indian vegetarian appetizers, entrées, and freshly baked breads. Dishes include samosas, baigan bhartha (baked eggplant), mushroom mutter (mushrooms and green peas in a sauce), and dal saag (yellow lentils with cooked spinach). Open daily for lunch and dinner. Full service, catering, $$.

MT. LEBANON

Aladdin's Eatery
630 Washington Rd., Mt. Lebanon, PA 15228   **(412) 344-4111**
Middle Eastern. This local restaurant chain offers great Mediterranean and Middle Eastern dishes, including many vegetarian and vegan options. These include lentil soup, vegetarian chili, hummus, tabbouleh, salads, stuffed grape leaves, falafel, and six vegetarian rolled pita options. Open daily for lunch and dinner. Full service, vegan options, fresh juices, smoothies, espresso/cappuccino, beer, take-out, VISA/MC/AMEX, $-$$. www.aladdinseatery.com

NARBERTH

Garden of Eatin'
231 Haverford Ave., Narberth, PA 19072   **(215) 667-7634**
Natural foods. This restaurant is in the rear of Narberth Natural Foods and offers various vegetarian dishes. **Open Monday through Saturday for lunch. Closed Sunday. Full service, fresh juices, take-out, VISA/MC, $.**

PHILADELPHIA

(For restaurant listings in the surrounding areas, see Ardmore, Bala Cynwyd, Fort Washington, Malvern, Narbeth, Southampton, West Chester, and Willow Grove.)

•• A-Free-Ya's
6108 Germantown Ave., Philadelphia, PA 19144   **(215) 848-5006**
Vegan. A-Free-Ya's offers an extensive menu of interesting and creative raw foods dishes. Some stir-fries, soups, and fresh-pressed solar wines are available during the winter. **Open Tuesday through Friday for take-out lunch only. Open Tuesday through Saturday for sit-down at other times. Closed Sunday and Monday. Full service, fresh juices, catering, take-out, VISA/MC, $$.**

Abyssinia Ethiopian Restaurant
229 S. 45th St., Philadelphia, PA 19104   **(215) 387-2424**
Ethiopian. Ethiopian vegetarian specialties are available. **Open daily for lunch and dinner. Full service, reservations recommended, non-smoking, espresso/cappuccino, wine/beer/ alcohol, VISA/MC/AMEX/DISC/DC, $.**

Adobe Café
4550 Mitchell St., Philadelphia, PA 19128   **(215) 483-3947**
Mexican. Adobe Café is a Southwestern bar and grill featuring a full vegetarian menu available with fire-grilled sandwiches, soups, salads, and more. Ask about hosting your next private party there. **Open daily for dinner. Full service, vegan options, reservations recommended, beer/wine/alcohol, VISA/MC/AMEX/DISC, $$. www.TheAdobeCafe.com**

•• Arnold's Way
4438 Main St., Philadelphia, PA 19127   **(215) 483-2266**
Juice bar. Arnold's serves up a variety of finely-cut salads and pies made without sugar, dairy, flour, or eggs. They also serve banana whips, smoothies, and protein shakes. **Open daily for lunch and dinner. Limited service, fresh juices, smoothies, soymilk, VISA/MC/AMEX/ DISC/DC, $.**

• The Basic Four Vegetarian Juice Bar
Reading Terminal Market
12th and Filbert Sts., Philadelphia, PA 19107   **(215) 440-0991**
Vegetarian. Located in the heart of Philadelphia, this is a food stand in Reading Terminal. Savor fast food vegetarian style, including sandwiches, salads, veggie steaks, veggie burgers, and mock chicken and tuna salads. **Open Monday through Saturday for lunch. Closed Sunday. Cafeteria, fresh juices, take-out, $.**

Ben's Restaurant
The Franklin Institute
20th and the Parkway, Philadelphia, PA 19103 **(215) 448-1355**
American. Ben's claims "an All-American menu with a nutritional twist." **Open daily for breakfast and lunch. Cafeteria, take-out, $.**

• Center Foods Natural Grocers
1525 Locust St., Philadelphia, PA 19102 **(215) 732-9000**
Vegetarian. Center Foods features a completely organic take-out counter with macrobiotic options available. **Open Monday through Saturday. Closed Sunday. Take-out, $.**

•• Cherry Street Chinese Vegetarian Restaurant ✪
1010 Cherry St., Philadelphia, PA 19107 **(215) 923-3663**
Vegan/Chinese. This smoke-free Chinese restaurant has an extensive menu, featuring vegetable, tofu, and mock meat dishes. Offerings include Sesame Lemon Beef, Watercress with Tofu Soup, Eggplant in Black Bean Sauce, and more. An upstairs banquet room is available for larger groups. **Open daily for lunch and dinner. Full service, vegan options, macrobiotic/ vegan options, take-out, VISA/MC/AMEX/DISC, $$.**

The Dining Car
8826 Frankford Ave., Philadelphia, PA 19136 **(215) 338-5113**
American. The Dining Car offers some vegetarian meals. **Open 24 hours daily. Full service, alcohol, take-out, $.**

Essene Café
719 S. 4th St., Philadelphia, PA 19147 **(215) 922-1146**
Natural foods. Located next door to a large natural foods store, Essene Café offers a wide variety of vegetarian dishes, including soups, salads, Gingered Tofu and Grilled Vegetables, Tempeh Burgers, Sautéed Tofu-Teriyaki Burger, Vegetable Lasagna, and a Macrobiotic Plate. **Open daily for three meals. Buffet, vegan options, fresh juices, take-out, VISA/MC, $$-$$$.**

Gianna's Grille
507 S. 6th St., Philadelphia, PA 19147 **(215) 829-4448**
Italian. Gianna's specializes in planet-friendly food, and they offer vegan versions of most of their items. This includes Monster-Sized Sandwiches; vegan lasagna; hearth-baked pizzas and calzones with homemade soy cheese and veggie pepperoni, chicken, ham, sausage, or bacon; gourmet salads; sides, such as vegan cheese fries; vegan cakes; vegan cookies; and vegan soft serve ice cream and toppings. **Open Tuesday through Saturday for lunch and dinner. Closed Sunday and Monday. Full service, vegan options, take-out, no credit cards, $-$$.** www.giannasgrille.com

• Gourmet To Go
1505 South St., Philadelphia, PA 19146 **(215) 985-0890**
Vegetarian. Gourmet to Go offers vegetarian versions of Kofta Subs made with vegetarian meatballs, Ham & Cheese Hoagies made with smoked soy, Chicken Salad Subs made with soy protein and soy mayonnaise, and more. Most sandwiches may be made with or without

cheese. They ask that you call in orders before pick-up. **Open daily for lunch and dinner.** **Take-out, vegan options, fresh juices, smoothies, catering, VISA/MC/AMEX/DISC, $-$$.**

•Govinda's Gourmet Vegetarian Cuisine
1408 South St., Philadelphia, PA 19146   **(215) 985-9303**
Vegetarian/Indian. Govinda's offers a wide range of Indian, American, and other international specialties created with soy proteins in lieu of meats. Sample the soy Shrimp, Scallops, or Chicken Fingers; the Copenhagen Pepper Steak made from strips of wheat gluten; or the Congo Asparagus, served with lemon ginger sauce and roasted cashews over basmati rice. Although Govinda's offers take-out every day, it offers full-service from Thursday to Sunday only. Reservations are recommended for these days. **Open Thursday through Sunday for full-service. Call for lunch and take-out hours. Full service, vegan options, fresh juices, smoothies, take-out, VISA/MC/AMEX/DISC/DC, $$-$$$.**

•• Harmony Vegetarian Restaurant ✪
135 N. 9th St., Philadelphia, PA 19107   **(215) 627-4520**
Vegan/Chinese. Any vegetarian who visits the City of Brotherly Love will undoubtedly hear, "Make sure you visit Harmony!" This highly-rated, completely vegan Chinese restaurant has a very extensive menu. Many delicious soups, appetizers, and countless vegetable, tofu, and mock meat dishes are featured. The service is friendly and the atmosphere is pleasant. Weekends are usually very busy. **Open daily for lunch and dinner. Full service, non-smoking, BYOB, take-out, VISA/MC, $$.**

•• K.C.'s Chuckwagon Inc.
3317 Rhawn St., Philadelphia, PA 19136   **(215) 543-9551**
Vegan. Enjoy a healthy and ethical twist on some traditional favorites at K.C.'s Chuckwagon Inc., where all meals are vegan. Dishes like the Unreal Veal Parmesan, the Kind Philly Cheese Steak, and the Barbecue Tempeh are made from whole grains, fresh produce and high quality plant proteins. Place your order one day before delivery. **Delivered on Tuesday and Thursday. Delivery only, vegan options, catering, personal chef service, nutrition counseling, $-$$.**

Kawabata
110 Chestnut St., Philadelphia, PA 19106   **(215) 928-9564**
2455 Grant Ave., Philadelphia, PA 19114   **(215) 969-8255**
Japanese. Dishes include vegetarian sushi and sukiyaki. **Open daily. Full service, vegetarian/ macrobiotic options, take-out, VISA/MC/AMEX, $$$.**

Keyflower Dining Room
20 S. 36th St., Philadelphia, PA 19104   **(215) 386-2207**
Natural foods. The Keyflower Dining Room offers self-service dining geared to vegetarians and the nutrition-conscious. You can dine on delicious protein dishes and homemade desserts. Smoking is not allowed in this natural foods restaurant. **Open Monday through Friday for lunch only. Cafeteria, take-out, $.**

•• The Kind Café
724 N. 3rd St., Philadelphia, PA 19123   **(215) 922-5463**
Vegan. Designed by a critical care nurse with a master's degree in nutrition education, The

Kind Café's menu offers seasonally-inspired foods made from organic produce, whole grains, and plant-based proteins. Choose from a variety of appetizers and entrées, including Butternut Bisque, Whole Wheat Vegetable Lasagna, Happy Chicken Salad served on Baby Endive, Whole Wheat Pierogies with Ruby Sour Kraut and Vegan Sour Cream, and Unreal Veal Parmesan with Baked Brown Rice Ziti. Or choose from a living foods menu called Super Kind Cuisine. The restaurant also has cooking classes on Wednesday nights, nutritional counseling appointments, and a Chuckwagon to bring hot food to local fairs and events. **Open Monday through Saturday for lunch and dinner. Closed Sunday. Limited service, fresh juices, smoothies, macrobiotic options, non-smoking, take-out, catering, VISA/MC, $$.** www.kindcafe.com

• Kingdom of Vegetarians Restaurant
129 N. 11th St., Philadelphia, PA 19107 (215) 413-2290

Vegetarian/Chinese. Kingdom of Vegetarians Restaurant's menu is a kingdom of vegetarian and vegan Chinese dishes. For a mere $10, try the all-you-can-eat dim sum, with such specialties as coconut triangles, scallion pancakes, and sesame chicken (imitation, of course). **Open daily for lunch through late dinner. Full service, vegan options, non-smoking, reservations required, discount to VegDining Card holders, VISA/MC/AMEX/DISC, $-$$.**

Lemon Grass Thai Restaurant
3626-30 Lancaster Ave., Philadelphia, PA 19104 (215) 222-8042

Thai. Request the vegetarian menu for an abundant selection of vegetarian items. **Open daily for lunch and dinner. Full service, take-out, VISA/MC/AMEX/DISC, $$.**

Mary's Restaurant
400 Roxborough Ave., Philadelphia, PA 19128 (215) 487-2249

Natural foods. Mary's Restaurant offers vegetarian selections, pasta, daily specials, fresh baked breads, and desserts. **Open Wednesday through Saturday for dinner. Open Sunday for brunch. Closed Monday and Tuesday. Full service, vegan options, take-out, catering, VISA/MC/AMEX/DC, $$.**

Natural Goodness Market & Café
2000 Walnut St., Philadelphia, PA 19103 (215) 977-7749

Natural foods. This mostly vegan café features vegetarian deli slices, a vegan Reuben, and daily specials, including Seitan and Mushrooms in Mirin Marinade and African Tempeh with Vegetables. **Open daily for three meals. Limited service, vegan options, fresh juices, smoothies, take-out, VISA/MC/AMEX, $.**

Rajbhog Vegetarian Indian Cuisine
738 Adams Ave., Philadelphia, PA 19124 (215) 537-1937

Indian. This Indian restaurant offers a large selection of soups, salads, appetizers, breads, and South Indian entrées. Selections include vegetable dishes, Bombay-style curries, and utthappams. **Open Tuesday through Sunday for lunch and dinner. Closed Monday. Full service, vegan options, fresh juices, special drinks, catering, take-out, VISA/MC/AMEX, $-$$.**

• Samosa Indian Vegetarian Cuisine
1214 Walnut St., Philadelphia, PA 19107   **(215) 554-7774**
Vegetarian/Indian. Enjoy several different varieties of samosas, soups, entrées, and Indian breads at this establishment. Open daily for lunch and dinner. Full service, vegan options, VISA/MC/AMEX/DISC/DC, $-$$.

•• Singapore Vegetarian Restaurant
1006 Race St., Philadelphia, PA 19107   **(215) 922-3288**
Vegan/Chinese. This wonderful vegan restaurant is located in Philadelphia's Chinatown. Both the food and service are outstanding. Open daily for lunch and dinner. Full service, fresh juices, take-out, VISA/MC, $$.

• Vegetable Garden
8225 Germantown Ave., Philadelphia, PA 19118   **(215) 242-5373**
Vegetarian/Chinese. This restaurant opened in 1997 and offers a fantastic vegetarian menu, including Scallion Pancakes, Miso Soup, Tofu and Vegetable Soup, Hot and Sour Soup, steamed or pan-fried dumplings, sizzling platters, tofu entrées, noodle and rice-based dishes, plus mock meat and mock fish dishes. Open Tuesday through Sunday for lunch and dinner. Closed Monday. Full service, vegan options, take-out, $$-$$$.

Wong's Gourmet
1699 Grant Ave., Philadelphia, PA 19115   **(215) 676-6220**
Chinese. They feature an extensive vegan menu. Open Monday through Saturday for lunch and dinner. Open Sunday for dinner only. Full service, vegan options, beer/wine/alcohol, take-out, VISA/MC/AMEX, $$.

Ziggy's
1210 Walnut St., Philadelphia, PA 19107   **(215) 985-1838**
Japanese. Ziggy's offers some vegetarian dishes on their menu. Open daily for dinner. Full service, take-out, VISA/MC/AMEX, $$.

PINE FORGE

Gracie's 21st Century Café
Manatawny Rd., Pine Forge, PA 19548   **(610) 323-4004**
Natural foods. Gracie's goal is to provide a place where both vegetarians and non-vegetarians can be comfortable and share a delicious meal. Offerings include Black Bean Chili, Middle Eastern Sampler, Saffron Curry, and Broccoli with Ravioli. The atmosphere has a Southwestern flavor with an outdoor dining terrace. Open Wednesday through Saturday for dinner. Open Friday for lunch. Closed Sunday through Tuesday. Full service, fresh juices, non-alcoholic beer, wine/beer/alcohol, take-out, reservations appreciated, catering, AMEX, $$$. www.gracies21stcentury.com

---

Restaurant codes: ✪ Reviewers' Choice   • Vegetarian Restaurant   •• Vegan Restaurant
Restaurant prices: **$** less than $6   **$$** $6-$12   **$$$** more than $12
Credit Cards Accepted: VISA - VISA   MC - MasterCard   AMEX - American Express
DISC - Discover   DC - Diner's Club

(For restaurant listings in the surrounding areas, see Mt. Lebanon and Shadyside.)

Aladdin's Eatery
5878 Forbes Ave., Pittsburgh, PA 15217   **(412) 421-5100**
Middle Eastern. See description under Mt. Lebanon, PA.

Ali Baba Restaurant
404 S. Craig St., Pittsburgh, PA 15213   **(412) 682-2829**
Middle Eastern. Located in the Oakland section, Ali Baba offers a variety of vegetarian Middle Eastern dishes, including a noteworthy couscous dish. **Open Monday through Friday for lunch and dinner. Open Saturday and Sunday for dinner. Full service, vegan options, beer, take-out, VISA/MC/AMEX/DISC, $$.**

Janet's Café
901 E. Carson St., Pittsburgh, PA 15203   **(412) 381-5308**
Middle Eastern. Delicious vegetarian salads, sandwiches, and more are offered at Janet's. **Open Monday through Saturday for lunch and dinner. Closed Sunday. Full service, vegan options, take-out, $.**

• Sree's Veggie Café
2107 Murray Ave., Pittsburgh, PA 15217   **(412) 781-4765**
Vegetarian/Indian. Though the Sree family owns several establishments in the area, this is the only one that is entirely vegetarian. The menu includes Spinach Tofu, Masala Tofu, Mixed Vegetable Curry, Menthi Carrots, Green Beans with Lentils, Beets with Lentils, Chickpeas, and Potatoes, and a variety of creative chutneys. All are made with vegetable oil, the samosas are sealed with water (not eggs), and the breads are vegan. **Open Monday through Saturday for dinner only. Closed Sunday. Counter service, vegan options, take-out, catering, $.** www.srees.com

Star of India
412 S. Craig St., Pittsburgh, PA 15213   **(412) 681-5700**
Indian. There are several vegan dishes, plus many other selections using dairy offered daily. **Open Monday through Friday for lunch and dinner. Open Saturday and Sunday for dinner. Full service, vegan options, special drinks, VISA/MC/AMEX, $$.**

Taj Mahal, Inc.
7795 McKnight Rd., Pittsburgh, PA 16066   **(412) 364-1760**
Indian. Informal atmosphere serving typical Indian entrées. **Open daily for lunch and dinner. Full service, special drinks, catering, VISA/MC/AMEX/DISC/DC, $$.**

• The Zenith Vegetarian Café and Antique Gallery
86 S. 26th St., Pittsburgh, PA 15203   **(412) 481-4833**
Vegetarian. The Zenith offers a different menu each week. Options often include grape leaves, a Greek platter, Caribbean rice salad, a Scandinavian apple soup, West African groundnut

stew, tofu pepper steak, spinach and cashew casserole, and vegan desserts. In addition to the menu, this restaurant features antiques, an art gallery, and a tearoom in an informal setting. **Open Wednesday through Saturday for lunch and dinner. Open Sunday for brunch. Closed Monday and Tuesday. Full service, vegan options, fresh juices, smoothies, soymilk, special drinks, take-out, VISA/MC, $$.** www.zenithpgh.com

SHADYSIDE

Jen's Juice Joint
733 Copeland St., Shadyside, PA 15232   **(412) 683-7374**
Natural foods. In addition to fresh juices, the menu here includes homemade soups, meatless chili, and veggie sandwiches and wraps. **Open Monday through Saturday for three meals. Open Sunday for brunch. Counter service, vegan options, fresh juices, smoothies, take-out, no credit cards, $$.**

SOUTHAMPTON

•Blue Sage Vegetarian Grille
772 2nd St. Pike, Southampton, PA 18966   **(215) 942-8888**
Vegetarian. Blue Sage carries a small but delightful menu offering items such as crispy herb-crusted portobello filets and grilled polenta. **Open Tuesday through Sunday for dinner. Closed Monday. Full service, vegan options, reservations not needed, take-out, $$.**

STAHLSTOWN

•• Maggie's Mercantile
Rte. 711 S., Stahlstown, PA 15687   **(724) 593-5056**
Vegan. Maggie's is home to a deli and resaturant where you can choose from a pay-by-weight selection or from items in the freezer case. They have a buffet every Saturday night with dishes such as misos, Asian yam tarts, and basil broccoli quiches. In addition, they have a grocery with homemade soy ice cream and 95 percent organic produce. **Open Tuesday through Sunday for lunch and early dinner. Closed Monday. Limited service, fresh juices, organic coffee, take-out, VISA/MC/AMEX, $$.**

STROUDSBURG

Everybody's Café
905 Main St., Stroudsburg, PA 18360   **(717) 424-0896**
Natural foods. Everybody's offers Polish and Italian dishes, as well as other European-style fare, including Mushroom Picata and many other creative entrées. This restaurant is located in a huge Victorian house. **Open daily for lunch and dinner. Full service, take-out, AMEX, $.**

WEST CHESTER

Hunan Chinese Restaurant
Town and Country Shopping Center
1103 W. Chester Pike, West Chester, PA 19382   **(215) 429-9999**
Chinese. Hunan has an extensive vegetarian menu with numerous appetizers, soups, and

entrées, including a large selection of tofu dishes and mock meats. The food is excellent, and the staff is very friendly. This is a real treasure for vegetarians, especially those living in southeastern PA! **Open daily for lunch and dinner. Full service, take-out, VISA/MC/ AMEX/DISC, $-$$.**

Senora's Authentic Mexican Cuisine
505 E. Gay St., West Chester, PA 19380   **(610) 344-4950**
Mexican. Senora's maintains a dedication to its customers and can prepare most dishes, besides those already vegetarian, "vegetarian style" such as its tacos, burritos, and nachos. All of the fried dishes are made with low-fat, cholesterol-free canola oil. **Open Monday through Saturday for lunch and dinner. Call Sunday for hours. Full service, reservations recommended, wheelchair accessible, BYOB, VISA/MC/DISC, $. www.westchesteronline. com/restaurants/casual/senora/index.htm**

WILLIAMSPORT

Freshlife Café
2300 E. 3rd St., Williamsport, PA 17701   **(570) 322-8280**
Natural foods. This establishment offers whole foods cuisine with many ethnic dishes, such as baked eggplant with feta, Mexican black bean pie, a tempeh stir-fry, and incredible baked goods. Most ingredients are organic, especially during the summer. **Open Monday through Friday for breakfast and lunch. Closed Saturday and Sunday. Full service, fresh juices, smoothies, soymilk, special drinks, macrobiotic options, VISA/MC/AMEX/DISC, $.**

WILLOW GROVE

• Horizons Café
101 E. Moreland Rd., Willow Grove, PA 19090   **(215) 659-7705**
Vegetarian café. Horizons Café offers tantalizing dishes like Jamaican Barbeque Seitan Wings; Smoked Tofu, Mushroom, and Spinach Quesadillas; Grilled Seitan Roast Beef; Pecan and Sage Baked Seitan; and Hazelnut Tofu Scallops. For those daring - or crazy - enough, try the spicy Red Chile and Wasabi Grilled Tofu. And save room for a choice from their all-vegan dessert menu. **Open Tuesday through Saturday for lunch and dinner. Closed Sunday and Monday. Full service, vegan options, VISA/MC/AMEX, $$. www.horizonscafe.com**

Restaurant codes: ✪ Reviewers' Choice • Vegetarian Restaurant • • Vegan Restaurant
Restaurant prices: **$** less than $6 **$$** $6-$12 **$$$** more than $12
Credit Cards Accepted: VISA - VISA MC - MasterCard AMEX - American Express
DISC - Discover DC - Diner's Club

Puerto Rico

AGUADA

•• Buena Mesa Restaurant
Carr. 2 Km. 138.5, La Cadena, Aguada, PR 00602   **(787) 252-1158**
Vegan. Come relax at Buena Mesa's table for delicious vegan fare. Open Monday through Saturday for breakfast and lunch. Open Sunday for brunch. Cafeteria, fresh juices, VISA/MC/AMEX, $-$$.

AGUADILLA

(For restaurant listings in the surrounding areas, see Aguada.)

• Long Life Deli Company
Carr. 2, Km. 129.5, Plaza Victoria, Aguadilla, PR 00603   **(787) 891-0380**
Vegetarian. This restaurant offers a changing lunch menu with salads and sandwiches. Hot lunches are served between 11:30 and 2 only. They offer at least one vegan option at all times. Open Monday through Saturday for breakfast through mid-afternoon. Closed Sunday. Cafeteria, vegan options, fresh juices, smoothies, soymilk, take-out, $.

CAGUAS

• Restaurante Vegetariano La Salud Al Natural
37 Ave. Rafael Cordero, Esq. Calle Vizcarrondo
Caguas, PR 00725-2835   **(787) 745-5640**
Vegetarian/natural foods. This restaurant is located next door to a natural foods store and near Monaga Park. Open Monday through Friday for lunch only. Closed Saturday, Sunday, and holidays. Full service, vegan options, soymilk, VISA/MC, $.

CAROLINA

• Freshmart Natural Market and Café
Carolina Commercial Park, Carretera 887, Km. 8
Carolina, PR 00926   **(787) 762-7800**
Vegetarian/natural foods. Though the store here is not completely vegetarian, the café here is. Among their offerings are Spanish soups, salads, and much more. Open Monday through Friday for breakfast and lunch. Closed Saturday and Sunday. Full service, take-out, VISA/MC/AMEX/DC, $$.

FAJARDO

• Vegetariano A Lo Criollo
4 Munoz Rivera #57, Fajardo, PR 00738   **(787) 863-7060**
Vegetarian. Vegetarian dishes in the Criollo styles. Open daily for three meals. Limited service, vegan options, non-smoking, fresh juices, soymilk, special drinks, take-out, VISA/MC, $.

HATO REY

• Freshmart Natural Market and Café
Calle Calaf Esq. Federico Costa Plaza Montemar
Hato Rey, PR 00917 **(787) 282-9106**
Vegetarian/natural foods. See description under Carolina, PR.

• La Zanahoria Vegetarian Restaurant
214 Ave. Eleanor Roosevelt, Hato Rey, PR 00918-3007 **(787) 274-0058**
Vegetarian. Enjoy Puerto Rican-style vegetarian food at this mostly vegan restaurant. It is located next to a natural foods store that is under different ownership and is not fully vegetarian. **Open Monday through Saturday for breakfast and lunch. Closed Sunday. Full service, vegan options, VISA/MC, $$.**

HUMACAO

• A Lo Natural
Ba-3 26 St. Villa Universitaria, Humacao, PR 00791-4349 **(787) 852-0945**
Vegetarian. A Lo Natural offers a unique blend of Puerto Rican cuisine and international accents in an eclectic, relaxing atmosphere. **Open Monday through Saturday for breakfast and lunch. Closed Sunday. Limited service, fresh juices, smoothies, soymilk, espresso/cappuccino, non-alcoholic beverages, non-smoking, VISA/MC, $$.**

Nutrilife
9 Calle Miguels Casillas, Humacao, PR 00791 **(787) 852-5068**
Natural foods. This health foods store and mostly vegetarian restaurant offers fruit shakes and other healthy options. **Open Monday through Saturday. Closed Sunday. Cafeteria, fresh juices, beer, take-out, catering, $.**

MANATI

• Freshmart Natural Market and Café
Manati Plaza, 10 Carr. 149, Ste. 290, Manati, PR 00674 **(787) 854-7800**
Vegetarian/natural foods. See description under Carolina, PR.

MAYAGUEZ

• Bella Vista Hospital Cafeteria
Bella Vista Hospital, P.O. Box 1750, Mayaguez, PR 00681 **(787) 834-6000**
Vegetarian. This cafeteria at a Seventh-day Adventist hospital serves only vegetarian food for all meals. **Open daily for three meals. Cafeteria, take-out, $. www.bvhpr.com**

OLD SAN JUAN

Café Berlin
407 Plava Colon, Old San Juan, PR 00901 **(787) 722-5205**
Natural foods café. Café Berlin is located near the Columbus Monument. Be sure to try their

tofu steak dishes and other sandwiches offered daily. **Open daily for three meals. Full service,** vegan options, espresso/cappuccino, wine/beer, VISA/MC/AMEX, $$-$$$.

• Gopal's

201B Calle de Tetuan, Old San Juan, PR 00901   **(787) 724-0229**

Vegetarian/Indian. This Krishna establishment serves Indian and Puerto Rican vegetarian cuisine buffet- and cafeteria-style. **Open for lunch Monday through Friday. Closed Saturday and Sunday.** Cafeteria, vegan options, fresh juices, soymilk, take-out, VISA/MC/AMEX, $.

RIO PIEDRAS

•• All Natural Plaza

370 Ave. 65 de Infanteria, Rio Piedras, PR 00926   **(787) 754-1499**

Vegan. Located near the airport, this informal restaurant offers all types of vegan breakfast items, entrées, and desserts. **Open Monday through Friday for breakfast and lunch. Open Saturday and Sunday for brunch.** Cafeteria, fresh juices, coffee drinks, VISA/MC, $$.

•• Buena Mesa Restaurant

El Tune Car Care Mall, Ave. 65 de Infanteria
Rio Piedras, PR 00923   **(787) 753-7908**

Vegan. See description under Aguada, PR.

• Salud Con Sabor

Parana 1668, El Cereza 1, Rio Piedras, PR 00926   **(787) 765-2183**

Vegetarian. With a different menu daily, Salud con Sabor provides "health with flavor" each and everyday. **Open Monday through Friday for lunch. Closed Saturday and Sunday.** Full service, vegan options, fresh juices, smoothies, soymilk, VISA/MC, $$.

SAN JUAN

(For restaurant listings in the surrounding areas, see Carolina, Hato Rey, Old San Juan, and Rio Piedras.)

Country Health Foods

53 Calle Robles, Rio Piedras, San Juan, PR 00925-3005   **(787) 763-7056**

Natural foods. Located near the University of Puerto Rico, this informal restaurant offers sandwiches and entrées made from tofu or mock meats. **Open Monday through Saturday for breakfast through early dinner. Closed Sunday.** Limited service, vegan options, fresh juices, take-out, VISA/MC/AMEX, $.

•• El Lucero de Salud Vegetarian Restaurant

1154 Avenida Americo Miranda, San Juan, PR 00921-2213   **(787) 273-1313**

Vegan. El Lucero de Salud, which means "The Health Guiding Star," is a small restaurant in a natural foods store that offers rejuvenating dishes, such as energy soup, sprouts salad, smoked tofu, lasagna, and stir-fry vegetables. The chefs do not use any refined sugar, eggs, meat, fish, or dairy products in any of their dishes, including desserts. There are free lectures about natural foods on Thursdays at 10 A.M. Located near the Medical Center of

Puerto Rico. Open Monday through Saturday for breakfast and lunch. Closed Sunday. Cafeteria, vegan options, non-smoking, fresh juices, smoothies, soymilk, take-out, catering, VISA/MC/AMEX/DISC/DC, $. www.alimentovivos.com

• Vida Health Food and Restaurant
Ave. Esmeralda #15 Urb. Munoz Rivera, San Juan, PR 00921   (787) 720-2480
Vegetarian. Located in the back of a natural foods store, Vida Health Food and Restaurant celebrates life with a commitment to providing all natural and healthful products and food. Open Monday through Saturday for lunch. Closed Sunday. Full service, VISA/MC, $-$$.

TOA BAJA

• GLB Natural Nutrition and Restaurant
Ave. Dos Palmas 2766, Toa Baja, PR 00949-4104   (787) 795-5590
Vegetarian/Caribbean. This restaurant serves Puerto Rican-style versions of traditional vegetarian and health food dishes. Open Monday through Saturday for breakfast through late lunch. Open Sunday for brunch. Full service, vegan options, take-out, VISA/MC, $$.

Rhode Island

EAST GREENWICH

Pick Pockets Deli
431 Main St., East Greenwich, RI 02818   (401) 884-0488
Middle Eastern. Dine on vegetarian options including falafel, hummus, tabbouleh, baba ghanouj, stuffed grape leaves, and other dishes at Pick Pockets. Open daily for lunch and dinner. Limited service, catering, take-out, VISA/MC, $$.

NARRAGANSETT

Crazy Burger Café & Juice Bar
144 Boon St., Narragansett, RI 02882   (401) 783-1810
American. The décor at Crazy Burger is predictably fun, with pale-green walls, paper lanterns, and ornaments hanging from the ceiling. Among the offerings here are veggie soups, sandwiches, veggie burgers, and a vegan tofu scramble. Open daily for three meals. Full service, vegan options, fresh juices, smoothies, BYOB, VISA/MC/AMEX/DISC, $$.

NEWPORT

Harvest Natural Foods
1 Casino Terrace, Newport, RI 02840   (401) 846-8137
Health foods store deli. Harvest Natural Foods carries health food, nutritional products, and more. Open Monday through Saturday for three meals. Open Sunday for lunch and early dinner. Limited service, catering, VISA/MC/AMEX/DISC, $-$$.

• Garden Grille Café and Juice Bar

727 East Ave., Pawtucket, RI 02860   **(401) 726-2826**

Vegetarian. Garden Grille serves delicious soups, vegetable chili, salads, wood-grilled sweet potatoes, soy chicken strips, grilled burgers and veggie dogs, wraps, rice noodle hot pots, and vegan desserts, including a tofu cheesecake with raspberry sauce. On weekends, breakfast options include organic, free-range egg dishes, breakfast burritos, vegan pancakes and muffins, and grilled tofu or tempeh. **Open Monday through Friday for lunch and dinner. Open Saturday and Sunday for three meals. Limited service, vegan options, fresh juices, soymilk, smoothies, special drinks, BYOB, catering, VISA/MC/AMEX, $-$$.**

(For restaurant listings in the surrounding areas, see East Greenwich and Pawtucket.)

Curry in a Hurry

272 Thayer St., Providence, RI 02906   **(401) 453-2424**

Indian. Curry in a Hurry offers several vegetarian dishes. Diners must place their orders at a counter upon arriving, then their meals are brought to their table. **Open daily for lunch and dinner. Counter service, take-out, $.**

Hot Pockets

285 Thayer St., Providence, RI 02900   **(401) 751-3251**

Middle Eastern. Hot Pockets has a whole menu section devoted to vegetarian foods. Their wrap sandwiches include Phil's Falafel, the Potato Pocket, vegetarian kibbe, grilled marinated vegetables, and more. Side items like stuffed grape leaves, baba ghanouj, and fresh homemade tabbouleh salad are also available. **Open daily for lunch and dinner. Limited service, take-out, VISA/MC/DISC, $.**

Kabob and Curry

261-263 Thayer St., Providence, RI 02900   **(410) 272-3463**

Indian. Kabob and Curry serves a range of classic Indian dishes, with a number of vegetarian items. Choose from baigan bharta (eggplant with onions and tomatoes), tandoori vegetable kabobs, veggie pakoras (fritters), and more. Those who can't decide can order the Maharani, the big vegetarian combination plate! They are happy to accommodate those with food allergies. **Open daily for lunch and dinner. Lunch buffet on Sunday. Full service, take-out, wine/beer/alcohol, VISA/MC/AMEX/DISC, $$.**

O-Cha

221 Wickenden St., Providence, RI 02903   **(401) 421-4699**

Thai. This restaurant offers six vegetarian Thai dishes, including Sautéed Veggies in Chili Sauce, Vegetables with Peanut Sauce, mock vegetarian duck made from tofu, and noodle dishes. They do not use MSG in food preparation. **Open daily for lunch and dinner. Full service, vegan options, take-out, $$.**

Taste of India
221 Wickendon St., Providence, RI 02903   **(401) 421-4355**
Indian. A vegetarian section on the menu lists several options at Taste of India. **Open daily for lunch and dinner. Full service, vegan options, take-out, $$.**

Thai Star
1088 Chalkstone Ave., Providence, RI 02908   **(401) 421-5840**
Thai. Located near the intersection of Chalkstone and Academy Avenues, Thai Star has a variety of appetizers, like fried tofu, and main courses, such as Pad Thai. Practically every entrée can be prepared with tofu, including four different curries. Don't forget to ask that the fish sauce be left off. This restaurant is a smoke-free environment. **Open daily for lunch and dinner. Full service, vegan options, take-out, VISA/MC, $$.**

WAKEFIELD

Pick Pockets Deli
231 Old Tower Hill Rd., Wakefield, RI 02879   **(401) 792-3360**
Middle Eastern. See description under East Greenwich, RI.

South Carolina

CHARLESTON

(For restaurant listings in the surrounding areas, see North Charleston.)

Doe's Pita Plus
334 E. Bay St., Charleston, SC 29401   **(843) 577-3179**
Middle Eastern. Doe's offers sandwiches made with freshly-baked pita bread and a variety of fillings, as well as salads, stuffed grape leaves, hummus, and other Middle Eastern foods. **Open daily. Counter service, vegan options, take-out, $.**

Raspberry's Natural Food Store
1331 Ashley River Rd., Charleston, SC 29407   **(843) 556-0076**
Natural foods store. Raspberry's deli serves some fish, but all of its cooked meals are vegetarian. Their menu includes two vegan soups daily, salads, sandwiches, fresh-baked breads, and vegan pastries. Organic produce is used whenever available. **Open Monday through Saturday for breakfast through early dinner. Open Sunday for brunch. Counter service, vegan options, take-out, VISA/MC/DISC, $. www.raspberrysnaturalfoods.com**

COLUMBIA

The Basil Pot
928 Main St., Columbia, SC 29201-3964   **(803) 799-0928**
Natural foods/macrobiotic. This is the home of the original Southern Vegetarian Hunting
Lodge's kitchen. Soups and salads, chili, a tofu burger, sandwiches, pizza with tempeh sausage,
a tofu loaf, daily specials, and a breakfast menu are featured. **Open daily for three meals.**
Full service, vegan options, fresh juices, non-alcoholic beer, take-out, VISA/MC, $-$$.
www.metromark.net/basilpot.htm

Miyo's Fine Shanghai and Szechuan Cuisine
922 S. Main St., Columbia, SC 29201   **(803) 779-6496**
Chinese. Voted "Best of Columbia" for three consecutive years, Miyo's lets you create your
own plate with choices from more than 30 kinds of fresh vegetables; dishes can be steamed
with no oil, starch, and/or MSG. Or choose from vegetarian appetizers, like spring rolls and
dumplings, and entrées, such as American and Chinese versions of Buddhist Delight. **Open
Monday through Saturday for lunch and dinner. Closed Sunday.** Full service, vegan options,
non-smoking, reservations recommended, macrobiotic options, fresh juices, wine/beer/
alcohol, VISA/MC/AMEX/DISC/DC, $$.

Nice-N-Natural
1217 College St., Columbia, SC 29201   **(803) 799-3471**
Natural foods. Just south of the Capitol Building, this mostly vegetarian establishment offers
soups, fruit and green salads, and sandwiches, like the highly recommended veggie Reuben.
Open Monday through Saturday for lunch. Closed Sunday. Counter service, vegan options,
fresh juices, special drinks, take-out, no credit cards, $.

The Orient
Decker Plaza, 1735 Decker Blvd., Columbia, SC 29206   **(803) 738-0095**
Chinese. Be sure to request The Orient's vegetarian menu, and you'll find Chinese Broccoli
in Barbecue Sauce, Chinese Eggplant, tofu dishes, and more. **Open Monday through
Saturday for lunch and dinner. Closed Sunday.** Full service, vegan options, wine/beer/
alcohol, take-out, VISA/MC/DISC, $$.

Rosewood Natural Foods Market & Deli ✪
2803 Rosewood Dr., Columbia, SC 29205   **(803) 256-6410**
Natural foods deli. Located near State Fairgrounds & Midlands Technical College, Rosewood
features both a natural foods store and a deli. Their chef, who has more than 20 years, expe-
rience with vegetarian cooking, serves up such vegan or vegetarian options as as Seaside Cakes,
Jerk Tofu, Seitan Pâté, and a tofu-based cream-filled Crumb Cake or Cheesecake. They even
make prepared pizzas to be baked at home. Special dietary needs are readily accommodated.
Open Monday through Saturday for three meals. Open Sunday for lunch and early dinner.
Deli-style, macrobiotic/vegan options, take-out, VISA/MC/AMEX/DISC, $-$$. www.
RosewoodMarket.com

GREENVILLE

Garner's Natural Foods Market & Café
60 E. Antrim Dr., Greenville, SC 29607   **(864) 242-4856**
Natural foods. Connected to the natural foods store, Garner's Café offers excellent vegan baked goods made from scratch on the premises. Hot lunches and veggie-bar drinks are available, as well as vegetarian and vegan deli salads. **Open daily. Cafeteria, vegan options, limited catering, VISA/MC/DISC, $-$$.** www.garnersnatural.com

India Palace
59 Liberty Ln., Greenville, SC 29607   **(864) 271-8875**
Indian. India Palace serves vegetarian specialties including appetizers, curries, and vegetable and rice dishes. **Open Monday through Saturday for lunch and dinner. Open Sunday for dinner. Full service, VISA/MC, $-$$.**

Pita House
495 S. Pleasantburg Dr., Greenville, SC 29607   **(864) 271-9895**
Mediterranean. Pita House offers excellent traditional Mediterranean vegetarian dishes, including hummus, baba ghanouj, falafel, fresh-baked pita bread, and a vegetarian plate. **Open Monday through Saturday for lunch and dinner. Closed Sunday. Full service, take-out, no credit cards, $.**

• SWAD
1421 Laurens Rd., Greenville, SC 29607   **(864) 233-2089**
Vegetarian/Indian. This vegetarian Indian restaurant offers friendly service and Bombay-style cooking, including samosas, rice dishes, and curry dishes. **Open Monday through Saturday for lunch and dinner. Closed Sunday. Limited service, VISA/MC/AMEX/DISC, $.**

MURRELLS INLET

New Life Natural Foods
2749 S. Hwy. 17, Murrells Inlet, SC 29576   **(843) 651-5701**
Natural foods. This natural foods store and café offers a menu including Thai, Indian, and Vietnamese dishes, organic peanut butter and jelly sandwiches, a hummus and veggie pita, a veggie burger, a Fakin' Bacon Sandwich, and grilled cheese sandwiches made of dairy, soy, or rice cheese. **Open Monday through Saturday for three meals. Open Sunday for brunch. Counter service, vegan options, fresh juices, smoothies, take-out, $.**

MYRTLE BEACH

New Life Natural Foods
1209 38th Ave. N., Myrtle Beach, SC 29577   **(843) 448-0011**
3767 Renee Dr., Myrtle Beach, SC 29579   **(843) 236-1950**
Natural foods. See description under Murrells Inlet, SC.

NORTH CHARLESTON

•Soul Vegetarian South
3225-A Rivers Ave., North Charleston, SC 29405   (843) 744-1155
Vegetarian. Considered a must for all visiting the area, this primarily vegan establishment serves great vegetarian versions of traditional soul cuisine. Highly recommended items include the Split Pea Soup, Carrot Salad Sandwich, Gyros, Pizzas, BBQ Kalebone, and Almond Ice Kream. Honey is used in the BBQ sauce and some drinks, but these are clearly marked on the menu. **Open Tuesday through Friday for lunch and dinner. Open Saturday and Sunday for three meals. Closed Monday. Full service, vegan options, special drinks, take-out, VISA/MC/AMEX/DISC, $-$$.**

South Dakota

RAPID CITY

Hunan Chinese Restaurant
1720 Mt. Rushmore Rd., Rapid City, SD 57701   (605) 341-3888
Chinese. Vegetarian appetizers, soups, and entrées are available at Hunan. **Open daily for lunch and dinner. Full service, wine/beer, take-out, VISA/MC/AMEX, $$.**

••Veggies
2050 W. Main St., #7, Rapid City, SD 57702   (605) 348-5019
Vegan. Located in a natural foods store, this highly affordable vegan restaurant and bakery offers soups, salads, veggie burgers, wraps, Chiquen Salad Sandwiches, whole grain rolls, muffins, cookies, and their own version of non-dairy ice cream. They also offer entrées of the day, such as Chickpea á la King, Veggie Lasagna, Veggie Stroganoff, and Harvest Nut Roast, and serve food based on themes, like Mexican Mondays, Fajita Fridays, and "All You Should Eat" Sunday buffets. **Open Monday through Thursday for three meals. Open Friday for breakfast and lunch. Closed Saturday. Open Sunday for brunch. Limited service, fresh juices, take-out, $.**

SPEARFISH

Bay Leaf Café
126 W. Hudson St., Spearfish, SD 57783   (605) 642-5462
Ethnic foods. Wow! Another restaurant in South Dakota with great vegetarian options. Try the Garden Burger, Black Bean Burger, Bean Burrito, Tempeh with Sautéed Veggies, or one of the other vegetarian selections. **Open daily for three meals. Full service, vegan options, espresso/cappuccino, catering, delivery, VISA/MC/AMEX/DISC, $-$$.**

Restaurant codes: ✪ Reviewers' Choice   • Vegetarian Restaurant   •• Vegan Restaurant
Restaurant prices: **$** less than $6   **$$** $6-$12   **$$$** more than $12
Credit Cards Accepted: VISA - VISA   MC - MasterCard   AMEX - American Express
DISC - Discover   DC - Diner's Club

| YANKTON |

Body Guard
2101 Broadway Mall, Yankton, SD 57078   **(605) 665-3482**
Natural foods. Experience a natural foods bakery with a lot of specialty and non-allergenic baked goods in a quaint atmosphere. **Open daily. Limited service, take-out, $.**

Tennessee

| BARTLETT |

Golden Garden
6249 Stage Rd., Bartlett, TN 38134   **(901) 372-2012**
Chinese. Be sure to request the special vegetarian menu, which features soups, appetizers, and entrées, many made with mock meats. **Open daily for lunch and dinner. Full service, wine/beer/alcohol, VISA/MC/AMEX/DISC/DC, $$.**

| CHATTANOOGA |

(For restaurant listings in the surrounding areas, see Collegedale.)

• Wildwood Country Life Vegetarian Restaurant
809 Market St., Chattanooga, TN 37402   **(423) 634-9925**
Vegetarian. At Country Life, enjoy an all-you-can-eat vegan buffet with a salad bar, soups, seasonal vegetables, beans, brown rice, cornmeal rolls, fresh baked desserts, and soft-serve soy ice cream. There are different choices for entrées each day, which may include a mixed-grain casserole, potato-mushroom chimichangas, tomato-asparagus stuffed potatoes, or zucchini, pepper, and tomato couscous. The only thing that keeps this establishment from being completely vegan is the occasional use of honey. **Open Sunday through Friday for lunch. Closed Saturday. Buffet, vegan options, take-out, VISA/MC, $-$$.**
www.wildwoodlsc.org/Restaurant/Restaurant.htm

| COLLEGEDALE |

• Village Market Deli
5002 University Dr., Collegedale, TN 37315   **(423) 238-3286**
Vegetarian/natural foods store deli. This ultra-affordable deli, in a natural foods store catering to the Seventh-day Adventist community, offers hot foods for lunch, such as cheese enchiladas and Spanish lentils and brown rice. Grab-and-go items, a pay-by-weight salad bar, and soups are available until 6 on weekdays. They can also make vegan cakes to order. **Deli open Monday through Friday for lunch. Store open Sunday through Thursday for three meals. Open Friday for breakfast and lunch. Closed Saturday. Deli-style, vegan options, take-out, VISA/MC/DISC, $.** http://vm.southern.edu/main.php

KNOXVILLE

El Charro
6701 Kingston Pike, Knoxville, TN 37919   **(423) 584-9807**
University Of Tennessee Campus
    811 22nd St., Knoxville, TN 37916   **(865) 525-9808**
10420 Kingston Pike, Knoxville, TN 37922   **(865) 693-9660**
Mexican. This Mexican establishment offers veggie burritos, enchiladas, tacos, beans without lard, and rice. Open daily. Full service, non-alcoholic wine/beer, wine/beer/alcohol, take-out, VISA/MC/AMEX, $-$$.

Falafel Hut
601 James Agee St., Knoxville, TN 37916   **(423) 522-4963**
Middle Eastern. Falafel Hut offers vegetarian grape leaves, hummus, tabbouleh, lentil soups, salads, kabobs, and deli sandwiches. Meatless items are clearly indicated on the menu. Open daily for three meals. Full service, non-alcoholic beer, special drinks, take-out, catering, VISA/MC/AMEX, $-$$.

The Tomato Head
12 Market Square, Knoxville, TN 37902   **(423) 637-4067**
Italian. Feast on gourmet pizzas, vegetarian and vegan sandwiches, a hummus pita, and tofu enchiladas in Tomato Head's dining room, which doubles as an art gallery. Open Tuesday through Sunday for lunch and dinner. Open Monday for lunch only. Full service, vegan options, VISA/MC/AMEX, $.

MADISON

Tennessee Christian Medical Center Cafeteria
500 Hospital Dr., Madison, TN 37115   **(615) 865-0300**
Hospital cafeteria. This Seventh-day Adventist-run cafeteria serves mostly vegetarian food, including cheese manicotti, burritos, cashew casserole, and quiche. There's also a great salad bar. Open daily. No breakfast on Saturday and Sunday. Cafeteria, take-out, $.

MEMPHIS

(For restaurant listings in the surrounding areas, see Bartlett.)

Brother Juniper's College Inn
3519 S. Walker Ave., Memphis, TN 38111   **(901) 324-0144**
American. Be sure to try Brother Juniper's scrambled tofu, granola with rice milk, Greek salad, and unique sandwiches made on Armenian cracker bread. Open Tuesday through Saturday for three meals. Closed Sunday and Monday. Full service, vegan options, catering, take-out, $.

Cravings
764 Mt. Moriah Rd., Memphis, TN 38117   **(901) 374-0600**
American. Enjoy a huge selection of vegetarian items from Cravings, including Middle Eastern appetizers and sandwiches, salads, pasta, gourmet pizza, and more. Open Sunday

through Thursday for lunch and dinner. Open Friday for lunch only. Open Saturday after sundown. Full service, vegan options, catering, take-out, VISA/MC, $$.

La Montagne Restaurant
3550 Park Ave., Memphis, TN 38111   **(901) 458-1060**
Natural foods. La Montagne offers several vegetarian options, including veggie burgers, vegetables alfredo, pizza, and burritos. **Open daily for lunch and dinner.** Full service, espresso/capuccino, take-out, VISA/MC, $$.

Squash Blossom
5022 Poplar Ave., Memphis, TN 38117   **(901) 685-2293**
Natural foods. Enjoy a tofu and tempeh vegetable stir-fry, oat burgers, linguine marinara, and other dishes in Squash Blossom's smoke-free environment. **Open daily.** Cafeteria, vegan options, fresh juices, smoothies, espresso/cappuccino, take-out, VISA/MC/AMEX/DISC, $-$$.

NASHVILLE

(For restaurant listings in the surrounding areas, see Madison.)

• Grins Vegetarian Café
Ben Schulman Center for Jewish Life, Vanderbilt University
2421 Vanderbilt Pl. at 25th Ave., Nashville, TN 37212   **(615) 322-8571**
Vegetarian café. Grins is pronounced "greens," like the Yiddish word for vegetables. This kosher, vegetarian café on the Vanderbilt campus offers daily entrée and panini specials, as well as a Curried Tofu Wrap, Hummus Wrap, Veggie Sandwich on Maple-Wheat, and other sandwiches. Options include soy mozzarella, and sandwiches that can be made vegan are clearly marked on the menu. The café also offers salads, sides, soups, cookies, muffins, and desserts, many of which are vegan. **Open Monday through Thursday for lunch and dinner. Open Friday for lunch. Closed Saturday and Sunday.** Cafeteria, vegan options, take-out, catering, VISA/MC, $.

Sunshine Grocery
3201 Belmont Blvd., Nashville, TN 37212   **(615) 297-5100**
Natural foods deli. Buy various ethnic vegetarian dishes at Sunshine's deli counter, located inside a natural foods store. **Open Monday through Saturday for three meals. Closed Sunday.** Take-out, fresh juices, smoothies, VISA/MC, $.

Restaurant codes: ✪ Reviewers' Choice   • Vegetarian Restaurant   •• Vegan Restaurant
Restaurant prices: **$** less than $6   **$$** $6-$12   **$$$** more than $12
Credit Cards Accepted: VISA - VISA   MC - MasterCard   AMEX - American Express
DISC - Discover   DC - Diner's Club

Texas

AMARILLO

Back to Eden Snack Bar and Deli

2425 I-40 W., Amarillo, TX 79109   **(806) 353-7476**

Natural foods. Described as the healthiest place to eat in Amarillo, Back to Eden features fresh baked goods and salads, homemade salad dressings, and fresh soups made without MSG. **Open Monday through Saturday. Closed Sunday. Limited service, catering, take-out, VISA/MC/AMEX/DISC, $-$$.**

AUSTIN

• Bouldin Creek Coffeehouse

1501 S. 1st St., Austin, TX 78704   **(512) 416-1601**

Vegetarian/coffeehouse. This coffeehouse has a good selection of dishes, including many vegan offerings that are marked as such on the menu. Choose from baked oatmeal, tofu scramble, hummus, salads, a vegetable plate, and vegetarian Sloppy Joes. There is a deck in the back for outdoor seating, and there are board games available for customers to pass the time. **Open daily for three meals and late night service. Limited service, vegan options, smoothies, take-out, VISA/MC, $-$$.**

Casa de Luz

1701 Toomey Rd., Austin, TX 78704   **(512) 476-5446**

Macrobiotic. This restaurant is mainly vegan and about 90 percent organic. The menu changes daily, but you'll usually find such items as soups, salads, brown rice, raw vegetables, steamed greens, beans, buckwheat pancakes, tofu dishes, burgers with yam fries, or the Guatemalan (tortilla with tofu stir-fry). They also offer vegan desserts and a great weekend brunch buffet. Patio dining is available, as well as natural cooking classes, yoga, massage, and much more. **Open daily for lunch and dinner. Full service, vegan options, no credit cards, $-$$.**

Changos

3023 Guadalupe St., Austin, TX 78705   **(512) 480-8226**

Mexican. Their limited menu does include vegetarian sides and entrées, and mushrooms may be substituted for meat in some dishes. All of their sauces are made from scratch. **Open daily for lunch through late evening. Limited service, take-out, non-smoking, special drinks, beer, smoothies, VISA/MC, $.**

• Madras Pavilion

9025 Research Blvd., Ste. 100, Austin, TX 78758   **(512) 719-5575**

Vegetarian/Indian. This restaurant serves up kosher, vegetarian South Indian cuisine, including idly, vadas, samosas, kabobs, lentil soup, naan, parathas, more than 10 kinds of dosais, utthapams, curry and rice dishes, thali, and desserts. Check out their popular lunch buffet as well. **Open daily for lunch and dinner. Full service, vegan options, fresh juices, special drinks, suitable for business entertaining, take-out, catering, VISA/MC/AMEX/DISC, $.** www.madras-pavilion.com

• Mother's Café and Garden
4215 Duval St., Austin, TX 78751 (512) 451-3994

Vegetarian. Mother's international vegetarian food includes enchiladas, stir-fry, veggie burgers, lasagna, soups, salads, and desserts. **Open daily for lunch and dinner. Full service, vegan options, fresh juices, wine/beer, take-out, VISA/MC/DC, $$.**

• Mr. Natural
1901 E. Cesar Chavez St., Austin, TX 78702 (512) 477-5228

Vegetarian/Mexican. Mr. Natural features a whole-wheat bakery, a juice bar, veggie burgers, and an array of Mexican food, such as Breakfast Tacos with Veggie Chorizo (sausage), Veggie Ceviche, vegetarian fajitas, and veggie tamales. **Open daily for three meals. Cafeteria, fresh juices, take-out, $.**

• Veggie Heaven
1914A Guadalupe St., Austin, TX 78705 (512) 457-1013

Vegetarian/Chinese. Veggie Heaven is a university hot spot serving healthy, Asian-style vegetarian and vegan cuisine that won't leave your stomach or your wallet empty afterwards. Try the Hawaiian Luau, which is a tantalizing combination of chewy vegetable protein, vegetables, and pineapple in a sweet and sour sauce. **Open daily for lunch and dinner. Full service, vegan options, take-out, reservations not taken, VISA/MC, $.**

• West Lynn Café
1110 W. Lynn St., Austin, TX 78703 (512) 482-0950

Vegetarian. Enjoy a delicious selection of vegetarian Southwestern, Mexican, Indian, and other international specialties here. Soups, sandwiches, light fare, and pasta are offered in an eclectic, historic neighborhood close to downtown. **Open daily for lunch and dinner. Full service, vegan options, fresh juices, espresso/cappuccino, wine/beer, take-out, VISA/MC/AMEX, $-$$.**

DALLAS

(For restaurant listings in the surrounding areas, see Fort Worth, Plano, and Richardson.)

• Follow Your Heart
600 N. Pearl St., Ste. G103, Dallas, TX 75201 (214) 953-0411

Vegetarian. Located in the arts district of downtown Dallas, Follow Your Heart carries healthy vegetarian and mostly vegan cuisine from all over the world. In addition to a juice bar, the café offers Texas chili over rice, curried tofu, and Italian rice balls. **Open daily for breakfast and lunch. Counter service, catering, take-out, soymilk, smoothies, reservations not needed, macrobiotic/vegan options, VISA/MC/AMEX/DISC/DC, $.**

• Francis Simun's
3106 Commerce St., Dallas, TX 75226 (214) 741-4242

Vegetarian. Francis Simun's offers a large selection of vegan muffins, cookies, cakes, and pies on a daily basis. **Open daily for lunch and dinner. Full service, vegan options, fresh juices, wine/beer, catering, take-out, AMEX/DISC/DC, $-$$$.**

Genghis Grill

1915 Greenville Ave., Dallas, TX 75206   **(214) 841-9990**

Mongolian. Select your vegetables from a salad bar and take them to a chef who will stir-fry them Mongolian barbecue-style for you. **Open Monday through Saturday for lunch and late dinner. Closed mid-afternoons. Closed Sunday. Full service, vegan options, VISA/MC/ AMEX/DISC/DC, $$.**

• Kalachandji's Restaurant and Palace

5430 Gurley Ave., Dallas, TX 75223   **(214) 827-6330**

Vegetarian/Indian. Vegetarian Times rated this restaurant, at a Krishna temple, the #1 vegetarian restaurant in the Southwest. All menu items are free of preservatives and refined sweeteners. A House Tamarind Tea and fresh homemade breads are featured. An Indian gift shop and indoor or outdoor dining are available. **Open Tuesday through Sunday for lunch and dinner. Closed Monday. Buffet, catering, VISA, $-$$.** www.kalachandjis.com

La Valentina de Mexico

14866 Montfort Dr., Dallas, TX 75240   **(972) 726-0202**

Mexican. Not just the average serving of tortillas and beans, La Valentina de Mexico delights customers with sophisticated choices from Crepas de Champinones (crepes with mushrooms and a poblano sauce) to Caldo Xochimilco (a corn kernel broth with poblano pepper stripes). Their bar is open until 1 a.m. **Open weekdays for lunch and daily for dinner. Full service, catering, reservations recommended, espresso/cappuccino, special drinks, beer/wine/alcohol, VISA/MC/AMEX/DISC/DC, $$$.**

Queen Of Sheba

3527 McKinney Ave., Dallas, TX 75204   **(214) 521-0491**

Ethiopian. This traditional Ethiopian menu will entice both the meat-eater and herbivore alike. Most of the salads and vegetable dishes are topped with exotic and spicy sauces. **Open daily for lunch and dinner. Full service, vegan options, espresso/cappuccino, non-alcoholic beer, beer/wine/alcohol, special drinks, reservations recommended, VISA/MC/AMEX/ DISC/DC, $$-$$$.**

Roy's Natural Market

130 Preston Royal Shopping Ctr., Dallas, TX 75230   **(214) 987-0213**

Health foods store deli. Roy's is a deli, bakery, and juice bar offering salads, sandwiches, and entrées, such as lasagna, brown rice and stir-fry vegetables, and calzones. **Open Sunday through Friday. Closed Saturday. Buffet, fresh juices, take-out, VISA/MC/AMEX/DISC, $.**

• Sankofa Vegetarian Café

1908 Martin Luther King Blvd., Dallas, TX 75215   **(214) 421-0013**

Vegetarian. This restaurant carries a great variety of dishes, such as soups, chili, salads, tacos, pasta dishes, veggie burgers, sandwiches, mock meats, and vegan desserts. It also hosts live music performances and poetry readings. **Open Tuesday through Friday for lunch and dinner. Open Saturday for lunch through late night service. Open Sunday for dinner only. Closed Monday. Full service, vegan options, fresh juices, smoothies, take-out, catering, VISA/MC/AMEX, $.**

• Strictly Vegetarian Inc.
243 Wynnewood Shopping Cntr., Dallas, TX 75224   **(214) 941-0540**

Vegetarian. This casual deli offers healthy and nutritious vegetarian alternatives, such as "veggie fish," "veggie barbecue chicken," and a "veggie meatball sub," along with an array of soups, salads and desserts. Open Monday through Saturday for lunch and early dinner. Closed Sunday. Deli-style, non-smoking, take-out, catering, reservations not taken, macrobiotic/vegan options, $-$$.

Thai Lotus Kitchen
3851 D Cedar Springs Rd., Dallas, TX 75219   **(214) 520-9385**

Thai. Thai cooking classes are offered in this smoke-free restaurant. Open Friday and Saturday for lunch and dinner. Full service, take-out, VISA/MC/AMEX, $-$$.

DENTON

Cupboard Natural Foods
200 W. Congress St., Denton, TX 76201   **(940) 387-5386**

Natural foods. The Cupboard offers delicious soups, salads, and sandwiches made fresh in its café and sells organic produce, packaged vegetarian and vegan meals, and unique pastas and bread at the market. However, it is more than a natural foods market and café; it also has a full gift shop, alternative magazines, chair massages, and cruelty-free, environmentally-friendly cosmetics. Open Monday through Saturday for three meals. Open Sunday for lunch and dinner. Limited service, catering, take-out, macrobiotic/vegan options, fresh juices, smoothies, soymilk, espresso/cappuccino, beer/wine/alcohol, VISA/MC, $. www.cupboard naturalfoods.com

Mr. Chopsticks
1120 W. Hickory St., Denton, TX 76201   **(940) 382-5437**

Thai. Half of the menu is vegetarian, and the vegan items are marked with stars. The Denton Area Vegetarian Organization said the owner of Mr. Chopsticks has been wonderful about accommodating vegetarians. In fact, one of the baskets from the meat and seafood fryer accidentally contaminated the vegetarian one, so he bought a new vegetarian fryer specifically with baskets that would not fit the other fryers. Open daily. Full service, vegan options, outdoor seating, beer, take-out, VISA/MC, $. www.mrchopsticks.com

Siam House
909 S. Ave. C At I-35, Denton, TX 76201   **(940) 382-5118**

Thai. The menu includes some vegetarian items, such as spring rolls and soups, but the staff will accommodate any special requests. One member from the area says that the Garlic Tofu is particularly excellent. Open Monday through Friday for lunch and dinner. Open Saturday for dinner only. Closed Sunday. Full service, vegan options, non-smoking, beer/wine, VISA/MC/AMEX/DISC, $$.

• Tara Pherma
1306 W. Hickory St., Denton, TX 76201   **(940) 387-9222**

Vegetarian. Located behind Voyager's Dream, this mostly vegan restaurant serves soups, salads, hummus, raw foods, veggie wraps, sandwiches, and herbal tea. You can sit at tables or on pads on the floor in a tea room. The adjoining center houses a store and offers massage, yoga classes, apothecary, and more. **Restaurant open Monday through Saturday for lunch. Call for store hours. Full service, vegan options, smoothies, take-out, VISA/MC/AMEX/ DISC, $-$$.**

EL PASO

Ardovino's
206 Cincinnati Ave., El Paso, TX 79902   **(915) 760-6000**
865 N. Resler Dr., El Paso, TX 79912   **(519) 760-6000**
Italian. Established in 1961, Ardovino's originally opened as a gourmet and Italian food mart and has since expanded to include a pizzeria. The menu includes soups, salads, a Vegetarian Sandwich, and an assortment of traditional and gourmet pizzas, offered with or without cheese. Unique vegetarian pizzas include Sun-Dried Tomato & Pesto, Spinach & Garlic, Artichoke & Red Pepper, and the Mediterranean (mushrooms, garlic, tomatoes, and capers). **Open daily for lunch and dinner. Full service, vegan options, espresso/cappuccino, beer/ wine, take-out, VISA/MC/AMEX/DISC, $-$$. www.ardovinospizza.com**

The Bistro
7500 N. Mesa St., El Paso, TX 79912   **(915) 584-5757**
Café. This quaint, European-style restaurant offers some vegetarian items, such as Grilled Vegetables over Sun-Dried Polenta; Southwest Portobello Pasta with corn, black beans, and roasted red peppers (vegan); a Vegetarian Napolean; Three-Cheese Portobello Lasagna; and Vegetarian Soft Tacos. **Open Monday through Friday for lunch and dinner. Open Saturday for dinner only. Closed Sunday. Full service, vegan options, reservations recommended, espresso/cappuccino, wine, take-out, catering, VISA/MC/AMEX/DISC/DC, $$.**

Delhi Palace
1160 Airway Blvd., Ste. E1, El Paso, TX 79925   **(915) 772-9334**
Indian. Delhi Palace offers many vegetarian options. **Open daily for lunch and dinner. Full service, vegan options, take-out, VISA/MC/AMEX/DISC/DC, $$.**

Greenery Bakery, Café & Grill
Sunland Park Mall, 750 Sunland Park Dr., El Paso, TX 79912   (915) 584-6706
American. The menu here includes Vegetarian Tamales (with cheese), Garden Pitas, Pasta Primavera, Portobello and Eggplant Lasagna, veggie pizzas (with or without cheese), and salads. **Open daily for lunch and dinner. Full service, vegan options, VISA/MC/AMEX/ DISC/DC, $-$$$.**

Mediterranean Cuisine
4111 N. Mesa St., El Paso, TX 79902   **(915) 542-1012**
Mediterranean. This restaurant carries several vegetarian dishes, including tabbouleh, hummus, falafel, baba ghanouj, and vegetarian lasagna. Or simply ask the staff for dishes suitable for vegans. **Open Monday through Saturday for lunch and dinner. Closed Sunday. Full service, vegan options, VISA/MC/AMEX/DISC, $-$$.**

Sura Café
1421 N. Lee Trevino Dr., El Paso, TX 79936 **(915) 590-2424**

Thai. This informal restaurant offers many vegetarian Thai and Southeastern Asian dishes. They can substitute tofu for meat in any recipe, and they offer vegetarian dishes like Vegetarian Pad Thai, Nasi Goreng, and Broccoli Tofu. **Open Monday through Saturday for lunch and dinner. Closed Sunday. Full service, vegan options, wine/beer/alcohol, take-out, VISA/MC/AMEX, $$.**

FORT WORTH

The Back Porch
3400-B Camp Bowie Blvd., Fort Worth, TX 76107 **(817) 332-1422**

Sandwich and salad shop. Located across the street from the museums and Omni theater, The Back Porch offers a salad bar with items sold by weight, vegetarian sandwiches and burgers, and low-fat ice cream. **Call for hours. Limited service, $.**

•• Spiral Diner & Bakery
1401 Jones St., Fort Worth, TX 76102-6576 **(817) 332-8834**

Vegan. Spiral Diner, the first vegan restaurant in Tarrant County, offers salads, burgers, tempeh sandwiches, Mediterranean foods, burritos, Tofu Rancheros, Spinach Lasagna, and vegan soft serve floats. The owner donates a portion of the restaurant's profit to local grassroots organizations that are fighting for human, animal, and environmental causes. **Open Monday through Saturday for lunch and dinner. Open Sunday for lunch through early dinner. Full service, smoothies, soymilk, VISA/MC/AMEX/DISC, $-$$. www.spiraldiner.com**

HOUSTON

• Anand Bhavan Restaurant
6662 Southwest Fwy., Houston, TX 77074 **(713) 977-0150**

Vegetarian/Indian. This restaurant specializes in South Indian dishes, such as masala dosa and sambar. Lunch is offered buffet-style, and outdoor seating is available. **Open daily for lunch and dinner. Full service, vegan options, take-out, VISA/MC, $.**

• Bombay Sweets & Vegetarian Restaurant
5827 Hillcroft St., Houston, TX 77036 **(713) 780-4453**

Vegetarian/Indian. As the name implies, you can indulge in a variety of Indian sweets and snacks at this establishment. **Open daily for lunch and dinner. Counter service, take-out, VISA/MC/AMEX, $.**

Butera's Fine Foods and Deli
4621 Montrose Blvd., Houston, TX 77006 **(713) 528-3737**

Deli. Butera's has become a staple in Houston cuisine, serving items from their gourmet deli to overflowing crowds. In addition to classic sandwiches, they offer vegetarian soup, salads, and fresh fruits and vegetables. **Open Monday through Saturday for lunch and dinner. Closed Sunday. Cafeteria, catering, wheelchair accessible, outdoor seating, VISA/MC/AMEX/DISC/DC, $$-$$$.**

•• Garden Bistro
9013 Westheimer Rd., Houston, TX 77063   **(713) 783-6622**
Vegan/Asian. One block east of Columbia Medical Center, Garden Bistro was formerly Green Planet Vegetarian Café. Its friendly, knowledgeable staff serves up dishes such as dumplings, garden fried rice, mock beef or mock shrimp entrées, and much more. Save room for some soy ice cream for dessert. **Open Thursday through Tuesday for lunch and dinner. Closed Wednesday. Full service, non-smoking, take-out, delivery, VISA/MC/AMEX/DISC, $.**

• Madras Pavilion
3910 Kirby Dr., Houston, TX 77098   **(713) 521-2617**
Vegetarian/Indian. See description under Austin, TX.

A Moveable Feast
9341 Katy Fwy., Houston, TX 77027   **(713) 365-0368**
American. Vegetarian offerings include five different kinds of veggie burgers, an eggless Caesar salad, vegetarian "Texas barbeque," chili tempeh burgers, blue corn enchiladas with black beans, cheeseless florentine lasagna, vegan spinach enchiladas, vegetarian chicken fried steak with roasted potato sticks, vegetarian fajitas, pita pizzas, and more. Desserts made fresh daily. Eggless mayonnaise available upon request; organic produce used when available. **Open daily for lunch and dinner. Limited service, take-out, informal atmosphere, non-smoking, vegan/macrobiotic options, fresh juices, smoothies, soymilk, special drinks, wine/beer, non-alcoholic wine/beer, VISA/MC/AMEX/DISC/DC, $-$$.**

• Quan Yin Vegetarian Restaurant
10804 E. Bellaire Blvd., Houston, TX 77072   **(281) 498-7890**
Vegetarian/Asian. Quan Yin offers a wide variety of dishes daily, many using mock meats and fish. **Open daily for lunch and dinner. Full service, vegan options, non-alcoholic wine/beer, VISA/MC, $$.**

•• The Raw Truth Vegetarian Café
3815 Live Oak St., Houston, TX 77004   **(713) 523-9755**
Vegan/raw foods. The raw foods offerings at this restaurant include salads, vegetable burgers, and veggie barbecue ribs. **Open Monday through Friday for lunch and early dinner. Closed Saturday and Sunday. Limited service, fresh juices, smoothies, VISA/MC/AMEX/DISC, $$.**

• Shri Balaji Bhavan
5655 Hillcroft St., Houston, TX 77036   **(713) 783-1126**
Vegetarian/Indian. Try Shri Balaji Bhavan's special crepe dishes and boiled rice patties. **Open daily for lunch and dinner. Limited service, MC, $.**

•• Soya Café
1304 M Blalock Rd., Houston, TX 77055   **(713) 464-2926**
Vegan/International. Soya Café offers many types of cuisines, including appetizers, salads, soups, Chinese dishes, sandwiches, veggie burgers, pasta dishes, and desserts. **Open daily for lunch and dinner. Full service, fresh juices, take-out, VISA/MC, $-$$.**

• Suprabhath
5600 Hillcrest Ave., Houston, TX 77036   **(713) 266-6684**

Vegetarian/Indian. Suprabhath carries authentic South Indian vegetarian cuisine for a fair price. Open Wednesday through Monday for lunch and dinner. Closed Tuesday. Counter service, catering, reservations not needed, non-smoking, VISA/MC/AMEX/DISC/DC, $.

Thai Pepper
2049 W. Alabama St., Houston, TX 77098   **(713) 520-8225**

Thai. We've been told this restaurant serves the best Thai food in Houston. Also, the staff is accommodating, and the cooks are willing to turn meat entrées into veggie entrées. Open Monday through Friday for lunch and dinner. Open Saturday and Sunday for dinner only. Full service, VISA/MC/AMEX/DISC/DC, $$.

• Thali Indian Vegetarian
6855 Southwest Fwy., Houston, TX 77074   **(713) 772-0084**

Vegetarian/Indian. This restaurant offers traditional Indian fare, including soups, curry dishes, and stuffed breads. Open Wednesday through Monday for dinner. Closed Tuesday. Full service, vegan options, VISA/MC/AMEX, $$.

• • Tien Ren Vegetarian Restaurant ✿
7549 Westheimer Rd., Houston, TX 77063   **(713) 977-3137**

Vegan/Chinese. Tien Ren's menu includes appetizers, soups, noodle dishes, rice dishes, chef's specials, and entrées. Try dishes like Braised Seitan Noodle Soup, Eggless Fu Yong, Vegan Beef and Chinese Broccoli, Tofu and Veggie Ham with seasonal greens, and Basil Tofu Crepes. The restaurant has lunch buffets on weekdays and all-day buffets each weekend. Open Tuesday through Sunday for lunch and dinner. Closed Monday. Full service, vegan options, take-out, VISA/MC/AMEX/DISC, $$-$$$.

• Udupi Café
Shepherd Plaza, 2121 Richmond Ave., Houston, TX 77098   **(713) 521-3939**

Vegetarian/Indian. This all-you-can-eat buffet often features items like curried vegetables, uthappam, dosas, palak paneer, samba vada (fried lentil donuts), and gobi (cauliflower) Manchurian. The service is highly rated. Open daily for lunch and dinner. Buffet, vegan options, VISA/MC/AMEX, $.

Ziggy's Healthy Grill
2320 W. Alabama St., Houston, TX 77098   **(713) 527-8588**

American. Ziggy's healthy American-style grill welcomes a relaxed and informal crowd to try its veggie burgers, salads, spinach and mushroom quesadillas, veggie platters, and pizza. The award-winning veggie chili and yam fries alone are worth the trip. Open Monday through Friday for lunch and dinner. Open Saturday and Sunday for three meals. Limited service, non-smoking, smoothies, espresso/cappuccino, beer/wine, non-alcoholic beer, take-out, VISA/MC/AMEX/DISC/DC, $-$$.

PLANO

Macro Broccoli
580 W. Arapaho Rd., Ste. 406, Plano, TX 75080   **(972) 437-1985**
Macrobiotic. Enjoy delicious cuisine served buffet-style, including Broccoli Quiche, Chickpea
Croquettes, Vegetable Stew, soups, tofu burgers, steamed vegetables, pasta dishes, lasagna,
baked goods, and more. **Open Monday through Saturday for lunch and dinner. Open
Sunday for lunch.** Cafeteria, macrobiotic/vegan options, VISA/MC, $.

RICHARDSON

• Food For Thought
581 W. Campbell Rd., Richardson, TX 75080   **(972) 889-3663**
Vegetarian/Indian. This restaurant serves both northern and southern Indian cuisine, includ-
ing soups, samosas, pakoras, and dosas. **Open Tuesday through Sunday for lunch and dinner.
Closed Monday.** Full service, vegan options, fresh juices, take-out, catering, VISA/MC/
AMEX/DISC/DC, $. www.fftdallas.com

• Gopal — Fine Indian Vegetarian Cuisine
758 S. Central Expy., Richardson, TX 75080   **(972) 437-0155**
Vegetarian/Indian. This restaurant offers both northern and southern Indian cuisine in a
lunch and dinner buffet. Feast on traditional soups, appetizers, breads, dosas, rice dishes,
and more. **Open daily for lunch and dinner.** Full service, vegan options, take-out, VISA/
MC/AMEX/DISC, $-$$.

• International Buddhist Progress Society
1111 International Pkwy., #300, Richardson, TX 75081   **(972) 907-0588**
Vegetarian. Healthy and light vegetarian and vegan lunch options available in this informal,
relaxed eatery. **Open Monday through Friday for breakfast through early dinner. Open
Saturday and Sunday for lunch.** Buffet, vegan options, cash or check only, $. www.ibps.org/
Dallas/index.htm

• Madras Pavillion
101 S. Coit Rd., Richardson, TX 75080   **(972) 671-3672**
Vegetarian/Indian. See description under Austin, TX.

Star Of Siam
708 W. Spring Valley, Richardson, TX 75002   **(972) 479-9542**
Thai. This down-to-earth, home-style restaurant prepares several meals for Dallas-area
Buddhist monks every week. They also offer 55 Thai-style vegetarian dishes and will
prepare meals with or without fish sauce. **Open daily for lunch and dinner.** Full service,
vegan options, soymilk, beer/wine/alcohol, take-out, delivery, VISA/MC/DISC/DC, $$.

•• Suma Veggie Café
800 E. Arapaho Rd., Richardson, TX 75081   **(972) 889-8598**
Vegan/Chinese. A simple, family-operated restaurant, Suma offers traditional dishes made
with meat analogs. No MSG is used in the food. They offer a lunch buffet from Monday

through Saturday. The owners are very sweet and accommodating. **Open Monday through Saturday for lunch and dinner. Full service, non-smoking, take-out, VISA/MC/AMEX/DISC, $$.**

• Udipi Café
35 Richardson Heights Ctr., Richardson, TX 75080 (972) 437-2858

Vegetarian/Indian. Udipi Café offers soups, more than 10 varieties of dosas, rice dishes, sambar, coconut chutney, idly, dahl, uthappams, and vada for both dinner and as part of a lunch buffet. **Open Wednesday through Monday for lunch and dinner. Closed Tuesday. Full service, vegan options, VISA/MC, $-$$.**

• • Veggie Garden
516 Arapaho Rd., Ste. #112, Richardson, TX 75080 (972) 479-0888

Vegan/Chinese. Located in the Northrich Village Shopping Center, Veggie Garden resembles a typical Chinese restaurant, except that all "chicken," "pork," "beef," and "shrimp" are vegetarian. Menu includes veggie fish with hot bean sauce, veggie pork with broccoli, veggie kung pao beef, and the house specialties, veggie lemon chicken and tofu hush puppies with brown sauce. **Open Tuesday through Sunday for lunch and dinner. Closed Monday. Full service, VISA/MC, $$.** www.lohla.com/veggiegarden

SAN ANTONIO

Adelante Mexican Food
21 Brees Blvd., San Antonio, TX 78209 (210) 822-7681

Mexican. Among the great vegetarian offerings here are tofu enchiladas and puffy tacos. **Open Tuesday through Saturday for lunch and dinner. Closed Sunday and Monday. Full service, take-out, catering, no credit cards, $-$$.**

Gini's Home Cooking and Bakery
7214 Blanco Rd., San Antonio, TX 78216 (210) 342-2768

Natural foods/American. Good old-fashioned foods are prepared in a healthy way and served in a totally smoke-free atmosphere. Menu choices for vegetarians include seasonal fresh fruit and whole-wheat pancakes. Pritikin-style meals are available, as are fresh baked breads, pies, and cookies. **Open daily. Full service, fresh juices, wine/beer, VISA/MC/AMEX, $$.**

Indian Oven
1031 Patricia Dr., San Antonio, TX 78213 (210) 366-1030

Indian. Indian Oven offers over a dozen different vegetarian dishes, including potatoes cooked with spinach, eggplant and potatoes sautéed in a tomato/onion sauce, and spicy garbanzo beans. Also, you can enjoy belly dancing the first Friday of every month at 7 p.m. **Open daily for lunch and dinner. Full service, vegan options, take-out, catering, VISA/MC/AMEX/DISC, $$.**

La Fiesta Patio Café
1421 Pat Booker Rd., San Antonio, TX 78148 (210) 658-5110

Mexican. Fiesta Patio's whole-grain brown rice is prepared Spanish-style. No lard is used, and foods are made with peanut oil. All food is prepared without preservatives, MSG, or other artificial ingredients. **Open Tuesday through Sunday. Closed Monday. Full service, wine/ beer, VISA/MC/AMEX, $.**

Thai Kitchen

445 McCarty Rd., San Antonio, TX 78216   **(210) 344-8366**

Thai. Enjoy soups, appetizers, and one of nine vegetarian entrées. Offerings include Spring Rolls, Hot and Sour Soup, Bean Curd with Hot Pepper, and Noodles with Vegetable Gravy. **Open Monday through Saturday for lunch and dinner. Closed Sunday. Full service, wine/ beer, VISA/MC/AMEX/DISC/DC, $$.**

Twin Sisters Bakery and Café

6322 N. New Braunfels Ave., San Antonio, TX 78209   **(210) 822-0761**

124 Broadway St., San Antonio, TX 78205   **(210) 354-1559**

Natural foods. The owners call this an "herbally influenced restaurant." Whole-wheat chalupas and quesadillas are samples of the natural foods choices. Oatmeal Special and tacos are included on the breakfast menu. **Open Tuesday through Saturday for three meals. Open Monday for breakfast only. Closed Sunday. Full service, macrobiotic/vegan options, fresh juice, wine/beer, $-$$.**

Zuni Grill

511 River Walk St., San Antonio, TX 78205   **(210) 227-0864**

Southwestern. Zuni Grill is in the heart of the Riverwalk tourist district and is only one block from the San Antonio Convention Center. Its menu includes vegetarian and vegan soups and three vegetarian entrées, and vegans may request that dishes be prepared without cheese. Both indoor and outdoor seating are available. **Open daily for three meals. Full service, vegan options, catering, take-out, VISA/MC/AMEX/DISC/DC, $$.**

SOUTH PADRE ISLAND

Naturally's

3112 A Padre Blvd., South Padre Island, TX 78597   **(956) 761-5332**

Natural foods. Naturally's features a salad bar, fresh juices, and full menu selection. **Open daily for breakfast and lunch. Full service, vegan options, fresh juices, smoothies, beer, take-out, VISA/MC/AMEX, $.**

U.S. Virgin Islands

ST. JOHN

•Katilady's Vegetarian Deli

Boulon Center, Cruz Bay, St. John, VI 00831   **(340) 693-8500**

Vegetarian deli. Katilady's offers numerous hot and cold vegetarian items, including sesame tofu, a feta-tomato salad, spicy lentil soup, a veggie nut burger, hummus, tabbouleh, vegan cornbread, and several desserts. The company also caters for weddings and other events, offers private chef services, and provides villa provisioning. **Open Monday through Friday** for lunch and dinner. Open Saturday for lunch. Closed Sunday. Deli-style, vegan options, fresh juices, smoothies, delivery, catering. www.katilady.com/vegetarian_deli_and_grocery.htm

ST. THOMAS

• Akasha Sweet Life
Smith Bay, St. Thomas, VI 00802   **(340) 775-2650**
Vegetarian. This is a small vegetarian café. Open daily for lunch and dinner. Full service, take-out only, VISA/MC, $$.

The Natural Choice
Wheatley Center II, St. Thomas, VI 00802   **(340) 714-1111**
Natural foods. At The Natural Choice, enjoy creative vegetarian dishes and fresh juices within a garden ambiance. Open Monday through Saturday for three meals. Open Sunday for breakfast and lunch. Limited service, vegan options, fresh juices, take-out, VISA/MC/AMEX, $$.

Natural Food Grocery & Deli
4 Basabe Subbase, Mardela Circle, St. Thomas, VI 00802   **(340) 774-2800**
Natural foods deli. You will find Middle Eastern dishes, veggie burgers, tofu spreads, smoothies, and more in this natural foods store deli. Open daily for breakfast through early dinner. Limited service, vegan options, take-out, $.

Wok and Roll
6200 Smith Bay, Red Hook, St. Thomas, VI 00802   **(340) 775-6246**
Chinese. This restaurant, located below the Warehouse Bar, offers four vegetarian entrées including Curry Tofu and Buddha's Delight. Though primarily take-out, it does offer some patio seating. It is located across the street from the ferry dock. Open daily for lunch and dinner. Take-out, $$.

Zorba's
1854 Hus, Government Hill, Charlotte Amalie
St. Thomas, VI 00802   **(340) 776-0444**
Greek. This casual, friendly restaurant offers several vegetarian and vegan options on their menu. Guests can sit out on the courtyard surrounded by banana and palm trees. Open Monday through Saturday for lunch and dinner. Closed Sunday. Full service, vegan options, take-out, VISA/MC/AMEX, $-$$.

Utah

BOULDER

Pole's Place
465 N. Hwy. 12, Boulder, UT 84716   **(801) 335-7422**
American. This restaurant is located across the street from Anasazi State Park. It offers a veggie burger and salads daily. Open daily. Counter service, $.

OGDEN

Bright Day Café
952 28th St., Ogden, UT 84403   **(801) 394-7503**
Natural foods. Bright Day features soups made from fresh vegetables, sandwiches on whole-grain bread, fruit shakes, and baked goods. **Open Monday through Saturday for lunch. Closed Sunday. Buffet, vegan options, fresh juices, take-out, $.**

Harvest Restaurant
341 27th St., Ogden, UT 84401   **(801) 621-1627**
Natural foods. Enjoy a wide variety of sandwiches, soups, and salads at Harvest Restaurant. **Open Monday through Saturday for three meals. Closed Sunday. Full service, fresh juices, smoothies, catering, take-out, VISA/MC/AMEX, $.**

PARK CITY

China Panda
1776 Park Ave., Park City, UT 84068   **(435) 649-5593**
Asian. China Panda offers vegetarian and vegan options and a large lunch buffet. Perhaps before or after a meal there, you can catch a movie at the nearby theater. **Open daily for lunch and dinner. Closed mid-afternoon. Full service, vegan options, beer/wine, reservations recommended, take-out, VISA/MC/DISC, $$-$$$.**

SALT LAKE CITY

(For restaurant listings in the surrounding areas, see Sugarhouse.)

Bangkok Thai
1400 Foothill Dr., #210, Salt Lake City, UT 84108   **(801) 582-8424**
Thai. Enjoy vegetarian "palace-style cuisine," such as Pad Tofu sautéed with chilies, garlic, broccoli, peppers, and basil; or Woon Sen Kai, which is glass noodles sautéed with bamboo shoots, egg, bean sprouts, onions, and Thai seasonings. Vegetable stock is used in all vegetarian dishes. According to the menu, most dishes can be ordered vegetarian upon request. Indicate to your server if you want your meal prepared vegan. **Open daily for dinner. Open Monday through Friday for lunch. Full service, vegan options, wine/beer, take-out, VISA/MC/AMEX/DISC/DC, $$.** www.bangkokthai.com

•• Evergreen House
755 S. State St., Salt Lake City, UT 84101   **(801) 328-8889**
Vegan/Chinese/Vietnamese. The menu here includes Spring Rolls, Curry Potatoes, Mock Chicken, Black Pepper Soy Beans, Szechuan Soy Beans, Kung Pao Tofu, and udon or rice noodle dishes. Sometimes, the fortune cookies do contain egg, though. **Open Monday through Saturday for lunch and dinner. Closed Sunday. Full service, non-smoking, take-out, VISA/MC, $-$$.**

• Long Life Vegi House
1353 E. 3300 S., Salt Lake City, UT 84106   **(801) 467-1111**
Vegetarian/Chinese. This vegetarian restaurant serves Chinese cuisine made from soy products

and wheat gluten. Try their spicy garlic eggplant and asparagus entrée. **Open Monday through Saturday for lunch and dinner. Open Sunday for dinner only. Full service, vegan options, non-alcoholic beer, beer, take-out, VISA/MC, $$.**

Oasis Café ✿

151 S. 500 E., Salt Lake City, UT 84106   **(801) 322-0404**

International. Called a "sanctuary in the city," Oasis Café is a mostly vegetarian restaurant featuring a unique, large menu (even for breakfast!) and an atmosphere of natural light and palm trees. All vegan selections are marked as such on the menu, including Farro Medallions, Mixed Grill Polenta, Roasted Portabello Carpaccio, and a Tempeh Gyro. **Open daily for three meals. Full service, vegan options, take-out, catering, beer/wine/alcohol, fresh juices, VISA/MC/AMEX/DISC, $$-$$$.**

•• Sage's Café ✿

473 E. 300 St., Salt Lake City, UT 84111   **(801) 322-3790**

Vegan. Patrons of Sage's Cafe are treated to a comfortable, unique atmosphere where they can enjoy original vegan creations, including Macadamia-Carrot Butter, Shiitake Mushroom "Escargot," and Vegan Philly "Cheesesteaks." Sage's also offers raw food items, macrobiotic options, and its own vegan pastries. Every Wednesday is "all-you-can-eat-vegan-pizza" night. **Open Wednesday through Friday for dinner. Open Saturday and Sunday for three meals. Closed Monday and Tuesday. Full service, beer/wine, take-out, VISA/MC/AMEX/DISC/ DC, $$.** www.sagescafe.com

SPRINGDALE

Panda Garden

8805 Zion Park Blvd., Springdale, UT 84676   **(801) 772-3535**

Chinese. Panda Garden, located near Zion National Park, offers eight vegetarian Chinese dishes, including several with tofu. **Open daily for lunch and dinner. Full service, vegan options, take-out, $$.**

Switchback Grille

1149 Zion Park Blvd., Springdale, UT 84767   **(435) 772-3700**

American. Near Zion National Park, Switchback Grille offers vegetarian and vegan options, such as Traditional "Checca" Pasta, Southwestern Veggie Burrito, and Vegan Linguine. A great assortment of vegetarian appetizers, juice bar beverages, and coffee drinks are also available. **Open daily for three meals. Full service, vegan options, catering, beer/wine/alcohol, VISA/MC/AMEX/DISC/DC, $-$$$.** www.switchbacktrading.com

Zion Pizza & Noodle Company

Town Center, Zion National Park
868 Zion Park Blvd., Springdale, UT 84767   **(801) 772-3815**

Pizza. Enjoy several different types of veggie pizza, as well as a veggie stir-fry with pasta and other dishes. **Open daily for dinner. Full service, take-out, $$.**

SUGARHOUSE

Wild Oats Deli & Store

1131 E. Wilmington Ave., Sugarhouse, UT 84106   **(801) 359-7913**

Deli. Conveniently located in the shopping district of Sugarhouse, Wild Oats is a grocery store emphasizing natural and organic foods. At its deli, customers can choose from a variety of hot- or cold-case vegetarian items, and a vegan dish is available at the deli every day. The Vegan Panini and the Vegetarian Pizza, sold by the slice, are both recommended. **Open daily for three meals. Deli-style, vegan options, fresh juices, VISA/MC, $-$$. www.wildoats.com**

TORREY

Capitol Reef Café

360 W. Main St., Torrey, UT 84775   **(801) 425-3271**

Natural foods. Capitol Reef Café is located next to an inn a few miles from Capitol Reef National Park. Their menu offers a wide variety of vegetarian dishes, including Fettuccini Primavera, Mushroom Lasagna, salads, sandwiches, stir-fry vegetables, and more. **Seasonal hours. Full service, fresh juices, espresso/cappuccino, take-out, $$.**

Vermont

BARRE

A Single Pebble

135 Rte. 302, Barre, VT 05641   **(802) 476-9700**

Chinese. This Chinese restaurant offers great gourmet dishes, including many vegan options. Recommendations include their Hot & Sour Soup, Napa Cabbage, Buddha's Sesame Beef, and the highly popular Mock Eel. Also, they are willing to replace the meat in any dish with tofu. **Open daily for dinner. Full service, vegan options, wine/beer, reservations recommended, VISA/MC/AMEX, $$-$$$.**

BRATTLEBORO

Brattleboro Food Co-op Deli

2 Main St., Brookside Plaza, Brattleboro, VT 05301   **(802) 257-0236**

Natural foods. The co-op has a salad bar stocked with organic ingredients. There is also an eat-in café serving fruit smoothies, organic juices, soups, and stews. **Open daily for breakfast and lunch. Limited service, take-out, macrobiotic options, fresh juices, smoothies, MC/DISC, $. www.brattleborofoodcoop.com**

• Common Ground

25 Elliot St., Brattleboro, VT 05301   **(802) 257-0855**

Vegetarian. A community-based, worker-owned cooperative, Common Ground emphasizes the use of local and organic foods. The restaurant strives to maintain a balance between business needs and social and environmental concerns. Stir-fry and seitan dishes are offered at every meal. **Open Wednesday through Monday. Closed Tuesday. Take-out, vegan options, wine/beer, $.**

• Istanbul Kitchen

74 Cotton Mill Hill, Ste. 357, Brattleboro, VT 05301   **(802) 254-3413**

Vegetarian/Mediterranean. Diners can enjoy a great view of the Connecticut River while they feast on vegetarian and vegan items, including a recommended leek and eggplant casserole, an artichoke casserole, stuffed grape leaves, and maple baklava. **Open daily for lunch and dinner. Deli-style, vegan options, catering, take-out, $.**

BURLINGTON

(For restaurant listings in the surrounding areas, see South Burlington.)

A Single Pebble

133 Bank St., Burlington, VT 05401   **(802) 865-5200**

Chinese. See description under Barre, VT.

City Market

82 S. Winooski Ave., Burlington, VT 05401   **(802) 863-3659**

Natural foods. This establishment is a natural foods and regular grocery store. **Take-out $-$$.**

Five Spice Café ✪

175 Church St., Burlington, VT 05401   **(802) 864-4045**

Asian. Near Burlington's Marketplace, this casual restaurant offers seitan, tempeh, and tofu substitutes upon request. A vegetarian special is available every night. Unique dishes include Indonesian-Style Mock Duck and Vegetarian Vindaloo. Take-out not available after 6 p.m. on Fridays and Saturdays. **Open daily for lunch and dinner. Full service, vegan options, take-out, suitable for business entertaining, special drinks, VISA/MC/AMEX/DISC/DC, $-$$.**

Loong Chat's Kitchen

169 Church St., Burlington, VT 05401   **(802) 651-9660**

Asian. This restaurant specializes in Thai, Vietnamese, and Chinese foods, all of which are available at different times. It is known for its fantastic sushi, and one of the area's most well-known chefs prepares the Vietnamese cuisine. The restaurant is around the corner from Flynn Theatre. **Open Monday through Saturday for lunch and dinner. Open Sunday for lunch only. Full service, non-smoking, reservations recommended, alcohol, non-alcoholic beer/wine, special drinks, VISA/MC/AMEX/DISC/DC, $-$$$.**

Parima Tai Restaurant

185 Pearl St., Burlington, VT 05401   **(802) 864-7917**

Thai. Located in downtown Burlington, Parima offers several of their dishes with tofu in place of meat. Options include woonsen soup (green beans noodle soup with black mushrooms), mixed vegetables with tofu, and tofu curry on jasmine rice. **Open Monday through Friday for lunch and open daily for dinner. Full service, reservations recommended, non-alcoholic wine/beer, wine/beer, smoothies, soymilk, $$$.**

• Stone Soup

211 College St., Burlington, VT 05401   **(802) 862-7616**

Vegetarian/natural foods. Located in downtown Burlington, Stone Soup is a community-based food establishment with cafeteria and counter service. This restaurant has a buffet and salad bar, and its menu includes hot and cold sandwiches, a vegan club, pizzas, vegan baked goods, and of course, soups with vegan rolls. They also offer a Saturday brunch. **Open Monday through Saturday for three meals. Closed Sunday. Buffet, vegan/macrobiotic options, beer/wine, special drinks, take-out, no credit cards, $$.**

KILLINGTON

Hemingway's ✪
4988 US Rte. 4, Killington, VT 05751   **(802) 422-3886**
American/international. Hemingway's has been voted one of America's top 25 restaurants by "Food and Wine Magazine." Located in a restored 1860 house at the foot of Killington mountain, the fine establishment offers many vegetarian selections, including a wild mushroom salad, fresh fruit soup, vegetable flan, fava bean ravioli, and a vegetable strudel. A specially-created four-course vegetarian meal is another option. Reservations are recommended. **Open Wednesday through Sunday for dinner only. Closed Monday and Tuesday. Full service, vegan options, wine/beer/alcohol, VISA/MC/AMEX/DISC/DC, $$$.** www.hemingwaysrestaurant.com

MANCHESTER CENTER

Bagel Works, Inc.
Routes 11 & 30, Manchester Center, VT 05255   **(802) 362-5082**
Bagel shop. More than 16 varieties of bagels are offered with various topping options, including cream cheeses, Tofutti spreads, salads, and other vegetarian combinations. Bagel Works is environmentally conscious and socially active in its community. **Open daily. Counter service, vegan options, fresh juices, $.**

MONTPELIER

(For restaurant listings in the surrounding areas, see Stowe.)

Coffee Corner
83 Main St., Montpelier, VT 05602   **(802) 229-9060**
American. This is a good, old-fashioned American diner with several vegetarian selections on the menu. The California Reuben—grilled tofu, sauerkraut, and provolone topped with Russian dressing on grilled rye—is a vegetarian favorite! Other options include a veggie burger, ratatouille, and a grilled eggplant sandwich. The staff is willing to fulfill special menu requests if possible. **Open daily for breakfast and lunch. Full service, $.**

•• The Evergreen Café
20-22 State St., Montpelier, VT 05406   **(802) 223-0120**
Vegan. The Evergreen Café, located in the back of a natural foods store, offers various stir-fries, Thai and Indian dishes, Middle Eastern and Mexican specialities, wraps, and egg- and dairy-free desserts. They give discounts to those who bring their own container and utensils for take-out. **Open daily for lunch through early dinner. Buffet, take-out, $-$$.**

• Hunger Mountain
623 Stone Cutters Way, Montpelier, VT 05602   **(802) 223-8000**
Vegetarian. With a riverside setting, this informal, family-style cooperative offers a self-serve

food bar that includes vegan baked goods. Sunday brunch is also available. **Open daily for three meals. Counter service, vegan options, beer/wine, VISA/MC, $-$$$.**

Mountain Herbals
7 Langdon St., Montpelier, VT 05602   **(802) 223-0888**
Natural foods. Patrons can enjoy a river setting near the Capitol building, as well as selections from the organic rice and veggies bar, salads, burritos, or a pesto dish, maybe followed by a vegan cookie or two. **Open daily for lunch and weekends for dinner. Limited service, vegan options, VISA/MC/AMEX/DISC, $-$$.**

Rhapsody
28 Main St., Montpelier, VT 05602   **(802) 229-6112**
Macrobiotic. With its emphasis on organic products, Rhapsody offers a natural foods buffet that includes miso soup, tempura, sushi, Japanese noodles, tofu and tempeh items, and maple-sweetened desserts. Thursday evening is "open-mike" night where customers might catch a poetry reading. Rhapsody is located next to the Savoy Movie Theatre. **Open Monday through Saturday for lunch and dinner. Closed Sunday. Cafeteria, vegan options, take-out, VISA/ MC, $-$$.**

State Street Market Grocery
20 State St., Montpelier, VT 05602   **(802) 229-9353**
Natural foods. Next to Evergreen Café, this grocery store specializes in natural foods items and supplements. **Open daily for lunch and dinner. Take-out, vegan options, $-$$.**

• Susan's Kitchen
209 Barre St., Montpelier, VT 05602   **(802) 223-8646**
Vegetarian. Susan's Kitchen offers take-out only and has a menu that changes weekly. Each night, two entrées from a specific country or region are served. The menu indicates which items are vegan. Past options have included moo shu pancakes and Cambodian noodles with red sauce and coconut. **Open Monday through Friday for dinner. Closed weekends. Take-out, vegan options, catering, reservations recommended, $$.**

NEWPORT

• Newport Natural Foods Bakery & Café
194 Main St., Newport, VT 05855   **(802) 334-2626**
Vegetarian. Several hot soups are available daily, plus sandwiches, salads, and freshly-baked goods. Located near Lake Memphremagog, Newport's chalkboard menu changes daily. **Open Monday through Saturday. Closed Sunday. Cafeteria, vegan options, take-out, $.**

SOUTH BURLINGTON

The Café at Healthy Living Natural Foods Market
4 Market St., South Burlington, VT 05403   **(802) 863-2569**
Natural foods café. This café within a natural foods store has an all-organic salad and hot entrée bar. Among its eclectic offerings from around the world are West African Yam & Peanut Stew, Seitan Stroganoff, Tempeh Cacciatore, and Hungarian Roasted Cauliflower.

It also offers sandwiches, tofu dishes, and desserts that are made daily. **Open Monday through Saturday for lunch and dinner. Open Sunday for brunch and dinner. Cafeteria, vegan options, non-smoking, fresh juices, smoothies, take-out, VISA/MC/AMEX/DISC, $$.** www.healthylivingmarket.com

STOWE

Food for Thought Natural Market
Old Farm Rd. (Rt. 100 S.), Stowe, VT 05672   **(802) 253-4733**
Natural foods. Besides being a market, Food for Thought has a café located inside with a salad bar and a steam bar with soups and salads. Hot daily lunch items vary, but past creations include tempeh burgers, burritos, and tofu noodle casserole. Non-dairy baked items are also available. All food is prepared fresh on the premises. **Open daily for three meals. Cafeteria, vegan options, fresh juices, smoothies, take-out, catering, VISA/MC/AMEX, $.**

Red Basil Thai Cuisine
294 Mountain Rd., Stowe, VT 05672   **(802) 253-4478**
Thai. This upscale casual restaurant with a wonderful atmosphere offers excellent gourmet Thai cuisine, including vegetable soup, cashew nut, shiitake and broccoli, and much more. Tofu may be substituted for all dishes on the menu. They are well-known for their sushi and martini bars. **Open daily for lunch and dinner. Full service, vegan options, wine/beer, VISA/MC/AMEX, $$$.**

WHITE RIVER JUNCTION

Tastes of Africa
191 S. Main St., White River Junction, VT 05001   **(802) 295-4250**
African. Tastes of Africa offers a unique dining experience set in an elegant dining room with flowing flora and vivacious music. The chefs here prepare low-fat, gourmet entrées, breads, and vegetable sides based on the customs of their region of Africa, including Ethiopia, Kenya, Nigeria, and Mali. Entrées include eggplant chickpea stew and groundnut vegetable stew. **Open Wednesday through Sunday for dinner. Closed Monday and Tuesday. Full service, take-out, catering, reservations recommended, fresh juices, wine/beer, VISA/MC, $$$.**

Upper Valley Food Cooperative
193 N. Main St., White River Junction, VT 05001   **(802) 295-5804**
Natural foods. This co-op has a deli and food bar that offers mostly vegetarian soups, salads, sandwiches, and plate dishes. Offerings include rice and pecan salad, an organic tempeh salad, baked tofu, and organic roasted root vegetables. **Open Monday through Saturday for three meals. Open Sunday for brunch. Deli-style, vegan options, take-out, $.**

Restaurant codes: ✪ Reviewers' Choice   • Vegetarian Restaurant   • • Vegan Restaurant
Restaurant prices: **$** less than $6   **$$** $6-$12   **$$$** more than $12
Credit Cards Accepted: VISA - VISA   MC - MasterCard   AMEX - American Express
DISC - Discover   DC - Diner's Club

Virginia

Bamboo Garden Restaurant

6331B S. Kings Hwy., Alexandria, VA 22306   (703) 768-2338

Chinese. Enjoy a varied menu with a considerable amount of vegetarian options, many of which include the restaurant's own vegetarian chicken, crafted from soy protein. **Open Wednesday through Sunday for lunch and dinner. Open Monday and Tuesday for dinner only. Full service, vegan options, beer/wine, take-out, delivery, VISA/MC/AMEX/DISC, $$.**

Bilbo Baggins Café Restaurant

208 Queen St., Alexandria, VA 22314   (703) 683-0300

American. Bilbo Baggins' vegetarian items include a Vegetarian Roll, a Vegetarian Plate, pastas, and salads. **Open Monday through Saturday for lunch and dinner. Open Sunday for brunch and dinner. Full service, espresso/cappuccino, non-alcoholic wine/beer, catering, VISA/MC/AMEX/DISC/DC, $$-$$$.**

Bombay Curry Company

3102 Mt. Vernon Ave., Alexandria, VA 22305   (703) 836-6363

Indian. Try the Vegetarian Curry, Vegetarian Thali, or Vegetable Biryani at Bombay Curry Company. **Open daily for lunch and dinner. Open Sunday for brunch. Full service, VISA/MC/DISC/DC, $$.**

Mediterranean Bakery and Café

352 S. Pickett St., Alexandria, VA 22304   (703) 751-1702

Natural foods café. This wonderful café features a Mediterranean décor, including arches, columns, and a terra cotta canopy. Dine on Middle Eastern vegetarian delicacies, including falafel, hummus, baba ghanouj, stuffed grape leaves, salads, spinach pies, and casseroles. All baked goods are prepared fresh on the premises. A grocery store offering Middle Eastern, Italian, and Greek items is also located here. **Open daily for three meals. Limited service, vegan options, take-out, $-$$.**

Whole Foods Market

6548 Little River Tpke, Alexandria, VA 22312   (703) 914-0040

Natural foods. Whole Foods is a chain of full-sized grocery stores specializing in health food items. Most stores have a salad bar and deli with hot and cold vegetarian and vegan options. **Open daily. Take-out, VISA/MC/AMEX/DISC, $.**

• Ambadi Café

4815 Lee Hwy., Arlington, VA 22207   (703) 875-9940

Vegetarian/Indian. This restaurant specializes in South Indian cuisine, such as masala dosas. **Open Tuesday through Sunday. Closed Monday. Full service, vegan options, VISA/MC, $$.**

Chico Rico
1700 N. Moore St., Arlington, VA 22209   **(703) 528-6996**
Mexican. Located in the Rosslyn Eatery on the second level above the Rosslyn Metro Station, Chico Rico has a classic Mexican menu with a wide range of vegetarian items. Vegetarian items are noted on the menu and the beans are made without lard. They offer a spinach burrito and a fresh steamed vegetable burrito platter. **Open Monday through Friday for breakfast and lunch. Closed Saturday and Sunday. Limited service, vegan options, catering, $.**

Delhi Dhaba
2424 Wilson Blvd., Arlington, VA 22201   **(703) 524-0062**
Indian. The menu offers an extensive variety of vegetarian and vegan items, such as samosas (turnovers), pakora (fritters), breads, bhindi masala (okra with onions and peppers), damalu (potatoes with fruit and nut sauce), and desserts, including homemade Indian ice cream with pistachios. **Open daily for lunch and dinner. Full service, vegan options, take out, VISA/MC, $.**

Kabab Masala
297 S. Van Dorn St., Arlington, VA 22304   **(703) 751-2500**
Indian. Try one of the many vegetarian curries found on Kabab's menu. **Open daily for lunch and dinner. Full service, vegan options, Take-out, VISA/MC/AMEX/DISC/DC, $.**

Lebanese Taverna
5900 Washington Blvd., Arlington, VA 22205   **(703) 241-8681**
Middle Eastern. Choose from an entire page of vegetarian appetizers, as well as a variety of vegetarian entrées and sandwiches at Lebanese Taverna. **Open Monday through Saturday for lunch and dinner. Closed Sunday. Full service, vegan options, espresso/cappuccino, take-out, catering, VISA/MC/AMEX, $-$$$.**

• Madhu Ban
3217 N. Washington Blvd., Arlington, VA 22201   **(703) 528-7184**
Vegetarian/Indian. Madhu Ban is located in the Virginia suburbs of Washington, D.C. It offers a wide variety of Indian breads, soups, salads, and entrées, including curry and rice, masala dosas, and more. **Open daily for lunch and dinner. Full service, non-alcoholic wine/beer, catering, take-out, VISA/MC, $$.**

Pamir Afghan Restaurant
561 S. 23rd St., Arlington, VA 22204   **(703) 979-0777**
Afghan. Pamir's vegetarian selection includes three vegetarian entrées, plus appetizers. **Open Monday through Saturday. Closed Sunday. Full service, vegan options, wine/beer/alcohol, take-out, VISA/MC/AMEX, $$.**

Primo Delicafe
4048 S. 28th St., Village of Shirlington, Arlington, VA 22206   **(703) 379-7573**
Deli. Primo Delicafe offers a tasty selection of typical deli sandwiches, including four vegetarian sandwiches, salads, side items, and fresh fruit. **Open daily for three meals. Limited service, vegan options, espresso/cappuccino, VISA/MC, $.**

• Saran Foods
5151 N. Lee Hwy., Arlington, VA 22207   **(703) 533-3600**
Vegetarian/Indian. Experience vegetarian Indian cuisine with such specialties as Chaat Papri (boiled potatoes and chickpeas, mixed with tamari and yogurt sauce), Malai Kofta Curry (vegetable dumplings stuffed with nuts and raisins), and Paper Masala Dosai (thin rice crepes with potato and vegetables) at Saran Foods. A lunch buffet is offered. **Open daily for lunch and dinner.** Limited service, vegan options, fresh juices, non-alcoholic beer/wine, take-out, delivery, catering, VISA/MC/AMEX/DISC/DC, $-$$$. www.saranfoods.com

Whole Foods Market
2700 Wilson Blvd., Arlington, VA 22201   **(703) 527-6596**
Natural foods. See description under Alexandria, VA.

BLACKSBURG

South Main Café
117 S. Main St., Blacksburg, VA 24060   **(730) 552-3622**
Ethnic foods. South Main Café offers a variety of delicious, international vegetarian entrées, including Lemon Grilled Tempeh Filet, Thai Eggplant, and Tofu and Pad Thai. **Open Monday through Saturday for lunch and dinner. Closed Sunday.** Full service, vegan options, fresh juices, wine/beer/alcohol, take-out, $-$$.

CHARLOTTESVILLE

• Integral Yoga Natural Foods
923 Preston Ave., Charlottesville, VA 22901   **(804) 293-4111**
Vegetarian. This health foods deli offers food by the pound, sandwiches, baked goods, knishes, lasagna, hummus, pasta dishes, and Indian and Mexican foods daily. **Open daily.** Buffet, vegan options, non-alcoholic wine/beer, take-out, VISA/MC, $.

Maharaja Indian Cuisine
Seminole Square Shopping Center
139 Zan Rd., Charlottesville, VA 22901   **(804) 973-1110**
Indian. The menu offers a myriad of vegetarian appetizers, soups, salads, entrées, and specialty breads. Lunch buffet available. **Open Tuesday through Sunday for lunch and dinner. Open Monday for dinner only.** Full service, vegan options, catering, take-out, VISA/MC/AMEX/DISC/DC, $$-$$$.

Ming Dynasty
1417 Emmet St., Charlottesville, VA 22901   **(804) 979-0909**
Chinese. This Chinese restaurant offers a huge vegetarian selection, including mock meat, fish, and poultry dishes; bean curd dishes; mixed vegetables; fried rice; spring rolls; steamed dumplings; rice noodles, and more. **Open daily for lunch and dinner.** Full service, take-out, VISA/MC, $$.

• Veggie Heaven
923 Preston Ave., Charlottesville, VA 22903   **(804) 296-9739**
Vegetarian. An organic salad and juice bar, a diverse deli section, and daily specials make

this a vegetarian's delight. Menu items include dishes from Europe and the Middle and Far East. **Open Monday through Saturday for lunch and dinner. Closed Sunday. Limited service, fresh juices, smoothies, soymilk, vegan/macrobiotic options, take-out, catering, non-smoking, VISA/MC, $-$$.**

FALLS CHURCH

Burrito Brothers
7505 Leesburg Pike, Falls Church, VA 22046   **(703) 356-8226**
Mexican. This restaurant offers an excellent selection of Mexican items (burritos, tacos, quesadillas). The menu notes that all non-meat items, including three types of beans, are suitable for vegetarians. **Open daily for lunch and dinner. Full service, vegan options, take-out, VISA/MC/AMEX/DISC, $.**

Neisha Thai Cuisine
6037 Leesburg Pike, Falls Church, VA 22041   **(703) 933-3788**
Thai. Rice noodles stir-fried with fresh mixed vegetables and crushed peanut, Thai eggplant with fresh basil leaves or sautéed fresh watercress in spicy light bean sauce can be yours to taste at the highly acclaimed Neisha Thai Cuisine Restaurant. **Open daily for lunch and dinner. Full service, vegan options, delivery, take-out, VISA/MC/DISC, $$.**

Panjshir Restaurant
924 W. Broad St., Falls Church, VA 22046   **(703) 536-4566**
Afghan. Panjshir, which advertises itself as "specializing in vegetarian dishes," offers creative vegetarian eggplant, pumpkin, and spinach items daily. **Open Monday through Saturday for lunch and dinner. Open Sunday for dinner only. Full service, wine/beer/alcohol, take-out, VISA/MC/AMEX, $$.** www.enterit.com/Panjshir4566/

Raaga
5872 Leesburg Pike, Falls Church, VA 22041   **(703) 998-7000**
Indian. The menu features a good selection of vegetarian authentic appetizers, soups, entrées, and desserts. A daily lunch buffet is also offered. **Open daily for lunch and dinner. Full service, beer/wine/alcohol, catering, VISA/MC/AMEX/DISC, $$.**

FREDERICKSBURG

Sammy T's Light Food and Ale
801 Caroline St., Fredericksburg, VA 22401   **(703) 371-2008**
Natural foods. Sammy T's offers both vegan and vegetarian options, some Middle Eastern and Mexican dishes, and a wide selection of beer. **Open daily for three meals. Full service, vegan options, wine/beer, take-out, VISA/MC/AMEX/DISC, $-$$.**

HARRISONBURG

The Little Grill
621 N. Main St., Harrisonburg, VA 22807   **(540) 434-3594**
American. This one-of-a-kind restaurant was established in 1930. To this day, it still offers

delicious, inexpensive homemade food, including a 'soup kitchen' feeding anyone in the world for free every Monday at noon. Its extensive, mostly vegetarian, menu includes items such as biscuits with mushroom gravy, tofu scrambler with soy sausage, veggie burrito, falafel in pita, veggie chili, and a portobello sandwich. Vegan items noted on the menu. **Open Tuesday through Saturday for three meals. Open Sunday for breakfast and lunch. Closed Monday. Full service, vegan options, fresh juices, espresso/cappuccino, soymilk, beer, $.**

HERNDON

Alahdin Kabab House
2415 B-3 Centerville Rd., Herndon, VA 22070   **(703) 713-9119**
Indian. The vegetarian portion of the menu includes dahl, Bhindi Masala (okra with onions and peppers), and Alu Gobi (cauliflower and potatoes cooked in masala spices). Vegetarian appetizers and rice dishes are also available. **Open daily for lunch and dinner. Cafeteria, vegan options, non-alcoholic wine/beer, catering, take-out, $.**

Asian Bistro
328 Elden St., Herndon, VA 22070   **(703) 742-8881**
Asian. An extensive vegetarian selection distinguishes the Thai and Southeast Asian cusine at the Asian Bistro. Many tofu, eggplant, and vegetable entrées are available, as well as appetizers and soups. **Open daily for lunch and dinner. Full service, vegan options, wine/beer/ alcohol, take-out, VISA/MC/AMEX, $$.**

Harvest of India
364 Elden St., Herndon, VA 22070   **(703) 471-8149**
Indian. Have a Vegetable Samosa, Vegetable Pakora, or one of the several vegetable entrées offered at Harvest of India. **Open daily for lunch and dinner. Full service, wine/beer/alcohol, take-out, VISA/MC/AMEX/DISC/DC, $$.**

Hunan East
2533 John Milton Dr., Herndon, VA 22071   **(703) 476-1666**
Chinese. Choose from several vegetable and tofu entrées. **Open Monday through Saturday for lunch and dinner. Open Sunday for dinner only. Full service, vegan options, VISA/ MC/AMEX, $-$$.**

The Tortilla Factory Restaurant
648 Elden St., Herndon, VA 22070   **(703) 471-1156**
Mexican. All meals are made with 100 percent canola oil, including vegetarian fajitas, meatless Mexican lasagna, and cheese enchiladas. **Open daily for lunch and dinner. Full service, vegan options, non-alcoholic wine/beer, take-out, catering, VISA/MC/AMEX/DISC, $$.**

LEESBURG

Andy's Pizza & Subs
9F Catoctin Cir., SW, Leesburg, VA 22075   **(703) 771-0277**
Deli. Many Middle Eastern favorites, such as falafel, hummus, baba ghanouj, and stuffed grape leaves, are offered daily. Andy will make Lemon-Tahini sauce for the falafel for vegans. **Open daily. Full service, vegan options, $.**

LURAY

Mindi's Mexican Restaurant
1033 US Hwy. 211 W., Luray, VA 22835   **(540) 743-7550**
Mexican. Enjoy several of Mindi's vegetarian Mexican dishes including tacos, burritos, enchiladas, and more. Kids are especially welcome! **Open Tuesday through Sunday for lunch and dinner. Closed Monday. Full service, vegan options, wine/beer, non-alcoholic beer, $.**

MANASSAS

La Tolteca
8412 Sudley Rd., Manassas, VA 20109   **(703) 257-7293**
Mexican. Authentic Mexican restaurant offering a number of vegetarian entrées as well as a variety of margaritas and mixed drinks. **Open daily for lunch and dinner. Full service, take-out, catering, VISA/MC/AMEX/DISC, $-$$.**

McLEAN

Neisha Thai Cuisine
7924 Tysons Corner Ctr., McLean, VA 22102   **(703) 883-3588**
Thai. See description under Falls Church, VA.

NEWPORT NEWS

Nawab Indian Cuisine
11712 Jefferson Ave., Newport News, VA 23606   **(757) 591-9200**
Indian. Nawab features a large selection of vegetarian and vegan appetizers and entrées. Sample vegetable patia (vegetables cooked with sweet and sour mangos and a touch of ginger), palak paneer (spinach with or without Indian cheese), mushroom broccoli krahi (sautéed with vegetables, garlic, and herbs), Bombay potatoes, egglant bharta (baked, then mashed and sautéed with garlic, onions, and tomatoes), and much more. Children's portions are often available for half the price of a regular entrée. **Open daily for lunch and dinner. Full service, vegan options, reservations recommended, beer/wine/alcohol, non-alcoholic beer, special drinks, take-out, VISA/MC/AMEX/DISC/DC, $$.** www.nawabonline.com

NORFOLK

• The Healthfood Center Juice and Smoothie Bar
1701 Colley Ave., Norfolk, VA 23517   **(757) 625-7283**
Vegetarian/juice bar. Located only a mile away from PETA headquarters, this smoothie bar blends fruits, juices, and other healthy ingredients to create its own original, delicious, and refreshing meals in a cup. However, they do not serve food. **Open Monday through Saturday for lunch. Closed Sunday. Counter service, vegan options, fresh juices, smoothies, soymilk, take-out, VISA/MC, $.**

Nawab Indian Cuisine
888 N. Military Hwy., Norfolk, VA 23502   **(757) 455-8080**
Indian. See description under Newport News, VA.

RESTON

Burrito Brothers
11690 Plaza America Dr., Reston, VA 20190   **(703) 478-6394**
Mexican. See description under Falls Church, VA.

Whole Foods Market
11660 Plaza America Dr., Reston, VA 20190   **(703) 736-0600**
Natural foods. See description under Alexandria, VA.

RICHMOND

Cactus Café
5713 Hopkins Rd., Richmond, VA 23234   **(804) 275-9030**
Mexican. This California-style Mexican café serves up a myriad of vegetarian options from the appetizers to the salads to the house specialties. Try the Mexican pizza made from a crispy flour tortilla and topped with salsa, cheese, black olives and jalapeños as well as the delicious stuffed peppers and/or burritos. **Open Monday through Saturday for lunch and dinner. Closed Sunday. Full service, vegan options, beer/wine/alcohol, non-alcoholic beer/wine, take-out, VISA/MC/AMEX/DISC, $-$$.**

The Café
4 N. Thompson St., Richmond, VA 23221   **(804) 359-7525**
Natural foods. Located inside Ellwood Thompson's Natural Market, this café has a rotating menu. New dishes are created on a regular basis by the chef, who is a graduate of The Culinary Institute of America and a registered dietitian. **Open Monday through Saturday for lunch and dinner. Closed Sunday. Limited service, vegan options, fresh juices, catering, VISA/MC, $.**

• Harrison Street Coffee Shop
402 N. Harrison St., Richmond, VA 23220   **(804) 359-8060**
Vegetarian/coffeehouse. This restaurant is a must for vegetarians visiting the area. Their breakfast menu includes a vegan breakfast burrito, veggie or vegan French toast, omelettes, veggie sausage and bacon, and bagels with vegan cream cheese. For lunch, try homemade soups and salads, a black bean hummus wrap, a BBQ tofu sandwich with vegan coleslaw, or the tempeh and artichoke sub. Call ahead for their daily specials. They also offer vegan banana and pumpkin breads. **Open Monday through Friday for three meals. Open Saturday and Sunday for brunch. Full service, vegan options, espresso/cappucino, beer/wine, $.**

India K' Raja
9051-5 W. Broad St., Richmond, VA 23294   **(804) 965-6345**
Indian. Feast upon authentic North and South Indian cuisine at India K'Raja restaurant, which offers various vegetarian appetizers and delicacies. **Open daily for lunch and dinner. Full service, vegan options, fresh juices, smoothies, special drinks, non-alcoholic beer/wine, beer/wine/alcohol, reservations recommended, catering, take-out, VISA/MC/AMEX/DISC/DC, $$.**

Ipanema Café ✪
917 W. Grace St., Richmond, VA 23220   **(804) 213-0170**
Café. This primarily vegetarian café offers delicious dishes, such as stuffed portobello caps, veggie pot pie, jerk seitan, burritos, pastas, and polenta with pumpkin sauce. The spinach enchiladas (with vegan sour cream) and the sweet potato fries are highly recommended. **Open Monday through Saturday for lunch and dinner. Closed Sunday. Full service, vegan options, VISA/MC, $$$.**

ROANOKE

•Eden's Way Vegetarian Café
104 Church Ave. S.E., Roanoke, VA 24011   **(540) 344-EDEN**
Vegetarian café. Eden's Way Vegetarian Café lets you explore vegetarian and vegan specialties, like their original pecan meatloaf, non-dairy lasagnas, and quiches, and more. **Open daily for breakfast through late lunch. Full service, vegan options, fresh juices, soymilk, non-alcoholic beer, non-smoking, take-out, VISA/MC/AMEX/DISC, $.**

Nawab Indian Cuisine
118A Campbell Ave., SW, Roanoke, VA 24011   **(540) 345-5150**
Indian. See description under Newport News, VA.

Wildflour Café and Catering
Towers Shopping Center
2143 Colonial Ave., Roanoke, VA 24015   **(540) 344-1514**
Natural foods. This small friendly restaurant opened in 1991. Enjoy excellent vegetarian soups, fresh baked goods and desserts, along with salads and sandwiches. Entrées include a Millet Grain Burger, rice and beans, quesadillas, burritos, and lasagna. **Open Monday through Friday for lunch and dinner. Open Saturday for lunch. Closed Sunday. Full service, vegan options, take-out, catering, espresso/cappuccino, wine/beer, VISA/MC/AMEX/DISC, $-$$.**

SOUTH ARLINGTON

Luna Grill & Diner
4024 28th St., Shirlington Village, South Arlington, VA 22206   **(703) 379-7473**
American/international. Luna Grill offers ample vegetarian options including salads, three bean vegetarian chili, veggie burgers, pasta, sandwiches, and desserts, including fresh fruit. Chili and soups are served in bread bowls. **Open daily for three meals. Full service, vegan options, VISA/MC/AMEX, $$.**

SPRINGFIELD

Taj Mahal
7239 Commerce St., Springfield, VA 22150   **(703) 644-2875**
Indian. Taj Mahal, which has the same owners as the Washington establishment by the same name, has a special section of the menu offering vegetarian cuisine from northern India. Vegetarian appetizers, soups, and desserts are also available. **Open daily for dinner. Open Monday through Friday for buffet lunch. Full service, vegan options, wine/beer/alcohol, take-out, VISA/MC/AMEX/DISC, $$.**

Whole Foods Market
8402 Old Keene Mill Rd., Springfield, VA 22152   **(703) 644-2500**
Natural foods. See description under Alexandria, VA.

VIENNA

• Amma Vegetarian Kitchen
344-A Maple Ave. E., Vienna, VA 22180   **(703) 938-5328**
Vegetarian/Indian. This small restaurant offers a number of Southern Indian specialties, such as dosa (a thin rice crepe served with sambar and coconut chutney), puri bhaji (fried breads filled with potato), and rasam (a spicy soup). **Open daily for lunch and dinner. Full service, vegan options, take-out, catering, special drinks, VISA/MC/AMEX/DISC/DC, $.**

Panjshir II Restaurant
224 W. Maple Ave., Vienna, VA 22180   **(703) 281-4183**
Afghan. See description under Falls Church, VA.

• Sunflower Vegetarian Restaurant
2531 Chain Bridge Rd., Vienna, VA 22181   **(703) 319-3888**
Vegetarian/Asian. Enjoy both Chinese and Japanese-style vegetarian cuisine, including Lily Flower Soup, wakame soup, miso soup, spring rolls, grilled vegetable salad, cold soba salad, udon or soba noodle dishes, rice-based dishes, tomato tofu, eggplant in basil chili sauce, and much more. Desserts include lemon tofu cheese pie, pumpkin tofu pie, and apple-nut cake. **Open daily for lunch an dinner. Full service, macrobiotic/vegan options, fresh juices, non-alcoholic beer, VISA/MC/AMEX/DISC/DC, $$.**

Whole Foods Market
14E. Maple Ave., Vienna, VA 22180   **(703) 319-2000**
Natural foods. See description under Alexandria, VA.

VIRGINIA BEACH

Azar's Natural Foods
108 Prescott Ave., Virginia Beach, VA 23452   **(757) 486-7778**
Natural Foods/Mediterranean. Known for its many tasty flavors of hummus, Azar's also carries both vegetarian and vegan specialties for lunch, dinner, and desserts, like herbal pizzas, baba ghanouj, and baklava. **Open Monday through Saturday for lunch and dinner. Closed Sunday. Full service, vegan options, espresso/cappuccino, beer/wine, reservations recommended for large parties, take-out, catering, VISA/MC/AMEX/DISC, $$.** www.azarfoods.com

Bangkok Garden
4000 Virginia Beach Blvd., Virginia Beach, VA 23452   **(757) 498-5009**
Thai. A separate vegetarian menu offers large portions of dishes, such as Coconut Soup, Spring Rolls, Tofu Red Curry, and Pad Thai Tofu. **Open Monday through Saturday for lunch and dinner. Open Sunday for dinner. Full service, vegan options, take-out, VISA/MC/AMEX/DISC/DC, $$.**

• Fresh Fare Café
700 19th St., Virginia Beach, VA 23451   **(757) 491-5383**

Vegetarian. A great find if you're near the Virginia coast, the veggie lasagna is rumored to be wonderful. **Open daily for three meals. Full service, vegan options, fresh juices, take-out, $.**

The Heritage Café Deli
314 Laskin Rd., Virginia Beach, VA 23451   **(757) 428-0500**

Natural foods. Many of The Heritage Café Deli's entrées, sandwiches, soups, and fresh baked desserts are prepared without wheat, dairy, sugar, or animal ingredients. **Open daily for three meals. Limited service, vegan options, fresh juices, smoothies, take-out, VISA/MC/AMEX/DISC, $.**

Nawab Indian Cuisine
756 First Colonial Rd., Virginia Beach, VA 23451   **(757) 491-8600**

Indian. See description under Newport News, VA.

Panda Garden
4624 Princess Anne Rd., Virginia Beach, VA 23462   **(757) 467-6698**

Chinese. This restaurant serves vegetarian and vegan versions of most traditional Chinese dishes. **Open daily for lunch and dinner. Full service, vegan options, take-out, catering, VISA/MC/AMEX/DISC, $$.**

Tandoor Indian Restaurant
5760 Northampton Blvd., Virginia Beach, VA 23455   **(757) 460-2100**

Indian. Vegetarian items offered at Tandoor Indian Restaurant include curry dishes, vegetable biryani, freshly baked Indian breads, and more. **Open daily for lunch and dinner. Full service, vegan options, take-out, $$.**

Terra Nova
1805 Laskin Rd., Virginia Beach, VA 23454   **(757) 425-5383**

Natural foods café. Terra Nova Natural Foods and Café gives you lots of ways to stuff yourself silly with overstuffed pitas and sandwiches, salads, and soups while you shop for your favorite organic, vegetarian, and/or vegan items in its store. **Open Monday through Saturday for three meals. Open Sunday for lunch and dinner. Full service, vegan options, fresh juices, smoothies, soymilk, take-out, catering, VISA/MC/DISC, $.**

WILLIAMSBURG

The Dynasty Chinese Restaurant
1621 Richmond Rd., Williamsburg, VA 23185   **(804) 220-8888**

Chinese. Dynasty's menu includes meatless eggrolls, Cabbage and Bean Curd Soup, Chinese Eggplant with Brown Sauce, and Bean Curd and Mushrooms. **Open daily for lunch and dinner. Full service, wine/beer/alcohol, take-out, catering, MC/AMEX/DISC/DC, $$.**

Nawab Indian Cuisine
204 Monticello Ave., Williamsburg, VA 23185   **(757) 565-3200**

Indian. See description under Newport News, VA.

Washington

BELLEVUE

• Nature's Pantry
15600 NE 8th St., # K15, Bellevue, WA 98008   **(206) 957-0090**
Vegetarian/juice bar. Enjoy various vegetarian salads, noodle dishes, baked potatoes, and more. Open daily for breakfast and lunch. Limited service, vegan options, fresh juices, take-out, $.

Pho An-Nam
2255 140th Ave. NE, Bellevue, WA 98005   **(425) 644-4065**
Vietnamese. This restaurant has two menus—one where tofu can be substituted for the meat in any dish, the other organic and vegetarian. Open Monday through Friday for lunch and dinner. Open Saturday for dinner only. Closed Sunday. Full service, vegan options, take-out, cash only, $.

Thai Chef
1645 140th Ave., NE, Bellevue, WA 98005   **(425) 562-7955**
Thai. A wide selection of Thai foods including vegetarian appetizer, soup, and entrée specialties. Open daily for lunch and dinner. Full service, vegan options, wine/beer, take-out, VISA/MC/AMEX, $$.

The Thai Kitchen
14115 NE 20th St., Bellevue, WA 98008   **(425) 641-9166**
Thai. This Thai restaurant offers many vegetarian options, including Spring Rolls, Corn Patties, Coconut Soup with Tofu and Mushrooms, Hot and Sour Vegetable Soup, Eggplant with Ginger and Black Bean Sauce, Steamed Spinach and Tofu topped with Peanut Sauce, and more. Be sure to request for them to omit the oyster sauce. Open daily for lunch and dinner. Full service, vegan options, take-out, $.

• Udupi Palace
15600 NE 8th St., Ste. 9, Bellevue, WA 98008   **(425) 649-0355**
Vegetarian/Indian. Located on the outside of Crossroads Mall, this all-vegetarian restaurant offers delicious authentic Southern Indian cuisine. Open daily for lunch and dinner. Full service, vegan options, VISA/MC, $.

BELLINGHAM

Casa Que Pasa
1415 Railroad Ave., Bellingham, WA 98225   **(360) 738-TACO**
Mexican. Casa Que Pasa's menu features fresh, creative and largely vegan or vegetarian burritos wrapped in vegan flour tortillas. It also offers combination plates, quesadillas, tacos, and chimichangas, and more than 77 choices of tequila. Open daily for lunch. Limited service, vegan options, fresh juices, alcohol, take-out, VISA/MC, $. www.casaquepasa.com

Old Town Café
316 W. Holly St., Bellingham, WA 98225   **(360) 671-4431**
Natural foods. The Old Town Café has a special philosophy regarding its staff: "The people who work here are a team. All jobs are equally important and all tips are shared equally by the cooks, dishwashers, and waitpersons." This social consciousness extends to recycling everything posssible, reducing use of non-recyclables, and supporting local food suppliers. Sandwiches, salads, soups, and vegetarian specials are offered. No smoking allowed. **Open daily for breakfast and lunch. Full service, vegan options, espresso, $.**

Thai House
3930 Meridian St., Bellingham, WA 98226   **(360) 734-5111**
Thai. Thai House has some vegetarian offerings, including spring rolls and rice and noodle dishes. **Buffet take-out, $-$$.**

COLLEGE PLACE

• Walla Walla College Cafeteria
204 S. College Ave., College Place, WA 99324   **(509) 527-2732**
Vegetarian. Choose from meat analogues, a Mexican food bar, pastas, soups, and deli selections. **Open daily during school year. Limited hours in summer. Cafeteria, vegan options, take-out, $.**

ELLENSBURG

• Peace Café
211 E. 8th Ave., Ellensburg, WA 98926   **(509) 962-9599**
Vegetarian. The Peace Café serves vegetarian and vegan food with organic ingredients, fair-trade coffee, tea, and homemade baked goods. All of the money collected from the sales at this small non-profit, which is mostly run by volunteers, go to the Peace & Justice Alliance of Central Washington. The café also serves as a local meeting place for the community and houses our progressive book and video library. **Open Monday, Tuesday, Thursday, and Friday for breakfast through early dinner. Open Wednesday for three meals. Closed Saturday and Sunday. Limited service, vegan options, non-smoking, fresh juices, smoothies, soymilk, take-out, no credit cards, $.** www.elltel.net/peacejustice/

Valley Café
105 W. 3rd Ave., Ellensburg, WA 98926   **(509) 925-3050**
Natural foods. This original Art Deco facility offers Pacific Northwestern cuisine, including some vegetarian options. **Open Monday through Friday for lunch and dinner. Open Saturday and Sunday for three meals. Buffet, take-out, VISA/MC/AMEX/DISC, $.**

EVERETT

The Sisters
2804 Grand Ave., Everett, WA 98201   **(425) 252-0480**
American. This funky family-owned and operated restaurant offers buttermilk hotcakes, salads, their own nut burger, hummus and pita bread, plus more in an environment decorated with

local artwork. **Open Monday through Friday for breakfast and lunch. Closed Saturday and Sunday. Limited service, espresso, VISA/MC, $.**

FEDERAL WAY

Marlene's Market & Deli
31839 Gateway Center Blvd. S., Federal Way, WA 98003   (253) 839-0933
Natural foods. This inviting deli/restaurant has an adjoining espresso bar serving only organic coffee. Marlene's is easily accessible to Interstate 5. **Open daily. Limited service, fresh juices, espresso, take-out, VISA, $.**

KIRKLAND

• Café Happy
102 Kirkland Ave., Kirkland, WA 98033   (425) 822-9696
Vegetarian/Chinese. This tiny Taiwanese-style restaurant has pictures of all the dishes to help you order. Dishes are made fresh and light, with more than 40 menu items to choose from. Seating is limited. **Open daily for three meals. Full service, vegan options, fresh juices, espresso, special drinks, no credit cards, $.**

Moung Thai Restaurant
12549 116th Ave., NE, Kirkland, WA 98034   (425) 821-0577
Thai. Menu contains a number of vegetarian items, including Tum Kah Tofu (hot and sour) soup, Yum Pug (mixed vegetables) salad, Rama Tofu (tofu and poached spinach with peanut sauce), and Rhud Thai (stir fried rice noodle with dried tofu). **Open Tuesday through Sunday for lunch and dinner. Closed Monday. Full service, non-smoking, wine/beer, VISA/MC/ AMEX, $$.**

Shamiana
10724 68th St., NE, Kirkland, WA 98033   (206) 827-4902
Indian. Shamiana's vegetarian specialties include vegetable curry, eggplant dishes, and more. **Open daily for lunch and dinner. Full service, vegan options, non-alcoholic beer, wine/beer, take-out, VISA/MC/AMEX/DC, $$.**

MOUNT VERNON

The Deli Next Door
202 S. 1st St., Mount Vernon, WA 98723   (360) 336-3886
Natural foods. Enjoy wholesome sandwiches, salads, specialties, hot entrées, and kids' plates. **Open daily. Limited service, fresh juices, espresso, $.**

OLGA

Doe Bay Café
Star Rte. 86, Olga, WA 98279   (360) 376-2291
Natural foods. Doe Bay Café is in a turn-of-the-century building that overlooks Otter Cove at the historic Doe Bay Village Resort and Retreat on Orcas Island. Serving dishes with an international flavor, Doe Bay has a casual and social setting. Mineral spring hot tubs, cedar

sauna, massage, and a daily guided kayak-trip help build appetites worthy of the meals there. Indoor and outdoor seating is available. **Open daily in summer. Open only for weekends and holidays after September. Full service, wine/beer, $$. www.doebay.com**

OLYMPIA

Olympia Food Co-op
3111 Pacific Ave. SE, Olympia, WA 98501   **(360) 956-3870**
Natural foods. This co-op restaurant features six different menu rotations with several vegetarian and vegan options, including Cilantro Pesto Pasta, Smoked Tofu Sandwich, Curried Tempeh, and Nori Rolls. Organic foods are used whenever possible. **Open daily for lunch and dinner. Cafeteria, vegan options, fresh juices, take-out, $.**

• Saigon Rendez-Vous Restaurant
117 W. 5th Ave., Olympia, WA 98501   **(360) 352-1989**
Vegetarian/Asian. Choose from appetizers, soups, and main dishes on this Vietnamese and Chinese restaurant's meatless menu. All meat dishes at Saigon are made with soy. **Open daily for lunch and dinner. Full service, vegan options, VISA/MC, $-$$.**

The Urban Onion
116 Legion Way, Olympia, WA 98501   **(360) 943-9242**
Health foods store deli. The Urban Onion is located in the Hotel Olympian across from Sylvester Park and features a vegetarian, health-conscious cuisine. Espresso and delicious desserts are also offered. **Open daily. Full service, fresh juices, espresso, wine/beer, take-out, VISA/MC/AMEX/DISC, $$.**

• Voyeur Vegetarian Café
404 4th Ave. E, Olympia, WA 98501   **(360) 943-5710**
Vegetarian. This restaurant offers a good selection of dishes, including soups, sandwiches, and salads. **Open daily for lunch through late night. Full service, vegan options, take-out, VISA/MC/AMEX, $$.**

PORT ANGELES

(For restaurant listings in the surrounding areas, see Sequim.)

Café Garden
1506 E. 1st St., Port Angeles, WA 98362   **(360) 457-4611**
Ethnic foods. Breakfast items are served all day, and there are creative salads, pasta, and Szechuan stir-fries offered for other meals. **Open daily. Buffet, vegan options, wine/beer, $$.**

Thai Peppers Restaurant
222 N. Lincoln St., Port Angeles, WA 98362   **(360) 452-4995**
Thai. Located one block from the Victoria Ferry, Thai Peppers offers authentic Thai cuisine with a large vegetarian menu. **Open daily for lunch and dinner. Full service, beer/wine, take-out, totally non-smoking, reservations needed for large parties, VISA/MC, $$.**

PORT TOWNSEND

Khu Larb Thai
225 Adams St., Port Townsend, WA 98368 **(360) 385-5023**
Thai. More than 15 vegetarian items are offered at Khu Larb Thai restaurant, including Broccoli with Garlic, Spicy Tofu, Sweet and Sour Vegetables, Tofu with Cashew Nuts, and curry dishes. Be sure to request that fish sauce is not used. **Open daily for lunch and dinner. Full service, vegan options, VISA/MC, $$.**

The Salad Café
632 Water St., Port Townsend, WA 98368 **(360) 385-6532**
Natural foods. At The Salad Café enjoy a Tofu Reuben Sandwich, Tofu and Vegetables, Tofu Stroganoff, quesadillas, tostadas, burritos, cheese blintzes, and breakfast specials, including Tofu Scramble, Tofu Sauté on an English muffin, Potato Sauté, and oatmeal. **Open daily for breakfast and lunch. Full service, vegan options, take-out, $-$$.**

REDMOND

Market Café
Larry's Market, 7320 170th Ave. NE, Redmond, WA 98052 **(425) 869-2362**
Grocery store. A grocery store within a grocery store, the Market Café in Larry's Market offers a complete selection of meat and dairy alternatives, organically grown food, non-toxic cleaning goods, and much more. **Open daily for breakfast and lunch. Take-out, vegan options, catering, delivery, $-$$$.** www.larrysmarkets.com

RENTON

• Pabla Indian Restaurant
364 Renton Center Way SW, # C60, Renton, WA 98055 **(425) 228-4625**
Vegetarian/Indian. This restaurant offers freshly prepared Indian dishes and special tandoori breads made with natural ingredients. Entrées include eggplant bhartha, mushroom masala, mattar paneer, and daal channa wali. Several rice specialties are also offered. Traditional Indian décor and music make the atmosphere warm and inviting. Lunch buffets available. **Open daily for lunch and dinner. Full service, take-out, catering, reservations required, special drinks, VISA/MC/AMEX/DISC/DC, $-$$.**

ROCKPORT

Cascadian Farm Organic Market
5375 Hwy. 20, Rockport, WA 98283 **(360) 853-8629**
Juice bar. This organic farm offers juices, espresso, freshly baked goods, and sorbet. There's a picnic area, and self-guided tours are permitted. **Open until dusk from May until October. Counter service, fresh juices, espresso, VISA/MC, $.**

Restaurant codes: ✪ Reviewers' Choice   • Vegetarian Restaurant   • • Vegan Restaurant
Restaurant prices: **$** less than $6   **$$** $6-$12   **$$$** more than $12
Credit Cards Accepted: VISA - VISA   MC - MasterCard   AMEX - American Express
DISC - Discover   DC - Diner's Club

(For restaurant listings in the surrounding areas, see Bellevue, Everett, Federal Way, Kirkland, Redmond, Renton, and Tacoma.)

•• Araya's Vegetarian Place
4732 University Way NE, Seattle, WA 98105   **(206) 524-4332**
Vegan/Thai. Enjoy 50 vegan Thai dishes at this Seattle restaurant that opened in 1994. Don't miss the fantastic all-you-can-eat buffet lunch on Saturdays. **Open Monday through Saturday for lunch and dinner. Open Sunday for dinner only. Full service, take-out, VISA/ MC/AMEX, $-$$.**

•• Bamboo Garden
364 Roy St., Seattle, WA 98109   **(206) 282-6616**
Vegan/Chinese. The extensive vegetarian menu features delicious vegan Chinese cuisine, including mock turkey and chicken dishes. **Open daily for lunch and dinner. Full service, reservations accepted, wine/beer/alcohol, take-out, VISA/MC/AMEX, $$.**

Bandoleone
2241 Eastlake Ave. E., Seattle, WA 98102   **(206) 329-7559**
International. Bandoleone is a romantic and charming restaurant with a European/Spanish flavor. Vegetarian options include roasted poblano stuffed with corn, vegan soups, and fresh salads. **Open daily for dinner. Full service, reservations recommended, soymilk, espresso/ cappuccino, wine/beer/alcohol, take-out, catering, VISA/MC, $$$.**

• Café Flora ✪
2901 E. Madison St., Seattle, WA 98112   **(206) 325-9100**
International vegetarian. Café Flora lets you savor fine international vegetarian food featuring the flavors of Mexico, Japan, and India. The many creative dishes include Portobello Wellington, Grilled Nutburger, Oaxaca Tacos, and Indian Chickpea Stew. **Open Tuesday through Sunday. Closed Monday. Full service, vegan options, fresh juices, non-alcoholic beer, take-out, VISA/MC, $$.**

• Carmelita
7314 Greenwood Ave., N., Seattle, WA 98103   **(206) 706-7703**
Vegetarian. Carmelita's menu has been influenced by locations around the Mediterranean. The restaurant is owned and operated by a husband-wife team, both of whom are artists. Garden seating is available. **Open Tuesday through Sunday for dinner. Closed Monday. Full service, vegan options, wine/beer, VISA/MC, $$.**

•• The Globe Café & Bakery
1531 E. 14th Ave., Seattle, WA 98122   **(206) 324-8815**
Vegan. This funky coffeehouse has monthly art shows, occasional acoustic music, poetry readings, baked goods, and a weekend brunch menu. **Open daily for lunch through late night service. Limited service, fresh juices, soymilk, espresso, take-out, no credit cards, $.**

•• Good Morning Healing Earth Vegetarian Restaurant
901 55th St., NE, Seattle, WA 98105   **(206) 523-8025**

Vegan. This restaurant is located in the University district of Seattle. Menu items include several salads, stir-fry dishes, veggie burgers, pasta dishes, soup, and more. They use organic ingredients when available. **Open Tuesday through Sunday for lunch and dinner. Closed Monday. Full service, fresh juices, take-out, $-$$.**

Gravity Bar
115 Broadway E., Seattle, WA 98102   **(206) 325-7186**

Natural foods. An extensive menu, including raw and macrobiotic choices, is offered in an intimate, eclectic atmosphere. The juice bar offerings are out of this world. **Open daily for lunch and dinner. Full service, macrobiotic/vegan options, fresh juices, take-out, VISA/MC, $.**

• The Green Cat Café
1514 E. Olive Way, Seattle, WA 98122   **(206) 726-8756**

Vegetarian. This community gathering place offers several salads and delicious entrées, including a vegetable curry dish served over brown rice, a linguini dish, and tofu scramble. **Open daily for three meals. Full service, smoothies, espresso/cappuccino, wine/beer, $.**

Hi-Spot Café
1410 34th Ave., Seattle, WA 98122   **(206) 325-7905**

Natural foods. Located inside a Victorian house, Hi-Spot Café offers a menu of various sandwiches, soups, salads, and beverages for vegetarians and non-vegetarians alike. It also has a bakery featuring low-salt, low-sugar, and whole-grain pastries. No smoking and no cellular phones are allowed inside! **Open Wednesday through Monday for breakfast and lunch. Closed Tuesday. Full service, vegan options, wine/beer, take-out, VISA/MC, $.** www.hispotcafe.com

•• Hillside Quickie's Vegan Sandwich Shop
4106 Brooklyn Ave., Seattle, WA 98101   **(206) 632-3037**

Vegan. Specializing in soy products, this establishment prepares an array of organic and vegan burgers, subs, sandwiches, and side salads almost always filled with tofu, tempeh, or the like. **Open Monday through Saturday for lunch and dinner. Closed Sunday. Limited service, espresso, non-smoking, $$.**

• Honey Bear Bakery
17171 Bothell Way, NE, Seattle, WA 98155   **(206) 366-3330**

Vegetarian. Honey Bear is a Seattle institution that specializes in mostly organic baked goods and pastries. It also offers black bean chili, soups, salads, and more in a homey and fun atmosphere. **Open daily for three meals. Buffet, vegan options, fresh juices, espresso, no credit cards, $.**

• Lucky Palate
307 W. McGraw St., Seattle, WA 98119   **(206) 352-2583**

Vegetarian. Primarily provides a home delivery service of delicious vegetarian or vegan meals through the Seattle area on a weekly basis. The storefront is open Mondays, Tuesdays, and occasionally at other times for grab-and-go meals and a selection of homemade groceries. They sell last week's menu items for $1 every Monday. **Call for hours. vegan options, take-out, catering, delivery, VISA/MC, $$. www.luckypalate.com**

New Orleans Creole Restaurant

114 S. First Ave., Seattle, WA 98104   **(206) 622-2563**

Creole/Cajun. The New Orleans Creole menu features a vegetarian section. It is located in historic Pioneer Square and offers live jazz and blues every evening. **Open daily for lunch and dinner. Full service, vegan options, wine/beer/alcohol, take-out, VISA/MC/AMEX/ DC, $$.**

Pioneer Organics

901 NW 49th St., Seattle, WA 98107   **(206) 632-3424**

Organic natural foods. Depending on where you live in Washington state, you can have fresh, organic packaged goods and produce delivered right to your door. Order online, over the phone, or by snail mail. **Delivery only vegan options, VISA/MC, $-$$$. www.pioneer organics.com**

• Silence-Heart-Nest Restaurant

5247 University Way, NE, Seattle, WA 98105   **(206) 524-4008**

Vegetarian. Fresh and delicious international cuisine featuring items such as Indian light meal (soup, salad, and warm chappati), curry platter, black bean enchilada bake, and the original "neat loaf," a savory blend of wheat cereals, eggs, tofu, rice, and herbs topped with a tangy sauce. Vegan items noted on menu. Daily specials, salads, and sandwiches also offered. **Open Thursday through Tuesday. Closed Wednesday. Open Sunday for brunch. Full service, vegan options, take-out, soymilk, VISA/MC, $-$$.**

Sound View Café

1501 Pike Pl., #501, Seattle, WA 98101   **(206) 623-5700**

Natural foods. This health-minded restaurant has an unusual variety of vegetarian specialities. **Open daily. Cafeteria, wine/beer, take-out, $.**

• Sunlight Café

6403 Roosevelt Way, NE, Seattle, WA 98115   **(206) 522-9060**

Vegetarian. Known for its eggless waffles and pastries, Sunlight offers many vegan options, including sautéed vegetables, desserts, and much more. **Open daily for three meals. Full service, vegan options, fresh juices, organic espresso, wine/beer, take-out, $$.**

•• Teapot Vegetarian House

125 15th Ave E., Seattle, WA 98112   **(206) 325-1010**

Vegan/Asian. All of the food at Teapot Vegetarian House is vegan and certified kosher. They specialize in delicious fake mock chicken, seafood, duck, and beef dishes and offer amazing vegan desserts. **Open daily for lunch and dinner. Full service, VISA/MC, $-$$.**

• Vegete

131 15th Ave. E., Seattle, WA 98112   **(206) 325-1733**

Vegetarian deli. This wonderful deli serves traditionally non-veg items using meat analog products to create a large variety of delicious breakfasts, burgers, soups, salads, and sandwiches. They strive to serve you the tastiest vegetarian food, using the freshest ingredients and as many organic products as possible. **Open daily for three meals. Full service, vegan options, take-out, VISA/MC, $. www.vegeterestaurant.com**

SEQUIM

Khu Larb Thai II

120 W. Bell St., Sequim, WA 98382 **(360) 681-8550**
Thai. See description under Port Townsend, WA.

SPOKANE

China Best

226 W. Riverside Ave., Spokane, WA 99201 **(509) 455-9042**
Chinese. In addition to 22 vegetarian menu items, China Best is willing to accommodate special diets. Every dish is freshly prepared to order. **Open Open Monday through Friday for lunch and dinner. Open Saturday and Sunday for dinner only. Full service, vegan options, wine/beer/alcohol, take-out, VISA/MC/AMEX/DISC, $$.**

• Mizuna

214 N. Howard St., Spokane, WA 99201 **(509) 747-2004**
Vegetarian. Mizuna serves an eclectic array of entrées pulled from many ethnic groups. Some of their dishes include Rustic Polenta, Spring Vegetable Curry, and Ginger Sesame Stir-Fry. Organic produce is used when available. The restaurant features live music in the evening, including classic guitar or Celtic harp music. Wine tasting is featured with dinner on Wednesday evenings, and organic wines are often served. **Open Monday for lunch only. Open Tuesday through Friday for lunch and dinner. Open Saturday for dinner only. Closed Sunday. Full service, vegan options, fresh juices, espresso/cappuccino, non-alcoholic wine/beer, VISA/MC, $$-$$$.**

Niko's

725 W. Riverside Ave., Spokane, WA 99201 **(509) 624-7444**
321 S. Dishman Mica Rd., Spokane, WA 99201 **(509) 928-9590**
Greek/Middle East. Niko's offers many vegetarian items and an all-you-can-eat lunch bar. Open Monday through Friday for lunch and dinner. Closed Saturday and Sunday. Full service, $$.

STANWOOD

Cookie Mill

9808 State Rd. 532, Stanwood, WA 98292 **(360) 629-2362**
Natural foods. The Cookie Mill offers baked goods, a gift shop, and a blackboard menu that features salads, veggie sandwiches, and fruit cups. **Open daily. Cafeteria, smoothies, take-out, no credit cards, $.**

TACOMA

Marlene's Market & Deli
2951 S. 38th St., Tacoma, WA 98049   **(253) 472-4080**
Natural foods. See description under Federal Way, WA.

VANCOUVER

•Nature's Northwest Vancouver
8024 E. Mill Plain Blvd., Vancouver, WA 98664   **(360) 695-8878**
Vegetarian. Come join the fun at Nature's Vancouver with their all-you-can-eat vegan brunch
every Sunday. **Open daily for three meals. Limited service, vegan options, $-$$.**

Thai Orchid Restaurant
1004 Washington St., Vancouver, WA 98660   **(360) 695-7786**
Thai. Thai Orchid offers more than 40 vegetarian dishes, cooked in a traditional Thai
manner with no MSG or hydrogenated oil added. Options include Pra Ram stir-fry (with
broccoli and topped with peanut sauce), Pad Kai Yad Sai (a Thai Omelette made with
ground tofu, onions, tomatoes, and bean sauce, wrapped in scrambled eggs), Evil Jungle
Noodles (medium rice noodles on a bed of steamed cabbage with bean sprouts and curry
sauce), soups, salads, curries, and more. **Open daily for lunch and dinner. Full service,
vegan options, VISA/MC/AMEX/DISC, $$. www.thaiorchid.citysearch.com**

West Virginia

HUNTINGTON

Calamity Café
1555 3rd Ave., Huntington, WV 25701   **(304) 525-4171**
Southwestern. Dedicated to welcoming artists, entertainers, and other walks of life, Calamity
Café is anything but ordinary. It serves comforting Southwestern soul food and offers an
additional vegetarian menu for those craving comfort without the meat. **Open daily for
lunch and dinner. Full service non-smoking, special drinks, beer/wine/alcohol, catering, live
entertainment, VISA/MC, $$. www.calamitycafe.com**

MORGANTOWN

Maxwell's
1 Wall St., Morgantown, WV 26505   **(304) 291-6131**
American. Maxwell's menu clearly labels all their vegetarian options, including Middle

---

Restaurant codes: ✪ Reviewers' Choice • Vegetarian Restaurant •• Vegan Restaurant
Restaurant prices: **$** less than $6 **$$** $6-$12 **$$$** more than $12
Credit Cards Accepted: VISA - VISA MC - MasterCard AMEX - American Express
DISC - Discover DC - Diner's Club

Eastern dishes, various salads, grilled tofu sandwiches, veggie burgers, stir-fry dishes, and much more. **Open daily for lunch and dinner. Full service, vegan options, take-out, $-$$.**

•Mountain People's Kitchen
1400 University Ave., Morgantown, WV 26505   **(304) 291-6131**
Vegetarian. This vegetarian restaurant, attached to a natural foods co-op, offers sandwiches, dairy and non-dairy entrées, and Sunday brunch. The casual and funky atmosphere is conducive to finding information on local events and concerts. **Open Monday, Tuesday, and Friday for breakfast through early dinner. Open Wednesday and Thursday for three meals. Open Saturday for breakfast through late lunch. Open Sunday for brunch. Cafeteria, vegan options, take-out, VISA/MC, $.**

MOUNDSVILLE

•New Vrindavan (Palace Of Gold) Restaurant
Rd. 1, Nbu #24, McCreary Ridge
Moundsville, WV 26041   **(304) 843-1812**
Vegetarian/Indian. This restaurant, on the grounds of a Krishna temple, offers authentic Indian cuisine. **Open daily. Full service, take-out, VISA/MC, $$.**

Wisconsin

GREEN BAY

Los Banditos
2335 W. Mason St., Green Bay, WI 54303   **(414) 494-4505**
1258 Main St., Green Bay, WI 54302   **(414) 432-9462**
Mexican. Their authentic Mexican fare features vegetable or guacamole fillings, but take note that their beans contain a ham-soup base. **Open Monday through Saturday for lunch and dinner. Open Sunday for dinner only. Full service, wine/beer/alcohol, take-out, VISA/MC/ AMEX, $-$$.**

Zimmani's
333 Main St., Green Bay, WI 54301   **(414) 436-2340**
Italian. Fresh pasta specials and homemade pasta salads are highlighted at this upscale restaurant with a full bar and complete deli/bakery. At least one vegetarian special is offered each day, and the staff is willing to accommodate special orders. **Open Monday through Saturday. Closed Sunday. Full service, wine/beer/alcohol, take-out, VISA/MC/AMEX, $-$$.**

LAKE GENEVA

The Cactus Club
430 Broad St., Lake Geneva, WI 53147   **(414) 248-1999**
Southwestern. The Cactus Club offers black bean or vegetable burritos, vegetable fajitas, and garden burgers. **Open daily for lunch and dinner. Full service, take-out, VISA/MC/AMEX/ DISC, $$.**

Himal Chuli
318 State St., Madison, WI 53705   **(608) 251-9225**
Nepalese. Authentic Nepalese cuisine is featured on a menu divided into vegetarian and non-vegetarian dishes. Vegetarian entrées include various vegetable stews and dumplings. Outdoor seating available. **Open daily for lunch and dinner. Limited service, beer, take-out, $-$$.**

Husnu's
547 State St., Madison, WI 53703   **(608) 256-0900**
Turkish/Italian. Sample hummus, falafel, eggplant, and vegetable couscous from Husnu's menu. **Open daily for three meals. Full service, non-alcoholic beer, take-out, VISA/MC, $$.**

Lulu's Restaurant and Deli
2524 University Ave., Madison, WI 53705   **(608) 233-2172**
Middle Eastern. Hummus, baba ghanouj, falafel, and other traditional Middle Eastern dishes are served. **Open Monday through Saturday for lunch and dinner. Closed Sunday. Full service, vegan options, non-alcoholic wine/beer, take-out, VISA/MC, $-$$.**

Monty's Blue Plate Diner
2089 Atwood Ave., Madison, WI 53704   **(608) 244-8585**
American. Step into the past at this 1950s art-deco diner featuring big band music. Although they have the usual diner staples, you'll have no trouble finding a vegetarian meal. Choose from several vegetarian sandwiches, including an artichoke sandwich, a grilled eggplant sandwich, and a black bean burger. Ask about the daily vegetarian dinner special. **Open daily for three meals. Full service, vegan options, espresso/cappuccino, take-out, VISA/MC, $-$$.**

Mother Fool's Coffeehouse
1101 Williamson St., Madison, WI 53703   **(608) 259-1301**
Coffeehouse. Mother Fool's coffeehouse, whose mission is to support the community that supports them, offers organic coffee, vegan treats, a relaxed atmosphere, art work, and good music. **Open daily for three meals. Counter service, vegan options, live music, fresh juices, espresso/cappuccino, take-out, $. www.motherfools.com**

Pasqual's Salsaria and Southwestern Deli
2098 Atwood Ave., Madison, WI 53704   **(608) 244-3142**
2534 Monroe St., Madison, WI 53711   **(608) 238-4419**
Mexican. Pasqual's Salsaria and Southwestern Deli offers a plethora of vegetarian options and variations on their typically meat-filled meals. **Open daily for lunch and dinner. Limited service, take-out, reservations not needed/taken, totally non-smoking, catering, VISA/MC/AMEX/DISC/DC, $.**

• Peacemeal Vegetarian Restaurant
115 State Street, Madison, WI 53703   **(608) 251-7687**
Vegetarian. Described in it's menu as "Madison's only vegetarian restaurant," Peacemeal offers meals made from "locally grown produce, cooperatively produced goods and organic items whenever feasible." All items on the menu are vegetarian and can be made vegan and

include Seitan Gyros, Tempeh Reuben, Lentil Loaf with Mashed Potatoes, daily specials, desserts such as Carrot or Chocolate Cake, and much more. **Open Monday through Saturday for lunch and dinner. Closed Sunday. Full service, vegan options, Equal Exchange coffee and teas, $-$$.**

Rocky Rococo

1618 W. Beltline Hwy., Madison, WI 53713   (608) 251-0304
1301 Regent St., Madison, WI 53703   (608) 256-0600
3001 N. Sherman Ave., Madison, WI 53704   (608) 241-4423
4002 E. Washington Ave., Madison, WI 53704   (608) 241-8001
7952 Tree Ln., Madison, WI 53719   (608) 829-1444

Pizza. Enjoy whole-wheat crust pizza, an excellent salad bar, and pasta dishes in a family atmosphere. **Open daily for lunch and dinner. Counter service, vegan options, non-alcoholic beer, beer, take-out, VISA/MC, $.**

SukhoThai and Thai Center Foods

1439 Regent St., Madison, WI 53711   (608) 255-1313

Thai. Located in a downtown university setting, SukhoThai and Thai Center Foods offers a full menu of vegetarian appetizers, salads, soups, entrées, noodle dishes, and rice dishes. The staff is also willing to modify its meat offerings to meet vegetarian and vegan needs. **Open Tuesday through Friday for dinner. Open Saturday through Sunday for lunch and dinner. Closed Monday. Full service, vegan options, reservations recommended on weekends, take-out, catering, delivery, beer/wine/alcohol, VISA/MC/DISC/DC, $-$$$.** www.foodspot.com/sukhothai/

Sunroom Café & Gallery

638 State St., Madison, WI 53703   (608) 255-1555

Ethnic foods. Several international vegetarian dishes and gourmet desserts are available at this European-style café and art gallery on the university campus. **Open daily for three meals. Full service, fresh juices, espresso/cappuccino, wine/beer/alcohol, take-out, VISA/MC, $$.**

MENOMONIE

• Blue Moon Café and Deli

815 E. Main St., Menomonie, WI 54751   (715) 235-8596

Vegetarian. Blue Moon Café has a relaxed, cozy atmosphere and offers patio seating in the summer. Menu options include fresh salads and soups, Greek spinach pie, various grains, and vegetables. A large selection of scones, muffins, cookies, and truffles tempt most anyone. They use organic products when possible. **Open Monday through Saturday for lunch and dinner. Closed Sunday. Limited service, take-out, fresh juices, $-$$.**

MILWAUKEE

Abu's Restaurant

1978 N. Farwell Ave., Milwaukee, WI 53202   (414) 277-0485

Middle Eastern. Sample spinach pies, hummus, eggplant casserole, lentils, baba ghanouj,

Egyptian chili, and many other interesting dishes at Abu's Restaurant. **Open Monday through Saturday for lunch and dinner. Closed Sunday. Full service, take-out, $.**

Au Bon Appetit

1016 E. Brady St., Milwaukee, WI 53202   **(414) 278-1233**
Lebanese. This family-owned and operated restaurant offers many Lebanese vegetarian dishes, including hummus, baba ghanouj, spinach pie, falafel, carrot soup, lentil soup, tabbouleh, couscous ratatouille, and more. **Open Monday through Saturday for lunch and dinner. Closed Sunday. Full service, vegan options, fresh juices, wine, special drinks, catering, take-out, VISA/MC.**

Bangkok Orchid

2239 N. Prospect Ave., Milwaukee, WI 53202   **(414) 223-3333**
Thai. Authentic Thai food is prepared by the chef/owner in a non-smoking environment. Bangkok Orchid offers vegetarian soups and 25 dishes with fresh vegetables and/or tofu. **Open daily for dinner. Full service, take-out, wine/beer/alcohol, VISA/MC/AMEX/DISC/DC, $$$.**

Beans & Barley

1901 E. North Ave., Milwaukee, WI 53202   **(414) 278-0234**
Natural foods. Vegetarian, Mexican, and Middle Eastern specialities, including homemade soups, salads, sandwiches, burritos, and stir-fries, are served. All foods are prepared using the freshest ingredients possible. **Open daily for lunch and dinner. Full service, vegan options, fresh juices, wine/beer, take-out, VISA/MC, $$.**

Comet

1947 N. Farwell Ave., Milwaukee, WI 53202   **(414) 273-7677**
American. This coffee shop's menu is about half vegetarian and has many vegan options. They offer a long list of unusual sandwiches, soups, salads, and specialty drinks. **Open daily for breakfast through late dinner. Full service, vegan options, $-$$.**

MINERAL POINT

Brewery Creek Brewpub

23 Commerce St., Mineral Point, WI 53565   **(608) 987-3298**
Brewpub. Located in a restored 1854 limestone warehouse building, this microbrewery and bed and breakfast offers limited but very high quality vegetarian fare, such as the "MLT" (mushroom, lettuce, and tomato sandwich), the Walnut Burger, Pesto Pasta, and more. **Open Wednesday through Monday from May through October. Closed Tuesday. Full service, take-out, reservations not taken, non-alcoholic beverages, beer/wine, non-smoking, VISA/MC/AMEX/DISC, $$.** www.brewerycreek.com

OSCEOLA

Organica Restaurant

Aveda Spa Osceola, 1015 N. Cascade St., Osceola, WI 54020   **(800) 283-3202**
Natural foods. Located in a spa near the St. Croix River, Organica offers vegetarian and vegan

dishes using local organic produce whenever possible. The menu changes daily. **Open daily for lunch and dinner. Full service, vegan options, fresh juices, reservations required, take-out, $$.**

SPRING GREEN

Spring Green General Store & Café
137 S. Albany St., Spring Green, WI 53588   **(608) 588-7070**

Natural foods. Located in a cheese warehouse by the Wisconsin River, Spring Green features a menu that changes daily and includes Mexican, Indian, and Italian specialties. Some regular favorites include West African Sweet Potato Soup, Pea-Potato Curry with Lime Rice and Raita, and Vegetable Stir-Fry with Hot Peanut Sauce. Most of the produce used in the summer is grown locally. **Open daily for breakfast and lunch. Limited service, espresso/cappuccino, take-out, VISA/MC, $.**

WISCONSIN DELLS

• The Cheese Factory
521 Wisconsin Dells Pkwy., Wisconsin Dells, WI 53965   **(608) 253-6065**

Vegetarian. The Cheese Factory combines the comfort of the jukebox and soda fountain generation, the taste of international cuisine, the humanity of vegetarianism, and the joy of music and dance. This quaint stop has a meals fit for all, from traditional American breakfasts (minus the meat, of course), to exotic curries and stir-fries. **Open Wednesday through Monday for three meals. Closed Tuesday. Full service, vegan options, catering, take-out, reservations not needed, espresso/cappuccino, smoothies, non-smoking, live entertainment, VISA/MC/AMEX, $$.** www.cookingvegetarian.com

• The Secret Garden Café
910 River Rd., Wisconsin Dells, WI 53965   **(608) 254-4214**

Vegetarian. Located at the White Rose Bed and Breakfast, the Secret Garden Café is a completely vegetarian restaurant that caters to meat-eaters and vegetarians alike. It has incredible edible meat substitutes like crab salad sandwiches, bacon cheese burgers, and a seafood pasta dish, as well as vegan dishes, such as Red Hot and Green Curry and a Thai stir-fry. The Secret Garden offers outdoor seating and an indoor Mediterranean grotto in the basement of the century-old bed-and-breakfast. In addition, there is often free live music in the evenings on weekends. **Open Wednesday through Monday for three meals during the summer. Open during the winter Friday for lunch and dinner, Saturday for three meals, and Sunday for breakfast and brunch. Full service, vegan options, espresso/cappuccino, take-out, VISA/MC/AMEX/DISC, $$.** www.thesecretgardencafe.com

---

Restaurant codes: ✪ Reviewers' Choice   • Vegetarian Restaurant   •• Vegan Restaurant
Restaurant prices: **$** less than $6   **$$** $6-$12   **$$$** more than $12
Credit Cards Accepted: VISA - VISA   MC - MasterCard   AMEX - American Express
DISC - Discover   DC - Diner's Club

Wyoming

CHEYENNE

Twin Dragon
1809 Carey Ave., Cheyenne, WY 82007   **(307) 637-6622**
Chinese. This Mandarin Chinese restaurant offers 10 vegetarian entrées, including tofu dishes, Broccoli and Garlic Sauce, Vegetable Lo Mein, Chow Mein, and Veggie Egg Rolls. **Open daily for lunch and dinner. Full service, wine/beer/alcohol, take-out, VISA/MC/AMEX, $.**

CODY

The Hong Kong Restaurant
1201 17th St., Cody, WY 82414   **(307) 527-6420**
Chinese. Enjoy vegetable and bean curd dishes here. **Open daily for lunch and dinner during the summer. Open Tuesday through Sunday for lunch and dinner during the winter. Closed Monday. Full service, wine/beer/alcohol, take-out, VISA/MC, $-$$.**

JACKSON

Harvest Organic Foods
130 W. Broadway Ave., Jackson, WY 83001   **(307) 733-5418**
Juice bar/café/bakery. Taste the organic goodness in Harvest's freshly-made subs and sandwiches, soups, waffles, and more. Wash your delicious meal down with one of their many refreshing smoothies or all-natural fruit juices. **Open daily for three meals. Limited service, vegan options, reservations not taken, fresh juices, espresso/cappuccino, soymilk, smoothies, VISA/MC, $.**

LANDER

China Garden
162 N. 6th St., Lander, WY 82520   **(307) 332-7666**
Chinese. Several vegetarian dishes, including Tofu and Mixed Vegetables, Noodles and Vegetables, and Stir-Fry Broccoli, are offered at this Chinese establishment. **Open Monday through Saturday for lunch and dinner. Closed Sunday. Full service, BYOB, take-out, $$.**

LARAMIE

• Sweet Melissa Vegetarian Café
213 S. 1st St., Laramie, WY 82070   **(307) 742-9607**
Vegetarian café. As one of the few vegetarian restaurants in this part of the cattle ranching West, Sweet Melissa's menu offers soups, salads, sandwiches, falafel, lentil loaf, pot pies, and desserts. **Open Monday through Saturday for lunch and dinner. Closed Sunday. Full service, vegan options, take-out, no credit cards, $.**

CANADA

Alberta

BANFF

Michael's Café
415 Banff Ave., Banff, AB T0L 0C0   **(403) 762-9339**
Natural foods. This very vegetarian-friendly restaurant offers items like Hearty Lentil Soup, Curried Tofu Veggie Crepes, Totini with Pesto, Tamari Ginger Tofu Stir-Fry, hummus, and whole-wheat spaghetti. Organically grown short-grain brown rice and, when available, organically grown produce is used. Menu items do not contain MSG or refined sugar. **Open daily for three meals. Full service, vegan options, wine/beer/alcohol, non-alcoholic beer, take-out, VISA/MC/AMEX, $$.**

CALGARY

•• Buddha's Veggie Restaurant
Southland Crossing Shopping Centre
9737 MacLeod Trail S., Calgary, AB T2J 0P6   **(403) 252-8830**
Vegan/Chinese. This gourmet vegan Chinese restaurant features more than 100 items on its menu, including Crispy Veggie Eel, Lemon Chicken, Dry Ribs, and Veggie Sweet & Sour Pork. Reservations recommended. **Open Wednesday through Monday for lunch and dinner. Closed Tuesday. Full service, take-out, delivery, VISA/MC/AMEX, $.**

Cedars Restaurant
Oakland Market
173 200 Barcley Parade SW, Calgary, AB T2P 4R5   **(403) 264-2532**
225 8th Ave. SW, Calgary, AB T2P 1B7   **(403) 263-0285**
Lebanese. Cedars offers many vegetarian and vegan options, including falafel, hummus, fatoosh, and tabbouleh. The owner is the author of several cookbooks. **Open daily for lunch and dinner. Full service, vegan options, wine/beer, take-out, VISA/MC/AMEX, $$.**

The King and I Thai Cuisine
822 11th Ave., SW, Calgary, AB T2R 0E5   **(403) 264-7241**
Thai. Enjoy the contemporary décor with soft jazz background music. The King and I's vegetarian selections include a Chili Club Tofu made with Japanese eggplant. **Open Monday through Thursday for lunch and dinner. Open Friday for lunch through late night service. Open Saturday for dinner and late night service. Open Sunday for dinner. Full service, wine/beer/alcohol, take-out, VISA/MC/AMEX/DC, $$.**

Meelen Lounge and Omar Khayam Restaurant
1935 32nd Ave., Calgary, AB T2E 7C8   **(403) 291-3188**
Indian. The Meelen restaurant features traditional family recipes. The very friendly staff will gladly cook without butter or ghee upon request. Reservations required. **Open daily for**

lunch and dinner. Full service, vegan options, wine/beer/alcohol, take-out, delivery, VISA/
MC/AMEX/DISC, $$.

Thai Sa-On
351 10th Ave., SW, Calgary, AB T2R 0A5   **(403) 264-3526**
Thai. Authentic Thai cuisine is featured here, including salads, homemade curries, pad
Thai, spring rolls, coconut rice, and desserts. **Open Monday through Friday for lunch and
dinner. Open Sunday for dinner only. Closed Saturday. Full service, vegan options, wine/
beer/alcohol, catering, $$.**

•Veggie House
303 Centre St. SW, #109, Calgary, AB T2G 2B9   **(403) 294-0626**
Vegetarian/Chinese. This all-day buffet features items like Veggie Ginger Beef, Coconut
Rice, and various wheat gluten dishes. Egg noodles can be substituted for rice noodles
upon request. **Open Thursday through Tuesday for lunch and dinner. Open Wednesday
for lunch only. Buffet, vegan options, non-smoking, reservations recommended, take-out,
delivery, VISA/MC/AMEX, $.**

EDMONTON

•Café Mosaics
10844 82 Ave., Edmonton, AB T6E 2B3   **(780) 433-9702**
Vegetarian. Saddle up to a large range of vegetarian and vegan dishes served amidst real
country music. Try tofu scramble, hash browns, salads, burritos, pasta, quesadillas, or the
infamous Triple Decker Tofu Clubhouse with a delicious array of sides. Local musicians
perform on Wednesday nights, and the restaurant displays the work of local artists. Patio
dining available. **Open Monday through Saturday for three meals. Open Sunday for brunch.
Full service, vegan options, non-smoking, fresh juices, smoothies, soymilk, espresso/cappuc-
cino, beer/wine/alcohol, take-out, VISA/MC, $$.**

High Level Diner
10912 88 Ave., Edmonton, AB T6G 0Z1   **(403) 433-0993**
Natural foods. The High Level Diner is an environmentally responsible natural foods eatery
furnished with antiques and decorated with local artwork. Vegetarian options include salads,
vegan chili, sandwiches, spinach pie, enchiladas, and mushroom stroganoff. Patio dining
available. **Open daily for three meals. Full service, vegan options, fresh juices, wine/beer/
alcohol, take-out, VISA/MC/AMEX, $$.**

The King and I Thai Cuisine
8208 107 St., Edmonton, AB T6E 4K7   **(780) 433-2222**
Thai. The owners emphasize healthy cooking, and special requests will be cooked to order.
The Vegetarian Bird's Nest entrée is a must! **Open Monday through Friday for lunch and**

dinner. Open Saturday for dinner. Closed Sunday. Full service, wine/beer/alcohol, take-out, VISA/MC/AMEX, $$.

New Asian Village Restaurant
10143 Saskatchewan Dr., Edmonton, AB T6E 4R5   **(403) 433-3804**

Indian. In an atmosphere of Indian decor and music, vegetarian options are provided by a friendly staff. Open Monday through Friday for lunch and dinner. Open Saturday and Sunday for dinner only. Full service, wine/beer/alcohol, take-out, catering, VISA/MC/AMEX, $$.

• Oriental Veggie House
10586 100 St., Edmonton, AB T5H 2R6   **(780) 424-0463**

Vegetarian/Chinese. From the most familiar vegetarian spring rolls to the exotic veggie oysters, Oriental Veggie House is a mostly vegan restaurant specializing in "meat-like" dishes made primarily from bean-based, mushroom-based, or wheat gluten. Try the shark fin soup or the very popular curry veggie lamb hot pot. Open Wednesday through Monday for lunch and dinner. Closed Tuesday. Full service, vegan options, reservations recommended, non-smoking, soymilk, take-out, delivery, VISA/MC/AMEX/DC, $$.

British Columbia

COURTENAY

• Bar None Café
244 4th St., Box 3093, Courtenay, BC V9N 5N3   **(250) 334-3112**

Vegetarian. Opposite the Library, the Museum, and the Civic Theatre, Bar None Café offers a mostly vegan buffet with a 20-item salad bar, soups, breads, hummus, lasagna, nut butgers, wheat-free desserts, an espresso bar, and much more. Open Monday through Saturday for three meals. Closed Sunday. Cafeteria, vegan options, fresh juices, espresso/cappuccino, take-out, catering, VISA/MC, $-$$.

GOLDEN

The Kicking Horse Grill
1105 9th St. S., Golden, BC V0A 1H0   **(250) 344-2330**

American/international. The Kicking Horse Grill offers several vegetarian dishes, including spiced lentil soup, portabello pizza, lasagna, veggie skewers, tofu gyros, and some vegetarian optional entrées. They will also prepare dishes based on individual needs. Open daily for lunch and dinner. Full service, beer/wine/alcohol, take-out, MC/AMEX, $$. www.kickinghorsegrill.com

RICHMOND

• Bo Kong Vegetarian Restaurant
80-8100 Ackroyd Rd., Richmond, BC V6X 3K2   **(604) 278-1992**

Vegetarian/Chinese. Bo Kong diners will find more than 100 unique Buddhist Chinese dishes, including 10 soups, congee (thick rice soups), spring rolls, bean curd dishes, hot clay pot dishes, noodle and rice dishes, and desserts. One VRG member raves about the quality, originality, and service at this restaurant. **Open daily for lunch and dinner. Full service, vegan options, non-smoking, take-out, VISA/MC, $$.**

•• Le Veggie
#105-4600 No. 3 Rd., Richmond, BC V6X 2L2   **(604) 303-9987**
Vegan. Enjoy Chili Eggplant, Sweet and Sour Crispy Delight, Hot and Sour Soup, and more at this non-smoking, vegan Chinese restaurant. **Open daily for lunch and dinner. Full service, vegan options, fresh juices, non-alcoholic wine, take-out, catering, VISA/AMEX, $$.**

VANCOUVER

(For restaurant listings in the surrounding areas, see Richmond.)

Afghan Horseman Restaurant
445 W. Broadway Ave., Vancouver, BC V5Y 1R4   **(604) 873-5923**
Afghan. Enjoy Afghan soups, salads, and entrées, such as Hummus, Badenjan Borani (baked eggplant), and Dahl (lentil stew). **Open Monday through Saturday for dinner only. Closed Sunday. Full service, wine/beer/alcohol, take-out, VISA/MC/AMEX, $$.**

• Bo Kong Vegetarian Restaurant
3068 Main St., Vancouver, BC V5T 3G5   **(604) 876-3088**
Vegetarian/Chinese. See description under Richmond, BC.

• Buddhist Vegetarian Restaurant
137 E. Pender St., Vancouver, BC V6A 1T6   **(604) 683-8816**
Vegetarian/Chinese. With almost 100 appetizing Chinese-style vegetarian and vegan dishes, Buddhist Vegetarian Restaurant is an ideal destination. They can make dishes without salt, wheat, or oil, and they do not use MSG. **Open daily for lunch and dinner. Full service, vegan options, non-smoking, take-out, VISA/MC/AMEX, $$.** http://members.home.net/buddhistveg

Capers
2496 Marine Dr., Vancouver, BC V7V 1L1   **(604) 925-3374**
Natural foods. A wide variety of vegetarian foods, such as Capers' Falafel, assorted salads, and an organic stir-fry are offered. **Open daily for three meals. Full service, fresh juices, wine/beer, take-out (deli only), catering, VISA/MC, $$.**

• Evergreen
4166 Main St., Vancouver, BC V5V 3P7   **(604) 879-3380**
Vegetarian/Chinese. Evergreen's menu is completely vegetarian, and all foods are prepared without preservatives. Choose from Sweet Tofu Cake, Lo-Hon Mixed Vegetables, and other dishes. **Open Monday through Saturday for lunch and dinner. Closed Sunday. Take-out, vegan options, $.**

The Green Room Café
204-345 Robson St. At Hamilton (Library Square)   **(604) 688-5565**
Vancouver, BC V6B 6B3
International. The Green Room Café, located downtown at the new public library, can satisfy the vegetarian with simple sandwiches and pastas to exotic sushi rolls and stir-fry. Open Monday through Friday for three meals. Weekend hours vary. Full service, vegan options, non-smoking, fresh juices, espresso/cappuccino, smoothies, soymilk, beer/wine, take-out, catering, VISA/MC/AMEX/DC, $$.

• Greens and Gourmet
2681 W. Broadway Ave., Vancouver, BC V6K 2G2   **(604) 737-7373**
Vegetarian. Greens and Gourmet features a self-service hot and cold buffet where food is sold by weight. Items included on their extensive menu are cooked with purified water, which is also served for drinking. Open daily for lunch and dinner. Full service, non-smoking, macrobiotic/vegan options, fresh juices, take-out, catering, VISA/MC, $-$$.

Habibi's
7-1128 W. Broadway Ave., Vancouver, BC V6H 105   **(604) 732-7487**
Lebanese. Experience traditional vegetarian Lebanese cuisine served in a warm, inviting atmosphere for a reasonable price. Choices include the falafel sandwich, tabbouleh, hot jalapeño or basic garlic hummus, bulgur dishes, and more. Open Monday through Saturday for dinner. Closed Sunday. Full service, vegan options, beer/wine, take-out, catering, delivery, packaged products in local grocers, no credit cards, $. www.habibis.com

Hon's on Robson
1339 Robson St., Vancouver, BC V6E 1C6   **(604) 685-0871**
Chinese. Hon's on Robson is unique because it houses a special Vegetarian Cooking Facility that ensures that meat products are kept separate from all vegetarian dishes. Its extensive vegetarian menu includes a variety of noodle soups, an impressive offering of dim sum, rice rolls, congees, and desserts. Unique offerings include a Vegetarian Goose appetizer; Sautéed Vegetarian Chicken and Prawns with Broccoli; Straw Mushroom, Melon, and Bean Vermicelli Casserole; Steamed Rice Rolls with Vegetarian BBQ Pork; and Chilled Almond Bean Curd Pudding. Open daily for lunch and dinner. Full service, vegan options, take-out, delivery, VISA/MC, $$. www.shinnova.com/hons_on_robson

•• Le Veggie
1096 Denman St., Vancouver, BC V6G 2M8   **(604) 682-3885**
Vegan/Chinese. See description under Richmond, BC.

•The Naam Restaurant ○
2724 W. 4th Ave., Vancouver, BC V6K 1R1   **(604) 738-7151**
International vegetarian. Founded in 1968, this funky, casual restaurant offers a wide assortment of dishes. Offerings include tofu scrambles, vegan pancakes, veggie sausage, salads, hummus, pita pizzas, veggie burgers, Mexican dishes, a veggie-nut steak platter, and much more. All foods are made on the premises, and live music is provided at lunch and dinner. Open 24 hours daily. Full service, macrobiotic/vegan options, fruit juices, smoothies, soymilk, cappuccino/espresso, wine/beer, take-out, VISA/MC, $-$$. www.thenaam.com/naam

Noor-Mahal Restaurant
4354 Fraser St., Vancouver, BC V5V 4G3   **(604) 873-9263**
Indian. Noor-Mahal offers several vegetarian appetizers, a choice of dosas, and other vegetable dishes. Open daily for dinner. Full service, take-out, VISA/MC, $-$$.

Nyala African Restaurant
2930 W. 4th Ave., Vancouver, BC V6K 1R2   **(604) 731-7899**
Ethiopian. Choose from six vegan options, including Shuro Wat and Yeshebera Asa. Nyala also offers a few salads, as well as cooking classes and vegetarian/vegan buffets every Wednesday and Saturday. Open daily for dinner. Full service, vegan options, wine/beer/alcohol, take-out, catering, VISA/MC/AMEX, $$.

Picasso Café
1626 W. Broadway Ave., Vancouver, BC V6J 1X6   **(604) 732-3290**
Natural foods. Beside having items like Vietnamese Spring Rolls, a Peacock Burger made from vegetable protein, and the Moosewood Mushroom Walnut Paté on the menu, another great aspect of this restaurant is that it is run by the non-profit Option Youth Society, which provides on-the-job culinary training to students involved in its Youth Career Development Program. Open Tuesday through Friday for three meals. Open Saturday for dinner. Open Sunday for brunch. Closed Monday. Full service, vegan options, fresh juices, espresso/cappuccino, VISA/MC/AMEX, $$.

• Planet Veg
1941 Cornwall Ave., Vancouver, BC V6J1C8   **(604) 734-1001**
Vegetarian. Explore the out of this world tastes at Planet Veg which boasts a menu of fresh soups, rice pots, samosas, roti rolls, curry specialties, and veggie burgers. Open daily for lunch and dinner. Limited service, vegan options, beer, take-out, $.

• Raw
1849 W. 1st Ave., Vancouver, BC V6J 5B8   **(604) 737-0420**
Vegetarian/raw foods. Voted Best Vegetarian Raw Food in 2001 and 2002 by "The Vancouver Sun," Raw has a great menu, about half of which is raw living foods. Choose from items like Breakfast Banana Splits, Raw Spring Rolls, Mock Salmon Rolls, the Raw Falafel Burrito, Chickpea Pesto, Pizzas, Raw Chocolate Cake, and much more. Open Monday through Saturday for three meals. Closed Sunday. Full service, vegan options, fresh juices, smoothies, soymilk, special drinks, take-out, $-$$. www.vancouverrestaurant guide.net/van_west/raw

• Sweet Cherubim Natural Foods Limited
1105 Commercial Dr., Vancouver, BC V5L 3X3   **(604) 253-0969**
Vegetarian café. This natural foods store and vegetarian café offers international cuisine, including salads, samosas, dahl, tofu veggie roll, non-dairy lasagna, nut loaf, vegan desserts, and much more. Also enjoy music and the art gallery. Open daily for three meals. Limited service, macrobiotic/vegan options, fresh juices, smoothies, espresso/cappuccino, non-alcoholic beer, VISA/MC, $$.

Eugene's Greek Restaurant

1280 Broad St., Victoria, BC V8W 2A5 **(250) 381-5456**

Greek. Eugene's specializes in traditional Greek food. The menu includes Vegetarian Souvlaki and Hummus, among many other dishes. **Open Monday through Saturday for lunch and dinner. Closed Sunday. Buffet, take-out, $.**

•• Green Cuisine

560 Johnson St., Victoria, BC V8W 3C6 **(250) 385-1809**

Vegan. In the Market Square area, this restaurant offers a hot buffet and a salad buffet that changes daily. Among their offerings are soups, bean and grain dishes, shepard's pie, spanikopita, paella, curries, Thai noodles, falafel, and desserts made without white sugar. Organic items are used whenever possible. **Open daily for lunch and dinner. Buffet, vegan options, fresh juices, soymilk, espresso/cappuccino, non-alcoholic beer, take-out, catering, VISA/MC, $.** www.greencuisine.com

India Curry House

506 Fort St., Victoria, BC V8T 4P6 **(604) 384-5622**

Indian. This formal restaurant's menu includes 10 vegetarian main courses. No MSG or preservatives are used in food preparation. Free parking is available. **Open Monday through Saturday for lunch and dinner. Open Sunday for dinner. Full service, reservations recommended, wine/beer/alcohol, non-alcoholic wine/beer, take-out, VISA/MC/AMEX/DISC, $$-$$$.**

•• Lotus Pond Vegetarian Restaurant

617 Johnson St., Victoria, BC V8W 1M5 **(250) 380-9293**

Vegan/Chinese. Located downtown, Lotus Pond Vegetarian Restaurant is a vegan Chinese Buddhist restaurant. They offer many dishes, including Crispy Taro Rolls, Black Moss Shredded Vegetables Thick Soup, Seaweed Tomato Vegetable Tofu Soup, Shiitake Delight (battered shiitake mushrooms sautéed in a basil sauce), Mock Salmon in Peking Sauce, and Lily Bulb Delight (pan-fried lily bulbs, lotus roots, mushrooms, and snow peas). They also serve chow mein, chow fun, udon noodle dishes, and three flavors of tofu ice cream. Their pay-by-the-pound lunch buffet is a bargain. **Open Tuesday through Sunday for lunch and dinner. Closed Monday. Full service, reservations recommended, VISA/MC, $$.**

• The Parsonage Café

1-1115 N. Park St., Victoria, BC V8T 1C7 **(250) 383-5999**

Vegetarian. This café offers a wide range of vegetarian dishes, including samosas, lasagna, quiche, vegetable and bean burritos, and more. Be sure to sample their delicious soups, desserts, and renowned coffees. About a third of the menu is vegan. **Open Monday through Saturday for breakfast and lunch. Closed Sunday. Limited service, vegan options, non-smoking, take-out, espresso/cappuccino, $.**

Re-Bar

50 Bastian Sq., Victoria, BC V8W 1J2 **(250) 361-9223**

Natural foods. Re-Bar is mostly vegetarian, with fish served once a week. Unique offerings include cranberry maple granola; Greek tofu scramble; a roasted pear salad; butternut squash, caramelized onion, and sage ravioli; an almond burger; and coconut-brown basmati rice pudding. Soups are made with 100 percent vegetable stock, the tortillas do not contain animal fats, and all eggs used are free-range. All baked goods are made daily, with minimum use of refined sugars and flours. The restaurant uses filtered water, and organic produce is used when available. **Open daily for three meals. Open Saturday and Sunday for brunch. Full service, vegan options, fresh juices, smoothies, soymilk, wine/beer, non-alcoholic beer, take-out, VISA/MC, $-$$.** www.rebarmodernfood.com

• Rising Star Wholefoods Bakery, Ltd.
1320 Broad St., Victoria, BC V8W 2A9   **(250) 480-0021**
Vegetarian/natural foods. Enjoy the wonderful taste and smell of freshly baked traditional, gluten-free, wheat-free, or yeast-free breads at this café and bakery that also serves veggie burgers, soysage rolls, sandwiches, pizza, falafels, salads, and desserts. **Open daily for breakfast and lunch. Cafeteria, fresh juices, espresso/cappuccino, take-out, catering, $.**

Taj Mahal Restaurant
679 Herald St., Victoria, BC V8W 1S8   **(250) 383-4662**
Indian. Taj Mahal serves vegetarian dishes from all regions of India, including samosas, rice dishes, curried vegetables, and breads. All foods are prepared without MSG or preservatives. **Open daily for dinner only. Full service, wine/beer/alcohol, catering, take-out, VISA/MC/ AMEX, $$.**

Wild Fire Bread and Pastry
1517 Quadra St, Victoria, BC V8W 2L3   **(250) 381-3473**
Bakery. In the center of downtown Victoria, Wild Fire Bakery offers organic naturally leavened breads baked fresh daily in their own wood fired brick ovens. Sample one or all of the varieties, like three seed, rye, ciabatta, or raisin walnut. **Open Tuesday through Saturday for three meals. Closed Sunday and Monday. Limited service, vegan options, non-smoking, soymilk, espresso/cappuccino, take-out, $.**

Manitoba

WINNIPEG

• Affinity Vegetarian Garden
208 Edmonton St., Winnipeg, MB R3C 1R7   **(204) 943-0251**
Vegetarian/Chinese. One block north from the Convention Center, this casual, mostly vegan restaurant marks the items that do contain dairy or eggs clearly on the menu. Their menu offers an entire page of noodle and fried rice dishes, including thick Shanghai Fried Noodles and Garden Special Chow Mein. They also offer entrées like Crispy Black Mushroom, Chili Eggplant, and Sweet and Sour Veggie Fish. Brown rice is available, and no MSG is used in any of the food. **Open Monday through Friday for lunch buffet and dinner. Open Saturday for dinner only. Closed Sunday. Full service, vegan options, fresh juices, special drinks, take-out, catering, delivery, VISA/MC, $-$$.**

•• Delicious Vegetarian Restaurant
1467 Pembina Hwy., Winnipeg, MB R3T 2C5   **(204) 477-1530**

Vegan/Chinese. Enjoy delicious vegan Chinese cuisine at this restaurant, such as Hot & Sour Soup, Tofu with Lemon Grass, and imitation chicken, turkey, pork, beef and fish. Lunch specials are also offered. No MSG. **Open daily for lunch and dinner. Full service, beer, take-out, VISA, $$.**

Desserts Plus
1595 Main St., Winnipeg, MB R2V 1Y2   **(204) 339-1957**

Kosher dairy. All food in this smoke-free restaurant is homemade without additives. Pastries, vegetable soups, blintzes, knishes of all types, and vegetarian egg rolls are typical vegetarian selections. Catering is the main business at Desserts Plus. **Open Monday through Friday for lunch. Open Thursday for dinner. Closed Saturday and Sunday. Full service, reservations recommended, take-out, catering, VISA/MC, $$.**

Falafel Place and Deli
1670 Corydon Ave., Winnipeg, MB R3N 0J7   **(204) 489-5811**

Middle Eastern. The owner claims that customers say his is the best apple strudel and baklava in town! You can also try the hummus, veggie burgers, couscous, potato pancakes, meatless soups, and foul (fava beans). **Open Monday through Friday for three meals. Open Saturday for breakfast through early dinner. Open Sunday for breakfast and lunch. Counter service, vegan options, fresh juices, non-alcoholic wine/beer, take-out, catering, $.**

•• Mondragon Bookstore & Coffeehouse
91 Albert St., Winnipeg, MB R3B 1G5   **(204) 946-5241**

Vegan/International. This coffeehouse, located in the historic Exchange District, is completely vegan except for the option of cow's milk for the coffee drinks. The menu features home-made organic soups, African Peanut Stew, samosas, a vegan Caesar Salad, a Fake Bakon BLT, a Southern Fried Tofu Sandwich, Lasagna, Spanakopita, and much more. Desserts include chocolate-walnut-caramel cake, tofu cheesecake, cookies, muffins, pies, and soy ice cream sundaes. **Open Monday for lunch. Open Tuesday through Saturday for three meals. Closed Sunday. Counter service, non-smoking, fresh juices, soymilk, espresso/cappuccino, catering, VISA/MC/AMEX.** www.a-zone.org/mondragon/

Stone Ground Daily Bread
1399 Pembina Hwy., Winnipeg, MB R3T 2B8   **(204) 474-5900**

Bakery. This unique bakery grinds their own organic flour before each bake and maintains excellence in style, ingredients, and service. They also offer specialty products free of wheat, dairy, egg, yeast, sugar, oil, animal fats, and more. Try their multi-grain, hand-formed bagels or the vegan cookies and cinnamon buns. **Open Tuesday through Friday for lunch through early dinner. Open Saturday for breakfast through mid-afternoon. Closed Sunday. Take-out, vegan options, non-smoking, fresh juices, soymilk, special drinks, $.**

Restaurant codes: ✪ Reviewers' Choice • Vegetarian Restaurant •• Vegan Restaurant
Restaurant prices: **$** less than $6 **$$** $6-$12 **$$$** more than $12
Credit Cards Accepted: VISA - VISA   MC - MasterCard   AMEX - American Express
DISC - Discover   DC - Diner's Club

New Brunswick

MONCTON

•Calactus Vegetarian Café
179 Mountain Rd., Moncton, NB E1C 2L1   **(506) 388-4833**
Vegetarian café. This mostly vegan café specializes in North American, East Indian, and Italian cuisine. Though the menu changes regularly, you can often choose from salads, soups, a homemade veggie burger, burritos, tabbouleh, dahl, and desserts. **Open daily for lunch and dinner. Full service, vegan options, espresso, special drinks, take-out, VISA/MC, $.**

Healthy Bites
Highfield Square, 1100 Main St., Moncton, NB E1C 1H4   **(506) 855-1787**
Variety. Healthy Bites, located conveniently in the mall, will not serve anything "greasy." Vegetable Lasagna, vegetable soup, salads, and sandwiches are among the vegetarian choices on the menu. **Open Monday through Saturday for three meals. Open Sunday for lunch and early dinner. Counter service, take-out, $.**

SUSSEX

The Broadway Café
73 Broad St., Sussex, NB E0E 1P0   **(506) 433-5414**
Café. Located across from the beautiful historic train station, Broadway has been serving food and coffee for more than 10 years. Many vegetarian items are available, such as soups, sandwiches, curries, pizzas, and tasty desserts. The staff is also very friendly. **Open Monday through Saturday for three meals. Closed Sunday. Full service, espresso/cappuccino, VISA/MC, $.**

Newfoundland

CLARENVILLE

Pasta Plus
Restland Motor Inn, Box 237, Clarenville, NF A0E 1J0   **(709) 466-2287**
International. This is a great restaurant to get good food at low prices. Some dishes include Vegan Black Bean Chili, Black Bean or Chick Pea Quesadillas, Mediterranean Vegetable crepes, vegetarian curries, and, of course, dishes made with fresh pasta. **Open Monday through Saturday for lunch and dinner. Closed Sunday. Full service, vegan options, espresso/cappuccino, wine/beer/alcohol, VISA/MC, $.** www.wordplay.com/pasta_plus

---

Restaurant codes: ✪ Reviewers' Choice • Vegetarian Restaurant •• Vegan Restaurant
Restaurant prices: **$** less than $6 **$$** $6-$12 **$$$** more than $12
Credit Cards Accepted: VISA - VISA   MC - MasterCard   AMEX - American Express
DISC - Discover   DC - Diner's Club

ST. JOHN'S

Bamboo East Restaurant
136 Princess St., St. John's, NF E2L 1K7   **(506) 634-1661**

Chinese. This restaurant, located behind the Imperial Theatre, is one of the last restaurants in Saint John offering fine dining. Bamboo has several vegetarian options, such as Vegetable Chop Suey, and will make any of its dishes vegetarian if you ask. Reservations are recommended on the weekends. **Open Monday through Friday for lunch and dinner. Open Saturday and Sunday for dinner only. Full service, wine/beer/alcohol, take-out, VISA/ MC, $$.**

India Gate
786 Duckworth St., St. John's, NF A1C 1G9   **(709) 753-6006**

Indian. You can enjoy fine dining in downtown St. John's at India Gate. There are 13 vegetarian dishes on the menu, such as Baigan Masala, Navrattan Curry, and Dahl Makhni. There is an excellent lunch buffet on the weekends. Reservations are recommended. **Open Monday through Friday for lunch and dinner. Open Saturday and Sunday for dinner only. Full service, wine/beer/alcohol, take-out, catering, VISA/MC, $$.**

Kenmount Restaurant
75 Kenmount Rd., St. John's, NF A1B 3P8   **(709) 753-8385**

Chinese. Conveniently located near The Avalon Mall, Kenmount offers an authentic Chinese setting for dining. Stir-fried Vegetables, Spring Rolls, and Deep Fried Bean Curd are some of the dishes offered. Reservations are recommended for large groups. **Open daily for lunch and dinner. Full service, wine/beer/alcohol, take-out, VISA/MC, $$.**

Pasta Plus
Avalon Mall, St. John's, NF A1E 4N1   **(709) 722-6006**
Terrace On The Square, Churchill Square, St. John's, NF A1B 4J9 (709) 739-5818
223 Duckworth St., St. John's, NF A1C 1G8   **(709) 739-6676**
Village Shopping Centre, St. John's, NF A1E 4N1   **(709) 368-3481**

International. See description under Clarenville. **Duckworth location open Sundays as well.**

Quintana's de La Plaze
57 Rowan St., Churchill Square, St. John's, NF A1B 2X2   **(709) 579-7000**

Mexican. Great fiesta décor makes dining at Quitana's a treat. There are a few vegetarian items, such as black bean soup and burritos. With most of the dishes, you can substitute vegetarian black beans or vegetarian refried pinto beans. Reservations are recommended for dinner. **Open Monday through Saturday for lunch and dinner. Open Sunday for lunch only. Full service, wine/beer/alcohol, take-out, VISA/MC, $$.**

Taj Mahal
203 Water St., St. John's, NF A1C 1B4   **(709) 576-5500**

Indian. Taj Mahal is located in the heart of downtown St. John's. Some of the dishes offered include Vegetable Korma, Shahi Paneer, and Aloo Gobhi. Lunch time buffet available on weekdays. **Open Monday through Friday for lunch and dinner. Open Saturday and Sunday for dinner only. Full service, wine/beer/alcohol, VISA/MC, $$.**

The Wild Carrot Café
City Market, 47 Charlotte St., St. John's, NB E2L 3H8　　　　　**(506) 632-1900**
Café. The Wild Carrot serves up homemade and fresh foods daily. There is a 20-item salad bar, in addition to hummus, veggie-wraps, quiches, and vegetable dips. You can enjoy dining in the beautiful solarium. The City Market is also a smoke-free zone. **Open Monday through Saturday for three meals. Closed Sunday.** Cafeteria, espresso/cappuccino, VISA/MC, $.

Zapatas
10 Bates Hill, St. John's, NF A1C 4B4　　　　　**(709) 753-6215**
Mexican. Zapatas offers several vegetarian dishes, such as salads, nachos, burritos, and cornmeal crepes. Reservations are required on weekends. After you dine, you can enjoy the piano bar available upstairs. **Open Monday through Friday for dinner. Open Saturday and Sunday for dinner only.** Full service, wine/beer/alcohol, take-out, VISA/MC, $$.

Northwest Territories

INUVIK

Peppermill Restaurant
288 MacKenzie Rd., Inuvik, NT X0E 0T0　　　　　**(403) 979-2999**
Fine dining. The great view is only one of the many special features of Peppermill. This restaurant flies in fresh fruits and vegetables for their dishes. Veggie items are available, including a lunch time veggie burger, as well as polenta and fresh pastas. The restaurant hosts a Sunday brunch. **Open daily for three meals.** Full service, espresso/cappuccino, wine/beer/alcohol, take-out (phone ahead), catering, VISA/MC/DC, $$$.

YELLOWKNIFE

Grandma Lee's
38-5014 49th St., Yellowknife, NT X1A 3R7　　　　　**(867) 920-7325**
Cafeteria. This small sandwich shop/café offers a few vegetarian items, such as salads, vegetarian quiches, and sandwiches. This is a cozy place to sit back and enjoy a latte. **Open daily for breakfast and lunch.** Cafeteria, espresso/cappuccino, catering, take-out, $.

Monkey Tree
483 Range Lake Rd., Yellowknife, NT X1A 3R9　　　　　**(867) 669-9623**
Chinese. A few vegetarian dishes are available at the Monkey Tree, such as stir-fries and salads. This restaurant is suitable for business entertaining. Reservations are strongly recommended on the weekends. **Open daily for lunch and dinner.** Full service, take-out, VISA/MC, $$.

Nova Scotia

ANTIGONISH

Sunshine Café
322 Main St., Antigonish, NS B2G 2C4   **(902) 863-5851**
Natural foods café. Sunshine Café offers simple breakfasts, such as coffee and bran muffins. For lunch, the café features pizza, burgers, hearty whole-wheat sandwiches, vegetable stir-fries, chili, and salads, including tabbouleh. Desserts in this smoke-free café are made with local maple syrup. **Open daily for three meals. Full service, take-out, catering, VISA/MC, $-$$.**

HALIFAX

• Dofsky's Grill
1583 Brunswick St., Halifax, NS B3J 3P5   **(902) 425-4278**
Vegetarian. Dofsky's Grill offers all types of dishes, such as veggie burgers, gourmet veggie pizza, veggie wraps, spring rolls, and stir-fries. **Open daily for lunch and dinner. Full service, Reservations recommended, $$.**

• Satisfaction Feast Vegetarian Restaurant
1581 Grafton St., Halifax, NS B3J 2C3   **(902) 422-3540**
International vegetarian. The mostly vegan, often organic menu includes a large selection of appetizers, soups, sandwiches, salads, and entrées. Specialties include the tofu salad, chili, burritos, curried panir with rice, lasagna, curries, stir-fries, casseroles, macrobiotic rice supreme, and vegan cheesecakes. Partly thanks to its Buddhist affiliation, the restaurant has a relaxing atmosphere, complete with soft music and a fountain. **Open Monday through Saturday for lunch and dinner. Closed Sunday. Full service, vegan options, non-smoking, fruit juices, take-out, catering, VISA/MC/AMEX, $-$$.**

WINDSOR

• The Herbal Shoppe & Café Yummy
102 Gerrish St., Windsor, NS B0N 2T0   **(902) 798-9256**
Vegetarian café. This vegetarian café offers daily specials, including soups, pastas, salads, and baked goods. **Open daily for three meals. Full service, vegan options, fresh juices, soymilk, smoothies, espresso/cappuccino, take-out, VISA/MC, $. www.geocities.com/herbsshoppe**

Ontario

BRAMPTON

•• Brar Sweets and Restaurant

199 Advance Blvd., Unit 12, Brampton, ON L6T 4N2   **(905) 799-1625**

Vegan/Indian. Enjoy vegan Indian snacks, desserts, and other items at Brar Sweets. Open Wednesday through Monday for lunch and dinner. Closed Tuesday. Limited service, VISA, $$.

CONCORD

East Moon Restaurant

2150 Steeles Ave., W., Concord, ON L4K 2T5   **(905) 738-1428**

Chinese. The menu lists vegetarian egg and spring rolls, as well as approximately 10 vegetarian entrées. Open Monday through Friday for lunch and dinner. Open Saturday and Sunday for dinner only. Full service, wine/beer/alcohol, take-out, catering, VISA/MC/AMEX, $$.

ELORA

The Desert Rose Café

130 Metcalfe St., Elora, ON N0B 1S0   **(519) 846-0433**

Natural foods. Enjoy an eclectic blend of international cuisine, including homemade soups, salad dressings, entrées, baked goods, and more. The café features stained glass, antique furniture, and occasional live music. Open daily for three meals March through December. Closed January and February. Full service, vegan options, wine/beer/alcohol, VISA/MC, $$-$$$.

ETOBICOKE

• Rajdhani

2658 Islington Ave. (At Albion Rd.), Etobicoke, ON M9V 2X5   **(416) 748-7108**

Vegetarian/Indian. This restaurant specializes in South Indian cuisine, including vegan pakoras, channa garam masala, curried spinach, thali, and more. No eggs are used in any of the dishes. Open daily for three meals. Full service, vegan options, take-out, no credit cards, $.

GUELPH

(For restaurant listings in the surrounding areas, see Elora and Kitchener.)

•• Café Aquarius

33 MacDonell St., Guelph, ON N1H 2Z4   **(519) 766-1268**

Vegan/International. Though small, this restaurant offers friendly service and large servings at reasonable prices. The menu includes soups, sandwiches, hummus, burritos, rice bowls, and good desserts. Tuesday is International Buffet night, Thursday is Vegan Pizza & Pasta night, and Sunday offers a vegan brunch with Scrambled Tofu, Tofu Quiche, and Vegan French Toast. Open daily for lunch and dinner. Counter service, non-smoking, take-out, catering, $. www.cafeaquarius.com

• The Cornerstone

1 Wyndham St. N., Guelph, ON N1H 4E2 **(519) 827-0145**

Vegetarian. This homey restaurant with a coffeehouse atmosphere offers bagels, appetizers, hummus, salads, soups, wraps, tofu dishes, pastas, pizzas, a three-bean burrito, a black bean burger served with a side salad and pilaf, dairy-free desserts, and an extensive tea menu. Live jazz is performed Sunday nights. **Open daily for breakfast through late night. Full service, vegan options, special drinks, cappuccino/espresso, take-out, VISA/MC, $-$$.**

HAMILTON

(For restaurant listings in the surrounding areas, see Oakville.)

• Maharajah's Asian Grocery and Take-Out

425 King St., E., Hamilton, ON L8N 1C5 **(905) 521-2744**

Vegetarian/Indian. Call in your order and enjoy vegetarian Indian cuisine from Maharajah's. **Open daily for lunch and dinner. Take-out only, $-$$.**

KITCHENER

• Muses Café and Vegetarian Dining

10 King St., Kitchener, ON N2G 2K6 **(519) 742-3087**

Vegetarian. This restaurant offers terrific homemade food, including fresh soups and meatless chili made daily. **Open Monday through Saturday for three meals. Closed Sunday. Full service, fresh juices, smoothies, take-out, no credit cards, $$.**

MARKHAM

• Graceful Vegetarian Restaurant

Market Village Shopping Centre **(905) 479-8381**
4396 Steeles Ave., E., Markham, ON L3R 9W1

Vegetarian/Chinese. Graceful Garden offers Cantonese-style vegetarian fare. Mock meats and mock fish are available. **Open daily for lunch and dinner. Full service, vegan options, reservations required, soymilk, special drinks, VISA, $$-$$$.**

• Kamal's Bombay Chowpatty

7200 Markham Rd., Markham, ON L3S 3R7 **(905) 472-0111**

Vegetarian/Indian. Enjoy a wide variety of Indian vegetarian dishes in a comfortable environment at Chowpatty restaurant. **Open Thursday through Tuesday for lunch and dinner. Closed Wednesday. Counter service, vegan options, take-out, catering, $.**

• Pearl Vegetarian

8362 Kennedy Rd., Markham, ON L3R 9W5 **(905) 415-8368**

Vegetarian/Chinese. Enjoy vegetarian Chinese and fast foods at Pearl Vegetarian. **Open Tuesday through Saturday for lunch and dinner. Open Sunday for lunch. Closed Monday. Take out only, $.**

• Saravana Bhavan

4559 Hurontario St., Mississauga, ON L4Z 3L9   **(905) 290-0769**

Vegetarian/Indian. Featuring South Indian vegetarian cuisine, this restaurant serves masala dosas, idlies, utthappams, curry dishes, and much more. **Open Tuesday through Sunday for lunch and dinner. Closed Monday. Full service, vegan options, special drinks.** www.saravanabhavan.com

• Village Of India Sweets & Restaurant

1011 Eglinton Ave. E., Mississauga, ON L4W 1K4   **(905) 290-0769**

Vegetarian/Indian. This restaurant offers a daily buffet of 30 items, including fresh Indian breads like naan and roti, curries, chapati, and more. **Open daily for lunch and dinner. Buffet, vegan options, take-out, $$.**

• Xin Vego Café

4939 Victoria Ave., Niagara Falls, ON L2E 4C7   **(905) 353-VEGO**

Vegetarian/Chinese. Located on the Canadian side at Niagara Falls, this restaurant offers a mixture of cuisines from Hong Kong, Japan, China, and Thailand. Dishes utilize mock meats, including Seafood Bird Nest, Stuffed Vegetarian Fish, Thai Curry Mock Chicken, Sizzling Vegetarian Pork Cutlet, and Olive Garden (string beans with minced soy meat in olive leaves). Most dishes are vegan, with the exception of desserts. Vegan desserts can be special-ordered in advance. **Open Thursday to Monday for lunch and dinner. Closed Tuesday and Wednesday. Full service, vegan options, fresh juices, soymilk, espresso/cappuccino, special drinks, take-out, $-$$.** www.xinvego.com

Fans Court Chinese Restaurant

135 Queen St., Niagara-On-The-Lake, ON L0S 1J0   **(905) 468-4511**

Chinese. Vegetarian options include spring rolls, vegetable soup, and several vegetable entrées. **Open daily for lunch and dinner. Full service, vegan options, take-out, VISA/MC, $$.**

•• Counter Culture

4700 Keele St., York University, 305 Lumbers Bldg.   **(416) 736-2100 x22642**
North York, ON M3J 1P3

Vegan. Voted "Best Hangout at York University" in November 2002 by "NOW Magazine" (free weekly newspaper/entertainment guide), Counter Culture is the only vegetarian/vegan place on campus and takes the college's Student Meal Card. It offers bagels, samosas, lentil/bean pockets, organic fruit, salads, chili, potato and veggie pizzas, and pastries. Patrons can enjoy eating in the bright, friendly Environmental Studies Lounge on a hodge-podge of couches, or they can check out the ever-changing student artwork on the walls. Also near

Black Creek Pioneer Village. **Open Monday through Thursday for breakfast through late afternoon. Open Friday for lunch. Closed Saturday and Sunday.** Cafeteria, soymilk, special drinks, take-out in reuseable containers, catering, $-$$.

La Mexicana Restaurant
3337 Bathurst St., North York, ON M6A 2B7   **(416) 783-9452**
Mexican. This restaurant features authentic Mexican cuisine, Latin American music, and an open outdoor patio. Choose from several vegetarian dishes, including Vegetable Enchiladas, Chilaquiles (Mexican Lasagna), Chili Rellenos, and an eggplant casserole. **Open daily for lunch and dinner.** Full service, wine/beer/alcohol, take-out, catering, VISA/MC/AMEX, $$.

•Super Indian Cuisine
2400 Finch Ave. W., North York, ON M9M 2C8   **(416) 740-6665**
Vegetarian/Indian. Super Indian Cuisine offers a variety of three-vegetable combination plates with rice and bread. Choices include dishes with two kinds of lentils, cauliflower, and/or chickpeas, as well as a peas and cheese curry. **Open daily for lunch and dinner.** Full service, reservations recommended, take-out, $.

OAKVILLE

••Ruby's Organic Vegan Restaurant
325 Kerr St., Oakville, ON L6K 3B6   **(905) 842-6112**
Vegan/Caribbean. Ruby's offerings include soups, spaghetti with veggie meatballs, veggie chicken and seafood dishes, veggie burgers, and more. **Open Sunday for lunch and early dinner. Open Monday through Friday for three meals. Closed Saturday.** Limited service, vegan options, fresh juices, catering, VISA/MC, $$-$$$. www.rubysveganrestaurant.com

OTTAWA

Domus Café
85 Murray St., Ottawa, ON K1N 5M5   **(613) 241-6007**
Natural foods. The menu of eclectic gourmet foods here changes daily, but it is always prepared with fresh produce from local farmers. The restaurant is connected to a kitchen/housewares store. **Open daily for lunch and dinner.** Full service, wine/beer/alcohol, VISA/MC/AMEX, $$$.

•Govinda's Vegetarian Buffet
212 Somerset St., E., Ottawa, ON K1N 6V4   **(613) 565-6544**
Vegetarian. Govinda's, the oldest vegetarian restaurant in Ottawa, offers a wide variety of vegetarian dishes served buffet-style. **Open Monday through Saturday for dinner. Closed Sunday.** Buffet, vegan options, non-smoking, fresh juices, take-out, catering, VISA, $-$$.

•The Green Door
198 Main St., Ottawa, ON K1S 1C6   **(613) 234-9597**
Vegetarian/natural foods. The Green Door specializes in macrobiotic foods and organic foods; very few dairy products or eggs are used, and food is sold by the pound. They offer salads, soups, breads, quiche, lasagna, stir-fries, desserts, and much more. Items are clearly

marked as vegetarian or vegan. Organic flours are used in sourdough baking, yeast-free
baked goods, wheat-free breads, and sugar-free baked goods (no honey is used). **Open
Tuesday through Sunday. Closed Monday. Buffet, macrobiotic/vegan options, fresh juices,
wine/beer, take-out, catering, VISA/MC/AMEX, $.**

•Peace Garden Café
47 Clarence St., Ottawa, ON K1N 9K1   **(613) 562-2434**
International vegetarian. This small café offers salads, sandwiches, Indian dishes, lasagna,
baked potatoes, soy burgers, homemade desserts, and more. **Open daily for three meals.
Counter service, vegan options, fresh juices, smoothies, espresso/cappuccino, special drinks,
take-out, catering, VISA/MC, $-$$.**

•Perfection - Satisfaction - Promise
167 Laurier Ave., E., Ottawa, ON K1N 6N8   **(613) 234-7299**
Vegetarian. Across the street from the University of Ottawa, Perfection offers Indonesian
vegetables with peanut sauce and rice noodles, Japanese miso soup, Vietnamese spring rolls
with julienned vegtables in a soft rice wrapper, foot-long veggie subs, and much more. **Open
Monday, Tuesday, and Thursday through Saturday for lunch and dinner. Open Wednesday
for lunch and early dinner. Closed Sunday. Limited service, vegan options, fresh juices,
espresso/cappuccino, non-alcoholic wine/beer, take-out, catering, VISA/MC, $-$$.**

REXDALE

•Gagan Sweets and Restaurant
1050 Albion Rd. Rexdale, ON M9V 1A7   **(416) 747-0075**
Vegetarian/Indian. Experience pure vegetarian, Indian cuisine at Gagan Sweets, which offers
Thali, Chaat Papri, and Golgappa for lunch and dinner as well as a varied array of snacks
and sweets like samosas, pakoras and kaju rolls. **Open daily for three meals. Limited service,
vegan options, fresh juices, non-smoking, take-out, catering, VISA/AMEX, $.**

RICHMOND HILL

•Gourmet Vegetarian Restaurant
280 W. Beaver Creek Dr., Richmond Hill, ON L4B 3Z1   **(905) 886-0680**
Vegetarian/Asian. A relaxing and comfortable atmosphere with affordable new creative
veggie dishes. **Open daily for breakfast through late night service. Full service.**
www.gourmetveg.com

SCARBOROUGH

•The Buddhist Vegetarian Kitchen
3290 Midland Ave., #9, Scarborough, ON M1V 2Z9   **(416) 292-7095**
Vegetarian/Chinese. Enjoy a large menu of vegetarian Chinese cuisine dishes made from vegetables, tofu, wheat gluten, and more. **Open daily for lunch and dinner. Full service, vegan
options, take-out, VISA/MC, $$.**

• Lotus Pond Vegetarian Restaurant
3838 Midland Ave., Scarborough, ON M1V 5K5   **(416) 412-3140**
Vegetarian/Chinese. This restaurant offers more than 60 dishes, including Sweet & Sour Soup, Lemon Mock Chicken, mock meats, and other entrées. **Open Wednesday through Monday for lunch and dinner. Closed Tuesday. Full service, vegan options, non-alcoholic wine/beer, VISA, $$.**

• Pearl Vegetarian
3833 Midland Ave., Scarborough, ON M1V 5L6   **(416) 298-9322**
Vegetarian/Chinese. See description under Markham, ON. **Full service.**

ST. CATHERINE'S

Chon-Buri's Spicy Thai
208 Church St., St. Catherine's, ON L2R 3E9   **(905) 687-THAI**
Thai. This restaurant offers a very attractive menu for vegetarians. Also, almost any item on the menu can be prepared with tofu instead of meat. **Open Monday through Friday for lunch and dinner. Open Saturday and Sunday for dinner only. Full service, vegan options, wine/beer/alcohol, VISA/MC, $$$.**

Spice Of Life Restaurant
12 Lock St., Port Dalhousie, St. Catherine's, ON L2R 5B5   **(905) 937-9027**
International. Noted for its live jazz and blues, Spice of Life has a menu that changes seasonally, but it offers offers a vegetarian/vegan menu year-round. Choices include samosas, bruschettas, award-winning garlic bundles, salads, pizza, pastas, vegan fondues, and a special Sunday brunch menu. **Call for seasonal hours. Full service, reservations recommended, vegan/macrobiotic options, fresh juices, soymilk, espresso/cappuccino, beer/wine/alcohol, non-alcoholic beer/wine, catering, cooking classes, VISA/MC/AMEX, $$.** www.niagara spiceoflife.com

THORNHILL

Terra
8199 Yonge St., Thornhill, ON L3T 2C6   **(905) 731-6161**
Canadian. Though definitely not a vegetarian restaurant, this formal dining establishment recommends informing them of your dietary needs when you make reservations. Vegetarian items are clearly marked on the menu and includes six salads, Grilled Portobello Steaks, Pan Roasted Gnocci, and Wild Mushroom Risotto. Many of these dishes can be prepared vegan upon request. Terra also offers an extensive coffee, tea, and dessert wines menu. **Open weekdays for lunch, daily for dinner, and Sunday for brunch. Full service, vegan options, reservations recommended, special drinks, wine/beer/alcohol, catering, VISA/MC/AMEX/ DC, $$$.** www.terrarestaurant.ca

---

Restaurant codes: ✪ Reviewers' Choice • Vegetarian Restaurant • • Vegan Restaurant
Restaurant prices: $ less than $6 $$ $6-$12 $$$ more than $12
Credit Cards Accepted: VISA - VISA MC - MasterCard AMEX - American Express
DISC - Discover DC - Diner's Club

(For restaurant listings in the surrounding areas, see Brampton, Concord, Etobicoke, Markham, Mississauga, North York, Rexdale, Richmond Hill, Scarborough, Thornhill, and Willowdale.)

Alternative Grounds Coffee House and Roaster
333 Roncesvalles Ave., Toronto, ON M6R 2M8   **(416) 534-6335**

Coffeehouse. Strongly committed to working with the community, Alternative Grounds helps to promote trade relationships between farmers and businesses in a coffee shop selling more than just coffee—there's also vegetarian fare and a variety of desserts. **Open daily for three meals. Limited service, soymilk, espresso/cappuccino, MC, $.** www.alternativegrounds.com

• Annapurna
1085 Bathurst St., Toronto, ON M5R 3G8   **(416) 537-8513**

Vegetarian/Indian. Many vegan dishes are served at Annapurna, which has been specializing in southern Indian cuisine for more than 20 years. **Open Monday through Saturday. Closed Sunday. Full service, macrobiotic/vegan options, fresh juices, take-out, catering, $.**

• The Big Carrot Deli
348 Danforth Ave., Toronto, ON M4K 1N8   **(416) 466-2129**

Vegetarian deli. This deli is located in a large natural foods store. The pay-by-weight menu features soups, lentil stew, salads, samosas, grain-based dishes, baba ghanouj, hummus, falafel, Barbecue Tofu, Bean Curd in Black Bean Sauce, tofu burgers, plus much more. **Open Monday through Saturday for three meals. Open Sunday for lunch and early dinner. Limited service, macrobiotic/vegan options, fresh juices, take-out, catering, cooking classes, $$.** www.thebigcarrot.ca

• B.J.S. Vegetarian and Fine Food
550 Hwy. 7 E., Toronto, ON L4B 3Z1   **(905) 886-6930**

Vegetarian/Chinese. This take-out establishment offers bulk foods, including a huge number of freshly-made bean curd dishes like Sweet & Sour Bean Curd and Curry Bean Curd. They also offer dishes made with vegetarian 'pork,' 'chicken,' and 'duck.' **Open for lunch through late night service. Take-out, vegan options, $.**

• Bo de Duyen Restaurant
254 Spadina Ave., 2nd Floor, Toronto, ON M5T 2E2   **(416) 703-1247**

Vegetarian/Asian. Bo De Duyen offers vegetarian versions of many traditional and unique Chinese and Vietnamese dishes, including Diced Vegetables with Cashew Nuts, Stir-Fried Beef Slices on Chinese Broccoli, Sweet and Sour Shrimp Balls, Vegetarian Chicken or Golden Ham Platters, Vegetarian Eel in Black Bean Sauce, Hot or Cold Tofu Pudding with Coconut Milk, and more. **Open daily for lunch and dinner. Full service, vegan options, fresh juices, wine/beer, special drinks, take-out, $$.** www.bodeduyen.com

• Bombay Bhel Restaurant
1411 Gerrard St., E., Toronto, ON M4L 1Z5   **(416) 461-4125**

Vegetarian/Indian. Enjoy both North and South Indian vegetarian cuisine at this no-frills snack bar in Toronto's downtown Little India. **Open Tuesday through Sunday for lunch and dinner. Closed Monday. Limited service, vegan options, take-out, VISA/MC/AMEX, $$.**

•• Buddha's Vegetarian Foods
666 Dundas St., W., Toronto, ON M5T 1H9   **(416) 603-3811**

Vegan/Chinese. Buddha's traditional Chinese dishes feature gluten and soy products rather than meat and fish. Enjoy various soups, appetizers, rice and noodle dishes, and more. The mock duck and the yam rolls are highly recommended. **Open Wednesday through Monday for lunch and dinner. Closed Tuesday. Full service, take-out, $-$$.**

• Café 668
668 Dundas St. W., Toronto, ON M5T 1H9   **(416) 703-0668**

Vegetarian/Asian. Enjoy jazz music while you dine on Southeast Asian-inspired vegetarian cuisine. Choose from almost 100 different appetizers, soups, fried noodle dishes, congees, and rice dishes. Entrées include Spicy Fried Tofu with Coconut Cream, Curry "Veggie Fish," and "Veggie Chicken" Fried with Cashew Nuts (Kung-Pu Style). **Open Tuesday through Sunday for lunch and dinner. Closed Monday. Full service, vegan options, fresh juices, soymilk, cappucino/espresso, $$.** www.cafe668.com

Café Nervosa
75 Yorkville Ave., Toronto, ON M5R 1B8   **(416) 961-4642**

Italian. This establishment, located in the upscale Yorkville area, offers casual and trendy dining with vegetarian soups, salads, and pizzas. **Open Monday through Saturday for lunch and dinner. Open Sunday for brunch. Full service, take-out, private parties, beer/wine/alcohol, VISA/MC/AMEX/DC, $-$$$.** www.cafenervosa.ca

Epicure Café
512 Queen St., W., Toronto, ON M5V 2B3   **(416) 504-8942**

Natural foods. Enjoy items from the traditional, seasonal Italian and French bistro blackboard menu, which changes daily. **Call for seasonal hours. Full service, wine/beer/alcohol, take-out, catering, VISA/MC/AMEX/DC, $$.**

• Fresh By Juice For Life
521 Bloor St. W., Toronto, ON M5S 1Y4   **(416) 531-2635**
336 Queen St. W., Toronto, ON M5V 2A2   **(416) 599-4442**
894 Queen St. W., Toronto, ON M6J 1G6   **(416) 913-2720**

Vegetarian. Juice for Life offers gourmet salads, rice bowls, veggie burgers, sandwiches, and fresh juices in a casual environment. **Open daily for lunch and dinner. Limited service, vegan options, fresh juices, smoothies, espresso/cappuccino, wine/beer/alcohol, take-out, VISA/MC/AMEX/DC, $$.** www.juiceforlife.com

• Fressen
478 Queen St. W., Toronto, ON M5V 2B2   **(416) 504-5127**

Vegetarian/Thai. Fressen, near the heart of Toronto, is an upscale establishment that offers elegant vegetarian and vegan cuisine even the pickest meat eaters will love. Interesting appetizers include Grilled Asparagus with Blood Oranges and mock Crab Cakes with a Spicy Corn Salsa. For your main course, consider the Portabello Mushroom Steak, Veggie Kebab with Curry Sauce, or a pizza with a Carrot Cornmeal crust. Also, save room for the just-baked purple buns (infused with beet juice) and a dessert, perhaps a late summer pudding with fresh berries and créme anglaise. Sunday nights, the restaurant transforms into the Red

Beet Lounge, which offers dancing, discounted drinks, and free snack food without a cover. Open Monday through Friday for dinner. Open Saturday and Sunday for brunch and dinner. Full service, vegan options, suitable for business entertaining, VISA/MC/AMEX, $$-$$$.

• Govinda's
Hare Krishna Center, 243 Avenue Rd., Toronto, ON M5R 2J6   (416) 922-5415
Vegetarian. You'll find this all-you-can-eat buffet in downtown Toronto. A donation as small as $7 will get you any of the Italian and Indian dishes, including rice, dahl, and soups, that are featured daily. No eggs are used. **Open Monday through Saturday for lunch and dinner. Open Sunday for evening feast.** Cafeteria, vegan options, take-out, catering, $.

• Hey Good Cooking
238 Dupont St., Toronto, ON M5R 1V7   (416) 929-9140
Vegetarian. Hey Good Cooking's daily specials include Chickpea and Vegetable Curry, Texan Chili, Mushroom Nut Loaf, and Southern Spiced Tofu, as well as homemade veggie burgers, soups, and salads. **Open Monday through Saturday for lunch and dinner. Open Sunday for brunch.** Cafeteria, vegan options, take-out, $.

• Kensington Natural Bakery, Inc.
460 Bloor St. W., Toronto, ON M5S 1X8   (416) 534-1294
Vegetarian. This bakery offers fresh juices, vegetarian baked goods, and entrées. **Open daily for three meals.** Full service, macrobiotic/vegan options, non-smoking, take-out, catering, $.

• King's Café/Perfect Vegetarian
192 Augusta Ave., Toronto, ON M5T 2L6   (416) 591-1340
Vegetarian/Chinese. Overlooking Kensington Market, this restaurant offers noodle soups, sushi, some unusual mock meat dishes, and many other choices. Try the Asparagus Handrolls, the Crustless Quiches, or the Fried Udon with vegetables and tofu "beef." **Open Sunday through Friday for lunch and dinner. Open Saturday for three meals.** Full service, vegan options, fresh juices, cappuccino/espresso, take-out, $.

• Le Commensal
Minto Plaza, 655 Bay St., Toronto, ON M5G 2K4   (416) 596-9364
Vegetarian. Established in 1977, Le Commensal offers more than 100 items on the menu. The buffet is set up as a pay-by-weight system, so you can tailor the portions. In addition to a large selection of salads, guests can choose from tofu dishes, seitan dishes, pasta, and vegan desserts. **Open daily for lunch and dinner.** Buffet, vegan options, fresh juices, take out, catering, VISA/MC/AMEX, $-$$.

•• Live Health Café
258 Dupont St., Toronto, ON M5R 1V7   (416) 515-2002
Vegan café. Live Health Café is primarily a lunch place, offering take-out and a few small tables. Between 50 and 80 percent of their meals are made with raw foods, and all are vegan, organic when available, and wheat-, gluten-, and sugar-free. Examples include risotto, raw sushis, and veggie pies, which are made from broccoli, carrots, yams, and sunflower seeds served over a walnut date crust. Also, leave some room for their homemade nut milks and/or macrobiotic cookies. They are open for private events at night and on weekends.

Open Monday through Friday for lunch through early dinner. Closed Saturday and Sunday. Counter service, vegan options, smoothies, soymilk, special drinks, take-out, catering, $-$$.

•• Lotus Garden Vegetarian Restaurant
393 Dundas St. W., Toronto, ON M5T 1G7   **(416) 598-1883**
Vegan. This unique Vietnamese restaurant serves appetizers including spring rolls, salads, 12 different soups, delicious entrées, dumplings, noodle and rice dishes, mock meat and fish, and much more. **Open Wednesday through Monday for lunch and dinner. Closed Tuesday. Full service, fresh juices, non-alcoholic wine/beer, take-out.**

• Lucky Sweets & Restaurant
2985 Islington Ave., Toronto, ON M9L 2K9   **(416) 740-4494**
Vegetarian/Indian. Enjoy a fully vegetarian menu at this Indian restaurant, including Thali. **Open daily for three meals. Limited service, $.**

• Madras Durbar Restaurant
1435 Gerrard St. E., Toronto, ON M4L 1Z7   **(416) 465-4116**
Vegetarian/Indian. Savor the exotic tastes of South Indian vegetarian cuisine at Madras Durbar Restaurant. **Open daily for lunch and dinner. Full service, non-smoking, espresso, catering, VISA/MC/AMEX/DC, $$.**

• Narula's
1438A Gerrard St. E., Toronto, ON M4L 1Z8   **(416) 466-0434**
Vegetarian/Indian. Narula's offers vegetarian Indian cuisine, including masala dosas, poori, samosas, and aloo tikki, at some of the best prices in town. Plus, they sponsor $2 Tuesdays, when everything on the menu drops to that price. **Open Tuesday through Sunday for lunch and dinner. Closed Monday. Full service, take-out, $.**

• Naturally Yours Vegetarian Gourmet
P.O. Box 372, First Canadian Pl., Toronto, ON M5X 1E2   **(416) 368-0100**
919 Kingston Rd., Toronto, ON M4E 1S6   **(416) 691-7055**
P.O. Box 444, W. Commerce Court, Toronto, ON M5L 1G4   **(416) 364-7401**
Vegetarian. Naturally Yours offers three daily hot entrées, as well as a salad bar, veggie burgers, pastas, Chinese dishes, burritos, shepherd's pie, cauliflower bake, broccoli patties, and more. **Open Monday through Friday for lunch. Closed Saturday and Sunday. Take-out, vegan options, fresh juices, catering, VISA/MC, $.**

• Nature's Emporium
16655 Yonge St., Newmarket, Toronto, ON L3X 1V6   **(905) 898-1844**
Vegetarian/natural foods store deli. Located inside a holistic market, this café offers music, a 'weigh-n-pay' section, coffees, smoothies, a juice bar, and a vegan bakery. **Open for lunch, dinner, and late evening service. Full service, macrobiotic/vegan options, fresh juices, smoothies, $.**

• The Organic Buddha Café
443 Danforth Ave., Toronto, ON M4K 1P1   **(416) 406-3338**
Vegetarian/Chinese. The Organic Buddha Café is located on the Danforth, an area known

for its eclectic flavor. It offers a dynamic experience that invites you to elevate your awareness of the environment, while astonishing your taste buds wuth a cornucopia of exotic entrées, pastries, and coffees. **Open daily for three meals. Limited service, vegan options, non-smoking, fresh juices, smoothies, soymilk, espresso/cappuccino, take-out, $$.**

• Pulp Kitchen Juicebar and Eatery
898 Queen St. E., Toronto, ON M4M 1J3   **(416) 461-4612**
Organic café/juice bar. Pulp Kitchen serves up dishes that are fast, tasty, and healthy, as well as a full selection of fresh juices. Sample their daily soups, Roti Wraps, 'Shroom Burger, VLT, Mange á Trois, or hemp ice "cream." Or attend their recently added vegan brunch. They also carry gifts, natural pet foods, and organic herbal remedies. **Open Monday through Friday for three meals. Open Saturday and Sunday for brunch. Full service, vegan options, fresh juices, smoothies, soymilk, espresso/cappuccino, special drinks, take-out, VISA, $$-$$$.** www.pulpkitchen.ca

• Pure Juice Bar/Espresso Bar
12 St. Clair Ave. E., Toronto, ON M4T 1L7   **(416) 927-9863**
Juice bar. This juice bar, with a distinctive, brightly-colored floral décor, specializes in smoothies, juices, and shakes. They also offer organic, fair trade coffees and cocoas and vegan baked goods made in-house. **Open Monday through Friday for three meals. Open Satuday and Sunday for breakfast through early dinner. Limited service, vegan options, fresh juices, smoothies, soymilk, espresso/cappuccino, take-out, catering, $.** www.purejuicebar.com

• Simon's Wok
801 Gerrard St. E., Toronto, ON M4M 1Y5   **(416) 778-9836**
Vegetarian. Located in Chinatown, Simon's offers 100 different vegetarian dishes in a non-smoking and informal atmosphere. **Open for three meals. Full service, $$.**

Sunny Café
322 Bloor St. W., Toronto, ON M5S 1W5   **(416) 963-8624**
Natural foods. Sunny Café is located in Noah's Natural Foods Store. The café offers organic foods, soups, sandwiches, burgers, entrées, and more. **Open Monday through Saturday for lunch and early dinner. Closed Sunday. Counter service, vegan/macrobiotic options, fresh juices, take-out, catering, $-$$.**

• Surati Sweet Mart
4801 Keele St., #51, Toronto, ON M3J 3A4   **(416) 665-8545**
Bakery. Located near York University, Surati offers more than 70 snacks and sweets as well as hot fresh Gujarati Thalis and other meal items. **Open Wednesday through Monday for lunch and dinner. Closed Tuesday. Limited service.**

• Udupi Palace Vegetarian Indian Cuisine
1460 Gerrard St. E., Toronto, ON M4L 2A3   **(416) 405-8189**
Vegetarian/Indian. Udupi Palace offers a wide range of South Indian cuisine, including appetizers, soups, dosas, curries, rice dishes, and breads. Unique dishes include Cashew Pakoras, Tomato and Peas Utthapam, Pineapple Utthapam, and Bagala Bath (yogurt rice

garnished with mustard seeds and cucumber). Reservations required on weekends. **Open daily for lunch and dinner. Full service, take-out, catering, VISA/MC/AMEX, $$.**

•• Vegetarian Haven
17 Baldwin St., Toronto, ON M5T 1L1   **(416) 621-3636**

Vegan/Chinese. Health Haven's menu features soups, baked spring rolls, tofu dishes, veggie seafood, veggie cutlets, stir-fries, noodle dishes, rice dishes, non-dairy ice cream, vegan cakes, and more. A wheat-free menu is available, and they can accommodate special dietary requirements. A private party room upstairs seats 60. **Open daily for lunch and dinner. Full service, fresh juices, soymilk, non-alcohlic beer, take-out, catering, cooking classes, VISA/MC, $.** www.vegetarianhaven.com

• The Vegetarium Café
University Of Toronto, 33 St. George St., Toronto, ON M8Z 3Y6   (416) 838-9400

Vegetarian. The Vegetarium is a co-operatively-run non-profit that provides students fair and equitable job opportunities, as well as community awareness about food issues through educational outreach. Offerings include rice & dahl, veggie burgers, soups, salads, chilis, samosas, bagels, veggie pizza, veggie lasagna, stir-fries, sushi, pasta dishes, falafels, and more. The café strives to meet its patrons' dietary needs and can accommodate vegans, those adherring to Halaal and semi-strict Kosher diets, and those with food allergies. **Call for hours. Full service, vegan options, catering.** http://vegcafe.sa.utoronto.ca/main.htm

• Wanda's Pie In The Sky
7-A Yorkville Ave., Toronto, ON M4W 1L1   **(416) 925-PIES**

Vegetarian café. This small, mostly vegan café and bakery offers soups, gourmet pizzas, sandwiches, pies, desserts, and organic coffees. **Open Monday through Saturday for breakfast through early dinner. Open Sunday for lunch and early dinner. Counter service, vegan options, baking classes, VISA/MC.** www.wandaspieinthesky.com

WASAGA BEACH

Harvest Moon Natural Foods Restaurant
1080 Mosley St., Wasaga Beach, ON L0L 2P0   **(705) 429-4411**

Hotel restaurant. Located near the world's largest freshwater beach, this hotel restaurant offers fresh juices, natural ice cream, and gourmet international dishes. **Open daily for three meals. Limited service, fresh juices, smoothies, soymilk, non-smoking, VISA/MC/AMEX, $$.** www.donatohouse.com

WILLOWDALE

• Tov-Li Pizza and Falafel
5982 Bathurst St., Willowdale, ON M2R 1Z1   **(416) 650-9800**

Vegetarian/Kosher. Enjoy Middle Eastern cuisine and more at Tov-Li Pizza. **Open Monday through Thursday and Sunday for lunch and dinner. Open Friday for lunch. Open Saturday for dinner and late-night service. Limited service, vegan options, espresso/cappuccino, take-out, catering, $.**

Prince Edward Island

CHARLOTTETOWN

Shaddy's

44 University Ave., Charlottetown, PE C1A 4K6   **(902) 368-8886**

Lebanese. Shaddy's separate vegetarian menu includes a wide range of vegetarian Lebanese dishes, including salads, falafel, hummus, lentil soup, and more. **Open daily for three meals. Full service, vegan options, take-out, catering, $-$$.**

Québec

GREENFIELD PARK

•La Boulange Du Commensal

4817 Taschereau Blvd., Greenfield Park, PQ J4V 2J1   **(514) 676-1749**

Vegetarian. Established in 1977, Le Commensal offers more than 100 items on the menu. The buffet is set up as a pay-by-weight system, so you can tailor the portions. In addition to a large selection of salads, guests can choose from tofu dishes, seitan dishes, pasta, and vegan desserts. **Open daily for lunch and dinner. Buffet, vegan options, fresh juices, take-out, catering, VISA/MC/AMEX, $-$$.**

LAVAL

•La Boulange Du Commensal

3180 St. Martin W., Laval, PQ H7T 1A1   **(514) 978-9124**

Vegetarian. See description under Greenfield Park, PQ.

MONTRÉAL

(For restaurant listings in the surrounding areas, see Greenfield Park, Laval, and Pierrefonds.)

Formosa Gastronomie D'asie

2115 St. Denis St., Montréal, PQ H2X 3K8   **(514) 282-1966**

Thai. There is a vegetarian section on the menu with tasty-sounding dishes, but be aware that this restaurant also serves exotic and game meats. No peanuts or MSG is used in the food. **Open Monday through Friday for lunch and dinner. Open Saturday and Sunday for dinner. Full service, take-out, beer/wine/alcohol, VISA/MC/AMEX/DC, $-$$.**

Restaurant codes: ✪ Reviewers' Choice   • Vegetarian Restaurant   •• Vegan Restaurant
Restaurant prices: **$** less than $6   **$$** $6-$12   **$$$** more than $12
Credit Cards Accepted: VISA - VISA   MC - MasterCard   AMEX - American Express
DISC - Discover   DC - Diner's Club

Foxy's Kosher Pizza
5987 Victoria Ave., Montréal, PQ H3W 2R9   **(514) 739-8777**
Kosher/natural foods. Foxy's features kosher pizza. Open Sunday through Friday. Closed
Saturday. Cafeteria, beer, take-out, $.

• La Boulange Du Commensal
2115 St. Denis St., Montréal, PQ H2X 3K8   **(514) 845-0248**
1204 McGill College Ave., Montréal, PQ H3B 4J8   **(514) 871-1480**
3715 Queen Mary, Montréal, PQ H3T 1X8   **(514) 733-9755**
Vegetarian. See description under Greenfield Park, PQ.

• Manbo
81 Lagauchetiere W., Montréal, PQ H2Z 1C2   **(514) 392-7778**
Vegetarian/Chinese. Enjoy a wide variety of Chinese vegetarian cuisine at Manbo. Open
daily for lunch and dinner. Full service, vegan options, wine/beer/alcohol, non-alcoholic
wine/beer, VISA/MC/AMEX, $$.

Pizza Pita
5710 Victoria Ave., Montréal, PQ H3W 2X5   **(514) 731-7482**
Kosher/natural foods. Vegetarians can dine on a wide variety of pizzas, falafel, hummus, and
much more. Open Sunday through Thursday for three meals. Open Friday for breakfast
and lunch. Open Saturday for late dinner. Limited service, vegan options, take-out, $-$$.

• Pushap Restaurant and Sweets
5195 Pare St., Montréal, PQ H4P 1P4   **(514) 737-4527**
Vegetarian/Indian. Pushap is a family-run restaurant offering Indian vegetarian food, including a thali meal with rice, dahl, two side dishes, and your choice of bread. Open daily for
three meals. Full service, special drinks, take-out, $$.

• Restaurant Chuchai
4088 St. Denis St., Montréal, PQ H2W 2M5   **(514) 843-4194**
Vegetarian/Thai. The décor, music, and cuisine all contribute to Restaurant Chuchai's
authentic Thai feel. A mostly vegan establishment, offerings include spicy curries with
coconut milk and basil, cool vegetarian fish, and vegetarian beef, chicken, and shrimp
dishes. Open daily for lunch and dinner. Full service, vegan options, reservations required,
espresso/cappuccino, beer/wine/alcohol, take-out, catering, delivery, VISA/MC/AMEX,
$$$.

PIERREFONDS

• Pushap Restaurant and Sweets
11999 Boul. Goulin W., Pierrefonds, PQ H8Z 1V8   **(514) 683-0556**
Vegetarian/Indian. See description under Montréal, PQ.

Bouquinerie-Café' Mille Feuille

1405 Chemin Ste.-Foy, Québec City, PQ G1S 2N7   **(418) 681-4520**

Natural foods. Situated in a historic house with a fireplace, the café offers a primarily vegetarian menu with meatless chili, cauliflower with mushroom and cheese in tomato sauce,
millet pie, quiche, bread with cheese, salads, and spanakopita. Outdoor dining is available
in the summer, and you can also enjoy their art exhibitions. **Open daily for three meals in
the summer. Full service, reservations recommended, espresso/cappuccino, wine/beer/alcohol,
non-alcoholic wine/beer, take-out, catering, VISA/MC/DC, $$.**

• Le Commensal

869 St. Jean, Québec City, PQ G1R 1R3   **(418) 647-3733**

Vegetarian. See description under Greenfield Park, PQ.

• Le Commensal

360 Rue Sicard, Ste. Therese, PQ J7E 3X4   **(514) 433-0505**

Vegetarian. See description under Greenfield Park, PQ.

Saskatchewan

Alfredo's

1801 Scarth St., Regina, SK S4P 2G9   **(306) 522-3366**

Italian. The staff at Alfredo's prepares homemade pasta (with eggs) fresh daily, which
enhances such vegetarian entrées as Baked Zucchini Parmesan, Spinach Tortellini, and
Eggplant Parmesan. **Open Monday through Saturday. Closed Sunday. Full service, cafeteria
options, reservations recommended, espresso/cappuccino, wine/beer/alcohol, take-out,
catering, VISA/MC/AMEX/DC, $-$$$.**

• Heliotrope Organic Vegetarian Restaurant

2204 McIntyre St., Regina, SK S4P 2R9   **(306) 569-3373**

International vegetarian. This organic, vegetarian restaurant allows its patrons to explore the
flavors of Mexico, India, Asia, and more. Try the Thai Coconut Curry topped over brown
rice or the Green Enchiladas filled with smoky black beans and vegetables, all covered in
a creamy green pumpkin seed tomatillo sauce. Or try something from the full juice and
smoothie menu. **Open Monday through Friday for lunch and dinner. Open Saturday for
dinner only. Closed Sunday. Full service, vegan options, reservations required, non-smoking,
fresh juices, smoothies, soymilk, beer/wine, special drinks, take-out, VISA/MC, $$.**

SASKATOON

Taj Mahal Restaurant
1031 Broadway Ave., Saskatoon, SK S7N 1C1   **(306) 978-2227**

Indian. Regarded as one of the best Indian restaurants in Canada, Taj Mahal has quite a few vegetarian options. Choose from vegetable samosas, pakoras, chana (chickpeas), dahl, khumb bhaji (mushrooms in spinach and tomato sauce), alu gobi (cauliflower, tomato, and peas), alu bangan (eggplant), vegetable biryani, thali, side dishes, breads, and more. **Open Tuesday through Sunday for dinner. Closed Monday. Full service, vegan options, fresh juices, special drinks, beer/wine/alcohol, VISA/MC/DC, $$-$$$.** www.lights.com/tajmahal

Yukon Territories

DAWSON

Ruby's Shady Lady's
882 5th Ave., Dawson, YT Y0B 1G0   **(867) 993-5721**

Canadian. A great place for some home cooking, Ruby's offers several vegetarian items. With 24-48 hours notice, they can cater to any of your dietary needs. Some of the dishes available are jambalaya, quiches, and vegetarian subs. **Open daily for three meals. Open Sunday for brunch. Full service, wine/beer/alcohol, take-out (afternoons and early evenings only), $$-$$$.**

WHITEHORSE

Talisman
2112 2nd Ave., Whitehorse, YT Y1A 1B9   **(867) 667-2736**

Middle Eastern. Located in Yukon's capital, this very vegetarian-friendly restaurant has excellent services. Some of the dishes Talisman offers are burritos, veggie burgers, spring rolls, and tabbouleh. **Open daily for three meals. Full service, wine/beer/alcohol, VISA/MC, $$.**

Restaurant codes: ✪ Reviewers' Choice   • Vegetarian Restaurant   •• Vegan Restaurant
Restaurant prices: **$** less than $6   **$$** $6-$12   **$$$** more than $12
Credit Cards Accepted: VISA - VISA   MC - MasterCard   AMEX - American Express
DISC - Discover   DC - Diner's Club

VEGETARIAN VACATION SPOTS

"From Atlantic to Pacific, gee, the traffic is terrific!" It must be vacation time. Whether you choose to vacation on one of the coasts or any place in between, you'll find vegetarians now have a multitude of options. Choose one of the following spots for some tasty food and combine the experience with rafting, yoga, or simply a relaxing getaway.

UNITED STATES

ALABAMA

Uchee Pines Institute

30 Uchee Pines Rd., Seale, AL 36875   **(334) 855-4781**

A health-conditioning center for ambulatory people who have health problems, the institute operates within the framework of Seventh-day Adventist beliefs and is supervised by two M.D.'s. All meals are vegan. **www.ucheepines.org**

ARIZONA

Canyon Ranch Health & Fitness Resort

8600 E. Rockcliff Rd., Tucson, AZ 85715   **(800) 742-9000**

Each lunch and dinner menu includes the option of a vegan soup and/or appetizer and entrée. **www.canyonranch.com**

Healing Center Of Arizona

25 Wilson Canyon Rd., Sedona, AZ 86336   **(877) 723-2811**

Recycling, composting, and use of earth-friendly products are characteristic of this smoke-free center, which offers vegetarian and vegan meals to groups and allows individuals to use their kitchen. Enjoy the sauna, hot tub, massages, and more. **www.sedonahealingcenter.com**

Natural Bed & Breakfast

3150 E. Presidio Rd., Tucson, AZ 85716   **(520) 881-4582**

Enjoy the macrobiotic-style cooking and a desert environment at this bed-and-breakfast. Natural Bed and Breakfast provides whole foods breakfasts and can accommodate special diets. Also visit the nearby Sonoran Desert Museum. **www.tucsonnatural.com**

Tree of Life Rejuvenation Center
171 3rd Ave., P.O. Box 1080, Patagonia, AZ 85624   **(520) 394-2520**
This center stresses organic live foods. Meals have an international flavor and much of the food is grown in their own garden. Vegan options are always available. **www.treeoflife.nu**

ARKANSAS

Singleton House Bed & Breakfast
11 Singleton, Eureka Springs, AR 72632   **(800) 833-3394**
Singleton House is a vegetarian bed-and-breakfast situated in a restored 1890 Victorian home on a hillside in Eureka Springs' historic district. Each room has a private bath. Breakfast is served on the balcony overlooking a wildflower garden. Located one block from shops and cafés. **www.singletonhouse.com**

CALIFORNIA

Cal-a-Vie
29402 Spa Havens Way, Vista, CA 92084   **(866) 772-4283**
This health spa offers vegetarian and vegan options at all meals. The dishes are lowfat and have an international flavor. Enjoy casseroles, burgers, loaves, pasta, curries, and much more. **www.cal-a-vie.com**

Carole's Bed and Breakfast
3227 Grim Ave., San Diego, CA 92104   **(800) 975-5521**
This establishment gladly accommodates vegetarians and vegans for breakfast with fresh tropical fruit and breads.

The Cottage
3829 Albatross St., San Diego, CA 92103   **(619) 299-1564**
Built in 1913, this cottage is a redwood homestead-style home located in the heart of San Diego. Enjoy fresh baked goods, juice, and fruit at this bed-and-breakfast.

Doral Desert Princess Resort Palm Springs
67-967 Vista Chino, Cathedral City, CA 92234   **(888) FUN-INPS**
The chef at this resort's restaurant is more than willing to accommodate vegetarian and vegan diners, preparing dishes such as vegetable soup with tofu and a portobello mushroom salad made with wild rice and sprouts. Also, the establishment offers breathtaking views of the San Jacinto Mountains. **www.doralpalmsprings.com**

Joshua Grindle Inn
44800 Little Lake Rd., P.O. Box 647, Mendocino, CA 95460   **(800) 474-6353**
The innkeeper at this inn is vegan and serves vegetarian and vegan breakfasts. Their full breakfasts are served sit-down style on a long 1800's pine harvest table. On Sunday mornings they offer tables for two on the front veranda. The inn is located on two acres in a home built in 1879. The Mendocino coast offers a variety of outdoor activities from mountain bike trails and river canoe trips to whale watching tours. **www.joshgrin.com**

Land of Medicine Buddha
5800 Prescott Rd., Soquel, CA 95073   (831) 462-8383
Health retreats here include organic, vegetarian meals. www.medicinebuddha.org

Manzanita Village Buddhist Meditation Retreat Center
P.O. Box 67, Warner Springs, CA 92086   (760) 782-9223
This Buddhist retreat invites non-Buddhists to learn how to meditate. They serve vegetarian and vegan cuisine in a rustic environment.

Montecito-Sequoia Lodge
8000 General Hwy., Sequoia National Park, CA 93262   (800) 227-9900
Open year round, this vacation spot serves one vegetarian entrée at each meal. Price of meal is all-inclusive, including choice of salads, soups, desserts, and drinks (excluding beer, wine, or alcohol.) Cross-country and alpine skiing, snowshoeing, hiking, and more are all available to guests of the lodge.

Mount Madonna Center
445 Summit Rd., Watsonville, CA 95076   (408) 847-0406
The center is a community for the creative arts and health sciences within a context of spiritual growth. Campgrounds in redwood groves are located on the site. The center is strictly lacto-vegetarian but can accommodate vegans. www.mountmadonna.org

The Oaks At Ojai
122 E. Ojai Ave., Ojai, CA 93023   (800) 753-6257
This resident health spa located in the Ojai Valley serves vegetarian and vegan meals on an "alternative" basis. www.oaksspa.com

O'Brien Mountain Inn
P.O. Box 27, O'Brien, CA 96070   (888) 799-8026
This bed-and-breakfast that accommodates vegetarians and vegans is located off of Interstate 5 on 47 acres in the Shasta/Trinity National Forest. It is less than one mile from Shasta Lake. Enjoy hiking, swimming, and more, along with delicious vegan breakfasts featuring a fantastic menu. www.obrienmountaininn.com

The Palms
572 N. Indian Canyon Dr., Palm Springs, CA 92262   (800) 753-7256
The Palms calls itself one of the top ten health spas in the country. It offers vegetarian options at every meal, but it does not always accommodate vegans. www.palmsspa.com

Rancho La Puerta
P.O. Box 463057, Escondido, CA 92046   (619) 744-4222
The ranch prides itself on being the world's first fitness spa. Largely vegetarian since its opening 50 years ago, it does serve fish. They can accommodate vegans if meals are requested upon arrival. www.rancholapuerta.com

Royal Gorge Cross Country Ski Resort
P.O. Box 1100, Soda Springs, CA 95728   (800) 500-3871
The resort serves vegetarian food to its guests. www.royalgorge.com

Sivananda Yoga Vedanta Center
Sivananda Ashram Yoga Farm
14651 Ballantree Ln., Grass Valley, CA 95949   (800) 469-9642
The center offers a lacto-vegetarian menu and vegan meals upon request at all of its yoga retreats. It also conducts weekend workshops on vegetarian lifestyles. www.sivananda.org/farm/

Stoney Brook Inn
309 W. Colombero, P.O. Box 1860, McCloud, CA 96057-1860   (800) 369-6118
Seated at the foot of Mt. Shasta, Stoney Brook Inn offers indoor amenities like hot tubs and saunas, as well as access to wilderness areas like Mt. Shasta, McCloud Reservoir, Lake Siskiyou, and McCloud Falls. Vegetarian meals and some vegan meals are available. www.stoneybrookinn.com

Two Bunch Palms Resort & Spa
67-425 Two Bunch Palms Trail, Desert Hot Springs, CA 92240   (800) 472-4334
This resort and spa offers vegetarian options including soups, salads, bean and rice burgers, pasta dishes, and vegetarian and vegan specials daily. www.twobunchpalms.com

Vega Study Center's Summer Camp
1511 Robinson St., Oroville, CA 92240   (530) 533-7092
An annual affair in Tahoe National Forest, the program centers around macrobiotic living. www.vega.macrobiotic.net

We Care Spa
18000 Long Canyon Rd., Desert Hot Springs, CA 92240   (800) 888-2523
A holistic health group devoted to physical and mental wellness runs the center. It offers a wide variety of raw vegetable juices as part of its vegetarian regimen. www.wecarespa.com

Weimar Institute
P.O. Box 486, 20601 W. Paoli Ln., Weimar, CA 95736-0486   (530) 422-7933
A strictly vegan health resort, Weimar also offers a variety of health-related seminars. www.weimar.org

Wellspring Renewal Center
18450 Ray's Rd., Philo, CA 95466   (707) 895-3893
This spiritual retreat and conference center uses organic produce and products whenever available. Much of this produce is grown in their organic garden. Vegetarian meals are offered for groups of 14 adults or more. Individuals may join groups to use the main kitchen. www.wellspringrenewal.org

Zosa Ranch Bed and Breakfast
9381 West Lilac Rd., Escondido, CA 92026   **(800) 711-8361**

This bed-and-breakfast offers primarily vegan meals. The ranch, located on 22 acres of Monserate Mountain, offers eight fully furnished bedrooms, tennis, basketball, volleyball, and more.

COLORADO

Gray's Avenue Hotel
711 Manitou Ave., Manitou Springs, CO 80829   **(800) 294-1277**

This bed-and-breakfast was built in 1886 and serves a sit-down breakfast. Vegan food available upon request. Guests have access to a hot tub. **www.graysbandb.com**

Nada Hermitage
Box 219, Crestone, CO 81131   **(719) 256-4778**

The Hermitage is a monastic spiritual institute in the wilderness of the Sange de Cristo mountains. People may eat as they choose, but the institute is primarily vegetarian and accommodates vegans. **www.spirituallifeinstitute.org**

Red Crags Bed and Breakfast Inn
302 El Paso Blvd., Manitou Springs, CO 80829   **(800) 721-2248**

A vegetarian breakfast includes mushroom spinach quiche, waffles, green chili, or homemade breads. Vegan meals are prepared upon request. Perched on a bluff, the main house has views of Pike's Peak, Manitou Valley, Garden of the Gods, and the city of Colorado Springs. **www.redcrags.com**

Two Sisters Inn
10 Otoe Pl., Manitou Springs, CO 80829   **(800) 274-7466**

This bed-and-breakfast will gladly cater to vegetarians upon request. Enjoy fresh fruit, home baked muffins, a hot entrée, and more. **www.twosisinn.com**

FLORIDA

The Café at Safety Harbor Resort & Spa
105 N. Bayshore Dr., Safety Harbor, FL 34695   **(727) 726-1161**

Calling itself the "ultimate spa vacation," Safety Harbor offers a few vegetarian/vegan options on its regular menu. **www.safetyharborspa.com**

Hippocrates Health Institute
1443 Palmdale Court, West Palm Beach, FL 33411   **(800) 842-2125**

A strictly vegan health resort, the institute now offers a singles program. **www.hippocrates inst.com**

Regency House Natural Health Resort and Spa
2000 S. Ocean Dr., Hallandale, FL 33009   **(800) 454-0003**

This is a luxury-class beach resort offering gourmet vegetarian cuisine. **www.regencyhealth spa.com**

Rustic Inn
65 N. Main St., P.O. Box 387, High Springs, FL 32643   **(386) 454-1223**

This inn is located on 40 acres near a state park and can accommodate up to 24 people for conferences. Nearby is The Great Outdoors Café, offering vegetarian entrées.

HAWAII

Haikuleana
555 Haiku Rd., Haiku, HI 96708   **(808) 575-2890**

On the island of Maui, amidst the lush green foliage lies this luxury country inn. All food is prepared vegan to the individual's tastes. Less than fifteen minutes from the airport and the city, as well as a number of great beaches and hiking trails, this inn offers seclusion, and at the same time, proximity to a number of exciting activities. Crater walks, kayaking, snorkeling and scuba diving, helicopter rides, surfing, biking, hiking and more are all available to visitors. Other services offered at the Inn include massage, reflexology, herbal and nutritional counseling, cooking, yoga, tai chi, acupuncture, and more. **www.haikuleana.com**

Hana Accommodations and Plantation Houses
P.O. Box 489, Hana Maui, HI 96713   **(808) 248-7248**

This beach resort is operated by a vegetarian who was a founder of the Ecologically Conscious Host Network, and operates two Environmental Information Centers. **www.hana-maui.com**

Hawaiian Wellness Holiday/Kauai Yoga Vacation
P.O. Box 279, Koloa, Kauai, HI 96756   **(808) 332-9244**

Focus on total health and fitness in a tropical paradise. Vegetarian cuisine (fish is also served) with a vegan option is offered. **www.sunsignyoga.com**

Hyatt Regency Maui
200 Nohea Kai Dr., Lahaina, HI 96761   **(808) 661-1234**

Chefs at this hotel have expanded their vegetarian selections to include such items as Crispy Tofu with Three Asian Salad in a spicy Sesame Sauce, Vegetarian Wonton Tacos with Oriental Salsa, Potato Spinach Lasagna with Wild Mushrooms, plus much more. **maui.hyatt.com**

Kalani Oceanside Retreat
RR 2 Box 4500, Pahoa, HI 96778   **(800) 800-6886**

This conference and retreat center specializes in vegetarian and vegan cuisine, although fish and fowl entrées are offered. The center conducts a wide variety of workshops and festivals. **www.kalani.com**

IDAHO

Idaho Afloat
P.O. Box 542, Grangeville, ID 83530   **(800) 700-2414**

A white-water rafting organization in the Pacific Northwest, Idaho Afloat can accommodate vegetarians and would be happy to bring a local vegan cook for a group of more than 12. **www.idahoafloat.com**

ILLINOIS

The Heartland Health Spa
1237 E. 1600 N. Rd., Gilman, IL 60938					**(800) 545-4853**
Located 80 miles south of Chicago, this health and fitness retreat is situated on 31 acres of woods and farmland. The cuisine is "basically vegetarian supplemented with fish."

Maggie's Bed and Breakfast
2102 N. Keebler Rd., Collinsville, IL 62234					**(618) 344-8283**
Enjoy a rustic wooded area surrounding this bed-and-breakfast, which is located in a historic former boarding house. Dine on herbal tea, juice, fresh fruit, homemade granola, organic multi-grain cereal, homemade bread, vegetable omelets or quiche, fruit crepes, pancakes, and more for breakfast. Located minutes away from downtown St. Louis, Missouri.

IOWA

The Raj Hotel and Health Center
1734 Jasmine Ave., Fairfield, IA 52556					**(800) 248-9050**
This spa features rejuvenation programs, purification treatments, and exercise routines. Enjoy meals at their gourmet vegetarian restaurant. **www.theraj.com**

MAINE

Greenhope Farm
Castine Rd., Brooks, ME 04921					**(207) 722-3999**
At this women-only vacation farm that recently relocated to mid-coast Maine, the cooking is vegetarian/vegan. **www.greenhopefarm.com**

Park Place
1 Metcalf Rd., Camden, ME 04843					**(207) 236-0208**
Enjoy macrobiotic/vegan cuisine at Park Place. Organic ingredients are used when available. The resort is open June through September only. **www.parkplacebarharbor.com**

Poland Spring Health Institute
32 Summit Spring Rd., Rfd 1, Box 4300
Poland Spring, ME 04274					**(207) 998-2894**
This institute offers a lifestyle improvement program, including a vegan regimen.

The Roaring Lion
995 Main St., Waldoboro, ME 04572					**(207) 832-4038**
Open all year, this bed-and-breakfast caters to vegetarian and macrobiotic diets. **www.roaring lion.com**

West of Eden
Rt. 102 and Kelleytown Rd., P.O. Box 65, Seal Cove, ME 04674   (207) 244-9695
You'll find this small bed-and-breakfast on Mt. Desert Island, just outside of Acadia National Park. It is macrobiotic with a very strong vegan emphasis. **www.acadia.net/westofeden/**

MARYLAND

Gramercy Bed & Breakfast
1440 Greenspring Valley Rd., Box 119, Stevenson, MD 21153 (410) 486-2405
Located outside of Baltimore on 54 acres of forest, organic flower and herb gardens, Gramercy's facilities include a pool, tennis court, and hiking trails. Breakfast items include omelets, French toast, pancakes, cereals, and fresh fruit. Please note that several rooms have a hunting motif. www.gramercymansion.com

MASSACHUSETTS

Brook Farm Inn
15 Hawthorne St., Lenox, MA 01240 (800) 285-7638
This vegetarian bed and breakfast allows you to shop in appealing boutiques, discover antique treasures and fine art in many galleries or you can visit Edith Wharton's home, The Mount, as well as Chesterwood and the Norman Rockwell Museum. Attend Tanglewood concerts, local theater festivals, or go hiking, boating or skiing. In the morning, enjoy a breakfast buffet. English tea with homemade scones, for guests only, is served each afternoon. www.brook farm.com

Canyon Ranch in the Berkshires
165 Kemble St., Lenox, MA 01240 (800) 326-7080
Each lunch and dinner menu includes the option of a vegan soup and/or entrée. www. canyonranch.com/lenox/index.asp

The Kushi Institute
P.O. Box 7, Becket, MA 01223 (800) 975-8744
The Institute is a nonprofit educational resort located in the Berkshire Mountains. It is macrobiotic with a vegan emphasis. www.kushiinstitute.org

Maple House Bed and Breakfast
51 Middletown Hill Rd., Rowe, MA 01367 (413) 339-0107
This family farm and bed-and-breakfast that hosts retreats and reunions specializes in home-made vegetarian cooking. Can accommodate vegans. www.maplehousebb.com

Rowe Camp and Conference Center
King's Highway Rd., Box 273, Rowe, MA 01367 (413) 339-4216
This center offers all kinds of programs to aid in the revitalization of body and mind for all ages. It is surrounded by 1400 acres of protected forest, and the cuisine is "gourmet vegetarian." www.rowecenter.org

The Shady Hollow Inn
370 Main St., South Dennis, MA 02660 (508) 394-7474
Located in the historic village of South Dennis, this 1839 Sea Captain's House is an elegant Inn in the midst of Cape Cod. Enjoy any number of activities, including golf, bicycling, hiking, antiquing, whalewatching and kayaking. Eat a breakfast made only of the finest

fresh and, when possible, organic ingredients, served from their 100 percent vegetarian kitchen, in their spacious dining hall.

The Turning Point Inn
3 Lake Buel Rd., Box 148, Great Barrington, MA 01230   **(413) 528-4777**

A year-round bed-and-breakfast, The Turning Point is a 200-year-old inn in the heart of the Berkshires. The inn serves lacto-ovo vegetarian meals and can accommodate vegans. **www.turningptinn.com**

MICHIGAN

Circle Pines Center
8650 Mullen Rd., Delton, MI 49046-9751   **(269) 623-5555**

This cooperative recreation and education center provides vegetarian and vegan meals in a campground setting. **www.circlepinescenter.org**

MINNESOTA

Chatsworth Bed and Breakfast
984 Ashland Ave., St. Paul, MN 55104   **(877) 978-4837**

This bed-and-breakfast is located 10 minutes from downtown St. Paul. Enjoy meals including fruits, yogurts, breads, and special entrées like cream-cheese stuffed French toast in the company of other guests, in the privacy or your room, or, in the summer, on the porch. Vegans can be accommodated. **www.chatsworth-bb.com**

MONTANA

Boulder Hot Springs Bed & Breakfast
P.O. Box 930, Boulder, MT 59632   **(406) 225-4339**

This establishment is located 3 miles south of Boulder, Montana, on Highway 69. They offer vegetarian meals as an option all the time and will prepare vegan dishes on request. Enjoy their geo-thermal mineral pools as well. **www.boulderhotsprings.com**

Feathered Pipe Foundation
P.O. Box 1682, Helena, MT 59624   **(406) 442-8196**

Located in the Rockies, the foundation offers programs for those seeking a healthier mind and body. It also organizes international tours. The cuisine is primarily vegetarian and they enthusiastically accommodate vegans, but fish and chicken are occasionally served. **www.featheredpipe.com**

NEW HAMPSHIRE

Star Island Corporation
10 Vaughan Mall, Ste. 8, Worth Plaza, Portsmouth, NH 03801   (603) 430-6272

Summer conferences covering a wide range of topics are offered on Star Island off the coast of New Hampshire. Vegetarian meals are offered. **www.starisland.org**

The Tuc'Me Inn
118 N. Main St., P.O. Box 657, Wolfeboro, NH 03894 **(603) 569-5702**
Located in a quaint New England town on the Eastern Shore of Lake Winnipesaukee, this bed-and-breakfast serves vegetarian and vegan breakfasts. Enjoy swimming, boating, hiking, mountain-climbing, or skiing nearby. **www.tucmeinn.com**

NEW JERSEY

Appel Farms Arts & Music Center
P.O. Box 888, Elmer, NJ 08318 **(856) 358-2472**
This dormitory-style conference center accommodates vegetarians and vegans if meals are requested in advance. Some of the produce is organically grown on the grounds. **www. appelfarm.org**

Serendipity Bed and Breakfast
712 Ninth St., Ocean City, NJ 08226 **(800) 842-8544**
Of their six breakfast choices every morning, at least three are vegan. Near many Ocean City attractions. **www.serendipitynj.com**

NEW MEXICO

The Ranchette
2329 Lakeview Rd., SW, Albuquerque, NM 87105 **(505) 873-8274**
While staying in this desert adobe-style home, be sure to enjoy their hot tub, grand piano, and delicious breakfast burritos.

NEW YORK

Elat Chayyim
99 Mill Hook Rd., Accord, NY 12404 **(800) 398-2630**
This vegetarian resort is a center for healing and renewal. They serve kosher vegetarian cuisine with a fish option and offer various classes. **www.elatchayyim.org**

Brookton Hollow Farm Bed & Breakfast
18 Banks Rd., Brooktondale, NY 14817 **(607) 273-5725**
Located on a 130-acre organic farm near Cornell University and Ithaca College, this bed & breakfast includes a full vegetarian breakfast made with organic ingredients when available. The farm bed & breakfast, at the gateway to the Finger Lakes region, offers access to many hiking and biking trails as well as Sapsucker's Woods, a prime area for birdwatching. **www. brooktonhollowfarm.com**

Farm Sanctuary
P.O. Box 150, Watkins Glen, NY 14891 **(607) 583-2225**
This shelter for abused farm animals also operates a bed-and-breakfast serving a continental vegan breakfast. The bed-and-breakfast is open May through October, but the shelter is open all year. **www.farmsanctuary.org**

Full Moon Catskills Resort
12 Valley View Rd., Oliverea, NY 12410   **(845) 254-5117**
Full Moon Catskills Resort is home to Valley View House, a turn-of-the-century country inn that has been converted into an ecologically aware bed and breakfast. The neighboring Full Moon Café provides the menu, which may include yellow peppers stuffed with polenta, spinach, and artichoke or cabbage leaves rolled with Basmati brown rice and garlic tofu in red sauce. **www.fullmooncentral.com**

The Golden Guernsey
31 Mitchell Pond E., Cochecton, NY 12726   **(845) 932-7994**
This barn and breakfast is located in rural Sullivan County, just 90 miles from New York City. Guests are welcome to picnic on the patio, visit the Golden Guernsey cows that are the establishment's namesake across the street, or take a hike, bike ride, or drive through the countryside. The vegetarian/pescatarian menu includes freshly squeezed juices, organic coffees and teas, frittatas, quiches, grain scones, muffins, and homemade breads. **www.the goldenguernsey.com**

Mountain Gate Lodge
212 McKinley Hollow Rd., Oliverea, NY 12410   **(845) 254-6000**
This mini resort located deep in the Catskill Mountains, has 20 rooms with private baths, a swimming pool and hiking trails, and has the Mountain Gate Indian Restaurant on site. **www.mountaingatelodge.com**

New Age Health Spa
Rte. 55, Neversink, NY 12765   **(800) 682-4348**
This spa is located on 280 acres in the Catskill Mountains. It offers non-vegetarian, vegetarian, and vegan options, as well as a juice fast. **www.newagehealthspa.com**

Omega Institute
150 Lake Dr., Rhinebeck, NY 12572   **(800) 944-1001**
This conference and workshop resort "exists to encourage and promote a hopeful response to personal and cultural challenges...based on a belief that a sane world starts with healthy people." The institute also offers outdoor journeys and kids' camps. It is primarily lacto-ovo vegetarian, but it serves vegan options at all meals and some fish. **www.eomega.org**

Sivananda Ashram Yoga Ranch
P.O. Box 195, Budd Rd., Woodbourne, NY 12788   **(845) 436-6492**
At Sivananda Ashram Yoga Ranch, located on 77 acres of woodlands in the Catskills, a single yoga class can be enjoyed, or an intensive month-long yoga teachers training course is offered. An organic garden and greenhouse supply a good deal of the food that is used to prepare the vegetarian and vegan dishes available at every meal. **www.sivananda.org**

Vatra Mountain Valley Spa
P.O. Box F, Route 214, Hunter, NY 12442   **(518) 263-4919**
An affordable weight loss spa that lets guests cleanse the body, mind, and soul amidst the tranquility of beautiful mountains. It accommodates vegetarians and vegans. **www.vatraspa.com**

Wise Woman Center
Fishcreek Rd., P.O. Box 64, Woodstock, NY 12498   **(845) 246-8081**
Enjoy wild foods and seasonal fresh cooked vegetarian and vegan dishes at this retreat and workshop center. Wise Woman is located in a quaint village of the mountain region. **www. susunweed.com**

NORTH CAROLINA

Beaufort House Inn
61 N. Liberty St., Asheville, NC 28801   **(800) 261-2221**
Enjoy vegetarian, vegan, and macrobiotic breakfasts at this Victorian inn including juice, fresh fruit, homemade muffins, a breakfast pastry, and one entrée including Belgian waffles with strawberries, French toast with maple cream, etc. Organic ingredients are used when available. **www.beauforthouse.com**

The Duckett House Inn and Farm
P.O. Box 441, Hot Springs, NC 28743   **(828) 622-7621**
Located on five acres bordering the Pisgah National Forest, Duckett House offers activities like white-water rafting, hiking on the Appalachian Trail, and hot springs mineral baths. Vegetarian and vegan breakfasts, made with organic produce and grains, are served daily. Dinners are by reservation only. **www.bbonline.com/nc/ducketthouse**

OREGON

Breitenbush Hot Springs Retreat and Conference
P.O. Box 578, Detroit, OR 97342   **(503) 854-3314**
Enjoy both a lodge and private cabins situated amongst dozens of steaming hot mineral springs and a roaring glacial river. Three vegetarian buffets are offered daily. Guests have access to hot tubs, steam sauna, hiking trails, cross-country skiing, and much more. **www. breitenbush.com**

Portland's White House Bed and Breakfast
1914 NE 22nd Ave., Portland, OR 97201   **(800) 272-7131**
Portland's White House is located in a Victorian bed-and-breakfast at the edge of Portland's downtown district. They serve juice, coffee, fresh fruit, granola, hot cereals (soymilk available on request), and more at this pleasant resort. **www.portlandswhitehouse.com**

Shambhalla Retreats
Rogue National Forest, P.O. Box 446, Ashland, OR 97520   **(541) 941-0178**
Deep in the ancient forests of southern Oregon, this wilderness preserve is an hour east of Ashland. They serve gourmet, organic vegetarian cuisine for patio dining, campfires, and picnics. **www.ashlandweb.com/shambhalla**

PENNSYLVANIA

Himalayan Institute
RR 1, Box 1126, Honesdale, PA 18431   **(800) 822-4547**
The institute is devoted to teaching yoga and meditation and serves vegetarian meals. All

foods are clearly labeled as vegetarian or vegan. **www.himalayaninstitute.org**

Ten Eleven Clinton Bed and Breakfast

1011 Clinton St., Philadelphia, PA 19107 **(215) 923-8144**

This bed-and-breakfast includes several apartments with separate baths and kitchens. Each has a water filter. Macrobiotic kitchens upon request will have a steamer, woks, miso, organic oatmeal, etc.

PUERTO RICO

Hosteria Del Mar

1 Tapia St., Ocean Park, San Juan, PR 00911 **(787) 727-3302**

This lovely, beachfront guesthouse overlooks the ocean, and several suites have kitchenettes. All rooms have air conditioning, a television, and phone. The restaurant offers native and vegetarian meals that include hummus, falafel, and tofu sandwiches served on whole wheat pita bread with vegetables. A vegetarian soup is also served as well as salads. Main dishes include mashed plantains with eggplant and spiced spinach. Macrobiotic options available.

La Casa de Vida Natural

Box 1916, Rio Grande, PR 00745 **(809) 887-4359**

La Casa provides an incredible setting to enjoy nature. They are located in the Puerto Rican rainforest and visitors have views of both mountain peaks and the ocean. Enjoy hiking and swimming during the day, and fantastic vegetarian and vegan cuisine with an international flavor. **www.lacasaspa.com**

SOUTH DAKOTA

Black Hills Health and Education Center

Box 19, Hermosa, SD 57744 **(800) 658-5433**

This strictly vegan health resort is situated in the famous Black Hills. **www.bhhec.org**

TEXAS

Saint John's Retreat Center

Church Of The White Eagle Lodge
2615 St. Beulah Chapel Rd., Montgomery, TX 77316 **(936) 597-5757**

This spiritual retreat center is dedicated to the following and teaching of White Eagle's philosophy. It is lacto-ovo vegetarian and will accommodate vegans. **www.whiteaglelodge.org**

UTAH

Capitol Reef Inn

360 W. Main St., Torrey, UT 84775 **(435) 425-3271**

Located in southern Utah, a few miles from Capitol Reef National Park, this inn has ten units. It is also home to a natural foods restaurant, but they do not readily accommodate vegans. **www.capitolreefinn.com**

Snowbird Ski and Summer Resort

P.O. Box 929000, Snowbird, UT 84092   **(801) 742-2222**

This resort is home to 11,000-foot peaks that are open all year round and a conference facility. The menu contains a few vegetarian entrées. **www.snowbird.com**

VERMONT

Somerset House Bed & Breakfast

130 Highland Ave., Hardwick, VT 05843   **(800) 838-8074**

A vegetarian or vegan breakfast is available, made with ingredients from the house garden, local co-op, or nearby producers. It's located in Vermont's Northeast Kingdom, the most rural corner of the state. Enjoy country walks, mountain hikes, mountain biking, skiing clean lakes and rivers, and beautiful scenery. The local village center features a bookstore and a new cooperative café. **www.somersethousebb.com**

Sweet Onion Inn

Rte. 100, P.O. Box 66, Hancock, VT 05748   **(800) 897-6490**

Nestled in the Green Mountains, Sweet Onion offers all vegan breakfasts like Full-a-fruit Tarts and Sunrise Burritos made with veggie sausage. Dinners include Shepherd's Pie with tempeh, and Mountain Burgers made with brown rice, vegetables, and tahini. In between eating these wonderful vegan meals, take advantage of the surrounding country for skiing, hiking, canoeing, and visiting local historical sights. **www.sweetonioninn.com**

VIRGIN ISLANDS

Maho Bay Camps, Inc.

Cruz Bay, Box 310, St. John, VI 00830-0310   **(800) 392-9004**

Maho Bay Camps is strongly committed to environmental preservation. It consists of a community of tent-cottages within a national park. Every cottage has a propane stove and an ice cooler for food storage. A restaurant offers one vegetarian option at each meal. **www. maho.org**

VIRGINIA

Ballard House Bed & Breakfast

12527 Ballard Drive., Route 660, Willis Wharf, VA 23486   **(757) 442-2206**

Ballard House is located on the Eastern Shore of Virginia near the Chesapeake Bay and Barrier Islands. Vegetarian breakfasts are available upon request. Ballard House offers air-conditioned rooms. **www.ballardhouseesva.com**

Belle Meade Bed and Breakfast and Inn

353 F. T. Valley Rd., Sperryville, VA 22740   **(540) 987-9748**

Located near Shenandoah National Park, Monticello, caverns, and other attractions, Belle Meade is a restored Victorian farmhouse featuring a 60-foot pool, a hot tub, and organic flower and vegetable gardens. Each night, the staff serves gourmet, candlelit vegetarian dinners made with in-season organic produce to the guests. Request the Comfrey Cottage if you are traveling with canine companions. **www.bellemeade.net**

Satchidananda Ashram-Yogaville
Rte. 1, Box 1720, Buckingham, VA 23921   **(434) 969-3121**

This spiritual center offers a strictly lacto-vegetarian menu and has an annual summer camp.
www.yogaville.org

The White Pig Bed and Breakfast
5120 Irish Rd., Schuyler, VA 22969   **(434) 831-1416**

Located in the foothills of the Blue Ridge Mountains, The White Pig Bed and Breakfast is
a quaint and homey inn catering to those with a love of nature and animals. Wake up to a
refreshing fare of organic and vegan breakfasts, and dine on a vegan bag lunch or dinner if
you notify the staff ahead of time. Afternoon tea or wine with vegan cheese, crackers, and
fruit is also available. **www.thewhitepig.com**

WASHINGTON

Annapurna Center For Self Healing
538 Adams St., Port Townsend, WA 98368   **(360) 385-2909**

Views of snow-capped mountains surround the historic district of Port Townsend, where
Annapurna Inn is located. After enjoying a delicious vegetarian or vegan breakfast of Tofu
Scramble with herbs and almonds, or Tofu French Toast, try one of the several outdoor
activities available in the surrounding areas, like kayaking, hiking, or strolling the shores
of Puget Sound. Activities at the inn include ashtanga yoga, therapeutic massage, or cranio-
sacral therapy. **www.annapurnaretreat-spa.com**

Hoquiam's Castle Bed and Breakfast
509 Chestnut Ave., Hoquiam, WA 98550   **(360) 533-2320**

Located on the Olympic Peninsula, overlooking Gray's Harbor, this bed-and-breakfast has
vegan and vegetarian options at every meal. For example, they may serve vegan French toast
or oatmeal. **www.hoquiamcastle.com**

Palmer's Chart House
P.O. Box 51, Deer Harbor, WA 98243   **(360) 376-4231**

Located on Orcas Island, one of the scenic San Juan Islands, Palmer's Chart House features
sailing, a meatless breakfast - vegan by pre-arrangement - and rooms with private decks
overlooking Deer Harbor.

Towerhouse Bed and Breakfast
San Juan Island, 392 Little Rd., Friday Harbor, WA 98250   **(800) 858-4276**

Located on ten acres, Towerhouse offers vegetarian (vegan upon request) breakfasts. **www.
san-juan-island.com**

WEST VIRGINIA

Sweet Thyme Inn
Rte. 92/28, P.O. Box 85, Green Bank, WV 24944-0085   **(304) 456-5535**

This inn, built in 1870, is nestled in the Monongahela National Forest. Their organic vegan
menus change seasonally, but common offerings include Potato-Kale Croquettes or Biscuits

'n' Southern Gravy for breakfast and items like Herb and Walnut Ravioli or Mushroom and Seitan Stroganoff for dinner. **www.sweetthymeinn.com**

The Woods

P.O. Box 5, Mountain Lake Rd., Hedgesville, WV 25427 (800) 248-2222

This 18,000-acre resort and conference center, located near the Baltimore-Washington area, offers a few vegetarian entrées. **www.thewoodsresort.com**

WISCONSIN

Arbor House

3402 Monroe St., Madison, WI 53711 (608) 238-2981

Vegetarian and vegan meals are available, with advanced notice, at this bed-and-breakfast that bills itself as "an environmental inn." Across the street from Arbor House you can spend the day exploring the UW Arboretum, 1280 acres of ecologically restored woodland, prairie, and native communities. **www.arbor-house.com**

The White Rose Bed and Breakfast

910 River Rd., Wisconsin Dells, WI 53965 (800) 482-4724

The site of the Secret Garden Café, the White Rose offers a vegetarian bed-and-breakfast, as well as a motel and wedding and event facilities. Can accommodate vegans. **www.the whiterose.com**

CANADA

BRITISH COLUMBIA

Alive Health Resort For Wellness and Longevity

29 Square Valley Rd., Lumby, BC V0E 2G0 (250) 547-9433

This guesthouse is nestled among the rolling mountains of the North Okanagan and overlooks the Shuswap River Valley. A lifestyle program is offered, including cooking classes, vegetarian meals, lectures, natural remedies, exercise, and more. **www.aliveresort.com**

Bird Song Cottage B & B

9909 Maple St., Box 1432, Chemainus, BC V0R 1K0 (250) 246-9910

This bed-and-breakfast regularly offers vegetarian breakfasts and will prepare vegan meals upon request. Sample dishes include Vegan Lavender Rice Flour Pancakes with Blueberries. **www.romanticbb.com/birdsong_home.htm**

Golden Dreams Bed and Breakfast

6412 Easy St., Whistler Mountain Village, Whistler, BC V0N 1B6 (800) 668-7055

At this vegetarian bed-and-breakfast, rooms are tastefully decorated in Victorian, Oriental, and Aztec themes and feature sherry decanters, moccasins, and duvets. Relax in the private

Jacuzzi bath and awake to a nutritious, hearty breakfast including homemade jams and fresh herbs, served in a country kitchen. **www.goldendreamswhistler.com**

Hollyhock Farm

Box 127, Manson's Landing, Cortes Island, BC V0P 1K0　　　**(800) 933-6339**

Holistic-living workshops and retreats are offered, and camping is available. There is also a "Journeys Program." Fresh vegetarian and seafood fare are served buffet style. **www.holly hock.bc.ca**

The Salt Springs Centre

Box 1133, Ganges, BC V0S 1E0　　　**(250) 537-2326**

Situated in 69 acres of cedar forest, this center offers summer yoga retreats and personal retreats, among other programs. All programs include vegetarian meals. **www.saltspring centre.com**

Strathcona Park Lodge

Box 2160, Campbell River, BC V9W 5C9　　　**(250) 286-3122**

Located in the center of Vancouver Island in a wilderness area, the lodge offers outdoor expeditions that are mostly vegetarian. Special trips are offered for young students. **www. strathcona.bc.ca**

ONTARIO

Cozy Corners Health Retreat

15 Amelia St., Orangeville, ON L9W 2J2　　　**(519) 942-8941**

Cozy Corners is a health retreat and education center on the border of the Bruce and Trans Canada trails, tucked away in the rolling Caledon Hills and only one hour from "Big Smoke" Toronto. Among their offerings are meditation, Tai Chi, skiing, skating, canoeing, swimming, hiking, theater, and seminars on such topics as natural foods cooking and conversational French. The cost of a room includes an organic, vegetarian breakfast, and they offer packed lunch and dinner options. **www.cozycornershealthretreat.com**

The Dharma Centre of Canada

1886 Galway Rd., Kinmount, ON K0M 2A0　　　**(705) 488-2704**

The Dharma Centre of Canada is both a meditation retreat centre and a network of people involved in the practice of meditation and compassionate activity. The Kinmount facility provides mostly vegetarian foods, but you may also request a cabin with cooking facilities and/or bring your own food. **www.dharmacentre.org**

Forest Edge Bed & Breakfast

RR3, Durham, ON N0G1R0　　　**(519) 369-5661**

Enjoy a vegetarian breakfast at this bed-and-breakfast.

Hidden Valley Farm

RR2, Chatsworth, ON N0H 1G0　　　**(888) 624-0315**

Most of the food served on this farm is home-cooked and home-grown on 120 acres of organic farmland located close to many points of interest. Meals are vegan but dairy and eggs are available for those in transition. www.hiddenvalleyfarm.8k.com

A Home Away From Home
Chester Ave., Toronto, ON M4K 2Z9   **(416) 469-2033**

This guesthouse practices all-natural cleaning and uses all-natural linens. Yoga and holistic services available, as are refrigerators and stoves for vegetarian cooking. In addition, it is within walking distance of Toronto's largest all-natural foods store, The Big Carrot. Please contact the owner for more information and reservations.

Kukagami Lodge
Kukagami Lake, Wahnapitae, ON P0M 3C0   **(705) 853-4929**

Five hours north of Toronto, this lodge is set on Kukagami Lake and offers private log cabins, swimming, canoeing, hiking trails, and a sauna. However, there is no electricity or running water. Vegetarian meals are available, as well as picnic lunches to take along with you for a day of hiking or on the lake. www.yip.org/~erhard/kukagami/

Les Amis, A Vegetarian Bed & Breakfast
31 Granby St., Toronto, ON M5B 1H8   **(416) 591-0635**

Located in downtown Toronto, this bed-and-breakfast offers a rooftop patio, hardwood floors, and central air conditioning. Each morning, a full gourmet vegetarian breakfast is served, including homemade crêpes, waffles, and galettes made from home-milled organic wheat. Also offered are omelets, baked apples, a variety of breads, and homemade soymilk. There are lots of options for vegans as well. www.bbtoronto.com

MacRobiotics Canada
RR3, Almonte, ON K0A 1A0   **(613) 256-2665**

This bed-and-breakfast serves a macrobiotic-style vegan cuisine. Enjoy classes, yoga, and more. www.macrobioticscanada.ca

Maple Ki Forest Spirit Waters
P.O. Box 159, Tamworth, ON K0K 3G0   **(613) 379-2227**

All the meals served here are vegan, mostly organic, and gourmet. Enjoy hiking trails overlooking the Georgian Bay, waterfalls, or in a nearby forest. Massages are available during your stay. www.mapleki.com/home.html

Natural Choice/4 Nature Bed and Breakfast
263 McLeod St., Ottawa, ON K2P 1A1   **(888) 346-9642**

A vegetarian bed-and-breakfast with full spa services, including facials, yoga, iridology, and massage therapy. They also offer a wide variety of wedding services. www.vegybnb.com

Northern Edge Alconquin
P.O. Box 329, South River, ON P0A 1X0   **(800) 953-3343**

This retreat center serves delicious vegetarian cuisine made from organic and Fair Trade foods. They are willing to accommodate individual and group dietary needs for their guests. Practice no-trace camping, take yoga or drumming classes, and use showers and appliances powered by solar energy. www.algonquincanada.com

Still Point Bed and Breakfast and Retreat Center

Village of Northport, RR2, Picton, ON K0K 2T0   **(613) 476-8061**

This yoga and Tai Chi center offers vegetarian and vegan breakfasts upon request in a smoke-free environment. It is located on the shores of the Bay of Quinte. **www.angelfire.com/on/stillpoint**

Terrace House

52 Austin Terr., Toronto, ON M5R 1Y6   **(416) 535-1493**

This bed-and-breakfast is housed in a charming 1913 Tudor House in the upscale Casa Loma neighborhood surrounded by oak trees. The décor features hardwood floors, stained glass windows, North African rugs, antique furniture, and a backyard patio. Breakfast options always include fresh fruits, yogurts, freshly baked muffins or a fruit bread, coffee, tea, and hot chocolate. There is also a Dish of the Day, which may range from the lemon pancakes to a potato and saffron frittata to goat cheese and herbes of Provence scones. Bilingual French and English. Close to the St. Clair West subway station. **www.terracehouse.com**

The Yoga Spa

448 Old Wooler Rd., Codrington, ON K0K 1R0   **(888) 815-9772**

An hour and a half east of Toronto, The Yoga Spa is Canada's only Ayurveda spa destination. It has six elegant guest rooms decorated with the ornate textures and warm rich hues reminiscent of classical Indian art. All meals are vegetarian, and most are dairy- and wheat-free. Offerings include kamut pancakes with wild blueberry sauce, steamed cauliflower mung cakes with tomato sauce, mini tofu patties with sweet-and-sour pineapple sauce, and eggplant tofu ratatouille. Food is served buffet-style and is usually followed by dessert. **www.yogaspa.ca**

QUÉBEC

Chez Philippe

2457 Rue Sainte-Catherine Est, Montréal, PQ H2K 2J9   **(877) 890-1666**

Chez Philippe is a vegan bed-and-breakfast that offers four newly decorated rooms, two shared bathrooms, a large terrace, and full home-cooked breakfasts. They are careful that no animal products or byproducts are used in their room amenities (such as wool or silk) or bathroom toiletries. This establishment is less than a 10-minute walk to the Papineau Metro station and just a few stops from downtown Montreal. **www.chezphilippe.info**

Sivananda Ashram Yoga Camp

673 8th Ave., Val Morin, PQ J0T 2R0   **(819) 322-3226**

This Ashram has a lodge where guests are served lacto-vegetarian meals. Vegan meals are available upon request. Yoga, skiing, and various classes are offered to all guests. **www.sivananda.org/camp/**

AMERICAN VEGETARIAN TRAVEL TOURS & SERVICES

When you're smitten by domestic wanderlust, peruse this alphabetical listing of organizations; you're sure to find an expedition that will satisfy your needs.

Carnival Cruise Lines

327 E. 49th St., Hialeah, FL 33013   **(888) CARNIVAL**

Each menu offers at least one vegetarian option, and veggie burgers are available at buffets and in casual dining areas. Lacto-ovo vegetarians will find much to eat, though the vegan selection is rather limited. **www.carnival.com**

Celebrity Cruises

5200 Blue Lagoon Dr., Miami, FL 33126   **(800) 437-6111**

Vegetarian and vegan meals are served in the main restaurant only. **www.celebrity.com**

Country Walkers, Inc.

P.O. Box 180, Waterbury, VT 05676-0180   **(802) 244-1387**

Specializing in fine walking and hiking vacations around the country, and with an emphasis on natural history, Country Walkers donates some of its proceeds to conservation groups. The inns and hotels used by the group usually offer a vegetarian option. Upon request, vegans will be accommodated gladly.

Cunard Cruises

555 Fifth Ave., New York, NY 10017   **(800) 221-4770**

They meet vegetarian and vegan needs with two weeks' notice prior to the cruise. **www. cunard.com**

Equinox Wilderness Expeditions

2440 E. Tudor Rd., #1102, Anchorage, AK 99507   **(604) 222-1219**

Immerse yourself in a rainforest, kayak to a glacier, float a wild river, or hike. Explore the far north, where the summer sun never sets. Vegetarians and vegans accommodated. **www. equinoxexpeditions.com**

Escape Adventures

8221 W. Charleston Blvd., # 101, Las Vegas, NV 89117   **(800) 451-1133**

Escape accommodates vegetarians on mountain and road bike, multisport, and hiking tours throughout the Southwestern United States, Oregon, North Dakota, and Canada.

Green Earth Travel

7 Froude Cir., Cabin John, MD 20818   **(888) 2GO-VEGE**

Ask for or write Donna Zeigfinger who specializes in arranging travel plans for vegetarians. You may also e-mail greenearthtravel@aol.com. **www.vegtravel.com**

Hatch River Expeditions

P.O. Box 1150, Vernal, UT 84078   **(800) 342-8243**

Hatch River Expeditions specializes in white-water rafting trips down the Colorado River. Call in advance to request vegetarian/vegan meals.

The Macrobiotic Community

5 Frost St., #8, Cambridge, MA 02140   **(617) 497-0218**

The Macrobiotic Community Center of Cambridge arranges yoga macrobiotic vacations. Past retreat locations include Cape Cod; Sanibel Island, Florida; Fripp Island, South Carolina; and the Caribbean. Their menu is primarily vegan.

Newport-Mesa Travel

2043 Westcliff Dr., #110, Newport Beach, CA 92660   **(800) 223-0915**

Call Elda Caraco, who specializes in arranging travel plans for vegetarians. **www.newport mesatravel.com**

River Travel Center

Box 226, Pt. Arena, CA 95468   **(800) 882-RAFT**

River Travel specializes in rafting and kayaking in the American West and abroad. With proper notification most of its outfitters can accommodate vegetarians and vegans. **www. rivers.com**

Sea Quest Kayak Expeditions and Whale Watch Tours

P.O. Box 2424, Friday Harbor, WA 98250   **(888) 589-4253**

They offer international vegetarian and vegan meals as an option all the time on their kayaking excursions around the San Juan Islands, Baha Peninsula in Mexico, and near Alaska. **www.sea-quest-kayak.com**

Sierra Club Outings

855 Second St., San Francisco, CA 94105   **(415) 977-5522**

The club offers a wide range of outdoor expeditions. Most can accommodate vegetarians, and some can accommodate vegans. **www.sierraclub.org/outings/national**

VBT Deluxe Bike Vacations

614 Monkton Rd., Bristol, VT 05443   **(802) 453-4811**

On worldwide biking tours, this group serves vegetarian and vegan meals upon request. **www.vbt.com**

Wildland Adventures
3516 NE 155th St., Seattle, WA 98155   **(800) 345-4453**

Wildland Adventures sponsors ecotourism explorations to North America, Central America, South America, Africa, Turkey, Middle East, New Zealand, and Antarctica. All trips can accommodate vegetarians, and vegans may be accommodated depending upon the destination. **www.wildland.com**

INTERNATIONAL VEGETARIAN TRAVEL TOURS & VACATION SPOTS

The many ethnic foods described in this book may well give you a taste for foreign adventure. If so, contact one of the following groups or locations to assist with your vacation planning.

Adventure Associates Inc. of Washington
P.O. Box 16304, Seattle, WA 98116　　　　　　　**(206) 932-8352**
Offers co-ed and women-only expeditions around the world. The associates serve primarily vegetarian meals in the field; they can accommodate special requests but may ask the guest to supply some food. **www.adventureassociates.net**

Amazonia Expeditions
10305 Riverburn Dr., Tampa, FL 33647　　　　　　**(800) 262-9669**
Amazonia offers trips to the South American rainforests. Vegetarians and vegans are readily accommodated. **www.perujungle.com**

Auberge Santé Du Lac Brome
408 Lakeside, C.P. 616, Lac Brome, PQ J0E 1V0　　　**(450) 242-1567**
This establishment advertises itself as Quebec's premier vegetarianism and fasting center. **www.aubergesante.com**

Cultural Folk Tours International
5631 Lincoln Ave., Ste. B, Cypress, CA 90630　　　**(800) 935-8875**
Offering tours to Turkey for over a decade, Cultural Tours International can arrange for vegetarian meals in-flight and also in Turkey. **www.boraozkok.com**

D'Astros
Le Pin 82 340, Auvillar, France　　　　　　　**33 (0)-6395-9520**
This bed and breakfast offers vegetarian meals.

Exito Travel
108 Rutgers St., Fort Collins, CO 80525　　　　　**(800) 655-4053**
Focuses on travel to Latin America. Senstive to the needs of vegetarians and vegans. **www.exitotravel.com**

Forum Travel International
91 Gregory Ln., #21, Pleasant Hill, CA 94523   **(800) 252-4475**

Specializing in "classic and unusual travel" all over the world. Many tours, such as European biking trips, can accommodate vegetarians and vegans. **www.foruminternational.com**

Hi-Lo Travel
459 Rte. 79, P.O. Box 27, Morganville, NJ 07751   **(732) 591-9292**

Worldwide travelers themselves, staff members have had experience arranging trips for both diabetics and vegetarians. Ask for or write to Tema.

Hippocrates Health Center
Elaine Ave., Mudgeeraba
Gold Coast, Queensland, Australia 4213   **(07) 530-2860**

A guest described the center as a national park with luxuries. It offers raw vegan foods on Ann Wigmore's Wheatgrass Program.

Hotel and Inn at Coyote Mountain
San Francisco de Piedades Sur
San Ramon, Alajuela, Costa Rica   **+34-958-201-557**

This inn serves gourmet Creole-inspired vegetarian cuisine in a dining room open both to its vacationing guests and to the public. Menu offerings often include Chilled Tropical Fruit Soup, Garden-Fresh Artichokes á la Romana, Macadamia-Encrusted Wild Mushroom Cakes, and Mango-Macadamia Bread Pudding with Coffee Caramel Sauce. Call their New Orleans office at (504) 866-2931 for more information. **www.cerrocoyote.com**

Inverdeen House Bed & Breakfast
11 Bridge Sq., Ballater, Scotland AB35 5QJ   **(0044) 13397-55759**

This vegan guesthouse is nestled in the mountains near the River Dee. **www.inverdeen.com**

Inward Bound
4741 Reservoir Rd., NW, Washington, DC 20007   **(800) 760-5099**

Schedules both private and group retreats, often including vegetarian fare. **www.inward boundadventures.com**

Jackie's on The Reef
General Delivery, Negril P.O. Box, Negril, Jamaica   **(718) 469-2785**

Located on a secluded coral reef two miles past the oldest lighthouse in Jamaica, Jackie's on the Reef offers private cottages or accommodations in a stone house. Three vegetarain meals are offered each day. Yoga, meditation, Tai Chi, snorkeling, bird wacthing, and more are available. **www.jackiesonthereef.com**

Journeys International, Inc.
107 April Dr., Ste. 3, Ann Arbor, MI 48103   **(800) 255-8735**

This group offers trips around the world. The needs of vegetarian clients will be accommodated. **www.journeys-intl.com**

Kesher Worldwide Jewish Home Link
75 Solvent Rd., West Hempstead
London, England NW6 1TY   44 (0)1-7179-40073
An exchange and rental organization servicing the world, Kesher works only with vegetarian, kosher, and other Jewish families.

La Maison Du Vert
Hôtel Restaurant Végétarien, Ticheville
61120 Vimoutiers, Normandie, France   33 (0)2-3336-9584
Two hours from Paris, this hotel is close to the historic cities of Honfleur, Bayeux, and Caen, as well as the D-Day landing beaches and Monet's garden. There is always at least one vegan option on the menu, which may include veggie sushi, eggplant and sweet potato bake, or garden pears in local cider and almond cream. Organics are used whenever possible, and even the wines and ciders in recipes are vegan. **www.maisonduvert.com**

Lancrigg Vegetarian Country House Hotel
Easedale, Grasmere, Cumbria, England LA22 9QN   44 (0)1-5394-35317
This vegetarian hotel is located one half mile away from the Lakeland village of Grasmere. Enjoy nearby waterfalls and beautiful gardens. Sample breakfast menu includes whole grain cereals, fresh or dried fruit salads, juice, soymilk, whole wheat croissants and rolls, plus more. Evening menu items include Spinach Sesame Soup with poppeyseed rolls, or savory Stuffed Vine Leaves with a Tahini and Orange Sauce served with roast potatoes and three salads. **www.lancrigg.demon.co.uk**

The Lodge
P.O. Box 3540, St. George's, Grenada   (473) 440-2330
The Lodge is the Caribbean's first vegetarian and vegan resort. Converted into an intimate guesthouse that accommodates up to six visitors, this classic Caribbean-style plantation features a swimming pool, garden terrace, and wrap-around veranda with views of the Caribbean Sea. Full board includes three meals per day, as well as pre-dinner cocktails. Past choices have included pumpkin and ginger soup, plantain cakes, tofu kebabs with bulgar and hot pepper sauce, cashew nut loaf, mango or coconut sorbet, and "Death by Chocolate" cake. Vegan organic red and white wines are also available. **www.thelodge grenada.com**

Miranda's Veranda
Umaran 122, San Miguel de Allende
Guanajuato, Mexico 37700   011-52 (415) 152-2659
Miranda's is a smoke-free, vegetarian bed and breakfast that has a water treatment system.

Moshav Amirim
Bikat Beit Hakarem, Carmel, Israel 20115   04-6989213
Billing itself as a vegetarian/naturalist village, Moshav Amirim is located in the beautiful upper Galilee overlooking the Kinnert. Most of the foods and herbs are organically grown on the premises.

O'Reilly's Guest House

Lamington National Park Rd.
Via Canungra, Queensland, Australia 4275   **+61-7-5544-0644**

Located in Lamington National Park, O'Reilly's offers lacto-ovo vegetarian meals. www.
oreillys.com.au

Penrhos Court Hotel and Restaurant

Penrhors Court, Kington, Herefordshire, England HR5 3LH   44 (0)1-5442-30720

This non-smoking hotel is located on an old manor farm between England and Wales. It has
19 bedrooms, each with their own private bathroom. A vegetarian and vegan option is offered
at all meals, and many of the ingredients are organic. Visit nearby castles, stately homes,
gardens, golf courses, and galleries. www.penrhos.co.uk

Rio Caliente

480 California Terr., Pasadena, CA 91105   **(818) 796-5577**

This spa and mineral hot springs resort in Guadalajara, Mexico, is lacto-ovo vegetarian.

Royal Caribbean Cruise Line

1890 Park Marina Dr., #107, Redding, CA 96001   **(800) 852-3268**

The cruise line now offers vegetarian cruises to the Caribbean. www.rccl.com

Royal Court Hotel and Natural Health Retreat

P.O. Box 195, Montego Bay, Jamaica   **(800) 585-9437**

This hotel offers vegetarian meals and is located near a beach. Enjoy their pool, yoga classes,
massage sessions, steam room, hot tub, and more. They also feature a fresh juice bar.

Sivanda Yoga Vedanta Center

243 W. 24th St., New York, NY 10011

The center will connect you with Ashrams around the world.

Southwind Adventures

P.O. Box 621057, Littleton, CO 80162   **(800) 377-9463**

Vegetarian and vegan diets are accommodated on trips to the Andes and Amazon. www.
southwindadventures.com

Tigh-Na-Mara

The Shore, Ardindrean, Loch Broom
Wester Ross, Scotland IV23 2SE   **011-44-0854-85-484**

The guesthouse is close to many Scottish attractions and serves principally vegetarian meals.
Some vegan and seafood entrées are offered.

Tivoli Ltd.

Merkazimbuilding, P.O. Box 2045, Maskit St. 5
Industrial Area, Herzliya, Israel 46120   **011-972-052-557108**

This organization books hotels and tours that cater to vegetarians.

Tohum Travel
P.O. Box 972, Bernardston, MA 01337

Specializes in tours to Turkey with scheduled activities including yoga, shiatsu, and folk dancing. Whole foods, vegetarian, and macrobiotic teachings inspire the menu. **www. tohum.com**

Transitions Abroad Magazine
18 Hulst Rd., Box 344, Amherst, MA 01004   **(413) 256-0373**

Transitions is an international resource guide for educational and socially responsible travel. **www.transitionsabroad.com**

Vegesailing
408 Lakeside, C.P. 616, Lac Brome, PQ J0E 1V0   **(450) 242-1567**

Vegesailing offers all-inclusive vegetarian yachting trips in the Caribbean for groups of four or fewer. **www.vegesailing.com**

The Violin Bed and Breakfast
24 The Dee Grovehill, Hemel Hempstead
Herts, England HP2 6EN   **01442 -388977**

This vegetarian, homestyle bed and breakfast offers a vegetarian or vegan continental breakfast and, if arranged in advance, three-course evening meals. All of the toiletries are cruelty-free. Located 22 miles from Heathrow, this establishment is close to a train station and bus lines that will transport guests to central London almost hourly. **www.theviolinbnb.co.uk**

Local Vegetarian Groups to Contact for More Information

When traveling, you may want to contact the following groups for the latest information about restaurants in their area. Our thanks to many of these organizations for helping us secure information for this guide.

For updated information about local groups or to ask questions about vegetarianism, contact The Vegetarian Resource Group, P.O. Box 1463, Baltimore, MD 21203, or call (410) 366-VEGE (8343). Information is also available at The VRG website: <www.vrg.org>.

UNITED STATES

CALIFORNIA

Sacramento Vegetarian Society
P.O. Box 163583, Sacramento, CA 95816-9583
home.earthlink.net/~sacveggie

(916) 554-7090
info@sacvegsociety.org

The San Francisco Vegetarian Society
P.O. Box 2510, San Francisco, CA 94126-2510
sfvs.org

(415) 273-LIV1
membership@sfvs.org

South Bay Vegetarian Society
P.O. Box 865, Cupertino, CA 95015-0865
www.southbayveggies.org

southbayveggies@yahoogroups.com

Vegetarian Dining Club
440 Raymond Ave., #12, Santa Monica, CA 90405
www.happycow.net/vegetarian_dining_club

(310) 396-2826

Vegetarians in Paradise
17178 Goya St., Granada Hills, CA 91344
www.vegparadise.com

(818) 360-5821
vegparadise@vegparadise.com

COLORADO

The Vegetarian Society of Colorado
P. O. Box 6773, Denver CO 80206
vsc.org

(303) 777-4828

CONNECTICUT

Friends of Animals
777 Post Rd., Ste. 205, Darien, CT 06820   (203) 656-1522
www.friendsofanimals.org

DISTRICT OF COLUMBIA

Vegetarian Society of D.C.
P.O. Box 4921, Washington, DC 20008   (202) 362-VEGY
www.vsdc.org   vsdc@vsdc.org

FLORIDA

Tampa Bay Vegetarians
P.O. Box 7943, St. Petersburg, FL 33734-7943   (727) 392-0268
www.tampabayvegetarians.org   info@tampabayvegetarians.org

GEORGIA

Vegetarian Society of Georgia
P.O. Box 2164, Norcross, GA 30091   (770) 662-4019
www.VegSocietyOfGa.org   veggie236@earthlink.net

HAWAII

Vegetarian Society of Hawaii
P.O. Box 23208, Honolulu, HI 96823-3208   (808) 944-VEGI
www.vsh.org

ILLINOIS

Chicago Vegetarian Society
P.O. Box 223, Highwood, IL 60040   (847) 561-1302
www.chicagovegetariansoc.org   EdKugler@millardgroup.com

VegChicago.Com
c/o Protecting Animals USA/Earthsave Chicago
P.O. Box 25097, Chicago, IL 60625   (773) 463-2317
www.VegChicago.Com   dmarino@protectinganimals.org

MARYLAND

The Vegetarian Resource Group
P.O. Box 1463, Baltimore, MD 21203   (410) 366-8343
www.vrg.org   vrg@vrg.org

MASSACHUSETTS

Boston Vegetarian Society
P. O. Box 38-1071, Cambridge, MA 02238-1071
www.bostonveg.org

(617) 424-8846
BVS@ivu.org

MISSOURI

St. Louis Vegetarian Society
c/o 4734 Sunnyview Dr., St. Louis, MO 63128
www.geocities.com/thestlvs/

(314) 995-2699
thestlvs@yahoo.com

NEVADA

American Sanctuary Association
2308 Chatfield Dr., Las Vegas, NV 89128
www.asaanimalsanctuaries.org

(702) 804-8562
ASARescue@aol.com

NEW JERSEY

American Vegan Society
56 Dinshah Ln., P.O. Box 369, Malaga, NJ 08328
www.americanvegan.org

(856) 694-2887

Vegetarian Society of South Jersey
P.O. Box 272, Marlton, NJ 08053
www.vssj.com/vssjnn.html

(877) 999-8775
veggie@vssj.com

NEW YORK

Club VEG
P.O. Box 625 WVS, Binghamton, NY 13905
www.clubveg.org

(631) 286-1343
clubveg@clubveg.org

North American Vegetarian Society
P.O. Box 72, Dolgeville, NY 13329
navs-online.org

(518) 568-7970
navs@telenet.net

The Rochester Area Vegetarian Society
P.O. Box 20185, Rochester, NY 14602-0185
ravs.enviroweb.org

(716) 234-8750
drveggie@aol.com

The VivaVegie Society
P.O. Box 294, Prince St. Station, New York, NY 10012
www.vivavegie.org

(212) 871-9304
pamela@vivavegie.org

NORTH CAROLINA

The Triangle Vegetarian Society
P.O. Box 3364, Chapel Hill, NC 27515-3364   (919) 489-3340
trianglevegsociety.org

OHIO

Mercy For Animals
P.O. Box 363, Columbus, OH 43216   (937) 652-8258
www.mercyforanimals.org   info@mercyforanimals.org

Vegetarian Advocates
P.O. Box 201791, Cleveland, OH 44120   (216) 283-6702
vegetarianadvocates@yahoo.com

PENNSYLVANIA

Club VEG Philly
P.O. Box 81, Fort Washington, PA 19034-0081   (267) 481-0487
www.clubveg.org/philly   philly@clubveg.org

Letters For Animals
P.O. Box 7-Int, La Plume, PA 18440   (570) 945-5312
members.aol.com/letters4animals   Letters4animals@aol.com

The Pittsburgh Vegetarian Society
P.O. Box 44276, Pittsburgh, PA 15205   (412) 734-5554
pittsburghvegetariansociety.org   info@pittsburghvegetariansociety.org

Vegan Outreach
P.O. Box 38492, Pittsburgh, PA 15238-8492
www.veganoutreach.org   vegan@veganoutreach.org

TENNESSEE

Vegetarian Awareness Network/Veganet
P.O. Box 321, Knoxville, TN 37091-0321   (888) VEG-LINE

TEXAS

San Antonio Vegetarian Society
P.O. Box 791222, San Antonio, TX 78279   (210) 832-9293
home.satx.rr.com/savstx   SAVS@satx.rr.com

Vegetarian Society of Houston
2476 Bolsover, #231, Houston, TX 77005-2518   (713) 880-1055
www.vshouston.org   vshouston@bigfoot.com

Vegetarian Society of El Paso
6757 Gato Rd., El Paso, TX 79932   (915) 877-3030
utminers.utep.edu/vsep   VSoEP@aol.com

VERMONT

The Vermont Vegetarian Society
562 Pond Rd., North Ferrisburg, VT 05473   (802) 453-3945
vermontvegetarians.org   vvs@ivu.org

VIRGINIA

People for the Ethical Treatment of Animals
501 Front St., Norfolk, VA 23510   (888) VEG-FOOD
www.peta.org   info@peta.org

Vegan Action
P.O. Box 4288, Richmond, VA 23220   (804) 502-8736
www.vegan.org   information@vegan.org

WASHINGTON

Vegetarians of Washington
P.O. Box 85847, Seattle, WA 98145   (206) 706-2635
www.vegofwa.org   info@vegofwa.org

CANADA

EDMONTON

Vegetarians of Alberta Association
#201B, 10832 - 82 Whyte Ave., Edmonton, AB T6E 2B3   (780) 988-2713
www.planet.eon.net/~voa   voa@planet.eon.net

ONTARIO

Toronto Vegetarian Association
17 Baldwin St., 2nd Fl., Toronto, ON M5T 1L1   (416) 544-9800
www.veg.ca   tva@veg.ca

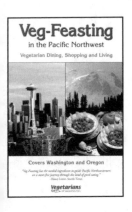

Also Available from The VRG

To order these or other resources from The VRG, mail the form on page 429 to P.O. Box 1463, Baltimore, MD 21203. Also, you can charge your order by calling (410) 366-8343 between 9 A.M. and 5 P.M. EST Monday through Friday or order on-line at <www.vrg.org/nutshell/materials.htm>.

Shipping and Handling Charges:

Orders under $25	$5 ($9 for Canada/Mexico)
Orders over $25	Free in continental U.S.
Other foreign orders	Inquire first

Simply Vegan

by Debra Wasserman and Reed Mangels, PhD, RD

These 224 pages contain over 160 quick and easy vegan recipes, a complete vegan nutrition section, and a list of where to mail order vegan food, clothing, cosmetics, and household products. Vegan menus and meal plans. Over 80,000 copies sold. ($13)

Meatless Meals for Working People

by Debra Wasserman

This 192-page book contains over 100 fast and easy recipes and tells you how to be a vegetarian using common, convenient foods. Spice chart, low-cost meal plans, party ideas, food info, and more. Over 90,000 copies in print. ($12)

Conveniently Vegan

by Debra Wasserman

Prepare meals with all the natural foods products found in stores today, including soymilk, tempeh, tofu, ... You'll find 150 recipes using convenience foods, along with grains, fresh fruits, and vegetables. Menu ideas, product sources, and food definitions included. (208 pp., $15)

426

Vegan Microwave Cookbook

by Chef Nancy Berkoff, RD, EdD, CCE

This 288-page cookbook contains 165 recipes, some of which take less than 10 minutes to cook and includes information for converting traditional recipes to the microwave, microwave baking and desserts, making breakfasts in a snap, and suggestions and recipes for holidays and parties. ($16.95)

Vegan Meals for One or Two

by Chef Nancy Berkoff, RD, EdD, CCE

Whether you live alone, are a couple, or are the only one in your household who is vegetarian, this 216-page book is for you. Each recipe is written to serve one or two people and is designed so that you can realistically use ingredients the way they come packaged from the store. ($15)

Vegan in Volume

by Chef Nancy Berkoff, RD, EdD, CCE

This 272-page quantity cookbook is loaded with terrific recipes serving 25. Suitable for catered events, college food service, restaurants, parties in your own home, weddings, and much more. ($20)

Vegan Handbook

Edited by Debra Wasserman and Reed Mangels, PhD, RD

Over 200 vegan recipes and vegetarian resources. Includes sports nutrition, seniors' guide, online resources, recipes for egg-free cakes and vegan pancakes, Thanksgiving ideas, feeding vegan children, vegetarian history, menus, and more. (256 pp., $20)

Vegan Menu for People with Diabetes

by Nancy Berkoff, RD, EdD, CCE

This 96-page book gives people with (or at risk for) diabetes a four-week meal plan, exchange listings for meat substitutes and soy products, and recipes for enjoyable dishes, such as Creamy Carrot Soup, Tangy Tofu Salad, Baked Bean Quesadillas, and French Toast. ($10)

No Cholesterol Passover Recipes

by Debra Wasserman

Includes 100 eggless and dairyless recipes. Seder plate ideas. Great for those on a restricted lowfat diet. (96 pp., $9)

The Lowfat Jewish Vegetarian Cookbook

by Debra Wasserman

Over 150 lowfat international vegan recipes with nutritional breakdowns, including Potato Knishes, Romanian Apricot Dumplings, North African Barley Pudding, and Russian Flat Bread. Also includes menu suggestions and holiday recipes. (224 pp., $15)

Vegan Passover Recipes

by Nancy Berkoff, RD, EdD, CCE

This 48-page book features vegan soups and salads, side dishes and sauces, entrées, desserts, and dishes you can prepare in a microwave during Passover. All the recipes follow Ashkenazi Jewish traditions and are pareve. ($6)

Guide to Fast Food and Quick Service Chains

This 24-page guide is a valuable tool for dining in many fast food and chain restaurants. It includes the menu items' ingredients from some companies and statements regarding vegetarian offerings from others. ($6)

Guide to Food Ingredients

This guide is very helpful in deciphering ingredient labels. It lists the uses, sources, and definitions of hundreds of common food ingredients. The guide also states whether the ingredient is vegan, typically vegan, vegetarian, typically vegetarian, non-vegetarian, or typically non-vegetarian. (32 pp., $6)

Vegetarian Resource Group *Order Form*

Name: _____ Phone: _____

Address: _____

City: _____ State: _____ ZIP: _____ Country: _____

Item:	Quantity:	Price:	Subtotal:
_____	_____	$_____	$_____
_____	_____	$_____	$_____
_____	_____	$_____	$_____

Payment:

☐ **Check or Money Order (enclosed)**

☐ **(circle one) VISA or MasterCard**

_____ Exp: __ / __

Signature _____

Subtotal: $_____

Shipping (see p. 426): $_____

In MD, 5% Sales Tax: $_____

Donation: $_____

Total: $_____

Send order information and payment to The Vegetarian Resource Group, P.O. Box 1463, Baltimore, MD 21203. Or fax this form to (410) 366-8804. You can order via telephone at **(410) 366-8343** Monday through Friday from 9 a.m. to 5 p.m. EST or online at **<www.vrg.org>**. Please e-mail **vrg@vrg.org** with any questions.

What is
THE VEGETARIAN RESOURCE GROUP?

The Vegetarian Resource Group is a national non-profit organization that makes it easier to be vegetarian. Our registered dietitians, educators, and activists assist consumers, businesses, health professionals, and food services. Our public policy work is creating new opportunities for future generations of vegetarians.

- Publishers of *Simply Vegan, Meatless Meals for Working People, Vegetarian Journal's Guide to Natural Foods Restaurants in the U.S. and Canada, Vegan Menu for People with Diabetes, Vegan Passover Recipes, Vegetarian Journal,* and more.

- On-line guide to vegetarian restaurants in the U.S.

- Fast food information

- Vegan recipes for individuals, families, and food services

- Vegetarian nutrition information that is both scientifically supported and practical

- Scholarships for high school seniors who actively promoted vegetarianism

- Sources for non-leather shoes, belts, coats, and other products

- Polls on the number of vegetarians

- Parents' e-mail list

- And much more…

The Vegetarian Resource Group
P.O. Box 1463, Baltimore, MD 21203
(410) 366-VEGE (8343) ◆ vrg@vrg.org

Don't forget to visit our website at www.vrg.org!

Restaurant Survey Form

Restaurants often change locations, new ones open, and others close. Please help us to update the next edition of this book by returning this survey with any new information we should have. Feel free to make copies of this form. Your help and support are greatly appreciated.

Return to Restaurant Survey, The Vegetarian Resource Group, P.O. Box 1463, Baltimore, MD 21203, or fax to (410) 366-8804. <u>Please include a menu.</u> Or fill out this form on-line at <www.vrg.org/travel/restupdate.htm>. Thank you!

RESTAURANT NAME: _____

STREET ADDRESS: _____

CITY: _____

STATE OR PROVINCE: _____ **ZIP:** _____

TELEPHONE NUMBER: _____

WEBSITE: _____

KIND OF RESTAURANT: (Circle if applicable) Vegetarian (no meat, fish, fowl) ✦ Vegan (no meat, fish, fowl, dairy, eggs, honey) ✦ Natural Foods ✦ Macrobiotic ✦ Raw Foods

IF NOT ONE OF THE ABOVE, WHICH OPTIONS DO YOU OFFER? (Circle all that apply) Vegetarian ✦ Vegan ✦ Natural Foods ✦ Macrobiotic ✦ Raw Foods

CUISINE: (Circle all that apply) Afghan ✦ African ✦ American ✦ Asian ✦ Baked Goods Barbeque ✦ Burmese ✦ Cajun ✦ Cambodian ✦ Caribbean ✦ Chinese ✦ Creole ✦ Deli Diner ✦ Eritrean ✦ Ethiopian ✦ European ✦ French ✦ Greek ✦ Indian ✦ Indonesian International ✦ Italian ✦ Korean ✦ Japanese ✦ Juice Bar ✦ Lebanese ✦ Mediterranean Mexican ✦ Middle-Eastern ✦ Mongolian ✦ Moroccan ✦ Persian ✦ Polish ✦ Regional Salad Bar ✦ Soul Food ✦ Southern ✦ Southwestern ✦ Thai ✦ Turkish ✦ Vietnamese Other: _____

ATMOSPHERE: (Circle all that apply) Formal attire ✦ Informal ✦ Casual ✦ Earthy Family-friendly ✦ Suitable for business entertaining ✦ Totally non-smoking

(Continued)

RESERVATIONS: Required ♦ Recommended ♦ Not Needed ♦ Not Taken

HOURS OPEN: (Please list) _____

_____

MEALS SERVED: (Circle all that apply) Breakfast ♦ Lunch ♦ Dinner
          Late Night Service ♦ Weekend brunch ♦ Sunday brunch ♦ Open 24 hours

TYPES OF SERVICE: (Circle all that apply) Full service (regular table service) ♦ Buffet
    Cafeteria ♦ Limited service (order at counter, but food taken to table) ♦ Counter service
          Take-out available ♦ Take-out only ♦ Delivery ♦ Catering

BEVERAGES: (Circle all that apply) Fresh juices (squeezed in the restaurant) ♦ Smoothies
Soymilk ♦ Espresso ♦ Cappuccino ♦ Beer ♦ Wine ♦ Alcohol ♦ Non-Alcoholic Beer or Wine
Special Drinks ♦ Other: _____

PAYMENTS ACCEPTED: (Circle all that apply) Visa ♦ MasterCard ♦ American Express
          Discover ♦ Diners Club ♦ No Credit Cards ♦ Travelers' Checks

COST FOR AN AVERAGE MEAL: Less than $6 ♦ $6-$12 ♦ More than $12

DESCRIPTION/SPECIAL FEATURES: (Examples of dishes, special foods, decor, music,
view, etc. In other words, what makes this establishment special?)

_____

_____

_____

IS THIS RESTAURANT WORTHY OF A REVIEWER'S CHOICE RATING? _____

Please feel free to attach any additional comments you may have to this questionnaire.

NAME OF READER: _____

STREET ADDRESS: _____

CITY: _____ **STATE/PROVINCE:** _____ **ZIP:** _____

PHONE: _____ **E-MAIL:** _____

JOIN THE VEGETARIAN RESOURCE GROUP!

Support Our Outreach and Receive *Vegetarian Journal*!

- For **$20**, you will get a basic **membership** and a year's subscription to the quarterly *Vegetarian Journal.*

- For a **$30** membership, we will send you the quarterly **Vegetarian Journal** and a copy of **Vegan Handbook.** This excellent 256-page book features over 200 great-tasting recipes covering the basics, feeding children, holiday cooking, breakfast ideas, international cuisine, desserts, and much more. You will also find a vegan meal plan, a one-week vegan menu, a 30-day menu for those who don't like to cook, as well as a collection of terrific articles from previous issues of *Vegetarian Journal* on topics, such as A Senior's Guide to Good Nutrition, Vegetarian History, A Shopper's Guide to Leather Alternatives, Vegan Sources of Omega-3 Fatty Acids, Weightlifting on a Vegan Diet, A Week of Vegan Diabetic Menus, Raw Foods Diets, plus more.

- For **$50**, you will receive the subscription to the quarterly **Vegetarian Journal** and a copy of **Vegan Handbook,** but you will also receive a copy of **Meatless Meals for Working People—Quick and Easy Vegetarian Recipes.**

Yes! I want to become a member of VRG!

Name: _____

Address: _____

_____ ZIP Code: _____

Phone: _____

Check Desired Membership Level: ❑ Member ($20)   ❑ Contributor ($30)
❑ Supporter ($50)   ❑ Life Member ($500)

Please note: In Canada and Mexico, add $12 per subscription. In other foreign countries, add $22 per subscription to cover additional postage and handling costs. Outside USA, pay by money order in US$ or by Visa or Mastercard.

Please check if this is a renewal: ❑

Send this form and a check or money order for your level of support to **The Vegetarian Resource Group, P.O. Box 1463, Baltimore, MD 21203.** For more information, call **(410) 366-VEGE**, e-mail **vrg@vrg.org**, or visit **<www.vrg.org>**.

Order Additional Copies of
Vegetarian Journal's Guide to Natural Foods Restaurants in the U.S. and Canada

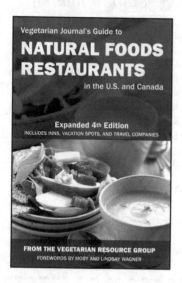

You can order additional copies of *Vegetarian Journal's Guide to Natural Foods Restaurants in the U.S. and Canada.* Just send a check or money order for $18 per book to The VRG, P.O. Box 1463, Baltimore, MD 21203. To pay by credit card, call us at (410) 366-8343 Monday through Friday between 9 A.M. and 5 P.M. EST. Or order directly from The VRG's website at <www.vrg.org/catalog/guide.htm>.

Join The Vegetarian Resource Group and Support Our Work!

The Vegetarian Resource Group (VRG) is a non-profit organization dedicated to educating the public on vegetarianism and the interrelated issues of health, nutrition, ecology, ethics, and world hunger. In addition to publishing this book, VRG produces and sells *Vegetarian Journal,* cookbooks, pamphlets, and article reprints.

Our health professionals, activists, and educators work with businesses and individuals to bring about healthy changes in your school, workplace, and community. Registered dietitians and physicians aid in the development of nutrition related publications and answer member or media questions about the vegetarian diet.

To join The Vegetarian Resource Group and receive a year's subscription to *Vegetarian Journal,* send $20 to The VRG, P.O. Box 1463, Baltimore, MD 21203, or call (410) 366-8343 Monday through Friday between 9 A.M. and 5 P.M. EST.

Visit VRG's Website at www.vrg.org

Updates to this restaurant guide are available at The VRG website, <www.vrg.org>. Also get travel tips, recipes, nutritional information, the application for our annual scholarship competition, and much more, with just a click of your mouse!